From The

Isle of Skye

to The

Isle of Maui

*A doctor's personal story including
Plantation Medicine
and the Cause of High Blood Pressure*

WILLIAM BENTON PATTERSON, A.B., M.D., F.A.C.O.G.

Published by
The Publishing Group, Inc.
609 Loulu Way
Makawao, Hawaii 96768

W.B. Patterson

Cover Photo:
The Patterson plantation home in Puunene, formerly occupied by Frank F. Baldwin, owner and manager. Haiku ditch in right rear. Aerial photo by Dr. Ralph Cloward.

To Bob and Pam Welle
in appreciation for what
they have done for
our daughter, Lois Uranga.

with much aloha

Bill Patterson

CONTENTS

FOREWORD

I have used an unusual format to present my story. I have combined my heritage with actual experiences that occurred during my life as I remember them or as they are recorded in my diary, which began at age 17. I have also recorded newsworthy world events of the time. I am sure some will find parts of my story boring. After dividing the material into 34 chapters, I found there was much information that I wanted to include that occurred in the time intervals between the chapters. Many events, such as visiting relatives, are repeated. Making a 10,000 mile round-trip is a major undertaking, and I felt I should include these trips. In between the chapters, I have listed the years. This will enable one to skip the parts that are of no interest to him or her.

The author at age 77
Photo by Elson-Alexandre

Some of my stories are related, but occurred several years apart. In many instances, I have grouped these together, which means that I get ahead of my diary, for instance, Dottie and I saw the play "The Tea House of the August Moon" on the stage in New York City. A few years later, it was made into a movie, and we saw it on Maui. About 20 years after this, we visited the area in Japan where the movie was filmed and actually had lunch in "The Tea House of the August Moon."

Another unusual feature of my story is to combine scientific information about my medical research along with a running story of my life. I have tried to use lay terms so that almost anyone can understand what I am trying to say. After studying this subject for 50 years, I cannot separate myself from it.

Another diversion I have made is to include a short summary of my wife's heritage with my story. Most of our ancestors were Scottish or English with some German on her side and French on mine. All of them came to America in the 18th century and helped build our great nation. In the Civil War, her forefathers were Yankees and mine were Confederates. Great-grandfathers on both sides fought in the Civil War, but on different sides.

It is my hope that my story will be of interest to some.

William B. Patterson

DEDICATION

This story is dedicated to my wife, Dottie, without whose love and encouragement I would never have written it. I "gave up" on my research project many times due to disappointment and fatigue. However, we had met when I was at the pinnacle of my success in the early phases of my research. She could not forget how determined I was at that time to see my work come to fruition. She continued to remind me that I had not finished my project. When I did finish it, she reminded me I had said I would write a story of my life and the research if and when it was accepted by my contemporaries. I finally realized this might be after my demise, and that is why I have gone ahead now.

In addition to Dottie, I dedicate my story to our seven grandchildren who are about to enter adulthood. I hope that my life experiences can help them choose a successful course of their own.

INTRODUCTION

For 50 years I pursued a medical research project on the cause of high blood pressure (hypertension) during pregnancy. This study began during the first week of July, 1936, when I started my internship at the Geisinger Medical Center, Danville, Pennsylvania. It ended during the first week of July, 1986, when I returned home from Valencia, Spain, where I had given two lectures at the XVIII International Congress on the Pathophysiology of Pregnancy. I have concluded my research, believing I have adequately explained the cause of hypertension during pregnancy. I have written 25 medical papers and five monographs on the subject. Lectures have been given at medical meetings on four continents, including three meetings in Europe and two in Japan.

In recent years it has occurred to me that if my theories prove to be correct and are generally accepted, it might be worthwhile to explain how one individual studying alone, isolated on a Hawaiian Island of about 50,000 population, could have unraveled the mysteries of the cause of hypertension during pregnancy. Because it may take several more years for my theories to be accepted, and I have already entered the last quarter of a century of life on this earth, I know that if I am to write such an explanation I must write it now.

My first thought about writing a life story was that only a braggart would do so unless he had achieved a real accomplishment in life that had been accepted by his contemporaries. I mentioned to my wife and four daughters the possibility of writing my memoirs when my research came to fruition. I referred to a daily diary I have kept for 60 years, including the World War II years in Hawaii. After reading parts of this diary to our daughters, they were fascinated and kept asking me when was I going to write my story. After much thought and self-analysis, I have decided that I should do it now.

This story is being written especially for our seven grandchildren because I feel it is important for them to know as much as possible about their heritage and background.

I entered medical school in 1932 and have witnessed the discovery and development of the miracles of modern medicine. My diary relates how I incorporated each new treatment in my medical practice.

Some aspects of my practice were unique. At times I was the only doctor on an island with a population of about 3,000. When I came to Hawaii, then a territory of the U.S.A., there was one neurosurgeon serving all the islands. On the outer islands we depended on a one-day-per-month visit by the Shriner's Hospital doctor for special orthopedic care.

For many years, I worked for the sugar and pineapple plantations, who gave their employees complete medical care including physician and hospitalization. I treated all types of illnesses. The training I received in my twelve months rotating internship before my two years training in obstetrics and newborn pediatrics became of great importance.

While my research project and medical practice were dominant factors in my life for 50 years, they were not the most important things.

During my formative years, I established goals and came to accept certain standards and principles that have remained with me and guided me through life: the need for a happy home; the need for work; the need for a code of conduct, ethics and morality; and a respect for God, which to me means that we must love our fellow men.

THE IMPORTANCE OF A HAPPY HOME

From my earliest years, the important thing to me was to have a happy home. This, no doubt, reflects the kind of home my parents had provided for me. I wanted a loving wife, several children, a comfortable house with all modern conveniences, and a yard large enough for flowers, fruit trees and privacy. I felt it was my duty to provide enough income to support my family and that my wife should not work outside our home. I envisioned that my wife and I would be partners in life, sharing all family responsibilities and decision-making, all joys and sorrows, and all successes and failures. I have held to this concept through 50 years of marriage. We have made errors; we have learned from them and have gone ahead. As has been said many times, the school of hard knocks is the best teacher and though some of us are able to learn from the experience of others, many are not.

THE IMPORTANCE OF WORK

As many teachings stress, mental work and physical activity are necessary to keep the mind and body in balance. Some people do not need to work because of inheritance; many are able to save money and retire, living on pensions and past earnings. Even for these people, when mental and physical activity are inadequate the mind and body soon deteriorate.

From the age of eight when my father died until the age of 67 when I retired, I had to work to survive. Very early in life I discovered that work was very rewarding. Efforts over and above what was required brought extra compensation and praise. This, in turn, would stimulate me to do more work. Although at times my work has failed to get the desired results, I never considered the effort to be a total loss. It not only made my next job easier, but it helped keep me normal mentally and physically so I could go ahead with something else. The axiom, no work is ever wasted, seemed to be true.

Most of us, I think, seek immortality. We have a desire to make this world a better place by our having lived. Some become great statesmen, political leaders, scholars and philanthropists, while others follow less illustrious paths. Both groups can achieve immortality by doing a good job. I think of my mother and my mother-in-law who both, as widows, reared seven children to become useful citizens. These women certainly will live forever through the various contributions to society made by their descendants.

I feel sure this desire for immortality is part of the driving force that kept me working on my research project for 50 years. I have spent much of our own money and a great amount of time on this project. If I had concentrated on making money perhaps I would be wealthy by now, but I would not be as happy as I am and possibly would have already succumbed to disease that so often ends the lives and careers of highly successful individuals. As a physician I have known how to prevent the development of certain diseases that have destroyed poets, musicians, scholars, business leaders and others when they were young. Even today, some of our most successful individuals die at middle age, apparent victims of their success.

I feel certain that I have inherited my love for work from my ancestors who had to work continually under adverse conditions to survive. Now that I don't have to work, I feel the need to discipline myself to do some physical activity each day before relaxing. I fulfill this need by maintaining our home and by cultivating our fruit trees and the flowers my wife so enjoys.

THE NEED FOR A CODE OF CONDUCT, ETHICS AND MORALITY

Ethics and morality are ever at center stage in our lives. From the earliest recorded history, standards of conduct have been established for civilized societies to live by. These standards are similar in most societies, though they may vary in some cultures. The Ten Commandments written by Moses form a basis for many ethical codes.

As a child, I learned what was right and wrong from my parents and other members of my family, from the teachings in Sunday school and church, from my school teachers and athletic coaches, from Boy Scouts, and from my associates. I vividly remember visiting a relative with my mother when I was four or five and taking a quarter that I had found on a bed. Later, failing to convince my mother that I had found the money in the yard, I had to return it and apologize. At age six, I visited a friend who owned a pair of wagon wheels on an axle with an attached tongue. When I left for home, I took these wheels with me without his knowledge. Sensing that I might be in trouble if I arrived home with them, I hid them nearby. Next day, when word reached home through my sisters that I had taken the wagon wheels, I had to return them and apologize.

For many years I wondered why I should have stolen things on these two occasions. After becoming a physician, I read in child psychology that it is normal for a young child to steal. When it happens, the parents have an opportunity to teach the child that it is wrong to do so. If the parents do this with love and understanding, the child will be apt to learn and not repeat. I also learned that it is normal for young children to fabricate stories and not always be truthful. Again, the parents must teach them with love and understanding. The examples parents set in their daily lives are the best teachers.

My parents were strongly opposed to the drinking of alcoholic beverages of any kind. Neither drank during their entire lives until the doctor suggested a glass of wine before dinner for my mother in her late 70s. Before I reached my teenage years, I had learned first-hand from close relatives the perils of drinking alcohol and taking drugs. Later in my medical practice on the sugar plantations, it was often necessary for me to treat both acute and chronic alcoholism and drug addiction. The lives of the individuals involved were always adversely affected. After a few years, most of them were self-destroyed, developing alcoholic related disease or intercurrent infections. When both parents in a young family are involved, it often means total disaster for their innocent children.

A RESPECT FOR GOD AND LOVE OF FELLOW MAN

As I have grown older, I have developed a greater respect for God. As a child, I went to Sunday school and church every Sunday. We were Southern Missionary

Baptists and they take their religion seriously. I joined the church at age 12 and was baptized (immersed) along with several others in the fishpond near our home. I have always believed in God as a Divine Power who controls the destiny of man, but only as man allows Him to do so. I follow the teachings of Christ and try to do unto others as I would have them do unto me. As a physician, I treated my patients as I would want a physician to treat me or any member of my family.

We children were allowed to play cards (finch, rook, old maid, etc.) and other indoor games, even on Sunday evening. We were taught that gambling for money with cards, or otherwise, was a sin and I still believe it is even if lotteries and other forms of gambling are legal in some states.

Our family did not work on Sunday except in emergencies. We celebrated Christmas as a religious holiday and our Christmas tree was a holly tree with red berries and no other decorations. We celebrated Easter Sunday and took Easter Monday as a holiday from school and work.

When I began my medical practice and encountered serious problems in my patients I would pray for guidance in my treatment. Eventually I prayed for guidance in the treatment of every patient, even the delivery of a baby when everything appeared normal. If an emergency did occur, I seemed to be able to choose the correct treatment more often.

During crises in my work, my personal life, and my research project, I would suddenly find the right solution to my problem as though some Great Power had been watching me and told me what to do. An example of this was the day I took a book off my library shelf and casually opened it. The first paragraph I read contained what I had spent years searching for - proof of the main theory of my research project. Many other research articles lending - support to my theory were found accidentally.

About twelve years ago while working in my yard, I became dizzy and had to stop. The next day, I had my blood pressure taken and it was 220/135. After a thorough check I was diagnosed as having physiological hypertension from too much work. I was given medications and my blood pressure returned to normal. However, whenever I worked all night and became tired, my blood pressure would go up again. I knew this was a warning that it was time to stop working. I resigned from the hospital staff and reduced my office hours to three hours daily for five days each week. At 67, I stopped the practice of medicine completely. Now, my blood pressure remains normal unless I am overactive in any endeavor, even the writing of this story.

CHAPTER I

HERITAGE

I do not recall a special search being made to trace our family heritage. In my youth I was told that our ancestors were from Scotland and that my paternal grandmother was Scotch-Irish. My maternal great-grandfather was Neill McLeod, a descendant of the MacLeod Clan of the Scottish Isle of Skye. His wife, my great-grandmother, died in 1916 at the age of 79 when I was three years, 10 months old. I remember her well.

After my maternal grandfather died in 1906, my grandmother moved from Broadway, North Carolina, to Coats, N.C., where her mother lived. My family moved to Coats in 1912, two months before I was born.

Coats is located in the Piedmont section of North Carolina about halfway between Raleigh and Fayetteville. When I lived there, almost every Caucasian family in the area had originated in the British Isles. The English and Scottish influences on the lives of the people were enormous. I am sometimes confused about stories I have heard; I cannot remember if they occurred in Scotland or in America.

My mother's maiden name was Fuquay. I was told that this, also, was Scottish. After studying French, I decided it could be of French origin and, sure enough, it proved to be.

The United States is now only slightly over two centuries old. Stories that date from a few generations before my birth reach a time before our country obtained independence from England. My ancestors on both sides have been traced to colonial days.

I am proud to have ancestors who helped build this great country of ours and am envious of those who can trace their heritage to the Pilgrims, who came here on the Mayflower in 1620. Most all the early settlers came for the same reasons: religious freedom, opportunity for work, and freedom from the tyranny of the governments in their homelands. However, not all came for these reasons. Just before the American Revolution, over 50,000 prisoners chose to be shipped to America rather than be hanged in England [1]. Many of these had committed only minor offenses, for which they were sentenced to death.

By 1630 the estimated population of the American colonies was 4,800, by 1650 it was 52,000, and by 1680 it was over 150,000. Between 1720 and 1775 over 250,000 Scotsmen settled in the Shenandoah Valley of Virginia, the Piedmont country of North Carolina and all along the Eastern seaboard. My Scottish ancestors were among these.

In 1973, my older sister, Velma Patterson Lawrence, compiled a history of our family that goes back to colonial days. She used all available sources of information such as birth, death, and marriage certificates, baptismal and church records, recorded wills, and inscriptions on tombstones in several cemeteries. She consulted with others who had written records about common ancestors on both sides of the family. Among these were Admiral Alex McLeod Patterson, U.S. Navy (Retired)[2] of Raleigh, and Larry Fuqua of Cary, North Carolina, who supplied her most of the information.

Dunvegan Castle, Isle of Skye   *Photo by British Travel Associates, London*

2

Grandma Fuquay's father was Neill McLeod, who died in a Union prisoner-of-war camp during the Civil War. We have in our family six letters written by him or by his brother-in-law to Neill's wife back home during the war.

The sources of the information listed below are: THE CLAN MacLEOD written by I.F. Grant[3]; the document my sister wrote on the heritage of our family in 1973; and a recent conversation I had with my brother, Harold McLeod Patterson. He and his wife entertained Dame Flora MacLeod of MacLeod, 28th head of the MacLeod Clan, while she was visiting in Honolulu in 1955. In 1965, they visited Dame Flora at Dunvegan Castle on the Isle of Skye. Likewise, my wife and I entertained Dame Flora in our home on Maui on February 13, 1955, and visited Dunvegan Castle on September 30, 1975.

According to my sister, MacLeod is a surname denoting descendants of Leod - from an old Norse personal name, Ljotr, meaning ugly. The prefix Mac is Gaelic, which means "the son of". From the 8th century, Norsemen traveled to the Western Isles of Scotland, first as raiders and then as settlers. A struggle between Norway and Scotland ensued and lasted for centuries. In the 12th and 13th centuries, the Norsemen became absorbed into Gaeldom in the great Gaelic revival.

According to legend, Leod, who lived in the 13th century, founded the MacLeod Clan on the Isle of Skye. He was the son of Olave the Black, the King of the Isle of Man, and through him descended from the Royal House of Norway. My brother told me that, according to Dame Flora, Leod's father was afraid his son would eventually become so strong that he, himself, would be dethroned. To solve the problem, Leod was given the Isle of Skye and married the daughter of the former Norse governor of Skye. Through her he laid claim to more land.

Leod had two sons from whom the two branches of the MacLeod Clan are descended. One was Siol Tormod, who owned Dunvegan, most of the Isle of Skye, and other territory. The other was Siol Torquil, who owned the Isle of Lewis and other lands. This gave rise to the MacLeods of MacLeod (Skye) and to the MacLeods of Lewis.

The headquarters and the stronghold of the MacLeod Clan was and is the Dunvegan Castle. This castle originated in the 8th century and was accessible only by a sea gate until 1748. It has been occupied by the MacLeods since the 13th century. Some of the walls and a primitive sea gate that date from that time are still present. Many renovations and additions have been made. It serves as the home of the head of the clan and is reputed to be the oldest structure in the world to have been continuously occupied as a home by the same family. Throughout the ages, many notable people were entertained there, including King James V of Scotland in 1536, and Boswell and Johnson in 1773.

The exact year the MacLeods arrived in America is not known, but they probably came between 1720 and 1775 when so many Scotsmen arrived. In America, the name was shortened to McLeod and this has been used ever since. The lineage of our ancestors is as follows:

My great-great-grandfather
Angus McLeod

My great-grandfather
Neill McLeod   married   **Elizabeth Matthews**
Born - Oct. 30, 1833   Born - Feb. 27, 1837
Died - Dec. 10, 1864   Died - Feb. 12, 1916

3

December the 21 Eth 1863

Dear wife I once more take my pen
in hand to inform you that I am well
at this time and hoping these few lines
may find you all well and harty and a plenty
to eat I recieved your letter dated December the

pleased with your riting I think Mary Jane
has ben mity smarte to lern her book and I hope
my tother two little ones will be the same way
when they get big a nuff to go to skool and I
recieved a letter from you dated December the 13
and was glad to here that you wer all well and
I wish I could here my boy call hogs and here

the sweat time with my babes I rote you one
letter sence the fite but I spose you had
not got it the 13 of the month I rote in that
I thought Cox wod go home this winter but
he haant ben seen sence the fight ef you see
eney of Mr Cones folks you can tell them
he was in the fite and he was kiled or taken

4

prisoner he heant ben seen nor heard from

on sence we are at the same camp where we was where I rote to you we have got splended shantes now I cant hardly tell when day comes onely by the drum but I am afrade we will have to moove a gin I here some talk of mooving nerer the railrode and I herd Rodes division moved yesterday I should be glad to get nere the railrode but I hate to bild a gin this winter I had like to forgot to tell you I was mite glad to git them stamps they come in a good time I was out and had bored 1 and could not find nun to by we have vary cold weather here now we wer on picket posts lately and we have Jest got back and I think I shal get a blanket in a day or two now the wagens is gon after them an some cloes and shoes it is geting nere crismas and I wish I could be at home and get a big potatoe and a dram nothing more at present onely my best wishes to you all Neill McLeod to Elisabeth McLeod

5

My grandmother

Mary Jane McLeod	married in 1873	**Richard Benton Fuquay**
Born - July 3, 1857		Born - Mar. 27, 1850
Died - Nov. 27, 1926		Died - Nov. 8, 1906

My mother (third of nine children)

Mattie Fuquay	married Feb. 11, 1902	**Neill Thomas Patterson**
Born - April 13, 1881		Born - April 14, 1878
Died - July 29, 1964		Died - Dec. 6, 1920

(See Patterson and Fuquay family histories below.)

The six Civil War letters referred to above were passed from Elizabeth Matthews McLeod upon her death to Mary Jane Fuquay, her eldest daughter. Then, upon Mary Jane's death, they were given to her daughter, Mattie Fuquay Patterson, my mother. She discussed them with my youngest brother, Col. Neill Theron Patterson, now deceased, and gave them to him. After her death, he compiled them into a document containing the following:

A photocopy of each original letter written in longhand, a typewritten copy of each letter, a transcribed copy of each letter in modern day language, and a brief of the campaigns of the Army of Northern Virginia for the period of Neill McLeod's enlistment. He had several copies made for the members of the immediate family and donated copies to Southern libraries.

Neill McLeod, my great-grandfather, enlisted in the Confederate Army on July 15, 1862, for the duration of the Civil War and was assigned to Company E, 3rd Regiment, North Carolina State Troops. After being wounded, he was furloughed and visited his family in 1863. He returned to duty and was captured on May 12, 1864, near the Spottsylvania, Virginia, courthouse when Union forces overran Confederate positions. An estimated 3,000 prisoners were taken including Neill McLeod. He was first confined to Point Lookout, Maryland, and then was transferred to Elmira, New York, where he died of pneumonia December 10, 1864.

The following is a typewritten version of the last letter that Neill McLeod's wife received from him. A photocopy of this letter is on page 4 and 5.

December 21st, 1863

Dear wife I once more take my pen in hand to inform you that I am well at this time and hoping these few lines may find you all well and harty and a plenty to eat I received your letter dated December the
pleased with your riting I think Mary Jane has ben mity smarte to lern her book and I hope my tother two little ones will be the same way when they get big a nuff to go to scool and I recieved a letter from you dated December the 13 and was glad to here that you wer all well and I wish I could here my boy call hogs and here
the Sweat time with my babes I rote you one letter sence the fite but I spose you had not got it the 13 of the month I rote in that I thought Cox wod go home this winter but he heant ben seen sence the fight ef you see eney of Mr. Coxes folks you can tell them he was in the fite and was kiled or taken prisener he heant ben seen nor hern fr om since we are at the same camp where we wer where I rote to you we have got splended shantes now I cant hardly tell when day comes onely by the drum beet I am afrade we will have to moove a gin I here some talk of mooving nerer the railrode and I herd Rodes division moved yesterday I should be glad to get nere the railrode

but I hate to bild a gin this winter I had like to forgot to tell you I was mite glad to git them stamps they come in a good time I was out and had bored 1 and could not find nun to by we have vary cold weather here now we wer on picket post latly and we have Jest got back and I think I shal get a blanket in a day or two now the wagens is gon after them an some cloes and shoes it is geting nere crisamas and I wish I could be at home and get a big potatoe and a dram nothing more at presant onely my best wishes to you all Neill McLeod to Elizabeth McLeod.

THE PATTERSON FAMILY

Apparently, my first Patterson ancestor to arrive in this country from Scotland was Duncan Patterson, who had received a land grant from the King of England. The exact date of his arrival is not known, although it is thought he arrived in 1740. A record written by his granddaughter, Decie McNeil, who arrived in 1742, states that when she arrived he was well settled near Fayetteville, N.C., where the Veteran's Hospital now stands, and had been there longer than anyone else in the region. In 1758, he moved to western Harnett County near Broadway, N.C., to an area that is known as the Barbecue section. Information about the immediate descendants of the original Duncan Patterson is sketchy and there is a long gap in the record. It could be that he had a son named Duncan, who was the father of the three sons about whom we have records. The sons were named John, Neill, and Daniel, and I am a descendant of John.

During the Revolutionary War, many Pattersons served in the Continental Line as Rebels. There is no record that any Patterson was a Loyalist. As early as 1769 a tax receipt signed by the sheriff of Cumberland County, N.C., notes that our ancestor, Duncan Patterson, was a Rebel. A Duncan Patterson who enlisted in the army in 1781 was killed in 1782, but this Duncan Patterson is not thought to be our ancestor as he would have been too old to serve at that time. After a few generations, there were many Pattersons with the same names, which leads to confusion.

The lineages of my Patterson ancestors and my descendants are as follows:

My great-great-great-grandfather:

Duncan Patterson   Wife, unknown

(He arrived from Scotland in 1740. He was among the second group of ruling elders of Barbecue Presbyterian Church, established in 1757. It is the oldest church in North Carolina.)

My great-great-grandparents:

John Patterson   married in 1813   **Margaret Buie**

(He helped supply land for the present Barbecue Church where sermons were preached in Gaelic for 100 years.)

My great-grandparents:

Archibald Buie Patterson   married March 4, 1834   **Clarky Wilson**
Born Feb. 17, 1814   Born Aug. 25, 1816
Died June 20, 1886   Died Feb. 20, 1892

(I have a photocopy of their marriage certificate.)

My grandparents:

William D. Patterson   married   **Mary Ann Thomas**
Born Mar. 20, 1847   Born Apr. 3, 1848
Died Oct. 25, 1920   Died Mar. 24, 1932

My parents:

Neill Thomas Patterson   married Feb. 11, 1902   **Mattie Fuquay**
Born Apr. 14, 1878   Born Apr. 13, 1881
Died Dec. 6, 1920   Died July 29, 1964

My brothers and sisters, including myself:

Orus Fuquay Patterson   married Feb. 3, 1921   **Verl Johnson**
Born Feb. 3, 1903   Born Apr. 14, 1902
Died Jan. 2, 1965   Died Aug. 27, 1980

Velma Patterson   married Aug. 1, 1928   **Marquis Wood Lawrence**
Born Apr. 19, 1905   Born Aug. 10, 1902
Died Apr. 2, 1986   Died Sept. 26, 1976

Maisie Jane Patterson   married Apr. 20, 1946   **Thomas Wiley Parker Jr.**
Born Oct. 5, 1907   Born Sept. 11, 1903
                                                    Died Aug. 29, 1958

                        married Oct. 17, 1981   **George Briner**
                                                Born Dec. 6, 1900

Harold McLeod Patterson   married Aug. 7, 1936   **Louise Weber**
Born Feb. 13, 1910   Born Sept. 14, 1914

William Benton Patterson married Aug. 17, 1938 **Dorothy Evelyn Graham**
Born Apr. 21, 1912   Born Apr. 15, 1917

Preston Cooper Patterson
Born Apr. 3, 1914
Died Apr. 5, 1917

Neill Theron Patterson   married Dec. 7, 1941   **Pearl Christen**
Born July 12, 1916   Born June 22, 1916
Died Aug. 31, 1978

Dorothy Kathleen Patterson   married June 1, 1942 **Jack Edwards Thornton**
Born Jan. 17, 1920   Born June 22, 1916

Our Children:

Lois Graham Patterson   married Aug. 6, 1966   **John Garcia Uranga**
Born Dec. 1, 1939   Born June 5, 1932

Ann Fuquay Patterson   married Apr. 30, 1966   **Michael Terrence McGovern**
Born Apr. 3, 1941   Born Apr. 20, 1937
                                                   Divorced 1971

Dorothy Jane Patterson   married Aug. 21, 1965   **Michael Isnardi Mote**
Born Sept. 18, 1943   Born Feb. 5, 1935

Carol Lynn Patterson   married June 21, 1969   **Peter Courtney Keck**
Born Apr. 21, 1946   Born May 21, 1945

Our Grandchildren:

William Patterson Uranga
Born Feb. 28, 1968

Carol Ann Uranga
Born Nov. 25, 1970

Michael Terrence McGovern II
Born Mar. 11, 1969

Timothy Isnardi Mote
Born May 29, 1970
Gregory Andrew Mote
Born Aug. 18, 1971
Adam Keck
Born Dec. 24, 1976
Todd Keck
Born Dec. 24, 1976

My grandfather, William D. Patterson, was born and lived near the original land holdings of the earliest Patterson settler, Duncan Patterson. After my grandfather was married, he bought a nearby plantation of 973 acres, as recorded in land records at the court house. The house was called Flint Hill and had a large ballroom on the third floor. This house burned before Papa knew Mamma and was replaced by a smaller house, which I visited. I remember the kitchen had a large fireplace which was used for cooking. I also recall the high poster beds with feather mattresses and pillows. A spinning wheel was in the parlor.

Cotton, corn, wheat, tobacco, vegetables for the table, and many other crops were grown on the plantation. Cows, pigs, sheep, chickens, turkeys and ducks were raised for meat for the family and to sell for income.

On uncleared land grew an abundance of oak and pine trees, which were cut for lumber and sold. Many of the pine trees were of the long-leaved variety and their trunks were tapped for resin similar to the way a maple tree is tapped for sap. The resin was converted to rosin and turpentine by distillation, a big industry in the area. I remember walking in the summer near some of the trees that had been tapped long before, but from which the resin (pine tar) was no longer collected. The resin would stick to my shoes, or to my feet if I were barefooted, and was difficult to remove. This is the origin of the word tarheel, which is a nickname for North Carolinians.

There were several barns on the plantation, all connected by a high fence, making a large inner court. This was used to exercise the horses and mules in the winter, when they were not working in the fields. The ground floor of the barns contained many stables and each animal knew which stall belonged to him or her.

My grandfather was a very industrious person. He soon had the plantation paid for and, in addition, he bought several hundred more acres of land. He and my grandmother, the former Mary Ann Thomas, had eight children, three sons and five daughters. When they married, each was given 50 acres of land and sold an adjoining 50 acres of the original plantation. Two roads divided the property and roughly formed a "T". There were three farms on the road that formed the top, short arm of the "T" and six farms along the lower, long arm of the "T". My grandparents lived about in the middle of the property, which extended one mile north and one mile south from their home. They could see four of their children's homes from their own home; the others were hidden by forest.

When my grandfather's estate was settled after my father's death, our family inherited 75 acres of land. This parcel, known as the Crow Land, was some miles away and east of the road between Lillington and Broadway. The soil was sandy and not very productive. Once a lumberman arrived at Coats, unannounced, and gave Mamma a check for $550. He had bought the timber on an adjoining tract of land belonging to an aunt and mistakenly cut the trees on our property. We eventually sold the land and I used part of the money I received to buy Dottie a string of pearls.

9

We still call them the Crow Land pearls.

I remember my grandfather sitting on the front porch of his home nursing a sore foot. He had gout, a condition I think I inherited from him.

My father's seven brothers and sisters lived their entire lives on the original farms their father gave them. Six of the farms are still owned and cultivated by my cousins.

Some of my cousins went to college and followed professional careers. One became a physician, J. Halford Patterson, M.D., and returned to Broadway, practicing medicine until he died.

The married names of my father's brothers and sisters with the number of children they had are listed below in the order of their births:

1. William Martin Patterson, 12 children.
2. Elizabeth Patterson Bird, 12 children.
3. Neill Thomas Patterson, 8 children.
4. Callie Patterson Buchanan, 10 children.
5. Lillie Patterson Thomas, 14 children.
6. Lulu Patterson Baker, 10 children.
7. John Dee Patterson, 3 children.
8. Florence Patterson Patterson, 7 children.

I seldom saw my Patterson relatives as they lived 26 miles from Coats. We visited them occasionally and in the summer, I would spend about two weeks with families who had boys near my age.

Aunt Lizzy Bird married a very successful farmer and I spent several vacations with them and their 12 children. They had many old-fashioned beehives. I remember Uncle Alec taking the honey out of the hives and giving us children some immediately. It was delicious. I fell in love with honey and eventually, in Hawaii, had my own bees.

Every Sunday when I stayed with these relatives, we attended church at the Holly Springs Baptist Church. My grandparents, William D. and Mary Ann Patterson, were among the 12 organizers of this church in 1874. The distance to the church, depending on which family I was staying with, was from one to three miles. We traveled on a wagon drawn by two mules. We first attended Sunday school at 10 a.m. and then church service. There always seemed to be more than one preacher and the worship service lasted about two hours. Afterward, a big Sunday dinner was served on tables in the churchyard under large oak trees. There was always an abundance of food that the families had brought. I remember the fried chicken, country-cured ham, biscuits, pies, cakes, all kinds of vegetables and always a half-gallon fruit jar full of honey unseparated from the honeycombs. Besides Aunt Lizzie's family, whom I usually came with, there would be several dozen other relatives present.

During one of my visits with the Birds, we went to Sanford and back in one day, a round trip of 26 miles. Traveling by mule and wagon, we carried a variety of farm produce to sell. We left two bushels each of wheat and corn at the wheat mill just outside Sanford. While we were shopping, these were ground into flour and meal which we stopped for on our way home. The mill kept about 20 percent as toll.

Several dozens of eggs, a crate of fryer-size chickens and two country-cured hams were brought along and sold to a grocery store, partly for cash and the rest in exchange for items such as sugar, spices, etc. We boys watched the mule while Uncle Alec shopped at a drug store and a dry goods store. Then, after giving the mule some water, we left for home.

The wagon seat was a board that stretched from side to side. We reached home after 6 p.m. and, after sitting for all those hours, I was uncomfortable and tired. This trip was routine for my relatives, but it was far from routine for me.

Aunt Callie Buchanan had 10 children. I liked to visit them as their children's ages almost matched ours. One of the girls married a man who worked for a tree-farming company in Louisiana. She and her husband visited us on Maui about 10 years ago.

Aunt Callie's family had lots of turkeys and when I was 16 they gave me a pair of young ones. Both of them proved to be hens, so I abandoned the idea of raising turkeys.

I visited Aunt Lulu Baker's home on several occasions. The first thing that comes to mind when I think of them is that all 10 of their children's names started with the letter "L". The next thing I think of is the Jersey bull that Uncle Everett owned. He kept this bull in a fenced area about 60 feet square that joined the regular barnyard on one side. The fence was six feet high and was constructed of eight strands of barbed-wire. At one time, there was an enclosed boarded area with a roof to protect the bull from the weather, but he had torn it down with his horns. He was very temperamental and we children kept clear of him.

One night when I was five or six, and before I had correctly figured out the biological facts of life, a cow in the barnyard gave birth to a calf. The bull became so excited he jumped the fence into the barnyard. The next morning the bull, the cow, and calf were together. My cousins and I were very interested in what had happened. I felt that this was proof that the bull was necessary for the cow to have a calf. Within a few years, I was breeding rabbits at home, the biological facts of life straightened out in my head.

When I was a teenager, Aunt Lulu's oldest son, Lewin, was a very good friend of mine. He worked as a bookkeeper in Orus's stores and owned a Model T Ford roadster. When I worked for Orus in the summer time, Lewin would generously loan me his car to go see my girlfriend.

Uncle John Dee and Aunt Bessie had three children, all sons. Their youngest son, Newell, was my age and became a school teacher. Their older two sons were H. Patterson as well as my brother McLeod, who used his first name, Harold, at that time. All three of the H. Pattersons attended Wake Forest College at the same time, causing frequent confusion. Two of them were H. M. Patterson.

Once when I was visiting in their home about 1922, we had homemade straw-berry ice cream. Uncle John Dee had bought a 30- pound block of ice in Sanford a few days before. It was packed in a wooden crate with a five-inch layer of sawdust for insulation. Very little of the ice melted on the journey home by mule and wagon.

THE FUQUAY FAMILY

The first of my mother's family arrived in this country 40 or more years later than the first of my father's family. On July 10, 1780, Count de Rochambeau landed from France accompanied by Guillaume Fouquet. This Guillaume Fouquet soon Anglicized his name to William Fuquay and was so known at the time of his marriage to Mary Hall in 1790 in Dinwiddie County, Virginia. He is my ancestor.

John Louis Fouquet, brother of William Fuquay, came to America with Lafayette. Both he and William were eyewitnesses to the surrender of Lord Cornwallis to General George Washington at Yorktown, Virginia, on October 19, 1781.

In 1810 William Fuquay and his family moved to Wake County, N.C., and settled near Sippihaw. Later, the name of this town was changed to Fuquay Springs because of nearby mineral springs that were discovered by the grandson of William Fuquay. In recent years, Fuquay Springs merged with nearby Varina and is now known as Fuquay-Varina.

William Fuquay and Mary Hall had several children. We have good information about one of his sons, but not our forefather. Therefore, the details of our family will skip one generation.

The lineage of my Fuquay ancestors is as follows:

My great-great-great-grandparents

William Fuquay   married in 1790   **Mary Hall**
(He came to America from France in 1780.)

My great-great grandfather

? Fuquay

My great-grandparents

James Fuquay   married   **Manassah Dickens**
Born Jan. 21, 1819
Died Aug. 21, 1875

My grandparents

Richard Benton Fuquay   married in 1873   **Mary Jane McLeod**
Born Mar. 27, 1850   Born July 3, 1857
Died Nov. 8, 1906   Died Nov. 27, 1926

My parents

Mattie Fuquay   married Feb. 11, 1902   **Neill Thomas Patterson**
Born Apr. 13, 1881   Born Apr. 14, 1878
Died July 26, 1964   Died Dec. 6, 1920

My Fuquay grandparents eloped when he was 23 and she was only 16. Her mother had remarried after her first husband died in a prisoner-of-war camp in the Civil War. She had several children from the second marriage and my grandmother, being the oldest child, had chores to do in the home besides field work. When Grandmother and Grandfather fell in love, they worked out a plan to run away and be married secretly, because she didn't think her mother would allow her to marry so young. Each day she fetched water from a spring in the woods and on each trip to the spring, she took some of her clothes and hid them nearby. According to plan, my grandfather met her at the spring and, packing her and her clothes on a horse, they rode off to be married.

This union produced nine children. After getting wet while working in the field, my grandfather developed pneumonia and died at age 56 in 1906. Soon after, my grandmother moved to Coats.

I knew Grandma Fuquay very well. She lived on the opposite side of town from us, but not more than a mile away. Her comfortable home had seven rooms, a well near the back porch, and a small, outside building for tools and storage. She owned half a city block and used the remaining land for a garden and to grow corn. A large chicken coop had a fenced yard, although the chickens were usually allowed the run of the entire yard.

From the time I can remember, about 1916, Grandma and her younger sister (Aunt Mag) lived there alone. Her youngest son, Uncle Leon, was already away working or in college. Unmarried, Aunt Mag spent her entire life helping Grandma care for her family. She was a very dear person and was loved by all. She developed blood poisoning from a sore on her arm and died within three days at age 71, in 1930. I was a freshman in college when she died and the emotional outpouring at her funeral was almost more than I could endure. I have been to less than a dozen funeral services. I spent my entire adult life helping the living who were sick and suffering, and I left it to others to comfort the relatives of recently deceased, loved ones.

On entering Grandma's house, the first thing seen was a hand organ the size of a small piano. To play it, the foot pedals were pumped while the key board was played like a piano. We children liked to attempt to play it, though we could only sound the notes.

Beside the organ was a spinning wheel. At the time Grandma was married, women used the spinning wheel to make thread from cotton or wool. This thread was woven on looms into cloth, which was made into clothing, as is demonstrated today in Colonial Williamsburg, Va.

From the time I was seven or eight years old, I visited Grandma to do odd jobs for her. I can't recall how much I was paid, if anything, but I do remember being praised for helping her. Later, when we got our horse, Mabel, I cultivated the corn field with a plow. When the corn was mature, I cut the stalk off above the ears and hauled the tops home for cow feed.

Fried chicken was famous in the South and it was almost always served for Sunday dinner at noon. My mother's recipe differed from today's fast food restaurants. She cooked it slowly in a pan with flour and milk until the pieces of chicken were nice and brown. There was plenty of gravy, eaten with hot biscuits or rolls.

Chicken fryers, weighing two to three pounds, were always plentiful in the spring and summer, but rare in late fall and winter. We depended on brood hens to hatch eggs from heavy-stock chickens such as Plymouth Rock or Rhode Island Reds. However, in the fall very few, if any, of our hens would sit on eggs to incubate them. It seemed that always in the fall, some of Grandma's hens would become broody. My job was to prepare a nest in a box and put in about 16 eggs. Then, after dark, I would bring Grandma's hen to our house and put her on the eggs in the nest in a corner of the washhouse. Being dark, she could not see to run away. By next morning, she had accepted the eggs and in 21 days they would hatch. These hens were good brood hens and often would remain on the nest too long. I would take them off the nest every three days for food and water, but they would always return to the nest within minutes. In this way, we could raise about 50 young frying chickens in the fall and winter.

Grandma Fuquay's schooling was interrupted by her father's death in the Civil War. When her mother remarried and had several more children, Grandma was needed at home and her schooling was neglected. She really did not learn to read and write well until she was 50 years old, according to my sister, Maisie. She and my grandfather had nine children. He died in 1906 leaving her with three sons under 15 years of age. One of these became a doctor, one a dentist and the other graduated from the University of North Carolina. He eventually was secretary of the Federal Power Commission for several years. Although Grandma was relatively poor, she helped her children financially as much as she could. More importantly, she knew the value of school and stimulated her children to get educations. The three brothers financed each other's schooling. Two worked while the third went to college until, eventually, all three graduated.

Sometime in 1923 Grandma Fuquay fell and broke her hip. The country doctor practicing in Coats treated her without taking x-rays first and recommended traction on her leg. A hole was made through the foot end of her wooden bed. A small rope was passed through this hole with one end attached to adhesive plaster that had been put on her leg and foot, and the other end attached to weights. Constant traction was maintained for many weeks, as I recall, and then she attempted to walk with crutches. About this time, she was taken for x-rays which revealed a fracture of the neck of the femur, which had not been reduced before it healed. The two ends of the bone were attached to each other on the side. Never again was she able to walk without crutches.

In 1926 when Grandma was 69 years old, she developed pernicious anemia. Although she received many transfusions from her sons, she died on November 27, 1926. At this time Minot and Murphy introduced a liver diet for the treatment of pernicious anemia. In 1927, Minot and Cohn developed a liver extract that was effective in curing the disease. The discovery of Vitamin B12 and its curative effects came a few years later. It is interesting that Grandma loved liver and ate it at every opportunity. She died just one year before liver extract was available commercially.

Aunt Ida, my mother's oldest sister, was born in 1875, two years after her parents were married. Like her mother, she married against the wishes of her parents. She bought a farm near Coats and paid for it with money that she and her 10 children made from growing cotton. She worked the fields herself on occasion, cultivating the cotton with a plow drawn by a mule. Her husband was a skilled carpenter-mason contractor who worked only sporadically. He and all five sons died before age 60, while most of the five daughters are still alive and married to successful husbands. One daughter died recently, in her 80s, after rearing a large family.

At age 78, Aunt Ida had a breast cancer removed. It had ulcerated through the skin and the lymph nodes in the axilla were greatly enlarged. She was told she had only six more months to live. Within three months, the operative site healed and the lymph node swelling disappeared. She lived to be 96 and had no further trouble with the breast cancer.

My wife and I visited Aunt Ida when she was 90 and found her busy sewing drapes for a daughter, who had an interior decorating business. She complained that it was a bit difficult to sew because her eyesight had weakened. She, like her mother, was fond of dipping snuff, a powdered tobacco that was applied to the gums. A special snuff brush was made by tearing a small branch off a particular forest shrub. When the base end of this branch was chewed on a bit, it became like a brush. After it was dipped into the can of snuff, it was placed in the mouth between the cheek and the gums.

Uncle Neill Fuquay, my mother's oldest brother, was born in 1878. He and his wife, Margaret, were delightful people with six or seven children about the ages of us Patterson children. The family lived in Lillington, where he was postmaster for several years. I spent several days as a guest in their home, and their children visited us for vacations.

Aunt Margaret's family owned lots of land. Some, by the Cape Fear River, was fenced and used as pasture for cattle, and Uncle Neill told Mamma she could put cows in the pasture for the summer if she wished. One year when I was about 12 years old, we had two heifers, four and five months old. These Jersey calves were named Esther and Jane. I can still see them: Esther was light tan and had no horns; Jane was dark brown and had horns. About the middle of April, Mamma decided we should put the calves in the pasture for the summer.

I put the high side rails on our wagon, lifted the two calves inside and left for

Lillington with our horse, Mabel, pulling the wagon. Lillington was 10 miles away and the pasture was two miles beyond. By the time I got to Uncle Neill's home, both Mabel and I were exhausted. We spent the night and returned home the next day. Six months later my brother, McLeod, went for the calves. They had grown much in six months and were fat.

I cannot recall exactly what we did with Jane, but I think she was slaughtered for beef. This was before the time of home freezers, so we probably sold part of the meat and stored the remainder at the butcher shop until we needed it.

Esther was fat when she returned from the pasture. Soon after, certain parts began to enlarge, a sure sign that she was pregnant. She was only a calf when we put her in the pasture and less than one year old when she came home. We knew there was a bull in the pasture, but young heifers normally are not mature enough for breeding. Now it was obvious that we would have a second milk cow in due time. We needed only one cow, so we could sell her.

Eventually, Esther went into labor. She still was only two thirds as large as a grown cow of her breed. After many hours of struggle, she was exhausted and could not deliver. The calf descended enough so that its head was outside, its eyes open, and it was breathing. There was no veterinarian in the area, but we engaged the services of a man who had had experience with similar cases. He got a rope around the calf's body and, with great force, it was extracted. Esther was in shock and the calf was alive and normal.

For days Esther barely ate or drank, lying on her side with feet outstretched. We changed her position daily from side to side, put new straw beneath her, and fed her fresh alfalfa. About the fifth day, she became very distended, her abdomen swollen like a barrel, and she could barely breathe. I thought this swelling was due to infection. The man caring for her said there was no hope and she would soon die. However, he said he could make her more comfortable by releasing the gas from her stomach so she could breathe easier.

After cleaning an area on her side, he inserted a large needle through the skin and, apparently, into the distended stomach. A large cloud of foul smelling gas escaped through the needle and the abdomen collapsed. She was able to breathe easier but was expected to die during the night.

Four hours later, Esther appeared much improved. She ate hungrily and drank water freely. She improved daily. She assumed a normal lying position and, within a few days, was able to stand. She accepted her newborn calf and nursed it.

In spite of our turning Esther from side to side daily, she had developed large ulcers on both sides. These were treated, but took several weeks to heal.

Finally, Esther had recovered and was producing over two gallons of milk daily. Her calf was growing normally. Mamma advertised that she had a cow and calf for sale, and one day when I returned home from school, they were gone. They had sold for $100.

I recently discussed this cow's illness with a rancher friend. He told me he had seen many similar cases not associated with calving. Apparently if a cow eats a large amount of fresh, green clover, it can sour in one of her two stomachs and cause distention. He told me he had treated many cows by putting a large needle through the skin into the stomach, just as was done by our attendant, and the cows would recover. So, the fresh alfalfa we generously fed Esther after her difficult calving may have caused her distention and near demise.

My Aunt Lilla, born in 1883, was two years younger than my mother and described as a very beautiful person. She died of pneumonia at age 22, unmarried.

My mother was grieved by her death and spoke lovingly of her all her life. In her later years, Mamma wrote the following poem:

My Sister

When she was five and I was seven,
We strolled the fields together,
With the trill of the bluebird o'er our heads,
No wild flower escaped our sight.

We made hats of leaves pinned with straws
And trimmed them with wild flowers gay,
Wild asters and goldenrod bedecked the hills
And strawberries grew by the way.

Thrift and industry reigned in our home,
Our mother was busy all day;
At the wheel and loom she toiled
While we went out to play.

This sister of mine so beautiful
And gentle beyond compare!
Had loving eyes of deepest blue,
And a crown of golden hair.

I want to go back to this childhood place,
And follow the stream as it glides
Through the rolling pastures green,
And gather wild flowers by its side.

My sister will not be there, I know
But I could stop by that quiet place
And spend awhile in the shade of the tree
That stands where her body rests.

Long years have passed since she left us
To live in a better clime,
But I shall not forget those parting words
"The Angels have come to take me home."

—Mattie Fuquay Patterson

My Uncle June, as we called him, was christened Junius Benton Fuquay. He was born in 1886. During his late teens or early twenties, he had a ruptured appendix which was not operated on. He survived, but continued to have much abdominal pain until, after World War I, he went to the Johns Hopkins Hospital in Baltimore and had a successful operation. Sometime after graduating from high school he took a one-year business course.

Uncle June never married. I remember his favorite saying about eligible girls he was courting: "She was feeding too fast so I had to ditch her." When he was about

16

30, he seriously considered marrying. He visited in his girlfriend's home for a week and became gravely ill, apparently from severe flu. His fiancee and her mother, worrying that he would die, suggested he give her his large diamond ring that he had planned to give her later. This was too much for him. After he recovered, he left and never returned.

In 1920, my father owned a lot of stock in the Ideal Brick Co. of Slocomb, N.C., near Fayetteville. Uncle June was manager of the brickmill. After the depression, the corporate structure of the company reorganized with Uncle June and Lloyd Langdon each owning 50 percent. They worked diligently building the company into a thriving business. Uncle June sold his share to his partner and moved to Mercedes, Texas.

He visited us only once in 15 years, driving a fancy Rickenbacker coupe that had the "Hat in the Ring" emblem on the radiator. The cover for the rear-mounted spare tire had two words painted on it, Adios Amigos. When he was ready to return to Mercedes, he suggested I accompany him. I think this was in August, 1928, when I was 16 years old. He offered to pay my expenses while I was with him. Then I was to hitchhike back to North Carolina paying my own way. After much hesitation, my mother agreed to let me go. Hitchhiking by college students was popular and relatively safe at the time.

I packed a small suitcase and we left. I had $70 in my pocket.

We hoped to drive the 450 miles to Atlanta the first day. After 10 p.m., a few miles outside of town, Uncle June fell asleep at the wheel and we went into a ditch. I was asleep as well and remember the rude awakening. We were uninjured, but the right side of the car was damaged and the front axle was bent.

After three days in Atlanta getting the car repaired, we were on the road again with Montgomery, Alabama, our next stop. I remember driving through Mobile and going across Lake Pontchartrain on a cement bridge 27 miles long. This is said to be the longest bridge in the U.S. and maybe in the world. We were soon in Texas and drove through Houston. From there to Mercedes, which is not far from the Mexican border near Brownsville, the road seemed endless. We would drive about 50 miles without a turn in the road. Then, we would cross the railroad tracks and drive another 50 miles without a turn. It was August and temperature was over 100 F. There was no air-conditioning in the cars in those days.

Finally, we reached Mercedes in mid-afternoon. Uncle June picked up his mail and a letter from my mother was waiting. She was concerned that I had gone with him and worried about my catching rides for the 2000-plus miles home. Uncle June made inquiries at the hotel where he was staying and learned that an older man and a college student were leaving the next morning for Alabama. They were driving nonstop and invited me to go with them. I would pay one-third of the expense for gasoline and oil and for my own food. This was almost too good to be true so I accepted.

Uncle June showed me around Mercedes and we drove to the border to see the Rio Grande River. He took me to a house that he owned in town where several grapefruit trees grew in the yard. He picked a ripe fruit and we ate it just like a sweet orange, unlike the Florida grapefruit.

The next morning at six, the three of us were on the road that I had come in on the day before. The day was hot and, although there was little of interest to see, I did see my first armadillo by the roadside.

The car was an older model Chevrolet touring car. Even though the owner would allow us to drive only 35 miles per hour, we drove continually and soon covered many miles. We took turns driving. Crossing the bridge over Lake Pontchartrain, it seemed longer this time because of our slow speed. Our route took us through Pensacola, the only time I have ever been in the State of Florida. The car owner's sister lived in an area near Andalusia, Alabama.

I spent the night in the sister's home and the next morning, after a good breakfast of fresh mangos, I was taken to the highway to catch a ride.

I do not remember my exact route, but I must have come back through Atlanta. I made good progress and spent my nights in small hotels. I do remember standing on a corner in Gainsville, Ga., and watching a Chevrolet touring car with two men pass me several times. When they finally picked me up, one man got in the rear seat where there was a shotgun on the floor. I sat in front beside the driver. When we passed a wagon being drawn by a mule, which I had noticed earlier while I was standing on the corner, I was told that there was a whiskey still on the wagon and it was being transferred from one side of town to the other. Well-camouflaged, it appeared that someone was moving household effects. The two in the car were watching to see that the police or anyone else did not interfere. This ride was for only a few miles.

My next ride was in a Model T Ford touring car carrying 330 dozen eggs. The driver bought fresh eggs from the farmers and took them to Asheville, N. C., where he sold them to grocery stores. Our route took us to Asheville without going through South Carolina. The pavement was white cement and the mountainous road, with its many curves, was steeply banked. The tires were not fully inflated, giving the eggs a softer ride, and the driver was in a hurry. As we rounded the sharp curves, the rims of the wheels would strike the cement pavement. We arrived in Asheville safely and went our separate ways.

I hitchhiked to Charlotte where I checked at the bus station and learned I had enough money to buy a ticket to Sanford, where I had been working for my brother. I took the bus and arrived about 9 p.m. Next day, I called Mamma, who was relieved I had returned safely.

We did not see Uncle June for a long time after that. In 1939, Mamma and my younger brother, Neill, drove to Mercedes on their way to California and Hawaii. They stopped to visit Uncle June and ended up taking him with them. They were on their way to visit my brother, McLeod, taking him a new Buick. He was practicing medicine near Hilo, Hawaii, and had purchased the car from the factory through the local dealer. My wife and I moved to Hawaii July 5, 1939, but Uncle June had already returned home by then.

After a few years, Uncle Garner got word from Mercedes that Uncle June was sick and destitute. Uncle Garner went to Texas and brought him home. He visited all his relatives and shortly afterward, committed suicide.

Aunt Edith was born in 1889. She married Carl H. Young, M.D., about 1915, and lived with him in Angier, N.C., about 10 miles from Coats. She had gone to business college for one year and worked for my father in the Bank of Coats before marriage. She was a delightful person and a smart businesswoman, a great help to her husband in his many endeavors.

Dr. Young, as we called him, was an exceptional country doctor. He had a strong influence on me before and after I decided to study medicine. Though he was a relative by marriage, I am including him in my heritage because of the enormous role he played in my family when I was young.

I remember Dr. Young as a short, fat man. He was only about 5 feet 5 inches tall and weighed about 200 pounds. When he had to make a house call in our vicinity, he often stopped in to see us. He had taught himself to play the piano using only the four fingers on each hand. His favorite number was "Turkey in the Straw" which he would always play for us children.

In 1921, two months after my father's death, my one-year-old sister, Dorothy, developed diphtheria. The severe infection was in the larynx. A thick membrane, formed by this infection, obstructs the larynx, resulting in a crowing sound when the child breathes. In fatal cases, the child dies of toxicity from the infection or chokes to death, or a combination of the two. About 5 p.m., the doctor caring for Dorothy told us it appeared she would not survive the night.

Because of a previous tragedy in our family, Dr. Young had alerted my mother to ask the doctor to call him for a consultation if any serious emergency arose. Dr. Young was called and came in the evening. He said my sister would have to be taken to Rex Hospital in Raleigh immediately, and that she might need a tracheotomy.

The current owner of the Paterson car was contacted and arrangements were made to leave for Raleigh. This was an open touring car, and it was a cold night in February. It was decided the open car would help my sister get more air. The driver, my mother and Dorothy left about 11 p.m. and arrived in Raleigh two hours later. The 30-mile route was unpaved and scarred with deep wheel ruts.

The doctors immediately put a breathing tube through my sister's larynx down into her trachea. A tracheotomy was not required. For about a week, diphtheria antitoxin was given in large amounts intravenously through scalp veins. My mother remained at the hospital until Dorothy recovered. Sixty-eight years later, my sister has had no residual ill effects from the diphtheria.

At home, the rest of us children were quarantined. A public health official posted a sign by our front door, throat cultures were examined, and we were each administered a large syringe full of toxin-antitoxin. I can still see the long needle being inserted deep into our thigh muscles. I cannot remember how long we were quarantined, but finally we returned to school.

My mother returned home with Dorothy, who looked a bit different because much of her scalp had been shaven. Both were smiling and happy. My mother had survived two catastrophic events within two months. She again demonstrated that she had nerves of steel and a heart of gold. She did not complain, but immediately shouldered her responsibilities and moved ahead. About 30 years later when she was in her seventies, she wrote the following poem about Dorothy's illness:

A Child of Prayer

There in that isolated room we stood
The doctor, the nurse, and I
While we watched as the color faded
From the face of my darling child.

"I have done all I can for your child"
The doctor said, and he left the room,
There was nothing left for the nurse to do,
But watch and wait for changes to come.

My thoughts went back to the children at home
They were praying for the child and me,
And waiting for some word of hope
And wondering when it would be.

19

I fell on my knees by the bedside
And there in that lonely room
I poured out my heart to the Saviour
And asked that "Thy will be done."

The nurse busied herself about the room
While I watched for a ray of hope
I felt that God was listening
To the prayers of the children back home.

The night wore on, I looked again at the child;
And it seemed that a light from Heaven shone over her face
And her beautiful eyes beamed wide.
Peace filled my soul, I would soon go home
With the little one close by my side

—Mattie Fuquay Patterson

In 1920, Dr. Young developed diabetes mellitus. Even on a low carbohydrate diet with gluten bread he lost weight. He was no longer the fat, jolly person that he had been and it appeared that he was succumbing to this disease.

In 1923, the discovery of insulin earned Banting and McLeod of Canada the Nobel Prize.

Insulin did not become commercially available immediately. Knowing he needed it, Dr. Young went to Canada to see Drs. Banting and Best. They gave him a supply of insulin for his own use 18 months before it could be purchased publicly. He took 40 units daily, recovered, gained the weight he had lost, and resumed normal activity. I remember that sometimes he would arrive at our home for a visit and remain in the car for 10 minutes before coming into the house. He had taken too much insulin and had had a mild reaction. He would eat some candy and wait for his blood sugar to return to normal.

Dr. Young didn't develop the serious complications of diabetes mellitus in spite of being severely ill at first. He was obese. Being a physician, he probably learned how to take care of himself properly before insulin was available and with insulin he could live a normal life. He worked doubly hard and lived 40 years after developing diabetes.

He had an office across the street from his home, but spent much of his practice in the patients' homes. He seemed to know when to send patients to Rex Hospital 20 miles away in Raleigh. He would not let patients die at home when possible lifesaving treatment was available at the hospital. After deciding to study medicine, I spent several days with him. I can recall making a call with him to see a man who had been vomiting for 12 hours. He had the cardinal symptoms of acute myocardial infarction, which was Dr. Young's diagnosis. After giving the patient morphine, we put him in our car and within an hour he was in the hospital under the care of a specialist.

Another house call, on a hot summer afternoon in August, involved three black boys who had typhoid fever. They had lost weight, their faces were gaunt, the whites of their eyes were large, and the eyes appeared to protrude from their sockets. I can still see them. If my memory is correct, they all recovered with treatment.

Dr. Young delivered many babies in the home, as many as 25 in one month. Rarely did he have to send a woman to the hospital for a cesarean. The women came to his office for prenatal checks. Sometimes, he would have two women in labor at the same time, 10 miles apart. I accompanied him on some of these home deliveries in the country. Immediately after arriving he would have his instruments boiled on the kitchen stove in case he needed them. I remember one patient, living 10 miles away, who was in labor for 48 hours before delivering. The baby's head was badly misshapen at first, from an occiput-posterior position, but it soon returned to normal.

Dr. Young practiced medicine through two severe depressions, one in 1920 and one in 1929. Many of the patients had no money to pay for his services, but he never refused to treat them. He told me that, in spite of being a busy doctor, he would be a poor man if he had depended upon income from the practice of medicine.

Tobacco farming is big in this area of North Carolina. Dr. Young inherited some farm land, then he and Aunt Edith bought more land as they were able, until they owned about 30 farms growing approximately 500 acres of tobacco. He furnished the land, farmhouse and fertilizer, and sharecroppers furnished the livestock and all the labor. At one time, Dr. Young was the biggest tobacco farmer in the State of North Carolina. When tobacco control legislation was being studied during President Franklin D. Roosevelt's administration, Dr. Young was invited to Washington to help the legislators formulate the rules for this control. I think these rules are still in effect today.

Uncle Lewis was born in 1892 and graduated from the University of Richmond Medical College. His younger brothers, Uncles Garner and Leon, worked in a munitions plant in Danville, Virginia, and financed his medical education. He received a commendation from President Woodrow Wilson after serving overseas in World War I.

After the war, Uncle Lewis married a nurse, moved to New Mexico, and worked for a mining company taking care of the employees and their families. The pay was good and they prospered. In school, he had been a good baseball pitcher and he continued playing on town teams after becoming a physician. In New Mexico, he pitched and won both ends of a double-header in one day.

Eventually, Uncle Lewis, his wife and three small children returned to Coats where he began practicing. He had an excellent bedside manner and his patients loved him. When I was 13, he took me in his blue and white Hupmobile roadster to Rex Hospital where I had a Baker's cyst removed from my right knee. He once treated me for a broken nose after a baseball struck me and when we left his office to go home, I fainted. By the time I recovered, I was home.

Two patients he treated stand out in my memory. One was a drunk who had fallen through the plate glass window of a store in Coats. With deep cuts on his neck and a severed jugular vein, he was taken to Uncle Lewis's office, which was nearby. The bleeding was quickly controlled and the cuts were repaired with hundreds of stitches. The whole town was impressed with the way Uncle Lewis had saved this man's life.

Another patient, who lived on a farm near our home, had typhoid fever when she was six months pregnant. He treated her at home and was justly pleased when she recovered and delivered a normal baby, also at home.

A chain cigarette smoker, Uncle Lewis developed cancer of the larynx and died at age 49.

Uncle Garner was born in 1894. During World War I, he worked in the munitions plant in Danville, then entered the Army. After the war, he worked to help send Uncle Leon to college. Eventually, Aunt Edith, Uncle Lewis and Uncle Leon helped underwrite his undergraduate work at the university at Chapel Hill. He studied dentistry at Emory University in Atlanta, and returned to Coats to practice. He was the only dentist in town and a very good one. He owned the only x-ray machine in town and often x-rayed fractures for the medical doctors. I remember riding bareback on our horse, Mabel, and falling off, injuring my right ankle. Uncle Garner x-rayed it for a possible fracture and, although none was found, I had to walk with crutches for several weeks. In 1932, he put a gold cap on one of my front teeth that had been chipped while I was boxing in college. It is still in place after 57 years and has never given me any trouble.

Uncle Garner and Aunt Gladys had two children. Cecil, their son, provided the above information about his father's and uncle's education. The daughter died of pneumonia at 18 months of age.

Uncle Garner and Aunt Gladys built a home in Coats which burned while they were away. A quiet and kind person, Uncle Garner was elected mayor of Coats several times, though he never sought the office. He was a great help to my mother after my father died. Sadly, he and Aunt Gladys were killed in an auto accident in 1948.

Uncle Leon was born in 1899. He had beautiful, blond, curly hair throughout his life. He married late and never had children. Aunt Ida, his oldest sister, was 24 years old when he was born, and was married, with several children of her own.

Uncle Leon graduated from the University of North Carolina at Chapel Hill, where he played second base on the baseball team. In the summer, he played second base for a Coats team on which Uncle Garner played shortstop, Uncle Lewis was pitcher, and Paul Green, who lived near Coats, played third base. In 1927, Paul Green won the Pulitzer Prize for "Abraham's Bosom", and won wide acclaim for his symphonic drama. His "Lost Colony" is presented as a pageant each summer at Fort Raleigh, near Manteo, North Carolina. In 1931, Paul Green was one of my professors at Chapel Hill.

Uncle Leon became the private secretary of Senator Simmons of North Carolina, the senior senator in the U.S. Senate. He remained with him five years, until the senator's death. After holding several positions in Washington, he became the permanent executive secretary of the Federal Power Commission, which position he held for several years and until his retirement. While working in Washington, he attended night school to study law, though he never achieved a law degree.

Uncle Leon was only four years older than my brother, Orus. He had moved to Coats about 1907; our family moved there in 1912. In close contact with us through-out his life, he married Page Leonard, a friend of my sister, Maisie. When I was in medical school in Philadelphia, I occasionally ran out of cash. Knowing it took three weeks to get money from McLeod in Hawaii, I would write Uncle Leon for a loan for a few weeks and he always obliged. After I was married and in a hospital residency in Philadelphia, I still found it necessary to call on him for small loans.

In 1955, Dottie and I, with our daughters, visited Washington and stayed at the Shoreham Hotel, close to Uncle Leon's home. Our two youngest daughters, Dottie Jane and Carol, ages 11 and 9, stayed with them one night. Next day, Dottie Jane said they didn't want to stay there, because they had to sleep with a large "poke chop". We learned that Uncle Leon had bought a large country-cured ham and had stored it on the dresser in the cool guest bedroom.

_____ *THE GRAHAM FAMILY*

(my wife's family)

Dottie's paternal great-grandparents came from Scotland.

Dottie's paternal grandfather, David Graham, was born at Blaine, Pennsylvania. At the age of 15, he joined the Union Army serving as a drummer boy in the Civil

War. He and his Irish wife, Elizabeth, had eight children. One of these was John Frederick Graham, Dottie's father.

Dottie's maternal great-grandparents were William B. Price and Elsie Ritter, from either the British Isles or Germany.

Dottie's maternal grandparents were Daniel Price and Jane Martin. Her grandfather was born September 28, 1854, the youngest of ten children. The Price family lived on a farm near Lewistown, Pennsylvania. Of five children, the fourth was Dottie's mother, Nellie Bertha Price.

Dottie's parents met while teaching at the same small school and were married in early 1900. They moved to a newly built home at 630 Highland Avenue in Lewistown, where they lived the rest of their lives. They had ten children.

John Frederick Graham   married in 1900   **Nellie Bertha Price**
Born Dec. 20, 1877   Born July 22, 1881
Died Dec. 31, 1930   Died Nov. 8, 1975

Children:

Clifford Price Graham
Born Sept. 25, 1900
Died July 12, 1960

Helen Mary Graham
Born Feb. 20, 1902
Died June 8, 1983

John Frederick Graham II
Born May 4, 1903
Died June 4, 1903

Martha Jane Harkinson
Born Sept. 13, 1904

Margaret Sara Graham
Born Dec. 28, 1907
Died Oct. 29, 1918

Josephine Graham Artman
Born Sept. 3, 1910

Lois Nell Graham
Born Mar. 17, 1913
Died June 17, 1930

Neff William Graham
Born Apr. 15, 1915

Dorothy Graham Patterson
Born Apr. 15, 1917

Pauline Graham Prough
Born June 8, 1919

CHAPTER II

My Parents

YOUTH AND SCHOOL YEARS

My father, Neill Thomas Patterson, was the third of eight children born to William D. and Mary Ann Patterson. He was born April 14, 1878, and died December 6, 1920. He was born and reared at the McCoy Place, about 10 miles north of Barbecue Presbyterian Church in Western Harnett County, N.C., five miles east of Broadway. This is the area where our ancestor, Duncan Patterson, had resettled in 1758. The McCoy Place is just north of U.S. Highway No. 421 that goes from Lillington to Sanford near Holly Springs Baptist Church.

Papa attended school in Broadway. He graduated from Broadway Normal School which taught regular high school courses and prepared its students to teach the elementary grades. He then took a one-year business course at Buies Creek Academy, Buies Creek, N.C., (now Campbell University) and taught school for a year or more.

My mother, Mattie Fuquay, was the third of nine children of Richard Benton and Mary Jane Fuquay. The Fuquay farm was located on Long Branch Road, three miles north of Broadway, and one and a half miles north of Juniper Spring Church.

Mamma may have attended Hickory Level School, a one-room school one mile north of her home. Later, she attended school in Broadway, and related many times how she walked three miles to school, sometimes in the rain and snow, if her father was unable to take her by horse and buggy.

In 1885, Broadway School had only one teacher. In 1890, after Professor Malcolm McLeod was hired as principal along with two assistant teachers, the reputation of the school spread and more teachers were added. The school eventually became Broadway Normal School, supported entirely by subscription. Later, it became a county-supported school for six months and a subscription-supported school for three more months. It had two dormitories for boarding students and a club where students cooked their own meals. Older students were taught English, Latin, and algebra to prepare them for college. Many became school teachers, qualifying as teachers for the first, second and third grades by taking examinations in 12 subjects. I have photocopies of the results of the examinations that Mamma took to teach the first grade in Chatham, Moore and Lee Counties. She was an excellent student, with perfect scores in spelling and definition.

Professor McLeod was an idol of my mother. His students were not only well-grounded in the rudiments of education, but he inspired them to better living and greater accomplishments.[4] Many became lawyers, doctors, teachers, and ministers.

After graduation, Mamma was accepted to attend the Woman's College of the University of North Carolina at Greensboro. However, when she was supposed to leave for college, a typhoid fever epidemic developed, and her father was afraid to let her go. Her new trunk, packed with school clothes, now belongs to my nephew. Giving up the idea of going to college, she became a first grade teacher. Her salary the first year was $21 per month; afterward, it increased to $25. She tutored her landlord's children, for which she received room and board.

Papa was exactly three years older than Mamma. They both attended Broadway

School, but apparently did not know each other when they were young as their homes were about four miles apart, on different roads leading out of Broadway, and they attended different churches.

_____MARRIAGE AND YEARS UP TO 1912

The first time Mamma saw Papa as an adult, they were attending a teacher's meeting and sitting on opposite sides of the room. Seeing Papa's bright red hair and blue eyes, she thought to herself that he would be the last person she would marry. When they met, her opinion changed. I have photocopies of letters Papa wrote to Mamma dated June 6, 1898, and August 17, 1901. After a courtship of over three years, they were married February 2, 1902.

Papa's father gave him 50 acres of land and sold him an additional adjoining 50 acres just north of the family homesite and across the road from a similar tract given to Aunt Lulu Baker. Aunt Lizzie Bird owned a similar farm just north of these two tracts of land.

Before marriage, Papa had already built and paid for a three-room house on his land and had started farming. Eventually, a second house was built for a tenant to live in and farm the land. In her 70s, Mamma wrote the following poem about her married life that started in this three-room cottage.

In Appreciation

In a little three-room cottage
Where the ground was not too smooth,
We started our quest for happiness
Out seaward on the boat of inexperience.

Here we learned the joy of toil and service
While children romped outside the door;
Music from little voices filled the air,
And flowers bloomed forevermore.

Years passed, and broader horizons were sought
To meet life's increasing needs;
Burdens were heavy - battles were fought,
As we felt we must succeed.

When I look back o'er the road I've traveled
It seems terribly dreary and long,
One by one my friends have departed,
There are only a few left behind.

Many times I have been near the brink
And the way seemed dark just ahead;
But an unseen Hand was guiding
And brightening the path where it lead.

It took faith and courage to travel
This road so lonely and rough;
But the ones who have come to my rescue
Are true and loyal - that is enough.

And now that the journey is ending,
And the goal is nearly in sight
The blessings received have been worthy
Of all efforts put forth in the fight.

Sons and daughters to comfort and cheer
Are more than I deserve, I confess;
But to their faithful work and cooperation,
I feel, I owe my success.

—Mattie Fuquay Patterson

My sister, Maisie, tells me that our family had the first telephone in the neighborhood and the only one for years. It hung on the wall in the kitchen and neighbors came often to use it.

Mamma described Papa as a visionary who always was looking ahead and investigating new business opportunities. He was not satisfied to be a farmer as most of his ancestors had been since coming to America in 1740. The business course at Buies Creek Academy had prepared him for a business career.

A staunch Republican, Papa served one term as clerk of the court at Lillington. After this term, the Republican Party was not in power in Harnett County for 35 years, until the late 1930s.

Apparently, Papa's first business adventure was a small country store that also served as a local post office. Broadway was five miles away by horse and buggy. Papa built a small building by the road on the corner of the family property and stocked it with commonly used staples. He was often away and, because the store was locked, customers would come to the kitchen door. Mamma would then unlock the store to serve them.

Papa worked in a general store in Broadway until the Bank of Broadway was founded in 1909. He worked there for three years, gaining experience in banking.

Four of my brothers and sisters were born while my family lived in their original home:

Orus - Feb. 13, 1903
Velma - Apr. 19, 1905
Maisie Jane - Oct. 5, 1907
Harold McLeod - Feb. 13, 1910.

Mamma told me that when she went into labor in the evening before Orus was born, a snow storm was raging. The doctor in Broadway was called, but because of the heavy snow, he wouldn't come until daylight. Orus was born during the night and the doctor arrived the next morning. Some months later, Mamma had to travel some 30 miles to Fayetteville by horse and buggy to have tissues repaired that were damaged during the delivery.

My four older brothers and sisters have always been amused by the names they were given. Apparently, my parents did not want to give them common names, feeling that, with an average of over nine children in each family, cousins would often have the same names. No one knows where they found the names Orus, Velma, and Maisie. Harold McLeod did not like his first name, and in recent years used H. McLeod. After some research, he found that Harold and Leod were the names of kings of Norway. Neill McLeod was my mother's grandfather as I mentioned in the section on my mother's heritage. It is apparent that my parents had researched the subject of names.

I was given the names of both my grandfathers, William D. Patterson and Richard Benton Fuquay. My brother, Preston, was named for a friend of my father, and Neill was named for our father. My older sisters chose the name Dorothy for our youngest sister. The name means a Gift of God and, after four consecutive baby brothers, she was indeed a welcome gift of God.

Patterson Home 1915, Coats, N. C.

_____MOVE TO COATS, N.C., IN 1912 TO NEW HOME

In February, 1912, our family moved to Coats, a distance of 26 miles. My sister, Maisie, was four and a half and remembers the cold and snowy trip by horse and covered buggy. Heated bricks wrapped in cloth kept their feet warm while they snuggled in woolen robes. The household effects and furniture were moved in wagons drawn by mules.

Our house was incomplete, so the family moved into the Whittington house, one block from Coats Baptist Church on one side and one block from Grandma Fuquay's home on the other. I was born in this house April 21, 1912. There was no doctor in Coats; one was called from Benson, 10 miles away.

When I was born, my parents had not decided on a name, so the doctor reported to the Bureau of Vital Statistics that a baby boy had been born to my mother on that day. When I went for a birth certificate 25 years later, I learned that my birth had not been recorded. Luckily, my mother was with me. She certified that I was the baby born to her on April 21, 1912, and I was issued a birth certificate. I have a birth registration card stating I was born April 21, 1912, my birth was recorded October 2, 1937, and the registration card was issued September 17, 1953.

By June 1912, our house was completed. My father had drawn the plans for a large stylish house. He envisioned a southern, colonial-type plantation house with columns, seven large rooms on the first floor, and a large hall about 10 feet wide. The second floor had four large rooms and a similar wide hall. Wide, covered porches ran along the east, south, and west sides of the house and small columns supported the roof. On the second floor, balconies about 10 by 12 feet extended out over the porch on the east and south sides. Gabled roofs above the balconies were supported by a pair of columns at each outside corner. The roof of the house was steep and covered with sections of tin creased together. It was leak-proof, but had to be painted about every three years. There was a tremendous amount of wasted space in the attic, enough for a third floor. My father got what he wanted, but he was not an architect.

The house was made of the best materials, primarily heart lumber from long-leaved pine, with a diagonal layer of tongue-and-groove storm sheathing beneath the outside wall. The inside walls were smooth, unpainted white plaster. The family room had a wooden wainscot three feet high.

Fireplaces in the two downstairs bedrooms, parlor, and family room provided heat, while the upstairs room had wood-burning heaters. The kitchen range burned wood or coal, producing adequate heat. A large kerosene heater, normally in the bathroom, sometimes had to be moved to the large pantry by the dining room to keep the jars of canned fruits and vegetables from freezing.

Aladdin lamps were used at first for light. They had special wicks that burned gasoline under pressure, giving off a very bright light.

The house was built with a large bathroom, but fixtures were not installed for some time. Water was drawn from the well on the back porch using a bucket on a chain attached to a pulley.

When the house was built, a small combination washhouse-smokehouse was erected about 100 feet behind it. The building materials matched the main house, and they were painted the same color. On laundry day, clothes were boiled in a large black pot over a furnace connected to a chimney.

Soon after we moved into our home, Papa made arrangements to pump water from a large spring on the Reverend Tom Coats' property a block away. An hydraulic ram pumped the water up a steep hill into a large elevated tank behind our house. No outside source of power was needed. Pressure from a large column of water in one part of the ram forced a smaller column of water up a pipe in another part. This action repeated as water continued entering the ram. Finally, water reached the tank.

With water now available, bathroom fixtures were installed as well as a large sink and sideboard in the kitchen. A wash basin was placed at the end of the hall by the entrance to the dining room and water lines were run to the washhouse and barn. A hot-water-jacket was installed by the firebox in the kitchen range and connected to an 80-gallon storage tank. Finally, we had hot and cold running water, the first home in town to have such.

As far as I can learn, this system worked well for about two years, until the water tank was blown over and destroyed during a storm. By this time, Papa owned a mill complex (sawmill, planing mill, and grain mill) in the center of town, six blocks

29

from our home. Water to run the steam engines in the mills was pumped from the spring near our home and stored in a large, high, water tank. A pipe connected this tank to our home, supplying us with adequate water. I cannot remember when the connecting pipe was installed, as I was too young, but I do remember its removal about 1918, after we began pumping water from our own well.

The front of the house was two feet above the ground, the rear about five feet. Cold penetrated the single layer of flooring and when the outside temperature dropped below freezing, the fireplaces could not adequately heat the house.

Papa continued to make improvements and about 1916, three major projects were started: a new heating system, an electrical system, and a new water system. A large basement was dug under the central part of the house. Access was through a door and down stairs built below the staircase that led to the second floor. The basement was large enough for a furnace with one large register in the back hall, an electrical generating plant with large two-volt storage batteries in series, and a tank to store water from our own well. The flue from the furnace connected to the fireplace in the back bedroom, which required it to be sealed. A brick wall was built underneath the house, enclosing the space entirely except for the area under the porch. A large coal chute opened to the outside of the house on the north side.

Our home was the first in town to have electricity. Two wires ran from room to room along the ceiling, and the generating plant came on automatically when the usage was high. A chandelier hung in the family room. An outlet in the kitchen supplied electricity for an iron and for an electric churn.

A pump was installed in a small enclosure by the well. A shaft was connected to a valve at the bottom of the well, 65 feet deep. The pump was driven by an electric motor connected to a wide, leather belt, and the motor was controlled automatically by the water pressure. Often the motor continued to turn after the pump had stopped, and the belt would then burn and have to be replaced.

Papa bought an automobile as soon as they were available in 1914. Both Maisie and McLeod say the family's first car was a Hupmobile. It had brass rods from the front of the top to the front fenders and a honking-type horn on the driver's side, outside the car. Papa took the family for a ride the day he bought it. Roads were sandy with deep wheel ruts, and on the way back, he lost control of the car and struck a tree.

A garage was built near the washhouse, with roof and walls constructed of sheets of galvanized iron. The floor was made of boards with a center pit almost four feet wide, enabling a mechanic to make repairs underneath the car. When my sisters learned to drive, they had difficulty avoiding the pit. As Maisie said, the hole in the center of the garage caused a lot of trouble.

Our second car was a Saxon, which I remember. It was a conventional-type touring car equipped with curtains to be used in rainy weather. After this came a seven-passenger Paterson, made in Paterson, New Jersey. It, too, was a touring car that had two folding seats behind the front seat. Papa then bought a second car, a Ford coupe which had only one seat. It was completely enclosed with glass windows, and had a trunk at the rear with a perfectly flat lid. A spare tire and rim were mounted behind the trunk. I have a picture of this car.

_MY FATHER'S BUSINESS ADVENTURES AT COATS

Papa was a planner and a dreamer. His father was a farmer with massive landholdings that he had bought with his own earnings. Papa and his seven brothers and sisters were each given a farm, but with an education in business, Papa was not content to be a farmer like his siblings. He had learned merchandising and banking at Broadway. There was no bank in Coats and there he saw an opportunity. After moving to Coats in 1912, he organized and founded the Bank of Coats and later opened a branch at Buies Creek. He also ran a fire insurance agency from the bank.

One of the small businesses that Papa attempted was raising rabbits. He had hutches built under the chinaberry trees near our home and stocked Belgian hares. The rabbits dug tunnels under the wire enclosures and soon roamed free in our yard and gardens. They chewed the bark off several young apple trees in the orchard, killing them. Papa promptly gave up the idea of raising rabbits.

Neill Thomas Patterson
circa 1918, age 40

The bank was a success from the start. In the surrounding area, many farmers needed cash in the spring to buy seed and fertilizer. In the summer and fall, money was needed to pay farmhands to cultivate and harvest the crops. Saving accounts paid three or four percent interest while loans cost eight percent. When the harvested crops were sold, the loans were repaid.

As cotton was the main crop grown in the area, Papa felt a cotton gin might by a good investment. This was one of the first businesses he started and it thrived.

There was much virgin forest in the region, especially long-leaved pine, so a sawmill and planing mill were his next enterprises. When trucks were available, logs were brought from as far as 10 miles. A railroad spur connecting with the Durham and Southern Railroad was installed by the planing mill and lumber was shipped to all parts of the state.

Steam engines were used to operate the mill's machinery. Water was pumped from the large spring near our home and stored in a large, elevated tank. Eventually, this turned into another venture, supplying water to other businesses and a few homes.

The pressures of all these enterprises were so great that Papa took in a partner on equal terms to operate the mills and cotton gin. He realized that with a partner he could devote more time to the bank and to developing other businesses.

Second to cotton in acreage in this area were corn and wheat. A mill was needed to process them into flour and meal, and this was Papa's next enterprise. A large building, about three stories tall, was constructed near the sawmill and cotton gin. The outside walls were corrugated iron, painted red. I remember taking corn to this mill and having it ground.

Another business Papa started was a yarn factory employing several women. I do not recall much about this operation other than its location on the second floor in a building on the main street of Coats.

I do remember a window shade factory Papa had on the second floor of another building. I recall visiting it and remember the different colored shades.

Papa owned a large block of stock of a large brick mill at Slocomb, N.C., near Fayetteville. After his death and the depression, the stock was almost worthless.

Mamma gave the stock to Uncle June, enabling him to own 50% of the brick mill.

Papa had another partner in the real estate business at Coats. They owned several farms operated by sharecroppers and, although McLeod thinks they had only one or two farms, I think they owned more.

In addition to these farms, Papa farmed some land himself, hiring most of the help to cultivate it. I remember he had a large field of cotton about three miles from our home. We children helped clean the grass from the fields and finally picked the cotton. I had malaria fever about this time, at the age of five or six. I remember having a chill one day and resting in the shade of a tree until the end of the day.

Papa was continually investigating new opportunities and making plans for the future. In 1919, he spent a lot of time with a new partner studying and making plans to build a railroad in North Carolina from east to west. This man spent two days at Christmas in our home. Unfortunately, a few months later, he was killed in an auto accident and the railroad plan was abandoned.

The last venture that Papa undertook was building a hosiery mill. About this time there was a boom in the textile industry in the South. Many of these early businesses went on to become massive enterprises and some still exist today. The development of synthetic fibers changed the industry. To survive, the old businesses had to develop new techniques to use the new materials.

Papa, along with his partner in the mills and cotton gin, built a small, modern hosiery mill. To eliminate the cost of fire insurance, the building was made to be fire-proof: The walls were solid brick; the windows and doors had iron frames with shatter-proof glass; the roof was corrugated iron with metal supports.

The hosiery mill was on a two-block section of land in the center of town near the other mills and cotton gin. This area was bordered on one side by the main highway and on the other by the railroad tracks. The space between the buildings was always covered by large stacks of new lumber curing in the sun. The sawdust from the mill was stored in a large pile away from the buildings. It was used to fire the boiler to make steam to operate the engines, but there was always an excess which was continually being hauled to a swamp two blocks away.

The front of the hosiery mill faced the highway and contained two large offices, one for the partner operating the mills and one for the mill secretary. Behind the office section, the building was essentially two stories. Inside, there were many large wooden vats used for dyeing the hosiery and a high wooden walkway from which the operation could be observed. A large workroom housed about 30 women who used machines to make the hose. The hosiery mill began operation in early summer of 1920 and offered employment to many. The hose were of superior quality and sales were good immediately. When my older brother left for college in September, my father told him that his financial position was bright and that, if business conditions continued to be good, he would be a wealthy man by the end of the year. However, there was a reversal in business conditions. By November, a general recession had begun. The hosiery no longer sold and the mill had to be closed. In the spring, cotton was selling for 40 cents per pound, but by harvest time, it brought only five cents per pound. Farmers did not even pick the cotton, allowing it to rot in the fields. They defaulted on their bank loans, which put the bank in jeopardy. All businesses were in recession, including the lumber industry.

Orus had to return home from college and went to work as a carpenter. Suddenly, Papa had no income. We children did not get new clothes for school in the fall. The large Paterson car had to be sold, which left us with only the Ford coupe.

One rainy morning in November, Papa took Maisie, McLeod and me to school in the car, passing by the hosiery mill. There was a crowd of people by the mill and smoke coming from the building. We were shocked when we saw what had happened. The interior of the building had caught fire about four o'clock in the morning.

Papa's partner lived directly across the street from the hosiery mill. When the fire started, he and his three sons came outside and fired many rounds of ammunition into the air, wild west style. His yard and the street by the hosiery mill contained dozens of shotgun shell casings and spent pistol cartridges. No one had bothered to inform Papa about the fire. Although we did not have a home telephone, we were only six blocks away.

Investigation showed that someone had forcibly entered the building and had strewn the boxes of packaged hosiery about the vats and walkway before starting a fire. No one had seen the arsonist, and investigation failed to unearth any clues as to the culprit's identity.

Later, it was learned that when the recession had started, Papa's partner had obtained a fire insurance policy on his half of the hosiery mill, unbeknownst to my father. The partner received the fire insurance payment, and Papa lost his half.

From this time on, business conditions went from bad to worse. Many banks in the state failed and many bank presidents committed suicide. There was a run on the Bank of Coats, but it survived when Papa put all his personal wealth, including home, furniture, car, and stocks and bonds into the bank to save it. However, a second run on the bank caused it to fail.

Neill Thomas Patterson, age 42, and Mattie Fuquay Patterson, age 38

Papa was an honest and trusting person. After the bank failure, he brooded over the financial losses of his friends and the clients of the bank. It had been his genius that organized the bank and made it prosper. It was impossible for him to eat or sleep. He devoted all his time and energy to trying to save the bank. I remember it all vividly. We children would eat supper at 6 p.m. Papa would come home about 7 or 8 p.m., and he and Mamma would sit alone at the dining room table. Mamma tried to comfort him, but great sadness prevailed.

I slept in the same bedroom with my parents. In the early morning of December 6, 1920, I heard my father get up and put on his clothes. The rattling of coins in his pockets wakened me. He went into the bathroom and then through a door that led outside.

Mamma got up as usual about 6 a.m. to prepare breakfast. It was still dark. When I got up about a half hour later, my father was not in his bed. I went to the kitchen and asked Mamma where he had gone during the night when I heard him leave. She had not missed him when she got out of bed and was immediately concerned. The 38-caliber pistol that always lay on the mantle in the bedroom was missing.

Uncle Garner and others were notified that Papa was missing. I recall going with Uncle Garner to the nearby fishpond in search of him. We all feared the worst. No trace of him was found for about three hours. Finally, someone went into the barn and found his body and the pistol lying on a pile of hay. He had put a bullet through his heart. His pocket watch had stopped at 2:20 a.m., though it was not broken.

A funeral service was held at the Coats Baptist Church, where we were members, and it was filled to capacity. The service was conducted by the Reverend J.A. Campbell, pastor of the church and a lifelong friend. Papa had been a deacon of the church and a Sunday school teacher. I was eight and a half years old and bewildered by this service. Due to the depression, I did not own a suit with pants and matching coat. The weather was cold, and I wore my overcoat, even in the church. We sat in the front pew. Everyone was sad; some were crying. Since that day, I have never been to church without a coat and tie, except when I had to wear a brace for a back injury.

A committee was formed by the church to send a letter of condolence to our family. In it the committee stated, "The church, the town of Coats, and neighboring communities have lost its best and most progressive citizen," and that our family had lost a devoted and Christian husband and father.

Another service was held at graveside with Masonic honors. This service was most impressive. Papa was a thirty-second degree Mason and a Shriner, a Past Master of Coats Lodge No. 622 A.F. and A.M. The Lodge sent our family a letter of condolence.

Obituaries appeared in several leading newspapers. The attendance at the funeral was described as probably the greatest ever witnessed in the County. One editor described Papa as follows: He was plain and unassuming. He moved among his people in the even tenor of his way in order that he might be counted a worker in the building of a progressive community, a servant to mankind who delights to make the world better from his having lived in it.

This same editor also said: In his friendship we tasted of that indescribable something that makes life sweeter. He was great and he was noble. That we know.

Papa was buried in the family plot at Coats Cemetery, which adjoined our homesite. A large granite tombstone about five feet high has since been placed at the foot of the grave. On it is carved the family name, PATTERSON, and below that is the Masonic symbol. A small, flat headstone gives his name and the dates of his birth and death. My brother Preston's grave, with its white marble angel tombstone, is beside my father's. When my mother died in 1964, she was buried next to my father and a similar headstone was placed by her grave.

Papa and Mamma had lived together only 18 years and 10 months, but during those years they had accomplished much. They had charted a course for the family and each of its members to follow in life. Mamma took control and carried on alone for 44 more years. Papa made one mistake in taking his own life, but other than that, no member of the family has faltered. Each has lived his or her life to the fullest and each and everyone has done his or her best to leave the world a better place by having lived in it. Papa and Mamma are together again and have been joined by four of their children. The time draws near for the rest of us, but, as my sister Velma said so many times during the last year of her life, there is no fear of the end. With the task of living successfully accomplished, we can enter eternity with peace of mind and tranquility.

CHAPTER III

My Youth - Ages Four to Seventeen

The earliest memory I have is visiting my great-grandmother, Elizabeth McLeod Bain. After losing my great-grandfather, Neill McLeod, in the Civil War, she married Grandpa Bain, as we called him. He had been a carpenter, but now worked as a cobbler. His shoe repair shop was in a small building on the main street of Coats at the edge of the business section. His home was on the same block around the corner, and Grandma Fuquay's home was on the same street, one block away. Although Grandma Bain died two months before my fourth birthday, she stands out in my memory, probably because she was blind and needed assistance.

Whenever my shoes needed new soles, I would stop by Grandpa Bain's shop on my way home from school and wait while he repaired them. Sometime after my father died, I learned to put new soles and heels on my own and my younger brother's shoes using shoe tacks, just as Grandpa Bain had shown me. We had our own shoe last (a metal form).

By nature, I am an introvert. At age four, I rarely spoke and my concerned parents took me to the doctor to determine if I was normal. The doctor said there was nothing wrong and that, in due time, I would talk if I had anything to say. I think I remember this visit, but I have heard others talk about it so many times I am not sure.

Actually, there was probably little need for me to talk when I was four. I was the fifth of seven children born every two years or so. Finally, after four years, an eighth child was born. The first child in our family was a boy, Orus. Next, there were two girls, Velma and Maisie. Four boys followed: McLeod, myself, Preston, and Neill. When Neill was born, Velma and Maisie were so disappointed that he was not a girl they would not speak to Mamma. They were tired of caring for little boys. Eventually they got their wish, as four years later my sister, Dorothy, was born.

When a new baby arrived in our home, Mamma's bed and the baby's crib were moved to the family room. It was next to the kitchen, allowing Mamma to run the household and still be near the baby. Apparently, she thought the bedrooms across the hall were too far away to leave the baby. Also, in the winter, there was always a fire in the family room, keeping it warm.

I was four years, three months older than my brother, Neill, and remember when he was born. When he was a few days old, I asked to hold him in my arms. I was allowed to do so, but, in the process of transferring him, we bumped heads. This upset me and I cried. When it was pointed out to me that Neill wasn't crying, I was soon consoled.

My brother, Preston, was born April 3, 1914, and died April 5, 1917. He had developed diarrhoea for some unknown reason. The family doctor treated him with paregoric and tea, but his condition worsened rapidly and within three days he was dead. I never forgot this and will relate how it affected my medical practice.

During my plantation practice, many of my patients were children with diarrhoea. I treated all of them vigorously and not one of them died. During an epidemic of dysentery at Puunene in 1943, we admitted 500 patients to Puunene Hospital, many of them children. Of these, 350 had stool cultures positive for Flexner dysentery bacillus. One child died in the emergency room 10 minutes after arriving and before treatment could be started. Untreated, many such patients die of electrolyte and fluid depletion. It was simple to give them salt solution beneath the skin of the thighs, but some of the sicker patients required blood plasma intravenously. The sulfa drugs were specific for the infection, and medication was needed to stop the diarrhoea. Usually, there was dramatic improvement within 24 hours, and the patients were well within five to seven days. The Board of Health traced the start of this epidemic to an unscrupulous food handler who did not wash her hands after going to the toilet. She had served food at a large Hawaiian luau.

Our family was grief-stricken by Preston's death. I was only five, but I can remember the sadness in our house. Preston's body was put in a casket in the formal living room, or parlor, as we called it. Our home was in the middle of one block and Coats Cemetery occupied an adjoining block. Next day, a short funeral service was held in the parlor, then six pallbearers took the small casket and walked to the cemetery. It was placed in a grave that had been prepared, and we walked back home.

Some months later, a tombstone was placed at Preston's grave. It was made of white marble and depicted an angel the size of a three-year old boy standing on a pedestal. It had outstretched wings and the right hand held a flower above its head. It is still there, 71 years later. Although Preston and I were only two years apart and played together every day, I don't recall much about him. I do remember that about one week before he became ill, we were cracking hickory nuts. He held a nut on a piece of cement and I hit it with a hammer to crack the shell. Once I hit his finger and injured it.

My brother, McLeod, is 26 months older than I am and an extrovert. He was a precocious child. At six and a half, he had already reached the fifth grade with the highest grades in his class. As long as he was home, I let him do the talking and I listened. Academically, I was four years behind him. At 14, he went away to Buies Creek Academy for his high school senior year and, again, received the prize for being the best student in school. This meant that from age 12 and for five years, I was the oldest male at home and carried much responsibility.

My mother had a wealth of knowledge about farming and raising farm animals and poultry. She had a background in business and had been a school teacher. She knew how to rear children. She was always in charge, but tried to let us children make our own decisions, especially about our own lives. She encouraged us, but would not tell us what courses to study in school or what we should prepare to do later in life. She expected us to do well and was proud of my brother's excellence in school.

SCHOOL YEARS

When I was a child, there were no kindergartens. We learned what we could from our older siblings, but were not really prepared for school. Until Dottie and I had our own children, I had the misconception that kindergartens were for lazy mothers who were trying to avoid caring for their small children. The public schools in Hawaii added kindergartens just before our second daughter, Ann, was five years old. We chose to send our oldest daughter, Lois, to a private kindergarten and soon learned the value of this early preparation for school. It was a joy to see how eager these little minds were to learn and to start a life of their own with new friends outside the home.

I remember my first day at school when events proved that I was not prepared. I had been outfitted with new clothes for the occasion. I knew some of my classmates from Sunday school, and the teacher was a neighbor of ours. Although I had no problem communicating with her, it soon became obvious that I did not communicate with her when I should have. My pants were soiled and wet. The teacher led me out of the room and told me to go home, a walk of about eight blocks. I have heard of the "long walk" from home plate to the dugout in baseball when a star hitter strikes out at a crucial time, but I don't think there has ever been a longer walk for me than the one I made that day.

I soon adjusted to the school routine and made many new friends. My brother, McLeod, had set an awsome precedent by always winning awards for being the best student in his class. I wanted to win this prize, but, try as I would, it eluded me for the first five years. A Sunday school friend of mine, James Lee, won the coveted prize the first four years, and I think we tied the fifth year. From the sixth year, I was the winner and, finally, in my junior and senior years in high school, I won the medal for being the best student in school. The award was a $10 gold coin and a certificate. By this time, my father had died, and I had to use the gold coin to buy clothes.

William B. Patterson
age 8, circa 1920

At first, I was not very selective in choosing my friends. I remember one in particular in the first and second grades who would take cigarettes from his father's supply and bring them to school. At recess, he and I would smoke the cigarettes until I became nauseated. I recall walking home after smoking and becoming very ill, barely able to reach our house. I can't remember if my parents or my brothers and sisters ever learned that I had been smoking, but they would have known if they had smelled my breath.

This same friend and his older brother were caught stealing watermelons from the Reverend Tom Coats' watermelon patch one night. The Reverend gave them a lecture about stealing and asked them why they did it. In response, one of them said, "Pa said to be sure to bring home two large ones." Later, when I returned home from college, I learned that my former friend was in jail for theft.

As a child, I had two very good friends. One was Bruce Langdon who was born in July, 1912, three months after me. Our families were friends and lived five blocks apart. My mother told me that when Bruce was one week old, she took me in a baby carriage to see him and his mother. My friendship with Bruce started that day and lasted until his death at about age 62.

Bruce's father and mine were business associates at Coats. Later, Mr. Langdon became Uncle June's partner in the brickmill at Slocomb, N.C.

My other good friend was James Lee, who won the prize for the best student the first four years. He, Bruce and I went to Sunday school together and afterward one of them would come home with me or I would go home with him. We would have Sunday dinner at noon, play all afternoon, and return home about five o'clock. This arrangement continued until high school. When we owned bicycles, we sometimes rode to Buies Creek or Erwin, both five miles away.

Apparently after the first day, I got through the first grade without incident. I do not recall any misadventures except smoking the cigarettes. I did get into trouble in the second and third grades, however. My teacher was the same for both grades and she did not seem to know how to manage mischievous little boys. I remember using rubber bands to shoot spitballs at other boys and flying paper airplanes across the room. Each time I was caught misbehaving, I would be disciplined in some way: Sometimes I would have to stand in the corner for 20 minutes; other times I was sent outside to stand behind a tree in the school yard. I can't remember if I was spanked or whipped with a switch in school, but it seems that I was.

With four older brothers and sisters in school, I rarely misbehaved without word reaching home about it. A standing rule in our home was made by my father: Any time we were disciplined in school, we would get a switching at home. It seems that I was in trouble often, and I can recall my father gently switching me many times.

In the fourth grade, things changed. We had a lovely teacher, and I was never in trouble.

Our school building was old and each room was heated separately with a wood-burning stove. The boys brought firewood in from outside. Once when I was chopping the wood into smaller pieces with an ax, a piece struck me on the chin making a cut one inch long. The family doctor repaired the cut with one stitch without using a local anesthetic. I can still feel the needle and thread going through my skin. He did not wear surgical gloves, and the wound became infected and drained for several days. In addition to the scar caused by the cut, the stitch left a scar, and I have since cut both many times while shaving.

A very sad thing happened the year I was in the fourth grade. The mother of my good friend, Bruce, developed appendicitis. This same family doctor treated her with ice packs to her abdomen, but after two days, the appendix ruptured and she developed peritonitis. Dr. Young, my uncle, was finally called in consultation, but it was too late. I can still hear him raving about how she should have been operated on a few days before and how her life could have been saved. Bruce was the oldest of four children, two boys and two girls. Their lives were changed by their mother's death. They went to live with their grandmother, and Bruce had to repeat the fourth grade.

The next year, the schools in the district were consolidated; the students were brought in from five miles around in Model T Ford school buses. There were almost a thousand students in school, whereas the town had only 520 residents. We moved into a new brick school building with classrooms on the first three floors, a large auditorium on the fourth, and steam heat. The auditorium was large enough to seat the entire student body for chapel. We would first sing a song, then the principal would make school announcements. Once, he told us how to brush our teeth. Finally, a prayer was said and we went to our classrooms.

The auditorium was also used for community gatherings, school plays, and music recitals. Traveling entertainers such as magicians would give performances there. Fiddler's conventions were one of the main events, well-attended by old and young. Many violin players, most of them middle age or older, would be on hand, playing solo as well as in groups. Turkey in the Straw was a favorite number. Other instruments played were the guitar, banjo, harmonica, and hand saw using a bow similar to a violin. Square dancing on the auditorium stage was very popular, with lots of audience participation.

A spelling bee usually would be the final event of the evening. Words to be spelled were taken from the Blue Back Spelling Book. Mamma won the spelling bee the first time I attended, and the next year the contest ended in a draw between Aunt Ida and Mamma. The director could not find a word in the book that they could not spell correctly. It had been their textbook in school at Broadway, N.C., many years before.

Our school year was only eight months and there were only seven years of elementary school. School children picked most of the cotton, the major farm crop. The cotton bolls opened between late August and mid-October, so school started about the tenth of October. For the first six weeks, classes began at 7 a.m. and ended at 1 p.m. with no time out for lunch, giving the children time to pick cotton after school. Repeated rains could knock the cotton to the ground where it would rot, so each field was picked two or three times.

In 1919, when the price of cotton was 40 cents a pound, we were paid two cents a pound to pick it, double the usual rate. I never picked more than 160 pounds a day; others, like my brother, McLeod, could pick 250 pounds or more.

When I was in the sixth grade, I decided I wanted to take piano lessons. My sisters had always taken lessons and my mother agreed it would be nice for me to know how to play. I took lessons for the last six months of the school year and played a solo at the annual recital, at which point, having no innate talent for music, I decided not to continue.

Sports were important to me in high school and the coach was an idol of mine. With only 100 students, including girls, we could not field a good team in anything. Almost every student lived on a farm and worked at home immediately after school, so we never practiced sports after school or on Saturdays. We practiced occasionally before school and always during the lunch hour break. We did not have a football team. The outdoor basketball court had a dirt playing surface and I played guard on the team. During one game, I sprained my right ankle severely and had to use crutches for two weeks. I was catcher on the baseball team in my senior year and manager. In a game against Dunn High School, I hit three doubles and one single in five times at bat.

Coats High School was not accredited for college entrance until my senior year when a science laboratory was added and a second foreign language was taught. I was judged the best student in school both my junior and senior years with a grade average of B+, and was valedictorian of my senior class. I applied for and received a tuition scholarship at the University of North Carolina at Chapel Hill. Of the 13 students in our senior class, I was the only one to go to college in the fall after graduation. Two of my classmates entered college the following year.

Coats High School had never had junior-senior proms or any kind of social activities for the students. I was president of our senior class and with the help of my sister, Maisie, organized a successful junior-senior party. We all helped prepare a buffet dinner and had canned music for dancing.

I was interested in the opposite sex and usually had a girlfriend, always dreaming about eventually having a girlfriend as my wife. I think my parents' example of their happy home kept this foremost in my mind, making it my number one priority. By having many girlfriends, I became wiser. I needed someone to love as my own, and during my search I met many nice girls. Some were not interested in me, while others who were interested in me did not have the qualities I wanted in a wife. Fate, or God, seemed to be guiding me, keeping me from making a mistake. When I met Dottie, I soon knew the search was over. At last, I had found the angel of my dreams and she has remained that for over 50 years.

My first girlfriend's family moved to town while I was in the third grade. With her bright red hair, I thought she was real cute. I walked an extra three blocks after school, walking her home and carrying her books. Her family moved away after two years.

For three years during high school, I dated a classmate who lived three miles out in the country. My family did not usually have a car for me to drive, so I caught rides with my friends to her home on Saturday or Sunday evening and then walked home about 11 o'clock. I still remember those long walks on cold winter nights in the moonlight.

BOY SCOUTS

Our Scout troop was organized when I was about 12 and I was made the patrol leader. The Scout master was the manager of the local bank and not very active in Scouting. He more or less left things up to me and, as patrol leader, I followed the Boy Scout Handbook. We had regular meetings and, in the summer, had many outings, cookouts, etc. We all bought Scout uniforms, knives and hatchets, studied the Handbook and took tests to advance in rank. Officially, I only reached the rank of second class though I had passed the tests for first class and had met the requirements for a merit badge in archery and cycling.

I attended a patrol leader's camp for six days one summer. All the patrol leaders from our district spent three days camping by a lake near Fayetteville to prepare for the last three days, which were spent at a state-wide Scout jamboree at Chapel Hill. At Fayetteville, we slept in pup tents among pine trees by the lake.

At Chapel Hill, we set up our tents along with several hundred other Scouts on Emerson Field, the baseball field. We continued cooking our meals in Boy Scout fashion. There was an organized program of Scout activities and contests, though I can't recall just what they were.

The next summer, the Boy Scouts of the eastern North Carolina district were invited to attend a Scout camp in the western North Carolina district near Marion. There was a two-week program of activities, which involved most all phases of Scouting. If my memory is correct, it cost $15 per week to attend, but my mother could only afford to let me go for one week. I was able to make arrangements with Scouts from Dunn to go with them to Marion, a distance of 200 miles or more.

Marion is in the Blue Ridge Mountains, which are three to four thousand feet high. This was the first time I had seen mountains and I found the scenery breathtaking. The Scout camp was near a lake between two mountain ridges. There was a large mess hall with a kitchen and about a half dozen cabins built on the side of the mountain with back doors at ground level. There were bunks, three layers deep, around the side of the cabins and another row in the middle. Some of the space underneath the cabins was used for workshops. One evening, a copperhead snake was caught near the back door of a cabin. Another night, a mountain lion raided the garbage container by the mess hall and we heard its blood-curdling cry.

I chose archery and a life guard course as my activities at camp. I won first place in an archery contest, using a bow and arrows I made from lemon wood. During the swimming drills we were required to retrieve a heavy weight from a depth of 15 feet, and I can still remember how cold the water was in the lake.

The highlight of the Scouting day was the story-telling around a large campfire about 9 p.m. The stories, told by the Scout leaders, were all scary and just at the climax, the cannon fired a blank 12-gauge shotgun shell. This week at camp was the highlight of my youth.

Later in life, when Dottie and I moved into a house, one of the first tools I bought was a Boy Scout hatchet. I have had it now for 49 years and use it often.

OTHER MEMORIES OF MY CHILDHOOD BEFORE MY FATHER'S DEATH

Occasionally my older sisters did the laundry. The clothes were boiled in the large pot in the wash house, rinsed in a tub of cold water, and hung on clothes lines to dry in the sun. One day, McLeod and I were playing nearby and managed to put some dirt into the tubs with the clean laundry. When my father came home for lunch we got a good switching for this prank.

We always had a good milk cow. My father once paid $150 for a Jersey cow that produced five gallons of milk daily. McLeod and I were responsible for staking the cow where there was plenty of grass. Once when we were not around, one cow became entangled with the chain around her neck and choked to death. Another cow died after getting into the vegetable garden and eating a large quantity of dried lima beans. We were told that the lima beans swelled in one of her stomachs, causing an obstruction.

I remember one year we raised four pigs weighing two to three hundred pounds each. When the temperature dropped below freezing about the middle of December, we had a "hog killing", which was quite an affair. Extra help was hired. Water was heated to boiling in the large pot in the wash house and transferred to a 50-gallon barrel. The pigs were slaughtered one at a time and brought to the back yard where they were put into the barrel of scalding water for a few minutes. After this, the hair scraped off easily.

When a pig was clean, it was put on a large table. The body was opened, all the organs were removed, and the carcass was cut into various parts - shoulders, hams, loins, etc. Nothing was discarded.

The meat was preserved by curing it in salt. The pieces were placed in layers in a large wooden box and each layer was covered with salt. The box was tightly sealed and put in the smokehouse where it was left for two weeks. The temperature would remain low only a few days and then might reach 50 degrees. The salt would permeate the meat and act as a preservative.

After two weeks, the box was opened and the meat removed. The excess salt was brushed off and each piece was treated with a mixture of dark molasses and black pepper. The meat was then hung from the rafters in the smokehouse, and oak stumps were set on fire on the earth floor. They burned slowly and the meat hung in the thick smoke for a week or more. After being smoked, the meat was left hanging or was brought into the house and stored in a cool place.

The parts of the pig that were not cured in salt were used in various ways. The feet were pickled in vinegar. Liver pudding and head cheese were made. The intestines were cleaned and cooked as chitlings, quite a delicacy for some people. Scraps of meat, both lean and fat, were trimmed off all the parts and were ground into sausage. I remember turning a meat grinder until my arms ached. Black pepper and sage from our graden were added for seasoning. My mother canned part of the sausage in fruit jars for use later in the year. The excess skin was cooked producing cracklings which were added to white flour dough and made into crackling bread, a delicacy. The excess fat was rendered into lard, the preferred fat for use in cooking. I still recall how delicious the fresh lean pork was when it was fried.

There was an influenza epidemic in 1918. Orus, age 16 at the time, contracted it and became very ill. He was in an upstairs bedroom and we children were not allowed upstairs. I remember his yelling during the night in his delirium and high fever. Luckly, he recovered. My wife's sister, Margaret, was not so fortunate and died of influenza at age 11 that year.

World War I officially ended at 11 a.m. on Thursday, November 11, 1918, and I remember the great celebration. Dynamite was normally used by farmers to remove large tree stumps while clearing land. In celebrating the end of the war, instead of putting the dynamite under the stump, several sticks were placed on top of a stump and detonated. The explosions could be heard for miles, starting in late afternoon and continuing past midnight. Orus was almost 16 and would have been drafted if the war had continued. Although sugar was in short supply and was rationed, my father had been able to buy 100 pounds, which we hid in the food pantry.

Sometime in our youth - I think I was five - my brothers and I contracted malaria. I am not sure if other members of the family were affected or not. It was August, with afternoon temperatures reaching 110 degrees. I recall sitting on the back porch steps in the afternoon sun and having a severe chill.

The doctor prescribed quinine dispensed in a chocolate-flavored milky mixture. We had to take three doses daily given to us by an older sister. I remember the medicine tasted so bad that I spit out several doses, unbeknownst to my sister. I learned what the saying "bitter as quinine" really meant. In spite of not taking all the medicine, I recovered and did not have any recurrence. For many years, the blood bank would not accept my blood for transfusions because I had had malaria.

Our family spent a week at Wrightsville Beach, N.C., in 1919. This was after Preston's death and before Dorothy was born, so there were only six children. At that time, we had the seven-passenger Paterson car, which had two extra foldaway seats. This was my first visit to the ocean and I remember the beach, the piers, and the women in their long bathing suits.

MEMORIES OF MY CHILDHOOD
AFTER MY FATHER'S DEATH

Our homesite consisted of two plots of land. The house was on a six-acre parcel that extended west from the last street on the west side of town. Two acres of this land were covered by trees and adjoined other wooded areas that extended for miles. A small stream, or branch as we called it, orginated in these two acres and flowed west. The other plot of land, one acre, was half a city block across the street from our home. This street has since been named Patterson Street.

After my father's death on December 6, 1920, my mother did not know what would happen to our family. We were totally bankrupt; we owned nothing except our clothes and household effects. We did not own the land, house or furniture. Orus had had to leave college earlier and was working as a carpenter. Mamma was apppointed executor of Papa's estate and was supposed to get $100 each month as salary but received little if any pay as the lawyer's fees took all the money that the estate collected. There was talk that we children might have to be put in an orphanage. We did not know if we would be allowed to occupy the house and use the furniture, or if everything would be sold.

Before the Bank of Coats went broke, Papa had put almost everything he owned into the bank to try to save it. However, he refused to cash in one insurance policy of

$25,000 and this was everything that Mamma owned. Everybody in Coats, including relatives and our minister, had lost money in the bank's collapse. Some people tried to convince my mother that they should be paid their money out of her insurance. She refused.

For several years, Mamma did not receive any pay from the estate, though we were allowed to live in the house and use the land free of charge. We did not know how long we would be allowed to stay, but we were never evicted. After seven years, Mamma was allowed to buy the house, furniture and land at a reasonable price.

From the start, Mamma decided to give each child $1000 for college education. Then, she loaned each child money as needed to finish college, to be paid back as soon as possible so the next child could go to college.

Orus decided not to return to school and, on his eighteenth birthday, married his childhood sweetheart. He and his wife, Verl, lived on the second floor of our home and, after a year, had a baby, Orus Fuquay Jr. Using his college money and more borrowed from Mamma, he opened a grocery store. From the start, the store operated at a loss and he sold it after a year or so. He promised his creditors and my mother that he would repay them, which he did.

We had no means of transportation, so Mamma bought a horse, a new buggy, and a wagon. On Sundays we all went to church crowded into the buggy. My oldest sister, Velma, fell off the horse and broke her arm at the elbow. It was treated and healed satisfactorily.

Before my father's death, we always had a large vegetable garden and grew much of what we ate. After his death, we planted an even larger garden and depended upon it amost entirely for our food.

We had lots of fruit trees - apple, cherry, peach and plum - and concord grape vines and two very large scuppernong grape vines.

In both 1921 and '22, we canned almost 400 jars - many half-gallon jars - of fruits and vegetables. We gathered wild blackberries, huckleberries, grapes and crabapples in the woods. The only drawback was a tiny mite-like red bug that produced a very itchy bite on our bare legs.

The scuppernong grape was juicy and delicious, particularly late in the fall after frost. Our two vines were trained on an overhead wire trellis covering about 1200 square feet. Mamma made grape jelly and preserves using the whole grape and juice. Occasionally, the seal on a jar leaked and air entered the jar, fermenting the juice and making scuppernong wine. Mamma never knew that we boys kept an eye on the juice and drank any wine that formed. She would have destroyed it if she had known.

The wooded area of our land was fenced with hog wire. It was originally used to raise pigs and later used for pasture for the cows. On the rest of the land we grew corn, oats, alfalfa and soy beans for feed for the animals and chickens.

The "we" I often use in this story refers first, to my mother, who knew how to farm. McLeod, the oldest boy was next in charge until he was 14. I was in charge from age 12 until I left for college at 17. My younger brother, Neill, took over in the summers when I began working away from home.

By 1923, the price of cotton had recovered from the depression and was selling for 20 to 22 cents a pound. We planted an acre or more and harvested about 2000 pounds, including the seeds. We put side rails on the wagon and piled the cotton inside. Mabel, the horse, could barely pull the wagon to the cotton gin, where we stood in line waiting our turn. Finally, a tin tube about 12 inches in diameter was lowered into the wagon and the cotton was sucked up into the gin, producing a bale of cotton lint weighing about 500 pounds. The seeds paid for ginning. The bale of cotton sold for $100 or more and, after paying for the seeds and fertilizer, we would have about $80 profit. Mamma kept the money and credited our account in her ledger. Later, when we were in college and needed money, she repaid us.

We boys had a contract with Mamma to raise pigs. We paid for the pigs and feed, then when one was slaughtered, Mamma would credit our accounts for its value. We butchered only one or two each year. There was a lot of profit in this, because we raised much of the feed. The pigs were kept in the mulberry orchard until three months before slaughter when they were put in a pen with a wooden floor. We boys and our friends spent much of the time in the mulberry trees ourselves, so I'm not sure if the pigs got more mulberries than we did. I have always thought of mulberries as pig feed but, actually, they can be used to make delicious jelly, jam, and pies.

Frequently, there was work available for us away from home. In the fall, there was always cotton to be picked, for which we were paid one cent a pound. At midsummer we earned 20 cents an hour working at tobacco farms when the tobacco was cured. This was hot work.

One summer, my friend, Bruce Langdon and I worked on his uncle's cotton and corn farm three miles from Coats. We stayed in his home. He had a beautiful horse named Tony and a young, very tempermental, Missouri mule. It was always my lot to have to plow with the mule. She walked very fast and when we got to the end of a row, she literally slung me and the plow around to start down the next row. The temperature was 100 degrees at times, but the heat didn't bother the mule. The horse, Bruce and I would be completely wet with perspiration and we had to be careful the horse didn't get too hot.

Early each morning, Bruce's uncle picked two melons from his watermelon patch and put them in a tub of cold water in the shade. Because of the heat at midday, we worked from 5 to 11 a.m. and then from 3 to 6 p.m. During lunch hour, each of us would eat half a watermelon, leaving the rind for the pigs.

By August, the cotton and corn were "hilled" or "laid by" and did not require any more attention until harvest. We then cut pine trees in the woods on the farm. The weather was hot and breezes could not get to us deep in the forest. This work was strenuous, using a crosscut saw to cut the logs into lengths of 18 feet. We hauled them to the saw mill on a log cart where they were cut into lumber to make new buildings on the farm.

During winter we kept a fire in the fireplace in our family room. In very cold weather we also kept a fire in the hot air furnace in the basement, which burned coal or wood. The kitchen stove was a large wood-burning range with a hot water jacket next to the fire box. Several times in extremely cold weather the fire went out during the night and the water in the jacket froze, bursting it. A new one then had to be installed.

One of the boys' duties was to keep a supply of wood in special boxes by the kitchen stove and in the family room. Mamma always cooked three hot meals a day, which included biscuits for breakfast and the noon meal, and usually corn bread for supper. Fast-burning pine wood was needed for the kitchen range, while long-burning wood, such as oak, was best for the fireplace. I can still hear Mamma warning us to be sure to bring in plenty of wood in case we had a blizzard. We had no daily weather reports, but she seemed to know when the snow storms were coming.

We bought pine slabs from the sawmill and had them cut into suitable lengths for the kitchen stove. Each year we bought several cords of oak for the fireplace.

46

Two men with a gas-powered saw cut the wood to the right lengths.

Sometimes we hired a man to cut trees on our own land which I hauled to our yard with our horse and wagon. When I was 13 I began cutting down the trees with an ax myself. Some of these were large gum trees growing in a swampy area. After cutting the trunks into lengths of eight feet, I chained them to the horse who pulled them out to an area where we could load them onto the wagon. Mabel, the horse, did not like standing in the water and once started too soon, catching my left thumb in the chains. I still have a scar where the thumb nail was torn off.

Cutting wood with an ax is good exercise, using almost every muscle in the body. I used an ax to cut wood until 10 years ago when my blood pressure rose and I had to buy a chain saw. I could cut down a eucalyptus tree 16 inches in diameter in 30 minutes with my ax.

Several months after my father died, our electric plant wore out and, because of the uncertainties of the future, Mamma would not replace it. This meant we had to use oil lamps for lights, no longer had running water, and used an outdoor toilet. We heated bath water on the kitchen stove and transferred it to the bath tub. A lot of water was needed for household use and for the animals to drink. Fortunately, our well had plenty of water, raised with a bucket attached to chain. I often rode Mabel bareback to the nearby fish pond for her to drink.

I remember doing my homework in the lamplight by the fireplace after the rest of the family had gone to bed. I had to be sure the fire in the fireplace was out before going to bed as sparks could set the house on fire. We always slept in cold bedrooms with windows open, having been taught that plenty of fresh air prevented tuberculosis. Obviously, during really cold weather, the windows weren't opened very wide.

About 1924, a public utility brought electricity to Coats. Our house was connected to it after being rewired. The old system was 32 volts and the wiring did not pass inspection. The new wires were put inside the walls and above the ceilings.

I suggested we buy a new electric motor for the water pump. Mamma agreed on the condition that I prove that the pump still worked after not being used for three years. I borrowed a small gasoline engine from a friend and connected it to the pump. It was soon evident that the leather washers in the pump's valve at the bottom of the well had disintegrated. Also, sand had accumulated at the bottom of the well until it reached above the valve intake.

The well was 65 feet deep. There were two sections of ceramic pipe, 30 inches in diameter and three feet long, at the bottom of the well. These prevented the walls from caving in. The water was three to four feet deep. It was obvious two things had to be done: The sand had to be removed and new leather washers had to be put in the valve.

When McLeod came home from school on the weekend and was able to help, I descended into the well holding on to the chain and sliding down the pump pipe. We hauled up several buckets of sand. The valve assembly was removed and new washers were installed. Suddenly, we had a problem. I weighed 20 pounds more than McLeod and gravity prevented him from hoisting me out of the well with the chain. To overcome this, I helped by bracing my feet and shoulders on opposite walls of the well and, with my hands, climbed up the pipe. I had the chain wrapped around my body so, together, we were able to get me out. Actually, I think I descended into the well two or three times before I got the pump fixed.

Again, the gasoline engine was started. The pump worked and the water pressure returned, pumping water throughout the system including the wash house and barnyard, and using most of the water in the well. Shortly afterward, Mamma bought a new electric motor with an automatic switch, controlled by water pressure.

When I was 12 and Neill was eight, we had our tonsils removed. A public health nurse visited our school and examined all the children's throats. She said my tonsils were buried and needed to be removed although I had never had trouble with my tonsils nor had I had throat infections.

In June, a temporary hospital was established in the school at Lillington, N.C., the country seat. Army cots were set up in the classrooms. A team of throat specialists, anesthetists and nurses from Raleigh removed the tonsils of several dozen children from all over the county. We children arrived early in the morning, without breakfast, and by the end of the day all our tonsils had been removed. We were given water and ice cream for supper and had to spend the night. Next morning, we were examined and sent home.

I preceded Neill to the operating room. Open drop ether anesthesia was used and the sensation I experienced was one of suffocation. Finally, my head seemed to explode and I was out. When I recovered, I was back on my cot, drowsy but quiet. Neill returned soon after and as he recovered he became delirious. Two nurses had to restrain him for about 30 minutes. I was embarassed by his behavior.

During the 2-week recovery period at home, I was miserable. My throat was so sore I couldn't eat. I was hungry but when I tried to swallow my throat muscles went into spasm. Neill, on the other hand, didn't seem to have much trouble eating.

The usual fee for removing tonsils at this clinic, including physician, anesthesia and room, was $25. My mother was charged only $25 for the two of us because she was a widow.

When I was 14 I began working for Orus in the summer and during Christmas vacation. He had recovered from earlier setbacks and now owned four grocery stores, two in Sanford, one in Jonesboro and one in Southern Pines. I worked for him for eight summers as a truck driver, clerk, butcher's helper, stock boy and general utility man. It took me one entire summer to paint a remodeled store, including all fixtures. All his stores had meat markets and clerks were used in all departments. The customers did not have access to the merchandise as they do today.

Sanford is located in a busy farming area. On Saturdays, the farmers would shop for the entire week so the sales on that day would total as much as for the previous five days. The store opened on Saturday at 7 a.m. and closed at 1 a.m. on Sunday. The last customers came about 10:30 p.m. and then, before we could go home, the shelves had to be restocked, perishable food had to be put in the cooler, and the working areas had to be thoroughly scrubbed. During the Christmas holidays, every day was like Saturday and the store closed at midnight every night.

Half the beef that he sold in the store where I worked, Orus bought from the local farmers, usually three carcasses each week. He also bought calves which were sold as veal. There was no abattoir in the county, so the butcher and a helper slaughtered the animals in the woods by a tree where the carcass could be hung. When the meat arrived at the store, a veterinarian inspected it before it was sold. For two summers I was the butcher's helper and then took over the butchering myself with a helper.

During my first summer, I was paid $12 a week, plus board, room and laundry; thereafter I received $15 a week.

After Papa died, I bought my own clothes when I was working. During a summer I would buy enough clothes to last through the school year and was still able to save about $60.

During my high school years I wore blue woolen bell-bottom sailor pants bought at an Army-Navy surplus store in Raleigh. Other boys soon began wearing them as well.

A merchant who owned a men's clothing store in Benson, N.C., owed my father money at the time of my father's death during the depression. Unable to pay it, he offered to have suits tailor-made for me as part payment on the debt. One fall, I got a good-quality, woolen suit with two pairs of pants. For the first time in my life, I was well-dressed.

During the 1920s many old coins came through the cash registers in Orus' store where I worked. I began collecting coins minted in the 1800s or before, and soon had over $30 in old coins, half my savings for the summer. When I had to cash them in I intended to save a few quarters and dimes from the late 1700s but, somehow, they were lost.

As a boy, I hunted with a gun. When I was eight I bought a Daisy air rifle that used BB shot which sold for 5 cents a pack. I remember buying several packs on credit. A row of chinaberry trees grew near our home and, in the winter, snow birds - as we called them - would perch in the branches. I would stand beneath the trees and pick them off with the air rifle. They were small, but their breasts were delicious when broiled over charcoal in the fireplace. I also shot sparrows and other birds, but never a bluebird.

When I reached high school age, I was permitted to hunt with my father's 12-gauge shotgun. It had a 30-inch choke barrel and was very effective against station-ary targets. My reaction time was slow, so I was not good with fast-moving targets. There were many bobwhite quail in our area. When they flushed out of the bushes their fluttering would startle me and they would be long gone before I could aim the gun. I never did shoot one. I was more successful in shooting large yellow-breasted woodpeckers and other birds as they ate berries in large gum trees.

I was most successful in shooting squirrels. Mamma would wake me early and by dawn I would be waiting underneath trees where the squirrels had nests high in the branches. As it began to get light, the squirrels emerged from the nests and I shot them. I also bagged several wild rabbits in the fields and woods near our home.

When I was 14 my mother agreed to let me have a dog. I paid $5 for a half-grown female bulldog with trimmed ears and a docked tail. Sometimes I rode my bicycle and led her on a leash. Once the leash became entangled around her and when I reached down she bit my finger. Rabies was prevalent in this area so the dog was observed closely for three weeks for any signs of the disease which could have been transmitted to me. When indicated, rabies vaccine was given by injection daily for 21 days. Luckily, she did not develop any sign of the disease.

I kept the dog tied on a leash or in her dog house and occasionally turned her loose to play around the yard. One Sunday when everyone else was away from home, I turned her out and forgot I had done so. I rode my bicycle to a friend's home and when I returned three hours later, I found dead chickens scattered around the yard. The dog had killed our rooster, eight of 15 hens, and 30 of 45 young chickens. I realized immediately that the dog could not stay in the yard with the chickens, a very important part of our food supply. I decided the dog had to go, the quicker the better, and knew I would be unable to give her away because she killed chickens. I got our gun and shot her, burying her and all the chickens in a common grave. When Mamma returned home, I had a lot of explaining to do.

In 1922 or '23, Mamma bought a secondhand Overland, a small touring car with a four cylinder engine. My sisters and McLeod soon learned to drive and I think I was drving by age 13. North Carolina did not rquire a driver's license until about 1935. With the car, we transported my sisters to college in Raleigh and McLeod to

Wake Forest, which at the time was located a few miles beyond Raleigh. Later, Velma taught school at Angier, 10 miles away. I recall driving her to Angier on Sunday evening and having two flat tires on the way home. The car carried a spare tire, but we were always prepared to patch an inner tube in case we had a second flat. The starter on the car locked at times so I learned to unlock it by lossening the bolts that connected it to the engine. Curtains attached to the windows when it rained. We used woolen buggy robes to keep warm in cold weather. In winter, we drained the water from the radiator to keep it from freezing when the car was not in use.

In 1926 Mamma traded the Overland for a small, secondhand Nash sedan. She learned to drive using a clutch and gear shift. I remember her driving us to Sanford, 35 miles away.

In 1927 when I was 15, I travelled with Mamma, Velma, Maisie, Uncle Neill and Aunt Margaret to Washington, Philadelphia and New York. This was a most successful trip and a highlight in all our lives. The car was crowded. Uncle Neill had been invited because Mamma thought he would know how to drive in the cities. The plan was that he, Velma and Maisie would share the driving. However, long before we reached New York City, it became evident that I was the best driver and the only one able to drive in city traffic. I recall the traffic cops in New York City: They would see the license plate and yell, "Come on North Carolina, speed it up!"

Maisie was majoring in art at Meredith so we visited every art museum in every city. This was almost more than I could endure. We also visited the Capitol, Mt. Vernon, Independence Hall and the Mint. I climbed the Washington Monument while the others waited in the long line for the elevator and we all reached the top at the same time.

Mamma put most of her money in a trust fund through a bank in Raleigh. This was recommended to her by her financial advisors and cost her several hundred dollars. About 1927, she became uneasy about the large public utility where the bank had invested her money. Against the bank's advice, she promptly removed it from the trust and re-invested it in government bonds.

A few months later, the public utility declared bankruptcy, to the surprise of almost everyone. I have often wondered how Mamma could have been so astute. We did not get a daily newspaper with financial reports, so I don't know how she could have determined the company was not financially sound. Mamma had lived for over 18 years with Papa, a financial giant, and she may have made the determination on her own intuition. As I have said before, sometimes God takes care of us in mysterious ways.

From the age of 12 to 17, I was the oldest child at home and had many responsibilities. There was always something to be done. During the school year, Mamma woke me at 7 a.m. After building a fire in the fireplace in the family room, I dressed and ate breakfast. Next, I fed and milked the cow. If she had a small calf, I left enough milk for it and later put the calf back in its own pen. I fed the horse and the pigs. If the temperature was near freezing, I stoked the furnace in the basement.

I rode my bicycle to school, which started at 8:30 and ended at 3:30. We lived about a mile from school, so I would be home before 4 to start my afternoon chores. First, I got firewood ready for the next day and brought it into the house. This included wood for the fireplace and the kitchen range. If there was a threat of a blizzard, I brought in a three-day supply. I also kept a supply under the porch where it would stay dry in case of continuing rain or snow.

In the afternoon, the eggs that had been laid during the day were gathered and the chickens were fed. The pigs and horse were fed again and given water. The morning routine of milking the cow and taking care of the calf were repeated. We had our evening meal, which we called supper, at 5:30 or 6.

There was always a lot of homework for school. I started studying before 7 p.m. and tried to spend at least one hour on each subject each evening. Frequently I was up until 10:30, long after everyone else had gone to bed.

On Saturdays, there were always special jobs to be done. Periodically I would put the high side rails on the wagon and haul a load of pine straw to be used as bedding for the horse and cow. Sometimes, trees in the woods had to be cut for firewood. I planted a field of rye in the fall to be used as cow feed in the spring. In early spring, the fields had to be readied for planting, especially Mamma's garden, and we spread cow and horse manure over the fields for fertilizer.

Corn shucking parties were social events that I frequently attended. In the fall after the cotton was picked, the farmers gathered the ears of corn from the fields and placed them in large piles near the barn. Often there were more than a thousand bushels of corn. All the neighbors and friends from miles around would be invited to the party. Contests determined who could shuck the most in a given time. Food and drink were provided and sometimes entertainment. Apple cider might be available, but no alcoholic beverages as this was during prohibition. Almost every farmer with a large corn crop would have such a party and a good time was had by all.

The shucks were used as cow feed. I recall making many trips to nearby farms to buy wagon loads of shucks for $3.

CHAPTER IV

College Years at Chapel Hill: 1929 to 1932

As all the members of our family were Southern Missionary Baptists, it was natural for us to choose Baptist schools. Orus attended Wake Forest College briefly and Velma graduated from Meredith College, where Maisie was a student at the time. McLeod was entering his second year at Wake Forest Medical School after three years as a premed student. He had noticed that the University of North Carolina at Chapel Hill had very few of the financial problems that plagued Wake Forest. He felt that the advantages of this outweighed any that Wake Forest offered and urged me to attend the University. I took his advice. Eventually, Wake Forest obtained adequate financing, moved to a new and larger campus, and became a full-fledged university.

Velma married Marcus Wood Lawrence August 1, 1928. He had taught school for five years and then became a Methodist minister. He joined the Eastern North Carolina Conference of the Methodist Church as a student minister and was assigned a circuit of churches along the Outer Banks near Manteo. He and Velma lived in the parsonage at Mann's Harbor - where bear and deer often visited their yard - and traveled to their other churches by boat. Their year there was a wonderful honeymoon and a good introduction to the ministry for both of them.

In September, 1929, Marcus entered the School of Religion at Duke University in Durham. He had graduated from Trinity College before the name was changed to Duke University. He also became the regular pastor of the Methodist Church at Carrboro, which adjoins the city limits of Chapel Hill. I entered the University at Chapel Hill in September, 1929, and lived with them for a year in the large parsonage. The distance to the center of the campus was about two miles. I rode with Marcus in the morning on his way to Duke and caught rides or walked home in the afternoon. I paid Marcus and Velma one-third of our living expenses with no charge for my room.

Marcus was named for his maternal grandfather, the Reverend Marcus Wood, who had been a bishop of the Methodist Church. He kept a daily diary during his adult life, including the years when he was bishop. Marcus' graduate thesis was based on the contents of this diary.

Marcus started keeping a diary himself. I thought it was a good idea and started my own diary on September 15, 1929, one day before I entered college. I continue this diary today, more than 59 years later.

FRESHMAN YEAR, 1929-1930

The freshmen entered college before the rest of the students for an orientation week. There were about 1,000 in my class and a total student body enrollment of 3,000. My schedule that first week was:

Monday. I arrived at Chapel Hill and had a physical exam in the gym at 7:30 p.m., along with 200 others. We were completely naked standing in line waiting to be weighed, our heights measured, and examined by the doctor. I weighed

159 pounds and stood 5 feet, 9 1/2 inches tall.

Tuesday. We all met in Memorial Hall for a general introduction. I was notified that I had received a tuition scholarship for one year. I met with a professor to arrange my classes, then took an English placement test at 7:30 p.m.

Wednesday. Registration was at noon. I signed up to play football, got my equipment and went to the first practice at 4. Our high school did not have a football team and, bewildered by what I saw, I promptly withdrew from football.

Thursday. We toured the library and learned how it functioned. We visited the Tin Can, a large building made of corrugated iron and used for all indoor sports. The gymnasium was small, inadequate for large student body activities. We met with the school dean at 8:30 p.m.

Friday. I attended my first classes and chapel, which all freshmen were required to attend. The Baptist Church had a special program. The movie theater management arranged a complimentary midnight show for the freshmen.

Saturday. A free day.

I survived freshman orientation week without incident and got into the routine of college. The University operated on a quarter system at that time, with three quarters during the regular school year and a fourth quarter in the summer. This summer quarter was divided into two six-week sessions. I had no idea what I wanted to study or what courses I should take. I entered the School of Liberal Arts, which required 36 units for graduation - normally, three units per quarter, three quarters per year.

My English placement test showed I needed remedial instruction, though I would get college credit for the course. I had had only one year of French in high school and had to take a second course, without college credit.

Because I lived off campus, I arranged my classes so I had three classes in the morning along with chapel. Each course met daily during the week and quizzes were usually given on Saturday.

I had some experience in boxing as Uncle Lewis had brought us boxing gloves from New Mexico. On October 3 I signed up for the freshman boxing team and began training from 4 to 6, five afternoons weekly.

Orus referred me to the manager of the "M" grocery store for possible part-time work. I was hired to start Saturday, October 5, and was paid 50 cents an hour, twice what I expected. I worked eight hours on Saturdays and from one to four on weekdays for a year, making from $10 to $12 each week.

Exams for the fall quarter were given before Christmas. I passed all my courses but made a 'D' in history.

I worked for Orus one week during the holidays, painting one of his stores.

I made the freshman boxing team and began stringent training, including five miles of track each morning before breakfast. Our first match was with Washington and Lee at Lexington, Virginia, on January 18. We traveled by train overnight from Durham, the first time I had slept on a train, and stayed at the Robert E. Lee Hotel. I won this bout by technical knockout.

We returned to Virginia for matches with VMI and the University at Charlottesville and then had bouts at Chapel Hill with N.C. State, V.P.I. and Oak

Ridge Academy. I lost all of these by decision. A slight "cauliflower" developed in my left ear and I had blood clots removed from it every day or so for several weeks.

Exams for the winter quarter were in mid-March and again I passed everything. I made a grade of B on the remedial English course.

The spring quarter ended June 5 and for the first time I had an average "C". This was important: A "C" average meant I could take an extra course in the next quarter.

Marcus got his Bachelor of Divinity Degree from Duke in June. Maisie graduated in art from Meredith College and McLeod got his B.S. in medicine from Wake Forest. He then transferred to the University of Pennsylvania in Philadelphia for his last two years of medicine.

Financially, I had done very well my freshman year. I started with $800 credit on Mamma's ledger and would also get $1000 from her for college. I had made $10 to $12 a week working during the year and living with Velma and Marcus was cheap. As a result, I was able to pay all my expenses without using any of my savings.

I was still undecided about what I should study. In a professional sense, I had been exposed only to teachers, ministers, doctors and dentists. With my innate mechanical skills, I thought maybe I should be some kind of engineer. I had experience in farming and working in grocery stores, but these did not appeal to me. Because of operations at 12 and 13 years under ether anesthesia, I had developed a strong dislike for medicine and the odors associated with doctors' offices. McLeod had known that he wanted to study medicine before he finished high school but, after my operations, I was strongly set against medicine as a career.

During my freshman year I had many conferences with McLeod about my studies and future plans. Finally, he recommended I take courses I could use in any field I might choose later, including medicine, teaching, dentistry, or others. It really surprised me that he thought I could become a doctor if I wanted to. My grade average was only a "C-minus" my freshman year but his encouragement was all I needed and things were to change.

Due to the economic depression, I was unable to make much money in the summer. McLeod suggested I take an extra course during the regular school year and also go to summer school. In this way, I could graduate with an A.B. degree in three years. If I decided to study medicine, having the degree would help me get into medical school.

Attending college was cheap at this time. I ate at a boarding house for $25 a month. Due to my poor grades, I lost my tuition scholarship but the University allowed me to sign a low-interest promissory note for my tuition, to be repaid after I graduated and started working.

I registered for summer school and completed two courses during each summer session with a grade average of "B". I continued living with Marcus and Velma and worked at the grocery store part-time through July.

My childhood friend, Bruce Langdon, and I reserved a room in Grimes Dormitory for the fall quarter. We chose a walk-up on the fourth floor, where the rooms were smaller and less comfortable. However, the rooms were also cheaper and provided a better environment for studying than did those on the first three floors.

During three free weeks between summer school and the fall quarter, I worked in Sanford for Orus one week, then spent two weeks at Coats. I built a chicken house and shed, did some painting and some plowing. I went to Fuquay Springs six times to see a girlfriend I had met at my high school commencement. She was the sister of my high school French teacher and I was smitten.

While I was at Sanford, Orus arranged a boxing match between me and a black college student who worked for him. We boxed in an open space in the warehouse on wood flooring. We were about the same size, though he had a longer reach. I have never been hit so many times in one round in my life. I think I lost the bout by decision.

SOPHOMORE YEAR, 1930-31

My sophomore year was the turning point in my life. I had done well in summer school, passing four courses, and was considering studying medicine. However, this would depend on how well I did in the science courses that premed students were required to take. My grades would also have to improve.

McLeod said the future of medicine was in biochemistry. He recommended that I get an A.B. degree in Liberal Arts with a major in chemistry and a minor in biology. My faculty advisor, Professor R.E. Coker, suggested I make biology my major and he later offered me a fellowship in biology for my senior year, which would have paid me substantially. I followed McLeod's advice. Ten of my 36 courses had to be in my major and three in my minor.

In my sophomore year, my attitude toward my studies had changed. I stopped working in the grocery store and used all my available time to study. I continued boxing, working out daily from 4 to 6 and running five miles before breakfast. The middleweight position on the team was filled by a senior, who was much better than I. There was no junior middleweight position at that time.

To get my degree, I needed a reading knowledge of two foreign languages. I continued French and started German. Then, on October sixteenth, my German professor attempted suicide and a new teacher started the next day.

When the quarter ended I had done well, with A in Zoology under Dr. Coker, B in Chemistry I, B in German, and D in French literature. This last course was taught by a native German professor who had little patience with nonlinguistic, American students.

In the winter quarter, I again made good grades in four courses.

I was doing better in boxing and had developed the kick of a mule in my right arm. Anyone I hit went down. When the football season ended, some of the players tried to make the boxing team. My right hand caught one of them on the chin and he was out for 15 minutes. I knocked out the varsity man and another opponent in my weight. Before I stopped boxing, I had knocked out everyone on the team, including the heavyweight. I was knocked down myself several times, but never for more than a count of three. However, I was a poor boxer; my reaction time was too slow and I took much punishment.

Participating in boxing was good for me. It gave me a sense of belonging and prevented me from studying too much. I trained from September through March and occasionally had my picture and write-up in the student newspaper, The Daily Tarheel. This was a big boost for me. I was looking forward to my senior year, when I would be the undisputed choice for the varsity middleweight position.

The spring quarter was about the same as the winter quarter. I took four courses and made good grades. During spring vacation, I helped Neill plant an acre of Irish potatoes and built a pig pen for him.

I continued seeing my girlfriend at Fuquay Springs. During the school year, I caught rides to Raleigh, visited her in the dormitory parlor at Meredith College, and then caught rides back to Chapel Hill after 10 p.m.

I went to summer school again for six weeks, taking two chemistry courses with afternoon labs. The weather was hot and the library was not air-conditioned. I remember the perspiration dripping off my face as I studied. My grades were A and B on the two courses in summer school and A on a food chemistry course I took by correspondence during the remainder of the summer. I had now finished enough work to be able to graduate in one more year, provided I passed an oral comprehensive exam in chemistry given by the department head.

During the rest of the summer, I built a clay tennis court at the side of our house at Coats using a scoop pulled by our horse to grade the area about 36 inches. The clay was hauled from another section of our property

The leather washers in the valve of the pump were worn out and, again, I replaced them.

I entered an amateur boxing event at an arena near Erwin. No decision was rendered, but many punches were landed on both sides. Afterward, I decided it had been a mistake to participate as I was not in proper training and had prepared for this bout only two weeks.

In early September, Mamma and I did some cleanup work in the graveyard where her father was buried at her old home near Broadway.

_____SENIOR YEAR, 1931-32

Bruce Langdon and I roomed together again in Grimes Dormitory.

The dedication service of the new Memorial Hall was held in October. Speeches were given by Governor Gardener and Josephus Daniels, former Secretary of the Navy and later Ambassador to Mexico.

One day, Walter B. Patterson, also a student at the University, brought me a letter from my girlfriend. Apparently he had been getting my mail for two years, reading it, then discarding it. Finally, he decided to locate me and give me this letter, which had not been addressed properly.

November 11th was Armistice Day, a holiday. I attended the inauguration of Dr. Frank P. Graham, the new president of the University who later became a U.S. senator of some note.

In November, I enjoyed my first airplane ride in an open cockpit biplane over Chapel Hill. The ride cost $5.

In December, I applied for an A.B. Degree in Liberal Arts in June. I also took a medical aptitude test and eventually was accepted in the two-year medical school of the University.

During the winter quarter, which started January 4th, I had a philosophy course under Paul Green, the famous playwright. However, before the quarter was over, he left for Hollywood to become a script writer for Will Rogers.

I had started boxing training as usual in September. During the Christmas holidays, I worked in Orus's grocery store for a week and then went home to find Mamma and Neill sick with mumps.

Back at school, we were preparing for our first boxing meet on January 16th. Each day we had a good workout on the bags and skipping rope, then boxed four, three-minute rounds. In the meets, we boxed only three, two-minute rounds.

On January 5th and 7th, I felt ill. On January 10th I recall that each time I was hit on the chin, my ears would ring for several seconds. That evening, I realized I had mumps; one side of my face was swollen. I was quarantined in the dispensary for a week.

On January 11th, mumps developed on the other side of my face and I was quarantined for another week. I returned to class on January 25th and the coach said I could continue boxing in another week.

I faced two serious problems. My attack of mumps was atypical in that I had a second attack after one week. There was the possibility that I would get orchitis if I returned to the strenuous activity of training too soon. Another problem was my classwork. I was taking two difficult science courses with labs and had to pass all courses with good grades to be able to graduate in June and get into medical school. It was clear I should stop boxing, which I did. I missed getting my letter in sports.

Now I realize I was lucky to have contracted the mumps when I did and how important it was to have stopped boxing. I have treated many patients with mumps orchitis, a serious illness. It often produces sterility which would have been a disaster for me as a happy home with wife and children was my first priority in life.

Of equal importance was the fact that varsity boxing was a tough sport. One of the members of our team, who was an excellent boxer, was already punch drunk by the time he was a senior. I was not a good boxer and took too much punishment. Each blow to the head causes a mild concussion and some brain damage. During the season, we boxed three or four rounds every day, and every punch had the potential to cause brain damage. If I had had a son, I would not have allowed him to box. Again, it seems that fate was taking care of me.

On February 19th, I took my oral comprehensive exam in chemistry from the department head and was among seven out of 14 who passed. Now I could graduate if I passed the remainder of my courses.

On February 20th I heard a lecture by physicist Professor Robert A. Millikin of the University of Chicago, entitled "The Changing World." He had won the Nobel Prize in 1923 for identifying the negative electron charge.

I took dancing lessons in the spring and began escorting girls to campus dances. I first wore a tuxedo (rented) at the junior-senior banquet at Meredith College.

My love affair was in trouble. My girlfriend and I became engaged after discussing the problems that might arise. She was the angel of my dreams and I thought I loved her; she was beautiful and I "melted" in her presence. She set the rules we were to abide by and then broke them, and our romance was on and off all spring. I finally sent her my last (souvenir) invitation to my graduation.

In May, I went to our junior prom and senior ball without dates and danced the entire time, enjoying myself immensely.

On June 4th commencement activities began with senior prayers and excercises in Gerard Hall. At 5 p.m. Bruce brought my girlfriend and her sister to Chapel Hill and we had a wonderful dinner and evening together. The next day, Dr. Hickman of Duke University gave the baccalaureate sermon. Commencement excercises were on Monday, the 6th, in Kenan Stadium. Mamma, Maisie, Neill and Orus saw me receive my diploma and a Bible, both of which I still have. In the evening, I went to the Alumnae Ball in the Tin Can.

After graduation, I went home for a while, worked on several projects, then went on to Sanford to work in Orus's grocery store.

On June 21st I listened to the Schmeling-Sharkey heavyweight boxing bout on the radio. Sharkey won, bringing the boxing crown back to the U.S.A.

On September 1st and 2nd, Neill and I painted the roof of the house at Coats using 22 gallons of paint.

Three days later I drove all night, hauling a truck load of chickens to Baltimore for Orus. Before returning, I bought a suit of clothes at Montgomery Ward.

CHAPTER V

Medical School Years: 1932 to 1936

Financially, I had done very well in my three years of college and 18 weeks of summer school. I had bought my own clothes and otherwise paid my own way. Starting with $800 credit on Mamma's ledger and using the $1000 that she loaned me for college, I still had $600 when I entered medical school. McLeod had graduated from medical school before I entered and was soon able to repay Mamma what he had borrowed and then loaned me money.

FIRST YEAR AT U.N.C.
MEDICAL SCHOOL: 1932-1933

Classes started on September 23rd. Paul Cameron had roomed on the fourth floor of Grimes dormitory for two years and we had become good friends. We roomed together during our first year in medical school, again on the fourth floor of the dorm. His was the most loyal friendship I ever had, lasting until his death at 62 of multiple myeloma.

During my medical school years, I studied until I was exhausted. For the first time in my life, I stopped going to church regularly. There was so much to learn, not enough time to study, and I was afraid I might not pass and be forced to drop out. Two of our class of 44 stopped school after four months because they could not grasp the work. I tutored one of these. One student developed pulmonary tuberculosis after four months and stopped medicine altogether. Another developed diabetes mellitus and tuberculosis, but recovered and returned after missing a year.

I realized I could not study all the time and survive. I participated in intramural sports and often went to the gym in late afternoon for a good workout. I tried to take a half-day off from study each weekend. Sometimes I went to campus events such as Playmaker productions, sports events, dances, and movies. I was still in love and saw my girlfriend every two weeks or so.

A few interesting events occurred during the first quarter.

On October 4th, the American Medical Association, through the local county medical society, gave a banquet in honor of the first year class.

Dr. Mangum complimented my partner and me on our dissection of the lower extremity of our cadaver and said we were the best in the class. I must admit that my experiences as a butcher helped me in my anatomy course. Our anatomy classes were three hours daily for six months, always working on cadavers preserved in formaldehyde.

I saw Paul Green's play, "The Cabin in the Cotton," at the Playmaker's theater and enjoyed it.

I took my first quiz in medical school November 2nd and made 98 (on materia med.)

November 8, 1932, was election day and the country went strongly Democratic, electing Franklin D. Roosevelt president. I welcomed this change, in spite of being a Republican.

Duke beat U.N.C. 7 to 0 in football on the 20th - the first time they had beaten us in the 20th Century.

I was having headaches due to eye strain and, on the 25th, was fitted for reading glasses.

I bought my first tuxedo on November 30th and paid $23.50 for a complete outfit that originally was priced at $37.50.

Classes for the fall quarter ended December 21st and I welcomed a two-week vacation. I had done well in my work.

In 1933, Dean Issac Manning, longtime dean of the medical school and professor of physiology, resigned and was replaced by Dr. Charles Mangum. Dr. Manning had been forced by the State Legislature to accept one more Jewish student into the medical school than the quota required. This quota was based on the percentage of Jews in the State's population. His resignation caused a furor among the doctors in the State, many of whom had been his students. He continued as professor of physiology and I was fortunate to be one of his students in my second year. As I recall, the student who was at the center of the controversy flunked out of school his first year.

On February 10th, my skin tuberculosis test was positive. A chest x-ray showed a Ghon tubercle, a sign of healed childhood tuberculosis, and no active disease. I do not know how or when I was exposed to tuberculosis. The x-ray also showed my heart to be abnormally enlarged and I was told I had an 'athletic heart.'

The medical and law schools joined forces and staged dances Friday and Saturday afternoons and evenings on February 17th and 18th. My girlfriend was with me on Saturday and we had a glorious time. The harmony in our love affair, however, was short-lived.

On March 4, 1933, I listened to the radio as Franklin D. Roosevelt was inaugurated as President.

Beer was finally legalized in North Carolina in April, 1933. By May 1st it was legal to sell beer in Chapel Hill for the first time in 100 years.

On the 9th of May, the U.N.C. baseball team beat Wake Forest 3 to 0. Andrews pitched a no-hit game against the notorious Lefty Barnes, who allowed eight hits.

The U.N.C. tennis team - the National Collegiate champions - won the Southern Conference championship on May 10th.

I took a co-ed to the junior prom and senior ball on May 12th and 13th.

I finished my freshman year on June 2nd with a B average.

Again, I spent the summer with Orus who had sold the grocery stores and bought a large farm. At first I did regular farm work. Then we began trucking fruits and vegetables from North Carolina to the large city markets on the East Coast. On our first trip, we hauled a load of dewberries (cultivated blackberries) from Vass, N.C., to Norfolk, Virginia, in nine hours on his Ford truck.

On June 10th, another driver and I left for the New York City market with a load of dewberries which are very perishable. They had to be delivered to the market within 24 hours. We left Vass at 5 p.m. planning to reach New York City, a distance of 475 miles, by 5 the next afternoon. The produce market opened at 11 p.m. for the following day. Our goal was to get there early, unload, and leave.

En route near Fredericksburg, Va., the front universal joint on the truck burned out. Luckily we were within three miles of a Ford agency that had a mechinic on duty all night. Within an hour, a wrecker had us in the garage, and three hours later we were on the road again. We were short of cash so I left Orus's Elgin watch in hock until we returned.

We reached the New York market at 10 p.m. Bedlam reigned. It is difficult to describe the noise and confusion at that hour. Our truck was half the size of most of the trucks and movement was very slow. Finally we delivered our load of berries in good condition and left.

We took another load of dewberries and a few crates of wild huckleberries to New York on June 15th. This time, we scorched a piston on the way home and had to drive slowly.

By then, the dewberry season was over. I worked on the farm for several days while Orus put a large body on the truck. With the addition of a second rear axle, the truck had six rear wheels.

On July 1st, a driver and I took 300 bushels of bellpeppers from Turkey, N.C., to the New York City market. A tire blew out near Petersburg, Va., but we were able to reach the market by 8 p.m. Another load of 320 bushels was carried on the 5th.

Starting on the 10th, we hauled three loads of cantaloupes of about 200 crates each to New York. The growers gave us a couple of crates of ripe cantaloupes to use as bribes for traffic cops who seemed to expect them. This certainly was better than paying for traffic tickets.

We had expected to haul peaches, but the market was flooded, resulting in no business for us. I next turned to watermelons.

Watermelons are heavy. They can't be trucked very far, nor be packed more than four deep without crushing the ones on the bottom.

Orus and I bought a load of watermelons from a farmer in Raeford, took them to Greensboro and sold them from the truck on a street corner in a residential area. The city inspector arrived to check on us. Truckers needed a special license to peddle fruits and vegetables, while farmers were allowed to sell their own produce without permits. Orus said we had grown the melons on our farm near Raefod. The inspector, sensing we were truckers and not farmers, asked Orus what county Raeford was in and got the correct answer, Hoke. Satisfied, he bought a melon and left.

There was a wholesale fruit and vegetable market at Candor, N.C., about 25 miles west of Southern Pines. Truckers from North Carolina, South Carolina, and Georgia, brought produce there and sold it to truckers from the large cities of the Eastern Seaboard. It was a busy market, but there was not much markup in prices.

I hired a black college student as a helper and we worked this market for the first two weeks of August. We worked, ate and slept together. Our bed was the floor of the truck if it were empty, with a folded blanket for a pillow and another to cover ourselves.

Grade A watermelons were long, uniform in shape and weighed 30 pounds. They were packed in box cars four deep and shipped to the city markets on the East Coast. I would buy 200 for 20 cents each, haul them to Candor and sell them for 30 cents apiece. We would eat and sleep at Candor and return the next day with another load.

If the weather was very hot for a few days, the ripe melons would get sunburned. An area up to six inches in diameter on the outside rind would get brown, although the inside of the melon was not damaged. This made the melons grade B and difficult to sell.

If the watermelons had abnormal shapes or were too large, they were also grade B, or cull., One day, I bought 200 of these culls for 5 cents each including loading them into the truck. They were guaranteed to weigh 40 pounds each and I weighed any melon that appeared too small. The profit on these grade B melons was much higher than on the grade A ones.

My final purchase of watermelons was to buy all the melons in a two-acre field without counting them. I peddled these in Greensboro and High Point, but had difficulty selling all of them. Finally, I exchanged the remaining melons for 50 gallons of gasoline, filling both tanks on the truck. I netted only $20 to $50 per week selling watermelons.

Mamma decided to live in Chapel Hill as Neill was entering college. Dorothy was beginning high school and I had one more year in medical school. I help locate a suitable house on the outskirts of town, three blocks north of the firehouse on the airport road. On August 14th, I moved Mamma's furniture to the house.

Mamma had always had a milk cow and wanted one at her new home. There was plenty of space at the back of the lot so I brought a couple loads of lumber from Orus's farm and built a barn and an exercise lot for the cow, with provisions for a calf. Orus sent Mamma a Jersey cow and calf. This cow produced an abundance of milk. My sisters are still amused that Mamma would insist on having a cow in Chapel Hill.

There was a small shed by the barn, where I enclosed a pigeon loft and raised squab for our table. This was my only experience with pigeons although I had raised chickens, ducks and rabbits.

The new home was heated by wood stoves, so I brought several loads of firewood from Coats and Sanford while I still had the truck.

SECOND YEAR AT U.N.C.
MEDICAL SCHOOL: 1933-34

I registered for the second year of medicine September 21st. My former room-mate, Bruce Langdon, was living with me in our home. He was now a senior in the School of Liberal Arts and planned to enter medical school.

Things were not much different in the second year. I studied almost all the time, trying to make good grades so I could transfer to the school of my choice for my third and fourth years.

We had some exposure to clinical medicine, but little compared to the students in four-year schools. I went to Duke Unviersity for several clinicopathological conferences, attended an eye clinic in Raleigh and saw four cataract operations, went to several clinical conferences at Watts Hospital in Durham, visited the State Mental Hospital in Raleigh and examined many patients, and saw at least two autopsies at Watts Hospital. One of these had arteriosclerosis with massive brain hemorrhage and died three weeks later. The other had been shot five times by the police.

I visited the State Tuberculosis Sanatorium, located in a rural area beyond Southern Pines. There, I was introduced to pneumothorax treatment, which I used in treating patients later in my practice.

I had a chest x-ray at the sanatorium which showed that my heart was still considerably enlarged. I had no symptoms or signs of heart disease and was again told I had an 'athletic heart' probably due to overtraining, though I was told how much to do by my coach. My heart is now normal size.

On November 8th, I saw Duke University beat U.N.C. 21 to 0 in football at the Duke Stadium with 30,000 other spectators. During half time, the two bands marched around the field in formation with U.N.C. in front. The Duke mascot, a blue devil with horns and tail, had a trident (spear) that he threw down the field as he cavorted in front of the Duke band. Once he threw it too far and speared a U.N.C. band member in the back. Luckly, the middle prong of the trident had been removed. An ambulance quickly came on the field and took the injured band member to the hospital. I never learned the outcome of this injury, although Maisie thinks he recovered.

On December 31st, Bruce and I went to a dance at Clayton, N.C., that lasted from 9 p.m. to 4:30 a.m. I recall that there were seven of us in a Chrysler Imperial, which had free-wheeling. The roads were level with few curves, and we were travelling at 85 miles an hour. When the accelerator was released on curves, the engine disengaged and we were rolling free. Luckily, the driver had not drunk much alcohol and we arrived safely. It still scares me to think that we went around those curves so fast.

Many four-year medical schools had room for a few junior student transfers each year. As a rule, we chose the best school we could get into, thinking that the big name schools in the large cities would give us a better education. Harvard and the University of Pennsylvania in Philadelphia were considered the two top schools. The University of Pennsylvania was the oldest medical school in the U.S., founded in 1765. Again, I depended on McLeod's advice. He recommended I apply to three schools: the University of Pennsylvania as first choice, Northwestern and Rush.

The dean of our school knew how many student transfers each school would accept and recommended the students to the schools of their choice if possible. Six students chose the University of Pennsylvania, but there was room for only five. Our dean refused to make the selection and had us all apply, leaving the decision to the dean at Pennsylvania. Luckily, I was accepted. McLeod had done well at Pennsylvania, a fact that I'm sure helped me. Also, I had a degree in Liberal Arts, whereas some of the other applicants did not. I heard of my acceptance on March 2nd and promptly withdrew my applications from Northwestern and Rush. Being accepted at the University of Pennsylvania was a dream come true.

On May 11th and 12th, I escorted a new girlfriend to the junior prom, senior ball and afternoon tea dances. Music was provided by Hal Kemp who had formed his orchestra while he was a student at Chapel Hill.

The Dionne Quintuplets were born May 18, 1934, the first quintuplets to survive. I saved a newspaper picture of them and their mother.

On June 7th I went to the final school dances at which Jan Garber and his band played and on the 11th I attended the Alumnae Ball.

I applied to the Queen's Hospital in Honolulu for an internship to start after my graduation in 1936. McLeod served his internship there and recommended I apply early. This was a good rotating internship which paid $1800 a month at a time when Mainland hospitals did not pay interns any salary.

On the 19th and 20th I took and passed the first half of the North Carolina State Medical Board Exams.

During the summer I worked for the Building Department of the University, starting at 20 cents an hour. Neill worked there part-time during the year and helped me get the job. Some of the workers were college athletes although most of them were ordinary laborers.

I started as a carpenter's helper and, on my first job, a carpenter and I replaced a wooden bridge over railroad tracks in the western part of town. The steel supporting girders were about 16 feet above the tracks. I soon became accustomed to the height and lost my fear of falling.

My next job involved digging a trench across a large cement area. One worker held a large steel spike while another drove it through the cement with a five-pound sledge hammer. After a few minutes, they changed places. Accuracy with the hammer was essential.

I was promoted to the position of tinner's helper at a wage of 25 cents an hour. The tin roofs and gutters of the houses owned by the University had to be repaired, as well as the tin flues for stoves. I really learned how to kill time at this job. We usually handled two small jobs in each four-hour period, when we could have done three or four.

I was again promoted, this time to plumber's helper at 30 cents an hour. I learned a lot at this work. One of our jobs was to replace a faulty trap in the sewer line six feet below the basement floor of the girls' dormitory. When everything was exposed and ready, an order was given to the girls not to use any of the plumbing from 10 p.m. to 6 a.m. We replaced the trap by the deadline. I worked continually except for meals for two days and the night between and was tired, though my paycheck was large. We were only paid straight time for the overtime.

My summer work ended August 20th and I then spent four days with Dr. Young in Angier. I attended a woman in labor with him and saw my first birth, a baby girl weighing eight pounds. Starting August 27th I was again with him for a week. He treated about 20 patients in the office and made several house calls each day. We took two patients to Rex Hospital in Raleigh. On the 27th and 28th I visited Atlantic Beach with the Youngs, where we went fishing.

On September 6th I repaired the sewer line at our house in Coats, which was rented at the time.

Aunt Edith loaned me $500 on a short-term basis. On the 17th I was in Philadelphia, preparing to enter the University of Pennsylvania.

THIRD YEAR, UNIVERSITY OF PENNSYLVANIA: 1934-35

Ralph Fleming, a classmate who lived near Durham, drove me to Philadelphia. During the first week, we looked for a suitable rooming house after asking several of McLeod's fraternity brothers for advice and help. Two other transfers from Chapel Hill arrived and all of us decided to stay at a rooming house on 38th Street. Before classes started, I went to several good shows and a burlesque for the first time.

On September 23rd I pledged Phi Rho Sigma Medical Fraternity. McLeod had been a member of this house since he was at Wake Forest. As there was no chapter at Chapel Hill, I waited and joined in Philadelphia. Becoming a member helped me in medical school and in getting adjusted to life in Philadelphia.

Our classes started on the 24th. Two days later I had my first patient assigned to me at the Pennsylvania Hospital on 8th and Spruce Street. This is the oldest hospital in the U.S., founded by Benjamin Franklin in 1752. I attended my first clinic at Philadelphia General Hospital on the 28th. At that time, this hospital had about 2800 beds and was one of the largest in the country. It has since closed. It was adjacent to the Hospital of the University of Pennsylvania and to the Medical School, and was supported by the City of Philadelphia. All the patients were indigent and, upon admission, were required to sign a permission for an autopsy in case of death. We students often spent Sunday mornings in the hospital morgue, watching 12 to 15 autopsies.

Our group could not endure the conditions in our rooming house, so we rented an apartment at 37th and Spruce Street. It was noisy because of street cars but otherwise excellent. Our former landlady raised hell with the dean when we broke our contract. The new apartment had a kitchen, so one of my roommates and I decided to prepare our meals. I bought and cooked the food and he washed the dishes. We occasionally invited girls in for dinner.

We had a telephone installed using all four of our names. There were 19 other William Pattersons listed in the directory at different addresses, while there was only one Shuford, our roommate, Jake.

I joined the John B. Deaver Surgical Society. Half its members were Phi Rho Sigma undergraduates and half belonged to Chi Phi medical fraternity. We had clinicopathological conferences each month presented by a prominent authority, usually not associated with our school. The meetings would alternate between the two fraternity houses. Dr. George P. Mueller, a former associate of Dr. Deaver, was our patron.

An international medical meeting was held at the nearby Philadelphia Convention Center from November 6th through 9th. I attended sessions every day and heard many world-renowned speakers.

I passed all my work in the first quarter and the second quarter began November 19th. On the 24th I was initiated into Phi Rho Sigma Fraternity. I invited a girlfriend to the formal banquet and dance at the Sylvania Hotel.

Ralph and I left for North Carolina November 27th for the Thanksgiving holidays. We saw U.N.C. beat Virginia in football 25 to 6 on Thanksgiving Day. George Barclay, an all-American from U.N.C., played.

In December, I saw my first mastoid operation at the University Hospital.

Just before Christmas, I met Uncle Leon in Washington and the two of us went to Chapel Hill for the holidays.

Philadelphia offered a great variety of entertainment and live shows starring prominent entertainers. Once a week we students usually got away from our studies to take in these shows. I saw Jack Benny and Mary Livingston at the Earle Theater, Guy Lombardo and his band at the Fox, Cab Calloway at the Lincoln, and many others.

In January, I visited Seny Bynum at the Women's Medical College in Philadelphia. Her home was in Chapel Hill and she had been a classmate of mine in medical school.

I applied to the medical school for a loan to pay my tuition for the second semester.

On January 14th, Dr. Piper of the obstetrical department died. He was famous for designing the Piper Aftercoming-Head-Forcep which has saved many lives and birth injuries.

I went to the Unversity of Pennsylvania Medical School Interfraternity Dance with a date and saw many old friends.

The Deaver Surgical Society had Professor Babcock of Temple Unviersity as a guest speaker. I was the only one to make the correct diagnosis for the case he presented.

Paul Cameron, who transferred to Temple Medical School, came to see me in February to borrow some money. This was most unusual as I was the one who frequently had to borrow from him.

I heard the famous Dr. Rosenow give a lecture at the Philadelphia College of Physicians on the new prophylaxis of pneumonia. At that time, pneumonia was one of the leading killers of young adults.

In March, I learned I had failed to get an internship at the Queen's Hospital in Honolulu for 1936.

World-famous Dr. Chevalier Jackson of Temple University Medical School spoke on hiatal hernia at the Deaver Surgical Society. He showed slides of pictures and made colored crayon drawings of his findings as seen through the esophagoscope. I will never forget the beauty of his drawings and the ease with which he made them; his artistic ability was phenomenal.

Easter vacation began April 18th and Easter Sunday was the 21st, my birthday. The two events have occurred simultaneously only twice since then. I was alone in the apartment for several days as my roommates had gone home. The landlady brought me a nice dinner and I received a telegram and a phone call from two of my girlfriends.

In May, I saw the Phillies and St. Louis Cardinals play a double-header with the brothers Paul and Dizzy Dean pitching for St. Louis.

I took my last exam on June 7th and left for Chapel Hill. The next day I went to the final University dance featuring Ozzie Nelson's band and Harriet Hillard. Those attending the dance seemed so young, almost like high school students. I was only 23 but the strain of three years in medical school was making me feel and look older.

On June 20th I left Chapel Hill for Philadelphia and Ocean City, New Jersey, where I had accepted work as a children's camp physician for the summer. Paul Cameron lived in Ocean City at the time, and got the job for me. The camp was a large two-story house on the beach about 34th Street. Over 100 children attended camp at one time, each child usually staying for one or two weeks. All kinds of beach activities were offered. The camp owned a motor boat and a rowboat, which were used on the inland waterway near the coast.

I spent the days with the children and in the evenings Paul and I usually went to the Boardwalk in Atlantic City, 10 miles away. There were always good shows and orchestras playing on the Steel Peir. Guy Lombardo's orchestra was there for a week. Unattached girls were everywhere, vacationing at the beach, so it was always easy to get a date.

I went deep-sea fishing three times. The first time Paul, one of his brothers and I chartered a 20-foot motor boat and went out so far we could not see land. Paul had a hangover from the night before and became seasick the minute we got out into the channel between Ocean City and Somer's Point. He begged us to return to land and we refused. The sight of my tuna sandwiches for lunch made him even sicker. I caught 33 fish weighing up to four pounds each which the camp directors were happy to get.

Uncle Leon and Maisie came to see me one weekend and we went fishing with about 50 other people on a 60-foot boat. That day I caught only two fish. When I went out again on this same boat I caught 44 fish weighing a total of 150 pounds.

I almost drowned one day. A young counselor and I tried to swim out to the camp's rowboat anchored to a buoy in the middle of the narrow channel south of Ocean City. The tide was coming in and the water in the channel was flowing like a raging river. We started swimming about 100 feet on the ocean side opposite the boat, but when I reached the boat area I was 10 feet beyond it and could not make any headway against the inflowing tide. The counselor reached the boat but could not untie the knot that held the boat to the buoy. He was a better swimmer than I and our plan was for him to come for me in the boat if I did not reach the buoy.

I realized the predicament I was in and began swimming with the tide to the nearest bank. Two boys on the pier were watching and quickly came to my aid in a rowboat. I grasped the side of the boat and my feet struck bottom as the water was only four to five feet deep at that point. I was so exhausted I could not get into the boat. Possibly, I would not have drowned if I had not been rescued, but it was a scary experience.

My work at the camp was primarily first aid for minor injuries and the treatment of colds. Impetigo was a real threat. If it got a foothold it would spread rapidly and possibly force the camp to close. There were no antibiotics or sulfa drugs at that time. I quickly learned that to cure impetigo I had to do two things: First I scrubbed the affected parts thoroughly twice dialy with hot, soapy water and then anointed the area with five percent ammoniated mercury cream for 20 minutes. I did this myself for each patient and the lesions healed in three days.

I was supposed to be paid $10 weekly for my work but for the first month, I received nothing. The camp owners claimed they were losing money. I gave them an ultimatum that if I were not paid $20 weekly thereafter I would leave. I was paid. Camp ended September 1st and I left for North Carolina.

During the first week of September I painted the roof of our house at Coats. On the 8th, Governor Huey Long of Louisiana was shot; he died two days later.

FOURTH YEAR, UNIVERSITY OF PENNSYLVANIA: 1935-36

I registered for my senior year on September 16th and started working on the wards at University Hospital. Ralph Fleming and I had an apartment and I took my meals at the fraternity house, two blocks away.

I was observing many operations in surgery by Drs. Ravdin, Eliason, Orr, and others. I saw Dr. C.H. Frazier, head of neurosurgery, inject the fifth facial nerve for trigemial neuralgia. He had devised this operation and was world-famous for it. He died of prostatic cancer during my senior year.

On October 4th I gave my first two general anesthetics. I also assisted in wiring the fractured jaw of one of my patients who had been in an auto accident. He was in a coma for three weeks and, when he regained consciousness, complained of leg pain. An x-ray showed a spiral fracture of the tibia. He eventually recovered. Later in my plantation work at Pahala, Hawaii, I wired a fractured jaw just as I had helped do on this patient.

For relaxation, Ralph and I spent a Sunday afternoon at the Philadelphia Zoo.

On the 28th I started night duty in the receiving ward at Episcopal Hospital. One patient with vaginal bleeding was found to have a stab wound in the vaginal wall. After suturing, the bleeding was controlled.

I attended the Penn-Navy football game at Franklin Field November 9th, which Navy won 13-0. It was a very colorful game, particularly the half-time show.

On the 15th I went to Chapel Hill and Durham with a friend to see a Duke-North Carolina football game. Duke won 25-0, knocking Carolina out of a Rose Bowl bid.

By the end of November, my feet became so painful I could hardly walk. An orthopedist prescribed special shoes with high tops and anterior and longitudinal arch supports. My feet soon improved. Since that time, which has been over 50 years, I have had sore feet. Thirty years after this original attack, x-rays demonstrated multiple gouty cysts in all my metatarsals. Probenecid therapy helped immediately. Gradually, over the years, my knees, back, neck and metacarpal joints became involved. I have had three attacks of acute gout with severely painful, hot, swollen knees, requiring Butazolidin therapy. My blood uric acid level has been only moderately elevated; the joint pains and attacks of gout have followed stress and strain, or exhaustion from any cause.

Mamma, Orus, his wife, Verl, and O.F. Junior came to Philadelphia December 1st for three days. I arranged an appointment with Dr. George M. Coates, head of the Department of Otolaryngology, to determine the cause of O.F. Jr.'s total hearing loss in one ear. His diagnosis was a nerve deafness due to mumps and no treatment was recommended. After a sightseeing tour of the city, they returned to North Carolina.

I applied to the Geisinger Hospital at Danville, Pennsylvania, for a 12-month rotating internship where my roommate, Ralph, had already been accepted. I was accepted on the 12th.

I spent the last two weeks before Christmas vacation at the Philadelphia Lying-In-Hospital and saw many babies born. One patient had an abruptio placenta and required a cesarean-hysterectomy.

Starting December 21st, I spent two weeks at the University's Southeastern Obstetrical Dispensary, giving up my Christmas vacation. Indigent obstetrical patients went there for prenatal checks. When labor began, two students and an obstetrical nurse attended the delivery in the home, travelling there by street car or on foot. An obstetrical resident from the hospital was on call for any emergency. After delivery, we visited the patients daily for a week and also took care of any patients who aborted at home. We had much night work. I remember walking in the ice and snow in the early morning hours carrying my medical bag. I had a delivery at 2:45 a.m on January 1, 1936, and as we walked down the streets, almost every home had a radio blaring out the song "The Music Goes 'Round and 'Round and Comes out Here."

We made calls on New Year's Day, stopping on Broad Street to see the wonderful Mummer's Parade.

Regular classes started on January 2nd. I heard a lecture on leprosy on the 4th by Dr. O.E. Kennedy from the leprosarium at Carville, Louisiana. Eventually, I used this information in Hawaii, where I encountered an occasional patient with this disease. It is now better known as Hansen's disease. Most new cases in Hawaii are found in recent immigrants.

I saw my first twins delivered on February 11th at Kensington Hospital. A beautiful display of northern lights (aurora borealis) lit up the night sky on the 14th. One of the babies I delivered, an 11-pound boy, was a native American, next in line to become chief of his people.

One day I borrowed a fellow-student's Model T Ford to drive to our clinic at Episcopal Hospital. The streets were covered with ice and snow. At an intersection I slid into the car coming from my right, learning right then that the car on the right has the right-of-way. I had no driver's license - North Carolina did not require one - but knew a license was required in Pennsylvania. The driver of the other car and I went to a garage where I paid $25 to have his car repaired. My borrowed car was not damaged. The accident was not reported to the police.

On March 31st I turned in my senior research paper, representing 100 hours of work. Each student was required to write a paper in both his junior and senior years. McLeod and Dr. Joseph McFarland, professor of patholgy, co-authored a paper on Odontoma, which was published in a national journal of pathology. I hoped to do as well.

The paper I wrote my junior year was entitled "The Toxicity of Dinitrophenol" and was not very noteworthy. For my senior paper, "A Classification of the Macrocytic Anemias," I consulted with all my professors of internal medicine and hematology. I wrote to Dr. George Minot of Johns Hopkins Medical School for additional information. He was an authority on this type of anemia (pernicious anemia) and had won the Nobel Prize for his work in this field. I had a special interest in this type of anemia because Grandma Fuquay died of it one year before the cause and treatment were discovered.

I got an A on my report. Dr. O.H. Perry Pepper, professor of medicine, told the entire senior class during a lecture that there were two outstanding senior papers, mine and one other. He recommended that all seniors read our papers and stated that they should be published.

A group of us went to Valley Forge on May 6th to see the historic sites and the dogwood trees, which were in bloom. The 7th was Undergraduate Medical Assocation Day and there were no classes so several of us drove to Atlantic City.

I heard Dr. C.H. Frazier give his last lecture, on brain abscess, on the 14th. He died soon after from cancer.

Dr. Farley, internist and former North Carolinian who had retained his Southern drawl, got me in the pit at Pennsylvania Hospital with a patient and grilled me on the treatment of iron-deficient anemia. He was stressing the use of ferrous compounds rather than ferric ones, which had been used before and were poorly absorbed.

About two months before, I was at a dance in the Mirror Room at the Sylvania Hotel and noticed that my reflection appeared pale compared to everyone else's. A hemoglobin check of my blood showed nine grams per ml compared to a normal of 15 grams. Obviously, I was not getting enough iron in my diet at the fraternity house. Thereafter, I took six Feosol pills (30 grains) daily and my hemoglobin level eventually returned to normal. I carried some Feosol pills loose in my coat pocket so I could take them with lunch.

Dr. Farley was not completely satisfied with my answers. He asked me the color of the Feosol pill - green - and then the shape - triangular. At this point, I took several Feosol pills from my pocket and showed them to him, explaining that I, myself, was taking them for anemia. He was satisfied and had gotten his point across to the class.

My last class was on May 23rd and I was exempt from taking the final exams in psychiatry and medicine. Ralph was exempt from all his final exams and was able to leave for home a week earlier than I.

May 30th, Maisie stopped in Philadelphia on her way home from Hawaii and spent two days with me. She had taken a year off from teaching and spent it at Hana, Maui, with McLeod, where he was practicing medicine on a sugar plantation. He was unmarried at the time. Maisie and I went to the Ringling Brothers, Barnum and Bailey Circus.

By June 2nd I had finished all my exams and left Philadelphia for Chapel Hill, choosing not to stay for commencement exercises a week later. My diploma was mailed to me.

The student transfers from the two-year medical school were not considered in the class rankings. I had done well in my two years at Pennsylvania with an average of 83.86, equal to about the 25th position in the original class of 144. Seventy was a passing grade. Ralph had an average above 90, which put him in the top ten in our class.

I took Maisie to the Alumnae Ball on the 8th. Then, for a week, I studied for the second half of the North Carolina State Medical Board exams, held in Raleigh for three days starting on the 17th. Following this, I went to Myrtle Beach, South Carolina, with Jake Shuford, a former roommate in Philadelphia, his fiance, and several other classmates and their girlfriends. We had R and R for five days which we needed before starting our internships.

On the 28th I went to Washington and stayed with Uncle Leon for the night. The next day I was in Philadelphia staying in the fraternity house. On the 29th I checked in to Geisinger Hospital in Danville. I was on duty with the retiring intern in obstetrics on June 30th and helped in the delivery of three babies.

CHAPTER VI

Hospital Training and Marriage

TWELVE MONTHS ROTATING INTERNSHIP AT GEISINGER HOSPITAL 1936-37; START OF RESEARCH PROJECT

Geisinger Hospital is located at Danville, Pennsylvania, halfway between Harrisburg and Wilkesbarre. The internship at Geisinger was considered one of the best. It was only twelve months, but gave the new physician experience in all the specialties before limiting himself to one, if he chose to do so. It was also good training if he decided to go into general practice. The interns were not paid, but received free board, room and laundry service. They had to furnish their own white uniforms.

Geisinger Hospital was considered a teaching institution. There was a fulltime staff of senior physicians and residents who instructed the interns and taught them how to treat patients. The goal was to give patients the best care without limitations, such as a lack of finances or the availability of specialists. This was group medical practice, begun in 1915 when the hospital first opened. At the time of this writing, the Geisinger system of group practice has expanded to many satellite hospitals and clinics in central and northeastern Pennsylvania. The hospital at Danville has over 600 beds and a clinic with all modern diagnostic and therapeutic facilities.

I had corresponded with the chief of obstetrics, Dr. Roy Nicodemus, before starting my internship and had expressed a special interest in obstetrics. I was assigned to his service first in my internship rotation. He did not have a resident and was the only staff member who did not work fulltime for the hospital. He had a busy gynecology practice at an outside office. He supervised the interns closely for about two weeks and then for four weeks usually allowed them to deliver the ward patients. The fee for the ward patients was $100 which included prenatal care, delivery fee and hospitalization. Patients who went into semiprivate rooms paid $125, while those who took private rooms paid $150. If cesarean was required, there was an extra $50 charge.

During my first week, we delivered only four babies; one of these was a cesarean for a 10-pound baby and another was the normal delivery of a 6-pound, 12-ounce baby in a 15-year old mother.

At the beginning of my second week, I worked all night. We delivered five babies in three and a half hours. One of the patients, the wife of a prominent citizen of Danville, aspirated her vomitus while under ethylene anesthesia and a chest x-ray failed to show any air in her lungs. For 48 hours it appeared she would die. She was forced to cough until she was exhausted, then her trachea and bronchi were aspirated with a bronchoscope. She was in critical condition for five days, then recovered.

During our internship, everyone was required to do a research project and write a report. Dr. Nicodemus had heard a paper read at a medical meeting in June in which it was claimed that there was a direct relationship between placental infarction and eclampsia. The placental infarction was said to be due to cholesterol endarteritis, which was very similar to cholesterol-induced endarteritis of the rabbit. It was suggested that hypercholesteremia, which is usually present during human pregnancy, could be the cause of placental endarteritis, infarction and degeneration.

In the first week of July, Dr. Nicodemus suggested I study this as my research project and I agreed to so do. I finished my study 50 years later, in July, 1986.

During the rest of my six weeks on the obstetrical service, I had many interesting patients and learned a great deal. I assisted in the delivery of one patient who was a multi-millionaire. I delivered a set of twins. One patient had multiple eclamptic convulsions, but recovered after delivery. In the 42 days I was on the obstetrical service, we delivered 47 babies. I delivered 27 of these myself, unassisted.

During this time I did not have a single date. My first time off duty was the evening of July 18th.

Dr. Nicodemus gave me the highest possible praise for my work on the obstetrical service. Later, he took a five-day vacation and asked me to supervise the intern in his absence.

My next service was Eye, Ear, Nose, and Throat. The three senior staff members and one resident were headed by Dr. Francis Davison. He had been one of Dr. Chevalier Jackson's first residents and, like Dr. Jackson, was an expert in bronchoscopy. I recall one patient with an obstruction of a main bronchus caused by tubercular granulation tissue. Dr. Davison fulgurated the lesions through the bronchoscope twice weekly for many weeks. The patient learned to accept the passing of the bronchoscope through her larynx without complaint.

On August 16th I assisted in the delivery of twins - a boy and a girl - to Dr. Nicodemus's wife.

I began studying my research project in the second week of July, going about the investigation methodically as I had been taught in medical school. The hospital had a good library, which had connections with other libraries giving me access to the world medical literature. I read everything I could find in medical literature on cholesterol metabolism, both in pregnant and nonpregnant humans and animals. I read the literature on arteriosclerosis and high blood pressure. I studied everything I could find on toxemia of pregnancy in humans and animals. I learned about the development of the placenta in humans and animals and also about placental degeneration, with and without infarct formation. I studied so much I had difficulty relaxing and sleeping and became ill at times. I still had my internship work to do.

On August 29th, I removed my first pair of tonsils, an operation that was most difficult for me at the time. I was required to take out two pairs of tonsils during my internship and I thought these would be my last. However, later in my plantation practice, I became very adept at tonsillectomy.

September 9th, I had a conference with Dr. Foss, surgeon-in-chief, Dr. Hunt, pathologist, and Dr. Nicodemus. We agreed that I would do my research project on toxemia of pregnancy, which would include a study of thyroid function in normal and toxemic pregnancies. Dr. Hunt agreed to do any laboratory work I needed and Dr. Foss offered me financial backing by the hospital. This encouragement stimulated me so that I slept less and, at times, could barely do my intern work.

I rotated to the Surgical Service in September and was very busy. On October 2nd, I had a patient die in thyrotoxic crisis after a thyroidectomy. The hospital was located in the 'goiter belt' of Pennsylvania, and about 10 thyroidectomies were performed each week.

I was off duty from October 5th to 9th and went to North Carolina with Ralph Fleming, my roommate again. He married his childhood sweetheart, Sue Thompson, on October 8th.

At the hospital staff meeting in October, I gave a talk entitled "Macrocytic

Anemia" based on the paper I wrote during my senior year in medical school. It was well received. Later in October and in November, I gave talks at staff meetings on my present research project.

On November 11th, the hospital decided to build me a private lab and furnish me any money and technical help I needed.

One of my surgical patients needed a transfusion. After 25 ml of blood had been given, the lab notified me that a mistake had been made: The blood was of the wrong type. I quickly discontinued the transfusion. There was a slight febrile reaction and albumin and casts appeared in the urine. The patient had no other ill effects.

Dr. Foss, a pilot, owned a four-passenger Stinson plane which he kept at Sunbury, Pennsylvania. In December, we went flying for an hour and landed twice. We also flew in a Piper Cub which he had used in flight training.

The hospital bought me 20 virginal adult rabbit does for my experiments. I was trying to determine the level of blood cholesterol throughout normal pregnancy in the rabbit and in the rabbit fetus at term. Once I had this established, I planned to remove the maternal thyroid gland at the end of the first trimester and determine the effects this had on the blood cholesterol levels during the second and third trimesters. The fetal thyroid would have developed by the end of the first trimester. I planned to study the effects that maternal thyroidectomy would have on the fetal blood cholesterol levels at term, and also the effects it would have on the histological structure of the fetal thyroid. The first rabbits were bred on January 3rd and my experiments were underway.

While the rabbit experiments were in progress, I determined what the average blood cholesterol level was during human pregnancy in 100 patients. Blood samples were taken at four-week intervals from the 2nd month of pregnancy until term. Fetal blood cholesterol levels were determined at birth. Some of the mothers developed toxemia with high blood pressure.

In another part of my research, the placentas of 180 consecutive patients were placed in a formaldehyde solution for 30 days and then studied, both macro- and microscopically. The results of this study were correlated with the clinical courses of the patients.

Another investigation was done to show the effects of thyroid medication on the blood cholesterol levels of pregnant patients. A group was given thyroid tablets by mouth for eight weeks about the middle of pregnancy. Their blood cholesterol levels were determined before, during, and after treatment. A sharp drop in the level occurred while a patient took thyroid, but it returned to the previous level when the medication was stopped.

January 10th, I started my internship rotation in Laboratory and Pathology, which meant I did not have patients to care for and had more time for my research. I removed the first thyroids from the pregnant rabbits on January 12th. My special laboratory assistant for three months began working on the 16th, which relieved me of some work. I was still working almost all the time, night and day. I had to do many autopsies and other lab work, especially emergency work at night when the lab technicians were off duty.

January 27th, I restandardized the reagents for making cholesterol determinations. The old reagents had been on the lab shelves for years and had become too concentrated through evaporation. I had complained to Dr. Hunt that all my cholesterol determinations were about 30 percent too low according to what I read in the literature. I think the solution of naphthol green was at fault. When I made a new solution, I tested the old reagent and found it was 30 percent too strong. This meant that the 600 cholesterol determinations I had done so far had to be raised 30 percent. I was relieved now that my findings were the same as others in the literature.

The gestation period of the rabbit is only 30 days, so my experiments moved along very fast. With limited time, I could do only one or two rabbits each day and had to develop techniques and choose the proper anesthetic. I first used sodium amytal intravenously and the rabbits died a few days postoperatively of toxic hepatitis and nephritis. I then used sodium pentobarbital by gavage and had no further problem. I had to establish what was normal in the fetus at term, so I performed cesareans at term on a group of controls.

Then the unexpected happened. One thyroidectomized rabbit was found dead on the 29th day of gestation. She had delivered stillborn fetuses whose placentas were still attached with both the maternal and fetal portions present. The next day, another thyroidectomized rabbit had a convulsion and died in my presence while I was working with other rabbits. She had not delivered her fetuses, but was at term. A week later, a third thyroidectomized rabbit at term died in convulsions. The placentas of all these rabbits were found to contain large infarcts and there was severe cholesterol endarteritis in the placental arteries.

I continued my experiments getting normal controls. I did a cesarean on one rabbit, kept two of her fetuses for blood and tissue samples and gave three fetuses to the mother to raise.

Dr. Hunt went south for a vacation in January and I was busy. I did an autopsy every day for a week while he was away.

February 8th, I gave another talk to the staff reporting the progress in my experiments. Most of those present were convinced I was on the right track to find the cause of eclampsia.

I started my final internship rotation on the Medical Service on March 10th and was very busy. Although I liked internal medicine and the problems it presented in diagnosis, I would remain in obstetrics because of my research project and my love for women.

I applied to the American Association for the Study of Goiter to give a paper at its annual meeting in Detroit in June. Dr. Foss, one of the leaders in this organization, was pleased for me to give a talk at the meeting and my application was accepted.

Dr. Foss thought I would benefit from a conference with Dr. David Marine, a pioneer in the study of thyroid disease and its relationship to iodine deficiency. In April I spent four days in New York, staying on Long Island with a friend of my sister and had a five-hour conference with Dr. Marine, who was very kind and helpful. I also visited Radio City Music Hall, World Fair exhibits, the Empire State Building, and other tourist attractions.

For several weeks, I prepared a report on my research, entitled "The Etiology of Eclampsia, a Preliminary Report." Dr. Nicodemus was planning to attend a national medical meeting in June and applied to present a talk based on my work. However, his application was not accepted. Dr. Hunt then volunteered to give a talk at the annual meeting of the American Society of Clinical Pathologists in Philadelphia in June. I was to write a paper on my work and make an exhibit to illustrate the research.

I prepared charts that showed all my research results. We had enlarged photographs made of the placentas of humans and rabbits showing infarcts and degeneration. Placental arteries could be seen that were clogged with cholesterol deposits.

The center of the exhibit was a large color drawing showing how the pregnant woman, if hypothyroid, absorbed fetal thyroid secretion through the placenta for her own use leaving the fetus deficient. The artwork for the exhibit was done by Mrs. Jean Bush, whose husband, L.F. Bush, was the assistant chief-of-surgery at that time. He later became surgeon-in-chief and president of the Geisinger Medical Center and the Geisinger Foundation.

Hypothyroidism is accompanied by hypercholesteremia. Fetal blood flows in the placenta vessels, which means that fetal hypercholesteremia produces cholesterol endarteritis, arterial occlusion and placental degeneration. I proved this in my experiments by doing thyroidectomies on pregnant rabbits. Pregnant rabbits, unlike humans, have a low blood cholesterol during pregnancy, even if the thyroid is removed. However, the fetuses of thyroidectomized rabbits have greatly elevated blood cholesterol. I had demonstrated the pathophysiology of placental infarction and degeneration, which is an integral part of toxemia of pregnancy. The causes of the high blood pressure and convulsions of toxemia eluded us and would not be known for 48 more years, when the relationship of calcium metabolism and high blood pressure was elucidated.

I went to the June meeting in Philadelphia with Dr. A.H. Sanford, head of laboratories of the Mayo Clinic. He had been Dr. Hunt's mentor in training and visited Geisinger Hospital before the meeting. Dr. Hunt read my paper on June 4th, and the president of the association, Dr. R.R. Kracke, announced that it was the most important paper of the entire meeting. The exhibit, which I spent three days explaining, won first place and the Gold Medal Award, now on exhibit at the Geisinger Medical Center. I was gratified.

Our paper and the exhibit received good coverage by the press. There were write-ups in the Philadelphia Ledger and the Evening Bulletin, New York Times, Time Magazine, Danville and Bloomsburg, Pennsylvania daily papers, and the Durham, North Carolina Morning Herald. Geisinger Hospital had received good publicity, which pleased Dr. Foss. Back in Danville, I received many compliments from the hospital staff. Our paper was eventually published in the American Journal of Clinical Pathology[5].

The annual meeting of the American Society for the Study of Goiter was held in Detroit in the middle of June. Dr. Foss hired a professional pilot to fly us to Detroit; the pilot then took the Stinson to the nearby factory for its first 100-hour check. We had a nice flight, arriving at 7 p.m. after stopping in Cleveland for fuel.

Dr. Foss had decided I should show my exhibit at this meeting. I displayed it for three days, gave my talk and illustrated it with slides. This was my first talk before a national group and it was well received. My paper was published three months later, in September, making it my first[6].

We had planned to leave Detroit at 3 on the afternoon the meeting ended, but the plane was not ready. We finally left at 5:15 and again stopped at Cleveland for fuel. Dr. Foss and the pilot sat in the front seat, using earphones to get weather reports and instructions from the airport towers as we flew across the country. I was in the rear seat without earphones. After dark, rotating beacons outlined our route. Suddenly at 9 p.m., when we were high above the Allegheny Mountains, the plane started descending rapidly. No one said anything to me, and I was really scared. Soon, I saw a landing field below outlined with lights. We circled it a couple of times at low altitude and when flood lights were turned on, we landed.

Afterwards, I learned that the static on the radio was so loud that Dr. Foss and the pilot could not hear the weather report which was given every 30 minutes. The airport at Sunbury was located on an island in the Susquehanna River where the weather was subject to rapid change. Pilots would not fly there without knowing the weather. We had landed at Kylertown, Pennsylvania, where an emergency landing field had been built to refuel commercial aircraft that were unable to reach Cleveland from New York City without refueling. The attendant did not hear us when we first arrived because of the static on his radio. He, too, could not get the weather report.

Although we soon learned that the weather was clear at Sunbury and we could land, Dr. Foss decided against continuing because of the mountains. We anchored the plane to the ground and obtained lodging at a nearby farm house.

Next morning, after a hearty farmer's breakfast, we went back to the airfield and took off. There were clouds over the mountains, but, as a whole, the weather was good. As we flew up the valley, the mountains on each side and ahead were enshrouded in clouds. We returned to the landing field, tied the plane down again and went home by car. As I recall, it was about 100 miles to Sunbury.

My internship was due to end soon. The hospital offered me a newly created residency position in obstetrics, paying $50 per month in addition to room, board, and laundry. Dr. Foss wanted me to accept a two-year residency in surgery under him, and Dr. Sanford offered me a residency at the Mayo Clinic. I still had much work to do on my research project. I decided to accept the one-year residency in obstetrics and then try to get into a two-year training program somewhere on the East Coast. Mayo Clinic seemed too far from home and was famous for medicine and surgery, not obstetrics. Dr. Nicodemus had trained at New York Woman's Hospital and said he would help me get a residency there. I also thought my research would help me obtain a good position somewhere.

FOURTEEN MONTHS OBSTETRICAL RESIDENCY, GEISINGER HOSPITAL: 1937-38

My residency began July 1st. I took the Pennsylvania State Medical Board exams in Philadelphia July 6th to 8th, as all residents were required to be licensed.

I helped Dr. Nicodemus operate on a patient who had been referred to him the previous afternoon. We diagnosed placenta previa, but when he opened the abdominal wall, he cut through the placenta which was attached to the abdominal wall between the bladder and the umbilicus. The baby was free in the abdominal cavity and was dead before we operated. The mother bled to death in spite of our efforts to stop the bleeding and replace the blood. The baby weighed eight pounds.

Years after I left Geisinger, Dr. Nicodemus told me he had a similar case in which he was able to remove the baby without disturbing the placenta. Two months later, he reoperated and removed the placenta, which had detached itself by that time. In this case, both the mother and the baby survived.

June 22nd, Mrs. Jean Bush, wife of the assistant surgeon, had her first baby, a boy. She was the artist who had created the artwork for our prize-winning exhibit.

Maisie visited me for two days in July following a trip she made to Washington.

My duties as resident were to supervise the work of the intern and to monitor the labors of private-room patients. By August, Dr. Nicodemus allowed me to deliver some of these private-room patients. I conducted two large prenatal clinics weekly, which Dr. Nicodemus and the intern usually attended. The big event of the day was morning rounds with Dr. Nicodemus. Many patients with complications were referred to him, some with prolonged, neglected labors. The service provided a good opportunity to see patients with all kinds of problems.

Now that I was a resident, I did not have to work all the time. Periodically, I was busy delivering babies, but at other times, I was free after surgery and morning rounds. I was still studying my research project and thought I would soon have the final answer as to the cause of eclampsia. A paper was being written for Dr. Nicodemus to give at the Pennsylvania State Medical Society's annual meeting. I also was preparing a paper, "Placental Infarction and Eclampsia", for Dr. Hunt to publish[7]. I felt an urgency in getting the papers published to establish priority in finding the cause of eclampsia. Although I thought the final explanation was nearer than it was, I was on the right track and never stopped studying.

With some free time, I resumed a normal social life, dating again after almost a year. I brought my boy scout archery equipment to Danville and practiced with other archers, mostly nurses, and played tennis with the doctors and nurses. I dated many nice and lovely girls though I could not think of marrying for years as I needed two more years of training after my present residency and had to pay off a large medical school debt.

McLeod had met Louise Weber in her father's surgical supply store in Honolulu when he was there on business. After a courtship of about six weeks, they were married on August 7, 1936. They came to the mainland in 1937 on their honeymoon and took delivery of a new Oldsmobile in Michigan. They arrived in Danville September 5th, and I met my beautiful new sister-in-law for the first time. I took time off and went with them to North Carolina, stopping in Baltimore to see Dr. A.J. Weaver, McLeod's classmate at Wake Forest. (We saw a lot of him later on Maui during the war.) We visited Uncle Leon in Washington and then drove to Roxboro, North Carolina, where Velma and Marcus were living. En route, we visited Luray Caverns and Natural Bridge, Virginia.

September 6th, we arrived in Chapel Hill and saw Mamma's new home at 205 Wilson Street. She had sold the house at Coats, had invested her money wisely, and finally was able to build a nice home in a good location. Maisie was teaching art in Chapel Hill public schools and had drawn the plans, a two-story brick house with eight rooms and a large attic which was later converted to bedrooms for students. The house was two blocks from the campus on one side and two blocks from the high school on the other, built on the last available lot near the campus. Mamma lived in it for 25 years.

Mamma no longer had a cow and chickens, but she did have a small vegetable garden and a pecan, a magnolia, and two apple trees. The pecan tree soon produced nuts, though the squirrels got most of them. The apple trees were prolific and Mamma became famous for her cinnamon apple pies. Her flower garden and shrubs were lovely, and I can still picture the beautiful crepe myrtle.

McLeod, Louise and I visited Sanford, Coats and Angier and saw all the relatives. I left for Danville at midnight on September 16th by train and was at work by 2 the following afternoon. On September 26th, we had seven babies in 22 hours and there were more women in labor.

At the Pennsylvania State Medical Society's annual meeting in Philadelphia in October, Dr. Nicodemus read a paper, and I showed an exhibit on our work. The paper was later published in the Pennsylvania Medical Journal[8].

That month, I started a new series of rabbit experiments, trying to duplicate my previous experiments and hoping to learn more about how eclampsia developed.

Dr. Nicodemus began a five-day vacation in late October. While he was away, one of our patients developed eclampsia with convulsions. I was able to treat her successfully, with recovery for her and her baby.

I joined the Montour County Medical Society in November, which included membership in the American Medical Association.

The hospital dining room served us sourkraut and pork on New Year's Day, 1938. This old Pennsylvania Dutch custom came about because the pig always moves forward when eating. It was thought to be a good omen to eat pork on New Year's Day so we would move forward during the coming year.

Dr. Nicodemus closed his outside office and became a full-time staff member of the hospital at the start of the New Year.

In early January, I heard from my fraternity brother, Jack Heyl, the senior resident in OB-Gyn at the Kensington Hospital in Philadelphia. He said I could get an appointment there for six months as junior obstetrical resident after my residency at Geisinger. Dr Edward Schuman, surgeon-in-chief, had taught me obstetrics in my junior year at the University of Pennsylvania and was one of the most outstanding teachers of the day. He was an original member of the American Board of Obstetrics and Gynecology. His uncle, Robert A. Schuman, was the famous German musical composer of the 19th century.

A heavy snowfall in Danville in January provided excellent sledding on the hilly terrain, and I was out every evening for a week during the full moon. On January 16th, I went sledding with a student nurse, Miss Graham, who became my wife eight months later. This was my first date with Dottie.

During the last week of January, I went to North Carolina to see my relatives and stopped for an interview at Kensington Hospital in Philadelphia on my way home.

In February, we had a patient develop eclampsia and convulsions after delivery. Any explanation of the cause of eclampsia would have to include such patients. It was not until 1973 that I fully understood how this could occur.

I sent my application on February 5th to the Woman's Hospital of New York City for their two-year residency in OB-Gyn. Dr Nicodemus had trained there, and a fraternity brother from the University of Pennsylvania was the first-year resident. I was interviewed by the doctors on February 23rd at a staff meeting and expected to get the appointment. However, though I had many letters of recommendation, I failed to get the position. This meant that I would take the appointment at Kensington Hospital. After that, I did not know what I would do.

We had a patient at term who developed type I pneumonia in March. Specific pneumonia serum was available, but the sulfa drugs and antibiotics had not been developed. Dr. Nicodemus had lost his first wife when she developed pneumonia at the 8th month of her third pregnancy and delivered a premature boy, her first son, who also died. I will never forget how apprehensive he was about this patient and how happy he was when she recovered.

I was still studying my research project. In March, I gave a talk at a staff meeting on placental fibrosis and infarction.

On April 5th, I delivered twins to an unmarried mother who had eclampsia.

Dr. Foss took me for a joy ride in his Stinson plane in April. I always enjoyed flying with him as he used good judgement in flying and avoided dangerous situations. Later, he persuaded the Federal Government to build a landing field at Danville and, thereafter, kept his plane there. During my internship, while I was on men's surgical service, we had a pilot as a patient who had had to make a forced landing. The plane's controls had torn through his peroneal tissues making a massive laceration. He finally recovered to fly again.

After Dr. Foss retired from most of his work, he told me he had stopped flying and had sold the plane. He felt he was too old and might make a mistake.

I took Dottie Graham to a semiformal dance in April and gave her a gardenia corsage, the first corsage I had ever given a girl. To this day, it is probably our favorite flower. Every gardenia I bring in from our garden reminds her of the first corsage. We have six gardenia plants that produce several hundred giant flowers from February to June.

I went to Washington in May to see a physician at the National Institute of Health who had read about my research work and invited me to come down for a conference. Nothing special developed from this, but I had a nice time. I stayed with Uncle Leon who owned a speed boat that would go 30 miles an hour, raising the front of the boat high out of the water. The speed made him too nervous, so he traded it for cruiser on which he could take his friends weekend fishing on Chesapeake Bay. The four-bunk cruiser arrived while I was there.

The next time I saw Uncle Leon, he said all I could talk about during my previous visit was a girl named Dottie. He knew I was in love. He still was a bachelor at that time.

McLeod sent me money in May so I could repay the tuition loan I had received during my senior year in medical school. He also paid Mamma all the money I owed her which upset Mamma. She felt it was her responsibility to loan me any money I needed to finish my education. McLeod knew she needed the money for her new home, so he absorbed my debt.

During May and June I played tennis almost every afternoon if I was not working. Dottie and I played often and I rarely beat her. I have many pictures of her in her white tennis shorts; she had a beautiful figure.

While playing tennis with Dr. Nicodemus on June 2nd, I sprained my right ankle and was on crutches for a week. I still worked and managed to be up all night on June third. Still on crutches, I joined a group of interns, residents, and nurses, including Dottie, for a cookout at a cottage in the nearby mountains. I have pictures of the party.

During the 12 months that I had been resident, we delivered 492 babies. Unless I was out of town, I was present at all deliveries.

Because of license requirements, the date of starting hospital residencies was changed to September 1st. Dr. Nicodemus made arrangements with Dr. Schuman for me to start at Kensington on September 1st, which meant I would have only four months there. My residency at Geisinger was 14 months instead of 12.

During my entire residency at Geisinger, I did only two cesareans with Dr. Bush assisting me in one when Dr. Nicodemus was away, and Dr. Nicodemus assisting me in the other.

MARRIAGE: AUGUST 17, 1938

Dottie Graham left for home on August 3rd for two weeks' vacation and we said goodbye on the phone. We had spent time together on 27 of the days between July 1st and August 3rd, often playing tennis in the afternoon and then going on a date in the evening. After she left, I missed her very much and wrote her a letter each day. On August 7th, I went to Lewistown with my fellow resident, Jess Gordner and his date to see her.

I had written McLeod about my love affair with Dottie, telling him I would marry her if I could arrange the necessary finances. Dottie and I had a plan. When we married she would necessarily drop out of nursing school and return to her former work as cashier in the Montgomery Ward Store in Lewistown. She would live at home while I continued with my training.

I got a letter from McLeod on August 13th saying he thought it was a good idea for us to marry. He said I did not have to repay him the money I owed him anytime soon and that he could loan me more money during the next two years. I immediately bought a pair of blue silk pajamas and called Dottie. I had told her that when we got married, I would buy silk pajamas for our honeymoon. This was my cue that I was going to propose to her when I saw her the next day.

I asked for time off to visit Dottie and take her to Chapel Hill to meet my family. I was up most of the night of August 13th delivering babies. Early Sunday morning, August 14th, I caught a ride to Amity Hall near Harrisburg and from there caught another ride to Lewistown arriving about 10:30 a.m. After an hour of visiting, I excused myself, went to my room and slept for two hours.

In the afternoon, Dottie and I sat in the back yard by a small pool and birdbath. I asked her to marry me as soon as we arrived in North Carolina and could make arrangements. She said she would.

Next day, we went into Lewistown and interviewed the manager of the Montgomery Ward Store who assured Dottie he would rehire her as bookkeeper. We sent a telegram to Marcus and Velma to prepare to marry us as soon as possible after we arrived.

On Tuesday, August 16th, Jess Gordner came for us early, and we drove to Velma and Marcus's home at Roxboro, North Carolina. En route, we traveled on the Sky Line Drive in the Blue Ridge Mountains of Virginia and stopped at Endless Caverns and Natural Bridge. The generator of the car burned out about an hour before we arrived but the battery was well-charged and lasted until we reached Roxboro. After we arrived, I telephoned Maisie in Chapel Hill, advising her to prepare for a home wedding the next day, August 17th at 4 p.m.

In the morning Jess took his car to a garage and had the generator repaired. He loaned me $35 to buy a wedding ring. We then went to Chapel Hill, arriving about 11 a.m. Neill had gone to Hillsboro for the wedding license and Maisie had bought a wedding bouquet of daisies and yellow roses to match Dottie's silk wedding dress.

The wedding was at 4 p.m. with Marcus officiating, Jess the best man and Maisie the maid of honor. Neill and Orus were witnesses listed on the marriage certificate issued by the Methodist Church. There were 14 guests present, five from Orus's family, four from Velma's family, four from Mamma's family, and Jess. The official marriage certificate issued by the Office of the Register of Deeds lists the witnesses as Mamma, Jess and Velma.

As the wedding ceremony was to begin, Jess and I were standing at the foot of the stairs, near the door to the living room. Dottie and Maisie walked down the stairs, and then Dottie and I walked over by the fireplace in the living room. Marcus read the marriage vows and announced that we were man and wife. Afterwards, we all had a wedding dinner in Mamma's home.

Marriage was a very sacred thing to Dottie and me. We were delighted that Marcus could marry us although we would have preferred to have been married in a church. As this was impossible, Mamma's home was the ideal place, and she felt honored for us to be married in it. These rushed wedding plans had slighted Dottie's family, but they forgave us.

Dottie was only 21 when I swept her off her feet in an eight-month courtship.

She accepted me for what I professed to be and I have never betrayed her. Our love for each other is greater than ever, and we have now celebrated our golden wedding anniversary.

As I have already said, my parents set a good example for me and were deeply devoted to each other. I had always had a girlfriend since the age of eight and looked forward to the time when I would have my own home, wife and children. I constantly dreamed about an angel whom I could love and who would love me. In my college days I thought I had found her but, after a third double-cross, I realized she was no angel and would not make a good wife nor a good mother for my children.

For five years I searched. I dated hundreds of girls, many of whom were beautiful and sweet, but I thought I could not marry because I was still in training and deeply in debt. Then I met Dottie and everything changed. We came from similar backgrounds and had similar goals in life. I am convinced that fate guided me to her, that we were created for each other and that our marriage was planned in Heaven.

Although I was dependent on McLeod for finances, it was easy to convince him to extend me more credit. After all, he had a similar experience when he met and married Louise.

Our honeymoon hotel for three days was the Carolina Inn, only two blocks from Mamma's home. The weather was hot and there was no air conditioning.

On Thursday, August 18th, Dottie, Jess, a friend of Maisie's and I toured the campuses at Chapel Hill and Duke. We then visited the Chesterfield Cigarette factory in Durham and were struck by its strong tobacco odor. Hundreds of factory workers made the cigarettes which, before processing, were about 20 inches long.

Next day, we visited Fayetteville, Fort Bragg and Lumberton. We saw the old slave market in Fayetteville and the tobacco market in Lumberton, where an auctioneer was selling tobacco. On our way home, we visited Laurinburg, Southern Pines, Pinehurst and Sanford, where we had dinner with Orus and his family.

Early the following day, Jess, Dottie and I left for Harrisburg, arriving at 3 p.m. Dottie and I spent the night at the Harrisburger Hotel and Jess returned to Danville. The next morning, I took Dottie to the bus station so she could return to Lewistown and begin work on Monday. I returned to my work in Danville.

We were very busy in the hospital in August and had the most babies of any month ever, 52 by the 25th. As soon as time permitted, I wrote thank you letters to all the members of my family in North Carolina. I also wrote to my new mother-in-law and apologized for marrying Dottie without her permission. Mother Graham, like my mother, was a widow with seven children. Her goal in life was to see that each of her children got a good education so he or she could make a living. Dottie told me her mother would not have agreed to her stopping nursing school before she graduated. When we were married, she accepted me as a son and was happy for us. Our relationship remained good until she died at 94. Dottie's brothers and sisters also accepted me as a brother and I love them just as I do the members of my own family. Including Dottie, five of the seven are still living.

During my last eight days at Geisinger, Dottie visited me once and I went to see her once. To make the trip, I borrowed an old Star automobile from one of the nurses. She warned me to check the oil often as it would probably need refilling before I got back to Danville, a 120-mile round trip. I stopped at 11 p.m. at a restaurant that also sold gas and oil. The car did not need oil, but the starter locked. I was stranded. Two young men saw the predicament I was in and offered to tow me 10 miles to their home, which was on my route, and fix the starter. They had a tow-rope in their car and soon we were underway. They fixed the starter and I arrived in Danville safely. Later, I sent them a check but couldn't have paid them nearly enough for their services.

A party was given by Dr. Bush on August 29th for three residents who were finishing their work. I left for Lewistown the next day and then for Kensington Hospital a day later.

FOUR MONTHS ASSISTANT OBSTETRICAL RESIDENT: KENSINGTON HOSPITAL

I arrived at Kensington Hospital and began my residency on September 1st at a salary of $20 per month. I felt very blue about leaving Dottie in Lewistown. On the 2nd, my sister, Dorothy, visited me for a couple of hours. We had lunch and looked at the pictures of our wedding that she had brought. I called Dottie on the 3rd and also wrote her a letter telling her that as soon as I could get money from McLeod, she was coming to Philadelphia to live. I then wrote McLeod for money.

The 4th was Sunday. I described it as a quiet day; I delivered only three babies. I felt better now that I had made the decision to bring Dottie to Philadelphia.

September 8th was a busy day; I saw 60 patients in obstetrical clinic and delivered four babies. I was also on 12-hour night duty and admitted a patient with irregular labor contractions at 6 a.m., just as I was to go off duty. The patient was only at her 8th month. I wrote on the chart that she complained of pain in the right side of her abdomen and was tender. Dr. Schuman made rounds and read my notes. He assumed the resident on day duty would follow-up on my observations and get a blood count and urinalysis. Then, an evaluation could be made regarding the pain and tenderness.

At 3 p.m. the patient developed more pain and board-like rigidity of the abdomen. The fetal heart sounds were normal. The assistant chief of staff examined her and diagnosed partial placental separation. He thought he should do a cesarean and notified Dr. Schuman. Dr. Schuman remembered that he had seen the patient at morning rounds and that she had pain and tenderness on the right side. He concurred, over the phone, with the assistant's diagnosis and gave permission for him to do a cesarean immediately. I was present at the operation. Dr. Schuman's technique was followed; a cesarean was done under local anesthesia. All appeared normal and the baby was normal, though premature. There was no placental separation, nor were there blood clots in the uterus.

Dr. Schuman was called again. He gave instructions to extend the incision and explore the cecal area. This procedure revealed a ruptured appendix. It was removed and a drain left in place. The patient recovered without further complications.

I went to Lewistown September 10th by train and spent two days with Dottie, returning Sunday evening. Next day, I attended the 3rd International Goiter Conference in Washington, D.C., and had a paper read by title at the meeting[9]. I returned in late afternoon and went on duty.

On September 14th, I delivered a multiparous patient at 5 a.m., barely arriving in the delivery room in time to catch the baby. In the afternoon, the patient developed generalized abdominal tenderness, pain and fever. Her white blood count was very high. There had been no excessive bleeding after delivery. Exploratory operation showed a rupture in the lower part of the uterus and a hysterectomy was done. Recovery was normal.

I was worrying about my future training and was discouraged. Dr. Nicodemus had talked with Drs. Norris Vaux and Clifford Lull at Philadelphia Lying-In-Hospital. They agreed to consider me for their two-year OB-Gyn residency starting July 1, 1939. I was interviewed by them and by Dr. Robert Kimbrough, my former teacher.

Dottie sent me a very good angel's food cake and I wrote her saying I would have her in Philadelphia by October 1st.

Dorthy Graham Patterson, December, 1938   *Photo by Brunel Photo, Philadelphia*

I rented an apartment at 2009 East Susquehanna Avenue, across a park from the hospital about two blocks away. Dottie arrived on September 23rd. So far as we can recall, I failed to meet her at the station when her train arrived and she waited until I eventually came.

On Saturday, September 24th, we bought kitchen utensils and a supply of groceries. Dottie then told me that she did not know how to cook. Growing up, the girls in her home always did the housework and washed the dishes while her mother did all the cooking. I was not much of a cook myself, as my sisters always cooked if Mamma was unable to do so. However, I managed to cook our first meal, a roasted hen, potatoes and green vegetables, and we both enjoyed it. We were extremely happy to finally be together. Needless to say, Dottie soon learned to cook and now is as good a gourmet cook as anyone.

I developed a severe chest cold and was hospitalized for three days in October. I found it a bit strange to be a patient in a women's hospital.

When I was not on call, I ate my evening meals at home with Dottie. When I was on call, she would visit me in the evening if I was not actively working. My room at the hospital was formerly a classroom in the school of nursing, which had been discontinued. A complete human skeleton hung in the room when I moved in and I relocated it to the closet. One evening, I asked Dottie to look into the closet and she almost fainted. Sleeping with skeletons nearby didn't bother me.

I was off duty for two days every other weekend, and Dottie and I partook of Philadelphia's fine cultural heritage. We visited the Art Museum, Franklin Institute, Aquarium, Planetarium, Museum of Natural History, Independence Hall, Betsy Ross House, University of Pennsylvania, and other historic sites.

In October, Paul and Vivian Cameron came to see us. He was my former roommate at Chapel Hill, now practicing medicine at Somer's Point, New Jersey.

We saw the University of Pennsylvania beat Columbia University 14 to 13 in football on October 22nd. Sid Luckman, the passer for Columbia, later became a great professional player. I think he is in the Football Hall of Fame.

Dottie's mother, her sister and brother-in-law, Josephine and Tony Artman, visited us in October. They walked in on Dottie, unannounced, while she was experimenting with dough, trying to make her first pie.

On October 30th, Dottie roasted her first chicken.

My fraternity brother, Jack Heyl, was the senior resident at Kensington Hospital. He and his wife, Mildred, lived nearby and we often played bridge with them. One evening we all went to a Phi Rho Sigma Fraternity dance.

On November 5th, I did my first cesarean at Kensington with Dr. Schuman assisting me. I followed his technique, using local anesthesia. He taught all his residents to do cesareans under local anesthesia and this proved to be very helpful to me later in my practice.

In November, I went to New York City to interview Dr. Aldridge about a residency. I also interviewed the Grace Shipping Line about becoming a doctor on a cruise ship but I was not accepted because I was married.

Dottie and I visited Paul and Vivian Cameron at Somer's Point for two days in November. I played my first 18 holes of golf at the Ocean City Country Club and scored132.

Dottie's brother, Clifford, was in Philadelphia on business on November 25th. He took us out to dinner and then to the Chestnut Opera House to see Fred Stone in the play "Lightening."

Dottie and I toured the Navy yard, going aboard the U.S.S. Phoenix and viewing the U.S.S. Nashville.

I accepted a six-month residency in newborn pediatrics at the Philadelphia Lying-In-Hospital starting January 1, 1939. I hoped to get the OB-Gyn residency afterwards. Besides the newborn work, the pediatric resident held two well-baby clinics and two sick-children's clinics each week at Pennsylvania Hospital, of which Lying-In was a part.

Mamma came to see us for a week in December. Dottie took her shopping and Mamma insisted Dottie choose all her Christmas presents for her. The three of us visited many of the cultural and tourist attractions. During casual conversation, Mamma asked Dottie how many children we planned to have. Dottie told her we were going to have four children, all girls, and this came to pass.

Dr. Nicodemus was in Philadelphia on December 9th and had lunch with us at the hospital. The highlight of the day at Kensington was the lunch hour. Dr. Schuman practically always had lunch there and he, of course, was the center of attraction. The others attending the lunch would be the two assistant chiefs, Drs. Clayton Beacham and Hanna, the three residents, the head nurse and one or two guests, often from out of town. A delicious meal would be served.

Dr. Schuman was a master teacher and story teller. The two subjects most often discussed were the American Board Exams in OB-Gyn, and music. He had helped create the American Boards and was anxious to teach the residents and staff what was required to pass. He, of course, did not examine any of his own residents or staff. He continually stressed the importance of the cardinal ligaments about the upper end of the birth canal and their support of the uterus.

There was often a lively discussion about music. Leopold Stowkowski was then the conductor of the Philadelphia Orchestra, receiving world-wide acclaim. There was great excitement when the opera season opened and most everyone, except poor residents, attended in formal dress. Jack and Mildred Heyl were musicians and could discuss music intelligently with Dr. Schuman. I knew nothing about classical music having never been exposed to it. This changed after I married, as Dottie loves music and is very knowledgeable. She has three text books on opera and classical music that are well worn from use. Rarely a day passes that we do not listen to classical music.

Dottie and I rented a studio apartment on Clinton Street, only one block from Lying-In. It had a bed that folded into the wall. We closed our apartment on Susquehanna on December 22nd, and Dottie went to Lewistown for Christmas. Just before I left to join her the next day, I delivered a baby by face presentation. It was born spontaneously without difficulty, much to my surprise. Since then I have had several more deliver spontaneously and easily, but I have had some difficult face deliveries, some requiring cesareans.

I spent two days celebrating Christmas with Dottie, then returned to work. On Saturday, December 31st, I moved our belongings to the new apartment. Again, because of the delay caused by moving, I was late meeting Dottie at the train station.When we arrived at the apartment and unpacked, everything was fine again.

RESIDENT IN NEWBORN PEDIATRICS: JANUARY TO JUNE, 1939

As I recall, 3000 babies were born at Philadelphia Lying-In Hospital each year. My duties included taking care of all the babies born to ward patients and patients in semi-private rooms. I was required to be present at all cesareans and all complicated deliveries. My chief was Dr. Ralph Tyson, a senior pediatrician and a professor at one of the medical schools (I think Temple). I also had four clinics weekly at Pennsylvania Hospital. My salary for this residency was $50 per month plus room, board and laundry.

A summary of all the births at the hospital was kept in a master ledger which had been neglected for some time. Dottie and I worked long hours in the evenings bringing it up to date. During my residency, I had many interesting patients. In the first week, a newborn died 36 hours after birth of adrenal hemorrhage and a ruptured stomach ulcer. In February, a 2-day old infant was operated on for a large mass in the right side of the abdomen that proved to be a blood clot originating in the right adrenal. The patient recovered. At that time I could not know that, 35 years later, I would publish a monograph on fetal adrenal hyperplasia, the cause of these hemorrhages.

We operated successfully on a newborn with intestinal obstruction due to a constricting band of tissue. Another patient died of tracheal obstruction due to an abnormality.

I gave 30 transfusions to newborns during my residency and had to cut down to reach the vein only five times. I usually used a syringe and a three-way stopcock to administer the dose of 10ml per pound of body weight. New equipment now makes transfusions of the newborn much easier.

Attendance of all doctors who worked in the hospital was required at the monthly staff meetings. The senior obstetrical resident presented a summary of the work of the previous month, nicely displayed on a large blackboard. All complications were discussed in depth. If there had been a maternal death, the discussion was lengthy. Very little was said about babies, usually only a statement indicating if they were at term or premature and if they survived or succumbed.

I thought there should be a summary for the newborns just like the one for the mothers. I suggested this to the attending pediatrician, who sent me to Dr. Tyson. He welcomed the idea as it would give him an active part in the staff meetings rather than just being present to answer questions.

My first month's report showed that the average temperature of the babies when they arrived in the nurseries was about 96 degrees. This meant some were much lower, a dangerous situation for a sick infant or a premature. The delivery rooms were on the ninth floor, as I recall, and the nurseries were on the four floors below. Greater care in keeping the babies warm while transferring them had to be taken.

I carefully examined every baby the day after birth and the day it was discharged and found a surprising number of fractured clavicles. Many of these were incomplete and showed a swelling from the callous at the time of discharge. About 95 percent of these babies were delivered by interns or residents. Treatment was the application of a figure-8 bandage across the back and through the axillae. There was usually complete recovery. My reports brought out many more interesting facts and became a permanent part of the monthly staff meeting.

Philadelphia Lying-In had one of the first Chappel Incubators. It was completely air-conditioned and a great asset in caring for prematures or sick newborns. Now all nurseries are equipped with similar and improved incubators.

Another great asset at Lying-In was the Mother's Breast Milk Bank, one of the first to be established. Excess breast milk was collected from the mothers before they went home and some brought in breast milk after being discharged. They were paid 20 cents an ounce. The milk was sterilized by heat, sealed in pint jars and stored in a refrigerator until needed. When I was there, some milk had been stored for two years and was still good. The milk that was brought in after the patients were discharged was tested to see if it had been diluted with water or cow's milk, which happened occasionally.

Any baby on formula who did not make normal progress was given canned breast milk. The results were usually startling with immediate weight gain and improvement.

During my residency at Lying-In, I attended the monthly meetings of the Infant Mortality Study Committee where unusual cases were discussed. The attending physicians were invited to these meetings. The cases were classified as preventable or non-preventable and suggestions were made as to treatment that might have altered the results. This was a great forum for learning.

In January, Dottie and I saw Catherine Littlefield and her ballet dancers on stage at the John Wannamaker Store. I remember going straight from work and watching the performance in my white uniform.

I had to borrow money from Orus in January, which I repaid in February when I got money from McLeod.

Dottie and I visited Paul and Vivian Cameron in Somer's Point one weekend. When I returned to work on Monday, 30 babies had been born, all of whom I had to examine.

Neill stopped by at 3 a.m. on March 23rd en route from Michigan with a new Buick that McLeod had bought. He was on his way to pick up Mamma in Chapel Hill and Uncle June in Mercedes, Texas, and then the three of them were going on to Hawaii.

When I accepted the residency at Lying-In, Dottie had hoped to find secretarial work in Philadelphia that would more than support us. This would take care of our finances through a two-year residency in OB-Gyn if I were accepted. She was well-qualified: She had taken an evening business course after high school and had two years' experience in the Montgomery Ward Store. Jobs were scarce. All prospective employers told her that by the time she became thoroughly acquainted with her work, she would move away with her doctor-husband. No one would hire her. I was becoming deeper in debt and had not yet been accepted for the two-year residency.

McLeod had written that he thought he could find work for me in Hawaii on a sugar or pineapple plantation if I did not get accepted in the residency. I could work two or three years, pay off my debt, and return to North Carolina where I wanted to live.

During the first week of April, Dottie became ill. She vomited everything I fixed for her to eat and lost many pounds. Finally, on April 10th, Dr. Kimbrough admitted her to the hospital with a diagnosis of hyperemesis gravidarium. She improved rapidly when given intravenous fluids.

On April 12th, I decided I should stop my training in June and go to Hawaii. I withdrew my application for the residency at Lying-In and wrote to McLeod and Dottie's mother of my decision. Dottie continued to improve. She spent her birthday, April 15th, in the hospital, then returned to our apartment the next day and improved on my cooking.

Dottie's mother, two brothers, Clifford and Neff, and nephew, Bob, came to see us later in April. Dottie had been eating and was doing well. However, following this visit, the vomiting recurred. She had lost a total of 20 pounds from the start of her illness. On May 4th, she was readmitted to the hospital, this time on Dr. Vaux's service as Dr. Kimbrough was out of town. She improved rapidly, but was in the hospital nine days. On the day she was discharged, I took her to Lewistown and left her there until we left for Hawaii. I returned to see her on May 20th and visited Geisinger Hospital on May 21st and 22nd.

I had received a letter from McLeod on May 4th telling me that the Hawaii Legislature had passed a law that prevented doctors from taking the Medical Board exams unless they had lived in Hawaii one year. The bill was on the governor's desk, but he had not signed it. I immediately applied by cablegram to take the exams on July 10th and was accepted.

I reserved an outside room, with a porthole, for two on the S.S. Matsonia sailing from San Francisco on June 30th and scheduled to arrive in Honolulu on July 5th. The one-way fare for two was $300. This would be the first ocean voyage for both of us. I packed our household effects and sent them to Dottie in Lewistown.

On May 23rd the U.S. submarine Squalus was lost off the Atlantic Coast with all aboard. On that day, I took tests for my first driver's license, though I had been driving for many years.

McLeod had Hawaii auto license plates sent to me for a new Chevrolet coupe he had purchased from the dealer in Hilo for delivery at the factory. We were to pick it up in Flint, Michigan, and drive it to San Francisco.

I surprised Dottie on Friday, June 2nd, by visiting her in Lewistown. Early next morning I left by train and visited Uncle Leon for an hour in Washington on my way to Chapel Hill. Mamma and Neill were already in Hawaii. Orus's and Marcus's families came to Chapel Hill to see me on Sunday. I visited Sanford Monday and Tuesday before leaving for Philadelphia late Wednesday. I was back to work Thursday morning.

I shipped my books to Neill in Honolulu and packed my bags, ready to leave any day. McLeod had arranged for Dr. Thomas Keay to interview me on June 21st in Detroit after we picked up our car in Flint. Dr. Keay practiced on a sugar plantation at Peepekeo on the Island of Hawaii and had indicated he might hire me as an assistant after an interview.

I checked out of the hospital on June 18th and went to Lewistown. The next day I got a wire from Dr. Keay setting up an appointment for an interview at his hotel. Dottie and I left by pullman for Detroit and Flint on June 21st. After picking up our car in Flint on the 22nd we drove back to Detroit and checked into the Sewara Hotel. We waited for Dr. Keay for three days. He never came, nor did we hear from him.

Later, sometime after we arrived in Hawaii, we learned that he had been delayed in Canada. Two of his children were very sick with measles so he could not come to Detroit for our appointment. I never learned why he did not leave a message at the hotel. When I finally saw him in Hawaii, he had decided not to hire an assistant for another year.

We had dinner with Dr. Glen Wible, a fellow-resident at Geisinger Hospital who was now at the Henry Ford Hospital. He died in the service in a plane accident during World War II.

At 5 p.m. on June 24th, we left for San Francisco. The S.S. Matsonia was scheduled to sail at 5 p.m. on June 30th and we were 1900 miles away. It was necessary for me to be in Honolulu to take the Medical Board exams on July 10th. If I missed the opportunity then, I would not be allowed to take them thereafter because of the new one-year residency requirement.

We drove our new car carefully to avoid engine trouble and to prevent Dottie - who was pregnant - from becoming ill. We spent the first night at the Hotel La Salle in South Bend, Indiana, and the second night at Boone, Iowa. The third night we were at Cheyenne, Wyoming, at the Plains Hotel. We thought the bellboys, who had brown skin, were American Indians and were surprised to learn they were Filipinos.

We reached Salt Lake City by the fourth night and stayed at the Temple Square Hotel opposite the Mormon Temple.

The next day we drove to Sacramento, a distance of 675 miles. The weather was hot and Dottie took off her maternity girdle and most of her clothes to be more comfortable. She was embarrassed at the California border when the agricultural inspector found her clothes in the car pocket. As it got dark that evening, we skirted Lake Tahoe and began the ascent to the Donner Pass. A full moon hung in the sky and the view looking back down over the lake was one of the most beautiful sights we have ever seen or will see.

We stayed at the Senator Hotel in Sacramento.

We arrived in San Francisco at 11 a.m. on June 29th, exactly 30 hours before the Matsonia was scheduled to sail. The car had operated perfectly and Dottie had had no problems.

We were tired from traveling, but we were relieved to be in San Francisco. We attended the San Francisco World's Fair in the afternoon, then checked into the Empire Hotel. Next day, we boarded the ship at 2 p.m. and watched as our car was loaded. We sailed at 6 p.m.

CHAPTER VII

Move to Hawaii, Plantation Medical Practice: July, 1939, to December 1, 1941

We had a pleasant trip to Hawaii on the Matsonia. The first evening after we sailed, we both felt dizzy and sick. Dottie could not retain her breakfast the next morning, but thereafter, we were both fine. The weather was cold the first day; by the third day it was much warmer. On the second day, we won the mileage pool of $18. The Captain's Dinner on July 4th was a gala affair, celebrating Independence Day. We still have the two small American flags - each with only 48 stars - that sat on our table.

The ship was to dock in Honolulu about 7 a.m. on July 5th so we were up and on deck at 5. We saw land as soon as it was visible and were surprised to see tall mountains. As we approached at dawn, there was a soft pink glow to the buildings and mountains. The Moana Hotel was the only tall building at Waikiki with the pink Royal Hawaiian Hotel nearby. As we entered the harbor, Hawaiian boys swam near the ship, diving into the clear waters for coins that were tossed overboard to them. When we docked, gentle tradewinds were blowing. On the piers, Hawaiian women were selling leis made of exotic flowers. The fragrant odors of ginger, plumeria and pikake permeated the air. Hundreds of people were on hand to greet the passengers and place leis around their necks followed by a kiss on the cheek. It was a beautiful occasion. Each visitor sensed that he or she was truly welcomed into a paradise, where the weather was perfect, the scenery and the flowers were beautiful, and the people were friendly. Neill was there to welcome us with leis.

As soon as we arrived, we went to the home of Mr. and Mrs. Eugene Weber, Louise Patterson's parents. We stayed with them until I took the Medical Board exams which started on July 10th. Their home was in lovely Manoa Valley with its verdant landscape and dazzling flowers. We got our car the day we arrived. Next day, I was interviewed by the members of the Medical Board and my credentials were in order. I met Dr. Nils P. Larsen, medical advisor to the Hawaii Sugar Planters' Association, who would help me find work. I used all my time studying for the exams, which lasted for four days and covered the entire field of medicine. I heard on July 21st that I had passed with an average grade of 86.2, the highest of anyone who took the exams with me.

On July 17th, we moved into a cottage at Waikiki and began unpacking our freight which had arrived from Pennsylvania. I met several Honolulu doctors who were friends of McLeod and followed every lead to try to find work. I had a conference with David Larsen, vice president of C. Brewer and Co. and a brother of Dr. Nils P. Larsen.

Mamma arrived by boat from Hilo in late July and stayed with us 27 days. We toured the Island of Oahu and the various attractions: the Dole Pineapple Cannery, where there were 13,000 employees; the hula dancers at the Kodak show at Waikiki. Each day, I swam an hour several hundred yards off the beach at Waikiki, where the clear water was eight to 12 feet deep.

We celebrated our first wedding anniversary at home with Mamma and Neill. I gave Dottie a pair of white silk pajamas.

Mamma boarded the S.S. Hualalai on August 22nd and went to Olaa to visit

McLeod and Louise for a while.

In late August, we moved into a two-bedroom cottage on Wilder Avenue owned by our former landlady; the rent was only $42.50 per month. We went to the piers early on August 30th and saw the liners President Coolidge, Monterey and Matsonia dock. Edgar Bergen and Charlie McCarthy were by the rail on A deck on the Matsonia, greeting everyone as the ship docked.

Germany attacked and bombed Poland on September 1st, which was the start of World War II in Europe. On September 3rd, England and France declared war on Germany and a German submarine sank a British ship with 400 persons aboard. Two hundred and fifty of these were Americans.

Dottie and I flew to Lanai on September 13th where I relieved Dr. Halpern who took two weeks' vacation. We flew on an Interisland Airway (now Hawaiian Air) Sikorsky S-38 amphibian aircraft, a twin-engine biplane, with the upper wing much larger than the lower. The cabin was mounted below the wings and engines and had a capacity of nine including the pilot. Entry was by a hatch that opened on the top side. The plane's maximum level speed was 125 miles per hour. It could land and take off from the water, though usually it landed on runways using wheels that folded into the side of the cabin during flight. The landing field on Lanai was unpaved and very crude.

We stayed at the Lanai City Hotel, about 1500 feet above sea level where the nights were cool compared to Waikiki. The streets were lined with hundreds of beautiful Norfolk Pines, which were unfamiliar to us.

There were almost 2,000 people on Lanai, as I recall, and I was the only doctor. I was able to take care of all the illnesses that occurred, but I had some uneasy moments. I sent two patients by plane to Honolulu to an eye specialist. They had deep lacerations of their corneas caused by the sharp ends of pineapple leaves.

Dr. Halpern had a patient with a streptococcal kidney infection, which he had correctly treated with sulfanilamide. However, the patient developed severe hemolytic anemia from the sulfanilamide. Following several transfusions, the anemia was corrected. After I arrived, the patient spiked a temperature of 105 degrees daily. The right kidney was acutely tender, and the right side of the abdomen became rigid, extending over to the midline. With the help of a good surgical nurse, I drained a large kidney abscess, an operation I had not done before. The patient recovered quickly.

Another male patient had urinary obstruction following repeated infections . During my internship, I had usually been successful in catheterizing such patients, but, after trying for three hours, I decided to do a cystostomy. I had never done one of these before, either. The uretheral sound I had been using penetrated something at one time but only blood clots came out. We put the patient on the operating table and prepared for surgery. Suddenly, there was a geyser of urine that reached the low ceiling of the operating room. I did not have to operate, and I think I was more relieved than the patient.

After I finished work each day, Dottie and I explored the island or fished at Manele Bay. Both of us caught several multi-colored fish. Most of the 14,000 acres of pineapple fields on Lanai are inside an extinct volcanic crater. At the bottom of the crater, the fruit grows very large and, as the fields extend up the crater walls, the fruit is small but sweeter.

We returned to Honolulu by plane on September 22nd. Mamma returned after spending a month with McLeod and Louise. She was nervous about the war in Europe and said it was time for her to return to North Carolina. We visited the

Bishop Museum and showed Mamma the rest of Honolulu, taking her shopping for gifts to take home. She sailed on the Matsonia for Los Angeles on September 29th after a royal send off with many leis. When we took her aboard, I could barely lift her luggage. Later, I learned she had collected several pieces of lava to take home with her.

Dr. Larsen assured me that, after two months, he would have permanent work for me as an assistant plantation physician. In September, I had an opportunity to go to Canton Island and work for Pan American Airways for six weeks. I wanted to go, but friends in Honolulu advised against it. They said there would be a war in the Pacific with Japan soon and that it was not wise to accept the offer.

On October 1st, Dottie and I ordered clothes and a special screened crib for our baby, due in two months.

I sailed on the S.S. Waialeale overnight to Hilo on October 10th to be interviewed by Dr. Jensen and the plantation managers at Pahala and Naalehu. Seasickness overwhelmed me and I was unable to eat my dinner. I met with Dr. Jensen and he spoke most favorably about my joining him. I toured the island, had a second conference with Dr. Jensen, and then sailed home on the S.S. Hualalai. Dottie met me at the pier and I was happy to know she had been fine while I was away.

I talked to Dr. Homer Benson of Molokai about relieving him while he was in Honolulu with his wife who was having a baby.

Dottie and I toured the U.S. Aircraft Carrier Enterprise in October with Dr. Clifford Phoebus, who was now in the Navy. He was a fellow intern at Geisinger Hospital and had married Bernadine Schultz, a nurse and friend of ours.

On October 26th, Dottie and I flew to Molokai just as we had flown to Lanai. Dottie was nearing term and had some trouble passing through the hatch into the cabin. I relieved Dr. Benson until November 12th, delivering several babies and doing much general work. We lived in his home and his maid continued working as usual.

While we were on Molokai, we became friends of Mr. and Mrs. Malcolm Clower. Later, they moved to Maui where he was principal of Maui High School for many years.

We saw a total eclipse of the full moon on October 27th. One day we rode to the pali and looked down on Kalaupapa Leper Settlement. At that time it was filled with patients. Today there are very few patients among the Hawaiians and the illness is known as Hansen's disease. Its progress can now be arrested with the sulfone drugs and isolation is no longer required. Former patients, many with deformities, prefer to continue living at Kalaupapa, which has been designated a National Historic Site.

I heard from Dr. Jensen that I had been hired as assistant plantation physician at Pahala and Naalehu. I was to work in the mornings at the hospital in Pahala and in the afternoons in the office at Naalehu, where we would live. The plantations would pay me $350 per month and provide a home for us. Dr. Jensen would add $50 per month from private practice. He assured me he would be able to give me a $50 per month raise after one year.

We left Molokai on November 13th. When we arrived in Honolulu, a letter was waiting for me, telling me to come to work at once. We packed and left for Hilo by boat the next day. I checked in with the plantation managers and Dr. Jensen on the 15th and went to work on the 16th. We were living in the manager's guest cottage in Naalehu until we could buy furniture. A nice house had been built for the doctor two years before and was waiting for us.

The sugar plantations gave their hourly employees complete medical care in addition to other perquisites, including housing and free fuel for cooking and heating water. All supervisors and anyone making over $100 per month had to pay their own medical expenses. The plantation laborers received $1 to $1.50 per day.

When I started working at Naalehu, I owed McLeod $10,000. Dottie and I owned a new car, a few dishes and pieces of silverware that we received as wedding presents. I was paying interest on my debt and was anxious to start paying it off.

I soon became adjusted to my new work, and Dottie and I were very happy. We were waiting for the arrival of our baby, who was due December 1st. James Beatty, the plantation manager at Naalehu, and everyone else welcomed us with open arms. Finally, the community had a much-needed doctor.

Dr. Jensen and I did three major operations the morning of November 28th, and I treated 28 patients in Naalehu in the afternoon. The plantation nurse at Naalehu, Mrs. Kapua Carter, was excellent. She was pure Hawaiian and had graduated in the first class of the School of Nursing at Queen's Hospital in Honolulu. For years, she was the only member of the medical profession living between Pahala and Kona, a distance of 75 miles. She treated many patients with minor illnesses and knew when to take patients with serious illnesses to the doctor. After I started working at Naalehu, the patients still called Mrs. Carter for any emergency at night and she called me. Her tentative diagnoses were usually correct.

Three miles beyond Naalehu was the village of Waiohinu, where the Kau district court was located. About 200 Hawaiians lived there and became my patients when they were ill. The plantation had a large cattle ranch at South Point, about eight miles beyond Waiohinu. Several cowboys and their families lived on the ranch and I had to make house calls there for any emergency. I carried supplies in my car, so I could treat some patients in their homes without bringing them into the office or hospital.

The belt road went directly from Waiohinu to Kona and passed over or through many lava flows. There were only a few people living in this area, who would be my patients in case of illness. Highway accidents did occur. If the victims were thrown out on the lava, they were usually severely injured.

When I started to work, the distance from Pahala to Naalehu was 16 miles. The road was an old wagon trail, paved, but with only one lane. It continually curved, first to the right and then to the left. The shoulders were narrow and cars could barely pass. The uncut grass on the shoulders hid many lava rocks. There was tall brush along the road, screening oncoming cars from view. I learned to quickly jerk the car off the road to avoid head-on collisions, although I hit several rocks on the shoulders, bursting three tires and breaking two rear springs. The tread would be worn off my tires at 4,000 miles and I would have them recapped at 5,000. I had some tires recapped as many as three times before discarding them. Driving on this road taught me to react quickly to oncoming traffic, which has probably prevented several accidents since then. When an approaching car veers into my lane, I pull off on to the shoulder without thinking.

In May, 1940, a new road opened between Pahala and Naalehu, cutting the distance from 16 miles to 12 and travel time from about 40 minutes to 20. One stretch of road traveled six miles over the lava flows without a curve.

Dr. Jensen announced soon after I arrived that I would have to remove all the tonsils. I remembered the difficulty I had had removing tonsils when I was an intern. We had an excellent nurse-anesthetist who encouraged me and actually told me how to take them out easily. The first operation took only 20 minutes and, thereafter, I had no difficulty.

Dottie had some labor contractions on November 29th and then all next day. Finally, at noon on December 1st, after 40 hours of labor, she was ready for delivery. However, the baby's face was looking forward instead of backwards, the normal position. Dottie was totally exhausted. Dr. Jensen did not know how to apply forceps and complete the delivery, so I took charge. The baby was born at 1:50 p.m. and weighed 9 pounds, 7 ounces, a healthy girl, just as Dottie had predicted. We hired a special nurse to take care of Dottie the first night, after which she recovered rapidly.

We named our baby Lois Graham after Dottie's sister, who had been struck and killed at age 17 by an apparent drunk driver while she and Dottie were waiting at a bus stop.

On December 6th, I went to Hilo, a distance of 60 miles, to shop. I bought Dottie a box of candy and a beautiful Cattleya orchid which I jokingly gave to Lois, because our first baby was not a boy as I had wanted.

Lois made normal progress. She was fed at breast entirely and was above birth weight by 10 days. Dottie was slow to regain her strength and fainted the first time she got out of bed. I brought them home on the 14th day.

Before we arrived in Naalehu, the manager's wife had hired a high school graduate to work for us as a maid. The usual wage paid to maids was $20 per month for a six-day work week. We thought this was too low, so we increased her pay to $25. Our maid, who was a delightful person, started work when Dottie and Lois came home from the hospital.

Our house got a coat of paint inside while we were waiting for our furniture. We started a garden and planted Chinese bananas which produced fruit in six months. We attended several Christmas parties and made many friends in Naalehu and Pahala. Many of the supervisors on the plantations had been born in Scotland and migrated to Hawaii. They were delightful people with customs unfamiliar to us.

I was busy in my work. Dr. Jensen and I alternated night calls and weekends off. I always spent my mornings doing clinic and hospital work in Pahala and some days made two trips back in the afternoon and evening to deliver babies or do emergency work.

When I received my first month's pay, I paid $50 on my debt to McLeod, although we had not yet furnished our home. I wanted to pay off the debt as quickly as possible and, also, I knew McLeod needed the money.

We borrowed two beds from the plantation club house and happily moved into our own home. The house had a kerosene hot water heater, but no other furnishings. We ate at the club house. The day we moved, January 9th, the slopes of Mauna Loa were covered with snow down to about the 8,000 foot elevation.

We ordered most of our furnishings from Montgomery Ward and Sears Roebuck on credit. The three-quarter-width twin beds we bought were solid maple, and we are still using them in my bedroom. Interestingly, the furniture was manufactured in North Carolina.

The plantation at Naalehu produced its own supply of electricity, some used in the sugar mill and the rest used for lights and small appliances, such as refrigerators, irons, etc. There was not enough electricity for kitchen stoves or for hot water heaters so we cooked with bottled gas.

The water was also furnished by the plantation and there was never enough. The domestic supply was turned off from 9 a.m. until 4 p.m. The sugar mill was at sea-level at Honaupo and the cane fields extended up to 3,300 feet. The cane was cut by hand, then washed down the hill to the mill in large wooden flumes. A large amount of water was needed for this. None of the cane was irrigated except a 50-acre field near the mill which used the discarded flume water.

The sugar mill produced unrefined raw sugar that was stored in 100-pound burlap bags. Every two to four weeks, a freighter anchored about 100 yards off shore, and the bags of sugar were transferred to it by lighters. The raw sugar was then taken to California to be refined.

Another interesting fact about the water system was that no cesspools or sewage treatment plants were needed. The whole area had lava tubes underneath and the sewer pipes were emptied into these tubes, which never filled up. When a truck traveled down the highway, three blocks away, a loud rumbling reached the dispensary through a lava tube.

The plantation operated a large general store and sold merchandise on credit to the employees. Beef from the plantation ranch was sold for 25 cents a pound for all cuts. The lean cuts were in great demand, which meant that there were always choice cuts available at 25 cents a pound.

On January 26th, we had dinner in Hilo with McLeod, Louise, Lee Burke and his wife. Lee had been on the boxing team with me at Chapel Hill and now owned the Singer Sewing Machine agency in Hilo. We bought a sewing machine from him, which we are still using 48 years later. The remainder of our furniture arrived on this day as well.

On Valentine's Day, I had to treat a seaman from the S.S. Manini who had fallen overboard while loading sugar off the shore at Honaupo.

About 3 a.m. on April 8th, Mauna Loa erupted. It was a beautiful sight. The eruption occurred at the top and there was also an outbreak on the Kahuku side, about eight miles behind our home. The sky was brilliant and it appeared as though the sun were rising behind the area. Dense clouds of volcanic smoke evolved. The eruption lasted many weeks.

Neill resigned from his job in Honolulu and came to see us for two weeks before his planned return to the mainland. We took him to all the attractions on the island. Mr. Beatty, the plantation manager, organized a party to go up Mauna Loa on horseback to see the eruption. He invited Neill to go along for the two-day trip. By the time they came back, Neill had a job on the plantation as assistant bookkeeper. He started work on May 13th.

We heard on the 6 p.m. news, May 9th, that Germany had invaded the Low Countries in Europe.

Dr. I.S. Ravdin spoke at the medical society meeting in Hilo, which I attended. He had been one of my professors of surgery at the University of Pennsylvania and was an outstanding authority.

On Kamehameha Day, June 11th, we went to horse races in Hilo with McLeod, Louise, Neill, and several friends from Hilo. We each bet a dollar on each race and drew a number from a hat for our horses. It was a lot of fun. The races were discontinued during the war and never revived.

Kamehameha I is considered to be the greatest Hawaiian of all times. He was an Alii, or king, much revered by the Hawaiians, and worshipped as a god.

Kamehameha I had, through hard-fought battles on each island, united the islands of Hawaii under one government by 1810. He was a large, tall man, invincible on the battlefield. He had a strong character and had been compared to Napolean. He was smart and, at times, ruthless. He had 21 wives and 24 children. A tall bronze statue of him stands in Kohala on the Island of Hawaii, where he was born. A larger replica of this statue stands opposite the Royal Palace Grounds in Honolulu. Its outstretched arms are draped with dozens of leis on all special occasions, especially on

Kamehameha Day.

Within a year after Kamehameha's death on May 8, 1819, the missionaries from New England arrived. Gradually, there was an abolition of the ancient Hawaiian religious tabu system and the worship of alii and idols was discontinued[10, 11].

A 20-minute earthquake shook the area on June 20th. We had had frequent small quakes every week or two. The seismographs at Kilauea volcano show smaller tremors almost daily. We became accustomed to them and did not worry about them. There are fewer of the tremors on Maui, but it is still upsetting to be awakened in the middle of the night by an earthquake. There is a rumbling of the earth, the house shakes, and one gets the feeling that the walls are collapsing. We, personally, have never had any damage from an earthquake.

We drove to Hilo on July 19th to see Gone With The Wind, which was the first movie we had seen in color on a wide screen. The show lasted to near midnight.

Dr. Jensen was preparing to take the American Boards in Urology. He had accumulated enough cases, so he resigned earlier than formerly planned, leaving at the end of June. He had told me of his plans when I was hired, and also that I was considered to be too young and inexperienced to be the head plantation doctor. Dottie and I were very happy. We loved the people we lived and worked with and they loved us.

We welcomed Dr. Jensen's replacement. During the first week, Dottie had a tea for his wife and we had a picnic at Punaluu Beach for his family. Then I was told that I would not be given the promised raise after one year and that none of the income from my practice belonged to me. I was developing an obstetrical practice and had attracted patients from the Kilauea Volcano area. All the supervisors at the Naalehu plantation were my patients as well as over 200 people living in and beyond Waiohinu. I was averaging $60 per month doing life insurance examinations. I assisted at all major operations and did some minor operations myself.

I was driving my own car 2,000 miles per month in my work and was paying for the oil, gas and tires. I paid my own malpractice insurance, car insurance, medical society dues, and expenses attending medical meetings. I took outpatient calls at the hospital, 12 miles away, every other night and weekend. If I were home, I would treat any patient in my district even if I were not on call. When I was away, the patients had to go to the hospital for care.

Again, I went to McLeod for advice. I then told the doctor, both plantation managers and David Larsen of C. Brewer and Co., who had hired me for the plantation originally, that the plan offered me in private practice was untenable. I could not afford to resign so I decided to bide my time. I developed diarrhoea, which lasted six months. I was very distraught and lost 10 pounds. Dottie tried to comfort me, but to no avail.

Neill was living at the bachelor's quarters, but we saw him frequently. On July 27th, McLeod, Louise, Dottie, Neill, Dr. Clifford Phoebus and I had dinner together at the Naniloa Hotel in Hilo. Dr. Phoebus, whom I have already mentioned, had been a fellow-intern and was now serving aboard the U.S. aircraft carrier Enterprise.

I saw a roundup of cattle on the Kapapala Ranch, a large ranch between Pahala and Kilauea Volcano.

On our second wedding anniversary, August 17th, I gave Dottie a silk bedjacket. We spent the day at home alone. My diary states that we were very happy and much in love. Dottie had not felt well recently, vomiting in the mornings occasionally. We soon realized she was pregnant; our babies would be only 16 months apart.

I was busy in my work doing a little of everything. One day, I had patients from two auto accidents, one with a broken back. Next day, I had to commit a patient to the mental hospital at Kaneohe. Two weeks later, I had another patient with a broken back. Three days after this, I saw a 21-year old girl with pulmonary tuberculosis that involved the upper third of her right lung. I had seen this patient three months before when she coughed up a small amount of blood. At that time, I thought I saw a small lesion in the x-ray behind the first rib and referred her to the chest clinic. The chest doctor did not agree with me. The patient was told to return in three months.

I treated a policeman for a stroke. Twenty-two patients were treated in the venereal disease clinic. Many of the plantation laborers were single men. Frequently, after an infected prostitute was in town, we would have four or more men come in with chancers. We had an excellent German-trained technician who could quickly demonstrate the infecting spirochetes using a dark-field microscope. This allowed us to start treatment immediately.

The port captain at Honaupo hit a pothole with his motor scooter and fell, striking his head on the pavement. I took him to the hospital in the evening and took x-rays, which showed a basal skull fracture. I observed him for several weeks and he recovered. A few days later, I took another patient to the hospital where we learned he had a lung abscess. I operated on a patient with an unruptured ectopic pregnancy.

I had a patient die with acute syphilitic myocarditis and heart failure. In the early spring, I had two patients with typical lobar pneumonia. I had thought this disease was associated with cold weather because, on the mainland, it usually occurred during or after a cold winter. In Hawaii there is no winter, but patients have pneumonia the same as on the mainland.

I had a 20-year old patient who developed acute rheumatic fever with carditis. She died of heart failure within a week. This is another illness I thought was usually associated with cold weather.

There was a military establishment near South Point called Morse Field, where a captain and several men were stationed. I was called to attend a very sick soldier who had a high fever. He proved to have acute epididymitis and was transferred to Honolulu.

As the end of my first year neared, I discussed my work with Mr. Beatty, plantation manager at Naalehu. He said I definitely would be allowed to work on the plantation a second year.

President Franklin D. Roosevelt was elected for an unprecedented third term on November 5, 1940.

Dottie and I were invited to a real Hawaiian luau in Waiohinu. A Hawaiian society put on the luau and we were the only non-Hawaiians present. It was a great honor for us to be invited and showed that the Hawaiian community had accepted us. As is customary at luaus, many danced the hula, including a 90-year old lady.

Numbers for the National Draft Lottery were drawn on November 13th. Neither my number nor Neill's were in the first 1250. My number was 5551 out of a total of 6500 in Hawaii.

The first anniversary of my joining the plantations was November 16th. I did not receive a raise from the plantations nor the head physician.

Dottie and I entertained 43 guests at the plantation club house on November 24th. Three turkeys were cooked, and Dottie made individual pumpkin pies. The dinner was said to have been the best ever served at the club.

In November, I examined my first draftee for the army.

A boxing card was held on November 7th at Naalehu, and my college boxing friend, Lee Burke, from Hilo, was there.

Lois had a party on her 1st birthday and began walking for the first time, taking a dozen steps at each attempt. That day, I had to go to South Point, where a man was killed in a truck accident.

I was called to the hospital one evening in December to see an 18-year old boy who had pain in his neck after doing jujitsu wrestling. An x-ray showed the odontoid process on the first cervical vertebra was fractured. He died later that night.

During the night of December 10th, I had a patient with two fingers blown off one hand. The next day, I took out an appendix with only the surgical nurse assisting me as the head physician was away.

Neill and one of the hospital nurses, Pearl Christen, had dinner with us on December 21st. They were married about a year later.

I went fishing in a motor boat with three plantation men from Honaupo. We caught six fish weighing 70 pounds total. One was a fighting, 25-pound barracuda, an edible game fish in Hawaii.

After I performed an appendectomy on Christmas Day, we had six guests in for dinner.

Dottie and I went to a dance at Pahala New Year's Eve. She was almost six months pregnant. She wore a long, blue evening dress and no one realized that she was pregnant. At this dance, we learned that our new Scottish friends celebrated the New Year in a big way.

McLeod and Louise were in Honolulu for the birth of their second child on December 20th. When McLeod heard that Dr. Gordon Lightner of Puunene, Maui, was looking for an assistant, he telephoned me on January 1, 1941. I immediately called Dr. Lightner and arranged to fly to Maui the next day and be interviewed by Dr. Lightner and Frank Baldwin, plantation owner and manager. I was hired as an assistant plantation physician at a salary of $400 per month plus $100 from Dr. Lightner for help in private practice. I would get suitable housing for my needs, and I would be furnished a car and gasoline by the plantation. Another young doctor, George von Asch, had been hired and had started working that day.

I returned to Hilo by boat and Dottie met me at the dock in the rain. We returned home and I resigned from all my work, effective the end of the month. By the time I left, I had worked fourteen and a half months without vacation or terminal leave pay. Actually, I was never put on the payroll or given a Social Security number. The people and the plantations had treated us well, and Dottie and I will forever be grateful to them. Dottie had stayed in the hospital 15 days when Lois was born, and the plantation cancelled her bill. Mr. Beatty gave me lumber to make shipping crates for our furniture and sent all the crates to Hilo by plantation truck without charging us for the service.

Dottie and I had been very happy in our first home. We had finally furnished it so we could entertain guests. We had planted beautiful flowers and two Norfolk pines in the front yard which we decorated at Christmas with multi-colored lights. The townspeople were amazed at our flowers and the care we took of our yard. We had a vegetable garden and already had harvested bananas. When we first arrived, we thought we would be there for years, but that was not to be.

Our neighbor, Bob Holloway, manager of the plantation store, had a large luau in his back yard on January 11th. He placed two turkeys, split down the back, on top of the pig in the imu before covering it with ti leaves, etc. After cooking, the turkey had a smoked taste like the pork and was delicious.

On January 12th, Dottie and I took a picnic lunch to Bird Park in Volcano National Park on the road leading up Mauna Loa. After lunch we drove up the road to the 6,700 foot level, which was about halfway to the top. The road cut through one lava flow after another. A small earthquake could have easily blocked our road and isolated us. Realizing this, Dottie made me turn around and drive down.

I had delivered a baby for a park ranger's wife and our families became good friends. Another ranger was studying bird life in the park, collecting the craws of quail and pheasants to determine what they were eating. He asked the other rangers to shoot quail and pheasants and keep a record of the time of day and at what elevation on the mountain the birds were taken. He would remove the craws and give the birds back to whomever brought them in.

My ranger friend told me to bring a shotgun and we would go bird-collecting. Hunting was not allowed in the park, but bird-collecting for scientific purposes was permitted. Hunting season outside the park had ended, so we kept our activities a secret. I borrowed a double-barreled shotgun and shells from a friend in Naalehu, without revealing what I was going to do.

As soon as we reached the hunting area, some quail flew up. I aimed my gun at one at close range and pulled the trigger. Out of a cloud of feathers dropped the quail's pulverized body. I had pulled the triggers to both barrels. In the past, I had hunted only with a single-barrel gun.

We drove up the mountain road in a pickup truck. When my friend saw a pheasant cock crouched by the road 20 feet away, he stopped the truck and shot the head off the cock while still sitting behind the steering wheel. I complained he was being unfair to the birds, but he disagreed. Obviously, the pheasants had not been hunted and were not very afraid of us. I preferred to walk and shot some on the ground and others in flight. One had been hit on the head by only one shot and was standing dazed when I reached him. We collected about 20 pheasant cocks and then checked in with the ranger who was making the study. There were plenty of birds for everyone to take several home.

Later, we invited Neill for a chicken dinner. He never admitted to being suspicious although he did comment about how delicious the food was and that it had a wild taste. Just as he noted that a thigh bone had been broken in the piece he was eating, I found a lead shot in my mouth and almost cracked up.

I did another appendectomy alone in January, as the head doctor was away again. The surgical nurse fainted and another replaced her.

Dottie and I went to Kalowala Landing in January to see cattle loaded onto a ship anchored 100 yards off shore. Kalowala was a few miles from South Point on the Naalehu side, near the plantation ranch lands. When cattle were ready to be shipped to the market in Honolulu, they were herded into corrals near the landing. A chute from the corral extended out over a cliff, 30 feet above the ocean. The cattle were brought down the chute one by one. The lead animal would stop to gaze at the water below, then it would be given an electric shock by a battery-operated instrument and would leap forward into the ocean. Cowboys in a lighter came alongside each animal to secure it with a rope around the horns or neck. The lighter with three animals on each side was then pulled out to the ship by rope. A sling was passed under each animal's body, and it was hoisted aboard. Today's good roads and large trucks make this method of loading cattle unnecessary.

During the month of January, I crated our furniture and sent it to Maui. We said goodbye to our friends and flew to Maui on January 29th. Our furniture arrived next day, and we were able to have dinner in our new home on the 31st. We had brought our maid with us. Our car, which was now Dottie's, arrived four days later.

I began work on February 1st and delivered one baby. Dr. von Asch and I alternated night calls and weekend duty.

Dottie and I were invited to dinner many times and we soon got to know the people. Over half of the Caucasians on the Island of Hawaii were native-born Scottish, while on Maui the percentage was much less. Maui seemed to be a suburb of Honolulu, whereas Naalehu was 65 miles from Hilo, which itself was rural. The Honolulu daily newspapers did not arrive in Naalehu until the day after publication. There was overnight boat service from Maui to Honolulu four times weekly, two from Kahului and two from Lahaina. There were many more plane flights to Honolulu, and the distance was just half as far as from Hilo.

Mrs. Bennie Lightner, Dr. Lightner's sister-in-law, had a tea for Dottie on Valentine's Day. Dottie again wore the long, light blue dress which hid her second pregnancy. When our daughter, Ann Fuquay, was born April 3rd, the ladies who had been present at the tea could not believe it; they had not recognized that Dottie was pregnant.

Dr. Lightner had dinner with us one evening, and Dottie served broiled grapefruit as a first course. He had never eaten hot grapefruit, and was relieved to hear that mine was also hot. He explained that when he first tasted the hot fruit, he thought maybe he had had too much to drink.

The two large sugar plantations at Paia and Puunene were owned and managed by the Baldwins. The managers' father, H.P. Baldwin, had started a plantation at Haiku and also had developed the East Maui Irrigation Co. that brought water from the Hana side for irrigation. He supervised the construction of the East Maui Irrigation Co.'s ditches and water conduits in spite of having recently lost his right arm in a mill accident.

H.P. Baldwin was the son of the Reverend Dwight Baldwin, a medical missionary who had come to Lahaina in 1831. He had lived in what is now the Baldwin Home Museum.

The advantages of having the owners manage and live on the plantation were quite obvious. They were cognizant of the laborers' needs and were able to do more for them. Hawaiian Commercial and Sugar Co. (H.C. and S. Co.) at Puunene was in the process of replacing the old camp houses with nice, new ones that had inside plumbing and other modern conveniences. About 100 new homes had already been built. When the supervisors got a new sport complex with swimming pool, tennis courts and bowling alley, the laborers also got the same with a regulation-size swimming pool. Several Olympic swimming champions developed there under Coach S. Sakamoto. Football fields and baseball diamonds were also provided.

Puunene Hospital was the largest and best on Maui with 120 beds and a management that insisted it be kept up-to-date. The hospital was fully staffed at all times, so the extra cost to the plantation for keeping a patient in the facility was only the cost of the food. In 1941, this was 72 cents a day. All children with high fevers and other significant illnesses were hospitalized, as well as adults who were so sick they couldn't work. Two field-nurses were provided, who visited each laborer's home weekly. There was no charge to laborers for hospital and physician care, nor for medicines. Specialists from Honolulu were provided when needed.

H.C. and S. Co. was more profitable than most of the other plantations, and its stock had paid a large dividend every year since the company was organized. I felt more secure in my work at Puunene, and I could easily see that everything was much better on Maui than on the Island of Hawaii, thanks to the Baldwins. Eventually, when labor was paid by the hour, H.C. and S. Co.'s employees were paid 10 cents an hour more than those on the majority of other plantations.

Dottie said I talked the entire month of January about the beauty of Maui. The thing that impressed me most was the relatively flat cane land with good soil and no lava. The roads were good with wide shoulders free of lava rocks waiting to burst tires and break car springs. There were miles of white, sandy beaches where it was safe to swim.

There were two large cinder cones in central Maui and several more on the side nearest the Island of Hawaii. There has not been an eruption on Maui since 1790 when lava formed La Perouse Bay near Makena.

The name, Puunene, was given to a large cinder cone located between Paia and Puunene. In the Hawaiian language, puu means hill and nene means goose and this particular cinder cone was shaped like a goose's head and beak. Soon, the whole area south of the cone was known as Puunene. In 1943 when the runways were built to make the Kahului Naval Air Station, the cinders from this cone were used to make the foundations for the runways. Today, the cone is gone and only a pit remains. The cinders from a similar cone at Maalaea, on the south shore of Maui, were used to make the runways at the Puunene Naval Air Station. A large pit remains where the cone was located. Chunks of lava from the edge of this cinder cone were used to make the rock walls in the yard of our present home. The contractor bought the lava from H.C. and S. Co. for 50 cents a cubic yard.

The Bulletin of the Hawaii Territorial Medical Association, forerunner of the Hawaii Medical Journal, published an article that I wrote entitled "The Importance of Complete Pelvic Examination in Obstetrics"[12]. This helped establish me primarily as an obstetrician, though it would be another 20 years before I could limit my practice to OB-Gyn.

Soon after I arrived on Maui, I did a cesarean on a patient who had a very abnormal pelvis. She had lost her first baby after a difficult delivery. In later years, I did two more cesareans on her. In 1987 I saw this lady in a supermarket. She told me how thankful she was that I had moved to Maui and had operated on her, giving her three healthy babies.

On March 5th, Neill visited us, arriving by boat at Lahaina at 2 a.m. He had decided to return to Chapel Hill, take a course in physics at the University and join the Army Air Force as a pilot trainee.

Dr. Lightner went to Honolulu on March 10th for a few days' vacation and to meet his wife, who was returning from the mainland. He put me in charge, as I had two more year's experience since graduation than Dr. von Asch. When he left, I had an infected hair follicle on my right third finger. The infection spread rapidly and within two days my whole hand and wrist were swollen. Dr. Lightner returned early and opened an abcess on my finger under general ethyl chloride anesthesia. I was given sulfadiazine for the infection, and my hand gradually improved. I spent six days in the hospital and had to continue hot packs at home.

Soon after arriving on Maui, I joined the Maui Country Club. The initiation fee was $50; now it is $5,000. I played golf for the first time in March, 1941, and continue to enjoy the game today.

Dottie and I played bridge with friends in Kahului on April 2nd. As we left, Dottie tripped and almost fell and, soon after, went into labor. Next evening Dr. Lightner delivered our second daughter, Ann Fuquay, weighing 7 pounds, 14 ounces. She and Dottie stayed in the hospital for nine days.

I was busy in my work, sometimes delivering three babies in one night. I started baby clinics in the plantation camps, and the field nurses made sure that every baby came monthly. Dr. Lightner had already started weekly obstetrical clinics at the hospital.

On April 26th, a patient came to the hospital with irregular labor contractions on her expected date of delivery. The contractions soon stopped, but she still had pain in the right side of her abdomen. I operated and removed an acutely infected appendix. I had seen a similar case during my residency at Kensington Hospital. Thirty hours after removal of the appendix, she went into normal labor and delivered normally. I reported this case five years later in the Hawaii Medical Journal[13].

A Navy plane with three men aboard crashed on the slopes of Haleakala about the 4,000-foot elevation, approximately 12 miles from Puunene Hospital. The police called for a doctor, and I went to the scene. I drove my car across the ranch land until the engine overheated, then walked the last quarter mile, carrying my medical bag. The plane had burned and there were no survivors.

There was considerable military activity at the Puunene Airport, where there was a special naval/aerial reconnaissance unit. Drone planes were sent into the air for target practice. We went to the airport in the evening of May 2nd to watch special night maneuvers.

Dr. von Asch and I took turns examining school children in Spreckelsville, Puunene, Kahului, and Kihei schools. Most of these were plantation dependents. We examined about 50 children each day and found many chronic diseases, such as diseased tonsils, draining ears, heart murmurs, hernias, scoliosis, etc.

The war in Europe was escalating. The British battle cruiser, Hood, was sunk on May 24th. President Roosevelt declared a national emergency on the 27th, the same day the British sank the German pocket battleship, Bismarck, in the South Atlantic. There had been great excitement throughout the world as the British, with its superior naval power, chased down and sank this German ship that had been preying on shipping in the Atlantic.

I saw Bill Smith compete at a swim meet on May 30th. He later became an Olympic champion under coach S. Sakamoto, who started his career at Puunene.

On June 7th, we performed four major operations and took out 27 pairs of tonsils. Dr. Lightner used the Sluter technique under general ethyl chloride anesthesia to remove tonsils. Only about five minutes were required for each patient, though many would bleed sometime afterwards. I became an expert at stopping bleeding after tonsillectomy. One of the major operations that day was opening a kidney abscess in a 500-pound Hawaiian woman, which Dr. Lightner did with great skill.

We operated on a sailor for appendicitis during the night of June 8th.

I sent in my Selective Service questionnaire on June 9th. Almost every day, a local person entered the service.

Pearl Christen and another nurse stopped on Maui to see us for two days. They were returning to the mainland from Pahala because a friend there told them there would soon be a war in Hawaii with Japan. Dottie and I met them at midnight in Lahaina. We were late arriving and as we drove onto Mala Wharf we saw them in a taxi and were able to get them. Pearl became my sister-in-law six months later, an event I had no advance knowledge of.

Malcolm Clower, whom we had met on Molokai, was now principal of Maui High School. Friends of his had sent him a leg of venison from Molokai, where deer were plentiful, and he invited us to his home for a venison dinner.

The Medical Preparedness Committee met on June 23rd and frequently thereafter. War seemed inevitable, and the medical community had to prepare for it.

Dr. von Asch called me from the hospital one evening and told me our maid was admitted following an auto accident. The car she was riding in hit a utility pole, and she was thrown out. She suffered a fractured skull, with a crack in the bone extending from ear to ear over the top of the head, and five fractured ribs. She remained in the hospital for two weeks and recovered. While she was in the hospital, her parents came to see her from Pahala and stayed in our home for several days. Recently, one of my golfing friends told me he had been in the car with her at the time of the accident.

There was a Navy plane accident near the airport on July 21st. As I remember, the plane stalled when it was about 50 feet off the ground. We treated the pilot, who had a broken leg and a deep vertical cut on the left side of his face from the forehead to the jaw. The eyelid was cut, but the eye was not injured. I was very pleased that, after healing, the scar on his face was barely visible.

We went to a formal dance at the Puunene Athletic Club. The monthly dance there was the biggest social event on the island. Mother Baldwin, the owner-manager's mother, had donated the money for the clubhouse with the stipulation that no alcoholic beverages were ever to be served. To get around this, the supervisors, most of whom lived within a block, had parties in their homes before the dance and during intermission. I remember that at one of these intermission parties, I entertained our guests by playing comic records on the phonograph such as "Hugh the Blue Gnu" and "Cocktails for Two" by Spike Jones.

I made a notation that I treated 100 patients in our clinic on August 14th. If one of the other doctors was sick or was away for any reason, I would have busy days like this. I would be so tired afterwards that it would take me two days to recover.

Dr. Lightner left for the mainland for 10 weeks in August and, again, left me in charge. We lived in his home on the beach in Kahului for a month and found it less desirable than our Puunene home. In the evenings, the trade winds stopped blowing and Kahului was just too hot. Puunene, at 45 feet above sea level, was much more comfortable.

Our head nurse was replaced by Miss Rose Littel, a nurse-anesthetist with whom I had worked at Pahala Hospital. Before this, a nurse without special training had given open-drop ether for all our anesthesia.

I admitted my first patient with poliomyelitis on October 1st. Later I admitted an army wife with a high fever, rigid neck and acute poliomyelitis. She was immediately transferred to Tripler Army Hospital in Honolulu.

The Maui County Fair was held October 9th to 11th at the fairgrounds in Kahului. This was the largest fair in Hawaii and was very similar to county fairs I had attended in North Carolina. There was great participation by the schools with students entering exhibits in arts and crafts, homemaking, etc. There was always a football game on Friday afternoon between Maui High and Lahainaluna High Schools. As the Maui High doctor, I always attended. Friday was children's day. Schools were closed and most every child went to the fair wearing new clothes and taking enough money to participate in everything. It was one of the happiest days of the year for them.

Horse races filled the grandstands on Thursday and Saturday afternoons during the Fair. There was always a good circus with elephants and other wild animals, just like circuses on the mainland. Each day there was a large main show and many smaller attractions.

The agricultural and livestock exhibits were outstanding. Maui was said to be the breadbasket for Hawaii and the farmers made the most of the opportunity to exhibit their produce at the fair. The flower show and flower arrangements, especially the Japanese cultural displays, were beautiful and exciting. Over the years, the

104

Hawaiiana exhibits and orchid show have received wide acclaim. People came from all the islands to visit the Fair, filling all the hotel rooms in Central Maui.

I treated my first case of tetanus in October. A plantation laborer had a small cut on his foot made by a cane knife and, although it had been sutured correctly, the infection developed. The patient had a few convulsions and lockjaw. The wound was opened widely and cleaned. Large doses of tetanus antitoxin were given and the patient recovered.

On Saturday, November 22nd, Dr. Jack Marnie, Allan Corell, Bruce Fleming and I went goat hunting on Molokai. We went in late afternoon on Bruce's boat from Lahaina and slept at an old landing on Molokai, just across from Maui. I became seasick as soon as we left Maui and had to lie down all the way.

We got up at 4 a.m. and climbed the mountain to the 3,000-foot level, only to find the goats were on another ridge with a deep valley between us. We could see them, but they were out of range of our 30-30 rifles. I still remember how tired I was after climbing the mountain carrying the rifle. Our goal was to be in the goats' grazing area before daylight. We returned to Lahaina in the afternoon.

I have often thought about this boat trip to Molokai, which occurred just two weeks before the Japanese attacked Pearl Harbor. The Japanese had a contigency plan to attack our fleet at Lahaina Roads if it were stationed there instead of Pearl Harbor. Submarines were probably in this area at the time of the attack.

CHAPTER VIII

World War II Years on Maui, Plantation Medical Practice at Puunene: December 7, 1941, to December 31, 1945

I was busy in the dispensary at Puunene Hospital on December 7th treating plantation patients, many of whom were Japanese aliens. A radio was on in an adjoining room, where the hospital laboratory was located. An American-born Japanese technician was busy with routine work. At 8:15 a.m. he called me to come and listen to the radio. The announcer was excited, reporting that planes with the rising sun painted on their wings had attacked many areas on Oahu. There were many casualties and great damage at Pearl Harbor.

Puunene is approximately 90 miles from Pearl Harbor. We could hear the rumbling noise of the explosions, like thunder in the distance. I listened to the radio a few minutes and returned to my work, treating Japanese aliens. Their reaction was one of disbelief, just like mine.

Both the American-born Japanese and most of the aliens on Maui were true Americans so far as I could discern, not only on December 7th, but throughout the war. The few pro-Japan aliens on Maui known to the authorities were taken into custody on December 7th. Some of these were kept in concentration camps, while others were later repatriated to Japan. In all of Hawaii, about 2,000 residents were put in concentration camps. I do not know of any spying or sabotage by the Japanese on Maui.

Dr. Lightner had an employee, a Japanese alien, whose salary was paid by the plantation. He worked in Dr. Lightner's office in Kahului, helping care for patients and also did yard work and miscellaneous jobs such as chauffeuring. He had a large family; his children were being educated in true American fashion. As a leader in the Japanese community, he always went aboard visiting Japanese ships at Kahului and entertained the officers. Many suspected that he was pro-Japan rather than pro-America and, when the war started, he was investigated. Dr. Lightner vouched for his loyalty and took responsibility for his actions. He continued to work and proved that he was loyal to America.

Minutes after the Japanese attack, I called Dottie who had also heard the news from our elderly Scottish neighbor. At the time, Dottie was bathing eight-month-old Ann. Without hesitation, Dottie asked our American-born Japanese maid to finish the bath, while she listened to the radio. There was never any doubt about the loyalty of the thousands of Japanese living among us. As I said before, the few who were known to be pro-Japan were taken into custody immediately.

The American-born Japanese were anxious to show their loyalty to the United States. It did not matter to them if their parents were pro-Japan; they were pro-America and wanted to prove it. Many of them wanted to join the army but, at first, they were denied. Finally, an army of Japanese-Americans, all volunteers, was formed (the 442nd Division) and fought valiantly in Europe. Its members received more decorations than did those of any other army unit ever. A laboratory technician from Puunene Hospital joined the 442nd Division and was killed in Italy. Later in the war, Japanese-Americans were drafted for duty, but they were not assigned to the western Pacific to fight against Japan.

One alien Japanese doctor who had raised a large family on Maui and owned much property here asked to be repatriated to Japan when he was interned early in the war. He was sent to Japan in an exchange for Americans and one of his sons, who had been reared in Japan, fought in the Japanese army. All of his other children were pro-America and remained here. One American-born doctor's son joined the famous 442nd Division and served in Europe until the end of the war. He was not quite five feet tall, and because of Army regulations in regards to height, had to sign waivers giving up all his rights. After the war, he returned to Maui to practice and, finally, along with six other doctors including me, helped organize The Maui Medical Group.

A second son also joined the 442nd Division and fought in Europe, while a third younger son later fought in the Korean War. A fourth son was classified 4F for physical reasons and was not allowed to join the army.

After World War II ended, the father was allowed to return to Maui and lived to be over 90 years of age. His property had been seized by the Federal Government and many years passed before the family regained possession of it.

During the week after December 7th, I was very busy. In fact, Dottie said I didn't come home for three days. The hospital had to be blacked out and many other emergency defense measures had to be taken. Dr. von Asch was in Honolulu on vacation and could not get home until December 12th so I had to help Dr. Lightner in surgery and defense preparations. Another attack was expected, and it was rumored that a Japanese beachhead would be established on Maui before they moved on to Honolulu. There was not a single shore gun to protect Maui. Things were in a state of chaos. The Maui County Medical Society met often, usually on Sunday, to formulate emergency procedures in case of an attack. Also, we doctors were busy teaching first-aid classes, although Dr. Lightner was often sick and unable to work.

On December 11th, Colin P. Kelly, a U.S. Naval airman, was credited with sinking the Japanese naval ship, Haruno, with a bomb. He became an instant national hero. Later, he was stationed at the Puunene Naval Air Station, and I attended several social gatherings with him. He died in another engagement with the Japanese Navy.

I had an afternoon off on December 13th, the first time off duty in two weeks. Homes had to be completely blacked out and there was a curfew from sundown to sunrise. Only emergency cars were allowed to travel at night, with headlights taped and only a slit, about 3/8 "x 2", letting light come through. There was a bank of dirt by the irrigation ditch which went along the constantly curving road between our home and hospital, a distance of about one and a half miles. When I felt my car begin to climb the bank on those dark nights, I knew I was off the road.

Just before dark on December 15th, a Japanese submarine attacked Kahului Harbor, firing ten shells. Several were duds, and when these were found, proved to have been made in the U.S.A. during World War I. Only one chicken was killed in this attack. One shell hit a large gasoline storage tank and went through the top. It did not explode and was removed later. Two shells fell into the harbor and three hit the Maui Pineapple Cannery, doing $700 worth of damage[14].

I was in Puunene, about two miles from Kahului Harbor, when this shelling started. I immediately climbed onto our garage roof, where I could see the ocean. With each shot, I could see a tongue of fire in the dark out on the ocean. Then I would hear an explosion when the shell hit, if it were not a dud. Two of the shells were fired toward the old Puunene Dairy, halfway between our house and the ocean. I could hear these shells whistle through the air.

After this attack, the people living on the beach in Kahului were afraid.

Mrs. William Walsh, wife of the manager of the harbor and the Kahului Railroad Co., spent the night with us in Puunene. Jack and Bennie Lightner and others spent three nights with us.

The Medical Society appointed me chairman of a committee to determine the blood types of all the civilians on Maui to give us a "walking blood bank." In case of a great emergency, a team at each hospital would draw 25 pints of blood and have it ready to use. This would keep the doctors free to do other things, saving much time. Thirty thousand civilians had their blood typed. I published a paper in the Hawaii Medical Journal describing the mass blood typing[15]. Very few errors were made, and these were discovered in the cross matching with the patient.

At 6:10 a.m. on Sunday, December 21st, I was called to the beach at Spreckelsville in front of Frank Baldwin's home, along with other members of the Medical Preparedness Committee. A 20-foot lifeboat with either 30 or 31 men aboard had come ashore (my diary states 31). They were survivors of the Matson freighter, Lahaina, which had been set ablaze by a surfaced Japanese submarine on December 11th, 800 miles from Maui. The entire crew escaped in a lifeboat, but two died during the ensuing days. Two others, crazed by the lack of food and water, jumped overboard 200 yards off shore and were drowned[14].

The survivors were given food and coffee on the beach and then transferred to Puunene Hospital to recover. Most of them left the hospital after a couple days, but I think one or two stayed a week or so. As I recall, Captain Mathewson recovered and went to sea again.

The Civil Defense Agency advised everyone to build a bomb shelter. Three of our neighbors joined us in digging a large shelter in our yard. The hole was about eight feet deep, large enough for all of us to get in, with a roof and stairs leading down. We stocked it with provisions and kept it ready to use for over two years.

All shipping to Hawaii was disrupted. Within a week or less, airmail was moving between the islands and to the mainland. Our first Christmas packages arrived by boat on December 28th while interisland boat mail from the Island of Hawaii first arrived on the 30th.

On December 31st at 2 a.m., Kahului was shelled again by a submarine. This time, shore batteries returned the fire in the brilliant moonlight. There were no casualties or damage. Jack and Bennie Lightner and daughter spent every night for a week with us after this second shelling.

January 2nd, I received a raise of $100 per month from the plantation after eleven month's employment. Dr. Lightner split the income with Dr. von Asch and me that he received for treating industrial accidents of the employees of a contractor who was building a road from Puunene to Kihei. This amounted to about $50 each per month. I was now receiving $650 per month compared to the $400 I would no doubt still be getting if I had stayed at Naalehu. In addition, I was furnished a car and gasoline by the plantation.

I played golf on January 10th at the Maui Country Club for the first time since the war started. Lines of cement posts placed close together were built about every hundred yards along the fairways to prevent aircraft from landing on them in case of an attack.

January 12th to 14th, I examined draftees in the armory in Wailuku. On one of those days, an airplane flew low overhead, the first plane I had seen since the war started, though planes had been landing at Puunene Airport. It was a twin-engine army plane from Oahu. If it had been an enemy plane, the armory would have been a likely target. Obviously, everyone had the jitters.

Colonel Lyman, ranking army officer on Maui, called a meeting of the Maui County Medical and Dental Societies to discuss the dispensing of liquor. There was no rationing of food or other merchandise on Maui. When the supplies were exhausted, we waited until more arrived by ship from the mainland. Hawaii raised much of its food, particularly fruits and vegetables, and we had plenty of raw sugar and even had a small sugar refinery at Paia Mill for wartime use. However, Dottie says she had difficulty buying refined sugar. An agreement was reached that each adult could buy a fifth of liquor per week. It was quickly explained that this amount would last to Thursday evening if one took two drinks before dinner each day. Many who did not drink received their allotment and gave it to those who thought they could not survive without it. As I remember, there was no real problem with the liquor rationing.

We had a dinner party on February 7th with eight guests. This was the first entertaining we had done since the war started.

A County Medical Society meeting was held on Sunday, February 8th, and a representative from the Army told us that Puunene Hospital, as well as Malulani Hospital in Wailuku, would have to be evacuated. The Army knew that the Japanese planned to land in central Maui. A line of defense had been established by the army and both these hospitals were in front of it.

Within one day, we had taken over the Baldwin Old Men's Home between Paia and Makawao and converted it into a temporary hospital. Dr. von Asch and I alternated nights on duty at the hospital with Dr. Lightner relieving us occasionally. It was about 10 miles from Puunene where the dispensary, x-ray and laboratory at Puunene Hospital were still operating.

The interisland freighter, Humuula, got stuck on the reef outside Kahului Harbor on February 20th. It was freed within 24 hours, as I recall.

A large contingent of mainland army troops arrived on Maui on March 13th. Eventually, there were over 30,000 army troops on Maui to defend us against invasion.

Practically no fruits or vegetables were arriving from the mainland, so on March 15th I dug up the lawn in our yard and planted a vegetable garden. Merchandise was not rationed on Maui as there was usually none to ration.

Ann got her first tooth and began walking on March 31st, three days before her first birthday.

I repaired a fractured patella on April 8th and got a good result. I had never even seen such an operation, but followed the directions in the surgical book.

Bataan Peninsula in the Philippines fell to the Japanese on April 9th. My lifelong friend and now a Navy doctor, Bruce Langdon, was among those captured.

We went to the wedding reception of Dr. Jack Marnie and Miss Cynthia Herbert on April 17th. Dr. Marnie, a dentist and our neighbor, had met Cynthia, a Puunene Hospital nurse, at a party in our home.

All the citizens of Maui were required to be revaccinated against smallpox. In four days in April, I vaccinated over 4,700 people. When the person to be vaccinated stepped in front of me, I applied a drop of vaccine to the arm and then punctured the area several times with a needle. The muscles of my back and arms became very tired and sore. Three times I accidently punctured my left index finger and thumb with the needle. I had been vaccinated two weeks before and had had a primary reaction. The new vaccine I was using had been supplied by the Army and apparently was much stronger than the old. I got three primary takes, and my left arm was so sore I could barely move it for a week.

Mauna Loa on the Island of Hawaii began erupting on the night of April 26th, illuminating the top of the mountain for several days. We were all worried that the light would aid the Japanese if they were ready to invade Hawaii.

An air raid alarm sounded on April 30th, but planes were never sighted.

In addition to smallpox, everyone was given typhoid vaccinations. One diabetic had a severe reaction and died. Two other patients developed a generalized bullous rash after smallpox inoculation and were very sick. Both recovered.

The Hawaii Medical Journal was established and Volume I, Number 1 was published January, 1943. Issue Number 5 was devoted to Maui, and we were asked to contribute articles. I wrote two papers. In the first, entitled "The Need for Autopsies in Stillbirth and Neonatal Deaths," [16] I described three deaths that occurred in Puunene Hospital in one month in which the diagnosis was unknown until autopsy. All three had conditions incompatible with life. The second paper was entitled "Trichonosis" and reported four cases from Puunene Hospital proven by muscle biopsy[17]. All four patients had eaten pork bought from the market. Live, moving larvae could be seen under the microscope in biopsy fragments of muscle tissue. These patients usually had a high fever, eye pain and general muscle pain and were often first diagnosed as having flu. The first white blood count would be normal. I learned to take a second blood count after four days; it would show an elevation with about one third eosinophils.

The pigs in Hawaii, wild or domestic, become infested with trichinae by eating infested rats. Thorough cooking of the pork will, of course, kill the larvae, while freezing for three months will do the same. Many of the plantation laborers were bachelors who did their own cooking and often ate pork that was not cooked enough.

The Puunene Hospital laboratory also served as the Public Health Laboratory for the County of Maui, doing water samples, milk samples, throat and stool cultures, and any other special work the doctors of the county requested. There was always a qualified technician on the staff, furnished by the Board of Health. Dr. Ozzie Bushnell, the technician in my early days at Puunene, later became a professor at the University of Hawaii.

The Army established a station hospital in the Makawao School building and often used the Puunene Hospital laboratory for special tests. We became friendly with the officers, some of whom visited every day. One of them, Lt. Field, had been a classmate of mine at the University of Pennsylvania.

On May 29th, according to my diary, some of these officers told us that U.S. Intelligence had broken the Japanese code and that a Japanese armada had left Japan on its way to invade Hawaii. Plans called for Midway to be taken first. On June 3rd the news announced the Battle of Midway was in progress[14]. Another news release on June 6th reported we had won the Battle of Midway. My diary states that two or three aircraft carriers were sunk, and that three battleships, three cruisers, two destroyers, and two aircraft carriers were damaged. There were rumors that several loaded Japanese troop ships were sunk. I was told that the sky over Honolulu was darkened by the numbers of Superfortresses (B29s) that left to take part in the battle.

Many of the wives of the civilians in Hawaii were evacuated to the mainland. Dr. von Asch's wife left on June 10th. Dottie and I decided that she and our two babies would stay in Hawaii unless we were told they should evacuate. After the Battle of Midway, we felt secure that we would not be captured by the Japanese.

June 21st, we entertained six soldiers. Before dinner, I took them to the Puunene Athletic Club to bowl and to go swimming.

Lt. Jack Dillahunt of the Makawao Station Hospital had dinner with us on June

25th. After the war, he and his wife visited us here, and Dottie and I visited them later in Albuquerque, New Mexico.

On July 21st, I played golf, the first time in a month. Frequently, Dr. Lightner was out sick for one or two weeks, leaving Dr. von Asch and me with more clinical work than we could do. In addition, we often had medical preparedness work to do such as first-aid classes, blood-typing, vaccinations, etc.

Dr. von Asch and I were both subject to the military draft. Every three months, I received a letter from the Selective Service stating I was class 3A and was deferred for three more months. They said my work on the plantation was considered essential and I was not allowed to leave. This continued even through the Korean war. McLeod, a captain in the Reserve when the war started, was told to resign his commission and to continue working as a plantation doctor.

We went to a farewell party in July for Lt. Jack Lightner, who had been serving as a supply officer for the Puunene Naval Air Station. He gave our children a miniature house that the Seabees had made for his daughter, who was the same age as Lois. It was very much admired by our children and their friends.

The large guns of our shore batteries fired many practice rounds on July 24th, making us think we had protection if we were attacked.

An announcement in July said there would be a 25 percent bonus paid to all plantation employees due to the rising price of sugar.

I took a week's vacation starting October 26th. Dottie and I went to Hana for two days and spent the night in the Hawaiian Telephone Exchange's guest room. I was their physician on Maui. We went as far as Kaupo and met Nicholas Y. Soon, a former Rhodes Scholar who operated a store at Kaupo. Later, two of his daughters lived with us at different times while they attended Baldwin High School. The military constantly patrolled this area in armored jeeps, as it was rumored that the Japanese had a plan to land there to invade Maui. I think the road was mined at the pali areas, which meant that it could quickly be made impassable.

I went to Honolulu by plane in October and stayed for four days. I had not been there in three years and could not believe how strange it felt to be in a big city again. I attended the Thursday morning clinic at the Queen's Hospital, visited several of my friends, and did some shopping.

Dottie went to Honolulu in November for six days, her first visit in three years. She stayed with friends and enjoyed herself until the last day when she became very ill after eating lunch at a downtown hotel. She was barely able to fly home the next day and did not recover for two more days.

We invited two soldiers to our home for Thanksgiving dinner.

I gave Dottie a gold ring with a large cultured pearl for Christmas, which I ordered from a catalog. Luckily, I got the mail the day it arrived and hid the ring in a coat pocket in our clothes closet. Dottie searched everywhere trying to find the package containing my Christmas present to her, but to no avail. She appeared upset, saying that I hadn't planned to give her anything. When she got the ring, she was delighted.

Not much happened in January, 1943. I was very busy with routine work and spending half of my nights at the evacuation hospital. I had my picture taken for an identification badge for the Navy which I needed when I went out at night, and when I had to enter restricted areas.

Dottie and I played golf and tennis as often as we could. My golf score was now usually below 100 for 18 holes.

We decided that we should have another baby. It appeared that we were safe from Japanese invasion, and that I would not be drafted into the service. I still owed McLeod money, but was making payments each month. It was evident that the war would be long and that we would not be able to travel for some time. Dottie began vomiting in February, a sure sign that she was pregnant as planned.

I heard from Neill in February. He was in the Army Air Force in North Africa flying a troop transport plane that towed a glider. Both his plane and the glider carried 25 troops. He said that for 18 months he had not slept on a regular bed, usually sleeping in the plane or on wheat straw beneath the plane.

After the war was over, Neill told me about the Allied invasion of Tunisia from North Africa. He was flying over the Mediterranean at night with his plane and a glider loaded with troops. As the formation of Allied planes flew over our fleet, someone from our fleet mistakenly opened fire on them. All our planes were shot down except Neill's plane and glider, which were the last in the formation. He had seen what was happening and turned around, landing back in North Africa. We had heard a news report about this.

In February, I diagnosed and operated on a liver abscess, the first of only three that I ever treated.

I had a bad time with a high-ranking plantation supervisor in February. He became mentally upset and fired many rounds of ammunition from his 38-caliber pistol through the ceilings in his home. I put the pistol in the pocket of my car, where it stayed for a week. He was hospitalized and, later, after causing more trouble, the plantation fired him.

We were notified on February 27th that the evacuation hospital was to be closed in March and Puunene Hosptial reoccupied. This was good news for Dottie and me as Dottie did not feel well. However, the hospital did not close until May 29th.

Dottie's Crow Land pearls, which I already mentioned, arrived in March. They were very beautiful and still are, 46 years later.

When Dr. von Asch's wife and daughter returned from the coast in March he took a week's vacation. I was on duty 24 hours a day for a week and spent my nights at the evacuation hospital.

Ann and Lois had repeated attacks of tonsillitis and ear infections, so in March, Dr. Lightner removed their tonsils. He used the Sluter technique and they had no post-operative bleeding.

Our neighbor, James Marnie, died of colon cancer in March. When Mrs. Marnie moved to Honolulu to live with her son, Jack, the plantation remodeled the Marnie home and allowed us to live in it. It had three bedrooms, two baths and separate maid's quarters. The yard was large enough for me to raise chickens and turkeys and to have a garden.

We flew to the Big Island in April to spend four days at Olaa with McLeod and Louise. This was our first trip with Lois and Ann. We also visited our friends at Naalehu and after three days, I felt rested and normal again.

On May 6th, I diagnosed a case of leprosy in a teenager and sent him to Kalaupapa where his father, brother, and maybe a sister were already patients. So far as I know, his mother never contracted the disease. Recently, he was on Maui and we discussed old times. He told me that when he was a teenager, I had given him a pair of shoes, the first he had ever owned. Today he is a very respected citizen at Kalaupapa and a leader in the community. He is not required to live there, but prefers to do so.

In early 1943, the Navy Seabees started building Kahului Naval Air Station and it was operational before the end of the year. This large base supported three air groups at one time. Much of the area used to build the station had been waste land covered with kiawe trees, but some good cane land was taken. After the war, it was converted to the Kahului Airport, which was about five miles closer to Kahului and Wailuku than the old airport at Puunene.

The civilian airport at Puunene was developed into the Puunene Naval Air Station, supporting two air groups in addition to the original reconnaissance unit. It continued to serve as the civilian airport. As the naval planes practiced take-offs and landings at the two air stations, they circled over our home at Puunene 24 hours a day. About 45 minutes before sunrise, we could hear the dawn patrol plane leave, searching for submarines that had surfaced to charge their batteries. As I remember, this was a noisy, single-engine, amphibian plane. I think there were about 30,000 Navy personnel assigned to the two air stations.

I was appointed to the interesting position of quarantine officer for the port of Kahului when Dr. W. Osmers retired. For several years, I boarded the ships from foreign ports about three miles outside the harbor along with Port Captain, Harold Stein. Grabbing the ladder and climbing aboard from the tug was dangerous if the weather was rough. Besides the quarantine work, I treated any sick seamen on board. On May 6th, I took out a seaman's appendix after transferring him to Puunene Hospital.

My diary states that on Sunday, June 5th, I was completely off duty for the first time in several months. I went to church and then to a movie with Dottie and Lois.

We invited Major Charles Wilbar for dinner in June in celebration of his appointment as President of the Territorial Board of Health. He was McLeod's classmate and a friend of ours since we arrived in Hawaii. On Maui, he had been in charge of the Army's Waikapu Dispensary.

On July 9th, we moved into the remodeled Marnie house. It was built about three feet off the ground and had high ceilings, making it much cooler and more comfortable than the bungalow across the street where we had been living. Tall trees in the yard helped keep it cool.

The hospital had a luau in July for its employees. On the same day, I helped Dr. Lightner remove Dr. von Asch's appendix.

We bought a rare blue Doberman Pinscher puppy in July and named her Patsy. She already had had her ears trimmed and her tail docked. I felt more secure leaving Dottie and the children alone with the dog there.

Dr. von Asch returned to work two and a half weeks after his operation and I took the afternoon off. While pruning the trees in our yard, I fell 12 feet but was not hurt.

Patsy became ill. The whites of her eyes became deeply yellow, and I called a veterinarian, Dr. Penfold, to see her. He thought she had contracted a viral liver infection when she was in a Honolulu hospital having her ears trimmed. He prescribed intravenous glucose as treatment. I gave her several liters of 10 percent glucose over a period of days, an easy treatment, as the veins in her front legs were large. She recovered quickly.

I completely forgot our wedding anniversary on August 17th; I made no mention of it in my diary.

August 19th was a busy day: I removed the tonsils of an adult under local anesthesia; I did an appendectomy; I was up all night delivering two babies and had one patient die of a natural cause. In between, I saw all the patients in the hospital and treated all the clinic patients.

September 13th was another busy day: I saw 70 patients in the clinic and admitted 15 of them to the hospital.

Dottie had a six-hour labor on the 18th and delivered a baby girl weighing 8 pounds, 12 ounces. She did everything this time herself, as the baby came just as we were wheeling her into the delivery room. Dr. Lightner did not reach the hospital in time. We named her Dorothy Jane, but called her Dottie Jane and she looked just like her mother. She was entirely breastfed and was above birth weight by the eighth day. They came home on the 10th day.

Dottie developed a breast infection and went back to the hospital after two weeks. When she came home, I took a week's vacation to help her. In spite of having a good maid, there was too much to do in taking care of two small children and a new baby.

In October I saw 5,000 troops land on the beaches in Kihei from three troop transports. They had full equipment including tanks, bulldozers, etc.

I planted a vegetable garden on October 27th. Our pullets, which were in a battery, laid four eggs for the first time and, within a month, were laying 10 eggs daily. We harvested grapefruit from our large tree.

Dottie Jane slept from 7 p.m. to 6 a.m. when she was one month and 22 days of age. When our babies were very young, Dottie and I alternated nights caring for them. Dottie was so tired she couldn't do it every night herself. Even when she was feeding them at breast, we followed this routine. I would get the baby for her to nurse, and then put it back in its crib. About 30 minutes later, I changed its diaper and then we all slept three or more hours. Dottie hardly woke up on my nights to care for the baby. I would be so tired the next night that I would not even wake up when the baby cried. Occasionally, my medical practice broke our routine. There was great relief when the new baby slept all night.

I lost a patient with tetanus in November according to my diary, although I do not remember any details.

As I was approaching Puunene Hospital a few weeks before Thanksgiving, a Navy plane flew overhead, at an altitude of about 500 feet. This was a common sight as they practiced from the nearby naval air stations. The engine of this plane began making an unusual noise, causing me to look up. Just as I did, there was an explosion. The pilot was thrown out of the cockpit and fell directly into the canefield below. The plane disintegrated and fell nearby. I rushed to the area, which was only a few hundred yards away, and went into the canefield to check the pilot. He had been killed instantly.

The day after Thanksgiving, a plantation laborer brought me a fountain pen which he had found in the field where the plane had fallen. It was a Parker pen that Dottie had given me, with a sterling silver cap and my name engraved on the barrel. The worker knew me very well because I had delivered two of his babies. He said although he would have liked to have kept the fountain pen, his conscience would not allow him to do so. I still have this pen.

On November 30th, I played nine holes of golf, the first time in several months.

We entertained as many military personnel as possible including two Army nurses for Thanksgiving dinner and two Marine officers for Christmas dinner.

I was told I would get another pay raise on January 1, 1944.

Dottie and I went to a formal party on New Year's Eve at the Grand Hotel in Wailuku. This was the first formal party we had attended since the war and we had to apply for a special permit to travel at night.

I was busy the first two weeks of 1944 when Dr. Lightner was sick and unable to work. I operated on a ruptured ectopic pregnancy and then repaired a hernia in a male plantation supervisor. Another day, I did four major operations. A patient had been in the hospital for a week with gallstone colic, waiting for Dr. Lightner. Finally, I took out his gallbladder myself with Dr. von Asch assisting me. It was completely filled with stones and there was one in the cystic duct. Dr. Lightner came into the operating room just as I was finishing the operation. This was the first gallbladder that I had removed completely on my own and the patient recovered without complications.

On January 20th, I made seven house calls to plantation supervisors' homes and to the homes of nonplantation patients. These were all private patients, and we were paid for caring for them. I usually made about 30 house calls per month. I remember reducing a dislocated shoulder in an 80-year old woman who had fallen out of bed. I gave her a few whiffs of ethyl chloride for anesthesia and reduced the dislocation just as we had been taught to do in medical school.

I operated on an infant with intussusception on January 21st.

A man was accidently electrocuted in the Puunene power plant on the 23rd. He was polishing the brass terminals of the transformers, when the electricity was turned on before the scheduled time.

Dottie and I drove to Haiku in February to see the site where barracks were being constructed to house the Fourth Marine Division and part of the Fifth Division. They would use this site as a rest camp between forays in the South Pacific to regain territory captured by the Japanese.

Dr. Pauline Stitt of the Board of Health had dinner with us. She had severe poliomyelitis as a child and wore braces on her legs and used a cane. Lois, who was four, could not understand that she was a doctor. Dr. Stitt asked Lois if she would like to be a doctor when she grew up to which she answered no, she wanted to be a woman.

The 4th Marine Division landed on Maui in late February and early March[14]. I got a call on March 10th from Dr. Andy Weaver, McLeod's classmate whom we visited in Baltimore in 1937. He was a highly trained surgeon and a Navy doctor assigned to the 4th Marines. I visited him that afternoon. There had been heavy rains and the camp at Haiku was a quagmire. Construction of the barracks was incomplete so everyone was busy erecting tents to provide dry places to sleep. Marines were everywhere, over 30,000 of them. In spite of the rain and wind, they were happy to be here. They had just returned from the Roi-Namur and Kwajalein invasions, where approximately 20 percent of their comrades were casualties. I will never forget this visit.

The next day, a Saturday, Dr. Weaver came to our home before noon. Dottie remembers that I went into the backyard and killed a chicken frier, which she prepared for lunch. He stayed for dinner and spent the night, sleeping on the punee in the living room. Sunday morning I took him to the top of Haleakala.

Andy was a true Southerner. His favorite drink was a mint julep and he always brought his own bottle of high-quality bourbon whiskey. We filled iced tea glasses with crushed ice, a teaspoon of crushed mint - fresh from our neighbor's garden - and about two teaspoons of sugar. Next, we poured bourbon whiskey over the ice, filling the glass. Within five minutes, the glass became frosted, and then we would sip the drink for 30 to 40 minutes. The mixture at the bottom of the glass, which had lots of mint and sugar in it, tasted the best. Andy usually enjoyed two of these potent drinks, although I quickly learned that even one was too much for me.

Andy told us about his activities as a doctor with the Marines. Immediately after an invasion, a field hospital would be set up near the beach. They carried the

necessary equipment to perform all kinds of lifesaving operations although they had
to choose their patients so that the greatest number of lives possible would be saved.
He said that immediately after an invasion, he would operate for 36 hours, sleep five
or six hours, then operate another 24 hours and so on, until all were treated. Andy
was the oldest child of a large family and had been reared on a farm in North
Carolina. I think he could adapt to this work and the long hours much better than
most doctors.

The 4th Marines made three separate invasions of Japanese-occupied islands,
and each time the casualties were great. After each invasion, the survivors returned
to Maui for R & R. In August they lost 6,600 men[14]. On Iwa Jima, about half their
members were casualties. Reinforcements brought their strength up to normal, and
they got ready to go again. In 1945, only 20 percent of the original 4th Marines were
alive.

Dottie and I could see a change in Andy after each invasion. After seeing so
many of our youth massacred he seemed to no longer have a zest for life.

After the second and third battles, Andy skipped the formalities when he arrived
on Maui and came directly to our home . Once he arrived at 9:30 in the evening. I
got the mint from our neighbor and we made mint juleps. After he sipped on one for
awhile, he seemed to relax and come to life.

Maui was proud of the 4th Marines. Everyone, from the County government, the
merchants and the residents, welcomed them and tried to make their stay as comfortable as possible. This was not the case on Oahu where there were so many more
troops. At one point there were about 100,000 troops on Maui including Army, Navy
and Marines. One of the reasons the troops were always welcomed in Maui homes
and at parties was because they always brought along a supply of good liquor and,
sometimes, choice steaks. The civilians often could not buy whiskey; when they
could, it was usually of poor grade. Five Island Gin was an example of a locally-
made, poor quality liquor.

The people of Maui could tell when an invasion of Japanese-occupied territory
was about to occur. The Navy fliers stopped practicing their take-offs and landings
and began flying in formations. Sometimes there would be a hundred planes in the
air at one time. Then, when it became quiet again, we knew the planes had landed on
their carriers at sea, ready for another invasion.

By word-of-mouth, we learned when a fleet of ships gathered off the south coast
of Maui. We would drive to Kihei or to the Lahaina pali, where we could see an
armada of ships extending over the horizon - more ships than could be counted. The
larger ones would be far in the distance, making it difficult to identify them. In a day
or so the ships would be gone. Within a week or 10 days, we would hear that there
had been an assault on Japanese positions. Two or three weeks after that, the 4th
Marines would return to Maui.

On different occasions, two of Dottie's nephews came to see us for a few hours.
One was from one of the ships in the convoy gathered off Maui and he telephoned us
the moment he got off the skiff that brought him ashore. The thing he wanted most
was fresh milk. We took him to Puunene Dairy, where he drank all he wanted and
got several gallons to take to his buddies on his ship.

In 1944 my brother-in-law, Lt. Jack Thornton, spent two days here on a freighter
that was being loaded with Army cargo. He was being transferred to a ship in the
South Pacific.

A dysentery epidemic hit Maui in 1944. This is the one I described when I told
of my brother, Preston, dying of diarrhoea at age three. I published a description of

this epidemic[18].

In May, I got a penicillin culture solution to be used to bathe skin ulcers. Penicillin by injection was available only for cases in which it was proven to be effective and the supply was very limited. Dr. N. P. Larsen of the Hawaii Sugar Planter's Association had grown the penicillin solution and made it available to plantation doctors.

I gave a talk entitled "Thyroid Disease and Eclampsia" at the 22nd Station Hospital at Makawao. My presentation was based on my research from 1936 to 39. I then read the world literature on eclampsia to date and again tried to find the cause. After a thorough search, I decided the answer was not known yet.

The European invasion at Normandy, France, began on June 6, 1944. We in Hawaii were very happy to hear about this knowing if the war in Europe ended, all the Allied effort could be concentrated in the Pacific to defeat Japan.

I did an autopsy in June on a plantation worker who had been shot in the chest with a service revolver and died three days later. An intruder (a soldier) cut a screen door and entered the victim's bedroom at 2 a.m. while he and his wife slept. When the man sat up in bed to confront the intruder, he was shot through the hilum of the left lung. The lung and the left chest cavity filled with blood. I transfused him many times but the blood merely drained into the chest cavity and out through the bullet wounds. Today, a pneumonectomy would save his life, but the technique for doing such had not been developed then. The gunman was arrested.

As I have stated, there were about 100,000 service personnel on Maui and, occasionally, one of them would lose self-control due to stress. Many civilians, including myself, owned guard dogs. The murdered man had owned a German Shepherd, but the day before the shooting, his dog was run over by a Kahului Railroad train which passed his home.

On June 17th, I noted in my diary that I had delivered seven babies in the past 48 hours, many more than my average of about 20 per month.

A patient had a partial prolapse of the uterus at the eighth month of pregnancy. With conservative treatment she delivered a 5-pound, 6-ounce baby who survived. I reported this case in the American Journal of Obstetrics and Gynecology[19].

I robbed my honey bees in July. I love honey and always wanted bees of my own. When we moved I was given two diseased hives by Mrs. Marnie. Then Mr. E. Kage of Kihei, who had hundreds of hives, gave me two good ones. When the kiawe trees flowered, the bees filled all the frames in the hives with delicious kiawe honey in two to three weeks. I was usually able to rob the same hive two or three times each season and gave the excess honey to our friends. On the above date, I got only one bee sting; I was not so fortunate later on.

I took a mentally disturbed patient to the hospital in Honolulu. I put him to sleep with sodium Amytal intravenously and had no trouble during the flight.

One of my patients, a 13 year old boy, had acute rheumatic fever. He had a heart murmur, friction rub, joint pains and fever. His mother, an intelligent woman, preferred to take care of him at home, so I had the laboratory technicians go to the house to take blood samples. He was kept at absolute bed rest for three months or longer. A cardiologist from the 22nd Station Hospital at Makawao saw him in consultation several times. The cardiologist, Dr. Johnson, was a former Rhodes Scholar and before the war practiced in the Boston area. He knew of Nicholas Soon of Kaupo, also a Rhodes Scholar, and I think he visited him.

My patient eventually recovered with no residual heart murmur or other problems. After high school, he attended Stanford University and joined the Air Force

ROTC, then served in the Air Force for three years, flying jet fighters. He is now married and has two children.

Dr. Andy Weaver returned on August 18th from the invasion of Saipan and Tinian Islands. We invited him frequently for dinner and other social gatherings.

In the fall of 1944, I conducted several experiments on pregnant guinea pigs in my search for the cause of toxemia of pregnancy. I catherized them to get urine samples and learned that they normally harbor a fast-moving microorganism in their bladder. My research did not prove fruitful.

In September I tried to rob my bees again, but got stung so many times I had to stop. Four days later, I tried again and got the honey. I was becoming allergic to the bee stings. My hands and arms would swell, preventing me from putting on surgical gloves to operate. The bees sensed that I had become afraid of them and would attack me, penetrating my protective clothing and head gear. Mr. and Mrs. Kage robbed them for me for several years after I had to stop.

I went to Lahaina in May to do an appendectomy for Dr. Dunn who was away in Honolulu. A nurse assisted me.

A pregnant diabetic patient was referred to me. She was 38 years old and progressed normally until one week before term when she developed mild acidosis in spite of a low blood sugar. I induced labor and she became severely acidotic with abdominal distention. She finally delivered a normal baby. I reported this case in the Hawaii Medical Journal[20].

Although there was a shortage of poultry feed I was able to raise a few turkeys. I killed a large one and invited Andy and two nurses for Thanksgiving dinner. On this day in 1944, 70 superfortresses (B29s) raided Tokyo from Saipan.

It is difficult to conceive of the damage these continuing raids did to Tokyo. I have a Japanese friend who was 11 years old at the war's end. He inherited a four-story medical building in the Ginza section, the main business district of Tokyo. Today, there is an enormous concentration of skyscrapers in this area. When we are in Tokyo, we use the one with the large Canon Camera sign on top as a landmark to find his building. My friend told us when we were there in 1979 that at the end of the war, if one stood in the center of the Ginza district, not a single building could be seen. They had all been leveled by U.S. bombs. The Imperial Palace and some other historical sites were spared.

Lt. Jim Bird of the 7th A.A.F. on Saipan was on Maui for R & R and spent three days with us at Christmas. Dottie prepared a delicious dinner for him and three Marine doctors.

During the first week of January, 1945, a doctor from the U.S. Public Health Service was on Maui to instruct me as to my duties as quarantine officer. Many army supplies were stored on Maui and later shipped to the South Pacific, so there was much traffic in and out of the port of Kahului.

We were getting more supplies now, including poultry feed, and the restrictions on raising domestic poultry were lifted. I had young turkeys hatch in January. When the turkeys were about three weeks old, they were vaccinated against fowlpox, an infection - spread by mosquitoes - which developed into head sores and resulted in death.

Our dog, Patsy, was now mature and I allowed her to be bred to Clipper, our neighbor's large Doberman. Clipper would sit by our gate, morning and evening, gently knocking on the gate with his paw. I would let him come inside for half an hour's visit and this continued for a week. There was only one complication: The dog house was beside the two beehives. The bees became disturbed one day and attacked both animals. After much yelping, activities soon resumed elsewhere in the yard and, thereafter, the dogs kept their distance from the bees.

Caudal anesthesia was introduced to relieve the pains of childbirth. I studied this procedure intently and administered it to a patient for the first time in January, 1945. I used it in selected cases for about three years and usually got good results without complications.

In January I killed a tom turkey that weighed 21 pounds dressed. He was almost too large to get into the oven, and our six guests enjoyed another of Dottie's fabulous dinners.

One of our field nurses, Louise Anderson, developed meningitis from an ear infection. She recovered after Dr. F. J. Pinkerton of Honolulu saw her in consultation and operated.

We saw a show in March, "Up in Arms," with Danny Kaye. He died in 1987.

I did a therapeutic abortion at the fourth month on a patient with severe heart disease. She was short of breath, even at complete bed rest, and lived only five months after the operation.

Patsy had eight puppies in March of which four males and three females survived. She nursed them for three weeks and then I became the nursemaid, feeding them a tremendous quantity of evaporated milk. Our neighbor got the choice of the litter for Clipper's services and I sold the rest - $40 for males and $20 for females. Although they were thoroughbred, I did not bother to get them registered.

In March I got a letter from Andy from Iwa Jima where half the assaulting force of the 4th Marines were casualties. On April 8th, we prepared another delicious dinner for Andy and other returning Marines.

I played golf with Lt. Caldwell Wyncoff of Gastonia, N.C., in March. Later, we had him in our home for dinner. About 1980, I received a letter from him in which he mentioned this golf game and other things I had done for him while he was on Maui. I have not heard from him since except for one Christmas greeting.

On May 8, 1945, victory over Germany was proclaimed, 11 months after the Normandy invasion.

There was another dysentery epidemic on Maui in May, but not as severe as the one in 1944.

I delivered a patient in June who had chronic thrombocytopenic purpura. Her mother, grandmother and great grandmother had been "bleeders." There were reports in the world literature of only 62 such patients to go through pregnancy. She bled excessively following delivery and I had to transfuse her. She recovered normally. Her baby weighed almost eight pounds at birth and was normal, except for a low platelet count. I reported this case in the Journal of the American Medical Association[21].

Dr. Andy Weaver operated on a patient with abdominal trauma on July 5th. I do not remember the details of this case. I asked him to see another patient, an 11 month-old infant, who had a massive intestinal hemorrhage from a Meckel's diverticulum, though intestinal x-rays were negative. Dr. Lightner and I operated on this patient and he recovered. Later, I reported a summary of this case in the Hawaii Medical Journal[22].

In 1987 I wrote to Andy and received an answer. After he left Maui, he spent eight months at the Naval Hospital at Bethesda, Maryland, and was promoted to the rank of full commander. In December, 1945, he married a girl who, I recall, he had met through the USO on Maui. He returned to his practice in Clarksburg, West Virginia, and retired at the end of 1986. By this time he was nearing 80 years of age.

He and his wife had four children, including twin boys. As I have already said, he had superior qualities that enabled him to survive the war on the front lines with the Marines. He also survived the aftermath of the war, apparently without psychological scars that have affected so many veterans. His longevity is proof of this. The letter I received from him mirrors the same person I knew 42 years ago. (I received a letter from Andy's wife at Christmas stating that he died on April 30, 1988).

Three of my close friends of college and medical school days, who were in the services throughout the war, succumbed in their early 60s from cancer and heart disease. I strongly suspect that the war-time stress that they experienced sped up their demise.

The curfew was lifted July 7th. It had been in effect since the start of the war, more than three and a half years.

McLeod, Louise and two children visited us for a week at the end of July. I took a week's vacation and we had a nice time playing tennis, golf, swimming, etc. We went to Hana for a day for them to see their old friends, and we had dinner at the Marine Officer's Club at Haiku with Andy.

I learned from the American Board of Obstetrics and Gynecology that I would be able to take the exams in obstetrics after limiting my practice to obstetrics for six months. I planned to return to the mainland after the war and needed to be certified. I began collecting and writing up my surgical cases, discussing all of this with Dr. Lightner and telling him I would eventually be leaving.

Dottie and I decided that, as soon as the war was over, we should make a visit to our families in Pennsylvania and North Carolina. We each had six brothers and sisters and our mothers were living. We had not been home for over six years or since any of our children were born. During this visit, I would make a survey and we would decide where we should live. We would return to Maui for approximately a year and then move to the mainland permanently in 1947.

Patsy was bred to Clipper again August 1st. This time they had no interference from the bees.

President Truman announced on August 6th that an atomic bomb had been dropped on Hiroshima. On the 8th, Russia declared war on Japan and, on the same day, an atomic bomb was dropped on Nagasaki. Two days later, the Japanese agreed to surrender with exceptions. The Allies would not agree. Finally, on August 14th, the Japanese accepted the Potsdam Ultimatum and President Truman announced the end of the war.

We had a holiday on the 15th, celebrating the end of the war.

I forgot our wedding anniversary on the 17th as I was busy getting my application to the American Boards signed and mailed. I also wrote to the War Manpower Board about my planned activities.

We invited Dr. Worley of Asheville, N.C., for dinner. Later, he spoke to the Maui County Medical Society on external, skeletial fixation of fractures.

On August 26th, there were horse races at the fairgrounds, the first since before the war.

Sunday, September 2nd, was V-J Day and a National holiday. Monday the third was Labor Day. There was a big victory parade in Wailuku in the morning and horse races at the fairgrounds in the afternoon.

I delivered our former Japanese maid a baby boy in September. He eventually graduated from college and did graduate work and now he holds a high executive position with the Department of Education. Most of the Japanese of Hawaii came here as laborers. Many of their children received good educations and now hold more of the responsible positions in the community than do those of any other race.

Soon after the war ended, I made ship reservations for our family to travel to the States for a visit, as we had planned. Not more than a week after this, Dottie realized she was pregnant. We had not planned this pregnancy at this time, though originally we had said we would have four children. Not wanting her to take such a strenuous trip while she was pregnant, we changed our plans. We decided to remain on Maui until our baby was born, then move to the mainland permanently three months later. I cancelled our reservations.

In September, we invited four Marine doctors for dinner. This was their last visit with us as they were leaving for the States and for discharge.

I diagnosed my first case of Weil's Disease since coming to Hawaii. This is an infectious disease caused by a leptospira, often accompanied by jaundice. In humans, the infection is usually acquired by coming in contact with contaminated urine. In Hawaii, cats, rats, dogs, pigs and mongooses are often infected. While working as a plantation physician at Olaa Sugar Plantation, McLeod reported one of the largest series of cases (61 patients) ever treated by one physician[23]. All patients are treated with penicillin G as first choice and A tetracycline as second choice. If patients are severely ill, they are also given whole blood transfusions from donors who have recovered from the disease. McLeod was the first to use penicillin in its treatment and is an authority on Weil's disease.

Dottie's nephew, Dick Graham, was with us for 24 hours in October. He was stationed on the aircraft carrier Hornet.

Patsy had 12 puppies in October, 10 females and two males. None had the rare, grayish-blue color similar to hers. I went through the feeding routine again and was glad to get rid of them.

I removed an eight-pound ovarian cyst from a 14-year old girl. Her classmates had assumed she was pregnant, but she had not even gone through puberty. Within a year after surgery she had developed into a beautiful young woman.

I did a second cesarean on a patient near term. When I opened the abdomen, I could see the baby's head and ear through a thin layer of peritoneum. The old uterine scar had opened, though there was no bleeding. The baby was normal and the mother recovered.

We ordered nice large dolls for our three daughters for Christmas, but they arrived three days late. When they did come, they were well received by our girls who were approximately two, four and six years of age. They loved the dolls dearly, made several dresses for them and treated them just like they had been treated as babies. They still have these dolls.

CHAPTER IX

January, 1946, to June 10, 1955:
Years of Catastrophies and Changes at the
Puunene Plantation

The new year got off to an ominous start. Chu Baldwin died on January 3rd. He soon would have been 37 years old, just three years older than I. He was in charge of personnel at Hawaiian Commerical and Sugar Company and many assumed that he was being groomed to replace his father as manager. I had many contacts with him and always found him to be a very likeable person. He, of course, was a major stockholder in H.C. and S. Co. and lived on the plantation. In the two generations before him, the Baldwins had created the two Maui sugar plantations which were so successful. He was to continue their work.

Likewise, Asa Baldwin, Chu's older brother, was assistant manager of Maui Agricultural Company at Paia. Apparently, he was being trained to become manager of that plantation when its present manager, his uncle Harry A. Baldwin, retired. H. A. Baldwin had no son to follow him. His son-in-law, J. Walter Cameron, was busy managing Maui Pineapple Company at Haliimaile.

Frank Baldwin, Chu's and Asa's father, had owned the Island of Lanai. A recent newspaper account stated that he sold it to James Dole for $1,100,000. However, since I first moved to Maui, I heard that he traded it some years before for Ulupalakua Ranch, a large cattle ranch on the southeast slope of Maui. Instead, he must have used the proceeds to buy the ranch. His oldest son, Edward, was a successful rancher and managed this ranch for years.

Frank Baldwin was president and a major stockholder of Baldwin Packers, a large pineapple plantation beyond Lahaina. He also was president and a large stockholder of Alexander and Baldwin in Honolulu, which helped the plantations manage their business affairs. He was 70 years old and was making plans for retirement. He had worked hard all his life, usually putting in more than eight hours of work each day, six days a week. He had made H. C. and S. Co. the largest and one of the most profitable sugar plantations in Hawaii. Besides growing sugar cane, it also owned the Kahului Railroad Company that managed the docks at Kahului Harbor, a vast network of wholesale and retail stores, a building supply business with a planing mill, and a rock crusher, as well as many other enterprises.

Frank Baldwin was the active manager of H. C. and S. Co. for the first seven years I worked for the plantation. His day started at sunrise when he went to the canefields with the labor force. Originally he rode one horse from sunrise until about 8 a.m., when he went home for breakfast. Afterwards, he rode a second horse until lunch. He spent the afternoons in the office attending to the many business affairs that confronted him. At first, he rode a third horse to the office in the afternoon, but had changed to an automobile before my arrival. After World War II, the plantation overseers stopped riding horses and began using jeeps or small trucks. Mr. Baldwin drove his car about the plantation. He was an excellent plantation manager, functioning through assistant managers (one at first and then two), his many department heads and five division overseers. From the first year of his management, 1906, H. C. and S. Co. paid a handsome dividend and did so for 42 years while he was in charge. A few years after he retired, the dividends stopped. The board of directors eventually took over the active management of the plantation from Honolulu and it began making a profit again.

The death of Chu Baldwin was a major setback for his father. Frank Baldwin had witnessed the genius of his own father, H. P. Baldwin, in helping to create East Maui Irrigation Company and the first Alexander and Baldwin plantation at Haiku. In 1876, H. P. Baldwin joined with Samuel Alexander in a great engineering feat. Through a series of ditches and tunnels they had brought water from the rainy Hana side of the island to the desert side across Maliko Gulch. The original Hamakua Ditch was 17 miles long, approximately six feet wide, and could carry up to 60 million gallons of water a day. It was owned by the following: Haiku Plantation (Samuel Alexander), 9/20ths; Alexander and Baldwin Plantation, 5/20ths; Grove Ranch, 4/20ths; and James Alexander, 2/20ths. It took two years to complete and cost $80,000 to build. Each of the owners paid its share of construction costs and received a like share of water from the ditch. Samuel Alexander was the brains behind the plans, having seen a similar one on Kauai 20 years earlier. However, it was H. P. Baldwin's genius that brought the plans to completion. He did not have a single trained engineer in his crew, which at times numbered 200. The final major problem was to bring the water across Maliko Gulch, 300 feet deep and 800 feet wide. This was done with an inverted siphon, 52 inches in diameter. There was great cooperation between Samuel Alexander and H. P. Baldwin, who were managers of the adjoining plantations at Haiku. They knew their plantations could not succeed unless they brought in water for irrigation. The first water from the Hamakua ditch reached the cane fields in July,1877.

From this beginning 112 years ago, many improvements have been made. Today, there are four major ditches bringing water from as far as Nahiku, a distance of about 35 miles. Sometimes the ditches run parallel. The water flows by gravity. There are 75 miles of ditches, with a total capacity of 420 million gallons daily. There are 50 miles of tunnels through the mountains and 25 miles of open ditches. All of this was done with private capital. In 1976, the replacement cost of such a system was estimated at $100,000,000. Today it probably would be twice that amount.

In due time, the Baldwins obtained control of the plantations at Haiku and eventually Maui Agricultural Company at Paia was formed, which included the Haiku plantations. A new mill was built at Paia. Harry Baldwin, another son of H. P. Baldwin, was the manager.

During the construction of the Hamakua Ditch, Alexander and Baldwin ran into another problem. Claus Spreckels returned to Maui from California and obtained a large land grant from King Kalakaua at the area now known as Spreckelsville. He planned to build his own ditch, 30 miles long, from the slopes of Haleakala. His grant stipulated that if Alexander and Baldwin did not complete the Hamakua Ditch in 1878 that it would revert to Spreckels. They beat the deadline.

Spreckels built a large sugar mill and plantation at Spreckelsville. Eventually, the Baldwins bought out Spreckels and his Hawaiian Commercial and Sugar Company. Frank Baldwin became manager in 1906. He developed more sugar land and finally merged all sugar operations from Spreckelsville to Kihei. A large double sugar mill was built at Puunene. He developed a system of wells to get enough water to irrigate the vast desert plains of central Maui. One of the wells (Well Seven) is known throughout the world and is written up in many hydraulic engineering textbooks. Capable of producing over 90,000,000 gallons daily, enough water for the city of San Francisco, it is the number one attraction of visiting engineers. I descended to the bottom of this well in an elevator to observe it in operation. The pumps are operated by electricity the plantation produces by burning the residue of the cane stalks after the sugar has been extracted. At the bottom of the well, water flows rapidly to a central point in three tunnels. From here it is continuously pumped out to reservoirs. Even during heavy rains in the winter months, the water must be pumped out to prevent flooding the equipment.

There is little doubt that Frank Baldwin wanted one of his sons to carry on his work just as he had forged ahead with the foundation his father had given him. With Chu Baldwin dead, changes would have to be made if this was to come about. The months ahead would bring more disasters and Frank Baldwin would soon choose how his empire was to be managed after his retirement.

Our fourth baby was due in April. I told Dr. Lightner I would be leaving the plantation by October 1, 1946, to return to North Carolina. Within a few weeks, he hired Colonel Edward Underwood to replace me after his separation from the Army. He would take a refresher course in clinical medicine before starting to work.

On February 1, 1946, I applied to the American Board of Obstetrics and Gynecology to take the exams in obstetrics. Also on this day, several hundred Filipino laborers and their families arrived to work on the plantation. There was a temporary labor shortage in Hawaii because many men had entered the services or were employed in service-related work.

The new arrivals had traveled to Hawaii on freighters, experiencing crowded conditions and poor ventilation. I cleared them through quarantine procedures. Many were sick. I admitted entire families to Puunene Hospital with fever and flu symptoms. A few developed pneumonia. Eventually they recovered and were assimilated into the plantation. They presented our field nurse a real challenge. Although the men could speak a little English, the wives and children often could converse only in a Filipino dialect. Some of our interpreters could not understand them.

I made visits to the homes of some of these new immigrants when the mothers were sick. I also visited their homes with the field nurses when we made camp inspections. Usually, there was very little furniture and little variety of food. There was always white rice and dried codfish (baccalreau). As soon as land was available, the Filipinos planted nice gardens with many vegetables, but this took time.

I remember one new mother with six small children under 10 years of age. They had been sick with fever, colds, ear infections, etc., and she was trying to take care of them. The field nurse helped her by taking the children to the dispensary to see the doctor, but finally, the mother was unable to handle the situation any longer. Her husband reported that he could not go to work because his wife could not get out of bed to care for the children. When I visited her, I found her bedridden and unable to move her arms or legs. I could find nothing wrong with her to account for the apparent paralysis. She, obviously, was exhausted and I decided I had to resort to psychology to help her.

We had an electric fulgurating machine in the dispensary that was used to cauterize small skin lesions after we anesthetized them. When the electrode was held near the skin, a visible spark jumped to the skin. If the electrode was removed within a second, the electric spark could be felt but did not cause a lot of pain or destroy any tissue. I explained to the husband what I was going to do, and he informed his wife in her native dialect. I told him I would give her three treatments, one each day, and that she would improve after each one. I said she would be able to walk after the third treatment.

We lifted her into my car and took her to the dispensary. She was put on the examining table and her arms and legs were exposed. I sparked each arm from the finger tips to the shoulder at one inch intervals and each leg from the toes to the hip. Then we took her home. After each treatment she improved, just as I had predicted. After the third treatment, she was able to walk and her husband returned to work the next day. The children had recovered by this time.

On February 2, 1946, I again made ship reservations for our family to return to the mainland and learned on the last day of February that we could leave August 1st.

A flu epidemic hit Maui in February and lasted about three weeks. Hundreds of cases were treated in our dispensary. We treated the patients symptomatically, but had to watch for complications. Most of the patients had high fevers. We had a flu epidemic about every three years on Maui.

On March 7th, I finished paying McLeod the money I had borrowed from him, 17 years after I had entered college. I shall ever be grateful to him for not demanding that I repay him as soon as possible. Because he was lenient, I was able to get married and Dottie and I were able to have our four children while we were young. I paid McLeod a low rate of interest on my loan. At times, supporting me was a real hardship on him, particularly during the three and a half months I did not work after arriving in Hawaii.

I had to send a patient, a top executive not associated with the plantation, to a psychiatrist in Honolulu. His wife and I had been unable to understand his behavior. Finally, she found two bottles that had both contained 100 capsules of Seconal; one was empty and the other almost empty. We never learned where he obtained the drug.

On April 1, 1946, a large tidal wave hit Hawaii at 7:15 a.m. As I recall it originated in South America. Very few people here had experienced a tidal wave and practically no one had provided any protection against one. I think the last tidal wave had occurred about 1925. The plantation had built a large home on the beach at Spreckelsville for Bob Hughes Sr., who had seen tidal waves. He did not disturb the sand dunes between his home and the beach, but planted coconut trees on them. These were now large. When the tidal wave came ashore, the water was diverted around the sand dunes and finally flooded the foundation and floor of the house. It did not do any structural damage. Many neighboring houses on this same beach were totally destroyed. The sand dunes in front of these had been removed and replaced by lawns. Typically, the front door steps, which were solid cement, were all that remained of many homes.

The wave hit the northeast side of Maui and caused damage from Kahakuloa to Hana. In lower Paia, a store building was washed across the highway and homes were destroyed. The four or five deaths on Maui occurred in Maliko Gulch, about five miles beyond Paia. Here, the walls of the gulch served as a funnel and, as the wave came in, the level of the water rose. The crest of the wave was over 30 feet high as it passed over the highway bridge and on up the gulch.

I received a call soon after the wave hit telling me to go to Frank Baldwin's home on the beach at Spreckelsville. Apparently he had been caught in the wave and was injured. When I reached an area about 500 yards from his home, I found the road was under water. Thinking it was not deep, I drove into the water and my car stalled. A moderately large truck came along and took me with my medical bag the rest of the way.

Mr. Baldwin had been in his living room when the wave struck. There were many large glass doors on both the ocean and mountain sides of the room. The wave seemed to have passed through the room, floating the furniture and Mr. Baldwin about the room in water eight to nine feet deep. He received a deep, three-inch cut on his forehead that required sutures. We took him to the hospital in the truck. The house was not extensively damaged, as I recall. My car was later retrieved and eventually had to be rewired due to saltwater damage.

Many fish were brought in on the wave and remained in the water beside the road at Spreckelsville when the wave retreated. I picked up a 12-pounder and we enjoyed a delicious fish dinner.

Dottie spent the night of April 10th in the hospital with mild labor contractions. These stopped and she came home the next day. She had chosen to have Dr. Tompkins deliver this baby at the Kula General Hospital. I knew the baby was large and probably should be delivered, but didn't want to interfere.

I started a 10-day vacation on April 18th so I could be home with the children while Dottie was away having our new baby. The plantation had hired Dr. James Marnie to relieve me.

April 21st was Easter Sunday and also my birthday. I gave Dottie two ounces of castor oil at 10:30 the evening before and labor started a few hours later. However, her labor was not short and easy like the last two had been. Finally, she delivered a beautiful 10-pound, 4 1/2-ounce baby girl at 10:30 p.m. on April 21st. The baby was so large that Dottie's coccyx (tail bone) was broken during the spontaneous delivery. I realized this had happened because of the pain she had during the following six weeks and then I forgot about it.

This was to be our last baby and we were happy to have another girl; we thought a boy would be out of place with three sisters. Originally we had hoped for two boys and two girls. We named our new daughter Carol Lynn and she, like her sisters, has been a joy to us. She and Dottie came home from the hospital on the 9th day.

We raised rabbits at the hospital for pregnancy tests. One day I discovered one of the mother rabbits had died, leaving five young ones about two weeks old. They appeared healthy, but hungry. I brought them home and Lois and Ann fed them with a nursing bottle they had for their dolls. Soon, they were large enough to eat on their own and I took all but one back to the hospital. We named this one Peter Rabbit and kept him on the enclosed back porch, allowing him to run through the house like a kitten. It was funny to see him slide across the slick floors. Then we discovered he had eaten a hole in the wool rug under the dining room table, so he too went back to the hospital.

I was preparing for our return to the mainland. I obtained many footlockers that the service men had left behind, to pack our belongings. I sold my chicken coops and egg battery. There was a great demand for used furniture, secondhand cars and most anything else. Very few, if any, household products had been manufactured during the war. We had promised everything we had to someone. I no longer owed any money except the tuition loan from the University of North Carolina that I had promised to repay when I was able to do so. I estimated that after paying for transportation, we would have $5,000 after we reached North Carolina. Certainly, we would have financial difficulties until I could get settled and to work.

Dr. von Asch left on May 3rd for a long vacation. Normally, we got two weeks off each year and then every three years we got three months for a mainland trip. Both of us had worked over five years but, because of the war, we were unable to take a long vacation.

I heard Dr. Chauncy Leake, professor of pharmacology at the University of California at San Francisco, speak at the County Medical Society meeting in May. He spoke on how drugs have their actions in the body and I have never forgotten his lecture.

In May we heard that we had reservations on Pan American Airways to return to the mainland on August 9th and, on June 3rd, I paid for the tickets.

The plantation had made arrangements with the Army for resident physicians from Tripler Hospital to work with us for about a month at a time while Dr. von Asch was away. This was necessary because Dr. Lightner often did not come to work, sometimes being out for one or two weeks. During this time, a plantation supervisor got a badly fractured leg when he was kicked by his horse while at work. Dr. Lightner treated him and put a cast on his leg.

About two weeks later, an orthopedic resident from Tripler started working for us. I asked him to check the fractured leg. He took x-rays and found that the fracture had not been reduced. Unless there was drastic treatment, we would surely get a bad result. This was an industrial accident and the plantation would have to pay dearly for any disability. I asked the doctor to try to fix the fracture, if possible.

The patient was put on the operating table with his leg hanging over the side. One side of a figure-8 sling was placed around the ankle and the doctor put his foot in the other side. The patient was anesthetized and then the doctor put all his weight on the sling. The callous that had formed about the ends of bone was broken. The fracture was then reduced and a new cast applied. X-rays showed perfect alignment. The fracture healed normally and the patient eventually walked without a limp.

When Dr. Lightner returned, he asked me why I had changed his treatment of this patient. I referred him to x-rays taken before and after the orthopedic doctor treated the patient. He had no further comment.

I was called to see Frank Baldwin at his home on May 22nd. Dr. Lightner usually treated him but he was sick and unavailable. A few weeks after his tidal wave experience, Mr. Baldwin developed pneumonia and had received treatment by Dr. Lightner in his office. He had improved and was thought to be well. Now, about two weeks later, he had developed fever, cough and a painfully swollen leg. There was redness about the superficial veins and also deep tenderness. The other ankle was swollen. Chest examination showed fluid in both lungs and rapid heartbeat. I admitted him to the hospital with diagnoses of thrombophlebitis following pneumonia and chronic heart failure.

He remained in the hospital for two weeks. I asked Dr. Emory Anderson of Haliimaile to help me treat his thrombophlebitis with Coumadin, which he took for several months. I also gave him penicillin for several days. I had to digitalize him to get rid of the water in his lungs and the ankle edema.

Dr. Lightner gave his annual party for all the hospital employees at his Kula home on June 16th. On this day I had a two- hour conference with Mr. Baldwin regarding the hospital. I had talks with him again on the 20th and 21st. Finally, on June 25th, Dr. Lightner's employment was terminated and I was made medical director of the plantation and head of Puunene Hospital. As head plantation physician, I also was the industrial physician for the Kahului Railroad Company, which paid a stipend and provided an office for private patients. The Kahului Railroad employees did not receive free medical care. Suddenly, my income would triple.

Later, I discussed Dr. Lightner's termination with him and he said he deserved what he got. He had worked for the plantation for 25 years. I told him I would call him in consultation in problem cases. Several months later, he bought an 830-acre Virginia estate called Bollingbrook Farm. On it was a magnificent Southern mansion, part of which was constructed before the Civil War. We visited him there and, after his death, visited his wife.

Before I could accept the position as medical director of the plantation and head of the Puunene Hospital, I had to resolve the following: I was not trained as a hospital administrator, nor was I an industrial surgeon. I could not do many of the surgical procedures that would be required in this work. My training was in obstetrics and my primary interest was research on the cause of high blood pressure of pregnancy.

By this time, I had been doing plantation medicine for over seven years. I had learned a lot. I knew I could do a better job than Dr. Lightner had been doing, because he was sick and on the job only about half the time. I knew I would be able to get help for the surgical procedures that I was not able to do.

I was a strong advocate of group practice and specialization and had spent 26 months at the Geisinger Medical Center, which was a large group of specialists working together with its own hospital. I had seen how group practice would give patients better care than single physicians working alone. Most physicians served as family physicians for their patients and treated minor illnesses. It was very easy for me to visualize the physicians at Puunene Hospital working as a group, with both plantation and nonplantation patients. If we added a few more specialists, we would attract more nonplantation patients. Then, all would benefit: the hospital, the plantation employees and the physicians.

When I was appointed head physician, Dr. von Asch was on vacation and did not return to work until late August. I was alone for two weeks and hired Dr. James Fleming to help me during this time. Dr. Underwood arrived on July 9th and soon was working. Our former nurse-anesthetist was now working at Malulani Hospital in Wailuku. I rehired her.

There were about 8,000 people living on the plantation and in Kahului. Most of these were plantation dependents with free medical care and many of the others came to Puunene Hospital and to the doctor's office in Kahului for care. Patients also came from other parts of Maui to us for care. I saw patients in consultation for obstetrical problems at the Kula General Hospital.

Recently, I talked to a man I had treated at this time before I had hired any specialists. He had had a fractured humerus just above the elbow when he was eight years old. I treated him with a hanging cast and he got a perfect result. By the time the Shriner's orthopedic surgeon made his monthly visit to Maui, this patient was well on his way to recovery and no consultation was necessary. The same was true with an eight-year-old boy with a fractured femur. The lower half of his body was suspended in bed, casts were applied to both legs and these were attached to a bar above the bed. He also got a good result.

Mr. Baldwin was readmitted to the hospital on June 29, 1946, with a recurrence of his thrombophlebitis. He was a very good patient and followed all instructions although it was very difficult for him to be inactive. He stayed in the hospital a week. His congestive heart failure was as much a problem as the thrombophlebitis. I had to rearrange his lifestyle so he could function with what heart reserve he had. I required him to stay in bed for 10 hours at night and for one and a half hours at noon. He had a chauffeur but preferred to drive his car himself. I did not allow him to drive for many months.

Dottie's brother, Neff, was a horticulturist. After he was discharged from the Army as a full colonel, he decided he wanted to live in Hawaii and applied for work to all the pineapple companies. Libby, McNeill and Libby hired him and after a year on Oahu, he was transferred to Haiku on Maui. We were happy to have him and his wife, Jane, here. Dottie and the children visited them in Haiku often.

During the ensuing weeks, I was very busy. I usually had some type of surgical procedure every day. I recall I did 30 operations in one month, most of them minor but in the operating room. On August 6th, I took out four pairs of tonsils in one hour, using the Sluter technique. We gave general ether anesthesia and waited in each case until all the bleeding had stopped or was controlled. Doing so much surgery made me feel essential, though I had always insisted that surgeons were no more important than other doctors.

Dr. von Asch returned to work on August 19th and announced the next day that he was leaving the plantation. I asked him to continue working, but he did not care to. He would have to be replaced.

Dottie went to Honolulu on August 18th for a week's vacation and to do necessary shopping. She stayed at the Young Hotel.

The sugar plantation labor force was organized into a union by the International Longshoremen's and Warehousemen's Union. An attempt to do this had been made a few years before, but had failed. A general strike was called for September 1st. Before it was settled the union had won most of its grievances. Afterwards, employees were paid by the hour and went on a 40-hour work week with paid vacations and holidays. They lost their perquisites of free housing, fuel and medical care but paid a small, monthly fee for medical care, which, as I recall, was only about one-third of what it cost the plantations.

I had discussed my ideas about group practice with Mr. Baldwin. He had given me permission to hire an eye, ear, nose and throat specialist who would be paid a salary in addition to any income from treating non-plantation patients. He would be furnished a special office in our dispensary. Dr. George Uhde began work in this capacity on September 25, 1946. We converted a nurse's aide's recreation room beside the dispensary into offices for him.

Our trip home had been delayed twice; first, when Dottie became pregnant for the fourth time, and then when I was made head plantation physician. Now, we had changed our plans and had decided to live in Hawaii indefinitely. However, we were anxious to see our families and have them meet our children. We had been in Hawaii over seven years and needed a vacation and change.

Another complication arose. There was a stevedore strike and the ship reservations I had made on the Matsonia were useless. Finally, at the end of October I was able to get reservations on Pan American Airways for November 5th. I had always been afraid to fly across the ocean but decided to take this chance.

Mr. Baldwin had another flare-up of his thrombophlebitis on October 4th and spent a few more days in the hospital. He had his office make hotel reservations for our family in San Francisco and train reservations to Chicago and Lewistown, Pa. He also gave me a letter of credit to use if I ran out of money, a useful item in those days before credit cards.

With Dr. von Asch leaving after I returned, I had to hire another physician. I advertised with a physician placement agency for a general surgeon and got many applications. I would interview them on my trip.

I bought a new sedan from the local Chevrolet dealer and arranged to take delivery of it in New York City. New cars were still difficult to buy and my mainland friends were amazed that I could get one. I took Hawaii license plates for the car with me.

November 5th was election day. Dottie and I voted in the morning during heavy rain and then our family left for Honolulu at noon. At 4:30 we left for San Francisco on a DC-4. The plane was old and, no doubt, had flown throughout the war. Near the

130

doors in the interior where there had been extensive wear, one could see that it had been painted three times. All the children became slightly airsick but, as a whole, they survived the flight very well. Carol was six months old and was fine until we started descending when she became very pale and sick.

I was nervous throughout the trip as this was my first overseas flight. We started to descend through dense clouds at sunrise. Suddenly, the clouds seemed to open and I saw the green hills about San Francisco, much to my relief. Our flight from Honolulu had taken 13 hours.

Katherine Hughes and Pat Walker from Maui met us at the airport with two cars and took us to the Mark Hopkins Hotel, where we had reservations. We had a very elegant suite on an upper floor, with a beautiful marble fireplace in the living room and marble bathroom fixtures. All of us were impressed, particularly the children. We rested most of the day and felt fine after 24 hours. The hotel employees were surprised to see baby diapers hanging throughout our beautifully decorated living room. This was before the day of disposable diapers.

The next morning, the older children and I went to the San Francisco Zoo. About 4 p.m., we took a ferry across the Bay to Oakland and boarded our train to Chicago. Again, the girls were impressed. We had three adjoining roomettes on the train and the toilets that folded away were the number one attraction.

There was a storm as we traveled across the Rocky Mountains and I remember stopping in Omaha and seeing the ground covered with snow. The service on the train was deluxe. We always ate in our compartments and the food was delicious.

We arrived in Chicago at noon on November 9th, about 42 hours after leaving Oakland. Carol happily went to sleep in the nursery in the train station. Unfortunately, just as we disembarked from the train, Dottie Jane became very ill; the traveling and excitement had been too much for her. I was able to visit my fraternity brother, Dr. Wayne Slaughter, in the Pittsfield Building. He was a plastic surgeon and a professor at the University of Wisconsin. Dottie and I also visited Ethel Wylder, our sister-in-law's mother.

We boarded another train at 6:30 p.m. and were met by Dottie's family in Lewistown, Pennsylvania, at 8 the next morning. It was a grand occasion but the children needed rest. Dottie Jane had improved and now Lois was ill. After a couple of days, all of us were rested and felt fine.

Dottie and I departed for New York City by train on November 14th and stayed at the Pennsylvania Hotel for three days. Carol, who was seven months old, was left with Dottie's sister, Jo, and the other three children with their grandmother and Aunt Helen. We picked up our new car the next day. That evening we had dinner with Bruce and Helen Langdon at the hotel. Bruce was now a urology resident physician at Columbia and appeared very tired.

Dottie and I went shopping the next day. We saw the Rockettes at Radio City Music Hall in the afternoon and the Broadway musical, Carousel, in the evening. We returned to Lewistown the following day in our new car.

On Friday, November 22nd, we drove to Chapel Hill, N.C., a distance of about 450 miles. All my brothers had arrived or were on their way to Chapel Hill for our first reunion since before the war. Neill and my brother-in-law, Jack Thornton, had both seen action throughout the war.

We attended the Duke-Carolina football game on Saturday, which Carolina won 22 to 7. Orus and his family visited on Sunday and we went to Sanford the next day to see them. Velma and Marcus were living in Durham and we had dinner with them on the 26th. McLeod, Neill, Marcus and I played golf the following day. Marcus's congregation had given him a set of golf clubs and, although he had never played golf, he soon established a handicap of seven, something I have never been able to do.

On Thanksgiving Day, we had a family reunion at Orus's home near Sanford. All 33 of Mamma's descendants were there. For three days we all gathered for dinner until the rest of the family had to leave for home.

For the next week, we visited relatives at Coats, Angier and Broadway, and Ralph and Sue Fleming in Durham. Dottie and I shopped and visited several furniture stores. A doctor came from Lexington, Kentucky, to interview me about the surgical position on the plantation.

On December 10th, we drove back to Lewistown, stopping on the way to see Bennie Lightner at Purceville, Virginia. Jack was still in the Navy. I left our family at Lewistown and spent eight days at Geisinger Hospital, observing all departments. I slept in the resident's quarters.

We had a nice, traditional New England Christmas with the Grahams. Dottie had often told the children about her Christmases as a child, so everybody tried to fix things as in the olden days when Dottie was young. The Christmas tree was brought into the house Christmas Eve, when all the children were in bed. A toy train and a miniature house with quaint furniture were placed under the tree. A turkey with all the fixings was served for dinner. Dottie's brothers and sisters and their families visited on Christmas Day.

About four inches of snow fell Christmas Day. The Grahams were horrified when they saw the Patterson girls in the yard barefooted playing in it just like they would play in the rain in Hawaii.

We drove to Philadelphia after Christmas to spend five days with my sister, Dorothy, and her family. I observed Dr. Franklin Payne, formerly my professor of gynecology, operate at the University of Pennsylvania Hospital for three days. Dottie and I did some shopping and, one afternoon, we drove to Somers Point, New Jersey, to see Paul and Vivian Cameron. On New Year's Day, we again saw the Mummer's Parade and then visited Jack and Mildred Heyl. When we returned to Lewistown, dense fog made driving hazardous. People who live in Hawaii forget what it's like to drive on roads covered with ice and snow and fog.

We planned to leave for Washington, D.C., on the 6th. I had made a timetable that would allow us another visit in North Carolina before driving across the country. We were to board the Matsonia at Wilmington, California, on February 7th. A snow and ice storm hit Lewistown on January 5th. Although I was afraid we would get snow-bound in Lewistown we left as planned the next day. The temperature was about 30 degrees. A three-inch layer of sleet coated the road and more was falling. I remember driving at 35 mph along the river towards Harrisburg and looking up at the tree branches heavily laden with ice, while the tires crushed through the ice on the road. I decided then that no one should live in a place with such foul weather as this, if he could live in Hawaii.

Before we reached Washington, the sleet had changed to rain. We spent the night in a hotel near Uncle Leon's home and had a nice visit with him. We phoned Maybelle Hughes and Matthew Horn, students from Maui. Next day, we took a sightseeing tour about the Capitol in the car and then left for Velma's and Marcus's home in Durham, N.C.

McLeod and his family were visiting in Chapel Hill, but they soon left for the West Coast. We moved in with Mamma again and Lois and Ann returned to school in the one-room, red school house they had attended earlier.

On January 12th, our family drove to Laurinburg, N.C., to see Maisie and her husband, Tom Parker, whom she had married during the war. They could not find a house to rent, nor were they allowed to build one, so they were living with Tom's uncle. He had a glass eye, which he would remove and show to our fascinated children.

This was a beautiful day in North Carolina in the middle of winter, so different from what we had left in Lewistown. The sun was shining and we sat on the front porch, visiting in the 70-degree weather.

We saw a Duke-Wake Forest basketball game at Duke in the evening on January 14th. Dottie Jane had left her small purse on the car seat with $1.20 inside. Someone broke one of the car windows and stole the purse while we were watching the game.

Marcus christened our four children in a private ceremony at the First Methodist Church in Durham, where he was the minister. Mamma and Velma were present as well. He had married us and we were so happy that he could christen our children.

We spent two more days at Sanford with Orus on his farm. When we returned to Chapel Hill, I finished my interviews by phone with applicants for the surgery position at Puunene Hospital. We prepared to leave for the West Coast just as the weather got cold with temperatures below freezing. It was difficult for me to adjust to the temperature changes and frequently I found myself outside without enough warm clothes.

We left Chapel Hill on January 23rd and drove through Asheville to Newport, Tennessee. We reached Nashville the next day and stopped at the Noel Hotel. Lois and Ann developed high fevers with deep coughs so we spent three nights in Nashville until they improved. I treated them with penicillin. During our stopover, Dottie shopped at Harvey's Department Store and I bought supplies from a sugical supply house. I also interviewed another surgeon.

We left on the 27th and drove through Memphis on our way to Little Rock, Arkansas. We stayed two nights at the Hotel La Fayette, allowing the children to completely recover. The clean city and the beautiful white capitol building were very impressive.

The next stop was Oklahoma City and, en route, we drove through a dust storm with winds 60 mph. Still many miles from the city, we could see smoke billowing up from an oil well fire. We eventually drove through the smoke as we approached the city. We stayed at the Black Hotel.

We reached Amarillo, Texas, on the 13th and stayed at the Amarillo Hotel. In my diary, I describe this as high plateau country with plenty of cattle. The temperature was 32 degrees. I remember that Uncle June would leave Mercedes in the summer because of the heat and come to Amarillo.

Albuquerque, New Mexico, was our next stop. We drove through Santa Fe, which we found to be a very quaint town surrounded by desolate, waste lands. In Albuquerque we stayed at the Franciscan Hotel.

The following day, we drove to the charming village of Flagstaff, Arizona, passing through the Petrified Forest and the Painted Desert National Parks. There was snow on the ground but, because of the elevation and low humidity, the water evaporated as fast as the snow melted and there was no run-off. We spent the night at the Monte Vista Hotel. Dottie bought beautiful silver jewelry with petrified stone mountings.

We spent almost the entire day of February 2nd in Grand Canyon National Park and spent the night in Williams, Arizona, at the Fray Marcos (Fred Harvey) Hotel. Next day, we passed through Kingman, Arizona, where several thousand decommissioned army planes were stored. For several miles as we approached we could see the planes and, not knowing why they were there, were puzzled at first. I doubt there ever has been or will be an accumulation of so many planes at one place. Later, I learned that the planes were dismantled and the parts sold.

We soon reached Boulder Dam and Lake Mead and crossed the Colorado River. The dam had been renamed Hoover Dam for former President Herbert Hoover, an engineer and a guiding force in its conception and construction. We descended to the bottom of the dam in elevators and saw the giant turbines.

We were now in Nevada and soon reached Las Vegas, where we spent the night at the Nevada Biltmore Hotel. When we got up for breakfast, the hotel casinos had just closed for the night.

On February 4th we drove to Los Angeles through the San Bernadino Valley, a spectacular sight after having driven through the desert. Thousands of acres of orange trees and vegetable farms filled the air with the fragrance of flowers and fruit.

In Los Angeles, we had reservations at the Clarke Hotel and were to leave for Honolulu on the 7th on the Matsonia. All of us were exhausted by the trip across the country. Dottie had lost 10 pounds, the children had been sick, and bad weather was only one or two days behind us all the way.

We rested the entire day after we arrived. Then we went sightseeing in Hollywood and visited the Los Angeles Zoo. Dottie and I went shopping and bought a piano among other things.

I interviewed my last surgeon applicant, Dr. Guy S. Haywood, in our hotel. He had been through a surgical residency at the Mayo Clinic and was now on the neurosurgical service at an army hospital in this area. He was from Montana and had developed a strong love for fishing, although I could not understand how he could have cultivated such a hobby in Montana. His great desire in life was to live where he could own a boat and fish often. He was married and had two children and would soon be discharged from the Army. We agreed that, as soon as he was separated from the service, he would come to Maui and then decide if he wanted to work for the plantation.

We drove to Wilmington on February 17th and boarded the Matsonia, including our new car. Our family, and McLeod and his family, had lanai suites, very nice and adequate for both groups.

We sailed at 5 p.m on Friday and were due to arrive in Honolulu at 7 a.m. on Wednesday. Early Saturday afternoon, we ran into a violent storm. Most of the passengers were seasick and no one went to dinner that evening. The storm raged on Sunday and Monday and only about 10 percent went to the dining room. By Monday and Tuesday, Dottie and the children were able to retain some food, but I could not. I had been seasick only once before and now was sicker than anyone else in either our or McLeod's families. I remained flat in bed all the time, my head feeling as big as a watermelon; I was very hungry.

Monday night we were in the worst part of the storm. The ship was tossed about in the 90-foot waves like a piece of cork. Half the time while I was lying in bed, I was looking down into the ocean. During the night a large wave slammed against the ship and broke open the door on B deck. No one had been allowed to go on A deck during the storm. In the middle of the night, one of the booms used to load freight broke loose and slammed to the deck.

The storm abated late Tuesday, and I was able to eat my first meal in three days. Playing Keno in the lounge on Tuesday and Wednesday evenings, Louise Patterson and I seemed to win every second game, either alone or together. We would put in

$4 and get back $124, $62 if we tied. Although I usually don't gamble, after being seasick for three days I was anxious to do something. Fate seemed to be repaying me for being so miserable and I did enjoy these last two days of our trip. We arrived in Honolulu on Thursday morning, one day late. The storm had driven us 300 miles off course.

Dottie's brother, Neff, and his wife, Jane, met us in Honolulu and spent the morning with us. We flew to Maui in the afternoon. I checked the hospital and saw Mr. Baldwin on Friday. I returned to work on Monday, after being away for three months and 10 days.

I received a telegram on February 18th from Dr. Haywood, saying that he would be coming to Maui for a trial period with us soon. He arrived March 12th.

The plantation strike officially ended December 30th, after 125 days. It had been settled in principle on November 14th, but could not be finalized until an assault and battery charge against eight or nine Lahaina employees had been settled in court.

When I returned, there was a tremendous amount of work to be done. The accounting system at the hospital had to be reorganized. The hospital jobs had to be classified and a job description made for each. I met with plantation officials several times and made a few trips to Honolulu to discuss all these things with officials at Alexander and Baldwin. The perquisite system had been discontinued. The employees and the union knew they had a good thing in their medical plan and they wanted to hold on to it. As I recall, each employee was required to pay $1.65 per month for his own coverage in the medical plan. If he had a family, he paid slightly more.

Puunene Hospital was the largest and most modern general hospital on Maui, with airconditioned operating rooms and private rooms. Some areas, particularly the employees' dining room and kitchen, needed to be modernized. I discussed these things with Mr. Baldwin before I went to the mainland and told him I would study hospital trends in the States and report to him. I had heard that there was Federal money (Hill-Burton funds) available to improve hospitals.

Indeed, in every area I visited, I learned that Hill-Burton funds were being used to modernize present hospitals or build new ones if they were needed. Central Maui had three old wooden-structure hospitals that were fire hazards. They varied in size from 80 to 120 beds. Lahaina, 25 miles away, had a similar hospital. Central Maui was an ideal location to have a large hospital serving all of Maui. It could be a community hospital with a managing board representing all major interests. Ideally, the board would have one representative from each plantation, the county government, the medical society and the labor union. The Federal Government would pay about 80 percent of the construction cost.

I discussed the possibility of organizing and building such a community hospital with Mr. Baldwin, recommending he support such a project instead of spending more money on improving Puunene Hospital. Persons in the county government knew about the Hill-Burton funds and already were trying to replace the County's Malulani Hospital,which was in a deplorable state in all ways.

Mr. Baldwin had lived all his life on Maui except while in school and had seen the County Government fail in its effort to operate a decent hospital. He had just been through a long labor strike and could not imagine that a representative from labor could help manage a hospital. He had built a good hospital at Puunene - by far the best general hospital on Maui - and continued improving it. He was proud of Puunene Hospital and of the medical care the plantation medical department provided for plantation employees. He was not about to close the hospital and support another to be managed by persons whom he did not control.

After a couple of discussions about a community hospital, Mr. Baldwin told me in simple words that if I mentioned the subject again, he would fire me. He said he was not going to close Puunene Hospital.

During the year since Chu Baldwin's death, there had been much talk about a plantation merger with Maui Agricultural Company. Even if this did not occur, it seemed wise to improve Puunene Hospital and close Paia Hospital, which was much older. Mr. Baldwin asked me to discuss a hospital merger with Dr. F. A. St. Sure Jr., medical director of Maui Agricultural Company.

We had discussions and worked on plans to enlarge and improve Puunene Hospital. I wrote a special report on my thoughts about what the future medical program of the two plantations should be and presented it to all concerned in late March. I was a proponent of group practice and had written articles for the Sugar Planter's Health Bulletin explaining its advantages. I already had the nucleus of a group at Puunene Hospital with a general surgeon, an eye, ear, nose and throat specialist, an obstetrician and a general practitioner. If the two plantation medical departments merged, there would be more expertise among the seven doctors involved. Then, as our patient load increased, we could add physicians in other branches. We would not need to call Honolulu specialists to come to Maui to check on seriously ill patients as I had had to do on March 25th when one of our deparment heads had a massive heart attack.

The plantations allowed their physicians to treat nonplantation patients to augment their income. By doing this, the plantations could attract higher-caliber physicians and their employees would benefit. Often, due to isolation, the plantation physician was the only medical doctor in an entire district. Management was very lenient with its physicians and allowed them to have large nonplantation practices. On a large plantation with several physicians, such as the one at Puunene, there were no rules about how much time was to be devoted to plantation work. Clinic patients were not given appointments. All patients who came to the dispensary each day had to be seen. If the physicians worked as a group with a prearranged division of income for both plantation and nonplantation patients, all would benefit.

The plantation bought me a green Super Buick sedan. I had been driving a Pontiac which was three years old when the war started and had frequent mechanical trouble. Twice I was stopped by the military police for breaking the 35 mile an hour speed although I was not fined because I was a physician. We checked the speedometer and found it registered 10 miles per hour too slow. Our head nurse, Rose Littel had friends at the Kahului Naval Air Station which was in the process of closing. She arranged for the Puunene Hospital to get a truckload of new surplus linen, free of charge.

Dr. Haywood's wife, Anita, and two children arrived in June. He had been impressed by our medical department, by the Maui Country Club and by the ocean for fishing. He had written Anita telling her about the beautiful greens at the country club, with a refrigerated water fountain at each hole (there are only two for nine holes). In Montana where he was reared, the golf greens were made of sand saturated with oil. I could understand why he was impressed.

Rotary was a big social club on Maui, but many of us were never invited to join. I attended an organizational meeting of the Kiwanis Club of Maui and became a charter member with perfect attendance for three years. I resigned because of the stress of work.

At a Maui County Medical Society meeting at the Wailuku Hotel, I was not allowed to eat in the dining room, because I was not wearing a coat. I usually wore a coat anytime I appeared in public - at work, in church, and on all social occasions.

The plantation gave a stag dinner at the Maui Country Club for all the supervisors to honor Jim Phantom and Jim Smith, two of the five division overseers who were retiring because of age. Both received a large silver tray. Mr. Baldwin and all other plantation officials were present. After dinner, someone told a slightly risque story, then Dr. Haywood told a story and he continued telling every second story for about an hour. He had been with us only four months but I felt if he proved to be as good a surgeon as he was a story teller, all would be fine.

I followed Dr. Lightner's tradition and gave the hospital employees a luau at the nurses' beach cottage in June. Caterers prepared a delicious Hawaiian feast with kalua pig.

On August 4, 1947, I was told that we might soon be given a larger, nicer home. We were still living in the three-bedroom house that had been remodeled for us in 1943. As a department head, I was supposed to have a larger home and be furnished a yardman.

I bought Dottie a green two-door Super Buick sedan in August. This was a good safety measure as the rear windows could be lowered only six inches, not enough for a child to get its head through. Once or twice each month, a child would be treated in the emergency room at Puunene Hospital after falling out of a moving car, and I didn't want this to happen in our family. Very pleased with her new car, Dottie took good care of it and logged 100,000 miles in eight years.

The stores on Maui offered very limited merchandise so Dottie spent a day in Honolulu shopping for school clothes for the girls. She returned in the evening.

Norene and Henry Alexander were married in September and Dottie Jane was the flower girl at their wedding. We had introduced them at a dinner in our home.

I was still the quarantine officer for the port of Kahului and met a ship direct from China. It was loading canned pineapple for the U.S. mainland.

In September, Asa Baldwin made a public announcement that Maui Agricultural Company and Hawaiian Commercial and Sugar Company would merge into one company in 1948. Harry and Frank Baldwin would retire and Asa would be the manager of the combined plantations. The new company would retain the name of Hawaiian Commercial and Sugar Company to simplify the legal transfer. The combined plantations would have more than 32,000 acres of sugar cane under cultivation and would use 126 billion gallons of water per year for irrigation. More than half of this would be supplied by East Maui Irrigation Company and the rest would come from wells.

When Frank Baldwin developed thrombophlebitis in 1946 and I became his physician, I advised him to stop smoking cigars. He told me he had been smoking them since he was eight years old but immediately complied, substituting Chicklets (candy-coated chewing gum) for the cigars. He had one in his mouth almost all the time. Within a year, all his teeth decayed and he had to have 13 teeth filled in September. Within a month, his dentist, Dr. Roy Stisher, decided all his teeth had to be removed. I accompanied him to Dr. Stisher's office because, by this time, his heart was more difficult to regulate. He survived the extractions and I called Dr. Harry Arnold Sr., internist from the Straub Clinic in Honolulu, to come to Maui to check him and to help me in my treatment of him.

Dottie and I went to see the home where Ward Walker, the assistant plantation manager, was living. He was moving to a new home at the beach and Mr. Baldwin wanted us to move into this house. Mr. Baldwin had built this house for himself in 1912 and lived in it for seven years when his three sons were small. The assistant managers had occupied it since 1920. It had been extensively remodeled in 1938 and a second story had been removed. The present house had 5500 square feet of floor space with six bedrooms, four bathrooms, a formal living room, a library and an enclosed lanai measuring 32 by 46 feet. The dining room was 26 feet square. There was a guest cottage in the yard with a bedroom-living room combination and bath. There was a large, deep swimming pool near the guest cottage and a shower and two dressing rooms at the rear of the cottage. Giant monkeypod trees, royal palms, Norfolk pines, shower trees and others grew in the four acres of lawn. The mango orchard had a dozen large trees and there was one macadamia nut tree, a breadfruit and other fruit trees.

In the back were four houses for servants, a five-car garage, stables for four horses, and a saddle room. The house was on a hill in the middle of a cane field overlooking Puunene and central Maui. It was about one and a half miles from the sugar mill and plantation offices and a half-mile from the hospital. The elevation was 75 feet above sea level, much cooler than at Puunene which was only 45 feet. Dottie and I gladly agreed to move into the house. It needed repainting and some minor repairs which the plantation would furnish along with yard service and water for the swimming pool.

Dottie's brother Neff, and his wife, Jane, moved to Maui in November. He was a horticulturist and would be working at Haiku for Libby's pineapple plantation. A new house had been built for them.

I took Mr. Baldwin on a tour of the hospital, showing him the new eye, ear, nose and throat offices and other improvements we had made and pointing out more changes I wanted to make. I had bought a large amount of new equipment, some of it Army surplus.

I attended the Plantation Physician Association's annual meeting at the Volcano House on Hawaii for three days in December. Dr. Bunnel talked on hand injuries and infections.

THE YEAR 1948

The year was very eventful. I continued my program of improving Puunene Hospital and advocating group practice for all the plantation doctors. I hired a registered record librarian and got our hospital approved by the American Hospital Association.

In February I delivered the baby of one of Maui's most prominent women. She had been trying to conceive for many months without success and had come to see me about seven months before. She had the symptoms of pregnancy. According to her husband's story, she told me she would not leave my office until I told her she was pregnant. I apparently replied in my usual, serious manner, "Well, if you were not pregnant when you came in, you will not be pregnant when you leave."

The Maui Philharmonic Society was very active. During the winter concert season, world-renowned artists who were performing in Honolulu were brought to Maui to perform at Baldwin High School Auditorium. It seated about 1300 and its acoustics were excellent. In March, Dottie and I attended a viola concert by William Primrose.

Dottie and I spent March 13th and 14th at Hotel Hana Maui. While there, we again drove to Kaupo to see Nicholas Soon.

Dr. Haywood operated on Dottie and removed her coccyx. It had broken two years before when Carol was born and the distal fragment healed at a right angle to the midline. Every time Dottie took a step, she had a pulling sensation in the area, particularly while playing golf. Actually, it was a major operation and several weeks were required for recovery.

The plantation merger took place about April 1st and many changes were made. Generally, the Maui Agricultural Company's department heads were put in charge of the new plantation departments. I had a good talk with Asa Baldwin and learned that I was to be second-in-command of the medical department. Dr. F. A. St. Sure Jr. was to be the medical director. I felt a great sense of relief knowing I no longer had to worry about administration except to help Dr. St. Sure. I could devote more time to medical practice and resume my research project on the cause of high blood pressure during pregnancy. I would have more time to be a normal husband and a father to our four children.

In April a plantation truck loaded with workers overturned and injured 21 persons, ten of whom had to be hospitalized. Luckily, all recovered.

We made many visits to our future home while it was being repainted and repaired. We bought a double stainless steel sink with sideboards and had it installed in the kitchen. We had the backyard and the pool enclosed with a wire fence, four feet high, and a lock was put on the swimming pool gate. We enforced a strict rule that no child was ever to climb over the fence. Several children on the plantation had drowned in irrigation ditches and we maintained a constant vigil guarding against such as there were irrigation ditches near our home on all sides. The three older children had already taken lessons and could swim. Carol was only two and I told her I would give her a dollar and would remove the fence around the pool when she could swim across it. She was able to do so soon after her 4th birthday.

I delivered Jane Graham, my sister-in-law, a baby with multiple congenital deformities, incompatible with prolonged life. She and Neff loved this child dearly and gave it the best possible care. He lived eight years. After two failed pregnancies, they had three beautiful babies who have since reached adulthood.

We moved into the large house on May 28, 1948. Dottie and I have discussed the value of this house in our lives. The most important event in our lives was finding each other and marrying. Next in importance were the births of our four healthy babies. The privilege of living in this grand home was next in significance. We had Frank Baldwin to thank for this gift. I did my best in taking care of his health and he provided us with the best home on the plantation. I also gave the plantation the best 18 years of my life. If I had left the plantation earlier I might have made more money, but that was not my goal.

Soon after we moved, Hannah Bonsey left for college. She had a pet donkey named Go Along, which she gave to our girls. She had trained the donkey and, like a puppy, it followed the children everywhere, even up on the lanai. We bought a saddle and all the children learned to ride. Sometimes all four rode her at the same time as pictured on our Christmas greeting in 1948. At first we did not tether her and, after five days, she wandered away. We put an ad in the newspaper and found her on the plantation at Camp 10. We kept her for years and finally gave her to Dr. Andrew's family at Kula. At Puunene, flies bit her legs producing ulcerations which would not heal; this did not occur at Kula.

I made six lawn chairs and a luau table for the backyard and bought a nice prefabricated grill made of hollow tile. The children often ate their lunches in the yard and Dottie cooked on the grill for large outside parties.

Louise Weber Patterson, McLeod's daughter from Honolulu, spent the first week of July with us and Dottie invited 45 children to a party for her. The yard and swimming pool were ideal for parties. McLeod Jr. spent the next week with us.

I ordered 100 day-old cockerels from Sears Roebuck in California. They came by airmail and all survived. When they weighed two to three pounds we killed and cleaned them and stored them in the freezer until needed. I also bought 18 egg-laying pullets.

We had a picnic in our yard for all the hospital employees and their families - about 100 people. The children played games and and swam while the adults played softball. This became an annual affair as long as I worked for the plantation. Dottie quickly became an expert at preparing delicious meals for a hundred or more persons.

I hired a plantation laborer, who was due for retirement, and his wife to work for us part-time. We called them mammasan and papasan, terms of endearment Japanese use for their parents. They lived in one of the servants quarters in the rear. The wife worked five mornings each week washing and ironing clothes while the husband took care of my animals as I acquired them, and cultivated a vegetable garden. In addition, the plantation mowed our lawn with their large tractor-mower and furnished us a yardman.

I asked papasan if he knew how to milk a cow and he assured me he did, saying that he had learned as a young man living in Okinawa. Since coming to Hawaii, he had worked on pineapple and sugar plantations and for a while was an independent pig rancher. He had won a prize for having a litter of pigs attain the weight of a ton sooner than any other litter in the Territory of Hawaii. He had a picture of himself, smiling broadly, holding the certificate telling of his accomplishments.

The head of Puunene Dairy sold me a cow that was producing about three gallons of milk daily. I prepared a milking stall in one of the stables and papasan attempted to milk her after I showed him how to cleanse the udder and teats. His hands and fingers were calloused from using a hoe and his fingers were arthritic; he simply could not get the milk out. I got up every morning at 5 and helped him milk the cow before he left for his regular work. Again I helped him at 6 each evening. After a week, it seemed to be a losing struggle. He was trying his best, but could not get the job done. He wanted very much to keep the cow so I told him we would try for three more days and, if he couldn't milk her by that time, I would have her returned to the dairy. On the last day he succeeded and had no problem thereafter. He kept two quarts of milk for himself and his wife and we took the rest.

There were three or four acres of unused land around our home on which kiawe trees were growing. They produced an abundance of flowers in the springtime - from which my bees collected honey - and then kiawe beans formed. These were excellent feed for cows and horses as were the koa hale plants and guinea grass growing under the kiawe trees. In the winter months, when we had good rains, there was plenty of feed. I enclosed all this land with barbed wire, digging the postholes myself and using redwood cross-ties for fence posts. The plantation had stopped using trains to haul cane from the fields and I bought discarded cross-ties for 50 cents each, delivered to my yard. The cow grazed in the enclosure. Later, our horses and steers also grazed there.

There was a large duck pen in the backyard so I immediately bought a pair of large white ducks. The hen would lay 18 to 20 eggs and all of them would hatch. I would force feed the young ducks and in three months the males would weigh seven to eight pounds. I would then cut their heads off, scald the carcasses with boiling water, quickly remove their feathers, and put them in the freezer.

When I finished the fences for the cow pasture, I built a pig pen beside the irrigation ditch. I ran a pipe with fresh water to the pen and we flooded the cement floor daily into the irrigation ditch. I bought our first pig for $5 and, within a year, had a deep freeze loaded with pork.

Papasan's good friend was the leading pig rancher on Maui. He often visited papasan and gave us piglets anytime we wanted them. We usually got the runt of the litter, but with good feed it soon grew large. Occasionally, a sow died soon after giving birth. If she lived for four days and nursed her piglets, they would survive on cow's milk. Once, he brought us eight at one time and they all survived. For a while, they were free and roamed all over the yard, eating the small figs that fell from the banyan trees.

My pig pen held only two pigs at one time so I had to build additional holding pens for the young ones. If space permitted, I would put the pigs in the cement-floored pen at three months of age and give them all the feed they would eat. We would always butcher them before their 1st birthday, usually at about 10 months. They were never on the ground after three months and ate only commercial feed, excess mangoes, coconuts, vegetables, breadfruit and our kitchen garbage. They never ate dirt or roots and, as a result, their meat was delicious and sweet.

Papasan usually butchered a pig every three months. They weighed between 150 and 300 pounds. He would get one-half of the good cuts of meat and all of the head, liver, kidneys, intestines, etc. I kept a record of the cost of the feed we bought which showed that no pig ever ate more than $15 worth of commercial feed. Chicken feed usually sold for six cents a pound but if it contained bugs I could get it for three cents a pound. I fed this grain to the pigs and steers. Often, I bought a ton at one time. Once I paid three cents a pound for a ton of powdered milk that had been slightly contaminated in a tidal wave.

Besides chickens and ducks, we raised many turkeys each year. I first bought day-old turkeys just like I bought chicks. Then I kept a few turkey hens and one gobbler weighing 25 to 30 pounds.

I watched the turkeys in February when they bred, then I dressed the gobbler and put him in the freezer. Three weeks later, the hens laid a clutch of 18 to 20 eggs, all of which were fertile. After the hens incubated them for 28 days, the eggs hatched. Usually at Thanksgiving we had 18 to 20 grown turkeys walking around the yard, some white and some black. I gave many of the dressed, frozen turkeys to our friends.

Someone gave our children a pair of bantam chickens which they immediately named Henny and Penny. The pair usually had two families of chicks each year and we gave them to our children's friends. Henny was not monogamous. He assumed any of the hens in the yard were his for the taking. Sometimes, the large hens just walked off with him aboard. Some of our baby chicks did not grow to be as large as their mothers.

There were many mongooses in the cane fields and they came into our yard to catch and eat the baby chicks and rob the hen nests of eggs. I prepared boxes with straw for nests and put them on top of 6-foot high tool cabinets in the garage, thinking they would be safe from the mongooses. The children used a ladder to climb up to collect the eggs each day. Once we saw a mongoose coming down the ladder with a large egg in its mouth.

I made a trap resembling a rabbit trap I had used in the South to catch cottontail rabbits. Baited with an old chicken head, it soon caught several mongooses. The next step was to empty the animal into a burlap bag and beat it to death. However, this was rather dangerous because the vicious mongoose could bite me through the bag. Instead, I used a frog gig to kill the mongooses, not a very pleasant task.

One of my friends gave me several pheasant eggs he had found in a cane field that was being harvested. I set them under Penny, the bantam hen, and they hatched giving me a blue pheasant cock, a ringnecked cock and several hens. The Board of Agriculture gave me permission to raise pheasants provided I made a monthly report of my inventory of birds.

Penny raised the baby pheasants just as though they were bantams. The hens laid lots of eggs in the pens, but would not hatch them so, again, I used Penny and she hatched many more. We ate some of them and they were delicious.

Finally, I decided to have a taxidermist friend mount the cocks. The afternoon before I had planned to take them to him, our family went for a two-hour ride. When we returned, we found that a pack of wild dogs had broken into the pens and killed most of the pheasants.

The hospital needed male Bufo toads to do pregnancy tests. Our yard had an abundance of them. The females laid their eggs in a lily pond in our yard and the males were on hand to fertilize the eggs as they were produced. The eggs were suspended in a mass of gelatinous liquid-like material that had an appearance somewhat like poppy-seed dressing. Soon afterwards, tadpoles hatched from the eggs and, a while later, small Bufos were everywhere.

The male Bufo is smaller than the female and can be identified by a rough sandpaper-like area on each side of his head. The hospital offered our girls 10 cents each for them. In the evening, they used a flashlight to catch the Bufos as they hopped about the yard in search of insects. They put them in paper grocery bags. When the Bufos became scarce the girls were paid 25 cents for each.

It is interesting to watch a grown Bufo devour a six-inch long centipede, which they do without ill effects from the centipede bites. The Bufo has a large amount of adrenalin stored in its body, usually fatal to a dog that eats one. They seem to know this and usually do not bother the toads. The sugar plantations originally imported Bufos to help with insect control.

When the plantation supervisors started using trucks and cars, the plantation had a surplus of riding horses. I bought two gentle, old ones for the children. The first was named Baby and was fifteen years old. She was a large horse and had been ridden by the assistant manager for 10 years. The second horse was smaller and was named Mele (Hawaiian for Mary). Four of us could ride at one time, Carol sitting behind me on Baby, one girl on Mele, and one on Go-Along. We rode along the roads through the plantation fields.

Mele had problems with swollen ankles, usually in the winter. She would be unable to walk for a week or so, and then would recover. Once when I was riding her at a gallop, she fell. Luckily, my feet came out of the stirrups and I was not hurt. After we had her for three years, three of her ankles swelled at the same time and she never recovered. The plantation disposed of her for me. We told the children we sent her to a pasture where old horses were allowed to live out their lives and not have to work. They were satisfied.

We replaced her with a four-year-old horse named Whitey. The owner of this horse kept her in a pasture at Kula but, because of a severe drought, there was little for her to eat. Finally, she was eating nothing but roots and considerable dirt along with them, grinding off her teeth so she could not properly chew her food.

She was very skinny when we got her. Her condition improved with good feed but she never got nice and fat. We grew cane grass for our horses and cows and they ate all of it, including the stalks. Whitey could not chew the stalks properly and got intestinal obstruction because of it. We found her down on the ground in the pasture with colic. The veterinarian worked with her for three days, but could not help her and she died Good Friday, a plantation holiday. One of the department heads sent a big crane and truck to haul her away.

When Carol was five years old, she and I went riding on Baby and Mele. Baby was very gentle and easy for Carol to manage. We trotted slowly at times, but never galloped. I was slightly in front of Carol when my cap blew off and flew past Baby. She became frightened by the sight of the cap and began running as fast as she could. Carol held on to the saddle while I galloped alongside and took hold of the reins until I could get Baby stopped. I thought she had calmed down but, when we started again, she resumed her running. I had to catch her again and restrain her, holding on to the reins until we were home.

Baby was a grand horse who lived to be 25 years old. Finally, her coat of hair became long and shaggy; she lost weight and I couldn't get her fat with extra feed. She became feeble and I had her put to sleep.

Frances Kinnison Ashdown and her husband were leaving Maui. She gave me her pet, a small Hawaiian horse named Skrippy she had raised from birth. He was adorable and liked to play like a kitten. I don't think a harsh word had ever been said to him or that he had ever been struck with a whip. Frances had worked for the plantation breaking horses and they seemed to understand her.

Skrippy was very gentle with our girls and they all rode him. However, when I was aboard it was a cue for him to act up. He would weave from one side to the other just like a cat playing with a mouse. Then we would run across our four-acre yard with him bouncing and throwing his heels up, not really bucking-just bouncing. I wore cowboy boots and hat and would yell "Hi-ho-Silver!" as we raced around the yard. This frightened Dottie and she would run into the house.

When we moved out of the plantation house, I sold Skrippy to a boy who lived at Kula. A few years later, Frances returned to Maui and bought him back. I am sure he lived his last years at peace.

Papasan became a good milker and took good care of the cow. The cow feed we bought from the dairy contained kiawe beans, pineapple bran (made from peelings), cotton-seed meal and other imported grains. There was a problem with the cow, however. She became extremely restless during her estrus period every 21 days. The dairy was less than two miles away. During the first cycle, she jumped the fence and soon was with the bull at the dairy. The dairy returned her in a trailer.

I then assumed all would be peaceful and she would have a calf in due time. I was wrong. Twenty-one days later she jumped the fence again and reappeared at the dairy. She was bred again and brought home.

I was planning to attend a medical meeting on the mainland and would be away during her next estrus period if she had not been bred successfully. I fortified the doors of her stable and left orders for her to be locked inside during her next cycle. This did not deter her. She knocked the door open with her head, using it like a battering ram. This time she avoided the dairy and was finally found at Kihei, about seven miles from home.

When I returned home, Dottie was very upset by this latest episode. I had the cow butchered and most of the meat was ground into hamburger. An ovarian cyst was found that had prevented her from conceiving.

I bought another cow from the dairy and this one had already been bred. She was a beautiful Jersey, seven years old. I was advised to have her slaughtered in a couple of years. One day our family drove to Hana on a Sunday and, when we returned, we found the cow had had a beautiful female calf. The children named her Hana. We reared her as an eventual replacement for her mother.

The cow was bred again and had a male calf about 15 months after Hana was born. We raised him as a steer and put him in the freezer when he was 18 months old.

Although I knew the cow was old, I decided we would risk breeding her one more time. When the time came for the calf to be born, papasan spent the entire night with her, thinking she would deliver momentarily. He fell asleep about 5 a.m. and when he awoke at 7 she was dead. He was very upset as he thought he could have completed the delivery and saved her if he hadn't fallen asleep. His friend, the pig rancher, came and took her away. For a few months we were without a milk cow.

In addition to our milk cow and her calf, we always had one or two steers in our pasture. We bought male calves from the dairy for $5 when they were five days old and taught them to drink milk from a pan. After a few weeks, they would survive without milk. Sometimes I fed them powdered milk. As they grew, I gave them any kind of grain. When they were mature, the dairy slaughtered them for me for the price of the hide. The Ulupalakua Ranch Meat Plant aged the meat and cut it up for a few cents a pound.

I bought a Holstein calf from the agricultural department of Lahainaluna High School. Its father was a Carnation bull from the Carnation Farms in Washington State. I kept the calf about 27 months and he grew to be enormous. When he was slaughtered, his hind quarters weighed 185 pounds each.

Soon after we moved to the large home, one of our daughters got a parakeet. This was about 1950 when they were selling for $7.50 each. The girls decided they wanted to raise parakeets to sell. I built a 6x6x12-foot cage with nesting boxes in one of the unused garages, keeping it a foot above the cement floor. All of us learned all we could about raising them. A friend gave us 15 for breeding stock and we bought more.

Soon we had baby parakeets and sold many to the stores. One day Dottie decided to help the girls take care of the birds and went into the cage, carelessly leaving the door open. Most of the parakeets flew out and up into the monkey pod trees. We were able to retrieve only a few of them. By the time we got our breeding stock built up again, the market was flooded.

Dottie and I assigned the girls various chores to do which they would rotate from week to week. They were paid one cent per coconut for hauling them to the backyard where I cracked them open with an ax for the chickens and pigs to eat. One girl was assigned to take care of the animals. She had to collect the eggs, feed the chickens and ducks, and feed the horses and dog. Dottie Jane's teacher once asked her what she did in the afternoon after school. He was amused to learn that, during the current week, she was the "animal girl."

Our large plantation house had 16 outside doors, all without locks, and most of which opened onto lanais. Before the war, hardly anyone on Maui bothered to lock doors. Guard dogs were necessary for protection in a house such as ours. We had our Doberman pinscher, Patsy, who was a good guard dog, though she was getting old.

Dr. Lightner's wife, Amelia, raised champion German shepherd dogs. She also had a male English setter. Unbeknownst to Amelia, her German shepherd bitch was bred to the English setter. The eight puppies were beautiful and all looked like German shepherds when they were young. She gave us the pick of the litter, a light tan pup that became dark brown when he was grown. His ears never stood erect like his mother's. We got him soon after we moved into the large house and named him Bonn for the new capital of Germany.

I brought Bonn home when he was about four months old. I fed him, took care of him and, although I never mistreated him in any way, he developed a mistrust of me and would not allow me to be near him. He loved all the girls. When his license tag on his collar had to be changed, it took two girls holding him for me to change it. He never became friendly with me or any other man. He had a loud bark and was an excellent guard dog.

The girls walked a half mile each morning to the school bus stop and Bonn was with them all the way. In the afternoon, he was always there on time to meet the bus and escort them home. He never wandered away from home for any reason.

When any of us rode the horses through the cane fields, Bonn was very happy. There were always pheasants in the fields and, in the winter time, plovers from Alaska. Instinctively, he could find the plovers from the sounds they made and he tracked down the pheasants. Although he looked like a German shepherd, he was half bird dog. As practically all dogs in Hawaii do, Bonn developed heartworm infestation and died when he was 12 years old. We replaced him with another German shepherd that we, again, named Bonn.

The plantation merger had taken place in April and we had two hospitals. By August, plans were ready to renovate Puunene Hospital and, when this was completed, Paia Hospital would close. During the renovation, we would treat all patients at Paia Hospital. I was busier than ever as Paia Hospital was about eight miles from the Puunene dispensary and our home. As an example, on the last day of August, I did a cesarean in the morning at the Kula Hospital which was 20 miles away and, later in the day, delivered three babies at Paia Hospital.

I lost a patient - the only one in 43 years - after a delivery at Paia Hospital. We did an autopsy and think she died of pulmonary embolism. I am still distressed over this loss. The family was wrecked; she left two babies, a girl and a boy, to be reared without a mother.

Donald Hughes, a plantation supervisor, married Mary Lawrence on September 18th. She was a nurse at Puunene Hospital. We had the reception in our home and even with 100 guests, there was no crowding.

Jan Peerce, one of the world's foremost tenors, gave a concert at the Baldwin High School Auditorium, which Dottie and I attended.

We furnished the large plantation home as soon as we could afford to do so, using traditional, early American furniture in the dining room, library, formal living room and bedrooms. Much of it was dark mahogany furniture from North Carolina, though we bought it through a store in Honolulu. I insisted we furnish the house with period-style furniture I thought was superior to more modern styles that, actually, were better suited to Hawaii.

Dottie and I each had our own bedroom, dressing room and bath, while each daughter had her own bedroom and shared a bath with a sister. Dottie furnished each bedroom according to the wishes of each child.

Dottie Jane's bedroom was the first on the bedroom wing with the door only a few feet across a passageway and steps to the ground. A door to her mother's room was across the passageway and Carol's room was connected to Dottie Jane's through the bathroom.

We finally got the bedrooms furnished and put each girl in her own room. Soon after, Dottie Jane began to stutter. I eventually guessed, and Dottie Jane admitted, that she was afraid to sleep in her room alone. We moved her back into Carol's room, which had twin beds, and the stuttering stopped. After about a year, she decided to sleep in her own room, which she did without any more trouble.

We met an architect, Haydn Phillips, through friends and commissioned him to design furniture for our huge front lanai. Four years passed before it was finished and delivered. The furniture was made by experienced craftsmen at the Kahului Railroad Company's planing mill. Teak and monkeypod woods were used primarily, though a light colored wood was used for the borders of all the table tops and Philippine mahogany for all the cabinet walls. We had a tropical landscape mural put on the inside wall.

A massive three-section punee sat in the right corner of the lanai. Another smaller, two-section punee faced the other end of the lanai just to the left of the front entrance. There was a large, Chinese design coffee table, 54 inches square with four matching monkeypod top sections and teak legs. There was a Chinese bench, six feet long with teak legs matching those of the coffee table. Two fancy end tables and two small cabinets sat at the ends of the punees.

There was a large buffet by the wall beneath the mural. It measured 114 inches long, 26 inches wide and 34 inches tall. A smaller, matching music cabinet occupied the rest of the inside wall between the formal living room and the door to my bedroom.

In the corner to the left of the entrance, there was a 40x40- inch fish pond made of monkeypod and lined with copper. On both sides stood monkeypod planter boxes with three fillers in each. There were three beautiful monkeypod card tables with teak legs. The floor was covered with a rug from the Philippines made of woven grass squares. Dottie had everything designed so it would be easy for her to entertain. There was a place in the buffet for all the pieces of silver, linen and dishes.

We knew we would not be in the plantation house forever and told the architect to design the furniture so we could use it in our own home when we built one. The architect spent most of his time designing commercial buildings and private homes and furniture designing was his hobby.

We ran into a problem. All the tropical fish I put in the pool died. Finally I realized that the copper dissolving from the lining of the pool was poisonous to the fish. I lined the pool with fiber glass and had no more trouble.

Coiled metal springs were made for the punees in Honolulu. They were barged to Maui and stored in the building at Pier Two, waiting to be delivered. A tidal wave struck Maui on November 4th and the boxed metal springs floated in the sea water that flooded the building. Three days later they were delivered to our home. I removed the cloth on the underside and thoroughly hosed the springs with fresh water and then dried them in the sun. This was over 35 years ago and the springs have not rusted.

I continued to be busy and delivered 22 babies at Paia Hospital in October. This was only about one-third of my work, as I had to take care of all the babies, work in the dispensary and treat many patients in the hospital.

On November 2, 1948, President Harry Truman, a Democrat, was elected in a great upset, defeating Alf Landon, a Republican. I could not believe that a haberdasher was going to be our President. I thought our country was doomed. Again, I was wrong. He was a product of the old political machine, without the frailties of many recent candidates for political office and some presidents. So far, history has given him a good mark.

I took out a large insurance policy on October 20th at age 36 and struggled to make the payments for the next 20 years. It not only gave my family protection, but I borrowed from it to help build our home and to send our children to college. At age 65, I converted it to an annuity which, to date, I have collected for over twelve years. I advise all young people to first start a good insurance program and, later, if they are able, invest in other things and take some gambles. When I was young, I was just too busy to study finances and invest intelligently. My father was a financial genius, yet he lost everything except his insurance in a national depression. Many of my friends criticized me for my investment choices. Today I have a baseline income to support us, even in a depression. If the economy is good, we have more than we need. My plan could not be wrong as my goal in life was not to become rich but to be independent.

Dottie and I heard Yehudi Menuhin give a violin concert at Baldwin Auditorium on November 3rd. He had already established himself as a world-renowned violinist, and today he is considered one of the top three. We last heard him on Educational Television about two years ago.

I admitted the wife of a plantation supervisor to the hospital between Christmas and New Year's Day for the treatment of chronic alcoholism. Her liver was enlarged so much that it filled the entire right side of her abdomen. She died a few years later before she reached 50 years of age. Treating alcoholism was one of the saddest parts of my practice, particularly in patients with young children.

THE YEAR 1949

I lost a newborn baby in January with erythroblastosis. The mother was RH negative and had been transfused as a child with RH positive blood before the RH factor had been discovered. Her only surviving child was a spastic. The technique of exchange transfusion had not yet been developed.

Mauna Loa, on the Island of Hawaii, erupted during the first week of January. We drove to the Lahaina pali one evening and could see the lava flowing from the top of the mountain down towards Waimea.

I did a cesarean on a patient that I had attempted to deliver with forceps. The head was wedged into the pelvis, but I could not deliver it due to a contracted, bony pelvic outlet. Both the mother and the baby survived without complications. No doubt, antibiotics had helped. This was my first cesarean after failed forceps and the good outcome made me feel more secure.

I treated over 100 patients in the dispensary, most of them with flu, on February 14th. As I said before, it always took me 48 hours to recover from such a day.

I had to sew a man's nose back in place after it had almost been torn off in an accident. Luckily, there was enough blood supply for it to heal.

We invited several guests to a suckling-pig dinner. Dottie put a cranberry lei around its neck and an apple in its mouth, and served it on a special pig board. She and the cook had some trouble getting the pig into the oven. This dinner was supreme. Our guests are still talking about it, 40 years later.

I was president of the Territorial Association of Plantation Physicians in 1949. The Hawaii Sugar Planters Association paid my expenses to attend the annual meeting of the Industrial Physicians Association in Detroit in April. It was my duty to organize our own annual meeting and to invite a guest speaker.

En route to Detroit I spent two days in Chicago. Mrs. Wylder, Jane Graham's mother, rented a car and took me sightseeing all day. I also visited my fraternity brother, Dr. Wayne Slaughter. Next day I visited Kiwanis International's main office and also the American College of Surgeons headquarters.

In Detroit I visited the Harper Hospital and the Henry Ford Hospital, where a fellow intern, Dr. Robert Horn, was pathologist. I attended all the lectures of the Industrial Physicians Association meeting and a meeting of the Board of Directors. They frowned on the fact that in Hawaii the plantation industrial physicians gave total care instead of just practicing industrial medicine, as was done on the mainland.

I was guest of honor at the meeting's banquet. After dinner I showed a color movie of Hawaii that the Hawaii Tourist Bureau had provided. It was well received.

There were two outstanding dynamic speakers present at the meeting, Dr. Edward Holmblad, managing director of the Industrial Medicine Association and Dr. Leonard Goldwater, professor of industrial hygiene at Columbia University. I discussed with both the possibility of their coming to Hawaii as guest speakers at our annual meeting. Neither was sure he could come. I extended an invitation to both and to their wives to be guests in our home, assuming that one would not accept and maybe neither. Within a few weeks, I got letters from both accepting the invitation. I knew now that we would have a good meeting, but I was putting Dottie under stress with four house guests.

I wrote an article entitled "Plantation Medicine in Hawaii" that was later published in the Journal of Industrial Medicine and Surgery[25].

After I left Detroit I spent two days with Dottie's family in Lewistown and one day with Dr. Nicodemus at the Geisinger Hospital. I continued on to New York City and attended the annual Tri-City (New York, Philadelphia and Boston) Obstetrical Society's meeting and banquet on April 12th. I visited the New York City Lying-In and Margaret Hague Maternity hospitals, where I observed surgery.

I spent April 13th with Bruce and Helen Langdon on Long Island. Bruce had developed minimal pulmonary tuberculosis when he was a prisoner of war in Japan, but was thought to have recovered. When he started his residency in urology at Columbia, he became worse and had a thoracotomy. He was now resting at home and recovering normally. He had two toy Schnauzer dogs that had won all obedience shows they had entered. Bruce was in great demand to give demonstrations with his dogs on television in New York City.

I was with my sister, Dorothy, and her husband, Jack, in Wilkesbarre, Pennsylvania, for one day. Jack had his own general insurance agency.

On April 15th I flew to Durham and went to Chapel Hill. All my brothers and sisters and their families came to see me during the next three days.

My friend, Ralph Fleming of Durham, was my mother's doctor. Mamma needed to have a hysterectomy and I wanted it done while I was there. Every gynecologist in Chapel Hill and Durham, except one, had gone out-of-state to a medical meeting. The one remaining was Dr. Eleanor Easley. Luckily, she was able to take Mamma as a patient and operated on her April 21st. Mamma was out of bed the next day and made a normal recovery.

Neill and his family lived in Maryland near Andrews Air Force Base. I drove to Washington with them and spent a night with Uncle Leon. I left for home at 11:30 a.m. on April 13th and arrived in Honolulu at 7:15 the next morning. I was on Maui at 1:45 p.m., having been away 30 days. I don't think I have ever done so much in any 30-day period.

I bought Dottie a 35mm Kodak camera for Mother's Day. She took about 1000 pictures of the children as they were growing up; most were color slides. When our grandchildren visit, I show them pictures of their mothers when they were young. This makes a big impression on them, particularly scenes of our plantation home, swimming pool, horses, turkeys, etc.

We had bought a small deep freeze but it was always full. We exchanged it for a commercial-type freezer, 18.5 cubic feet in size, which enabled us to store the meat of a steer along with the poultry and pork.

On Memorial Day, 1949, it is noted in my diary that I walked playing nine holes of golf, then went swimming and finally ended my day horseback riding. I am now over 77 years of age. I need rest after three to four hours of work. I get up early, but usually sleep 75 minutes before lunch each day. I have no complaints. I have enjoyed my many years of work and play and now must be satisfied with a diminished capacity for work and other activities. I am very grateful that my mind seems clear in the morning, which enables me to do such things as write this story.

Puunene Hospital reopened on June 9th with a new kitchen and employee's dining room. The completely new obstetrical department and a new wing of 16 private rooms were air-conditioned. Cement blocks were used to build the walls and a cement slab was poured for the floor. As I recall, the cost of the remodeling was $535,000.

The day after the hospital reopened, I delivered four babies with a total weight of 36 pounds.

Dottie Jane's and Carol's tonsils were removed in June. They had had repeated attacks of tonsillitis and ear infections. No doubt, they went swimming too much and this could have caused some of the ear infections. Too, I may have brought some infections home on my clothes.

I insisted that Dottie take a vacation and go to the mainland to see our relatives. She left on July 1st and was away the entire month. While she was away, Lois and Ann spent one week at Maluhia Girl Scout Camp and one week in Honolulu with their cousins.

Dottie stopped in Chicago with Mrs. Wylder for two days and did some shopping. She went to Lewistown and saw all her relatives, visited my sister at Wilkesbarre, Pennsylvania, and then went to North Carolina. My brother, Orus, gave her a car and she saw everyone just as I had done in April. She returned to Lewistown for another visit with her mother. The day before she was to come home, her sister, Helen, announced that she was coming with her. After several telephone calls, airline reservations were obtained. When they arrived on Maui, we were surprised to see Aunt Helen. She left on September 2nd, after a busy month meeting all our friends and seeing all of Maui.

At the hospital we had an 8-year-old boy develop intestinal obstruction while he had measles. At surgery, a Meckel's diverticulum was found that had caused the obstruction. He recovered.

On our 10th wedding anniversary I was too tired to celebrate after working many hours with a patient with a complete placenta previa. After almost losing her, I finally gave her four pints of blood.

McLeod Jr. and sister, Louise Weber, spent a week with us in August while Aunt Helen was visiting. They loved to visit us because of the swimming pool, horses, mangoes and the country life on Maui. It was far different from life in Honolulu.

One hundred and fifty people attended our annual party for the hospital employees and their families. Aunt Helen couldn't believe the day's activities.

Puunene Hospital emergency room was always busy. I was on call on Labor

Day and had one patient with a laceration on his cornea, another with a broken leg and a third requiring repair of a lacerated tendon. I was again on call Sunday, October 22nd, when a school teacher was admitted with a broken leg.

On Saturday, October 2nd, I admitted a patient about 10 p.m. who was said to have fallen off a horse in late afternoon. He had long, deep scratch marks on his chest and abdomen that were caused by barbed wire. He was in shock and had a rigid abdomen. I didn't like what I saw, so I called the police. They investigated and found that he had been in an automobile accident and was thrown out of the car on to a barbed wire fence. Dr. St. Sure was called to treat this patient and when he opened the lower abdomen he found it full of bile. This incision was closed and another made in the upper abdomen. We repaired the jejunum which had been completely severed. I got home at 4 a.m.

The next day, one of my patients who was six months pregnant developed acute appendicitis. When I operated I found the end of the cecum and the appendix were both under the uterus and inside the patient's pelvis. They had developed there from embryo time. It was a difficult operation, but the patient recovered normally. This was probably the keenest diagnosis I ever made and my most difficult operation.

A week later a Kahului Railroad employee's foot was cut off in an accident. I seem to have had more difficult cases than usual during this period.

Dr. and Mrs. Goldwater and Dr. and Mrs. Holmblad arrived on Tuesday, November 15th, for the plantation medical meeting. This was the Holmblads' first trip to Hawaii. Dr. Goldwater had worked as a merchant seaman after he finished high school about 1920, and had made a tour of Maui while his ship was docked in Kahului Harbor. The thing he remembered best was Puunene Avenue with the large, overlapping monkeypod trees. He enjoyed seeing them again.

Both the Holmblads and Goldwaters were our houseguests. On Wednesday I took them on a sightseeing tour to Hana, and we had lunch at Hotel Hana Maui. On Thursday we had an early dinner at home with several additional guests, as the first session of the meeting started at 8 p.m. After the meeting on Sunday, I took them to the top of Haleakala. They were lovely houseguests and were very appreciative. In return, the two doctors made our meeting a great success.

The medical meeting was held at Puunene Athletic Club for three days. We had only 30 members but 45 physicians registered for the program, entitled "A Seminar on Industrial Medicine." Sixteen doctors and plantation officials spoke, including Drs. Holmblad and Goldwater who were on the program many times. All phases of medicine were discussed, particularly those that often involved plantation employees. Puunene Athletic Club was ideal for the meeting: The hall was large and cool and the dining room allowed us to have breakfast round-table discussions and luncheon meetings.

The Maui County Medical Society Women's Auxiliary staged a teriyaki steak dinner at the Paia Baldwin Pavilion from 5 to 7 p.m. on Friday for all registrants and their guests. On Saturday evening, the Auxiliary sponsored a formal dinner dance at the Maui Country Club. Sunday was reserved for golf and sightseeing.

We had a busy meeting and it was the most successful one the association ever had.

We never saw the Goldwaters again. The Holmblads became close friends and spent two vacations with us later. Dr. Holmblad died at about age 80, but Mrs. Holmblad is living at 94. She is mentally alert and writes us a long letter occasionally. (She died May 3, 1989.)

The year got off to a good start and proved to be very eventful. In January, Dottie, Lois, Ann and I attended a concert by opera singer Gladys Swarthout at the Baldwin Auditorium. She was one of the leading sopranos of the Metropolitan Opera Company.

I had very few administrative duties, which meant I could devote some time to my research project. Although I was very busy with both plantation and nonplantation patients, I had some time off each week and could also study four hours or more each evening. I still delivered most of my plantation and all nonplantation patients even though I was off plantation call at the time.

For many years I was chairman of the program committee of the Maui County Medical Society. The Hawaii Medical Association brought outstanding speakers to Honolulu for graduate courses. If invited, these speakers gladly came to Maui for sightseeing and, while here, lectured to the Maui County Medical Society. The hotels on Maui were poor, so Dottie and I housed them in our guest cottage. One of these was Dr. Joseph Baer, professor of Obstetrics and Gynecology at the University of Chicago and president of the American Board of Obstetrics and Gynecology. He and his wife, Janet, liked Maui so much they stayed with us three days instead of two as originally scheduled.

Dr. Baer was a very dynamic person. He was actually the dean of American obstetrics and gynecology. He and my former professor, Dr. Edward Schuman, were founders of the American Board of Obstetrics and Gynecology. The Maui doctors were scheduled to meet with him for an hour on Sunday morning. After his lecture, he offered to answer questions. Sitting in a comfortable chair, he talked and answered questions for three hours.

In the evening, the doctor's wives had a party for the Baers at Dr. McArthur's home. Sliding glass doors separated the living room and the lanai. Dr. Baer walked straight into one of the closed doors, knocking his glasses off. Fortunately, he was not injured.

Mrs. Baer was a beautiful, gracious lady with silky, gray hair and a model's bearing. We became lifelong friends with her and her husband and visited them in Chicago.

Dr. Baer practiced medicine and lived in the center of Chicago. When he had to go to the office or make house calls, his chauffeur drove him. He was on the staff of the Michael Reese Hospital and, even at his advanced years, was still delivering babies and making house calls. His patients were generally wealthy, though he did much charity work at the hospital. I enjoyed discussing his practice with him.

When the Baers were ready to leave on February 13th, one of our younger daughters exclaimed that she thought Dr. Baer had planned to deliver our pregnant cow, due any day. This amused him very much. According to Mrs. Baer, he often told this story to family and friends. Sure enough, the calf was born on Valentine's Day. The children named him Valentine and he became a pet. They objected when we had him slaughtered and put the meat in the freezer.

On March 4th, Neff, Jane, Dottie and I went to the top of Haleakala to see the sun set as the full moon rose. There were no clouds in the sky to obscure this indescribable, beautiful sight.

I was busy in my practice and had started studying long hours at night on my research project. If possible, I would come home from work at 5 p.m. and go horseback riding with Dottie or one of the girls or by myself. I had gone to much expense to have two riding horses, but often no one would ride with me. Carol rode with me more often than anyone else.

By the end of March, I had made much progress in my studies and had come to many premature conclusions. I had learned about the hypothalmus-pituitary-adrenal axis and how a disturbance in the normal function of this axis could lead to disease, particularly to toxemia of pregnancy. This was before Dr. Hans Selye had published his monumental work, "Stress."

I took a week off from work and studied 20 hours a day. My family thought maybe I was going crazy. I wrote and published a monograph entitled "An Explanation of the Biological Functions of the Body in Health and Disease"[26]. Dottie typed the 63-page manuscript and I had 1,000 hardcover copies published by the Honolulu Star Bulletin. I spent $1,500 producing it.

My monograph was almost a complete flop. I distributed it widely and received many comments, most of them unfavorable. McLeod had tried to dissuade me from publishing it, but I wouldn't listen. A few respondents encouraged me and made suggestions. Recently, 30 years after publication, I got a very favorable, unsolicited commentary on it.

I finally reached the conclusion that it had been a mistake to publish the monograph and that I had been very immature and premature in my actions. However, I do not think I wasted my time and money. I decided I would not write anything else until I could support my opinions with accepted facts, and I have stuck to that decision. I learned how to publish a book and, 23 years later, published a second monograph that has been well received. The subject for my second monograph was taken from the original one. I distributed 500 copies of the first one and destroyed the other 500.

After my first monograph was published, I immediately engaged in a detailed study of all the aspects of my research project. I ordered Selye's new book and all the other books that he had written. I ordered six other new books on the adrenal, vitamins, hormones and human biochemistry. I was determined to find and explain the cause of high blood pressure during pregnancy. I couldn't know at the time that the answer was 23 years away and that it would depend on several new discoveries by other workers in human biochemistry and physiology.

I soon relaxed from the frenzied mental state that I had been in for months and began living a more normal life although I was still studying at night and plodding towards my goal.

Dottie and I had decided that we would probably live the rest of our lives on Maui, so we transferred our church memberships to the Wailuku Union Church on April 2, 1950. It was one of the original Congregational churches in the Islands and we had worshiped there for eight years.

On April 26th Dottie and I attended a party celebrating Mr. and Mrs. Frank Baldwin's 50th wedding anniversary. They were yet to celebrate nine more anniversaries.

Dr. Paul Dudley White, Dr. and Mrs. Warren White, and Dr. and Mrs. Edmund Tompkins had lunch with us on May 14th. Paul White was professor of cardiology at Harvard and a world authority on heart disease. He had treated President Eisenhower when he had a coronary occlusion. The Warren Whites were friends of ours and Paul and Warren were brothers.

Paul White was very lean. He was very careful not to eat any food containing cholesterol and he limited his total calories to the minimum that he thought he needed. Warren White was much shorter, rotund and overweight.

Dottie served chicken curry with white rice along with a large bowl of fresh Hawaiian fruit for lunch. Paul White ate sparingly of the fruit and refused to eat the curry and rice, scolding Dottie for serving them and telling her what awful foods they were. Mrs. Warren White was embarrassed at his comments. In spite of his remarks, we had a wonderful lunch and an enjoyable time. There was a great esprit de corps among us. We all knew about Dr. White's views and teachings on the causes of heart disease and respected them although we did not always adhere to them when we were hungry and there was good food before us. After lunch Paul White jogged around our yard to work off any excess calories he had eaten.

We had a Sunday school picnic in our yard at the end of May and we continued this each year. Our church did not offer Sunday school in the summer so this picnic came at the end of the school year. The picnic was similar to the hospital employee's picnic we hosted each year. Adults and children played games and went swimming. Dottie and I often furnished hot dogs or hamburgers for all, while the members brought the rest of the food. It was a fun day for everyone and we were glad to share our yard with them.

May was a busy month for me. I delivered 24 babies, more than the usual number.

Mauna Loa erupted again on June 1st. The following evening, Dottie, Ann, Dottie Jane and I drove to the top of Haleakala to see the molten lava flowing down the side of the mountain facing Maui. A group of our friends chartered a Hawaiian Airline's DC 3 in the evening of June 5th and for about 30 minutes flew over the erupting volcano. I refused to go, but Dottie eagerly accepted. She said they flew very low over the eruption which was on the flank of Mauna Loa. The Federal Aviation Administration had not yet established any rules governing these sightseeing flights. She could see large boulders being tossed several hundred feet into the air and several rivers of fiery molten lava flowing rapidly down the mountain. She took many beautiful pictures as the plane banked from side to side. Inside the plane she could feel the heat from the volcano and smell the sulfur fumes. Although the colored slides Dottie took are beautiful and spectacular, she says they fail to show the awesome spectacle they saw from the plane.

When the plane arrived back on Maui, the group went to the home of one of the sightseers for about an hour to discuss what they had seen. Dottie was not driving her own car, so she didn't come home until about 11 p.m. By this time I was worried sick, thinking the plane could have gone down. A telephone call would have relieved my concern.

The trade winds stopped blowing on June 13th. Dense fog-like fumes from the erupting volcano settled over all Hawaii and reduced visibility to almost zero. Within a few hours after the trade winds finally returned, the fumes disappeared.

I was on call on Sunday, June 8th, and we had friends in for lunch. I had one new patient with a broken leg, another patient died and I had to do an appendectomy on another.

I was not on call Saturday, July 1st, but delivered three babies early in the day. We had a garden party in the evening with 150 guests. I had gotten a large quantity of filet mignon steak from a friend, Al Rego, manager of Ulupalakua Ranch Meat Plant. After the guests had served themselves at a buffet table, they passed by the charcoal grill where I served them a steak in a hamburger bun. Most of them came back for seconds. I have never seen so many filet mignon steaks at one time. Dottie had become a master at serving large numbers of guests.

A Filipino man murdered another at Camp 4. The murderer had spent a year in Kula Sanitorium, recovering from tuberculosis. When he returned home he learned that his wife had been seduced. The wife claimed it was not her fault, as she was unable to resist the advances of the other man. The victim was approached from behind while he was sitting in his yard weaving a fish net. He continued his weaving and did not turn or look at his assailant. He was shot through the upper chest and died immediately. An autopsy showed that the main pulmonary artery had been severed. As I recall, the assailant was never sent to jail for his crime.

Dr. Charles Wilbar, president of the Board of Health of Hawaii, and Dr. and Mrs. Ira Hiscock spent two days with us. Dr. Hiscock, professor of Public Health at Yale University, gave a lecture to the Maui County Medical Society. He and his wife were charming people and of great stature. Our lives were enriched by their visit.

Dottie and I spent a week at the Royal Hawaiian Hotel in August and celebrated our 12th wedding anniversary. Rose Littel, head nurse of Puunene Hospital, stayed with the children. A Kona storm hit Oahu the second day and we couldn't leave the hotel. The sliding doors on the ocean side of the elegant Monarch Dining Room had to be closed. When we were able to go out we had dinners at several fancy restaurants, including Don the Beachcomber's. On our anniversary we had dinner and danced in the Monarch Room again and heard Ed Kinney sing, as I recall. He and a Hawaiian girl were dressed beautifully and had many pikake leis around their necks. They sang Ke Kali Nei Au, the Hawaiian Wedding Song, more beautifully than we had ever heard. We visited the zoo and the aquarium, swam in the ocean every day and drove around the island in a rental car. We had dinner with McLeod and Louise in their home. It was a wonderful vacation.

We had our annual picnic for the hospital employees and their families in August. There were 175 present this year. Even though I was not the medical director, Dottie and I wanted to continue these picnics. Everyone who came had fun and appreciated them. Even now, the employees and their children tell us when we see them how much they appreciated those picnics.

I treated three fractured elbows within one month. All three patients had been driving cars with the left arm out the window. Two of the cars were sideswiped by other cars and the third ran off the road on the left side, striking a dirt bank.

One day Ann was running in the laundry room and accidently struck herself in the solar plexus with a protruding mop handle. She was knocked unconcious and began convulsing, frightening everyone. She recovered after several minutes and had no ill aftereffects.

I attended the annual meeting of the Territorial Association of Plantation Physicians on Kauai in November and presented a paper entitled "Vitamin Deficiencies and Disease." It was later published in the Hawaii Medical Journal[27]. In this paper I point out how vitamins act as catalysts in enzyme systems inside the cell and are necessary for all physiological activity. If a deficiency exists, the hormone which controls the specific enzyme system will be produced in excess through negative feedback stimulation. This production of an excess of hormones may result in disease, not only in the gland producing the hormone but in tissue where the hormone acts.

I operated on another patient with acute appendicitis, who was five months pregnant. This was my third patient in nine years who was five or more months pregnant to develop this complication. All of them recovered normally.

I delivered one of our former nurses her second baby. She developed mild high blood pressure during each pregnancy and acute thrombophlebitis in her legs soon after each delivery. When she recovered, a decision was made that pregnancy was too dangerous for her to undertake again. She has had no recurrence of either disease for 38 years.

On the day after Thanksgiving, one of my patients developed convulsive eclampsia soon after delivery. She had been an executive and had worked until the 6th month, when she moved to Maui. She said she had ignored the advice of both her doctors and had eaten a lot of salt in her diet. This was my first case of eclampsia after delivery. She recovered normally.

We had heavy rains during the entire first week of December and there were floods in many parts of Maui, killing one person and many animals. Some homes in Iao Valley had water up to the ceilings.

THE YEAR 1951

We had a gala New Year's Eve party at our home. Many of our friends were tired of the New Year's parties at the Maui Country Club and the Puunene Athletic Club. Thirty of us joined efforts and finances and staged a real nice, no host dinner dance. There were streamers hanging from the three chandeliers on the lanai and balloons were everywhere. Five Norfolk pine trees of varying sizes were placed about the lanai and decorated with blue lights. Eddie Wilson and his Hawaiian group played music for four hours. The bass fiddle player wore the varnish off the floor under his right foot that he used to keep time. A table was set in the breakfast room with hors d'oeuvers and light food. At midnight the dining room doors were opened to a table filled with a lavish buffet and champagne. Everyone had a good time. I got to bed at 2:30 a.m. On New Year's Day, several guests came back at noon to help clean up. We ate the leftover food for lunch.

Mammasan and papasan decided to return to Okinawa to live out their lives. They had been replaced by Roy Tamanaha and his wife, who had two small children. Roy had a fulltime job as an electrician but would have time to do my work also.

Papasan and mammasan bought three used Singer sewing machines and had them crated for shipping. The machines would bring a good price in Okinawa. They went to Honolulu to board their ship but the voyage was cancelled due to the Korean War. They returned to Maui and moved into one of our servant's quarters to wait until they could get passage to Japan.

Papasan was disturbed by the change of plans. I did not have work for him and mammasan. He wanted to force Roy to leave, but I would not permit that. He developed a stomach ulcer and had some acute pain on New Year's Day. I examined him and decided he could remain home a few days, then we would admit him to the hospital for study.

When he was admitted he was found to have a large stomach ulcer. Dr. Haywood operated and discovered that the ulcer had ruptured. However, it had been completely sealed off from the peritoneal cavity. Most of his stomach was removed including the ulcer and he made a good recovery. Eventually, he and mammasan returned to Okinawa where he died two years later.

After two years, we replaced Roy and his wife with Robert and Thelma Tamanaha, who had five children. Robert was a crane operator on the plantation and was very happy to work for us part-time. He received free housing, milk, eggs, pork, chickens, vegetables and beef when we slaughtered a steer. There was always an excess of honey to share with his family. I had bought a small farm at Kula where he worked one day each week. I paid him $25 per month cash and Thelma received regular wages for her work. I taught Robert how to do yard work, how to farm and how to care for animals and poultry.

Just before we moved from the plantation some years later, Robert moved his family to Los Angeles. He had been with us four years. His youngest child was entering the first grade and the oldest was a sophomore in high school. He formed a landscape maintenance company and cared for over 30 residencies. Neither he nor Thelma completed high school, but all five of their children graduated from college. Now the children are married and have good jobs. Some are supervisors in large computer organizations and own expensive homes.

Robert visited us in the summer of 1987. We reminisced about the good times we had when he was with us. His children would help our children clean the swimming pool and then all would go swimming as the water filled the pool. I had a gallon ice cream freezer, operated by an electric motor. We raised strawberries on our Kula farm and had an abundance of fresh cream from which we would make a gallon of strawberry ice cream. The children of the two families would consume it at one time. Robert said he and Thelma tried to rear their children just like they had observed us rearing ours. They had no real problems with them and they have all succeeded. The yard work and farming I taught him formed the basis of his new avocation. He is now 67 years old and partially retired. He still is in charge of the grounds of Hollywood High School. Sadly, Thelma died two years ago.

On January 15, 1951, I had to re-register for the military draft. Again, I received a letter telling me that I was considered essential in my work on the plantation and that I was not to plan to leave.

One of my turkey hens hatched 17 baby turkeys from 17 eggs. This should have been enough for a year, though two months later a chicken hatched 12 more turkey eggs. There were many tricks to raising turkeys successfully, the most important of which was to vaccinate them for fowl pox before they were three weeks old. They were inoculated in the web of one wing.

I was very busy in my work. I was a member of the Hawaii Medical Association's Committee on Maternal and Infant Mortality and went to Honolulu each month to attend the association's meetings. Mr. Baldwin needed to be seen often because of his chronic heart failure. His wife called me frequently and I visited him in his home in the evening. I was studying my new books and formulating plans for a new paper on high blood pressure and pregnancy.

Bill Gimbel and wife, Odie, daughter of Mrs. Joseph Baer, and Mr. and Mrs. Sandy Cole of Chicago were with us for two days. They were most delightful guests. Mrs. Cole was one of the top models in Chicago. I took them to Hana on Saturday and to the top of Haleakala on Sunday.

Mildred Nordman, an artist-photographer whom we met while living on Hawaii, spent five days with us. Dottie and she visited many scenic areas on Maui for her to sketch for pictures. She painted us a beautiful, peaceful beach scene of a Kihei sight. Now the area is cluttered with hotels and condominiums.

I finished my new paper entitled "Adrenal Dysfunction; an Etiological Factor in Late Toxemia of Pregnancy." In it I point out how nutritional deficiencies and stress during pregnancy could cause adrenal gland disease and the syndrome known as late toxemia of pregnancy. It was published by the Western Journal of Surgery, Obstetrics and Gynecology[28].

Dr. and Mrs. Nicholas Eastman and traveling companions, Mr. and Mrs.

156

Harrison spent two days with us. Dr. Eastman was the professor of Obstetrics and Gynecology at the Johns Hopkins Medical School and the author of a widely used textbook on obstetrics. He spoke to the Maui County Medical Society. I took them sightseeing to the top of Haleakala.

I had the planing mill fabricate a diving board for our swimming pool from two-by-fours on edge, held together with glue. It had a good spring and was a big hit with everyone.

Dottie and I attended the garden wedding and luau of Jane Baldwin, daughter of Mr. and Mrs. Edward Baldwin of Ulupalakua Ranch. She was a grandchild of Mr. and Mrs. Frank Baldwin. Plans for the wedding extended over a year. The ranch house was nearly 100 years old, situated in a grove of large trees on the slopes of Haleakala at about the 3,000 foot level. The ocean, Kahoolawe and Molokini could be seen in the distance. The flowers in the yard were primarily blue agapanthus and yellow marguerites. They had been planted around the house, by the walks and in the flower gardens. The bridesmaids had dresses to match the flowers in color. The wedding ceremony was beautiful, with the ranch house in the background and flowers on every side.

Soon after the ceremony, there was a heavy downpour of rain. According to the Hawaiians, this was a good omen. Many friends and relatives of the bride and groom attending the wedding were representatives from the old missionary families in Hawaii. Because of the rain the luau was served indoors, but there was plenty room for everyone. This was certainly the most beautiful affair of its kind that we ever attended.

Dottie and I returned to the Royal Hawaiian Hotel for another week's vacation. We ate at many fancy restaurants including Lau Yee Chai, the Halekulani Hotel, Don the Beachcomber's and Queen's Surf. We visited the Bishop Museum and the Honolulu Art Academy and saw Neff and Jane and many of our friends in Honolulu.

I was on call July 13th and had a patient come in with a partial dislocation of his neck. He was still very much alive. Dr. Haywood put tongs in his skull and applied several pounds of traction. The displaced articular facets slipped back into normal position after the muscles relaxed. According to Dr. Haywood, the patient had no residual injury.

We drove to Lahaina July 14th on the new road across the pali. The old road had been built on an old wagon trail and was very hazardous to drive. The Kahului Railroad trucks and trailers hauling sugar to the harbor in Kahului could barely negotiate the curves. Once, the front wheels and the cab of one of these trucks went over the side, but the weight of the rest of the truck held it suspended in space until it could be retrieved. Another time, a loaded tour bus went off the road and over the cliff. It became wedged behind a large kiawe tree, which prevented it from falling into the ocean.

The new road was an engineering masterpiece with cuts 50 feet deep through lava ridges on the mountain side. There was one tunnel about 100 yards long, the first on a public highway in Hawaii.

Hawaiian Commercial and Sugar Company had an anniversary celebration as part of its public relations program. The mill was open to the public and employees and their families were urged to see it. Hot dogs and ice cream were served to all. Our family, including McLeod Jr. who was visiting us, took the tour.

Governor Oren Long appointed me to an advisory commission to the Board of Health. The commission's duties were to make recommendations regarding construction of new health facilities and the spending of public funds for the care of the

157

indigent, as I recall. We met once each month in the evening in Honolulu. I think I was the only doctor on the commission, though the Board of Health had one of its physicians present at all meetings. I enjoyed these meetings and the association with leaders in fields other than medicine.

I was on a week's vacation in August and took our family to Hana via Ulupalakua Ranch and Kaupo. The road was barely passable due to damage by recent floods. While we were away, our cow had a heifer calf that would eventually replace her mother as our milk cow. We named her Hana. I removed her horn buds when she was three weeks old.

The next day, our cow developed paralysis and couldn't walk. The veterinarian diagnosed her as having milk fever and treated her with a calcium solution intravenously. She recovered immediately. Thirty two years later, I published a paper showing that calcium deficiency was the cause of toxemia of pregnancy in the human. I did not know originally that high blood pressure and toxemia of pregnancy in the human were caused by calcium deficiency just as milk fever was in the cow.

I did an autopsy on a friend killed in an auto accident. A truck, entering the highway, struck the left front side of his car. The steering wheel post hit him in the center of his chest and ruptured his aorta. He died instantly.

I operated on an unruptured tubal pregnancy. It was always satisfying to find these and operate before the tube ruptured. If the tube ruptures, the patient may bleed profusely internally, go into shock and require several emergency transfusions.

I operated on a two and a half-year-old boy for acute appendicitis. This was my youngest patient to have appendicitis. It was not mango season, when children often develop right-sided abdominal pain and vomiting from eating the peels of green mangoes. Dr. Lightner taught me to treat these children with castor oil and enemas. I observed them in the hospital and never had one fail to recover.

I boarded a ship for quarantine inspection, along with the port captain, two miles off shore at the buoy which marks the entrance to the channel. Dottie had permission to go along on the tug, where she remained. Maui is very beautiful when viewed from two miles off port.

McLeod and his family spent Thanksgiving with us though he left for Honolulu in the evening. Louise and the children stayed until Sunday. On Saturday the children went horseback riding and swimming. Afterwards, we drove to Lahaina and had dinner at the Banyan Inn.

I delivered four babies on the last day of November, making a total of 30 for the month. This was a record.

Lois had a 12th birthday party on December 1st and invited 24 girls for the day. We allowed each daughter to have a big party on her 12th and 16th birthdays. The children had lots of fun with plenty of room to play. It was a joy to watch them.

Dottie went to a dinner party in Puunene alone as I was sick with a migraine headache. I had been up the entire previous night, finally doing a cesarean in the early morning. After nights like this I often had to go to bed and get a good rest before I could continue.

THE YEAR 1952

The year started as usual. I delivered the first baby on Maui at 12:01 a.m. There was always a baby derby on New Year's Day, with the first baby receiving many gifts from merchants. Dottie and I had attended a New Year's party at the Country Club and, as usual, I had to take time out to deliver the baby.

Life continued as usual at home. I had set a turkey hen with 11 eggs and she hatched 12 baby turkeys. This was the first set of twins I had ever had with any kind of poultry.

On January 25th, Carol became paralyzed from the waist down. Dottie and I were up all night with her. Next day, Dr. Haywood examined her and did a spinal tap which showed a normal result. There were many cases of poliomyelitis on Maui and we were relieved that the spinal tap was normal. I talked to Dr. Warren White of Shriner's hospital on the telephone about her. The right leg was very weak and she couldn't move the left leg. She had severe abdominal distention and pain and no control of any of her sphincters. She remained about the same for five days. Then Dr. Underwood told me about an article he had read in a medical journal recently about a similar case who had chronic potassium deficiency. We tested her blood potassium and it was very low. We gave her potassium chloride by mouth and within six hours she was much improved. She was able to stand, but could not walk. Her sphincters were resuming normal function. The next day she could walk and she improved thereafter. Thirteen days later, I made a notation in my diary that she was getting stronger slowly.

As many parents do, Dottie and I often served our children more food than they would eat. Each child got an iced tea glass of milk at each meal and sometimes they would drink milk between meals. Carol always seemed to have difficulty emptying her plate.We thought she should eat all the food that we put on her plate but, to get the meal over with, we would agree that if she drank all her milk she could be excused from the table. I think that her total fluid intake was too great. When she excreted this extra fluid she apparently excreted too much potassium with it.

Carol's illness occurred two months before her 6th birthday. She resumed normal activity and appeared to have escaped any permanent ill effects. However, when she reached adulthood, her left thigh and calf measured two inches less in circumference than those on the right. Both legs are of the same length.

Sam and Ellie Lebold of Chicago visited us on February 19th, and we took them to Lahaina for dinner. She was another daughter of Mrs. Joseph Baer. We became close friends, and they visited Maui a week each year for many years. We would play a round of golf with them at Kaanapali and then go to dinner. Later, they would play with us at Maui Country Club and then have dinner with us in our home or at a restaurant on this side of the island. Sam's wood pulp and paper business manufactured the cardboard cartons for Coca Cola and other items.

The Trapp family was on a world tour and gave a concert at the Baldwin Auditorium on February 29th, which we attended. Next day, we had the whole group at our home for lunch after Dottie and Bob Hughes Sr. had taken them sightseeing to Lahaina. They stopped at the lookout on the pali where they could see the whales cavorting. According to Dottie, it was a beautiful Maui day. They got out of the cars and sang a glorious native song acapella. They were dressed in their native costumes. Some years later, they again performed on Maui and visited in our home, some spending the night with us. Certain individuals who were with them on their first tour did not accompany them on the second visit.

On June 7th, Dottie and I left for the mainland. Mrs. Hall, Lois's school teacher, stayed with the children. She was a mother and a grandmother whom we could trust. We were flying with United Airlines on one of their Boeing Stratocruisers. When we were four hours from Honolulu and one hour from the point of no return, an engine failed. We returned to Honolulu, arriving after midnight. After a four-hour sleep in a hotel at Waikiki, we tried again on another plane, arriving in Los Angeles at 3 a.m. on June 9th. We flew low over the Grand Canyon en route to Chicago, where we arrived at 4:30 p.m. The Holmblads had had a party at the hotel for us on June 8th, which we missed. We were staying at the Sherman Hotel, where the American Medical Association was having its meeting. I registered for the meeting and attended several sessions.

We were invited to a fabulous dinner party by Dr. and Mrs. Joseph Baer in the Empire Room of the Palmer House on June 10th. Dr. Baer was giving a dinner for several members of the American Board of Obstetrics and Gynecology, of which he was president. Later in the evening, Bill and Odie Gimbel took us to the Pump Room at the Ambassador Hotel. Bill's mother lived in the Ambassador Hotel permanently. We had never seen such splendor as we saw in the Empire Room and the Pump Room.

Dr. Holmblad rented a car and took us sightseeing in the morning of June 11th, along with Mrs. Ethel Wylder. I attended the medical meeting in the afternoon and, after dinner, Dottie and I went to see the musical show "Guys and Dolls."

We had lunch with Dr. and Mrs. Baer on June 12th and then went shopping in the afternoon. Dr. and Mrs. Holmblad took us to dinner at the Swedish Club and introduced us to our first smorgasbord. The food was delicious. I still can't forget the smoked snake meat that was served although I did not eat any.

On June 13th, we flew to Pittsburgh and caught a train to Lewistown. Our visit in Chicago was too rushed, partly due to arriving a day late and partly because we had too many friends to visit. I spent many hours at the medical meeting, shopping required much time, and we attempted to do too much sightseeing.

We were in Lewistown for nine days and had nice visits with all of Dottie's family. I did many jobs around the house for mother Graham and Dottie was able to do a lot of shopping. Flower leis we had sent from Hawaii arrived while we were there as well as letters from our daughters.

We took a train on June 18th to Washington and spent a night with my brother, Neill. He was stationed at Andrews Air Force Base and lived nearby in Maryland. Uncle Leon, who was now married to Page Leonard, came to see us.

We flew to Chapel Hill next day and in six days were able to visit all my relatives in Coats, Angier and Sanford. I saw all my brothers and sisters and their ever-enlarging families. Even Maisie now had two nice sons born when she was 40 and 42 years of age. We went to Fayetteville to visit Bruce and Helen Langdon and to Durham to see Ralph and Sue Fleming.

We had invited Mamma to come home with us, but she had always refused to fly in an airplane. Finally, she remarked that she was old, all her children were married and if the plane wrecked, her death would not result in a hardship on anyone. She agreed to fly to Hawaii with us. This would be her second trip to the Islands.

We left from the Raleigh-Durham Airport on June 25th for Washington. The temperature was 98 degrees. We spent the night with Uncle Leon and Page and left the next morning for San Francisco. We were flying United Airlines in a DC 6 plane. As we flew over the Rocky Mountains, the air was very turbulent. We flew through the clouds and the plane shook and shuddered. I was sitting just in front of the wing and could see ice form on the front edge of it. Then I thought about what Mamma had said about the plane going down.

It was 5 p.m. when we arrived in San Francisco. The temperature was 57 degrees, 41 degrees cooler than it was the day before in Washington. We went to our

160

hotel on Union Square and to bed early, as we were tired.

The next morning we all felt fine. We took a bus tour of San Francisco and had lunch at Fisherman's Wharf. In the afternoon we went on a boat cruise in San Francisco Bay. Mamma was enjoying herself and did not let her age prevent her from taking in all the activities.

We left for Hawaii at 2 a.m. on June 28th, again with United Airlines in a DC 6. During the flight, the captain announced that since our departure, Kilauea Volcano had erupted. He said we would fly over the volcano and give us a good look if there were no clouds to interfere. When we arrived, visibility was good. We flew low over the volcano and could see the fountains of red, molten lava in Halemaumau fire pit. The plane circled the area several times, and Dottie was able to get good pictures. Then we flew around Mauna Loa. The surface of the mountain was made up of numerous lava flows of different ages. Some had come from Makuaweoweo Crater at the top, and others had broken out along the flanks. We had lived between old lava flows at Naalehu for 15 months. The lava rock had burst my tires and broken my car springs. I had learned to hate it. However, when viewed from high above, the lava flows created a beautiful mosaic pattern as they formed tongues going down the sides of the tall mountain. It appeared that Madame Pele, the volcano goddess who is respected as a grand old lady, was putting on a beautiful show for Mamma, another grand lady. We were fortunate to see Madame Pele's handiwork, both old and new, as the airlines no longer divert their flights from the mainland over erupting volcanos on the Island of Hawaii. We continued on to Honolulu.

We arrived in Honolulu at 10:30 a.m. and on Maui at 4 p.m. Everything was fine at home. Two girls were at Scout camp. Next day, I took another to camp and brought one home. Louise Weber, our niece, also was at camp.

I returned to work and was very busy as usual. As time permitted, we took Mamma to Lahaina, Hana, Ulupalakua, and to the top of Haleakala. We had all our film developed and the pictures of our trip were wonderful. The photos of Grand Canyon from the air were superb.

After three weeks with us, Mamma flew to Honolulu and spent two weeks with McLeod and Louise. She then returned to Maui and stayed with us another two weeks before leaving for the mainland. Dottie had a tea party for her and invited all her older friends, including Mrs. Frank Baldwin, Mother Burnett, and Mrs. Louise Boyum.

Mamma found that she had gained 10 pounds since arriving on Maui and wondered why. The answer was in our abundant crop of mangoes. She loved them. She would peel and eat one or two between meals.

Mamma flew home alone and had no problems. She was over 70 years of age, but this was her second trip home alone from Hawaii. She flew to Pittsburgh and was to go to Lewistown by train to visit Dottie's mother. During her stopover in Pittsburgh she took a city bus tour which was late returning. She missed her train and Dottie's family was upset when she did not arrive at the scheduled time. She took another train and arrived two hours late. A professor at the train station was going to Pennsylvania State College and would be passing by Dottie's mother's home. He took her to the door. She had a nice visit for a few days and then visited Uncle Leon in Washington on her way to Chapel Hill.

My work continued as usual. I delivered a nine-pound baby to a woman with active chicken pox. The baby did not contract it. We had the usual church and hospital picnics in our yard. We were busy in the backyard raising pheasants, parakeets, piglets, calves, chickens, ducks, and turkeys.

Mattie Fuquay Patterson, circa age 70

An agent of the Internal Revenue Service audited the books of my practice. She was in my office every day for five days. She explained that I should not be disturbed because this was routine. I told her she was welcome to investigate all she wanted to, and that I was not afraid of any of her findings, nor of any man or woman, dead or alive.

I had charged my country club dues as an expense of my private practice, and this alerted the I.R.S. to investigate me. I had reported all income from insurance exams and other income that some doctors overlook. In fact, I had reported a relatively large amount of income each year as taxable though it was not. This was almost enough to offset the country club expense that was not allowed. I had to pay $150 to cover underpayments for the previous five years.

At that time the Territory of Hawaii did not use tax forms similar to federal forms. The Hawaii tax agent told me they never made refunds for overpayments. There were no advance payments for estimated income at that time. When the I.R.S. reported its findings to the Territory, I was found to have paid $65 too much tax to the Territory for the five years that were audited. They refunded this to me and I have never been audited since. Now, I depend on tax accountants to determine how much tax I owe.

On Sunday, September 7th, our family went to the Kahului Union Church to hear the Reverend Abraham Akaka. He soon transferred to Hilo and later to Kawaiahao Church in Honolulu, which some lovingly call the Westminister Abbey of Hawaii. He recently retired. Dottie and I consider him almost a saint, certainly the greatest Hawaiian of recent times. I delivered his wife a son who is now a physician. Before he retired, the Reverend Akaka christened our grandson, Michael McGovern II, age 10, in the Christmas Day baptismal service at the Kawaiahao Church.

I gave my friend, Karl Heyer Sr., nine pheasants I had raised. He was a member of the Haleakala Gun Club and released the birds for hunting.

It was election year again, and Dottie and I attended several political rallies of both parties. These were very entertaining as well as informative, with musicians and hula dancers to put on a show. Often on Maui there were not enough qualified candidates to run for all the positions in each party, but, usually, someone would be encouraged to seek every office. Every candidate would have his say at the rallies. I can remember one who said he had been overworked by a sugar plantation and got a hernia as a result. As proof, he dropped his pants on the stage before a mixed audience to show the scar of the hernia repair. He wanted to be elected so he could protect the workers against abuses. He won.

I had a chance to buy a four-acre farm at Haleakala Acres in Kula, 12 miles from our home. We decided to buy it so we would be forced to save money. We knew eventually we would like to own our home and, when that time came, we would sell this farm and buy or build a home. There were many fruit trees on the farm, especially many varieties of plums. The elevation was 3500 feet above sea level. In the winter, the night temperatures would be in the low 40s. Temperate zone fruits such as apples, peaches, persimmons, plums, grapes, etc., grew and produced very well. I planted a large flower garden, which had many choice varieties of roses. One year we harvested 300 pounds of delicious Kula onions. I did much of the work on Wednesday afternoons and on the weekends. We often took papasan to the farm Saturday morning and went back for him in late afternoon. When Roy and Robert Tamanaha worked for us, they drove their own cars. One of the biggest problems we had was giving away all the vegetables, flowers, and fruit that we raised. It took about an hour after I returned home at sunset to distribute all my produce and flowers.

General Dwight Eisenhower was elected President on November 4, 1952. I had been a great admirer of his since he had been appointed Commander of the Allied Forces in Europe in World War II. He had shouldered the greatest responsibility of any human being ever, in my opinion. He waged a successful campaign and won the war in Europe. He was now president of Columbia University, where mankind would benefit through his actions and his writings. The stress of this position was miniscule compared to what he had already experienced.

I felt it was a great injustice to ask General Eisenhower to be President of the United States, which, no doubt, was the most stressful peacetime job in the world. The Korean War was in progress and he would have to find a way to terminate it. I thought he had done enough for his country and for mankind; to ask him to be President was making him a martyr to the cause. He deserved better.

Sure enough, he had a coronary occlusion (heart attack) during his first term and, luckily, recovered. He was urged to run for a second term and was told his country could not do without him. I was very sad when he agreed to do so. Again, he developed terminal ileitis (in my opinion, a result of stress) and recovered after operation. By the end of his second term, his face showed the effects of prolonged stress. He lived eight more years, dying at age 79.

On election day we had another tidal wave in Hawaii. There was not a lot of damage on Maui, though buildings in low beach areas were flooded. Again, I bought a lot of cereal and grain that had been damaged and fed it to my animals.

Hilo sustained severe damage by the tidal wave. All the buildings on the main street running parallel to the beach were totally destroyed. The force of the water was so strong that the steel pipes holding the parking meters were bent over. The wave was 30- feet high two blocks inland from the beach in a residential area. About 60 persons lost their lives.

My brother, Neill, spent eight hours with us on November 6th. There was a conference in Honolulu involving all the United States military forces in the Pacific and he participated in it. He was one of the pilots on the four-engine plane that flew the Chiefs of Staff from Washington, D.C. When their plane was about three hours off the West Coast and still about two hours from the point of no return, as I recall, one of the engines failed. The Air Force General aboard ordered the pilots to proceed to Honolulu on three engines. They had no further problems.

Neill was not his usual relaxed and jovial self. He showed me his hands. They had multiple blisters between the fingers, a sign of neurogenic dermatitis resulting from the long, over-water flight on three engines. He had flown throughout World War II in Europe and over the Atlantic and survived. He had just experienced another hazardous flight of several hours over the Pacific.

I attended a meeting of the Hospital Commission in Honolulu on the evening of November 24th. When I returned next morning, I found Dottie very upset about Ann's school teacher. She was exerting undue pressure on Ann who had lost seven pounds since school had started. I immediately went to see the school principal who told me that the parents of every other child in the room had already complained about the teacher. She said she would have her replaced at once, which she did.

We had one macadamia nut tree in the yard of our plantation home. If I didn't gather the nuts regularly, the mongooses or rats gnawed holes through the shells and ate the meat, just like a squirrel would have done. Dottie made delicious macadamia nut-chocolate fudge for Christmas. Now we have two macadamia nut trees of a superior variety in our yard, which produce 50 to 100 pounds of nuts each year.

The new Maui Memorial Hospital was completed in late 1952, built primarily with Hill-Burton Federal funds. Hawaiian Commercial and Sugar Company had given the County of Maui about 50 acres of land across the highway from Baldwin High School to be used as a site for a hospital and other health-related activities. I was appointed, as a representative of the Maui County Medical Society, to a committee to choose the site for the hospital on this large tract of land. The committee met with Senator Harold Rice and we toured the site. He wanted the hospital to be located directly across from the high school and near the highway. The committee chose the higher area at the rear of the property, where the hospital now stands.

The furniture that Dottie and I having made for our large lanai was delivered on December 24th. We were very pleased with it and so happy to have the lanai finally finished. It had been four years since we had moved into the house. If we built a home in the future, we planned to design it around this furniture.

I was on call as usual on Christmas Day and spent four hours repairing a badly mangled hand. A teenage boy had constructed a pipe-bomb using firecracker powder. It exploded in his hand and mutilated it leaving only the thumb and index finger undamaged. Half the middle finger was destroyed. The ring and fourth fingers as well as the fourth and fifth metacarpals were missing. I made a good repair that never needed any reconstruction. When I saw this person in 1986, he showed me the scarred remnant of his hand, which had good function.

THE YEAR 1953

We celebrated the New Year at the Maui Country Club and got home at 1 a.m. My work for the New Year started with a bang. I delivered one baby at 1:53 a.m. and another at 7:45 a.m. On the 2nd, I delivered two babies. On the 3rd, I did a ceserean at 3 a.m., delivered another baby at 10:30 a.m., and then saw many patients in the office. In the afternoon I took out an appendix. On the 4th, which was Sunday, I admitted two more women in labor.

Dottie prepared another delicious dinner with a suckling pig for 16 guests on January 10th.

On January 30th we attended a concert of chamber music at the Maui Country Club by a Hungarian Quartet. The attendance was small, but the music was wonderful.

In February, Dottie and Mrs. Lorraine Sanders won first place in a table setting contest open to the public on Maui. They represented the Maui County Medical Society Women's Auxillary. They also won first place the next year. Thereafter, they were allowed to enter the contest, but chose not to compete for any prizes.

Dottie and I attended a concert by the Honolulu Symphony Orchestra at the Baldwin Auditorium on February 21st. Two of the musicians were housed in our guest cottage.

On March 4th, we had dinner with Dr. and Mrs. Joseph Andrews at Kula and watched television afterwards. At that time, there were no relay stations atop Haleakala. The Andrews were able to get the signals direct from Honolulu.

Our daughter, Lois, joined the Wailuku Union Church on Palm Sunday at age 13.

Dr. and Mrs. Edward Holmblad of Chicago visited us again from May 1st to the 8th, during the Territorial Association of Plantation Physicians meeting. McLeod and

Louise also were here.

I took a two-week vacation starting on June 21st. Dottie and I went to Honolulu for two days to rest and do some shopping as many necessary items still could not be bought on Maui. The first evening we had dinner with Neff, Jane, McLeod and Louise at the Hickam Officer's Club. The second evening we ate at Don the Beachcomber's.

We returned home and next day left with our four girls for a six-day vacation on the Island of Hawaii. We toured the volcano area, which is 4,077 feet above sea level. Our first night was spent at the rustic Volcano House Hotel, located on the rim of Kilauea Crater. Halemaumau fire pit was inside the crater, about a mile from the Volcano House. We drove to a parking lot and walked the 100 yards to the fire pit. We could easily see the bottom of the pit, which was about 90 feet deep at that time. Smoke with a strong sulfur odor was coming from the bottom.

The volcanologist, Dr. Howard Powers, was a friend of ours. He showed us the seismographs in a room underneath the Volcano House Hotel. There were almost constant tremors in the area and fequently small earthquakes.

We drove down the Chain of Craters Road, passing seven dormant craters. Many fissures in the pavement extended out in the soil on both sides. Sometimes they were 12 inches wide; at other places, the pavement would be buckled 18 inches high. Each of the craters had a sign telling the time of the last eruption, usually several years past, and the depth of the crater, 100 or more feet. All had tall trees growing inside. One of these craters, Kilauea Iki, has since erupted several times with fountains of lava 1,500 feet high. A large cinder cone, several hundred feet high, has formed and lava has flowed out side fissures. Cinders have covered the surrounding area and the forest of native ohia trees has been killed. In recent years there have also been several eruptions in Halemaumau fire pit and along the flanks of Kilauea crater.

We drove through the tree fern forest with ferns growing 30 to 40 feet high, a beautiful sight. We walked through the Thurston Lava Tube - a tunnel through the lava, covered with forest and open at both ends. There were yellow sulfur banks nearby, which emitted clouds of sulfur fumes. The road leading up Mauna Loa passed through Bird Park where there were picnic tables. This is the area where I had helped collect pheasants and quail 13 years before for a ranger who was studying bird life in the park.

Next day, we drove to Kona through Pahala and Naalehu. We saw the hospital where Lois was born and the first home that Dottie and I ever had. We visited our friends in Naalehu.

We spent two days at the Kona Inn, sightseeing, shopping and swimming. We saw many acres of coffee trees on the mountain side, the branches loaded with red coffee beans. There were large sheds where the beans were dried in the sun. The many donkeys in the area - called Kona Nightingales because of their loud braying - were used to bring in the coffee beans after they had been picked by hand.

From Kona we went to Waimea and Parker Ranch. It is described as the second largest Hereford ranch in the U.S.A.; only King Ranch in Texas is larger. It covers the saddle area between Mauna Loa and Mauna Kea and extends to Waimea and the Kohala Mountains. On the southwest side it reaches Hualalai Mountain and Kona. Most of the area of Parker Ranch is high above sea level and the ocean cannot be seen from most of the property. Waimea's altitude is over 3,000 feet, with weather much cooler than at lower levels. The area has the feeling of ranch country in the western part of the United States.

We stayed at the old Waimea Ranch Hotel, which was a country style, western hotel. The girls complained bitterly. Actually, it was nice to stay at this old hotel without all the modern day luxuries. We had Parker Ranch steaks for dinner.

From our hotel headquarters at Waimea, we drove to Honakaa on the east coast of the island and then to Waipio. From the cliff where the improved road ended, we looked down into Waipio Bay and Valley. At that time, it contained many taro farms. The tidal wave of 1946 had caused extensive damage.

We went back to Waimea and drove along the Kohala Mountains to Hawi where we saw the original bronze statue of Kamehameha I, who was born there. We saw Haleakala and Maui, 40 miles away, across the Alenuihaha Channel.

From Waimea, we drove to Hilo over the Humuula Saddle road and spent our last night at the Naniloa Hotel. Hilo and the east coast of Hawaii are in the path of the tradewinds, which results in heavy rainfall, from 100 to 200 inches of rain annually. The sugar cane does not need to be irrigated. Due to the abundance of moisture, the foliage and flowers are beautiful. Anthuriums grow in profusion and are shipped commercially throughout the U.S.A. Orchids, also, do very well and many varieties grow wild.

A phenomenon found only in Hilo was a minibus called a sampan. The body of a standard sedan car was cut in half and a new body fabricated from metal. The new body was put on the chassis behind the front seat. It had a bench seat on each side and carried about eight passengers. These sampans roamed the streets of Hilo, picking up and discharging riders along the way. I think they have now been discontinued.

We saw movies on August 19th of the coronation of Queen Elizabeth II. She is still the reigning monarch of the British Isles. She and I celebrate the same birthday, April 21st.

On August 21st the plovers returned to Hawaii from Alaska where they breed and raise their young each summer. About the same time each year they return to Hawaii and apparently reside in the same area from year to year. We always had two or three in our yard in the winter and called them tweeter birds, because of their songs.

In August, I cleared the Norwegian Motorship, Fernbrook, from quarantine. It was here to pick up canned pineapple. Captain Apold had his wife and eight-year-old daughter aboard. Dottie and I invited them to our home for dinner after I received special permission for them to leave the ship. Only the Captain could speak English. I think they were awed by being in our home, but they seemed to enjoy themselves. Our family was invited to go aboard their ship the next day. It was spotlessly clean. They gave us some delicious Norwegian cheese.

I did an appendectomy on a woman in her ninth month of pregnancy. Two days later she developed severe abdominal distention and I was very concerned. After consultation with Dr. Haywood, I washed out her stomach with a large gavage tube and removed a large quantity of food. Her relatives had brought her food which she had eaten, unbeknownst to me or the nurses. Thereafter, she recovered normally and eventually delivered without further complications.

On October 4th, we prepared a 250-pound pig, kalua style, by cooking it underground in an imu (pit) with rocks. We invited 120 guests and had a grand feast, Hawaiian style. All of the pig, except the tough meat of the neck, was eaten. Actually, much of the weight of the pig is fat, which drains off while it is being cooked.

We saw the New York Giants baseball team play a group of service all-stars at the Maui County Fair. The Giants won 7 to 2.

Dr. Haywood and I did a simple mastectomy on one of my 80- year old patients who had had an ulcerating cancer of her breast for 15 years. She had been too busy taking care of a sick husband to get treatment herself until he died. She had no recurrence and died five years later of a heart attack.

Dottie and I attended the annual meeting of the Plantation Physicians Association on Molokai, November 13th to 15th. The first evening we had dinner and our meeting at the George P. Cooke home. Mrs. Cooke was most gracious. Next day, our sessions ended early so we could go sightseeing and then to a luau. We visited the Palaau State Park and saw the large, unabashed phallic rock. We walked several hundred yards over rough terrain to see a large, ancient heiau (an altar made of stones where Hawaiians of premissionary days worshiped many gods). We looked down from the precipice to Kalaupapa Leper Settlement, 1200 feet below on a flat peninsula only a few feet above sea level. The final day we visited Mr. Harry Larsen's home on the west end. He was the manager of the Libby Pineapple Plantation. We had a venison steak barbecue at Kaupoa beach for lunch. Axis deer abound in Molokai's wilderness and could be seen not only in the forest and pineapple fields but occasionally on the beaches. Sometimes they ate the ripe pineapple, which, if the damage was extensive, gave the plantation a right to shoot them out of season. Mr. Harry Larsen had quite an arsenal, which he showed me. He was able to shoot and kill an axis deer with a long, 22-gauge rifle bullet. He would aim at the deer's heart.

Finally, we left for home at 5 p.m. This was the first medical meeting ever held on Molokai and many people not connected with the medical profession helped make it a success. It was a real treat for all who attended. Dr. Frederick Reppun, who lived on Molokai, was president. He discussed this medical meeting of 35 years ago with me recently.

I delivered a normal baby boy to a woman who had recovered from metastatic choriocarcinoma to her spine three and a half years before. At that time, she had been told that she would be dead within six months. Later, she had two more babies and is still alive. There was no known cure for this cancer when she was afflicted. Patients were treated by removing the uterus, hoping to prevent the disease from spreading. This precluded future pregnancies, making this case probably the only one ever to have occurred. I reported a summary of this patient's case in the American Journal of Obstetrics and Gynecology[30].

I delivered a plantation manager's wife a baby at this time and later delivered her two more. I think I delivered about a dozen women whose husbands were middle-aged, top executives. Having a baby is a wonderful thing when it is wanted and should be the greatest event in a married couple's life. I have come to the conclusion that, when possible, couples should strive to have their babies when they are young. Then the children learn as they see their parents struggling to get ahead. Dottie and I followed this rule and had all our children while I was paying my school debts. However, it is usually better to have babies late in life than not at all.

THE YEAR 1954

The year got off to a good start with the plantation giving me a new Pontiac sedan. I was very busy with patients and with our farm at Kula.

A former Puunene Hospital head nurse, who had valvular heart disease and auricular fibrillation, had a second cerebral embolism. She was only partially paralyzed, but later had a third embolism and died. She would have been a good teaching case in a medical college.

Dottie and I planted eight pine trees on the edge of our property at Kula. Today they are about 40 feet tall and are very beautiful.

I cleared an Italian ship from quarantine. It had come from Japan and was loading canned pineapple for Europe.

I received a call that Dottie Jane had fallen at school and was injured. I went to the school immediately. She had been holding onto an overhead bar on a swing while other students pushed her back and forth, high into the air. She asked to get off when her hands and arms tired, but the boys would not allow her to do so. She then fell from the swing and injured her back. X-rays showed two transverse processes in the upper lumbar spine had been fractured as well as other damage to the vertebrae. She was put in a body cast for two weeks, which was very uncomfortable for her. I remember her in bed at home with her large blue eyes looking up at me. I tried to console her but she was resigned to her fate and did not complain. Finally Dottie took her to Honolulu for a brace, which she wore for 12 weeks. She recovered completely.

In the first week of March there was a storm with very rough seas. The breakwater at Kahului Harbor was partially destroyed and had to be repaired later. A ship was stranded inside the harbor. It could not be tied to the dock because of the high waves and it could not leave the harbor without great danger of going aground.

On March 15th, we had a heavy rain at night. The top of Haleakala was white with snow the next morning.

We had two cases of poliomyelitis in February, which was the beginning of an epidemic. Thomas Cole, a four-year-old son of one of my associates, developed acute bulbar poliomyelitis in March. I remember seeing him in bed in an isolation room at Puunene Hospital. He could not move any of his extremities. Luckily, he survived. He had severe residual weaknesses in his back and in all his extremities. One arm was in a sling for many months. He went to school in a wheel chair for years and was eventually able to walk with the aid of braces and crutches. He graduated from college and law school and, at the present time, is married and has two children. He has a very successful law practice on the Island of Maui. Recently, at a social gathering, I climbed a flight of steps behind him and found it amazing to see what he does with the few muscles he has in his extremities. One year after he developed polio, on April 12, 1955, there was a public announcement that an effective polio vaccine had been tested. Supplies became available and I began giving it to my patients on September 20th. I took it myself.

After eating fish one evening I became sick with extreme weakness, numbness and tingling in my extremities, nausea and vomiting. I continued working, but finally, after five days, had to go to bed for a day because of pain in my eyes. Fish poisoning in Hawaii is common. The fish eat a seaweed containing a poison which is stored in their flesh. It is not injurious to them, but is to humans. Fishermen often catch several hundred mullet or other fish with nets, and then go through the plantation camps, selling them. Often, several persons are affected at the same time when they eat fish caught from the same school although, sometimes, only some of the fish are affected. Six members in one family might eat different fish and only one or two would get sick.

I attended a meeting of the Maui County Medical Society at which Dr. Jerome Conn spoke on hypoglycemia. He was an authority on this subject and had written a textbook and many medical papers on it.

Our family drove around the Island of Maui in Dottie's car one Sunday. We had lunch at Hana and then came home by Kaupo. The road was barely passable and we had to drive so slowly the engine overheated and the water boiled out of the radiator. There was no water available so we poured a thermos of iced tea in the radiator, enabling us to continue our trip until we reached a cattle watering trough on Ulupalakua Ranch.

I admitted a baby with a temperature of 109 degrees to the hospital. Usually, a person with such a high temperature died of meningitis but, as I recall, this one recovered. On another occasion, we admitted a field laborer to the hospital with a temperature of 108 degrees. He had been found unconscious with heat exhaustion in the hot and humid weather. He had been pushing tall cane to clear irrigation ditches. We packed him in ice, his temperature returned to normal and he soon recovered.

Dottie was sick with the flu for several days and I took the children to see the show "Hans Christian Anderson," starring Danny Kaye. Ten days later, I saw this delightful show again with Dottie.

I had wanted to take the children to Kauai for a week to complete my plans to show them the four major Hawaiian Islands. However, they preferred to go back to Honolulu. It had been two years since we were there together on vacation. We again stayed at the Royal Hawaiian Hotel seven days and six nights.

There were always many celebrities at the Royal and the children thought it was wonderful to see them. The beach boys arranged for us to be near them on the beach with our spread of towels and umbrellas. Once, we were next to Danny Kaye; another time, we were beside the Shah of Iran with his entourage.

We visited all the tourist attractions including the Bishop Museum, Capitol, zoo, aquarium, Honolulu Art Academy, library, Mormon Temple at Laie and Pearl Harbor. We ate dinner at many of the famous restaurants including Fisherman's Wharf, Halekulani Hotel, M's Ranch and the Tropics. We lunched at the Young Hotel, the Outrigger Canoe Club and the Liberty House. Most popular with the children was breakfast at Stewart's Pharmacy in Waikiki, with its famous ginger-bread pancakes and syrups. The girls and I took a ride at Waikiki Beach in an outrigger canoe and caught a big wave back onto the beach. We visited McLeod and Louise at their home on Judd Hillside and Neff and Jane in their home at Wahiawa. We returned home refreshed.

I took Dottie out to dinner on our wedding anniversay, August 17th. I gave her an orchid corsage, a bottle of perfume and a nightgown.

The golden plovers returned from Alaska on August 27th, six days later than the previous year. The children were happy to see them again.

One of my patients gave me a rear quarter of venison from a Molokai hunting trip. We shared it with six guests at dinner.

I had a patient develop eclampsia on September 15th and, finally, delivered her safely at 4 a.m. on the 16th. Such patients must be watched constantly and I was exhausted by the time she had her baby.

I asked Dr. Haywood to assist me in operating on a pregnant woman who was in her eighth month. I had diagnosed acute appendicitis but, instead, she had an acute gall bladder infection and I asked Dr. Haywood to take charge. He left the appendix and gallbladder in place and treated her with antibiotics. She recovered without complications.

I had a patient deliver her second baby after an easy labor at term. It died of cerebral hemorrhage when it was 48 hours old. There was no way I could have prevented this death, but it is very disturbing to all concerned to lose a normal baby.

Dottie and I were invited to the home of Mr. and Mrs. Ray Allen to meet Faith Baldwin, an American novelist of great distinction. She was a friend of Mrs. Allen.

Dr. Franklyn Payne, my professor of obstetrics and gynecology at the University of Pennsylvania, and his wife arrived on October 15th for four days. He spoke at a meeting of the Maui County Medical Society. We drove them to Lahaina and had dinner at the Banyan Inn. The next day, we went to Hana. He was head of the section of obstetrics and gynecology of the Pan Pacific Surgical Association and would be back to its next meeting in three years. I promised we would have an Hawaiian luau for them if they would visit us again.

We attended a concert at Baldwin Auditorium to hear Nan Merriman, an American mezzo-soprano of international fame.

Carol had an attack of pyelitis, the first of many. Her temperature rose to 106 degrees. Since her paralysis due to potassium deficiency, she had had chronic constipation. I think this caused blockage of her ureters, which led to the pyelitis. She had these attacks every few weeks and missed as much as a month of school each year. She was a very good student and still made high grades. By the time she reached high school, she had no more attacks. However, the attacks left their mark.

Dottie and I attended a piano concert by Grant Johanason. He was considered by musical authorities as a promising American pianist who would gain international fame and he did. Dottie and I saw him again, on television, about three years ago.

On November 28th, there was an accumulation of commercial airplanes at Kahului Airport. Heavy rains in Honolulu prevented the planes from landing there. We again had snow on Haleakala.

I had a 42-year-old patient develop high blood pressure when she was eight months into her tenth pregnancy. One evening, she developed acute heart failure. Thick white foam from her lungs flowed out her mouth and nose. After consultation, I removed one pint of blood and her heart failure improved immediately. The blood was saved in case she needed it later. Digitalis was started for her heart and I gave her oxygen by nasal tube continuously. The next day, labor was induced with intravenous pitocin drip. She had one tube in her nose and one in her arm for a day. She delivered within 10 hours without further complications.

I was on call again on Christmas Day. About noon, I had to rush 18 miles out the Hana road to an accident. An old army jeep, loaded with children, had run off the road and overturned. The driver was drunk. Two children were still pinned beneath the jeep when I arrived. Neither of them were breathing or had heart beats and they could not be revived.

THE YEAR 1955

The year began uneventfully, but that changed as the year progressed.

A young patient was almost a year old before the mother and I noticed that there was something wrong with her legs. She had a congenital dislocation of her hip. I referred her to Dr. Ivar Larsen of Shriners Hospital who treated her with good results. Only the mother of such a patient who must wear body and leg casts for many months can know the added work that is required to care for such a child. Dr. Larsen also put casts on another patient of mine who had multiple congenital deformities including bilateral club feet. I changed the casts between Dr. Larsen's visits.

Our cow, Hana, had a calf in January ensuring us an abundance of milk again.

We attended a concert at Baldwin Auditorium by Tossy Spivakovsky, a noted violinist.

We entertained Dame Flora MacLeod of MacLeod at a luncheon in our home in February, which I have already discussed in the Heritage Section.

Ann joined the Wailuku Union Church on April 3rd, her 14th birthday.

Dr. William Kirby, professor of internal medicine at the University of Washington, spoke to the Maui County Medical Society. He and his wife spent three days with us in our home and we were to visit them later in the year. They were young and very delightful people with several small children.

I delivered 35 babies in April, seven for Dr. Burden who was away.

Dottie and I went to Honolulu and I attended the annual meeting of the Hawaii Medical Association. On the way to our hotel in Waikiki from the airport, we were involved in a traffic accident. The driver just ahead of me suddenly stopped in front of one of the piers and opened the wide door of a Mercury convertible without looking back. The door extended out into my traffic lane and was struck by the right front fender of the car I was driving. There was only slight damage. The police ruled that he was at fault and his insurance company had to pay for my car repairs. I telephoned the U-drive company and was brought another car. On the last day of the meeting, I played golf in the Medical Association's annual tournament at the Oahu Country Club.

CHAPTER X

Eleven Weeks Historic America Tour:
June 11 to August 26, 1955

Dottie and I had promised the children that, as soon as Carol was nine, we would take them on an historic America tour. Because of our isolation, we thought that the children should see some of our great country. We made many preparations. We left from the old Puunene airport for Honolulu at 8 a.m. on Saturday, June 11th. My pockets were bulging with thousands of dollars worth of tickets, reservations and cash. Our friends saw us off and put leis around our necks. I had told a patient I had five girls, so she brought us seven large carnationa leis. She thought I meant I had five daughters; Dottie was one of my 'girls.'

Our flight was delayed eight hours in Honolulu, as the United Airline's DC 6 that we were to leave on had to be completely inspected. It had a major overhaul just before the trip from Denver to Honolulu and required extra time for a thorough check, we were told. The day was spent with McLeod and Louise. We finally left at 7 p.m. and arrived in Los Angeles at 8 the following morning. I had assumed that because it was summer I would need only lightweight clothes and that is all I had with me. The temperature was 55 degrees in Los Angeles and all of us were very cold.

We checked into the Biltmore Hotel and slept all morning. In the afternoon, we took a limousine tour of the city, through Beverly Hills and by the homes of many movie stars. Several movie studios were on our route. We went down Hollywood Boulevard and saw the footprints of the movie stars in the cement in front of Grumman's Theater.

Our flight to Chicago Monday morning was on a DC 7 and took three and a half hours. We stayed at the Drake Hotel in Chicago. Our friends, Odie and Bill Gimbel, invited us to dinner at their town house. They had three sons about the ages of our daughters.

On Tuesday Dr. Holmblad took us sightseeing in the morning. We saw the Bahai Temple, which is one of the most beautiful buildings we have ever seen. Odie Gimbel was chairperson of a Chicago charity benefit drive that was held at the Riverside Amusement Park. She took our family to the park for dinner. Afterward, the children enjoyed the rides and other activities.

After breakfast at the Drake Hotel on Wednesday, we saw a live television show in the Tribune Building. Following the show, there was a sightseeing visit to the roof of the building. In the afternoon we attended the New York Giants-Chicago Cubs baseball game. Willie Mays hit a home run and played his usual stellar game much to the chagrin of our hosts, the Holmblads. The Giants won 7 to 2. In the evening we had dinner at the Swedish Club with the Holmblads.

Next morning, we went sightseeing and also visited the Rosenwald Museum of Science and Industry. I visited Dr. W. J. Dieckman at the Chicago Lying-In-Hospital. He was the leading authority on high blood pressure and pregnancy and I discussed some of my ideas with him. We had dinner at the Normandy House with the Holmblads.

We were up at 5 a.m. on June 17th and took an early flight to Flint, Michigan. We ran into a thunderstorm over Lake Michigan, which was a frightening surprise to everyone. We did not have our seat belts fastened and amid a flash of lightning and great turbulence we almost hit the ceiling of the plane. We could see storm clouds a few miles away.

We were in Flint to pick up our new car and got it by 2 p.m. We had ordered it in March through our dealer on Maui. I had looked at all the new cars and chose the one that I thought would best fit our needs on this trip. It was a beautiful, light blue Roadmaster Buick sedan; we named her Bluebelle. I had brought a set of Hawaii license plates with me. It proved to be a good car. We drove it 139,000 miles in 10 years without having the engine overhauled, valves ground or other major repairs. We did not have to change the muffler or radiator. Four daughters learned to drive using Bluebelle.

We drove direct from Flint to Lansing, Michigan, to see Warren Mason who was in a hospital there. He had been a supervisor on the plantation at Puunene and was our neighbor on Maui. He had bought a new car in Flint and, while driving across the country, had attempted to pass a large truck and trailer near Lansing. He hit an oncoming truck and his new car was totally demolished. Warren suffered a broken leg. When we saw him the weather was very hot. He was in bed with his leg in traction and appeared to be miserable. We visited him for 30 minutes. That evening I wrote his wife a letter.

We continued our trip and spent the night in Toledo, Ohio. We left early next morning and reached Dottie's home in Lewistown, Pennsylvania, at 10:40 p.m. Next day, I had a migraine headache from fatigue, but recovered with a day's rest.

We spent a week at Lewistown visiting Dottie's mother, four sisters and brother. During this week we went to a cheese factory at Belleville, in the heart of Amish country. The weather was very hot and I still remember the unusual, offensive odor in this factory. We also visited Juanita College at Huntington and Pennsylvania State College, and went to Danville and saw all our friends at Geisinger Hospital. We visited the zoo and amusement park at Hershey and toured the Capitol at Harrisburg. We had dinner with our friends, Dr. and Mrs. Charles Wilbar. He had been secretary of the Board of Health in Hawaii and now had this same position with the State of Pennsylvania.

Jo and Tony Artman, Dottie's sister and her husband, arranged a playday and picnic for all of us on the farm adjoining their home at Spruce Creek. All the neighbors's children were invited. A wagon loaded with bales of hay with the children on top, was pulled by a tractor across the farm and down a road through the Valley of Little Pines by Spruce Creek. This creek is famous for trout fishing and is where Presidents Eisenhower and Carter often went fishing. The children played baseball in a meadow. The local boys were surprised to see how well the Patterson girls could play and were horrified to see them barefooted in the grass. There were snakes in the area, but the girls had not been warned not to take off their shoes. After the ballgame, chicken was barbecued. We all enjoyed the night with the Artmans.

The next morning, Monday, June 27th, we drove on the Pennsylvania Turnpike to Valley Forge and toured the area. We went on to Philadelphia arriving in time to visit Independence Hall and the Liberty Bell. We saw Pennsylvania Hospital and the apartment on Clinton Street where Dottie and I lived when I was a resident at the hospital.

On Tuesday morning, I observed Dr. Payne do several operations at the University of Pennsylvania Hospital. In the afternoon our family visited the Ben Franklin Institute, the Museum of Natural History and the Philadelphia Art Museum. We had dinner with Dr. and Mrs. Payne at the Philadelphia Country Club.

The next morning, we visited the zoo and the Betsy Ross House, where the first American flag was made. After lunch, we drove to Ocean City, New Jersey, and saw the children's camp where I had been the doctor for 10 weeks when I was a senior medical student. I showed the children the narrow inlet south of Ocean City, where I almost drowned. We then drove to Somer's Point and spent the night with Paul and Vivian Cameron.

During the war, Paul developed tuberculosis in the lower lobes of both lungs. This was discovered just after he entered Paris when it was recaptured by our troops. His recovery was slow and required many years. While he was a patient in the hospital, someone gave him two tropical fish which fascinated him. He ordered books from the library and learned everything that was known about them. Finally, he was discharged from the hospital to rest at home for a year.

His home at Somer's Point had a basement under the entire first floor. He filled it with fish tanks and soon developed a thriving business raising and selling tropical fish although Vivian did most of the work. The public water supply did not agree with the fish so they put a large tank in their car and Vivian imported pure water. They flooded the New York City and Philadelphia markets with tropical fish, making enough money to support their family until he was able to return to work practicing medicine. As I recall, this was more than $1,000 per month.

On Thursday, June 30th, we left early for Atlantic City, only a few miles away, and spent two hours on the boardwalk. We saw the famous Steel Pier and other places of amusement where Paul and I had spent many evenings in 1935. The weather was hot and the children were anxious to go swimming in the Atlantic Ocean to cool off. They changed into their swim suits and went into the water. Five minutes were enough. They were shocked by the cold water, being used to the warmer Pacific Ocean. We then drove to Lewistown in six and a half hours.

On July 1st we were off early and soon reached Gettysburg, Pennsylvania, and toured the battlegrounds where the Confederate Army had retreated in disarray. We drove on to Leesburg, Virginia, and saw our friends, Bennie and Jack Lightner. Next morning, we drove to Upperville and visited Amelia Lightner, Dr. Lightner's widow. She was still operating the large farm, but had a manager to help her. Dr. Lightner had died a few years earlier of cancer that had developed from x-ray burns on his hands. We then drove down the scenic Skyline Drive in the Appalachian Mountains and reached Chapel Hill, North Carolina, at 9 that evening.

We spent nine days in North Carolina and visited many relatives and friends. The weather was hot with temperatures in the mid 90s. In Chapel Hill we saw a show at the Moorehead Planetarium. Ann and Carol were examined by the head of the dental school, to whom they had been referred by our local dentist because of the congenital absence of several teeth. The children saw the campus where I had gone to college and medical school for two years. We drove to Coats and saw the house on Patterson Street where I was reared, the cemetery on the next block where my father and brother, Preston, were buried and the school that I attended as a child. In Durham we went through the Chesterfield cigarette factory and visited Ralph and Sue Fleming.

We drove to Sanford and attended a stock sale at my brother Orus's meat packing plant. He bought and processed about one fourth of the cattle sold at these sales. We then went to Laurinburg, N.C., via Southern Pines, where we visited Dr. and Mrs. Robert McMillian. He was an intern at Geisinger Hospital while I was a resident and his wife had been a surgical nurse there. Tom Parker, my brother-in-law at Laurinburg, had had a stroke and now had footdrop. I measured him for a leg brace and, later, bought one for him in Durham.

We went to Kinston, N.C., for the weekend and I heard Marcus preach twice on Sunday. In Fayetteville we saw Bruce and Helen Langdon. We showed the children the old slave market located in the town square where, less than 100 years before, human beings were sold as slaves. Our children could not believe this had actually happened.

We spent the following weekend at Orus's beach cottage near Southport and Fort Caswell. To get there, we passed a factory that made fertilizer from fish. For two miles before and after, there was the most pungent odor in the air that I have ever smelled.

On July 19th we left for Williamsburg, Virginia, where we stayed for two days. We rented an entire small, restored house that was originally a boarding house. We went to Jamestown and in the evening saw the play, "The Common Glory." Next day in Williamsburg, we went into the eight historic buildings. This was my first visit to Williamsburg which had been restored after I became an adult. Every American youth should visit Colonial Williamsburg. It was the Capitol of Virginia, the largest and most populous of the original colonies. Here, leaders from all the colonies met and formulated the ideas that led to freedom from England and the birth of a new nation.

We drove to Yorktown on July 21st and saw where Lord Charles Cornwallis surrendered to General George Washington, ending the Revolutionary War. From there we went to Mount Vernon and took a tour of the home of George Washington. We next saw the Change of the Guard at the Grave of the Unknown Soldier at Arlington Cemetery and then visited Robert E. Lee's mansion nearby.

We spent three days and four nights in Washington at the Shoreham Hotel and visited with Uncle Leon and Page three of the evenings. On the first day we toured the White House, Lincoln Memorial, Washington Monument, Freer Art Museum, the Capitol and the Bureau of Engraving. At the mint we saw stamps and green dollar bills of different denominations being made. We visited Hawaii's delegate to Congress, Mrs. Betty Farrington.

In the evening, we had a picnic in a park with Neill and his family. He was stationed at Andrews Air Force Base and lived in Maryland. On the second day, we saw the Supreme Court building, Folger Shakespeare Library, Library of Congress, National Art Gallery and the Smithsonian Institute. In the Library of Congress the girls saw the original copies of the three great documents that form the foundation of the United States of America: the Declaration of Independence, the Constitution and the Bill of Rights. Uncle Leon had tickets for us to see the Ballet Russe de Monte Carlo at Rock Creek Park in the evening. On the third day, we visited the Franciscan Monastery and saw the Family of Man at the Corcoran Art Gallery. We had dinner with Neill and Pearl in their home and met a first cousin, Genevieve Patterson, from Broadway, N.C., who worked in Washington.

Early on July 25th we went into the Pan American Union Building and then drove to Annapolis, Maryland, where we saw the Naval Academy. We continued on to New York City and registered at the Statler Hotel. The first evening we attended the Broadway musical, "Pajama Game." The girls loved it and soon knew all the songs. They bought records of them, which they still have. The second day we went through the United Nations Building and were most impressed. Afterward, we went up to the roof of the Empire State Building for a panoramic view of New York City. In the afternoon we visited St. John the Divine Cathedral with its beautiful architecture. This building has not been completed, though construction began more than 50 years ago. In the evening we saw the Broadway musical, "Plain and Fancy," a story about the Pennsylvania Dutch.

In the morning of the third day we went shopping at Lord and Taylors where summer clothes had been put on sale. Dottie found each girl and herself beautiful dresses at greatly reduced prices. This was really a bonanza, as the clothes were suitable for wearing year 'round in Hawaii. In the afternoon we went to a baseball game between the New York Yankees and the Chicago White Sox, which the Sox won 7 to 2.

In the evening, we saw a play on Broadway, "Tea House of the August Moon." After many years on Broadway, this play was made into a movie which Dottie and I saw on Maui in 1957. The scenes for the movie were shot in Japan at the Fujiya Hotel in Hakone National Park, 56 miles (96 km) west of Tokyo. When Dottie and I were in Tokyo in May, 1985, our host, Dr. Yukie Nakaizumi, took us by taxi to this hotel for lunch which was served in the Tea House of the August Moon. We had delicious trout that had been caught in nearby Lake Ashi. We saw the exact scenes of the hotel that are shown in the movie and we took our own pictures of them. Dr. Nakaizumi had taken his family to this spa on vacation for many years. The proprietor led us on a personalized tour of the hotel, including its mineral baths and gardens. We then toured Hakone Park.

On the fourth day in New York City, we went shopping at Macy's Department Store and I bought a 50mm (2 in.) telescope. In the afternoon we took a scenic boat trip around the Island of Manhattan, passing by Ellis Island and the Statue of Liberty.

I had learned how to get theater tickets. By going to the theatre box offices a few days in advance I could usually get tickets. If they were sold out I would try the agent in the hotel. If I had no luck there, I would return to the box office at 5 p.m. on the day we wanted to go and, usually, some tickets would have been returned. Occasionally I would be told to come back at 6 or 7. This system has worked for me in many cities throughout the world where we have traveled. Frequently in New York we had to buy expensive box seats, but the girls loved sitting in these seats.

We had only five evenings in the city and wanted to make the best use of our time. On this fourth evening we saw "The Boy Friend" with Julie Andrews as the leading lady. Thereafter, she became a leading star and played in many movies including "The Sound of Music" in the 60s. In 1987 she was featured with Placido Domingo, the great Spanish tenor, and John Denver, a popular American singer, in "The Sound of Christmas," a wonderful Christmas presentation.

We went shopping at Altman's Department Store in the morning of our fifth day. We bought a rug for our library and had it shipped direct to Kahului, Maui, from New York City Harbor. We also bought a large, aquamarine-colored, glass fish, almost 24 inches long. It had been made in Florida. I brought it home in the car, which was fast becoming overloaded.

In the afternoon we took a tour of the Radio City building. That evening we saw the Rockettes perform on the stage in Radio City Music Hall and then saw the movie, "Mr. Roberts." Every evening at the theaters, ours were the only children we saw. Many people looked at us as though we didn't know that children should be in bed at this time of night. One taxi driver even told us so.

On our sixth and final day in the city, we visited the Metropolitan Museum of Art, the Museum of Natural Science and saw a show at the Hayden Planetarium. We left at 3 p.m. for Milford, Pennsylvania, to visit my sister, Dorothy, and her family. Her husband, Jack Thornton, owned an insurance agency there although he was planning to sell it and return to school for his Ph.D. in economics.

We left the next day for Connecticut, driving past the Military Academy at West Point, N.Y., in its beautiful setting on a bluff overlooking the Hudson river. As we drove up the East Coast from North Carolina to Maine and then across the northern U.S. border to the West Coast, we visited and took pictures of every State Capitol. We did not have hotel reservations along the way and avoided the large cities as much as possible. The first night we stayed at a motel near Hartford, Connecticut. The next morning, we drove through Providence, Rhode Island, and then Boston. The third day, we went through Concord, New Hampshire, and on to Augusta, Maine.

We spent the night in a motel at Lancaster, N.H. The temperature was cool compared to the weather we had had in the East. Next day there was an early morning mist covering the fir, spruce and hemlock trees on the rolling hills. It was a beautiful sight and reminded me of a Japanese painting. After suffering in the heat of the South and being in the busy cities of the East, we were enjoying ourselves tremendously in this beautiful, peaceful region.

We entered Vermont early next day and saw the Rock of Ages Granite Mines at Barre. We bought a gallon of famous Vermont maple syrup, adding more weight to our car. We were soon in New York State and reached Lake Champlain, which took an hour to cross by ferry. We landed at Fort Ticonderoga, the area in which the French and Indian wars had been fought from 1750 to '60. This is where General George Washington got the experience that readied him for his role in leading the colonists to success in the American Revolution.

I was anxious to get to Lewistown for a good rest before we left for the West Coast. After we toured Fort Ticonderoga we drove on to Lake George for the night. When we arrived at 5 p.m., we were rudely surprised. The town was teeming with cars and people from New York City. Not an empty hotel or motel room was to be found and we finally rented an entire four-bedroom house for the night. We were up and off early next morning and had breakfast in Albany, lunch at Binghamton and reached Lewistown at 7:30 p.m. During the previous four days we had driven through some of the most beautiful scenery in America. It was Grandma Moses country, which she depicted so well in her paintings.

We spent six days in the Lewistown area, the weather nice and cool for August. We visited all Dottie's relatives again and spent the last night with Jo and Tony at Spruce Creek. After dark, Tony took the girls and me in the car, turned off the lights and drove across an alfalfa field. When he turned on the lights, we saw about 20 deer eating the alfalfa. Needless to say, deer hunting was good in the winter.

We left at 7 on the morning of August 9th for the West Coast, driving on the Pennsylvania Turnpike through Pittsburgh and on to Oberlin, Ohio, where we toured Oberlin College. From there, we drove to Wakeman and visited Dr. and Mrs. Allan Cranston. He was the commanding Army medical officer on Maui when the war started and we had become good friends. We spent the night at Napoleon, Ohio.

The next day we drove across the states of Indiana and Illinois and reached Madison, Wisconsin, for the night. We saw the Capitol and the University and bought famous Wisconsin cheese to add to our load.

On August 11th we drove to Minneapolis, Minnesota, and spent one day with Rose and Pete Peterson. Rose had been the head nurse and nurse-anesthetist at Pahala and Puunene Hospitals. She was a very close friend and a second mother to our girls. Pete was the editor of the editorial page of the Minneapolis Star Tribune newspaper. He married Rose after his first wife, Rose's sister, had died. Their home was on Lake Minnetonka, where we went swimming. Wild rice grows in the marshes around the lakes in this region and we purchased some to bring with us. While there, we went to St. Paul and saw the Capitol.

The following day we reached Bismark, North Dakota, and stayed at the Bismark Motor Hotel. I can remember seeing the tall Capitol building standing high above the surrounding plains as we approached the city. It was beautiful country. We continued on to Forsyth, Montana where we had dinner with the Fred Zempel family, Anita Haywood's parents and visited Dr. Haywood's father, also a physician. Next morning we took a tour of Zempel's 17,000-acre ranch. He said at times he leased more ranch land from the government. We were able to drive our Buick across the ranch, sometimes where there were no roads.

I was interested to know how he could be a successful rancher in such a barren area that is sometimes subjected to extremely low temperatures. The land supported only one head of cattle for each 10 acres. He fenced in his land and divided it into highland and bottoms, or meadows, along the streams. In the summer there was always good grass on the highlands and he kept the cattle there. The bottom lands produced an abundance of hay, which he cut, cured and stored in haystacks. In the winter the cattle were kept in the low areas which were protected from the strong winds. If the ground was covered with heavy snow for long periods, he would feed the hay to the cattle. Sometimes, he would be forced to buy feed. When we were there, he said he had not used any of the hay from the haystacks for three years. He had kept hay as long as seven years. By this time, it begins to rot, but the cattle still relish it.

He showed me a small, four-inch tall cactus-like plant, called salt sage, that grew in large bunches throughout his ranch. It had a high protein and salt content and the cattle loved it. It did not die in the winter time. After the grass had been depleted, the cattle survived on salt sage. They knew how to find it, even under a few inches of snow.

As we drove across the ranch, an occasional group of antelope with white rumps bounced across the plain. Zempel said he would shoot one or two each year for meat, as well as an occasional deer. There was a high-powered rifle on the floor of his car, which I assumed was for this purpose. He explained that he was still in Wild West Country and on the frontier and needed the rifle for protection. There were cattle rustlers, both big operators with trucks and small operators, who would hit him occasionally. He had to be prepared for any encounter when he was alone and miles from the sheriff.

With such a large ranch, one would expect him to have many head of cattle, but he was careful not to overstock. Usually he had an abundance of feed. If there were a drought he would not suffer severely and could survive. If the winters were harsh he had enough feed for many months and needed to buy only a small quantity for each emergency. He always had less than 1,000 head of cattle, selling off the two-year olds in the fall and building up the herd with the birth of the calves in the spring.

From Forsyth, we drove to Red Lodge, Montana, for the night. That evening we attended a folk festival which depicted life in that area many years ago. Our girls won a prize for being the farthest from home.

On August 15th we entered Yellowstone National Park which was filled with tourists. I waited an hour in line to get a camper cabin, which I thought would be fun and a good experience for the girls. Finally I gave up and took the last two double rooms in Old Faithful Inn. Old Faithful Geyser could be seen from our windows.

We were up soon after daylight and went out to inspect Old Faithful. Suddenly, a storm developed with cracks of lightning nearby, loud thunder and a heavy downpour of rain and hail. The ground was soon covered with ice.

After we entered the park, we saw many wild animals, including bear, buffalo, moose, elk and deer. We observed the sulfur banks, steam vents, geysers, hot, bubbling, mud pools and other phenomenon in the park before leaving at the north entrance.

The day before we entered Yellowstone, a passing motorist pointed to one of our tires. I stopped and found it had a large blister on its wall so I put on the spare tire. We left Yellowstone and drove to Butte, Montana, where we saw the large, copper mine. There, I found a second tire defective and the other two had small blisters on them.

When we left North Carolina, Orus had given us a country-cured ham which we brought with us and I realized at this time that we had overloaded the car. The Roadmaster Buick was heavy itself. The six in our family plus the luggage was too much weight for the tires. We had bought items all across the country and added to our load. Finally, the tires gave out. I had to buy four new, nylon tires, which depleted my cash.

We drove on to Anaconda for the night and saw the large copper mine there.

Carol developed a slight temperature elevation and showed signs of illness. I gave her a course of Gantrisin and she soon recovered. We had been lucky she had not had a recurrence of severe pyelitis that had plagued her for several years.

We drove through Coeur d'Alene, Idaho, and went on to Spokane, Washington, stopping at a launderette to do our laundry. We spent the night in Ritzville. We were in the second half of August and fall was approaching. The temperature reached 85 to 90 degrees in the daytime, but dropped to 50 to 55 at night.

Next day we drove across broad, dry plains covered with wheat fields. I usually thought of Seattle and rain when Washington State was mentioned, though I knew much of Hawaii's grain for animal feed came from the state. We reached Seattle at 1 p.m. and got settled in a motel on the edge of the city. The sun was shining brightly, the first time it had been seen in Seattle for weeks. We rested in the afternoon and then had dinner with Professor William Kirby and his family, who had visited us at Puunene earlier in the year.

We visited an outstanding Indian museum the next day at the University of Washington. In the afternoon we took a boat trip on Lake Washington, that seemed to encircle Seattle. I remember seeing locks on a canal but I can't recall if we went through them. Again, we had dinner with the Kirbys.

On August 20th we drove to the upper level of the Mount Rainier Naitonal Park, travelling through beautiful rain forests of all shades of green and along rapidly flowing, pristine, mountain streams. Finally we were above the timber line and could see many glaciers. The children played in the snow at the side of the road. We could see silent Mount St. Helens in the distance. The scenery was breath-taking. In the afternoon we drove through Portland, Oregon, and on to Salem for the night.

Next morning we were soon in Eugene and took a good look at the University of Oregon. We drove on to Crescent City, California, where we spent the night. The weather was cool, the coastline was rugged and the ocean was rough. It was hard to believe this was California. This fishing village was more typical of those found on the North East coast. It had seen better days.

We had had a nice drive through Oregon and on to Crescent City, through beautiful redwood forests where we were awed by the tall trees. Driving the next morning was much different. It was Monday and this was timber country. Large trucks and trailers loaded with huge logs filled the highways. They could not go fast and there was very little opportunity to pass them. If one kept a safe distance behind them, an impatient driver would try to pass and get into the space. Our Buick had plenty of power, so I would not allow anyone to pass us and take my place. I would pass the timber truck at the first safe opportunity. It was a long day. When we finally reached Ukiah we stayed in a motel which was beside a drive-in theater. The screen for the picture was in plain view from our motel, which pleased the girls.

We arrived in San Francisco on August 23rd and our flight to Honolulu was not for another three days. I had not known when we would arrive, so I had not made hotel reservations. I felt sure we could get a room at the Cliff Hotel on Union Square, where we had stayed before, and, if not there, at the St. Francis. I was wrong. Every room was taken. We finally settled for a second-class hotel nearby and my family has never let me forget it.

We took a boat trip around San Francisco Bay the day we arrived and got a good look at the Golden Gate Bridge and the many large salt ponds.

Next morning we took a Grayline tour of the city. Later in the day we drove to Redwood City, where McLeod lived, and on to Aptos to see Mildred Nordman. She was the artist who had visited us in Puunene.

Finally on August 25th, we turned our car into the Matson freight office to be shipped to Maui. We spent the rest of the day shopping, buying two antique, hand-carved wooden Chinese wallpaper rollers from Gumps store. Both rollers had designs of leaves and flowers on them; one was of lotus. We had Gumps make them into table lamps which have become more beautiful with time.

McLeod came to the San Francisco airport to see us on August 26th. We left for Honolulu at 9:45 a.m. and arrived at 2:30 p.m. We finally reached Maui about four o'clock. We had been gone exactly 11 weeks and had driven our new car 10,500 miles. We had shown our daughters the most important historic parts of our country, some of which Dottie and I saw for the first time. I kept a diary of five lines each day, which was enough to help Dottie and me recall the things we had done. I did not keep a record of the money we spent, but I know that there was no better way that we could have spent it. All our children say this trip was the greatest event that occurred in their young lives. They have fond memories of every part of it. Carol was only nine years old, but seems to have remembered more of the trip than her older sisters.

CHAPTER XI

Plantation Medicine and Life at Puunene: September, 1955, to June, 1958

We arrived home Friday, August 26th, and I worked in the office Saturday morning. I played golf in the afternoon and also had the horses shod. By Monday I was back in the swing of work, delivering twins and two more babies that day. I went horseback riding after work.

The telescope that we bought in New York arrived. We first looked at the full moon but the telescope was too strong for this. Our 7x49 binoculars showed the moon better. Two nights later, I focused the telescope on one of the brightest objects in the sky, Saturn. The rings were plainly visible. This was a great thrill, the first time I had seen Saturn through a telescope. Thereafter, we invited many friends to our home to view the planets with us. Our front yard had two or more acres without obstruction and there were no street lights to interfere. Soon we could see Mars with its red spot on one side and its many moons. When we watched for about 10 minutes, we saw a moon come out from behind the planet and then another that had been visible disappeared. In December we were able to see Jupiter, the band that encircles it, and its four moons. We also saw Venus, which at times appeared just like our new moon. I had had a course in astronomy in college, so this was fun for me. The children also enjoyed using the telescope and learned something about the planets.

I was too busy to devote much time to astronomy. This was before the days of satellites, astronauts and the many uses of rockets. I loaned the telescope to young Don Hughes who pursued astronomy and physics on into college. Finally I gave the telescope to my son-in-law, Peter Keck, who taught school at South Kent School for Boys. He no longer teaches but has identical 12-year-old twin boys who enjoy using it.

I did a cesarean for placenta previa on Labor Day. The patient required five pints of blood to replace what she had lost. I also delivered two other babies on this day.

On September 20, 1955, polio vaccine became available for public use. I gave a talk on the radio regarding its value and use.

The plantation experimented with hundreds of young geese for grass control in the cane fields. I had seen geese used in cotton fields in the South for this purpose and they did a good job. After a few months the experiment was dropped and the geese were sold to the employees. I bought six. When they were grown we ate them although we did not care for the meat as it was too greasy.

The Plantation Physician Association's annual meeting was again held on Maui from November 10th to 12th. Dr. Compere was the visiting professor. He and his wife stayed in our guest cottage. We had a busy three days, which included a trip to Hana.

Dottie and I attended a viola concert by William Primrose, said to be the best viola player in the world at that time. He was Scottish and had been knighted by the Queen of England. He died in 1982.

The year got off to the usual start. I delivered the first baby of the year on Maui at 1 a.m. after having delivered two babies in the afternoon of December thirty-first. We had dinner with friends in the evening, which meant I started the New Year tired.

Lois, Dottie, Dottie Jane, Carol, Ann, Christmas 1956 .

All our family attended a piano recital given by Lois's piano teacher at Baldwin Auditorium on January 15th. Lois also played.

Bill and Odie Gimbel of Chicago were with us for two days. We had a dinner party for them Saturday evening. On Sunday morning, I arranged with a friend for us to use his private range for pistol target practice.

Our dog, Bonn, became ill with heartworm. In Hawaii the larvae of this worm are transmitted from infected dogs by mosquitoes. Eventually, the worms develop to a large size in the dog's heart and cause death from heart failure. Few dogs live more than 12 years after becoming infected although there is a medication that will kill the larvae in the blood stream if it is given continuously. Bonn died within a year.

On May 11th, we had Dr. and Mrs. Frederick Reichert, Dr. and Mrs. Al Burden and Dr. and Mrs. Mathurin Dondo for dinner. Dr. Reichert was the former professor of neurosurgery at Stanford. He had retired and built a large home on the beach at Kihei. Dr. Dondo had come from France originally and now lived on the beach at Maalaea. He had taught French at several American universities and had written a basic French grammar textbook that was used in Hawaii public schools for many years.

Dr. Dondo had taught at Pennsylvania State University for a while. To get there, he would go by train to Lewistown, Dottie's home town, and then by car the 40 miles to Penn State. Once his trunk of clothes was stolen from the train station at Lewistown. A few years later he was apprehended by the police after a person wearing one of his suits had committed a murder. Dr. Dondo had had the suit tailor-made in Paris and his name was on a label in the inside coat pocket. The police

184

traced him through the tailor in Paris. He was not charged with the murder.

The use of marionettes was one of Dr. Dondo's hobbies and he was very skillful with them. He introduced them wherever he went in the United States. He put on a show in his home for our children whenever we visited him.

Dr. Dondo was very much influenced by the French Impressionist School of Art. When he was a young man, he knew Monet who was one of the originators of this new art form. He decided he would develop his own technique of brush strokes and worked many hours daily developing his own methods. He painted many beautiful pictures which graced the walls of every room of his home. He became so possessed by the technique that he had to give up painting, saying he would have gone mad had he continued.

An interesting anecdote he told was about the first time he was introduced to eating corn-on-the-cob. He had been invited to dinner soon after he arrived in the United States and was served corn-on-the-cob. He said in France corn was only fed to livestock and he couldn't believe that animal food had been served. He did not know what to do with it. When he saw the other diners take an ear and bite off the corn, he was shocked. In later years, he enjoyed relating this story.

I did an autopsy on a 30-year old minister. While preaching in the pulpit, he complained of headache, sat down, and died within a few minutes. He had a ruptured aneurysm of the Circle of Willis at the based of his brain.

Dr. Michael De Bakey, a pioneer in arterial surgery, was invited to lecture to the Maui County Medical Society. He and his wife spent two days with us. Instead of going sightseeing with his wife, he preferred to just relax in the peace and quiet of our home. I asked him to examine a patient who came to our home. Later, he operated on the patient in Dallas, putting an arterial prosthesis in his leg The patient made a complete recovery and was able to walk and play golf. However, five years later, he died of a heart attack.

There were rumors that Puunene Hospital and Dispensary would close due to the rising cost of operation. The doctors would be provided land in Kahului to build their own office building and would then contract their service to the plantation, including laboratory services, x-ray and drugs. I saw there was a good opportunity to start a real group practice with all the doctors participating rather than working individually in association with the other doctors, as we had been doing. I suggested we call ourselves the Maui Clinic and get on with the organization of the group. We had our first meeting in June to discuss these possibilities.

Dottie and I had our last hospital picnic on June 24, 1956, with over 300 present. It was a joy to see everyone have so much fun. Over 30 years later, some of those who attended still tell us about the good times they had at our home.

The last patients were admitted to Puunene Hospital on July 17th. I delivered my first baby at Maui Memorial Hospital on July 21st. It had been slightly over nine years since I had recommended to Frank Baldwin that he join other community agencies and build and operate a community hospital using Hill-Burton funds. Instead, the plantation had spent $535,000 to renovate and build additions to Puunene Hospital. Now, seven years later, the hospital was closed. The older structures could be demolished, but some new use would have to be found for the new permanent buildings.

Instead of having a community-operated hospital, we now had the County of Maui operating our only hospital. In the past, the County had done a poor job operating Malulani Hospital and now, with a new building, it continued its inefficiency. Eventually, the hospital was operated by the State Board of Health. There was no end to the bureaucratic red tape and the problems that this created. Even as I write this, there is agitation to establish a community agency to own and operate the hospital but this seems impossible.

I did my first operation at Maui Memorial Hospital on July 27th. I offered to be chairman of the medical records committee after discovering there were no medical records of the patients that had been treated. There were a few nurse's notes, depending on the conscience of the nurse. There were laboratory reports, but no x-ray reports. Within six months I had the records improved so they could pass inspection by the American Hospital Association and the American College of Surgeons.

On August 4th our close family friend, Maybelle Hughes, married Dr. Phillip Helfrich, a marine biologist. We had the reception in our home. Dottie had arranged beautiful floral decorations and it was a lovely occasion.

Our farm at Kula was very productive, though it required a lot of work. I brought home two bushels of plums once and, at another time, two gallons of strawberries. I brought home a car load of flowers twice weekly. It was a chore getting rid of everything.

I took a two-week vacation starting on August 13th. I still delivered any of my nonplantation patients who went into labor. By the 21st, I had delivered nine patients since the 13th. Dottie and I then went to Honolulu for five days and stayed at the Princess Kaiulani Hotel. We saw some shows, spent time on the beach, visited friends, went shopping and ate at many fancy restaurants.

One of my patients who was six months pregnant had an appendiceal abscess. I operated on her and she recovered. It appears that I had many pregnant patients develop appendicitis. Actually, the average would be much less than one half of one percent of the women I delivered. Only one proved not to have appendicitis. She had an acute gallbladder infection which I have already described.

Dottie and I attended a piano concert at Baldwin Auditorium by Leonard Pennario. He was a brilliant young American pianist, who won international acclaim.

On October 13th, the Brooklyn Dodgers baseball team played a group of all-stars at the Maui County Fair.

President Eisenhower won his second term by a landslide on November 6th. As I have already said, I felt he was being a martyr to the cause. He had earned retirement and rest, but our country felt he should continue as President. Many people thought the job was too strenuous for one who already had suffered one heart attack.

I went to the annual meeting of the Plantation Physician's Association on Kauai in November. I gave a talk on high blood pressure and pregnancy (toxemia of pregnancy). I had nothing new to offer, but reviewed my theories as to its cause.

I heard Dr. R. J. McArthur, a Maui physician, preach at the Wailuku Union Church on alcoholism from the viewpoint of a recovered alcoholic. His sermon was excellent, as only a recovered alcoholic could give. The Reverend Richard Ritter had counseled him. He also counseled our children as teenagers, when they were groping for ethical and moral codes to live by. Dottie and I, and others, consider him a saint. He died on March 19, 1989, at age 94.

The Reicherts owned a very old Steinway grand piano which had a marvelous tone. As I recall, it was made about 1880. Because it was being damaged by the salt spray in their home at the beach, Mrs. Reichert suggested we keep it in our home. We paid the Reicherts the $200 freight charge for sending it from California to Maui. We kept it about four years during which time Dottie Jane and Carol were taking piano lessons and enjoyed playing this piano.

I went to Honolulu in December and bought a beautiful 6.27 carat opal, which was used as a setting for a ring for Dottie. It had six diamonds on the sides. Luckily, it arrived on December 24th and I gave it to her immediately. I had never been financially able to give her a large diamond, but this was a good substitute.

THE YEAR 1957

The new year was routine with nothing exciting happening early. Later, my diary states, I delivered a baby in the home of a mother who had chicken pox. I had forgotten about this and always said I had never intentionally had any home deliveries. Some accidentally delivered at home before they could leave for the hospital but we transferred those to the hospital as soon as possible.

Sunday, January 27th, was Youth Sunday in our church and Lois preached the sermon. She described her life up to age 17 and what a happy home-life had meant to her.

Lois played in another piano recital at Baldwin Auditorium given by the students of Mrs. Claire Nashiwa.

On March 9th, we had another tidal wave. The water rose several feet and came across the streets in Kahului, but there was little damage.

We had dinner with Karl and Pansy Heyer. Karl had started working for the plantation stores at the time I joined the plantation and was one of my best friends. He had never been promoted in 17 years, though there was now a job opening for which he was well qualified. He resigned and, with his brother-in-law, developed Hawaii Casuals clothing firm into a national business. They manufactured clothes only of superior design and quality. His clothes were marketed in the sunbelts, particularly in Florida, California and Hawaii and also in New York City. He had one manufacturing plant on Maui and another in Honolulu. Together, they employed about 150 seamstresses. Unfortunately, he and his brother-in-law died within 10 years and the company was liquidated. I miss him very much. Pansy, an accomplished person, is still living at age 83.

Dottie Jane joined the Wailuku Union Church on April 14th at age 14. I was always very proud when I went to church with my beautiful wife and four daughters. Originally we sat on one pew, but when they all wore crinoline petticoats, one pew was not enough. Once, when we stood to sing the last song, Dottie Jane fainted. I stretched her out on the pew and by the time the song was finished she had about recovered. Her fainting was hardly noticed by any one in the congregation.

The plantation continued talking to the doctors about contracting for the care of its employees. Talks were proceeding about the doctors constructing and owning their office building in Kahului.

My ideas about group practice were not accepted. My work load was ever-increasing. I treated my plantation and nonplantation patients the same, giving all of them the best care I could and treating all just as I would have members of my own family treated. Finally, I had more work than I could do. More plantation patients came to me than I could care for. My private practice had grown and I could not take care of all of it. The plantation had enough physicians, but there was no equitable distribution of the patients among them. If a physician practiced good medicine and was charismatic, he was penalized by having more patients than he could care for. I had frequent migraine headaches from overwork and no rest. At times I was barely able to get out of bed at night and go see sick patients. I had some half days and weekends off, but I delivered most of the plantation babies and cared for other emergencies whether I was on call or not.

I was elected to the Council of the Hawaii Medical Association for a three-year term. These meetings were interesting and kept me abreast of happenings in the medical community. I attended the annual meeting of the association on Kauai in May.

I did a quarantine inspection of a three-masted sailing ship that had just come from Japan and was a training ship of the Japanese Navy. The doctor aboard could not speak English but could speak German. I got my friend, Dr. Wolfgang Pfaeltzer, a native German, to entertain him.

Lois graduated from Baldwin High School on June 11th. Two days later, Dottie Jane graduated from the 8th grade at Kaunoa School. For the next 12 years, we would have daughters in college for a total of 21 years.

Wild blackberries grew in the Olinda area and we tried to pick some each year. Sometimes, for five dollars we could buy five gallons of blackberries that had been picked by prisoners at the Olinda honor camp. Dottie would make jam and jelly and also several pies for the freezer. When I was a child, I went blackberry picking every summer and we would have jams, jellies and pies. The main difference in picking blackberries in Hawaii was that there were no red bugs to get on our legs and cause severe itching.

Dottie, Lois and I left for San Francisco on July 6th. I had enrolled for a two-week refresher course in obstetrics at Harvard and Boston Lying-In-Hospital. En route, we planned to visit several colleges where Lois had applied for admission. We also planned to visit our families and some friends.

Our first stop was in Pittsburgh, where we toured Chatham College. This was a woman's tutorial college that offered a good education to girls who were eager to learn. We also toured the University of Pittsburgh campus before leaving by train for Lewistown.

While in Lewistown, we visited all the relatives. We drove to Spruce Creek to see Jo and Tony and, on the way home, went over the campus of Penn State University. We went to Geisinger Hospital and saw all our friends there. Next day, we had dinner with Dr. and Mrs. Charles Wilbar in Harrisburg.

On Sunday, July 14th, we left by train for Boston at 9:30 a.m. There was standing room only for me until Philadelphia, though Dottie and Lois had seats. We arrived in Boston at 7:30 p.m. and registered at the Statler Hotel. We immediately went to the Shell on the Charles River to a concert by the Boston Pops Orchestra with Maestro Arthur Fiedler conducting. With daylight-saving time, it did not get dark until 9. We sat on the grass by the river.

I checked into Boston Lying-In-Hospital the next morning and every morning thereafter for two weeks, travelling from the hotel to the hospital by street car. I enjoyed the instruction at the hospital. On Monday evening, we saw our first cinerama wide-screen movie. It was entitled "The Seven Wonders of the World," and was a good picture.

While in Boston we ate at many good restaurants, including Pironi's Parker House, Statler Hotel and Jimmy's. The latter, a most outstanding seafood restaurant, was in the harbor area and we ate there twice. Its desserts were delicious. Reservations were not accepted and it always seemed to be full, with a long line waiting outside the door.

We visited the Museum of Fine Arts on Saturday afternoon after I returned from the hospital. On Sunday, we attended services at the Park Street Congregational Church. This was the church that had sent the first missionaries to Hawaii around Cape Horn in sailing ships in 1820. That trip took 180 days. Dr. Dwight Baldwin, grandfather of Frank Baldwin, came in the fourth company of missionaries and arrived in Hawaii in 1831. He moved to Lahaina where he lived from 1835 to 1870. His home still stands and is now a museum. Its walls are 18 to 30 inches thick and are made of coral.

Another missionary, the Reverend Jonathan Green, came to Wailuku in 1833 and built a home that is now known as the Bailey House. It was occupied by the Reverend Edward Bailey from 1840 to 1885. The Reverend Richard Armstrong came to Wailuku in 1837 and built the large, two-story parsonage that is still used by the current minister of the Wailuku Union Church. It is known as the Alexander House and also has thick coral walls. We have attended the Wailuku Union Church since 1942, which is over 47 years.

On a Sunday afternoon while in Boston, we visited the Frigge Museum of Harvard University to see the glass botanical exhibits. Flowers from all around the world are reproduced in glass, appearing very real and lifelike. We saw many flowers that are common in Hawaii, such as orchids, bird of paradise, cup of gold and others.

We went to a night baseball game between the Boston Red Sox and the Kansas City A's. Boston won 1 to 0. Two days later we saw another game against the Cleveland Indians.

We flew to New York City on Saturday, July 27th, and registered at the Roosevelt Hotel. On Sunday my sister, Dorothy Thornton, and her family spent the day with us. We went sightseeing around the city and visited the United Nations and Staten Island. In the evening, Dottie, Lois and I went to Radio City Music Hall and saw "Silk Stockings," featuring Cyd Charisse with either Gene Kelly or Fred Astaire, I am not certain which. On Monday, Dottie and Lois went shopping for Lois's college wardrobe. In the evening, we saw a musical comedy on Broadway, "The Most Happy Fellow."

On Tuesday we went to Yankee Stadium and saw the Yankees beat Kansas City 10 to 4. In the evening, we saw a Broadway show, "Bells Are Ringing," starring Judy Holliday. We flew to Chapel Hill on Wednesday.

While in North Carolina, we visited Mamma in Chapel Hill, Orus and family in Sanford, Velma and Marcus in Durham, and Maisie and her family in Laurinburg. We went fishing and swimming with Pat and Tommy Parker, who were seven and nine years old. We visited Ralph and Sue Fleming in Durham. We went to Raleigh for Lois to see Meredith College. While in Raleigh we visited the State Art Museum which had been built and filled with outstanding art since I had left North Carolina. We went to a show featuring the planet Venus at the Planetarium in Chapel Hill.

On August 9th, we flew to Washington and then went to Lewistown by train. After we visited relatives for five days, we left Lois with Jo and Tony, and went to Pittsburgh to tour Chatham College again. The next day, we flew to San Francisco. We were with McLeod and Louise overnight and then flew to Honolulu and on to Maui.

I was back to work on August 19th and had to meet a foreign ship for quarantine inspection at 6:30 in the morning.

The doctors soon had two meetings about the proposed new office building in Kahului. Under the proposal, each doctor would be required to own a share of the building. The bank would require a large cash down payment from each doctor and would loan us the rest of the money that was needed.

Dottie took our remaining three daughters to Honolulu on August 27th for a three-day vacation.We had been away for six weeks and they needed some extra petting. They also needed new clothes for school.

Sunday, September 8th, was a busy day. I delivered three babies, circumcised three babies and did an autopsy, then played 18 holes of golf.

Dottie and I attended a reception for the Reverend and Mrs. Richard Ritter. He was retiring from our church. He had been our minister for about 12 years and had had a great influence upon our children as well as many other people, old and young. Our church was filled each Sunday morning including the two morning services on Easter Sunday.

I gave a talk at the hospital staff meeting on the pearls that I had gleaned during my two-week postgraduate course at the Boston Lying-In-Hospital.

I had a talk with Dr. Frank St. Sure, head plantation physician, and told him I was seriously considering leaving the plantation.

I was very tired and barely able to work on October 27th. During the previous 27 hours I had delivered seven babies.

Two days later, the doctors met again to discuss the new building. I had decided it would not be wise for me to go deeply in debt to own part of the building. I was required to take care of too many patients, especially male patients not in my specialty. The doctors would not enter group practice, which I felt was the best way for a group of physicians to work together. I wrote management a letter stating that I was resigning as of the end of June and gave Dr. St. Sure a copy. I further discussed the issue with him. I had offered to work part-time for the plantation in my specialty, but this offer was rejected. A few days later, the assistant manager came to see me and tried to convince me to change my mind. He felt I should continue working for the plantation in spite of my reasons for resigning.

When Frank Baldwin visited me for a blood pressure check, I discussed with him all that had happened. I told him I had resigned, which he already knew. He still wanted me to be his doctor. I told him I would open an office on Maui and build a home as soon as I could.

Maui Memorial Hospital finally put a double-decker bed in the doctor's room in the obstetrical department. Previously, there was only a hard couch for the doctors to use while waiting for deliveries. Sometimes there would be three of us waiting at one time.

I was able to go to our Kula farm on November 13th, the first time I had been free in 11 weeks. Besides having a full patient load myself, Drs. Haywood and St. Sure took vacations at the same time, which greatly increased my work load.

Dr. and Mrs. Franklyn Payne visited us again for two days following the Pan Pacific Surgical conference in Honolulu. We had a Hawaiian luau for them and had 125 guests. The pig, that we had raised, was not yet one year old and weighed 300 pounds. We had a Hawaiian caterer prepare all the food and serve it in our back yard by the swimming pool. He came for the pig at 5 a.m., slaughtered it and put it in the imu at 10:30. It was well-cooked by 5 p.m. Dr. Payne watched the pig go into and come out of the imu and took many pictures. The large Hawaiian caterer, who was nicknamed Calagoose, stood by the end of the table with the roasted pig on top. As each guest came by with a plate, Calagoose sliced off a large piece of the succulent meat. Many returned for seconds. Most of the meat was eaten.

Hurricane Nina came near the Islands in early December. There were heavy rains throughout Hawaii and the perimeter of the hurricane actually hit Kauai.

Damage was not extensive, but one poultry farm was totally destroyed by the strong winds.

THE YEAR 1958

This year was to be very eventful for me. I had resigned from the plantation and had to secure a new office within six months, and rent, buy or build a home.

An announcement of my resignation appeared in the plantation newspaper.

I was on call January 1st and operated on a patient with a ruptured ectopic pregnancy. Next day I delivered two babies. Later in the month, one of my women patients had a ruptured stomach ulcer. Both my plantation and nonplantation practices continued to be very active.

Carol's Girl Scout Troop had a camp-out in our yard. They put up tents behind the guest cottage, cooked their meals outside and slept overnight. Isabelle Cushnie, wife of the Wailuku Sugar Company's manager, was their leader and stayed with them.

Dr. Robert Kimbrough and his wife spent two days with us in April. He was one of my professors of obstetrics and gynecology at the University of Pennsylvania and had been Dottie's doctor when she first became pregnant. He spoke to the Maui County Medical Society on Saturday evening. We drove them to the top of Haleakala Sunday morning.

Dotty Jane played in her first piano recital at Baldwin Auditorium on April 27h. She was a student of Claire Nashiwa.

I attended the annual meeting of the Hawaii Medical Association on Oahu in April. I played two rounds of golf at the Oahu and Waialae Country Clubs in addition to playing in the Medical Society's annual tournament.

On May 20th, Sputnik III was scheduled to pass over Hawaii from north to south. The sky was clear. Dottie and I looked for it for a while and then I went into the house. Soon after, at 8:21, Dottie saw it and called me. A light inside the satellite could be seen as it tumbled in space. Seeing Sputnik III was a great thrill.

Lois arrived home on June 9th from Chatham College. Her plane from California had had to turn back twice and land, resulting in her arriving home one day late. This day was also my last day of work at Hawaiian Commercial and Sugar Company, as I had three weeks terminal vacation.

Fred Zempel, Anita Haywood's father, and I drove around the island on June 10th. He was the rancher we visited in Montana, as I mentioned earlier. We first drove through Hana and saw the beautiful ranch lands covered with well-fed, white-faced Hereford cattle. He commented many times about how few problems Hawaii ranchers had compared to him. There seemed to be an abundance of feed and water, there was no cold weather to contend with and apparently few droughts. He couldn't believe what he was seeing.

We stopped at Kaupo Ranch and had lunch with Boy von Tempsky, its current manager. He had more problems than other Maui ranchers, but produced excellent cattle. It was interesting for me to listen to these two seasoned ranchers talk.

Soon after lunch we reached Ulupalakua Ranch and finally Haleakala Ranch. There seemed to be no end to the beautiful ranches on Maui. Zempel enjoyed every mile of travel.

Dottie and I went to Honolulu in June for a five-day vacation and business trip.

We visited the registrar of the University of Hawaii and made arrangements for Lois to enroll there in September.

We met our architect, Haydn Phillips, about our future house plans and visited several homes in Honolulu he had designed. We went to Tripler Army Hospital to see Dr. Bob Cole, one of my associates, who had a chronic nerve disease and was becoming paralyzed.

This ended my employment at H. C. and S. Co., except for a few more days of terminal vacation. I had worked for the plantation for 17 years and five months. Luckily, the plantation had established a pension plan exactly five years before. I had made maximum contributions to the plan, which meant I would receive a small pension when I reached 65.

I made arrangements with the plantation to rent the house we were living in until we could buy land and build our own. We agreed to maintain the yard. I bought a small tractor-mower and the girls cut the lawn. I hired a yardman for three half days per week. I was charged only $125 per month rent, which included water for the pool. I feel very sure that Frank Baldwin intervened in my behalf.

CHAPTER XII

We Build Our Home, Hōmĕ Pilialoha:
June 16, 1958 to March 30, 1960

When Dr. Rockett went on leave to obtain more surgical training, I replaced him at the Wailuku Sugar Company's dispensary on the corner of Central Avenue and Mill Street in Wailuku. I started working there on June 16th. I owned the furnishings and equipment of the Kahului dispensary, which I moved to Wailuku. I also continued to employ my excellent nurse-bookkeeper, Mrs. Modesta Singlehurst. The staff at the dispensary now consisted of two nurses, one nurse's aide and one receptionist-clerk. I was busy from the start. There were fewer than 20 doctors on Maui to treat a population of about 44,000. Many of Dr. Rockett's patients came to me and my own patients followed me. More than half the patients who came to the dispensary were Wailuku Sugar Company employees or their dependents. I treated 44 patients the first Saturday morning. Frequently, I treated 60 or 70 patients a day in the office, as well as hospitalized patients. Frank Baldwin made a visit every two weeks.

During the first week, I approached Wailuku Sugar Company to sell me land in Wailuku for a homesite. Because of our lifestyle at Puunene, it was thought that we would want enough land for a small farm and I was offered land in Iao Valley with plenty of extra space. I quickly pointed out we only wanted enough land for a house, flowers and fruit trees in a location that would give us privacy. Alec Butchart, of Wailuku Sugar Company, found eight lots at Wailuku Heights that were for sale. This location was two to three miles from central Wailuku and the hospital. It would be ideal. Our architect, Haydn Phillips, came from Honolulu to advise us. He chose a large, nice lot down by the cane field that was relatively flat. Dottie and I had lived in the middle of a dusty cane field for several years and wanted our new home to be as far away from cane fields as possible.

We chose the last two adjoining lots at the end of Alaneo Place. The owners had been unable to sell them and had joined in efforts to find a buyer, thinking that maybe someone might use both lots for one home. The grade on the lots was 25 to 35 percent, which meant that extensive changes would be required. A Wailuku Sugar Company supervisor owned a third lot just below our lot on the north side. He offered to sell it to us for what it had cost him. The elevation of the lots extended from 900 to 958 feet above sea level. After grading the upper lots, there was a large flat plateau 944 feet above sea level and at least 150 feet above the sugar cane fields which were two blocks away. The prevailing trade winds were deflected by the mountain on the left, the Iao Valley side, which meant they moved from north to south. They blew the dust from the cane fields away from our property. The steep mountains on three sides precluded any more development and we would own one lot in front.

On July 21st we agreed to buy the three lots and I paid for them on July 31st. There was a total of 46,780 square feet for which we paid an average of 25 cents a square foot. Statehood soon followed and land prices have escalated rapidly ever since. With the improvements we have made and the privacy of our location, the market value of this land is now more than $10 per square foot.

We had to sell our farm at Kula to pay for the lots. I would have to spend all my spare time preparing to build our house and could not do the work needed on the farm. It would have been nice if we could have kept it, as it was very productive. On June 18th I brought home an Easter lily plant with 75 blooms on it. It was late for Easter but still a beautiful sight. On another day I gathered 10 pecks of plums.

All three of our Wailuku lots were covered with koa hale plants and a few large eucalyptus and ironwood trees. We had these knocked down with a bulldozer and burned most of the trash, saving some wood to use in the fireplace.

The woody roots of the koa hale plants were only partially removed by the bulldozer. I worked with a mattock for one to three hours each day for two months to remove the rest of them. If I were needed for an emergency, I could be reached by telephone through a neighbor. Finally, the lots were clean and ready for grading.

Before grading and further plans could be made, the architect needed a contour map. I engaged the Wailuku Sugar surveyor for this but he could do it only on weekends. It rained three consecutive weekends, so no progress was made. When I finally sent the contour map to the architect he proceeded with the plans.

My friend Jack Walker, an engineer, offered to help by overseeing the grading and the actual construction of our house. The architect would come to Maui once or twice each month to check the progress. We hired Henry Fong, contractor, to do the grading and, later, to prepare the drive and parking area for paving with asphalt.

Henry had lived in Kula for years among eucalyptus trees and knew they were brittle. He strongly advised me to cut down many huge trees just outside our property before we built, saying they would surely fall on our house during a storm. I owned a good ax and could cut down the eucalyptus trees, 12 to 18 inches in diameter, in 15 to 20 minutes. They were leaning and would break when cut about two-thirds through. I cut them into suitable lengths and then split the logs with wedges for firewood. I had cut firewood with an ax since childhood. It was good exercise and used all the muscles of the arms, legs and back. I had to stop using the ax when I was 65 and then I bought a chain saw.

THE YEAR 1959

The public water supply for our subdivision is pumped from a lower reservoir to one on the mountain above us at 1,100 feet elevation. One six-inch water main leads to the reservoir about two feet north of our property. Another six-inch main descends from the reservoir on the line between our two upper lots. It then passes down the middle of the street, supplying the houses on both sides. It is buried six feet below the surface. When our lots were graded, this main was exposed so that it was six feet above the ground. In January the County of Maui lowered the main to six feet below the new surface at a cost of $531 to me. The grading could now be finished.

While our lots were being prepared we had two rainstorms. The soil had been graded and moved forward, but the final surface of the plateau had not been established. We had 16 inches of rain in 25 hours. The newly moved soil became mud and much of it slid down the bank to the lot below on the south side. A week later we had nine more inches of rain in 15 hours and lost more soil.

Eventually, the grading was completed. It was designed so that during heavy rains the water drained from the front edge of the plateau back towards the mountain and then into drainage ditches on both sides. When we bought the property, adequate drainage ditches were already in place above and on the sides of the lots.

Hōmĕ Pilialoha

After six months of work and many conferences with Dottie and me, Haydn Phillips had the house plans complete and ready to be submitted to contractors for bids. It was interesting to watch this architect work. He kept a record of everything that we told him. He had studied our location in relation to the sun, winds, rain, etc. Dottie and I wanted more than we could finance, so he was ever-mindful of costs. We had provided him with one of the best building sites and commissioned him to plan a home for us. He was enjoying creating a masterpiece. He would use the massive furniture that he had designed for our plantation home. He would take full advantage of our view, which was superb. Facing east, we looked down on Wailuku, Kahului, the harbor and airport (five miles distant). Beyond this were the vast cane fields and ranch lands, which extended to about 7,000 feet up Haleakala. The top of the mountain, clearly visible, was 10,000 feet above sea level and 40 miles away.

I did not want a flat roof but Phillips explained a high roof would have wasted attic space. Also, overhanging eaves would obstruct the view. Our home would be at the highest elevation in the subdivision and no one one would look down upon us except from airplanes. We agreed on a butterfly roof. He suggested plate glass windows to take advantage of the magnificent view. We had the entire front and sides of the house enclosed with glass, including a plate glass window in the front bedroom. Every room has a beautiful view.

There are 3,200 square feet of floor space in the house, including the garage and a small workshop. A foyer on the west (mountain) side is separated from the living room by shojii doors. A hallway on the left of the foyer leads to two bedrooms and a door on the right opens into the kitchen. Both of the bedrooms have large dressing rooms and baths.

Across the east or ocean side of the house, from left to right, are the master bedroom, library, living room and dining room. These are cantilevered six to eight feet above the ground and are supported by 10x10-inch wooden posts set atop cement supports with footings in virgin soil. The latter two rooms are separated only by a partial, fixed decorative screen. The library and living rooms are separated by a fireplace which opens into each room. On both sides of the fireplace is a passage between the two rooms. Beside the fireplace are cleverly designed cabinets for a sophisticated music system with speakers and storage areas. Space is provided for a television.

The entire house was wired for music by Professor Charles Barbe of Maunaolu College. There are two speakers in the library, living room and both bedrooms.

There is one speaker in the laundry room that can be heard in the kitchen and one under the eaves outside the front door that can be heard in the entry walkway. There are also two speakers outside in the utility area, so our guests in the guest house are able to enjoy the music too. Switches control each speaker.

The library walls and all the cabinets are made of beautiful, native koa wood.

On the west side of the kitchen are the laundry and breakfast rooms. There is an open space and counter between the breakfast room and kitchen. The outside wall of the breakfast room is entirely glass with a view of the guest house, the mountain and the valley. Outside the kitchen door and by the garage is a third bedroom with a half bath that is entered from a small, open corridor leading to the yard toward the guest cottage. We call it the maid's room but use it for storage.

The plans were distributed to the contractors and became a topic of conversation. A copy of the blueprints later reached the vocational school, unbeknownst to the architect or to us, and was used by the school to demonstrate types of construction, especially the roof.

We opened the bids from the nine contractors on April 9th. One contractor, C. Nagamatsu, bid $9,000 less than the next bidder. He had built some of the nicest homes on Maui and we considered him the best. It was strange to me that his bid was so much lower than the others. We could not have afforded the next higher bid. Mr. Nagamatsu was bonded by A & B Commercial Company. Two days later, we signed a contract with him to build our house.

Work was supposed to start within three weeks and be completed within a reasonable time. However, nothing was done for six weeks after the contract was signed. The contractor apparently accepted a lucrative contract to build another house without having to bid on it, so he postponed starting ours. Work began six weeks later.

I began moving plants and trees from our Puunene home as time permitted using a small trailer I owned which I had used to transport cows and horses. I gave it to my yardman, Shun Toyama, and put a hook for it on his car. It would be his to keep after we finished moving. We had six rainbow shower trees about 12 to 15 feet tall which I topped at six feet and transplanted to our property. They all survived. I will not forget the work I had to do to dig them out and put them in the trailer. We moved a 4-year-old magnolia tree and planted it at the front of the plateau where there is about 12 feet of top soil. It grew broad and tall. Horticulturists tell me it is one of the most beautiful magnolia trees they have ever seen. It now has hundreds of blooms for six months in the spring and summer. We also moved plumeria trees, bird of paradise and many other plants. Mr. Toyama, who owned a nursery, gave me a choice, grafted tangerine tree, four Naval orange trees and a Hayden mango tree.

I brought our banker up to our homesite so he could see what we were building. He was impressed and gave us a larger loan. I planned to borrow on my insurance any additional money that I needed.

By August 3rd, the house was about half built. The cement slab for the rear half was in place with the main sewer lines underneath. The two-by-four studs for the walls were standing upright. At this time the carpenters went on strike. The building trades on Maui had never been unionized. They remained on strike until September 17th, six and a half weeks, and when they returned they had a good contract. There were many rains during this period. It was most disturbing for Dottie and me to see our dream house half completed and deteriorating in the rain, but there was nothing we could do about it. After 10 days, many carpenters began working in earnest and the roof was finished on October 5th. The drive and parking area by the entrance were paved on November 11th.

Although the roof was finished, there was much work to be done. The contractor had A & B's planing mill make all the cabinets. The electrical work was done by an outside contractor. Dottie and I had bought all the electrical, plumbing and hardware fixtures in Honolulu. These were installed.

The painters took several weeks to paint the house, but finally it was completed. I took apart and resewed the Philippine grass-rug squares we had on the large lanai floor at Puunene. We used them in our dining room, living room, library, foyer and hall. We used other rugs in the bedrooms and bathrooms.

We moved into our new home on March 30th. We had bought the lots in July, 1958, and it had taken 20 months to get the land ready and the house built.

Our plans included a guest cottage. The main house was situated on the larger of the two upper lots, on the north side. The guest house was built on the upper lot on the south side. The drive to the house entrance, which faced west, came up the north side on the property line between the two north lots. The three lot boundaries were left intact, so any lot could be sold individually if desired.

The architect, at our suggestion, drew plans for a two-bedroom, Japanese tea house with oriental moon window, shojii doors, etc. There was one bath, a large living room and a bar with stools between the kitchen and living room. The contractor offered to build it at a reasonable price, so we signed a new contract to include both houses. The guest cottage contained a total of 572 square feet. It was built on the south side of the lot leaving about 65 feet between it and the main house. Plans were drawn for a kidney-shaped swimming pool to be put in this area. Actually, we doubted we would ever build a pool, but a future owner would have space for one if he wanted it.

Tea House of the Maui Moon

We named our guest house "The Tea House of the Maui Moon." It has become a favorite spot for our daughters and grandchildren to vacation. When our Mote grandsons, Timothy and Gregory, were four and five years old, they coined new names for the two houses. The guest house was the "Tea Cup" and the main house was the "Tea Pot."

The Tea House of the Maui Moon is authenic Japanese in all details. Several objects of art from Japan, all gifts, are displayed, including a Japanese doll with obi, kimono and fan in a glass showcase. Our friends from Tokyo were impressed with the guest house and borrowed a set of blueprints to copy. They plan to build one like it in Japan.

We gave our home a Hawaiian name, Hōmĕ Pilialoha, as suggested by Lily Alameda, a friend of ours of Hawaiian descent who is now over 90 years of age. She speaks Hawaiian fluently and formerly gave the sermons in Hawaiian at our church on special Hawaiian Sundays. She says Hōmĕ is Hawaiian for home and denotes a feeling of warmth. Pilialoha means devoted togetherness as a couple with family and friends; it also means loving and bosom closeness. She said she thought this described Dottie, me and our children and would be a suitable name for our home.

CHAPTER XIII

Launching the Maui Medical Group; A Very Difficult and Traumatic First Year: 1961

I resigned from H. C. and S. Co. in October, 1957, to be effective June 30, 1958. I had assumed I would be able to buy or lease a lot in Kahului and build an office, but when I applied to the plantation for land I was flatly refused. This upset me. Although Frank Baldwin was still president of the plantation, Alexander and Baldwin and the Kahului Railroad Company, I knew he wanted to let his son, Asa Baldwin, manage all the business affairs without any interference from him. I talked with Herbert Jackson, manager of the Kahului Development Company, and he said there was no chance of my ever getting land in Kahului for an office. He had recently been a state senator and in his campaign for office had talked to members of many families in central Maui. He said the people had a great aloha for me and he knew I would have a big practice if I opened an office in Wailuku. He suggested I talk with his doctor, Louis Rockett, about joining him in his practice at the Wailuku Sugar Company.

With this encouragement, I had many conferences with Dr. Rockett. We discussed forming a group practice and invited a number of doctors to our meetings, including Drs. Joseph Andrews, Harold Kushi, Guy Haywood, Mamoru Tofukuji, Clifford Moran and Seiya Ohata. The possibility of forming a group seemed to be good.

At this time, a new office building on Lono Avenue in Kahului was available for rent and I could have established a solo practice. My preference for group practice was so strong, and chances for forming a group were now so good, I chose not to rent this office.

Drs. Rockett, Ohata, Andrews, Tofukuji and I decided to form a partnership, obtain land and build an office building. We hired Haydn Phillips as our architect and Tom Ogata as our legal counsel. We approached Pacific Chemical and Fertilizer Company (now Brewer Chemical) for a lease of the land at the corner of Kaahumanu Avenue and Lower Beach Road. They were agreeable and told us on January 3, 1958, that we could lease it. Our architect drew preliminary plans for a building at this site. The proper document was prepared for a 50-year lease and their Board of Directors approved it on March 4th. We were to have a joint signing of the lease the next day and take possession of the land. At this point, H. C. and S. Co. learned we were leasing the land for a medical building and were able to block the lease. They did not want competition for their doctors in Kahului.

This was a blessing in disguise for us although we could not understand it at the time. Ten years later, it was clear that fate had protected us from what might have been a bad lease. Wailuku would provide us a better location, just one mile from the hospital. However, there was no way for us to know this at the time. I was very tired and confused. I had the pressure of finding an office within three months and was very busy in my practice. On March 9th and 10th I delivered six babies in 36 hours.

I went to see Erling Wick, a realtor and friend, who offered to help us find land in Wailuku. Dr. T. M. Behrmann, dentist, and Dr. Roy Ohata, orthodontist, wanted to join us. We bought a long, narrow lot on Wells Street opposite the former Kress Store's parking lot. When our architect studied it, he said building a long, narrow building was too expensive. He recommended we try to find another site. Soon we were able to buy three adjoining parcels of land at the corner of Wells and Market Streets, providing room for a medical building. We could use our other, nearby land on Wells Street for additional parking.

By this time, we had run out of money. We could borrow some from the bank, but not enough. We approached Drs. Edward Shimokawa and William Iaconetti of Lahaina and they agreed to join our partnership. This would give us a much larger operation as Pioneer Mill Sugar Company agreed to contract its medical care to us. All of us would benefit.

Dr. Rockett had not been content doing general practice. He applied for the four-year surgical residency at the Queen's Hospital in Honolulu beginning July 1, 1958, and was accepted. He had a wife and three children to support and thought finances would allow him to be away for only one or two years. There was a possibility he might be allowed to return to Maui to operate on patients for me. If so, he might be able to stay away longer. Actually, for six months in 1958 and all of 1959 and '60, I had him return for a day every one to two weeks to do one to three elective operations. Most of these patients were not in my specialty, though some were. One was a ruptured duodenal ulcer that I diagnosed at 7 a.m. on one of the days he came. I had the patient ready for surgery when he arrived at 8. With this help and that of his wife, Natalie, who worked as a dietician at the Queen's Hospital, he was able to complete his four-year residency. He qualified for the American Boards in surgery, which he took and passed at his first opportunity.

Wailuku Sugar Company had approved of my being their physician until our group could begin functioning. Then they planned to contract with our group for medical care. This arrangement provided me with an office. I would attempt to take care of Dr. Rockett's private practice, my own patients and do the Wailuku Sugar work. At last, it appeared that temporarily I had an office and that we would get a medical group started.

Now that we had secured land, we commissioned our architect to go ahead and draw plans for our medical building using the lists of needs furnished by the doctors and dentists. We included plans for two doctors in a medical department which we would add later.

The Honolulu Medical Group, through Dr. Nils P. Larsen, helped us organize our group. They loaned us copies of their partnership agreement and sent their manager, Bob Millar, to Maui for several days to help us. We had many conferences with Wailuku and Pioneer Mill Sugar Companies to discuss the terms of contracts for medical care of their employees and their dependents.

Dr. Joseph Andrews announced at a meeting of our new group in June, 1959, that he had decided to resign. He had determined that because of retirement benefits, he should remain at the Kula Sanitarium for the remaining years of his medical practice. We returned the money he had invested in the building corporation.

Dr. Marion Hanlon, pediatrician of the Kamehameha School in Honolulu, came to Maui at my invitation in April to discuss the possibility of joining us in the Maui Medical Group. He returned in June with his family and agreed to join both the Maui Medical Group Partnership and the Maui Medical Group Building Corporation. He was the first and only pediatrician to practice on Maui. He began practicing medicine with me at the Wailuku Sugar Company's dispensary on July 20th. I agreed to pay him $1,000 per month of my own money, assuring him that as soon as the income from his work rose above this amount, I would pay him accordingly. He was to take care of Wailuku Sugar Company's dependents in his specialty to pay for his part of the overhead expenses. After five and a half months I raised his salary to $1,200 per month, based on his current input. I did not recover the money I paid him the first few months. My income fell $6,500 in 1960 after I made this arrangement. This is what I had anticipated, because he was taking care of all my pediatric patients. After the Maui Medical Group began functioning on January 1, 1961, I gave Dr. Hanlon all the money we made on work that he had done, though, according to our agreement, this belonged to me. This amounted to $2,321 for the first three months alone.

The Maui Medical Group Building Corporation and the Maui Medical Group Partnership had meetings about every two weeks during the remainder of 1959. We met with the architect frequently. We bought a new, modern x-ray machine in August, 1959, and the specifications of the building were modified to accommodate it.

The plans for the medical group building were given to the local contractors for bids on November 25th. The bids were opened on December 16th and on December 21st a bid from Muneo Yamamoto was accepted. On January 6, 1960, the legal papers were signed by our architect. Construction of our building could start as soon as we got a bank loan. The building would cost $23 per square foot, which was very cheap considering the type of construction and the number of rooms. We were very pleased with the low cost.

We had nine doctors and dentists in our building corporation and thought it would be easy for us to get money from the bank. At the recommendation of our banker at First Hawaiian Bank, we applied to the Small Business Administration for a loan. He thought we would qualify. Lee Burkland of the S.B.A. came to Maui on January 12th to process our loan. We heard on April 12th that our application had been rejected because two of our members had too many financial assets. They were able to finance our building themselves with some help from the bank but for personal reasons, they refused to do so.

It is interesting to note that within a few years, group practice and community health plans became very popular as a way for the public to obtain health care. The Federal Government encouraged the formation of medical groups and offered loans at low rates through the Small Business Administration. This came too late to help us. By then, we had gone through some very difficult times because of the lack of proper finances.

After we failed to get a loan from the S.B.A. or First Hawaiian Bank, Shizu Mizuha of the Wailuku Branch of Bank of Hawaii offered us the money we needed at a reasonable rate. We got our loan officially on May 10, 1960, and the contractor started work. The first cement was poured on June 8th.

On the morning of October 20th, a sudden downpour of rain ruined the new cement floor in one section of the building. The cement had to be shoveled out and replaced.

On November 4th the roof was completed and we had a topping-off party for the workers. Mr. Phillips was there.

The doctors' and dentists' offices and all waiting rooms had to be furnished by the Building Corporation. Our architect recommended a decorator, whom we hired.

The Maui Medical Group Medical Partnership began functioning on January 1, 1961. We could not occupy our building for several weeks, but we pooled our incomes and expenses. We hired an accountant, a friend of one of our members, to start a bookkeeping department.

We moved into our building on Tuesday, February 28, 1961, and began seeing patients March 1st.

We had commissioned a famous artist, Hon Chew Hee of Honolulu, to paint a mural to be hung in our main waiting room. Dr. Nils P. Larsen had related to him how the kahunas (doctors) in ancient Hawaiian times had prepared their medicinal potions from herbs and plants and administered them during a ritual accompanied by hula dancers. He created a beautiful, authentic picture, four by twelve feet, that depicts early Hawaiian medical practices. On March 10th the mural was hung. The waiting room had a large skylight over a Hawaiian garden containing tree ferns and other plants. The garden floor was about 30 inches higher than the multicolored, terrazzo tile floor. Its walls were made of beautiful lava rock to match the other walls in the waiting room.

On Sunday, March 12th, we had a dedication ceremony with the Reverend Kukahiko blessing the building. Mr. Phillips came from Honolulu and was introduced to the audience of several hundred people. Muneo Yamamoto, the contractor, also was introduced. All the members of the Maui Medical Group Partnership and the Building Corporation were presented. I gave a talk outlining how the Maui Medical Group had come into being and stressed that our goal in practicing as a group was to give our patients the best medical care available rather than to make more money. At that time, we did not know that for several months the founding members would be supporting the Maui Medical Group instead of it supporting them.

The Maui Medical Group Partnership agreement stipulated that, after all expenses had been paid, the remaining income would be divided equally among all partners. Each member was to receive a cost-of-living allowance monthly. Every six months, the books would be balanced and the profits distributed. New doctors would be paid a salary for one, two or three years and then either be terminated or made a full partner. These rules could be changed by a specified majority vote of the partners. This agreement remained in effect for about 12 years, when we found it necessary to make a change. We found we could not attract new physicians in the higher income brackets under the old agreement.

One complication arose just as we moved into our new building. Our contract with Wailuku Sugar Company stipulated that any income generated by treating employees or their dependents and paid for by a third party would belong to Wailuku Sugar Company and not to the Medical Group. This applied to patients who had automobile accidents in which an insurance company was liable for the costs. Pioneer Mill Sugar Company's contract allowed the Maui Medical Group to collect physician fees. All the doctors except one agreed to practice under the proposed contract for a year, when a new contract would be negotiated. This one doctor said the contract was against his ethics and he refused to sign it. As a result, we lost the Wailuku Sugar contract.

When our group was organized, we had depended upon the two plantation contracts to generate enough income to get us started. It would take approximately three months for us to send out bills and have a steady income. We had about 25 employees with a large payroll. To pay their salaries the first month, each member of the group had to advance $300. Supplies such as drugs for our pharmacy and special equipment had to be paid for.

The loss of the Wailuku Sugar contract cost each physician of the group $550 each month for the duration of the year-long contract. All of us were young with meager finances, except for two as pointed out by the Small Business Administration.

The physician who refused to sign the Wailuku Sugar contract was one of these. He appeared to have few monetary problems and was not concerned about the other members' financial stress.

This setback was just the beginning of our problems. Our partnership agreement stated that each member was to put in $7,200 working capital, on which he would receive eight percent interest. This share of the working capital could be paid in monthly installments if the entire amount could not be paid in immediately. I did not ask the members for working capital until March, when we needed money for payroll and to pay for supplies and equipment. I put all my working capital in at once and was the only one to do so. The member who refused to sign the Wailuku Sugar contract flatly refused.At one of our weekly meetings, he said he would wait until he determined if the Maui Medical Group would be a success before he committed himself, and most of the other doctors followed his example. At this time we owed one supplier $12,000 and had no money. We got a short-term loan from the bank to pay it.

None of the members of the Medical Group except one, Dr. Ohata, could understand that after we paid current expenses, the remaining income of the Group had to be divided among the members. Because of lack of working capital, most of them thought we could just use the income to pay for drug inventory and equipment without having to pay income taxes on each partner's share. I finally had our lawyer explain this to them.

I was overworked. Also, I was harassed because the members would not follow our partnership agreement. I had started the Maui Medical Group with the help of the other members, but I could not continue being the manager and carry on a large medical practice. I insisted we hire a business manager to relieve me, which we did. An apparently suitable person, whom I did not know, applied and we hired him.

Another problem soon appeared. The accountant whom we hired as a book-keeper had not set up a bookkeeping system and he had not dropped his outside accounts. We found bills had not been sent out for three months except medical insurance claims sent out by a clerk. Sometime in April, I demanded that the manager and the bookkeeper prepare a report on our gross income, expenses, etc, so we would know how we were doing financially. The bookkeeper walked out in the middle of the afternoon and never returned. He had most of the vital information about our accounts recorded on scraps of paper. It took the manager several weeks to straighten out the mess.

All the doctors except two were under great financial stress because we had no income. Everyone became very irritable. I had talked them into joining me in forming the Maui Medical Group, so they blamed me for much that went wrong. It was claimed that I paid my nurse too much at $400 per month, which was within our pay scale for nurses. Yet, a younger nurse in Lahaina with less experience received $480 per month. I probably had more patients than anyone else and was supposed to have two employees in my office to help me. Every other department had two nurse employees, yet I was not allowed to hire a second helper when I asked for one.

I had recommended we hire Haydn Phillips as our architect, as he had drawn plans for our home. He had done a wonderful job in creating a medical building just as we had instructed. Yet, many of the members insinuated he was dishonest. They also said the same about the contractor. They criticized the interior decorator, whom the architect had recommended, and threatened to take her to court. They found fault with the landscaping and caused it to be unduly delayed.

I had worked very hard for three years to create the Maui Medical Group. I had neglected my family and had lost much income because of the group. Up to this time, only one member, Dr. Tofukuji, had thanked me and said he appreciated what I had done. I wrote the group a letter on March 31, 1961, stating my position and that their attitudes would have to change if the group was to continue.

On May 15, 1961, Dr. Hanlon wrote the group stating that he had to resign because of no income, and asked for a waiver of the six month's notice requirement to resign. He had bought a home on a large lot and could not make the mortgage payments. He had tried to sell part of the lot for eight months without success until Dr. Ohata came to his rescue and bought the property. This gave him relief so he could remain with us.

Things did not change. On June 18th, I wrote the group a letter in which I resigned, effective December 31, 1961. I said I would continue to practice in the building and mentioned three agreements under which this could be done. I suggested we wait for the first six months' accounting report and then discuss this.

I wrote the group another letter on July 4th and stated it was not too late to salvage the Maui Medical Group. I pointed out what the problems were and what we would have to do to correct them. After my last letter, I had been threatened with expulsion from not only the Maui Medical Group but also the Building Corporation, of which I owned one-ninth interest. I responded to this by saying we would let the judge decide if my part in the building corporation could be taken from me.

Our primary current problem was in the bookkeeping department. I arranged a business meeting in which all the members met with the manager and made a tour of the bookkeeping department to review the system as he had set it up. One member, the one who would not sign the Wailuku Sugar contract and also threatened to have me expelled, refused to attend this meeting, saying he had more important things to do. I offered to stay with the group and to do all I could to make it succeed if all the members would adhere to our partnership agreement.

Finally, early in July, the manager gave us a report for the first six months of operation so far as he could determine. Each doctor was paid $1,000 , the first income for six months. We had to contribute $300 each to make the first payroll, so our net was $700 each. The remainder of the earnings of each doctor was accredited to his working capital and began accruing interest. I had put more into working capital than was required, so the excess was returned to me.

Our business had improved by July and the manager was able to pay most of our bills without working capital as such. The doctors received another payment of $1,000 for July and monthly thereafter. We decided to have an outside auditor check our books and help set up a proper bookkeeping system. It was decided to invite Bob Millar of the Honolulu Medical Group to make a survey of our operations. He had helped us get organized and the members had confidence in him. He came on September 14th and met with us for two days. Thereafter, things improved in general.

We decided to terminate our manager at a group meeting on October 3rd. I do not recall the exact reasons for this action. He had done his best to get things straightened out but he was not an accountant and bookkeeper and that was what we needed.

On October 9th we hired Tomio Mukai as our business manager. He was an experienced accountant about 35 years old. Thereafter, we had no problems in this department. His wife was a patient of mine and, by coincidence, I did a cesarean on her four days after he started working.

On my Wednesday afternoon off October 24th, I painted lines for parking stalls on our lot on Wells Street. I used regular traffic line paint and a form with double lines. It seemed easier for me to do it myself rather than hire someone. However, it proved to be very hard work.

Dr. Rockett met with the Maui Medical Group on December 28th. He was returning to Maui in six months to live, after finishing his four-year surgical residency. We made a special financial agreement to fit his situation and he accepted it.

Forming the Maui Medical Group had been a severe financial burden for me and I did not recover for about 10 years. I had just built an expensive home and already had three daughters in college with one more to follow. My income for 1958, when I left Hawaiian Commercial and Sugar Company, was $33,225 plus prequisites; in 1959 it was $37,160; in 1960 it fell to $30,651 when Dr. Hanlon was with me the full year; in 1961, the first year in the Maui Medical Group, it fell to $20,651; in 1962 it rose to $24,234; and 1963 it was $31,070. When we changed our system of distribution so that members were paid in proportion to their input, my income rose considerably. As I have already stated, my goal in starting the Maui Medical Group was to improve the quality of medical care for my patients. From the above summary, it can be seen that forming the group and its first year of operation produced great emotional stress for me and cost me dearly financially. In retrospect, I still think it was worthwhile. My equity in the Building Corporation increased each year. With property values in Hawaii escalating rapidly, I was able to recoup some of the early losses when I retired and sold my shares in the Building Corporation. This was seventeen years after we began practicing as a group.

CHAPTER XIV

Other Significant Events:
June, 1958, through December, 1961

We made preparations to move out of the plantation house at Puunene though it took much longer to build our home than we planned.

We sold our cow in July and I removed the wire fences and redwood posts surrounding the pasture. I also removed 32 two-by-four redwood timbers I had used in the greenhouse as shelves for our plants. I used some of this material to build a large dog house with a yard eight by twelve feet. The redwood posts (old railroad crossties) I used as benches under the eucalyptus trees for my orchids.

On July 25, 1958, John Cushnie, manager of Wailuku Sugar Company, had a dinner party in our honor at his home. All the plantation supervisors were present.

Robert and Thelma Tamanaha and their five children had dinner with us on August 4th just before they moved to Los Angeles. It would have been a great help if he could have stayed with us one more year, but I had advised him to leave at this time. It proved to be a good move for him.

Lois left for the University of Hawaii on September 14th. She was back home after the first semester.

We heard on September 19th that Tom Parker, my sister's husband, had died. After his stroke, he developed diabetes and died after a second heart attack. Their sons were eight and ten years of age. Maisie continued operating their furniture store and her interior decorating business, and had enough income to rear her sons.

I attended the annual meeting of the Association of Plantation Physicians in Hilo in November. Dr. Sam Wallis of Kauai and I played golf at the Honokaa Country Club and the Volcano Golf Course with Merrill Carlsmith who had been National Seniors Golf Champion two years in succession. We went sightseeing and visited Pahoa, a former plantation village in the Puna district that had been completely destroyed in a recent lava flow. All that was left of the houses were a few pieces of corrugated iron that had been part of their roofs. Sugar cane had grown in this area for 50 years without a lava flow.

When we returned to Maui, I had to visit a sick seaman aboard a ship in Kahului Harbor. The sea was so rough the ship could not be tied up at the dock.

On December 5th, I examined a nine-year-old boy with a high fever. I could find nothing wrong, which was not unusual in my busy practice. For some reason, at the first visit I decided to send him to the hospital for a complete blood count. Dr. Moran diagnosed aleukemic leukemia. He lived only four more weeks. He was a very brilliant child, the son of a plantation supervisor. Fate had led me to get a blood count and make a diagnosis early.

I had been appointed president of the hospital medical staff. We were striving to meet the requirements of the American Hospital Association for accreditation. Dr. Vickers came in February and examined every department. A few weeks later we learned we had received full accreditation.

We had a dinner party on February 14th in our home at Puunene for the Wailuku Sugar Company's supervisors and their wives.

Carol won first place in the Science Fair of elementary schools on Maui. She had demonstrated that guinea pigs would die if they ate only sterilized foods, proving that they needed the bacteria in their intestinal tracts to digest their food. Dottie took her and the exhibit to the State Science Fair in Honolulu.

Saturday, March 21st, proved to be a busy day. I delivered five babies in 28 hours. Then we went to Baldwin High School Auditorium to hear Ann play trombone in a band concert.

On April 4th, we attended a farewell party for John Cushnie, who was retiring as a manager of Wailuku Sugar Company.

Lois enrolled at Maunaolu College on Maui, starting the second semester in the winter of 1959. She lived in the dormitory. This college was located at Sunny Side, about halfway between Paia and Makawao. The faculty consisted primarily of older professors who had retired from mainland universities. The enrollment varied between 200 and 300 students and most of them transferred to Mainland colleges after graduation.

Charles Barbe was head of the music department and his wife, Jane, taught voice. He had graduated from Westminster Choir College at Princeton, New Jersey, and was a genius in choir organization and music in general. He had had a severe heart attack and was left a cardiac cripple. He was forced to limit his activities and that is how Maunaolu was able to attract him as a faculty member.

Lois had been in our church choir and had taken piano lessons for years. She joined the Maunaolu Choir and both Mr. Barbe and his wife recognized that she had a better than average voice. Soon she was taking private voice lessons from Mrs. Barbe and continued for two and a half years. We first heard her sing in the choir on May 29th.

Ann graduated from Baldwin High School in June, 1959. She was accepted in the honor's program of the first-year class at the University of Wisconsin in the fall and attended for one year. She returned to Maui and went to Maunaolu College with Lois during the next year. Following this, she enrolled again for one semester at the University of Wisconsin. Thereafter, she went to San Francisco and easily qualified for a good executive secretarial job with Kennedy Engineers.

In July, I again robbed my bees. There were plenty of kiawe flowers and lots of honey. Luckily, I had lost my sensitivity to bee stings and had no problems.

I delivered a baby with an omphalocele, in which all the intestines were outside the abdomen due to a defect in the abdominal wall at the umbilicus which allowed the intestines to come through. It is a great surprise to see this in a newborn. I delivered only two of these in forty years. I immediately got a surgeon to repair the defect, knowing that a wait of more than three or four hours would have allowed bacteria to enter the intestines, which would become distended with gas. Then it is impossible to replace them into the abdomen.

I took a two-week trip to the mainland, leaving on November 29th. I went directly to Dallas and attended the winter meeting of the American Medical Association. One evening I attended a concert by the Dallas Symphony Orchestra. I took a city bus tour in the afternoon and remember the guide telling us that 55 percent of the population of Dallas was Southern Missionary Baptist. I went Christmas shopping at the Neiman Marcus store and was pleasantly surprised by the store's variety of merchandise. There were plenty of items that I could afford to buy for presents for Dottie and our four daughters. I had all of them carefully wrapped in Neiman Marcus-marked packages. They caused a lot of excitement when I distributed them. I had told a shopping guide about our family, and she helped me choose the presents. They were luxurious. Everyone was delighted and I am still occasionally reminded about these gifts.

I left Dallas on the 6th and flew to North Carolina. When I arrived the temperature was 33 degrees. I spent five days with Mamma at Chapel Hill and, while I was there, Orus and his family, Maisie and her two boys, Marcus and Velma, and Dorothy and Jack Thornton visited. We had Ralph and Sue Fleming come from Durham for dinner one evening.

I left North Carolina for Chicago and Madison, Wisconsin, on December 8th. Soon after leaving the Raleigh-Durham airport, the landscape was covered with a fresh blanket of snow.

Dottie had taken Ann to Madison in September when she started school, and now I was visiting her. We were trying our best to help her get a good start.

I spent two days in Madison, staying at accommodations available to parents. I visited Ann's dormitory. It was a long walk from the center of the campus to the dormitory and the calves of Ann's legs had enlarged from the amount of walking she did. I made plane reservations for her to spend the Christmas holidays with her Patterson relatives in North Carolina. I left Madison on December 10th after having breakfast with Ann in the college dining room, overlooking a lake. At dinner the evening before, waves on the lake were about six inches high. At breakfast the waves were still in place, frozen solid overnight.

I flew to Chicago, spent one night with Neff and Jane at Downers Grove, then went to Kansas to see Neill and his family. There was dense fog, which forced us to circle the area for two hours before we landed. This was a new experience for me, though I had heard others discuss being caught in similar situations.

Neill was stationed at a missile base in this area. He and Pearl had five children at that time. Their baby, Sonja, less than one year old, and I slept in the same room. She awakened during the night with a wet diaper. I made a quick change and we both went back to sleep. I had had plenty experience with our own babies. Recently, she, her husband and daughter spent a few months on Maui while he was doing some special work at the airport.

From Kansas City, I flew to Los Angeles. The plane was late, which resulted with me missing my flight to Honolulu. I was rerouted to San Francisco and spent three hours at the airport with McLeod until my plane left for Honolulu at 9 p.m. I arrived at 9 a.m. the next day and played golf in the afternoon.

On Sunday, December 20th, our family attended Makawao Union Church and heard Lois sing Handel's Messiah with Maunaolu College Choir. She sang the soprano solo. She had a beautiful voice and had made good progress. It was a joy to hear her sing. It appeared that music was to become her career.

THE YEAR 1960

We attended a St. Andrew's Society celebration in January, commemorating Robert Burn's birthday. Lois sang a solo.

I was called to see Frank Baldwin at his home about 7 a.m. on January 26, 1960. When he got out of bed to go to the bathroom, he became dizzy and fell. He had struck the back of his head on a bench and complained of pain in his neck, arms and legs. He was fully conscious and no longer dizzy. It was obvious he had seriously injured his neck. I had him transferred to the Maui Memorial Hospital by ambulance and asked Dr. Guy Haywood to help me treat him. X-rays showed a fractured cervical vertebra. We immediately discussed his case with Dr. Ralph Cloward, neurosurgeon. There was no improvement after a week of observation, so Dr. Cloward operated on him, hoping to relieve the pressure on his spinal cord. He withstood the anesthesia and surgery very well in spite of his chronic heart disease. However, his condition worsened. He died on February 6th while I was with him. When I had visited him on the previous day, he could tell by the expression on my face that I was very worried about him. He, himself, knew his condition had worsened. He scolded me for having such a depressed countenance; I knew there was nothing anyone could do for him and was sad that he would die this way. I had tried to comfort many patients in their last days or hours by smiling and talking about things they wanted to hear. Now I was at a loss as what to say and he knew it. He had been my patient for 12 years and had been very good to me and my family. He was a great man and a great philanthropist. He had probably done more for Maui and the Hawaii sugar industry than any other individual. He had helped many young Mauians get an education and had contributed to many charities without publicity.

Dottie became ill with vomiting on March 4th and was admitted to the hospital for a week. She had x-rays taken, and it was thought that she had a stomach ulcer. There were many situations that worried her: problems getting our house built, obstacles getting the Maui Medical Group started. The children had problems at school. All these situations were a strain on Dottie. I was conscious of this, but I had so many things to do that I could not always help her when she needed it.

We were completely moved into our new home by March 30th. I still remember being utterly frustrated and exhausted, at times unable to help Dottie do simple things that had to be done. Too much was required of her, including preparing meals for the family. By April 1st, she was sick again with exhaustion. She visited the doctor and gradually improved. Our friends, including Dr. and Mrs. Hanlon, sent us many prepared meals.

Dottie Jane was Queen of her Junior Prom. She wore a long white dress and was very beautiful. She was slightly over five feet 10 inches tall. The King was Hinano Kaumeheiwa, a tall, handsome Hawaiian boy. On April 8th, Dottie, Carol and I went to Baldwin Auditorium to see her crowned.

Dottie continued to be ill. We had some friends in for dinner on her birthday, April 15th, but she was too sick to enjoy them. Easter Sunday was on the 17th, and I went to church alone. I had to admit Dottie to the hospital in the evening because of vomiting and weight loss. She improved slowly, but stayed in the hospital for 10 days this time. My birthday was on April 21st, and we had a small party at home after which I took some of my cake to the hospital for Dottie.

I had many things to do getting settled in our home. We had the brown rug from our library put in wall-to-wall in one of the bedrooms in the guest cottage. I learned how to install rugs and fitted our dark green rug in the remainder of the guest house. It was a good quality, wool rug we had bought in 1943.

Lois continued her voice lessons and frequently sang solos in addition to singing in the Maunaolu Chorus. We went to Makawao Union Church again on May 1st to hear her sing.

Dottie and I were in Honolulu for four days in May while I attended the annual meeting of the Hawaii Medical Association. Dottie and I went shopping and also visited several friends. I took Dottie to see Dr. Stevens, a psychiatrist, to see if he could help her get over her worries and depression. We spent our last day on the beach at Waikiki.

On May 20th, we attended a special show put on by the Maunaolu Chorus. Professor Barbe and his wife had prepared a special program for a U.S. mainland tour by the chorus which left on May 21st. After giving a show in California, they travelled by chartered plane, giving performances in many cities and finally in Florida. Their program contained hula dances, Hawaiian chants, chorus singing, and special solos. Lois was the leading soprano. Their basso, Gene Cleeland, was outstanding, and I can still remember his unusual voice. They returned home June 15th, having been away 25 days.

We had a tidal wave on the night of May 23, 1960, and 34 people were killed in Hilo, which I have already mentioned. There was little damage on Maui.

I played golf on May 29th, the first time in six months. Dottie was not improving and often suffered periods of severe depression.

Neill wrote that he had $5,000 from an insurance policy that had matured and would be glad to lend it to us. He thought we might need a loan. It was phenomenal that he should be able to lend me money. During his younger years, he was always spending more money than he had and always had difficulty making the payments on this policy. I had not known he still had any insurance. After he and Pearl married, his life changed. I accepted the loan and paid him the same interest I would have had to pay the bank. The loan was a great help to us at that time.

Ann returned home from Wisconsin on June 4th for the summer. It was several days before we learned about her progress there.

Carol graduated from the eighth grade at Kaunoa School on June 7th. She won the D.A.R. medal.

Our faithful yardman, Shun Toyama, took a three-month vacation in Japan. He brought us a beautiful laquered plate, 15 inches in diameter, that he had made especially for us by craftsmen in the district where he was born.

Dottie continued to have problems. The doctors here tried many medicines to help her, but with little success. She continued to manage our home and had a good maid to help her.

On July 3rd and 9th, Dottie, Carol and I again picked blackberries at Olinda, which Dottie processed into jam, jelly and pies. There is nothing as good as a blackberry pie.

Dr. Haywood operated on one of my patients Sunday, July 10th for acute gall bladder disease. She had been my immediate neighbor for the first seven years we lived in Puunene. I spent the entire morning getting her ready for surgery. It took about two hours to remove the infected gall bladder, which was filled with stones. Following the surgery, she did not recover from the anesthesia or breathe spontaneously for three hours. We learned later that she had been treated for arthritis with cortisone by a Honolulu doctor. She had continued taking the cortisone for more than a year without his knowledge, and neither did she tell me about it. Luckily, she finally began breathing on her own and had a normal recovery from the operation.

Dottie's oldest brother, Clifford, died of cancer of the colon on July 12, 1960, at 59 years. He had been the president of the Lewistown Trust Company in Pennsylvania.

Dottie entered the Maui Memorial Hospital on July 14th for six days of tests. Her condition remained the same and nothing significant was found in the tests.

Mildred Mooneyhan, a school principal from Chapel Hill, visited us from July 22nd to the 25th. She was a very good friend of Maisie's and had lived with Maisie and Mamma for several years before Maisie was married.

Dottie's condition did not improve. We decided she needed a change of scenery, so I made arrangements with my friend, Dr. Sam Wallis of Kauai, to admit her to the Wilcox Hopital in Lihue for a week's rest. I took her to Kauai on Sunday, August 7th and returned to Maui the same day. After a week in the hospital, she spent 11 days with our friends, Agnes and Mac Clower. I sent her flowers on our wedding anniversary, August 17th and later went to Kauai myself to spend five days with her and the Clowers.

Lois continued her voice lessons at Maunaolu College during the summer. Professor Barbe and his wife wanted her to continue at Maunaolu for two more years of college and voice training. Then they would consider sending her to Westminster Choir College where he had his musical training.

Dottie did not improve after the Kauai trip. I took a week's vacation and we tried to play golf. Dottie was unable to play. The next day, August 30th, I took her to the Queen's Hospital in Honolulu for psychiatric therapy by Dr. Steven and I came home alone.

The movie, "The Devil at Four O'Clock," was filmed in Lahaina at the site of the Pioneer Inn, the court house, and a nearby old fort. There was much excitement and activity resulting from the filming. I took the children to Lahaina on Labor Day to see all the action.

On September 18th, I went to Honolulu to see Dottie and spent four hours with her. She had been in the hospital for three weeks and was much improved. I was overjoyed. Two days later, she phoned me.

Our four babies had all been large at birth and the first and last deliveries had been very complicated. Carol weighed 10 pounds and four ounces at birth. Dottie had had no specialists to deliver her, and I had to deliver the first baby in an emergency. As a result, she had extensive injury and needed much repair work. Dr. Robert Hunter operated on her on September 27th while she was recovering from her psychiatric treatment. I was present and he made me scrub and help with the surgery. I was back on Maui at 5 p.m. I talked with Dottie on the phone on September 29th and 30th and went to Honolulu to see her on October 2nd. I returned to Honolulu and brought her home on October 4th. We shall ever be grateful to Drs. Stevens and Hunter for their wonderful treatment of Dottie which restored her health to normal. In 1960, she spent 60 days in the hospital in addition to 11 days with the Clowers on Kauai.

On October 15th we again drove to Lahaina to see the movie set. This time, Dottie went with us.

I bought lumber on November 2nd to make a Christmas star to put on our roof. It was 12 feet high and had 43 15-watt, white lights on it. I had had a special socket installed under the eaves for electricity for the star and bought an electric timer to turn the lights on and off. I have now put the star on the roof for two to three weeks every year at Christmas since 1960. In early December the neighborhood children begin asking me when am I going to put the star on the roof. When they see it, they know Christmas is not far away.

Senator John Kennedy, a Democrat, was elected President of the United States on November 8, 1960. He was only 39 years old. To me it seemed that a person this young could not have the wisdom to hold this high office.

Dottie gradually grew stronger and recovered normally. She went to church and played golf for the first time on November 13th.

We had two Micronesian boys, students at Maunaolu College, for Thanksgiving dinner, and they were very appreciative. It was probably their first visit in an American home.

We did not celebrate New Year's Eve, choosing instead to have a quiet evening at home. On New Year's Day we went to church, in spite of a downpour of four inches of rain, and visited friends in the afternoon.

I attended a meeting in Honolulu of the Maternal and Infant Mortality Study Committee on January 6th. Dottie accompanied me to Oahu and we bought a dining room table which we used for 25 years. It was eventually replaced with a table made of beautiful Hawaiian koa wood.

On January 11th, a patient of mine lost control of her car and drove directly into a large monkeypod tree near Waikapu, two miles from my office. I was on the scene quickly, but the police and I had great difficulty extracting her from the car. She received multiple fractures and lacerations when part of the accelerator had gone through her right foot. I worked four hours repairing lacerations and then got help to fix the fractures.

Dr. Roy Nicodemus, my former chief of obstetrics at Geisinger Hospital, his wife and daughter visited us for three days. We had a party for them and invited the members of the Maui Medical Group and their wives.

Each day of their visit we went sightseeing. Dr. Nicodemus did not like the drive up Haleakala because, at that time, the road had only one lane of pavement and there were no guardrails. Within a mile of the summit, we encountered a herd of about 25 wild goats walking up the highway. They moved off the road and allowed us to pass. In the 48 years I have lived on Maui the many times I have been up Haleakala, this is the only time I have ever seen goats en route.

The next day we drove to Lahaina. Along the pali, about 100 yards offshore, a pod of about a dozen whales were swimming slowly along towards Lahaina, frequently blowing air and spray from their nostrils. We drove on beyond Lahaina along the ocean and saw another large pod a few hundred yards off shore. It seemed the whales and goats were putting on a special show for our guests.

Mrs. Joseph Baer, of Chicago, visited us for three days in February. Dr. Baer had died, but we had kept in touch with Janet and had visited her in Chicago. We had a dinner party for her and invited the friends that she had made on her previous visit.

We had a birthday-dinner party for Dottie on April 15th with all four daughters present. We realized this might be the last time we could all celebrate a birthday together.

Dr. and Mrs. Edward Holmblad arrived for a nine-day visit. We had a party for them and attended other parties given in their honor by their many friends. We were very busy for the entire time they were with us.

We attended Makawao Union Church on May 9th to hear the Maunaolu Chorus of which both Ann and Lois were members. The Chorus had been invited by the State Department and the U.S. Department of the Army to entertain our troops in the Far East. Arrangements had been made by Maunaolu College president, Dr. Karl Leebrick, and by U.S. Senator Hiram Fong. The group left for Tokyo via Honolulu on May 11th, traveling in Air Force planes. They entertained troops first at Hickam Air force Base in Honolulu, then at several bases in Japan - including Tokyo and Okinawa - in Korea, Taiwan, the Philippines, and on Guam. Mamasan Oshiro, who had lived with us in Puunene, saw Lois and Ann when they entertained on Okinawa. Sometimes, they gave three performances in a day. They were given the red-carpet-treatment wherever they went and, also, a per diem allowance. Ann told me they were able to get a suitcase- full of clothes laundered for 25 cents. They returned home on June 23rd.

Ann met a Naval officer, Jeff White, when they entertained at Sasebo Naval Base in Southern Japan. They corresponded and, after his discharge, became engaged. Dottie and I met him in Philadelphia where he was attending the Wharton School of Business of the University of Pennsylvania. He was a very fine person. However, Ann fell in love with an engineer where she worked in San Francisco and married him before Jeff finished school. She was 24 years old and I could not interfere with her decisions.

Dottie Jane graduated from Baldwin High School on June 13th and celebrated with a large party at home with many of her friends. She had decided to become a nurse and applied to San Francisco State College and was accepted. However, there was no dormitory room available. McLeod and Louise searched for a suitable room for her, finding one finally on August 22nd. Dottie and I took her to Honolulu early on September 6th and, after doing a lot of shopping, she left for San Francisco alone at 11:30 p.m. She was finally on her own and was very happy. We found it much better to have a child in school on the West Coast rather than in the Mid-West and East. When she became homesick - and children always do - we could talk more on the phone, and she could come home for Christmas holidays.

We had dinner at the Hukilau Hotel on July 19th. Lois's music professor had arranged for her and a fellow chorus member to sing the Hawaiian Wedding Song after dinner.

We attended a first-birthday luau on August 5th for our neighbor's son, Kimo Kaiama, at Yabue's Beach beyond Lahaina. I had delivered him when he was born. First birthdays merit great celebrations and are very important to the Hawaiians because, in olden days, few babies lived beyond the first birthday. When one did live this long, a feast was held in celebration. At the time of this luau, there was only one house on Yabue's Beach. Later, the crescent beach and the property between it and the road were sold for a large sum of money. Now, the site contains 50 or more condominiums.

I gave Dottie a corsage and took her to the Maui Palms Hotel for dinner on August 17th, our 23rd wedding anniversary.

When Lois graduated from Maunaolu College, Professor Barbe recommended her for Westminster Choir College and she was accepted. She left for Princeton, New Jersey, on September 17th.

Dottie and I saw the show "The Devil at Four O'Clock." It had been filmed in Lahaina although the town was barely recognizable in the movie.

Professor Charles Barbe died on October 30th. As usual, he was at work helping put a roof on one of the college buildings. He had been told not to undertake much physical activity, but would not obey his doctor. We will always be thankful that he had discovered Lois's hidden talents and directed her into a career of voice and music. It was beautiful to watch her blossom.

Heavy rains and strong winds hit Maui the first week of November. Twenty-five inches of rain fell in Lahaina in three days, causing much flooding and damage.

Dottie and I had a party for all the Wailuku Sugar Company's supervisors in our new home, to reciprocate for the many times they had entertained us. Although we lost the Wailuku Sugar contract, we thought we should repay them and I'm sure the manager was surprised at the invitation.

We now had three daughters in college at one time and I honestly don't know how I was able to pay all their expenses.

CHAPTER XV

My Life: January, 1962, through August, 1970

FOUR DAUGHTERS COMPLETE SCHOOL
AND MARRY

The new year got off to a slow start with the first baby on Maui arriving at 11:13 a.m. on January 1st. I was the doctor.

The Maui Philharmonic Society sponsored a concert on January 17th with the famous pianist, Firkusny, making his second appearance on Maui. We had six guests in for an early dinner before the concert. The Philharmonic Society sponsored another concert on St. Valentine's Day with a famous violinist as guest artist. Again, we had four guests for an early dinner before the concert. It was unbelievable that we could hear and see so many famous international artists here on Maui. They were attracted to Hawaii, especially in the winter and, after Honolulu, would come to Maui if invited. The audiences on Maui were small but appreciative and we had an excellent auditorium.

On February 17th there was a heavy rainstorm all night. Next morning, Haleakala was covered with a blanket of snow. Snowcaps on Haleakala usually melted within a few days, though occasionally they lasted one to two weeks.

Mrs. Ethel Wylder, Jane Graham's mother, visited for 11 days on her way home from a trip around the world. I drove her up Haleakala where we found zero visibility due to rain and clouds. Now we call the park ranger about the weather before starting this trip.

We heard on March 26th that my brother, Orus, had an operation for cancer of the colon. Although he appeared to be well when we saw him later in the year, he had a recurrence and died within two years, just before his sixty-third birthday. Dottie's oldest brother, Clifford, had died from the same disease at fifty-nine. Both had climbed to the top in the business world, but neither lived to retire and enjoy their successes.

The Hawaii Medical Association had its annual convention on Maui in 1962. A year before, the nominating committee had asked me to accept the position of president-elect. I had had the usual preparation, having been president of Maui County Medical Society, delegate to the Hawaii Medical Association, and a member of the Council of the Hawaii Medical Association for the three previous years. If I accepted the position, I would be required to go to Honolulu often. I had to decline the nomination because of my work load and Dottie's illness. I practiced alone as an obstetrician and was very busy in my practice. I devoted all of my extra time and energy to making the Maui Medical Group a success. It would have been an honor to be president of the Hawaii Medical Association, but helping Dottie more and success of the Maui Medical Group were of greater importance.

Dottie and I hiked into Haleakala Crater for the first time. We had lived on Maui for 21 years but always were too busy to go on this hike. Dottie Jane, Carol and two of their friends were with us. We spent the first night at Kapaloa cabin. It was delightful. The air was crisp - the temperature about 40 degrees that night - the skies were clear and the stars seemed to be nearer. We were away from all the noises and lights of civilization. All we could hear was an occasional bleat from a wild goat.

The second day, we hiked to Paliku cabin in the morning, had our lunch, and then took an hour's rest on the cots in the cabin. In late afternoon we reached Holua cabin where we spent the night. During the day we became hot while hiking and needed a shower by the end of the day. A water tank behind Holua cabin provided an outside shower which I used although I still remember the cold water. The girls heated water on the stove for their baths. One of the girls refused to carry her backpack, although it weighed only 15 pounds, and this meant my load increased. In the afternoon on the third day we hiked up the 2,000-foot Halemauu switchback trail in two hours. Our car was waiting for us, and we reached home at 4:00.

Dottie and I had enjoyed our crater trip so much that, two weeks later, she and I hiked into the crater alone for one night. We reached Holua cabin by 3:00 p.m. and explored the surrounding area, including the long lava tube. We had brought a steak, three inches thick, which I cooked over charcoal. It was so nice living away from everything for just one day.

On September 17th our medical group hired Dr. Wolfgang Pfaeltzer as a junior partner. He was an obstetrician practicing on Maui, but had agreed to also help us in general practice in our Lahaina office until we could afford more help there. It was my idea to hire him, as I could not do all the work in my department and I thought we could get along. I had hoped that finally I would be able to live a normal life and be on call only half the time. However, our arrangement with Dr. Pfaeltzer was to last less than three years and end with bitterness.

I went to the mainland alone for 23 days, leaving Maui on September 21st. During four days in San Francisco with McLeod, Dottie Jane, and Ann, I went over the San Francisco State College campus with Dottie Jane, and decided she was well-situated.

I then flew to North Carolina and visited all my relatives. I was particularly anxious to see Orus after his cancer operation and discussed many things with him, advising him to work less so his chances for full recovery would improve.

In Fayetteville, N.C., I saw my friend, Bruce Langdon, who was busy in his urological practice.

On October 3rd, via television, I saw astronaut Shirra take off and walk on the moon, the first man to do so.

I went to Princeton, N.J., on October 4th to visit Lois at Westminster Choir College and stayed with her for three days. I was very impressed with the school and her work.

During my week's stay in Philadelphia, I reported to the University of Pennsylvania Hospital daily for three days at 7:30 a.m. and watched Dr. Payne operate. He had a dinner party for me at the Faculty Club and invited several of my classmates and friends.

I attended the annual meeting of the American College of Obstetrics and Gynecology, which I planned to join soon. I also attended the banquet of the meeting with my former chief, Dr. Roy Nicodemus, and his wife.

The meeting finished on Saturday morning, October 13th. Lois came from Princeton and we attended the University of Pennsylvania-Navy football game. Dottie's nephew, Bob Graham, was an assistant football coach at the University and his wife, Dot, sat with us at the game. Lois, Jeff White and I had dinner together that evening.

On October 14th, I left for home. I saw Neff and his family at the Chicago airport, and Ann, Dottie Jane, McLeod and his family at the San Francisco airport. I arrived in Honolulu at 6:00 and was home at 8:00 p.m.

I played in the first Makule (Hawaiian for 'old' - 50 years-plus) Golf Tournament and came in second with a 68 net. I won a clock-radio which I still use when I need an alarm to get up early.

My family gave me a Bulova watch, engraved with my name and the date, for Christmas. I used it for 26 years.

On December 13th, Dottie and I hiked into Haleakala Crater with Carol and seven of her friends. The weather was clear with no clouds, and we could see Hana from the trail. We came out the next day.

Carol was a junior in high school at this time and would be home only one more year. We had had children with us for 23 years and soon would be alone, just as we were when we married 24 years before. As of this writing, we have been alone for 25 years and will celebrate our golden wedding anniversary in a few months. All our 50 years together have been golden, but particularly the last 25. We have seen our dreams come true; we have accomplished what we set out to do when we married. Now we are enjoying memories of the past as well as our present lives in our Hōmĕ Pilialoha. Our children are mature and settled in their careers. We join them in hopes and plans for our seven grandchildren. We hope we can see all of them develop and be productive in the generation of tomorrow.

THE YEAR 1963

Our medical group was functioning more normally by the beginning of 1963. Business was improving gradually, we each had a fixed monthly income, and we all looked forward to the distribution of net profits every six months. I no longer had to be chairman, chief finance officer, personnel director, etc. Every member had put in his share of working capital. We organized ourselves into a democratic group with committees to manage different activities. When we had organized five years before, I was the only one who had had any experience with group practice. Now, everyone was beginning to see how it worked and how it could benefit all. Dr. Tofukuji was made chairman of the group and I was chairman of the personnel committee. After a few years, I was appointed chairman of the long-range planning and recruitment committee. Although every one of the original members had his own ideas on how to run the group, a consensus eventually prevailed. A chairman's opinion might be accepted at first, only to have to be reversed later.

The year got off to a routine start. I had a patient who fell from a tree and fractured his jaw. I last treated such a fracture in 1940 but now could refer this patient to others in our group.

Dr. Robert Wilson, professor of Obstetrics and Gynecology at Temple University, and his wife were our house guests for two days. They were on their way home from a trip around the world and were stopping in Hawaii for lectures to each county medical society. I took them to Hana one afternoon and to the top of Haleakala the next morning. They gave us a temple rubbing of an ancient Chinese dynasty horse. It now hangs on a living room wall beside a love poem written in Chinese characters.

We had a storm on January 16th and 17th, with winds up to 70 miles per hour and heavy rain. The two plexiglas skylights in our dressing rooms were blown out, one coming to rest on the drive in front of the house. When the skylights had been installed, they were supposed to be secured with four screws, but were not. The rain caused some damage to the rugs and paint. Luckily, our insurance reimbursed us for repairs. It took about a week to clean the yard after the storm.

On February 3rd, I was made a deacon in our church. I assumed the appointment was for a year, but found it was for three years. Although I did not have much time to devote to this responsibility, I did the best I could.

I got a call from my friend, Paul Cameron, who was vacationing in Honolulu and planned to come to Maui. We had roomed together, one year in college and one year in medical school. His wife, Vivian, refused to fly, so he brought a friend, a supermarket manager, with him. They had a week in Hawaii and planned to play golf on all the islands. They quickly changed their plans and stayed with us for five days and on Oahu for two days. We played golf every day and bridge in the evenings. I took them up Haleakala one day. As I have said before, he was probably my best friend. Dottie and I played golf with him and Vivian during one of our later trips to New Jersey.

I operated on a patient for acute appendicitis on February 23rd, but found instead acute diverticulitis of the cecum.

On the 25th, a 75-year old patient asked for medication for constipation. Just to be complete, I had her put on the examining table and found a large abdominal mass, which had caused the constipation. At operation, it proved to be an eight-pound ovarian cyst.

We had our home refinanced so that we would have enough money to educate the girls. I paid only six and a half percent interest on our mortgage, which was very low. Interest rates would more than double in the next few years.

Sam and Ellie Lebold were on Maui for two days of golf and dinner parties with us. A week later, Ellie's mother, Mrs. Janet Baer and her friend, Mrs. Weil, were with us as house guests for three days.

I received a letter from the American College of Obstetricians and Gynecologists on March 21, 1963, stating that I had been elected a fellow. This is one of the highlights of my professional life, finally being accepted as a specialist in the medical profession. My medical training had been interrupted and I never did take the American Boards. Drs. Robert Hunter and Herbert Bowles of Honolulu had sponsored me after seeing the type of work I had done during my 24 years in Hawaii. Being a fellow of the college had many advantages, especially in postgraduate education.

Carol had written an essay in a school contest on Employment of the Handicapped. It came in first in the state and won her a free trip to Washington, D.C., to compete nationally. On May 7th the winners from the four counties were invited to a special luncheon in Honolulu hosted by Governor Burns. Later in the day, Carol and Dottie left for the mainland. They received the red-carpet-treatment all the way. Senator Inouye's aide, Henry Giugni, met them with a limousine at the airport in Washington and helped them throughout their stay. The senator had arranged a special meeting for Carol and Vice President Lyndon Johnson but it had to be cancelled due to the state of emergency caused by the racial disturbance at Selma, Alabama. President Johnson's secretary took Carol and Dottie on a tour of the Oval Office and other private areas of the White House. An awards banquet was arranged for all the contestants. The handicapped student of the year attended and gave an inspirational speech. All were given a grand tour of the White House, Senate and House chambers, the Supreme Court, the Lincoln Memorial, and other government buildings.

Carol had seen all of this on our 1955 tour and had remembered much. This surprised the other contestants, most of whom had never been out of their home states.

The dirt bank at the back of our yard presented a problem. It was 14 feet high and, as the dirt continuously slid down, I hauled it away. Finally I built a wall at the base of the bank with slabs of discarded cement faced with lava rock. It is 30 inches thick and 50 inches high in the center. I had planned to make it 36 inches higher later. The wall is 225 feet long and, at each end, only 15 inches high. Moss now covers the lava rock. The wall is a masterpiece of masonry. It took me six months to finish it and my back still hurts as a result of the hard work. Some of the pieces of lava and cement weighed 150 pounds each. I planted wedelia on the bank to hold the top soil and roots from the trees in the forest have penetrated the bank and also help hold the soil.

Our daughters were all very musical. All four sang in the Wailuku Union Church Choir. The three younger ones took piano lessons from Mrs. Claire Nashiwa. Dottie Jane and Carol excelled in her classes and always played in her music recital at Baldwin Auditorium. Dottie Jane's recital number was "Moonlight Sonata" by Beethoven, which she played beautifully. Carol memorized her music after she had played it two or three times, even a piece 20 minutes long. I could not understand how she was able to do this. The adjudicators always gave her a high mark and even recommended that she make music a career.

Dottie Jane played the flute, and Carol and Ann were both the first chair trombonist in the Baldwin High School Band. I bought a good trombone for Ann, which Carol used later. She was appointed the manager of the band her senior year, the first girl to ever hold this position at Baldwin High. She left with the band on May 29th to give concerts in Hilo and Kona under the direction of the band teacher, Saburo Watanabe. He spent about one-third of his class period lecturing to the band members on general conduct and morality. He had two children of his own and was genuinely interested in all his students. He had a great influence on them and they all loved him, as did we parents. Dottie and I shall ever be grateful to him for help in rearing our children.

Carol returned home alone from Washington, D.C., on May 19th. Dottie visited Lois at Westminster Choir College and then spent several days with her mother in Lewistown, Pa. She went on to San Francisco and stayed about two weeks with Dottie Jane and Ann, finally arriving home on June 23rd.

Our friends, Jack and Bennie Lightner from Virginia, were with Carol and me from June 12th to 18th. Carol prepared a few of our meals, though we ate lunch and dinner with friends most of the time.

A patient was referred to me immediately upon her arrival from Chicago. She had been sick with a chest problem since the birth of her son six years prior. She also had a 12-year old daughter. This was the second marriage for her 70-year-old husband.

A routine chest x-ray taken when her last child was born showed a small lesion similar to an early tuberculosis infection. However, many sputum tests were negative and neither she nor her husband would accept the fact that she probably had pulmonary tuberculosis. Her doctor and the Board of Health of Chicago recommended she be treated for tuberculosis, but she refused. Instead, she and her husband ignored her problem. Finally she became so sick she decided to come to Hawaii, thinking the sunshine might help her. The family arrived with a new Corvette convertible.

I examined her in mid-afternoon and it was easy to determine that she had advanced lung disease. I admitted her to the hospital, got a chest x-ray, and had her sputum examined for tuberculosis. All parts of both lungs were riddled with tuberculosis and the sputum smear was loaded with tuberculosis bacilli. She died early the next morning before I could transfer her to the Kula TB Sanatorium. Her husband took the body and their 6-year-old son back to Chicago. Dottie kept the 12-year-old daughter and the car for several weeks until he returned. It was a very sad situation.

I got a call from McLeod on July 29th that Mamma had died during the night. She had broken her hip in a fall and her heart was so weak the doctors refused to operate. They put her in a body cast instead which was very uncomfortable and she could not rest. She died during her sleep, at age 83. Her own mother had broken her hip in her early sixties and it never healed. She had to use crutches until she died at 69 of pernicious anemia. I feel sure that the prospect of being crippled with a broken hip like her mother had depressed Mamma. It was some comfort to me to know that she died in her sleep without prolonged pain. She and I struggled for nine years at Coats and a year at Chapel Hill to eke out a living and to make a better future for ourselves and for my younger brother and sister. There is nothing that can replace a loving mother.

In a recent letter from Maisie, who was the third of eight children, she had the following to say about Mamma: "She would churn (milk) with one hand, nurse a baby and read at the same time. She studied nutrition for our sakes and always had a milk cow. She attended county administration courses that were brought to Coats. She really had a thirst for life at its best. I wish she had gotten to college for one year. However, coming to Chapel Hill made up for the loss somewhat. She took a part in things here. She was the first treasurer of the Women's Garden Club. Mrs. Eubanks drove her to the meetings. She attended programs on the campus with me. We could walk from Wilson Street."

Maisie became a student at the university and got a second degree. All the cultural activities of the university were available to Mamma through Maisie and, in this way, Mamma received some of the fringe benefits of a college education.

I gave Dottie a silver bracelet on our 25th wedding anniversary, while she, Carol and I were visiting the Wallises on Kauai. We played golf, cribbage and bridge with the Wallises.

President Kennedy was assassinated on November 22nd in Dallas, Texas, and Vice President Lyndon Johnson took over as president. He was sworn into office aboard the presidential plane on the way to Washington. Monday, November 25th, was set aside as a day of mourning for President Kennedy. He had been in office less than three years and was actively carrying out the duties of the president. His death was a very tragic event in our country's history.

Carol, Dottie and I had Thanksgiving dinner at home alone. I cannot remember any other Thanksgiving that we did not invite guests for dinner.

Dottie Jane arrived home on December 14th for the Christmas holidays. I took a two-week vacation, and we drove to Hana via Kaupo. We had our Christmas dinner on Christmas Eve with only Dottie Jane, Carol, Dottie and me present. The year ended quietly except for the neighbor's firecrackers.

THE YEAR 1964

On January 13th, Ann telephoned from Honolulu on her way to Tokyo for a vacation. She had received a bonus at the end of the year and felt she had to spend it. The inn where she stayed in Tokyo had a wood burning stove, and she became very ill from carbon monoxide poisoning. Luckily, she recovered. When she returned to San Francisco she began working as executive secretary for Admiral Thomas Hamilton, commissioner for the Big Eight Athletic Conference.

Cassius Clay, later known as Muhammed Ali, won the world heavyweight boxing title on February 25th, beating Sonny Liston by technical knockout in the 6th round. It is interesting that as of this writing, Ali has advanced deterioration of parts of his nervous system, probably due to the trauma of boxing. Even though he made millions of dollars, in my opinion he continued long after he should have stopped.

On March 8th, Dottie and I had 31 guests in to meet Dr. and Mrs. Bertram Weeks, a new member of the Maui Medical Group. Dr. Weeks had been an army colonel and had bought a home on Maui on his retirement. He was the first specialist in internal medicine to establish a permanent residence and practice on Maui. His knowledge of internal medicine was astounding and he instilled the greatest of confidence in his patients, both in his office and at bedside in the hospital. We were fortunate he chose to join us. My dream of having a medical group with specialists to care for our patients was becoming a reality. So far, we had added a pediatrician and now an internist. Dr. Rockett had returned as a second general surgeon.

We had a county medical society meeting at Kula Sanatorium on March 22nd. Smoking and emphysema were discussed. I remember seeing the microscopic slides of tissue taken from the lungs of smokers who had died of emphysema. The walls of the alveoli were thickened with inflammatory cells, and the alveoli themselves were mostly obliterated. It is beyond my comprehension that supposedly intelligent individuals will smoke and destroy their lungs, leading to protracted illness and death.

Smoking also produces cancer of the lung, a disease that was almost unheard of when I was a student. I saw only one case while I was in school. Now, it is one of the leading causes of death, due to widespread cigarette smoking.

When I joined the American College of Obstetrics and Gynecology I met Mr. Don Richardson, its executive director. He had heard about goat hunting on Maui and asked me to arrange a hunting trip for him and his 14-year-old son. A friend of mine owned a four-wheel-drive jeep and knew a cowboy at Ulupalakua Ranch who had a hunting lodge on the south slopes of Haleakala above the round-the-island road. This cowboy also had a four-wheel-drive jeep. I made the necessary arrangements and, when Don's family visited us for a few days, Don, his son and I left with my friend for the hunting lodge. We all had 30-30 caliber rifles. We arrived about 5 p.m. and our host prepared a good dinner of beef stew. He had many stories to tell about the area in olden times when many Hawaiians lived there.

The whole mountainside was honeycombed with lava tubes and caves. Our host worked only three days a week maintaining the watering troughs for the cattle and spent much of his spare time exploring the caves and lava tubes.

Noisy, wild peacocks made weird sounds all night. The next morning we were up at 4:30 and, after a good breakfast, we left for the top of the mountain. We immediately ran into dense clouds and rain. We arrived near the top of the south side of the crater rim, about 8,000 feet above sea level, by 6 a.m. This was the area where goats were usually found. It continued to rain. It seemed that the goats had left the mountain to avoid the rain as we could not find them. After a couple of hours waiting, my friend, Don and his son drove down the mountain and found goats near the shoreline. However, they were out of range.

While they were gone, my cowboy host and I explored several caves and lava tubes. The Hawaiians had used the caves as shelters, storage areas, burial places, etc.

A large outrigger canoe was in one cave. It was in good condition and apparently had been there a long time. In heavy rainstorms, some of the lava tubes become rivers, and the water covers the cave contents with sand and dirt. I did not see any human bones, though my host said he had seen skeletons.

We left the lodge about 4 p.m. and arrived home two hours later. We had a nice day exploring, but failed to accomplish our mission.

A few days later Don and his son went sheep hunting on the Island of Hawaii, and the son got a large ram with long horns. He sent me a picture of himself holding the ram's head.

I gave Dottie a gold necklace and matching earrings on our 26th wedding anniversary, August 17th.

Carol had been accepted at the University of Washington and left Maui for Seattle on September 17th. She was an honors student and loved her schoolwork, amassing 30 credits in high school when only 20 were required to graduate. She had gone to summer school for two years while she was too young to work in the pineapple cannery. She loved English composition and complained when certain teachers failed to require several dissertations. Her counselor recommended she study journalism in college, and that is why she chose the University of Washington. Her college counselor came to a different conclusion. He suggested she choose occupational therapy as a career. This was a five-year course including a one-year internship. She completed the requirements and became a licensed occupational therapist. Since graduation, she has always been employed and now is considering going back to school for a graduate degree. Besides getting her degree from the University of Washington, she met Peter Keck, whom she fell in love with and later married.

My partner in obstetrics, Dr. Pfaeltzer, and the Maui Medical Group were having problems with his contract, so - at his suggestion - he was put on terminal leave. This meant I would be alone again until I could find a replacement for him. I had already made plans to attend the meeting of the American College of Obstetrics and Gynecology in San Diego in September.

Dottie and I left for San Francisco on September 8th. Dottie Jane and her boyfriend, Michael Mote, met us next morning at the airport. He was studying for his master's degree at San Francisco State College and was one of Dottie Jane's teachers. They took us to the University of California-Missouri football game and, later, we had dinner with McLeod and Louise. The next day, we attended a baseball game between San Francisco and Pittsburgh.

We were staying with Ann in Oakland and learned to ride the commuter buses into San Francisco. Ann worked all day Sunday at the office of the Big Eight Athletic Conference, but was off duty on Monday when she went shopping with us in San Francisco. In the evening, we were invited by Michael's parents, Dr. and Mrs. Clayton Mote, to the Olympic Club for dinner. Dottie Jane and Michael also were guests. It was easy to see that plans were being made for us to be in-laws.

Tuesday was our last day in San Francisco and again we went shopping. Dottie Jane drove to Oakland in the evening, and we enjoyed a good dinner with our two daughters.

On Wednesday we left for San Diego. I attended medical meetings every morning for three days. We played golf twice at Coronado Golf Club and almost froze in the 60 degree-weather. We were wearing shorts; others were playing in warmer attire.

We went sightseeing one afternoon to Tijuana, which was our first visit to

Mexico and, needless to say, disappointing. We returned home on September 27th.

Dr. Frank Lock, professor of Obstetrics and Gynecology at Wake Forest University Medical School, and his wife, Bonnie, were our house guests for two days. He spoke to the Maui County Medical Society on Sunday morning, November 8th. In the afternoon, we took them up Haleakala, but we couldn't see the crater as it rained the entire time. On Saturday, we had taken them to The Whaling Spree in Lahaina and to a luau at the old prison. Someone had dropped a large bowl of poi in the grass by the luau tables, and Bonnie stepped in it with her beautiful silk shoes. It was just as though she had stepped in fresh cow manure in a barnyard. She was upset at first, but relieved when we told her what it was. After Dr. Lock and I cleaned her shoes, we ate the luau, including some poi, and they enjoyed it all very much.

Bonnie wanted to buy some oriental art to decorate their new condominium in Florida. She asked Dottie to help her and signed a blank check for her to use. Dottie called a department store manager on Sunday morning. He opened his store for her, and she bought several scrolls, screens and oriental paintings which, Dottie says, would be worth a fortune at today's prices.

The Locks were some of the most enjoyable guests we ever had. Dr. Lock has since died.

The Canada Cup matches in golf (now the World Cup) were held at Kaanapali Golf Course in Lahaina the first week in December. Dottie was a scorer and walked 18 holes each day. She returned home at 9 p.m. the last day, tired, sunburned and thoroughly saturated with golf. I saw some of the play on the third day. Arnold Palmer and Jack Nicklaus were playing with the two Canadian entries. The four of them made three eagles and one birdie on the same hole.

Carol arrived home on December 16th for the Christmas holidays, and Dottie Jane came on the 19th. She was wearing a large diamond, placed on her finger by Michael.

We had Christmas dinner on Christmas Eve and Ethel Ige, our former maid, ate with us. She was a great friend of our daughters, and they were glad to see her again.

We had 36 guests at a dinner party on December 28th, announcing Dottie Jane's engagement. It was a glorious evening, and we served champagne. I had written the following poem as a toast, which I read at the party. It was a big hit. When Michael read the toast later, he began to wonder if I loved Dottie Jane too much.

Toast to Dottie Jane by Her Father
(upon the Announcement of Her Engagement to Michael Mote, December 28, 1964)

Here's to my sweetheart named Dottie Jane,
Who was born twenty-one years ago and received that name.
She was as beautiful as any angel could be
And a replica of her mother, it was easy to see.
 Her eyes were as large as saucers and so blue,
 That one could hardly believe it was true.
 Her smile was so dear and sublime
 That I knew she would not forever be mine.
When she was small, she called me "Bull,"
But the meaning of that word was not known in full.

Each little word that she did say
Would cheer me up at the end of the day.
    And then, up and up she began to grow,
    But how far no one could know.
    While playing, she fell and broke her back.
    The fracture healed and from her height did not detract.
Finally, she grew and became so tall
That she would not stand beside me at all.
In school her beauty was seen at a glance
And she was selected Queen of the Junior Class Dance.
    As a musician she was very astute . . .
    She joined the band and played the flute.
    The piano she learned to perfection
    And played "Moonlight Sonata" as her best selection.
Her disposition was so sweet and kind-
One knew her career would be easy to find.
When she decided that nursing would be her fate,
She matriculated at San Francisco State.
    And the name that I had loved so dearly
    Then lost its second half, but surely.
    And now when she comes home to visit me,
    I have two Dotties as you can see.
I went to visit her last fall,
But she hardly saw me at all.
She introduced me to Michael when I arrived
And it was plain to see a plot had been contrived.
    Finally, after much visitation, he did plead
    For Dottie's hand in marriage, indeed!
    After due and timely consideration,
    I said "yes" with great elation.
All my daughters I trust and love
And know they have been guided by God above.
Whomever they choose for their partners to be,
I will love and hope they will love me.
    Dottie came home Christmas to celebrate,
    But her hand is so heavy her wrist will hardly articulate.
    Upon her finger a diamond does shine
    And, after next August, she will not be mine.
With friends gathered together, old and new,
A celebration certainly is due.
And now upon this joyous occasion,
Let us drink to her happiness without persuasion!

THE YEAR 1965

I got a sad telephone call on January 2nd from McLeod, telling me that Orus had died. He had had a horrible year in 1964 with multiple metastases of his rectal cancer. His maxilla and mandible were involved, and his teeth had come out. Dottie sent him a large box of vanda orchids while he was in the hospital. They arrived in perfect condition. He gave many of them to his nurses and other friends who were very appreciative and this made him feel good temporarily. I had lived and worked with Orus for eight summers. He helped me in every way he could, and without his help I might not have gotten a college education. He was proud of McLeod and me, whom he had encouraged and helped. He died one month before his 62nd birthday. I doubt many his age had done more work than he. He learned the grocery business by trial and error. In the late 1920s, we worked a six-day week with 16 hours on Saturday, and he succeeded as a groceryman, eventually owning four stores. Then he bought a large farm and started a meat packing plant, becoming a very successful meat processor, packer and distributor. He always went to church on Sunday morning, even if he had worked 16 hours on Saturday. He was a leader in his community. He had an outstanding record of racial harmony in his meat packing plant, where his two top foremen were blacks. It is really sad that he did not live longer to enjoy the success he had achieved. He inherited the business mind of my father, as has his son, Orus Jr. He will live on through his several grandchildren who are doing well in their endeavors.

The American College of Obstetrics and Gynecology had its annual meeting in San Francisco in April and a post-convention meeting for four days at the Sheraton Hotel at Kaanapali, Maui. As the only member living on Maui, I was the local chairman and also chaired the last session. Dottie and I were given our choice of rooms, and we chose one in a cottage by the golf course. We both had our cars and parked them near our cottage. We also had free meals including the breakfast buffet, a gourmet's delight I will never forget.

I helped the tour operator set up the meeting facilities at the hotel, and Dottie and I helped him with a social program and entertainment for the wives. The meetings were held each morning, Monday through Thursday, from 8 a.m. till 1 p.m. The attendance at the meetings was good and every seat - about 150 - in the meeting hall was occupied. The afternoons and evenings were free so I played golf the first three afternoons. We had a Hawaiian luau one evening. Everybody seemed to enjoy himself and the meeting was a great success.

On April 24th, Michael McGovern arrived on Maui for a 24-hour visit with Dottie and me. He was Ann's friend from San Francisco and was passing through Hawaii on his way home from the South Pacific. While there, he had been a consultant for an engineering project working for Kennedy Engineers where Ann had formerly worked. We would see more of him in the future.

Also on April 24th, Dr. William Kroutil, his wife and three children arrived on Maui to join the Maui Medical Group. He had just finished his four-year residency in obstetrics and gynecology, and we had hired him to begin work in June. We were short one physician in Lahaina, so he agreed to come one month early to help us out there temporarily. The Medical Group had a party for him and his wife the day he arrived.

Curiously, some members of the Maui Medical Group treated Dr. Kroutil like a beginning intern in general practice. He was doing my backlog of major gynecological surgery and had demonstrated that he was not only capable, but was well-liked by the patients.

Dr. Kroutil saw that the Maui Medical Group had double standards for its doctors. By August 1st, he realized he did not want to be a part of it and resigned, agreeing to stay with us until the end of October so that I could get a vacation. He sent his family back to California before school started in September and lived in our home while we were away.

I had been frustrated with the members of the Maui Medical Group for six years and was grossly overworked. Dottie and I could take this no longer. I wrote a letter to the Group in August stating that, unless I could get an associate soon, I was resigning and entering solo practice. This letter was to serve as my six months' notice. I had written a possible associate and would make every effort to find one so I could remain in the Group.

Dottie Jane and Michael Mote had set their wedding date for Saturday, August 21, 1965. She returned from San Francisco, where she had been working as a nurse, on August 1st, and Dottie met her in Honolulu. They stayed for three days, buying Dottie Jane's trousseau. From then until August 21st, everyone was busy making preparations for the first wedding in our family. I took two weeks' vacation, starting on August 16th. Ann had arrived home on August 14th. A large contingent of Michael's relatives, family and friends and members of the wedding party were arriving from California for the prenuptial activities and the wedding.

August 17th was our own wedding anniversary. Our daughters took us to the Royal Lahaina Hotel for dinner, though Lois did not arrive on Maui until two days later.

It had been decided by Dottie Jane and her mother that it would be a large wedding and reception with all the frills. Nothing was to be denied. With so many out-of-town guests, this was an ideal time to have a large celebration.

The guests arrived on Maui early, many of them by August 18th. Michael and his friends had to go through the Watts riot area on their way to the Los Angeles airport and were barely able to get through. Our friends, the Pat Walkers, loaned Michael's two brothers their beach cottage at Kihei. One brother had a family of four, while the other had his girlfriend. There was also the best man and several more young friends of Michael's. Some slept on the floor.

There was one complication. Kihei was overrun with field mice at that time. The ecosystem had been disturbed so that predators such as owls and cats had not kept the mouse population under control. Each evening when the young folk returned home, they would have a mouse polo game, using brooms and mops for mallets. Several mice were destroyed.

On August 19th, we had a dinner in our home for 36 wedding guests. This was the beginning of the celebration, and there was much activity thereafter, particularly for the young adults.

We had the wedding rehearsal on Friday, August 20th, and afterwards, Michael's parents hosted the rehearsal dinner in the Sky Room of the Wailuku Hotel.

The hotel was new and nice, and many of the guests were staying there. None of the staff knew much about wines although the hotel had a wine cellar. Dr. Mote was a connoisseur of wines and visited the wine cellar to choose suitable ones for dinner. As I recall, we had a red wine with dinner and brandies and liqueur were served after dinner. We had a very enjoyable evening.

The dinners on Thursday and Friday ended about 10:30 and we older people went to bed. However, the younger guests were not satiated. Lahaina, with its night life, was only 25 miles away. Kui Lee, a native Hawaiian boy from Honolulu, as yet unrecognized as a serious Hawaiian composer, was performing in night clubs there. He had developed a type of modern Hawaiian melody that retained the beautiful melodies of old Hawaii and combined them with the newer sounds. He wrote many lovely songs which he played nightly. Our daughters and the young guests were simply enthralled by his music and went back to hear him over and over. Sadly, he developed a fatal illness and died the following year. Jack DeMello has recorded an album of his music, which everyone who loves Hawaiian music should own.

Dottie Jane and Michael were married at the Wailuku Union Church by the Reverend Emerson Sanderson at noon on Saturday, August 21, 1965. The church was filled. I proudly walked down the aisle and gave her in marriage. She wore a beautiful, white dress and was a lovely bride.

Following the ceremony, we had a wedding reception luncheon at the Maui Country Club for 300 guests. Champagne punch was served as well as fruit punch. After going through the reception line, the guests served themselves from a buffet in the upstairs dining room.

During the luncheon, music was played by Earl Apo, Eddie Wilson and Henry Long. Alice Johnson was the vocalist. She and Earl sang the Hawaiian Wedding Song, Ke Kali Nei Au. Finally, the wedding cake, which had been made by Beth Behrmann as a gift, was served. Activities had to end by 3:00 p.m. so that the newlyweds could catch a plane to Kauai at 4:00. The Motes and the Pattersons had had a wonderful day.

The Motes were members of the Sierra Club and were avid mountaineers. I had reserved Kapalaoa Cabin in Haleakala Crater for the night of August 22nd. Dr. Clayton Mote and wife, Lula, Pete Mote and his girlfriend, Taffy, Cookie Knoles (maid of honor) and I started hiking in the crater on the Sliding Sand trail late Sunday morning. We cooked our dinner in the cabin and all slept in one large room. I remember Dr. Mote going to bed with nothing on above his waist except his underwear. He slept soundly and didn't mind the temperature, which was about 50 degrees. I could never sleep well on the cots (no springs) due to my gouty arthritis.

Next day, we prepared breakfast and then hiked out of the crater, taking the long route so we could see more. Lula was very frail and weighed less than 100 pounds. She was unable to keep up with the rest of the group, so I stayed with her to be sure she didn't fall and get hurt. It rained as we came out of the crater, but we had a very successful trip.

Michael McGovern arrived on August 24th and stayed for 12 days. The newlyweds stayed on Kauai for two days, and then returned to Maui to stay in our guest cottage. Carol had a friend also named Michael. On August 27, Dottie and I took our three youngest daughters, all with escorts names Michael, to the James Lodge at Kula for dinner.

Dottie Jane and Michael left for Los Angeles on August 28th. Michael was studying for his Ph.D. degree at the University of California, and Dottie Jane would begin working in a doctor's office to help support them. It was Labor Day, September 6th, before all the guests had left, leaving only Carol, Dottie and me at home.

Dottie, Carol, Michael Walker and I spent the night of September 18th in the crater at Holua Cabin. We loved the peace and quiet. On this trip, we saw several goats.

MAINLAND TRIP 1965

Dottie, Carol and I left for Seattle and the University of Washington on September 23rd. We arrived the next morning and toured the campus after getting Carol settled in her dormitory. On Sunday, the 25th, the three of us took the last ferry of the season to Victoria, where Dottie and I planned to stay at the Empress Hotel. As soon as we arrived, we took a tour of the world-renowned Butchart Gardens. We attended our first formal British tea at the hotel at 4 p.m. and were served scones.

Carol was very amused at the little old British ladies and the tea. She caught the ferry back to Seattle at 5:30 p.m., which was near sunset, and planned to take a taxi from the dock to her dormitory.

Dr. Tim McCoy and his wife, Marge, met us in their car at the Empress at 1 p.m. the next day. He had known Dottie's family at Lewistown, Pa., when he was a resident physician in the hospital there in the 1930s. He was one of the original owners of the Napili Kai Beach Hotel on Maui and we had become close friends. They lived in the City of Vancouver and had been to a medical meeting in Victoria. We toured the city and I remember a beautiful golf course by the ocean. Finally, we drove the car onto a ferry and had a very pleasant journey to Vancouver, about 70 miles away.

Dottie and I spent the night in the beautiful new Four Seasons Hotel in Vancouver. The next day, the McCoys took us on a tour of the city including Stanley Park and zoo. We visited their home and met two of their children.

Their son, Bryant, was a young teenager, busy at the time with a roomful of toy trains. At present, he is co-owner of Maui Gold Manufacturing in Lahaina and is a successful gemologist and goldsmith. He also owns a banana and macadamia nut farm in the Napili area.

Dottie and I boarded the Canadian Pacific Railway train at 8:40 p.m. and left for Calgary, Alberta. We had a bedroom on the train and had a good sleep although it was sad that we missed so much beautiful scenery during the night. We were up early next morning and went to the car with the sightseeing dome. I saw a black bear on the bank near the tracks. At one point, we could see the train tracks at three levels as they went in and out of tunnels climbing the Rocky Mountains. We arrived at Calgary at 5 p.m. and stayed overnight at the Palliser Hotel. There was snow on the ground.

We left for Toronto next morning by Air Canada and finally reached New York City at 6 p.m. We checked into the Americana Hotel at 7:15 , where I would attend a section meeting of the American College of Obstetricians and Gynecologists.

From our hotel room window, we could see the marquee on the theater advertising the show, "Funny Girl" with Barbra Streisand. I went to the box office immediately and was able to get two good seats. I had learned in 1955 that often unsold theater tickets would be returned about 7 p.m. Again, I was lucky.

On September 30th, I attended medical meetings in the morning. Dottie and I visited several stores on Fifth Avenue in the afternoon and also went to Central Park and Lincoln Center. In the evening, we returned to hear the New York Philharmonic Orchestra with Leonard Bernstein conducting.

Next day, I attended medical meetings all morning and afternoon. In the evening, we went back to Lincoln Center to see the New York City Ballet in Don Quixote. The choreographer was George Balanchine. The stage designs were a perfect background for the ballet.

The medical meeting ended after the morning session on Saturday, October 2nd. We went to the World's Fair in the afternoon and evening. The enormous crowds made it difficult to get tickets to see the exhibits. We arrived back at the hotel at 10:30 p.m., exhausted.

On Sunday, we took an elevated train to Shea Stadium and saw a double-header baseball game between the Phillies and the Mets. The score for both games was three-to-one in favor of the Phillies. I don't think I have been so cold in my life. We had lightweight coats, not nearly adequate for temperatures in the upper 40s. In the evening, we saw the show, "The Great Race," at Radio City Music Hall and then had dinner at Radio City Plaza.

Before we left Maui, we had bought a new car from the local General Motors dealer for New York City delivery. It was late in the year and the next year's models would be available within a week or so. I told the dealer I would take any two-door model he could find. He was able to get us a black Chevrolet Impala Super Sport Coupe with red upholstery. I was to report to General Motor's Export Headquarters in New York City on October 4th to get the car. There, I learned the car was at a dealership in New Jersey, and that we would be transported there for delivery. Pope Paul was visiting in New York City that day and passed the General Motors building while we were there. We saw him, but had to wait 30 minutes until he had come and gone before we could leave for New Jersey. Finally, we took possession of our car, put on Hawaii license plates and left for Lewistown. We loved the car and still own it. Dottie has taken good care of it and the upholstery still looks like new. It has been driven 123,000 miles and is now classified as an antique. There is just one other like it on this island, a white one.

We stayed in Pennsylvania for five days and visited all the relatives. We were with Roy and Jerry Nicodemus for one night in Danville and saw Dr. Harold Foss for the last time. He was in his 80s by then. Dr. Henry Hunt was a patient in the hospital with emphysema, and this was the last time we would see him. These three men had supported me during my two years of research at the Geisinger Hospital 29 years before.

We left Lewistown October 9th and briefly visited our old Honolulu friend, Mildred Wilbar, in Harrisburg. We drove on to Round Hill, Virginia, where we spent one night with Jack and Bennie Lightner. We arrived in time to play 18 holes of golf with them.

Next morning we went to see Amelia Lightner, our friend who had lived on Maui, on her farm at Upperville, and then drove to Richmond to see Dottie's niece, Marjorie Shearer. From there we continued on to Williamsburg, arriving at 5 p.m. at the Heritage Motel. We stayed there two days, spending an entire day touring the town and visiting all the buildings and exhibits. A new visitor orientation facility with a theater had been completed, and we saw a movie of about 30 minutes that explained everything. We had great nostalgia about Williamsburg because of our visit in 1955 with the children, but we could not relive the past or feel the thrill we had had before. The eagerness and anticipation a child experiences when visiting such a place cannot be recaptured by adults. The fond memories of our visit in 1955 far outshone anything that we gleaned from this visit, but we had to visit it again.

We drove to Coats, N.C., and saw my mother's grave. We visited many relatives briefly en route, spending one or two nights with each of my sisters and with Sally and O.F. Patterson Jr.

My brother-in-law, Dr. Jack Thornton, was professor of economics at the Citadel, and my sister, Dorothy, taught at a college in Charleston, S.C. We arrived there on a Saturday and saw a football game between the Citadel and Arkansas State. On Sunday morning we toured Charleston and saw the mansions that dated from Ante-bellum times. The architecture had been influenced by the Spanish and French. In the summer, the weather is often hot but the air is cooled by sea breezes. Most of the houses are two stories with a screened porch on both floors where the occupants sleep to keep cool. The yards of most homes had several large magnolia trees.

We left for Asheville at 1 p.m. and reached there before dark, an easy drive on the Interstate Highway. When I was living in the area in the early 1930s, it would have taken all day to drive this distance. Next morning we drove around Asheville, which is a beautiful city. I remember the tunnel in the middle of town. From Asheville we went to Waynesville, N.C., where Velma and Marcus owned a mountain house on Lake Junaluska which we saw only from the road. We then toured the Great Smoky Mountain Park, driving west to Tennessee. These mountains are completely covered with trees, and it was the season for the leaves to change color. A whole mountainside would be a flaming yellow, gold or red color. It is impossible to imagine the beauty without actually seeing it. There is nothing in the West that compares with it.

After one night in Tennessee, we reached St. Louis and saw the Great Arch by the Mississippi River. As I recall, it was not entirely completed, so we could not go up on it in the elevator. We spent the night in East St. Louis, Illinois.

On October 20th, we drove to Sedalia, Missouri, where my brother, Neill, was stationed at a missile base. We had dinner with Neill and Pearl and spent the night in the officer's guest quarters.

Next day, we drove across the State of Kansas, stopping in Abilene at the Eisenhower Museum, which was the former President's childhood home.

According to the road map, we could reach Cheyenne Wells, Colorado, by dark. When we arrived, we found a crossroads in ranch country. There was a gas station and a small motel where, luckily, one room was available. We asked about the small restaurant across the road but the proprietor of the motel was noncommittal. However, we were able to get a good steak dinner that night and a good breakfast the following morning. We ordered pancakes, which came either in a 'small stack' or a 'large stack,' terms Dottie and I have used ever since whenever we have had pancakes. At night the temperature was in the low 30s. On October 22nd, we drove through Denver without stopping. We went on to the Air Force Academy, arriving just before noon. We were fortunate to see the cadets in a precision drill as they crossed the courtyard to enter the mess hall. It was a beautiful sight. We took a tour of the Chapel, one of the most beautiful buildings I have ever seen. It has very high ceilings and beautiful, stained glass windows on all sides. The light seemed to pour in from the Heavens. There were sections for all faiths to worship. It was a great surprise to find this architectural giant sitting between the Rocky Mountains and the great plains of the West. I was very proud that the leaders of our country had seen fit to build this masterpiece. The architect was Frank Lloyd Wright, who created many magnificent buildings in the U.S.A. and other countries.

From the Air Force Academy, we drove south to Pueblo and then turned west. We reached the Continental Divide at Monarch Pass, which is 11,312 feet above sea level. A large variety store there was a beehive of activity with many tourists buying all kinds of things. However, most of the people were deer hunters. Hunting season had opened east of Monarch Pass the day before. The next day, it would open on the west side. As we approached this area the previous day, we saw hundreds of deer strapped to hoods and roofs of hunters' cars going east. All the activity was very interesting to us. We drove on to Gunnison for the night.

The temperature was 19 degrees when we got up next morning, and our car was covered with ice. It took me about 20 minutes to get the ice off the windshield and rear window. We went through the Gunnison National Park, passing by a roadside geyser. We spent the night in Panguitch, Utah.

Next day, October 24th, we drove through Bryce Canyon and Zion National Parks. The splendor that Nature had created in these parks was unbelievable. We reached Las Vegas for the night and registered at the Sahara Hotel. I attended the American College of Obstetricians and Gynecologist Section VIII meetings each morning for three days. Hawaii belongs to this section.

While I attended meetings, Dottie went on a tour of homes in Las Vegas. Some belonged to physicians and others to casino owners and all of them she described as ostentatious. One afternoon, we went on a tour of the inside operation of the Mint Casino. The pay-off odds were given to us and we were shown how the croupiers and the players at the card tables were watched from the ceiling through one-way mirrors. We went to shows each evening and, on the final day, a second show starting at midnight.

The first evening, Polly Bergen, a popular singer, was entertaining at the Riviera. We sat at the junction of two aisles about in the middle of the theater. As the show started, Polly came down an aisle, stopped by us and, with spotlights on us, sang a song to me. She then kissed me and proceeded onto the stage. Another evening we saw Donald O'Conner in his dance routine and Sharri Lewis with her puppet, Lamb Chop.

Dottie wanted to go to a midnight show, so we chose to see the Lido at the Stardust Theater. When the girls dropped out of the ceiling on chandeliers and had essentially no clothes on, Dottie was surprised. We gave the free drinks that came with our tickets to two young ladies sitting at our table.

We left in late morning October 27th for Yosemite National Park and reached Lee Vining for the night. Next morning, we drove through Yosemite and saw the beautiful sights again. We arrived at Saratoga by 6 p.m. and spent the night with McLeod and Louise.

We were just on schedule as our car had to be at Pier 32 the next day for shipment to Hawaii. We first drove to Alameda to Lois's apartment and unloaded the car. Then, all of us drove to Oakland to see Ann. On our way back, we left the car at the pier and took a taxi to Alameda.

The next day was Saturday. Lois was the minister of music at the Methodist Church in Alameda. After her choir practice, we went into San Francisco to shop and met Ann. The four of us came back to Lois's apartment for dinner. On Sunday we heard Lois sing in church and met one of her choir members, John Uranga. She would marry him the following year. After church, Michael McGovern, Ann's friend, took us to the airport and we flew to Hawaii. We had been away five weeks and three days. I was back to work Monday, November 1st, and Dr. Kroutil left. I had attended two medical meetings, and we had visited all our close relatives. We had had a glorious trip and visited many places for the first time. I was indebted to Dr. Kroutil for giving us the time to make this trip.

THE YEAR 1965 CONTINUED

After I returned from the mainland, I found a letter that had arrived soon after we had left on our trip. It was from Dr. Larry Allred, who planned to retire on Maui and had bought a lot at Kula Kai. He had decided to move to Maui now while he was young enough to take the medical boards for a license and offered to join me in practice if I were still looking for an associate. When he did not hear from me in several weeks, he thought I was not interested. I had expected to see him at the meeting in Las Vegas, but for some reason he could not come. I wrote him immediately and sent him an application form. I suggested he come for an interview, which he did from December 6th through the 9th. Finally, on January 4th, we voted to hire him. It would take him some months to close his practice in Stockton, California, and move to Maui.

Again, fate had been kind to me. I would not survive long if I tried to continue to do the amount of work I was doing. I was considering leaving the group. In six successive days, besides seeing many patients in the office, I had, on day one, operated on a patient with cancer of the ovary; on day two, operated on a patient with cancer of the uterus; on day three, delivered two babies; on day four, delivered five babies in 21 hours; on day five, tried to play golf but had to stop and deliver a baby; and finally, on the sixth day, which was Sunday, I had to do a cesarean. It appeared that Dr. Allred was the answer to my prayers.

THE YEAR 1966

Dr. Edward Shimokawa, our oldest original partner, had hypertensive-heart-disease and died in February. I think he had six children. His loss was sorely felt, professionally and personally, in our Lahaina office. Since his death over 23 years ago, no partner of our group has died.

We had a party at home announcing the engagement of Ann and Michael McGovern. Ann was not home at the time.

For the first time, on March 13th, I shot an even par 37 on the first nine holes at Maui Country Club. Also on this day, my partner and I came in first in a duplicate bridge game.

Dottie went to Honolulu on April 11th to meet Ann, who was coming home for her wedding on April 30th. They bought her trousseau.

During the next three weeks so many things happened, I barely managed to keep my sanity. First, Dr. Allred arrived on April 15th. His wife, Bernice, was scheduled to arrive at a later date. He was allowed to practice medicine for one year without a Hawaii license, though I would be responsible for his work. He stayed in our guest cottage for several days and then rented a house in Kihei. He planned to build his house at Kula Kai as soon as time permitted.

Dr. Pfaeltzer had a financial grievance with the Maui Medical Group and took us to court to get it settled. This suit had been in progress for many weeks during which time he had the bank accounts of all the members frozen. Our lawyer countered this successfully. It was decided the grievance should go to arbitration and Bob Millar of the Honolulu Medical Group was chosen as the arbitrator. He came to Maui for two days in February to review the case. Finally, on the morning of April 30th, Ann's wedding day, there was a court hearing, and I had to testify. The outcome was accepted by both sides.

Dottie's birthday was April 15th, the same day Dr. Allred arrived. I had been busy delivering babies and doing surgery and apparently forgot it. My birthday was on the 21st, and I had a birthday dinner at home. I had also been busy during this day and delivered a baby.

I delivered a premature baby in the breech position on April 25th. The delivery had been spontaneous and rapid following very strong uterine contractions. The cervix and lower part of the uterus were torn at the time of delivery and although I repaired them from below, the bleeding continued. The patient received several transfusions. The following day, I did a hysterectomy on the patient and thought I had tied off the bleeding artery. However, the bleeding continued. Three days later, I re-operated and tied off the hypogastric arteries. She then recovered, after receiving a total of 24 pints of blood.

Michael's father and mother, Mr. and Mrs. Terrence McGovern, and his uncle and aunt, Dr. and Mrs. Richard Bagley, arrived on April 28th for the wedding. Dottie Jane arrived the next day. We had all the guests for dinner in our home on the 29th.

Ann was married at 4 p.m., April 30th in the Wailuku Union Church with only family attending. Immediately following, we had a reception for 60 guests in the Sky Room at the Wailuku Hotel. After the reception, the bridal party had a formal dinner at the hotel.

Mrs. Bagley had diabetes mellitus and Addison's disease, which rarely occur in the same person at the same time. Her diabetes got out of control, so she had to spend a few days in the hospital on Maui before returning home.

We had had two weddings in nine months, and soon learned that there would be another before long. Lois telephoned on Mother's Day, announcing her engagement to John Uranga, a World Airlines pilot. They were to be married on August 6th, which meant that we would have three weddings in less than one year.

John's brother, Joel, his wife, Ann, and his mother arrived August 4th from El Paso, Texas. On August 5th, Ann Uranga and I drove to Kaenae to pick fresh ginger flowers to be used as decorations for the wedding. We had a dinner party for all the guests at the Wailuku Hotel that evening.

Lois and John were married at the Wailuku Union Church at noon on August 6th. We had a formal luncheon for 30 guests in our home after the service. All were seated at tables in the living room. Lois had invited young and old friends who had played an important role in her life.

John flew a freight plane from California to Kawajalein Island with stopovers in Honolulu. He rented an apartment in Honolulu, where he and Lois lived for several months.

When Dr. Allred joined me, I decided that because of our night work, he and I deserved to have every second Saturday and Sunday free except when an emergency arose that required the presence of both. The other members of the Maui Medical Group disagreed. We all were taking a half day off during the week. They finally agreed that we could be off every second weekend if they, likewise, could be off. We had no objection. I had my first free weekend in May, after 30 years of practice (except during vacations). I played golf Saturday morning and did yard work in the afternoon.

Nancy Patterson, Neill's daughter, had a roommate in college whose home was on Kauai. She had gotten Nancy a job as a waitress in a restaurant there for the summer. Before returning home, she visited us for five days and we took her on the usual visitor's tour of Maui. She had enjoyed the summer in Hawaii and had made a lot of money, especially from tips.

Ann wanted to live in Hawaii. I referred Michael, who was an hydraulic engineer, to a friend of mine in C. Brewer and Company, and he was hired. They lived in Hilo for about a year and then he was transferred to Honolulu, where they bought a home.

Dottie and I attended the Pan Pacific Surgical Conference in Honolulu in September. We stayed at the Princess Kaiulani Hotel, whose guests had privileges to play golf at Waialae Country Club on certain days. We played there twice and I also played once at Oahu Country Club with my friend, Dr. Ralph Cloward. One evening we had dinner with Dr. Franklyn Payne, my former professor. Another evening, Dr. Herbert Chinn invited us to the most fabulous Chinese dinner that we had ever eaten, at the Red Rooster Restaurant. He, himself, was an excellent Chinese cook and had planned the menu.

The medical meetings were excellent and I attended many, especially in the Obstetrics and Gynecology section. One lecture at a general meeting was particularly noteworthy. If I recall correctly, the lecturer was Dr. Burkitt from South Africa. He pointed out that peoples of more civilized societies eat more processed food, which results in a higher incidence of chronic constipation. The incidence of colon and rectal disease, such as cancer, diverticulosis and others, was shown to be directly proportional to the amount of constipation. He studied the stools of hundreds of successful businessmen from a large city, on a daily basis for a long period. Then he traveled all over the world and studied the stools of native, primitive peoples, who ate local, unprocessed foods. He made photographs of the stools and had lantern slides of the pictures to show us. He told how he met a camel train in Africa and got pictures of the drivers' stools. After a dinner of vegetables and whole grain bread, the drivers would go outside the camps and have a large, soft, bulky stool. They would have another such stool next morning after breakfast. At night Dr. Burkitt took a picture of the stool using a flash bulb. Then he scooped the stool into a container and weighed it. The camel driver's stools weighed twice as much as the highly educated businessmen's stools. Also, the camel drivers had two stools daily compared with one for the businessmen. He explained it was the undigested fiber in the camel driver's stool that absorbed an abundance of water, resulting in two, large, bulky stools daily. Everyone was impressed with this report. I had usually eaten whole grain cereals for breakfast, but, after hearing this lecture, I have never failed to do so. Some of the whole bran cereals on the market are more like pig feed than human food. However, some of the raisin bran flakes and other whole grain cereals are delicious.

The Maui Medical Group bought land on Prison Street in Lahaina and built a new office building with offices for four doctors and a separate dental suite. I had wanted to hire Haydn Phillips as the architect because of the good work he had done in creating our building in Wailuku and because he was very cost-conscious. The rest of the members preferred a local architect and friend, whose experience was primarily in government-owned buildings, where cost was not a factor. The cost of our Wailuku building was $23 per square foot. Five years later, the cost of the Lahaina building was $41 per square foot. No one seemed to be concerned about the cost, though we had difficulty borrowing money. The opening ceremonies were on Tuesday, October 4, 1966.

Dottie and I went to Hilo and spent Thanksgiving with Michael and Ann, our first visit in any of our daughters' homes. It rained for two days, which is normal for Hilo. We visited the volcano while there.

Carol came home for the Christmas holidays and brought her roommate with her. Shadan Itemadi was from Tehran, Iran, and was in the school of architecture at the University of Washington. Although she was a Muslim, Shadan partook of all our Christmas activities and went to church with us. She was a very lovely person. Carol heard very little from her since she returned to Iran, and nothing now for several years.

_____*THE YEAR 1967*

Dr. Allred went to Honolulu on January 8th for three days and took the State Medical Board exams. He passed them and by the end of the month received his license.

George and Rose Peterson arrived in January and stayed with us for 25 days. She was our former head nurse and anesthetist at Puunene Hospital, and he was the former editor of the editorial page of the Minneapolis Star Bulletin. She was recovering from a recent heart attack. While they were here, Sam and Ellie Lebold spent a few days at the Royal Lahaina Hotel. The six of us had dinner at Napili Kai Beach Hotel on February 14th, with Dottie and me as hosts. Another day, we had a dinner party in our home for the Petersons and Lebolds.

The Up With People group, consisting of prestigious American teenagers who, through dance and song, accentuated the positive in the United States, put on a performance at Baldwin Auditorium. Two of the boys stayed in our guest house. On March 2nd the Honolulu Symphony Orchestra presented the opera, "Il Trovatore," at Baldwin Auditorium, which we attended and enjoyed.

I had resumed my study of high blood pressure during pregnancy and its relation to placental function. I was trying to determine if the placenta actually did produce the hormone, human chorionic gonadotropin (HCG), or merely utilized it in its production of estrogen and progesterone. After my abortive efforts in 1952 on this subject, I had said I would not study this again until I retired. However, something drove me to resume my investigations. I went to Honolulu to see Dr. S. Waxman at the University of Hawaii to try to get him to do placental tissue cultures, which would prove the point. Such cultures had been done by others, but my interpretation of the results was that they proved that the placenta did not produce the hormone. This was the opposite of the author's conclusions. My efforts were unproductive. I continued my study, reading everything on the subject I could find, and corresponding with researchers in this field.

Dottie developed acute, severe pain in her lower back radiating down the left leg. I had her rest in bed for three days and the pain subsided. She returned to playing golf, but, after a rough ride in a golf cart, the pain recurred. She could not walk.

Dr. Ralph Cloward had his neurological clinic on Maui on Wednesday, May 12th, and did a myelogram on Dottie. There was complete blockage between the fourth and fifth lumbar vertebrae, and he recommended a disc operation. I took her to the Queen's Hospital in Honolulu by stretcher on a Hawaiian Airlines Convair, using the space directly across four seats. They did not charge me any extra fare. She had an emergency operation Saturday morning. I stayed with her for two days, returned to Maui to work for three days, and then went back to see her.

The annual meeting of the Hawaii Medical Association began on Wednesday evening, and I attended each morning and evening for three days. Each afternoon I played golf with Drs. Sam Wallis and Ralph Cloward and pharmaceutical representatives. We played first at Makaha, then at Waialae in the Medical Society Tournament, and finally at the Leilehua Army Course. I saw Dottie twice daily and had dinner with her in her room.

Dottie was able to come home on the 8th day and could walk. Ann came from Hilo and spent about two weeks with us, then Lois arrived from Oakland on June 12th and stayed for a month. Dottie improved day-by-day, but had pain and muscle spasms in her back. Only one who has had this type of trouble can know the agony these patients are in. Finally after a month, she was able to ride to Lahaina and have dinner. She started riding in a cart and playing golf after three months.

I had not been feeling well and was tired. I had my blood pressure checked and it was 150/100. This was the first time in my life that my systolic pressure had been as high as 100. An electrocardiogram was normal. I felt fine after a few days, and my blood pressure dropped to 120/80.

I was an usher at church for the first time in July. Since then, I have continued taking my turn at ushering about every two weeks for over 20 years.

Michael McGovern and Arturo Zavala were with us for two days. Arturo, a very delightful and intelligent person, was making an inspection of the sugar operations of C. Brewer and Company, and Michael had been given the task of escorting him. Arturo's family owned the largest sugar mill in Mexico. As I recall, each year the mill processed over 300,000 tons of sugar cane grown by many independent farmers.

I took a week's vacation and Dottie and I went to Honolulu to do some shopping. Dottie got a special back brace, which she wore for months. After three days, we went to Hilo and stayed with Michael and Ann. We met their golfing friend, Paul Seidel, of Miko Meat Co. While on Hawaii, I played golf four times, twice at the municipal course, once at Hilo Country Club and once at Mauna Kea.

The Maui Medical Group met with Mr. Jenkins of Hawaiian Trust Company, and we started a Keogh pension plan with them. Later, the group switched to another company, though I kept my funds with Hawaiian Trust for the 12 remaining years that I worked.

A new patient was found to have an intrauterine contraceptive device free in her abdomen among the intestines. I removed it at the time I did a cesarean.

I went to a section meeting of the American College of Obstetricians and Gynecologists in Denver. Dottie and I left on October 20th and spent two days in Fremont with Lois and John. McLeod and Louise had dinner with us one evening.

In Denver, I attended meetings all morning on the 23rd. In the afternoon, Dottie and I took a tour to the Air Force Academy where we saw the beautiful chapel again. On our way home we stopped at Cherry Hill Country Club and had dinner. Some of the doctors, who had chosen to play golf instead of going on the tour, were caught in a wind and rain storm and could not finish their golf.

I went to meetings the next day, then we attended a dinner dance at the Hilton Hotel, where we were staying. I attended meetings in the morning of the final day, and in the afternoon Dottie and I toured the famous Denver Jewish Children's Hospital. Carol was to spend a three-month internship there as part of her training in occupational therapy. We met her superiors. That evening we saw a show at the auditorium in which Maurice Chevalier appeared on stage. As usual, he put on a wonderful performance.

We spent two more days in Denver, as this was our first visit to the mile-high city. Our hotel was across the street from a small park in front of the capitol building. The 'hippy' movement was very active at this time and I can remember looking down from our hotel at daybreak and seeing hippies sleeping on the grass in the park. Their sleeping bags were partially covered with fresh-fallen snow.

In the morning of the first day, we climbed the steps to the capitol and saw that one of the steps is exactly one mile above sea level. We then visited the U.S. Mint, where all denominations of coins are made. I remember seeing pennies being stamped out of large sheets of bright, shiny copper. I think the copper in a penny is now worth as much as the penny. I have seven pennies in my pocket at this moment, all of which have a small D just below the date, which signifies that they were minted in Denver. It is interesting to note that on this same date in 1965, we took a tour of the Mint Casino in Las Vegas.

In the afternoon we went on a mountain tour that took us to Lookout Mountain and to Buffalo Bill's grave. I remember it was at a high elevation among pine trees. We continued on to Red Rock Theatre, a beautiful amphitheatre carved out of red rock on a hillside overlooking a valley. Sounds from the stage below were said to reach all the seats and surrounding area in the stillness and quietness of this desert setting. In the summer, concerts and drama productions are presented here.

In the evening in Denver, the temperature was below freezing. Dottie and I walked to Larimer Square, an area that has been restored as it was many years ago, and had dinner in a quaint restaurant. We became very cold walking back to the hotel in spite of wearing topcoats.

On our final day we took a city tour and also went through the Colorado Museum. We visited an art gallery that was featuring a Chinese artist who was present and actively painting. It seemed so easy for him to create his beautiful artwork. We bought one of his paintings, depicting two birds sitting on a branch. When we left in late afternoon for Los Angeles, our new painting was in the cabin of the plane with us. Dottie Jane and Michael met us at the airport. Michael was studying for his doctorate at the University of California, and Dottie Jane worked in a doctor's office. We were with them for eight days.

Dottie Jane and Michael had a party for 24 friends the second day we were there. They were all graduate students and it was stimulating to be with them. Michael had borrowed a barely working slide projector to show pictures of their hiking trip through Yosemite. When I came home, I bought a Kodak Carousel projector and sent it to them.

The weather was beautiful in Santa Monica where they lived, and Dottie and I just relaxed for two days. We played bridge in the evening.

One evening, we all had dinner at the Los Angeles Music Center and afterwards saw the musical drama, "Showboat," at the beautiful, new Dorothy Chandler Theatre. Both the music center and the musical drama were very impressive. The center was just as beautifully designed as New York's Lincoln Center.

We drove to Disneyland the next morning and spent the entire day and still were not able to see everything. I thought we would go back some day but, so far, we have not returned. Dottie Jane, Dottie and I visited the Farmer's Market on Friday and bought many items, especially imported teas. I bought six nylon shirts and gave three of them to Michael as we wore the same size. I gave mine away after wearing them for ten years.

Early the next morning, we were off to Honolulu and had four hours there before our Maui flight. Michael and Ann had bought a new home on Kaneohe Bay, and we had time to visit it. We arrived home at 4:45 p.m., having been away for 16 action-packed days.

_____*THE YEAR 1968*

On New Year's Day, we were invited to the home of our neighbor, Toshi Nitta, for midday dinner. This is the most important day of the year for the Japanese who usually celebrate the day with a feast shared with their friends. They are careful to have their homes and yards spotlessly clean on this day. They pay all their debts. If available, sashimi (raw fish) is served in addition to an abundance of other delicious foods. This year, we saw the Rose Bowl Parade and football game in color for the first time, through the satellite, Telstar.

Dr. Sam Wallis of Kauai organized a golf safari to Mauna Kea on the Island of Hawaii every year, with 16 men and 16 women. We played 18 to 27 holes of golf in the early part of the day and then played cribbage. In the evening we had a delicious dinner in the elegant dining room at the Mauna Kea Hotel. The members of the safari were mostly Dr. Wallis's friends from Spokane, Washington, but often included Mr. and Mrs. Merrill Carlsmith of Hilo, Dr. and Mrs. Ralph Cloward of Honolulu, and Dottie and me. I remember the first time we went, the room rate per couple on the mountain side of the hotel was $65.00 per day and the oceanside $75.00, including breakfast and dinner.

I played golf on Maui with Dr. Tom Harper of Reno, Nevada, in January. He was stationed on Maui during the war. In school in Reno, he had been a classmate of Katherine Hughes of Maui. Her stepson, Donald Hughes, asked me to play golf with him. Besides being a good golfer with a handicap of seven at the time, he was a wonderful person. He and his wife return to Maui each year for a short vacation, and we usually have several golf games. I remember his comments about Afghanistan when the Russians first invaded it. He had spent a month in Kabul as a medical volunteer and said the Russians had not gotten anything of value when they invaded it. He predicted that they would have trouble there, which seems to be true as the Russians have now left.

When Lois and John learned they were unable to have a baby of their own, I contacted fellow obstetricians in Honolulu to help find a baby for them to adopt. I got a call on February 29th that a baby boy was available for them. Lois flew to Honolulu and took the baby home with her on March 7th. He has just had his 20th birthday, is over six feet tall and weighs 200 lbs. He is a junior in college, an honors student, and an outstanding person. He is my namesake.

The Reverend Martin Luther King Jr., the black leader of the Civil Rights movement in our country, was slain on April 4th, and our country went into mourning. He was a leader of the oppressed and used nonviolent tactics to improve their lot. He was a martyr to the cause. No doubt, the untimely death of this great leader set back the Civil Rights movement many years. I compare him in greatness to President Abraham Lincoln, both of whom could see beyond the horizon of current politicians and leaders.

MAINLAND TRIP, 1968

Dottie and I took a five-week trip to the mainland, leaving on May 4th. This was another action-packed trip, and I will mention only the highlights. En route to Chicago, we saw Ann and Michael in Honolulu and Dottie Jane and Michael at the airport in Los Angeles. I attended the annual meeting of the American College of Obstetricians and Gynecologists for four days at the Palmer House in Chicago, where we were staying. We had dinner with the Holmblads at the Swedish Club. Preston Williams, whose wife had died the day after she arrived on Maui about two years before, took us to dinner at the Tavern Club. Dr. and Mrs. George Finola took us to dinner at the South Shore Country Club, and I played golf with him there the next day. I played golf with Sam Lebold at Lake Shore Country Club and, afterward, we had dinner again at the Tavern Club with the Lebolds, the Bill Gimbels and Mrs. Joseph Baer.

On May 11th, Dottie's brother, Neff, and his wife, Jane, picked us up and took us to their home in Downer's Grove for two days. We played golf at Downer's Grove Country Club. We then flew to Pittsburgh, got a U-drive and drove to Jo and Tony's home near Penn State University. Dottie and I played golf at the Nittany Lion's Golf Course. The temperature was below 50 degrees, and we could barely grasp the golf clubs. After two days we visited Dottie's sister, Polly, and her husband, Paul Prough, at Mt. Union. We played golf there at the American Legion Golf Course. There was a par-six hole with a fairway over 600 yards long, uphill. I reached the apron in three, but had to settle for a par. We then drove to Lewistown and visited Mother Graham, Helen and Dottie's sister and her husband, Martha and Ed Harkinson.

The Ex-Residents Association of the Geisinger Hospital met on May 18th for its 25th anniversary. We spent three days and two nights in Danville as guests of Dr. and Mrs. Nicodemus, and I attended the meetings. It was very interesting to see the changes in the appearance of people after 30 years. We played golf twice with Dr. Nicodemus at the Frosty Valley Country Club. When I was a resident, the land that is now a golf course was a farm owned by the hospital.

We were back with Mother Graham for several more days. We golfed at the Lewistown Country Club where play did not start until mid-morning because of the heavy dew and cold weather.

In Linwood, New Jersey, we spent a week with Paul and Vivian Cameron. We golfed everyday except one, when it rained. We played at Wildwood, Linwood and Atlantis Country Clubs. Each evening we had dinner in fancy seafood restaurants in the area. We walked on the Boardwalk at Atlantic City where the temperature was in the low 50s, which was uncomfortable for us.

I turned in our U-drive when we arrived at the Camerons. After a week, they drove us to the Philadelphia Airport and we caught a plane in mid-morning to San Francisco. It was raining when we left but, after about five minutes, we were above the clouds in blue skies. McLeod and Louise met us in San Francisco, and we were with them at Saratoga overnight. Next day, they took us to Carmel and Pebble Beach Golf Course. We took the Seventeen-Mile-Drive at Monterey and saw and heard the famous seals at the rookery by the shore. We had dinner at Cannery Row in Monterey.

The next day, we went to Fremont and spent several days with Lois, John and Baby Bill.

Michael's parents, Dr. Clayton and Lulu Mote, lived at Sausalito. We spent a weekend there, staying at the Alta Mira Hotel. Clayton and Lulu had a big dinner party in their home for us and, as a surprise, brought Dottie Jane and Michael from Los Angeles. The next day was Sunday, and all the younger people took a walk through Sausalito. In late afternoon, we ate again with Clayton and Lulu, before we took Dottie Jane and Michael to the airport. We then returned to Lois's home at Fremont.

After two days, we left early for Hayden Lake, Idaho, and were guests of Ada and Jim Blankenship. We played 18 holes of golf the day we arrived and 36 holes the next. Along with Ada and Jim, we played golf with Eddie and Ruth Page and Grant and Grace Dixon, whom we had met on Kauai.

Finally, we went to Seattle to attend Carol's graduation from the University of Washington. On our arrival, she showed us the diamond on her finger and introduced us to Peter Keck, to whom she had become engaged. We spent three days in Seattle, took a tour of the University and met many of Carol's friends and their families who had come for graduation.

Barbara Keck, Peter's mother, had come from Long Island, New York. We had a dinner party at the Windjammer Restaurant on Puget Sound to celebrate the announcement of Carol's and Peter's engagement. On commencement day, we had breakfast at Carol's apartment with the family of her roommate, then attended a luncheon at the Occupational Therapy Department in the hospital. There were many graduates and thousands of visitors at the graduation exercises. Afterward, a reception was held on the grounds outside the auditorium. Many pictures were taken of the graduates in their caps and gowns. This was our third visit to Seattle in 13 years, and it had never rained while we were there, a phenomenom we were told was most unusual.

Next day we were taken to the airport by our friend, Dorothy McArthur, who previously lived on Maui. We arrived in Honolulu at noon, spent the afternoon with Ann in her home, and arrived on Maui at 6 o'clock.

_____THE YEAR 1968 CONTINUED

I was invited to a luau at the War Memorial Gymnasium put on by the International Longshoremen and Warehousemen's Union in appreciation to management and other friends for their cooperation. The relationship between this union and management had not always been so amicable. I was pleased to be invited and I accepted.

When I read my diary, I am amazed at how busy I was at times. On June 30th, I went to church, delivered three babies, and played 18 holes of golf with Dottie. The babies must have been delivered during the night. On July 7th, Admiral Tom Hamilton called, and I arranged a golf game for him and Bren Moynahan, who lived on Maui. Ann had been Admiral Hamilton's secretary when he was head of the Big Eight Athletic Conference in San Francisco. As I recall, he and Bren had been friends at the Naval Academy, and both had been captain of the aircraft carrier Enterprise during their careers. Doc Lyons of Maui also had been one of Admiral Hamilton's friends at the Naval Academy.

My sister and her husband, the Reverend Marcus Lawrence, visited us from July 12th to the 18th. I had lived with them for 12 months when I started college. Marcus had married us and had baptized our children and we had visited in their home on numerous occasions. I took a week's vacation and we entertained them in every way possible. We went sightseeing, had picnics and parties, played golf, toured the pineapple cannery, etc. On the final day, I went to Hilo with them and toured the volcano. I came home at 5:00 p.m., and they took a night flight to California. We were so happy we were finally able to return some of their kindness to us.

My nephew, O.F. Patterson Jr., and his wife Sally, visited us for four days in August, their first trip to Hawaii. I took them on the usual sightseeing tours of Maui. Friends invited the four of us to two dinner parties. O.F. Jr. remarked that everyone we were with talked golf, so he knew I was an avid golfer.

At the August meeting of the hospital staff, I gave a talk on "Severe Postpartum Hemorrhage," a condition that is always a threat to obstetric patients. My presentation included lantern slides depicting the anatomy involved and a discussion of treatments.

When Carol left for college, Dottie moved into the vacant bedroom, claiming that 25 years of telephone calls had disturbed her sleep. With the help of my friend Tom Nichols - a master carpenter - I removed an old dresser and installed a large window providing Dottie with a full view of the lovely entrance garden.

Richard Nixon was elected president and Spiro Agnew vice president on election day, November 5th.

Dottie and I spent Christmas with Ann and Michael at Kaneohe.

1969 had a quiet beginning. Dottie and I played rubber bridge with the Rocketts until 2 a.m. We joined our neighbors, the Nittas, to watch the Rose Bowl Parade and football game on color television, and enjoy a midday feast.

In late January, we enjoyed another four-day golf safari at the Mauna Kea Golf Course and Hotel with our friends from Kauai and Spokane. The days were the same: 18 to 27 holes of golf after breakfast, lunch at the pro shop, cribbage during the afternoon, cocktails in one of our rooms, and dinner at the hotel.

The men and ladies had their own tournaments with a jackpot split among three winners after four days of play. Eddie Page was tournament chairman each year.

In late February, we hosted a small golf safari on Maui, playing at three courses. Four of the couples stayed with us and the others stayed at the hotel. It rained for three days with winds up to 50 miles per hour. The ladies were literally blown off the Waiehu Golf Course. Seven of the eight men hit their drives out-of-bounds on the eleventh hole because of the wind.

My good friend, Dr. Paul Cameron, died in February. He developed multiple myeloma (cancer of the bone marrow) when he was about 60 but continued practicing medicine until he became disabled. He had served in the Army throughout World War II and developed pulmonary tuberculosis near the end of the war. I suspect the strain of the war years and his slow recovery from TB contributed to his developing cancer.

Michael Terrence McGovern II was born to Ann on March 11, 1969. Dottie stayed with Ann for five days, helping her adjust to the rigors of new parenthood. Little Michael was a joy to all, especially his father.

I had a draining sinus on the right second toe over the distal joint. It had started while I was wearing golf shoes that were too tight. I suspected I had gout, but my blood uric acid levels were only in the high normal range. When the sinus would not heal, I had the gelatinous, sunovial-like fluid examined several times for uric acid crystals but none were found. My internist said I could not have gout without a higher blood uric acid level. Finally, x-rays of my feet showed typical gouty cysts and tophi in all the bones of both feet. Several radiologists and one of the leading rheumatologists in the United States saw the x-rays and said they showed the typical changes of chronic gout. I started taking probenecid medication, and my joint pains (all joints) quickly improved. The sinus healed and for 20 years has not reccurred while I have been taking probenecid. I tried adding colchichin, but this was more of a liability than a help as it produced chronic diarrhea, which could not always be controlled. I tried adding allopurinol, but found no difference. If I stopped the probenecid, the sinus on my toe would begin draining again while I was taking allopurinol so my internist had me discontinue it.

On three occasions, I have had acute gouty arthritis in my right knee following excess fatigue from prolonged hours of yard work or other maintenance work in our home. I usually worked 16 or more hours a day on special jobs. Then, about 10 years ago, after painting for long hours for three days, my knee swelled and became hot. When it did not improve after three days of rest, my orthopedist prescribed phenylbutazone on a short-term basis. The knee improved within 12 hours, and I was able to play golf within 24 hours. After three days the swelling and pain were gone, and I discontinued the medicine. I took this medicine on two other occasions for acute gout. Now I limit any strenuous work to four hours a day. I do have pains in my knees and other joints after playing golf or doing heavy work, but not acute gout.

Ann visited us on Maui with little Michael for eleven days. He was a handsome, healthy baby.

I took a three-day vacation to help with the preparations for Carol's wedding on June 21st. We had a rehearsal on the 20th, followed by dinner at the Kula Lodge. Several of Peter's relatives, including his mother, came for the wedding, which was held in late afternoon at the Wailuku Union Church. Immediately afterwards, we had a reception in our yard under the beautiful magnolia tree near the tea house. The weather was perfect, and the scenery was spectacular. We looked down on the cane fields, the harbor and airport and, beyond, 10,000-foot Haleakala Mountain, whose summit was clearly visible.

Following the reception, at which champagne flowed, a buffet wedding supper was served in our home for 66 guests. The full moon rose directly opposite the plate glass windows in the dining room, living room and library. It was a beautiful sight.

Carol and Peter had rented a cottage on the beach at Kihei, where they spent a few days of their honeymoon. Carol immediately lost her wedding ring in the sand and never found it. A new one was purchased. A similar story occurred one evening before the wedding, when three carloads of family and friends had a beach picnic at Kihei. We cooked steaks over a large bonfire and everyone had a wonderful time. The Pattersons had similar picnics every summer.

After we had eaten, I enlarged the bonfire and everyone sat around it telling stories. The moon was almost full and was very bright. Peter had driven Dottie's car. He removed his shoes and left them, with the car keys inside, on the beach well above the water. Just after we put out the fire and prepared to leave, a large wave came in and covered the shoes with sand. The tide had come in, and Peter did not realize the shoes were no longer above the high water line. We recovered the shoes, but the car keys were not inside. After some searching, I was ready to drive the 24 miles round trip home to get another set of keys. As I was standing at the edge of the water, another large wave came up high on the shore. When it receded, I saw a reflection in the sand in the moonlight, which proved to be the keys.

Dottie had had a recurrence of pain in her back and legs. After another myelogram, the doctors decided she needed another lumbar disc operation. She was operated on for a herniated disc between the last lumbar vertebra and the sacrum. Her previous operation was for a disc just above this level. I remained with her for two days and then came home to work. I telephoned her each day and went to see her on my Wednesday afternoon off, but was back on Maui in the operating room at 8 a.m. the next day. She came home alone on the 13th post-operative day with the same pain and muscle spasm she had had after the first operation. Lois and Bill Uranga spent three weeks with us to help Dottie during her recovery. At the end of one month she was able to go out to a restaurant for dinner. She played golf for the first time after seven weeks.

On July 20, 1969, we saw Schirra walk on the moon. It was unbelievable that our knowledge of physics and our technical development had advanced so far. Although I watched it on television in my living room, it seemed more like science fiction to me than reality. This event will remain a major milestone in man's probe of space.

THE MAUI MEDICAL GROUP
BUYS A LARGE OFFICE BUILDING

The Maui Medical Group building at 99 South Market Street was overflowing with doctors. Although we had plans and space available for an additional unit for two doctors, if more doctors were added we would have to consider adding a second story. The bookkeeping department also needed more space.

The seven-story, 5-year-old Wailuku Hotel on the corner of Main and High Streets was for sale. Because it was not a beachfront hotel, it did not attract enough tourists to make it profitable. The owners were willing to sell it for the $1.5 million it had cost to build. It would cost $300,000 to convert it to an office building. The Maui Medical Group would need less than half the space in the building, and the remainder could be rented for income. As the group grew in the future, there would always be enough office space to meet its needs.

Luckily, a buyer was found for our existing building and we sold it for more than it cost. We negotiated a loan from the American Security Bank (now First Interstate Bank) and on July 24th, we bought the hotel building and proceeded to convert it to meet our needs. Our manager had done most of the business negotiations in selling our old building and in buying the new one. I had been the leader in creating our first building and decided I had done enough. Dr. Allred made plans for the new obstetrics and gynecology department. Needless to say, getting this building in the heart of Wailuku was a great boom to the Maui Medical Group.

McLeod and Louise arrived on July 28th for six days. I took more time off for golf and sightseeing. They spent one day and one night in Hana, where he had worked from 1935 to 1939.

I had developed hay fever, which prevented me from resting well at night. My nasal passages would swell shut in the evening. When I slept in the air-conditioned doctor's room in the obstetrical department at the hospital, my nasal passages opened and I could breathe normally. I had an air conditioner installed in a window in my bedroom, and this relieved my problem. I used it for a few years and then found I seldom needed it. Now, I use it only in the morning in the summer when it is too hot at my desk.

Dr. Allred was away for the month of August, and I delivered 33 babies. After that, I was ready for a vacation.

MAINLAND TRIP, 1969

Dottie and I flew to Spokane on September 1st, and Ada and Jim Blankenship met us. They drove us to Hayden Lake, Idaho, where we were their house guests for six days. I played in the Hayden Lake Country Club Member-Guest Tournament with 63 other member-guest teams. On the first day, my score was two under par for the first nine, the best I had ever scored. The 10 guests with the lowest net scores played in a horse race with the 10 members with the lowest net scores. I qualified for this playoff but my partner and I lost on the third of five holes. Later, I introduced the game of "horse racing" in our golf tournaments at the Maui Country Club, and it has been very popular.

On one morning of the tournament, the temperature was 52 degrees and it was raining. My tee-off time was 8 a.m. so I rushed over to the pro shop and bought a pair of rubberized long pants. By 11 the rain had stopped and the temperature had risen 20 degrees. I was not accustomed to playing in such weather.

After five days of golf, three of which were in the tournament, Dottie and I left for Minneapolis to see Rose and George Peterson. We had two lovely days with them and then flew to New York City. We took a bus to New Haven, Connecticut, where Michael Mote was doing post-doctoral studies at Yale University. We stayed with Michael and Dottie Jane for three days and nights. On one of these days, we drove to South Kent, Connecticut, where Pete Keck was teaching at South Kent School for Boys. Carol was an occupational therapist.

We rented a U-drive and drove to Lewistown, Pennsylvania, where we visited Dottie's family for three days. Our next stop was Albuquerque, New Mexico, where I was to attend a section meeting of the American College of Obstetricians and Gynecologists for three and a half days. Our favorite side trip was to Santa Fe, a beautiful, old, historic Spanish town filled with relics from the past.

While in Albuquerque, we had dinner with Dr. and Mrs. Jack Dillahunt. He had been stationed at Waikapu, Maui, during the war. I played golf one afternoon, and we attended the New Mexico State Fair one evening.

We flew to Fremont, California, on Sepember 20th and spent two days with Lois and John. On the 22nd we flew to Honolulu and had two hours with Ann before returning to Maui after a very busy 22-day vacation.

THE YEAR 1969 CONTINUED

For some months before our trip, I had been actively studying my former research project on the cause of high blood pressure during pregnancy. Each morning I got up early and studied from 4 to 8 a.m., seven days a week. I read everything in the world medical literature on the adrenal gland, both adult and fetal; everything on high blood pressure in women, pregnant and nonpregnant, and in men; everything on the placenta, both in normally pregnant women and in those with high blood pressure; and everything about nutrition during pregnancy. I studied the effects that maternal high blood pressure had on surviving infants and the autopsy findings in stillbirths and in neonatal deaths. My study also included research that had been done on pregnant animals, especially primates. I studied the adrenal glands of fetuses born with abnormalities incompatible with life, particularly those in anencephalics. I had begun writing a monograph on this subject, a project that took a long time to complete.

Dottie and I spent Thanksgiving with Ann and Michael in Kaneohe. Michael and I played golf twice at the Pali Golf Course. I came home early on Friday to work in the office and Dottie returned Saturday.

We had a Christmas open house for 200 friends. Half were invited to come from four to six and the others from six to eight o'clock. Dottie decorated the house beautifully. There were two Christmas trees, about eight feet tall, made of dried, gold-painted sisal blooms and decorated with beautiful silver, gold and crystal ornaments. Some guests still remember these original and lovely trees after 20 years. A table was set up as a bar in the foyer by the kitchen door. As guests arrived, Harry and Ann Nishimura had each person's favorite drink ready by the time he or she was inside. Patsy Kinoshita catered the party which was a gourmet's delight. Seafood was served on the large buffet in the dining room. The piece de resistance was a 25-pound opakapaka fish baked in coconut milk. On the dining table was a large turkey, a ham and numerous vegetables. A separate table held many wheels of imported cheeses. Petit fours were served for dessert. Two and three each of the fish, turkey, and ham were consumed before the evening was over.

Parking was a problem and the guests' coming and going created traffic jams. Parking attendants put many cars on Ekoa Place, a block from our home and sixty feet below, and used our cars to shuttle guests back and forth.

We still had straw rugs in our living areas and wanted to have a big party before good rugs were installed. No one worried about spilling food and drink. One of the wonderful things in life is that we tend to quickly forget our hardships and remember the good things that happen to us.

THE YEAR 1970

Again, it was nice to start the New Year with our neighbors, the Nittas. After Christmas turkey and trimmings, Japanese food was a treat, and they served an abundance of it.

On January 2nd, I had a delivery with a prolapsed umbilical cord, but the baby was alive and normal. Another baby I delivered appeared normal but had no esophagus. I had delivered one other with this condition; it died at 13 days from starvation. I sent this one to a chest surgeon in Honolulu, but it also succumbed.

We were scheduled to go to Mauna Kea for a golf safari the third week of January with our Kauai and Spokane friends. Dr. Allred's father died, and I was unable to go until the last two days. Several of our friends then came to Maui, and we continued our golf at Kaanapali Golf Course in Lahaina for two days. We had a big dinner party at the Royal Lahaina Hotel.

We attended a formal dinner dance at the Maui Country Club as guests of Mr. and Mrs. Ira (Loretta) Keller the last day of January. This became a very enjoyable, annual affair until both of them died. Mr. Keller had been very successful in the wood pulp business in the Northwest and supported many charities. He had been named the Portland, Oregon, Man of the Year several times and was known as Mr. Portland.

I was spending more time on my research and frequently worked all day long during the weekend. Dottie was typing the manuscript, which would soon be ready to present to editors. I hired our group's medical secretary to work on the weekend to make the final copy. The title of my manuscript was "Correlation of Fetal Adrenal Cortical Hyperplasia with Toxemia of Pregnancy."

Dottie and I drove to Hana and on to the Seven Pools on April 20th. There had been a heavy rain all night and all the waterfalls along the way were flowing. It was a very beautiful sight that can be seen only after heavy rains.

I took Dottie out to dinner on her 53rd birthday, April 15th, and gave her a gold ring with three large baroque pearls. She still wears this beautiful ring.

I sent my manuscript to three medical journal editors, and all rejected it. Then I sent it to my former professor, Dr. Franklin Payne, and he liked it. He had a friend on the editorial board of an obstetrical journal, and he thought he could get it published for me. Again, I was refused, but this contact would help me later. I continued to study and kept improving my manuscript.

I was on emergency call at the hospital the night of May 3rd and was very busy taking care of people injured in the Whaling Spree in Lahaina. The Whaling Spree was a three-day celebration, reminiscent of the past when Lahaina was the whaling capital of the world. The doctors in Lahaina also were busy. So many injuries and so much property damage occurred during the annual event that the Whaling Spree was discontinued. The Merrie Monarch Hula Festival was established about the same time in Hilo and it has just celebrated its 25th anniversary. It has become one of the great cultural events in Hawaii today and is helping to perpetuate Hawaii lore. It is so sad that the Whaling Spree could not have developed in a similar way. The work of a few dedicated leaders made the difference.

We moved into our new offices in the converted Wailuku Hotel building the first week of May. Dottie helped me buy pictures for my office and get it functional. Finally, Dr. Allred and I had a complete department with only women patients. We had a beautiful view of the West Maui Mountains and Iao Valley from the fourth floor.

Dottie and I attended the Hawaii State Medical Society meeting in Honolulu from May 7th to 10th. We stayed with Ann and Michael in their new home on Kaneohe Bay and I played golf at Mid Pacific Country Club with friends.

I continued my studies and was totally involved in my research, confident I was on the right track to learn the cause of high blood pressure during pregnancy. The more involved I got, the more absent-minded I became. My busy medical practice left me with very little time to devote to Dottie on a daily basis. She became depressed at times and required some medications.

Dottie Jane had her first baby, Timothy, on May 29th. He weighed 8 pounds, 13 ounces and was healthy. Also on this day, Ann and baby Michael came for a two-week visit.

I had my first tooth pulled since I was 12 years old, which had been 46 years, and had it replaced with a denture. I had only 28 permanent teeth originally and now was down to 26.

Barbara Keck, Carol's mother-in-law, arrived on July 27th for a week's visit. Dottie was sick during most of the time she was with us, though she did have a luncheon at the Country Club for her.

Dottie's doctor came to see her on August 5th at my request and failed to recognize that she had phenothiazine poisoning. He prescribed more of the medicine that was making her sick. I had never seen a patient with this condition, so I did not recognize it either. When she was worse on August 6th, I called one of my partners, an internist, who recognized her problem immediately and sent her to the hospital. She lapsed into a deep coma for five days and was near death. I could only pray, which I did continually. Ann came from Honolulu, and either she or one of my nurse friends stayed with Dottie continuously. On the sixth day, Dottie said one word and moved her hand. This was her first muscle movement in five days, except for breathing and her heartbeat. She improved rapidly. Ann went home on August 17th, and Carol arrived on the 18th, the day Dottie came home from the hospital. Carol helped rehabilitate her mother during the 12 days she was with us, and then had to return home and to work. Dottie continued the program of exercises that Carol had started, and she gained strength daily.

CHAPTER XVI

Europe, U.S. Mainland and Mexcio Trips

_____SEPTEMBER 4 TO OCTOBER 15, 1970_

Dottie and I had never been to Europe or any foreign country except to Tijuana, Mexico, to Victoria, and the train ride from Vancouver to Calgary, Canada. Most of our friends had already taken several trips abroad and seemed to always talk about them. We decided it was time for us to go to Europe. All four daughters had finished their education and had married and I had no debts except the house mortgage. I had a good equity built up in my insurance program. We made reservations for a 22-day tour of Europe on Pan American Airway's Going Great Tour which left Honolulu on September 4th. We had decided that a guided tour of Europe would be best for our first trip. Our return reservation was to New York City, from where we would visit Michael and Dottie Jane and then Peter and Carol. After visiting Dottie's relatives in Pennsylvania and mine in North Carolina, we planned to go to Mexico City for one week. While there, I would attend organizational and scientific meetings of the American College of Obstetricians and Gynecologists for four days. We would spend the rest of the time sightseeing in or near Mexico City.

The problem now was Dottie's health. Would she be able to travel? She needed a change of scenery, and the trip would be good for her if she could physically endure it. We decided she could. We left Maui September 4th to start the tour in Honolulu with 23 other Hawaii residents.

Our flight from Honolulu was scheduled to leave at noon, but left two and a half hours late. We arrived in Los Angeles after midnight. We had to be at the airport at 10:00 a.m. to check in for our London flight via the polar route. Again the plane was over two hours late. The Boeing 747s had just been put into service and it seemed there were always delays. Also, the cabin crews were unaccustomed to so many passengers and had not yet learned how to get everything done. Every seat on the plane was filled. By the time the plane reached London at 8:10 a.m. the following day, the hostesses were completely exhausted and frustrated. Their faces were flushed. One dared not ask for a second cup of coffee.

In London, we registered at the Washington Hotel. Although we were tired, we were advised not to go to bed until evening so we would adjust to the time changes in one day. We were furnished a bus with a guide to tour parts of London and also had time to explore on our own. We saw many famous landmarks including Piccadilly Circus, the House of Parliament, Big Ben, St. Paul's Cathedral, and the Changing of the Guards at Buckingham Palace. We visited Windsor Castle.

We had dinner at Kettner's Restaurant and were introduced to the famous English steak and kidney pie. We were not impressed. I took pictures of every statue we passed and when we got home, I did not know what many of them were. I quickly learned not to take so many pictures.

Dottie withstood the trip very well. She slept almost eleven hours the first night and felt fine. However, her ankles and legs had swollen up to her knees on the long flight and even wearing elastic support hose, she did not get rid of the swelling until we returned home.

On the second day we visited the Tower of London, where the royal jewels are displayed, and the London Bridge spanning the River Thames. It was disassembled in 1971, moved to Lake Havasu in Arizona and reconstructed, becoming one of the most popular tourist attractions in Arizona.

On the third day, Dottie rested in bed all morning. We left for Frankfurt, Germany, at 4:30 p.m. and were met by our Swiss courier who would be with us for about two weeks. She took us by bus to Wiesbaden where we spent the night at the Nassauer Hof Hotel.

The next day, we took a tour of the Rhine River Valley. I remember the many vineyards on the river banks. The grapes from the side with the most sun reportedly produced much better wine.

At 10 a.m., we boarded an excursion boat at Rudesheim. We were aboard about four hours, as I recall, getting off at Koblentz after lunch. Although we knew nothing about choosing wine, we thought we should try some from the local winery. It tasted like vinegar.

The traffic on the river was very interesting. I remembered studying about this river commerce in school. We were continually meeting loaded boats and others were overtaking us, the noise of their engines droning monotonously. I was particularly interested to see boatloads of logs from Norway and Sweden that were being shipped to Germany.

Our bus driver had driven across country and met us at Koblentz. We returned to Wiesbaden for the night. Next morning, we left by plane from Frankfurt and arrived in Zurich, Switzerland, soon after 10 a.m. We had some time for shopping and I bought Dottie two Bucherer wrist watches. We crossed the famous Student's Covered Bridge in the middle of town.

Another motorcoach and driver met us and we left for Lindau, crossing Lake Constance en route. We were to tour Switzerland, Austria, and Italy with this driver and courier.

Lindau was infamous for atrocities committed there during World War II, and it was no pleasure visiting it. Our hotel, the Bayerischer Hof, was nice.

In Switzerland, we saw many cows, each wearing a bell which prevented them from straying from each other in dense fog and cloud. We also saw women harvesting hay in fields by the road. The hay was placed on wooden frames, so it would cure in spite of the frequent rains.

On September 11th, we drove through scenic southern Germany into Austria and saw the beautiful Neuschwanstein Castle from the outside. We toured a nearby old castle with many crown jewels and memorabilia of former Bavarain rulers. Arriving at Innsbruk, Austria, in late afternoon in a cold rain, we checked into the Tyrol Hotel. The city is surrounded by mountains. We saw many ski slopes and lifts, including where the ski jumping competition was held in past winter Olympic Games. When we got up the next morning, I had a migraine headache and was vomiting. I recovered barely in time to leave on our bus. I think I had gotten too cold during the night.

Next day, we drove through the high Alps and the Brenner Pass into Italy. Along the winding road through the Dolomite Alps are many ski lifts and chalets for winter sports enthusiasts. Summer activities were still in progress and there were dozens of hikers with backpacks. We arrived in Venice in late afternoon, passing through a green farming belt that produced an abundance of vegetables and fruits.

The bus was parked and we took a water taxi to the Luna Hotel near St. Mark's Square. We were not accustomed to the water taxis, and some of the older ladies almost fell into the canal as we got out in front of our hotel. We were told that in the winter, the water in the canal rises several feet and engulfs the first floor of the hotel, including the lobby. St. Mark's Square is also inundated.

We were in Venice two nights and a day. During our touring we went to St. Mark's Square, less than a block away, and saw the thousands of pigeons. We visited St. Mark's Church and the Doge's Palace. We took a water taxi to the Murano Glass Factory across the canal and bought many items. One was a ruby-colored pitcher, 22 inches tall, made by an elderly glass blower. It is a masterpiece of Venetian glass and adorns a prominent shelf on our etagere in the corner of our living room.

In the evening we went on a gondola cruise through the canals under the full moon. The day before we arrived, there had been a sudden thunderstorm, and one of the gondola boatmen was drowned. The rest of the boatmen were in mourning and would not sing during our cruise, as they normally did.

The next day, we drove to Rome, where we stayed for three nights. The weather was hot and we were tired when we arrived. That evening we took a moonlight ride from 9 to 10:30 and visited the Seven Hills of Rome.

The final day in Rome, we had a special guide who showed us many of the most important highlights. We saw the remains of the Roman Forum and visited the Coliseum and were allowed to walk inside the ruins. This is no longer permitted. We toured St. Peter's Cathedral, a magnificent architectural giant and one of the most beautiful buildings I have ever seen. In it, we saw the Pieta sculpture, which we had seen before at the New York World's Fair, and Michelangelo's sculpture of Moses. In the evening we drove to Tivoli and saw all the water fountains in the bright moonlight.

On our last day we visited the Sistine Chapel in Vatican City and saw the beautiful frescoes of Michelangelo on the ceiling. We also visited the Pantheon.

We got an early start the next morning and arrived in the ancient town of Siena by noon. The bus was not allowed to enter the center of town, and we had to walk several blocks to reach the town square. The square is surrounded by buildings including the city hall and other administrative buildings, many restaurants and other businesses. Each year, a chariot horse race is held in the square in full, Roman splendor. Following the race, there is a great celebration. We ate lunch at one of the restaurants on the square, sitting at canopy-covered sidewalk tables. There was a uniqueness about Siena that we saw nowhere else in Italy. It was as though we reverted to a culture as it was thousands of years ago.

Soon after lunch, we boarded our bus and drove to Pisa. Beside the Leaning Tower of Pisa, which I climbed, there was a beautiful cathedral. Since our visit, the tower has leaned to an ominous degree and tourists are no longer allowed to climb it.

After visiting Pisa we drove on to Florence for the night. In the evening we visited a leather factory where I bought a belt made of alligator skin. I still have it.

The following morning was spent touring Florence and visiting Uffizi Art Gallery and the Midici Chapels. We saw Michelangelo's sculpture of David and many more of his works. Less than two years before, Florence was flooded when a dam broke in the mountains above the city. The art gallery was flooded. We could see the water marks on the walls, reaching a height of eight to ten feet as I recall. After the flood, people came from all over the world to help clean up and restore the paintings and books. When we left Florence we drove by the dam that had broken.

In the afternoon, we drove to Milan where we spent the night. Here there was a modern, magnificent shopping arcade with high glass roofs covering the sidewalks. We had not seen anything of its kind before on this trip. We drove by the La Scala

Opera House and saw the statue of Leonardo da Vinci. As we left in early morning, we passed the Gothic-styled cathedral which was bathed in bright sunlight. It was beautiful and so different from the buildings in Venice and Rome.

We soon reached the Italian-Swiss Lake District and Lake Lugano. The sun did not get above the high peaks of the Alps until about 9 a.m., leaving the valleys below in shadow. We got off our coach at a landing by Lake Lugano, and our driver left with our coach to have it serviced. We were to take an hour's cruise on the lake and stop en route for a hot drink at a lakeside snack shop. While we were waiting for our excursion boat to arrive, we explored the dock area. I went out on a walkway made of a single, wide board. Because of my bifocals I did not see where the second board overlapped the one I was on. I tripped and fell into the lake. The water was only three feet deep, but very cold. Naturally, the lower part of my body was soaked. I held my camera high to protect it. The traveler's checks in my pocket got wet, but I was able to cash them when they dried out. Our driver was not due to return with the coach and my luggage for an hour so there was nothing for me to do except wait. We went on the excursion, but I did not go into the restaurant. By the time we returned, the sun had risen over the mountain and I was not as cold. Eventually, my clothes dried.

We went through St. Goddard's Pass which was over a mile high in the snow-covered Alps. We reached Lucerne in late afternoon and stayed at the Astoria Hotel, which had a training school for chefs. It seemed that all hotels in Switzerland had similar schools. It was interesting to watch the instructors teach the apprentice chefs, who eventually traveled over the world with their culinary knowledge. The United States was lacking in this form of instruction in its schools, though this is no longer true in Hawaii.

The next morning we went shopping, and in the afternoon took a cable car up Mt. Pilatus, which was 7,000 feet high. From the summit, we could see snow-covered mountain peaks for many miles. In the evening we went to Le Chalet Restaurant, and, after dinner, saw authentic folk entertainment. Dancers were in native costumes and one of the features was the blowing of a long alphorn.

The next day, Monday, September 21st, provided some sobering news. A Boeing 747 passenger plane had been destroyed in the desert by terrorists, with the loss of many lives. The terrorists announced that an Air France plane would be their next target. We were scheduled to leave nearby Zurich Airport at noon on an Air France plane for Paris.

When we arrived at the airport, we said goodbye to our faithful bus driver and to the very efficient courier. She was multilingual, and it was interesting to watch her get us through customs as we traveled from country to country. Often, we did not have to show our passports or be inspected. She made our trip very pleasant.

When we checked in, we were advised that we could take only one piece of hand luggage into the cabin and that it would have to be inspected. There was rapid consolidation of hand luggage among the members of our group. When we left the terminal, we were taken to a table halfway to the plane, 100 yards from the terminal building. There, each piece of hand luggage was thoroughly inspected and every passenger was frisked. It was amazing what some passengers (not in our group) had in their carry-on luggage, and some of it was not allowed. After the inspection, we boarded the plane for the hour flight to Paris. We arrived in mid-afternoon, in very hot weather.

We had almost two days for sightseeing in Paris and briefly saw many of the highlights. On the morning of the second day, Dottie and I rented a taxi and saw many places our official tour had not included. The most notable places we visited were Versailles Palace, Napolean's Tomb, and the Eiffel Tower. We passed the Louvre Museum, but it was closed for the day, and also saw Notre Dame Cathedral from the outside.

We were impressed by street after street of apartment houses, all six or seven stories tall. Usually the streets were beautiful boulevards with tall trees. We saw hundreds of dogs being walked on leashes, particularly in the evening. It was obvious from the sidewalks that there were many more dogs than we saw and too few street cleaners.

Dottie and I took a walk in the evening. Near our hotel, a college student from Africa was selling artifacts he had brought from his country. He said he was supporting himself this way. We bought a beautiful ebony madonna statue, carved by an outstanding artist. Dottie displays it all the time in our living room and makes a special display with it at Christmas. We also bought a small bongo drum to give to our son-in-law, Michael Mote. We purchased a specially decorated black fertility mask for Carol and Pete Keck who had no children at the time. Eventually they had twins, the first in our family. We thought we would return to Paris someday for a long visit, but so far, we have not.

We left for Lisbon, Portugal, and arrived in our hotel, the Mundial, before 6 p.m. I still remember the large table of food in the dining room, a display of every type of seafood, including large baked fish and the largest prawns I have ever seen. Melons were in season and were delicious.

Our hotel was near the main shopping center. Next morning, I walked down the nearby streets where all varieties of vegetables, fruit and seafoods were openly displayed. I had never seen so many fish and other exotic seafoods.

We took a scenic bus tour of the city in the morning. A huge white cross stood on a high hill across the river from the city. The cross itself must have been 100 feet high. In the afternoon we drove to Sintra in the country and back along the coast to Lisbon.

While Dottie was resting after the tour, I went back to the shopping area where there were many linen stores with beautiful, hand-embroidered linens. I wanted to buy a large tablecloth and napkins, which sold for less than $100, but would not trust my own judgement. Instead, I bought two bridge-table-size linen cloths with matching napkins. Dottie was very pleased with them.

One day when we were on the main street near our hotel, the President of Portugal passed in his limousine. His car, sporting a license plate with number 1 on it, was accompanied by several secret service cars.

We were surprised to see an Arch of Triumph in Lisbon, similar to the one in Paris. Later, we saw others in different parts of the world. There was much evidence of the invasion of Portugal by the Moors.

The last evening after dinner, we enjoyed a fado, a very colorful folklore show with dancing and singing. This ended our European tour.

The next day we left the tour group and boarded a plane to New York City on the first leg of our trip home.

Our flight to New York took eight hours. Carol and Peter met us and drove us to Philadelphia, where we stayed with Dottie Jane and Michael for two days. We visited Dr. Franklyn Payne and also Jack and Mildred Heyl.

On Monday, September 29th, we rented a U-drive and visited Dottie's family in Lewistown. From there we drove to Richmond, Virginia, and spent the night with my sister, Dorothy, and her husband, Jack Thornton. Next day, we arrived in Chapel

Hill, N.C., where we stayed for three days. Maisie now owned my mother's former home, where she lived with her son, William. We visited Ralph and Sue Fleming in Durham, and Orus's family in Sanford.

On October 4th, we left the Raleigh-Durham Airport on Eastern Airlines at 9 a.m. After stopping in Atlanta and New Orleans we reached Mexico City at 1:40 p.m. We stayed at the Maria Isabella Sheraton Hotel near the square with the Gold Angel statue, our landmark when we got lost.

Next day, I attended meetings of the American College of Obstetricians and Gynecologists all morning, and we took a guided tour of the city in the afternoon. On the second day, I attended meetings all morning, and then we visited Guadelupe Shrine and the Pyramids. After morning meetings on the third day, we took another city tour which included the University of Mexico. Seeing the seven-story library building with the mosaic murals by Diego Rivera on all the outside walls was the highlight of this tour. This is certainly one of the most beautiful buildings in the world. Many other mosaic murals appear on buildings throughout the city. These are unique to Mexico City and typified the artistic nature of the people.

In the evening we attended the Ballet Folklorico de Mexico. Amalia Hernandez, its dynamic founder, director and choreographer, had developed it into one of the leading ballets of the world. The production, depicting the songs and dances of the peasants in Mexico, had been performed throughout the world, winning acclaim and awards wherever it was presented. Two ballet companies were formed - a traveling company and a resident company. The haunting ballet was unforgetable.

The medical meetings lasted three days, leaving three and a half days free to explore the wonders of Mexico. We spent one entire day in the National Archaeo-logical Museum and the Museum of Modern Art. There is no doubt in my mind that the Archaeological Museum is the most outstanding museum of its kind in the world. New and modern in all respects, and beautifully designed, it contains Mexican art from ancient times to the present. On display is a large Aztec stone medallion about six to ten feet in diameter and two feet thick, as I recall. Carvings on it depict information about the Aztec civilization, which our guide said was more advanced than Egyptian or any other civilization. Small replicas of this medallion are available throughout Mexico.

In the evening we ate at Del Lago Restaurant. This was the most elegant restaurant we visited and it served the most delicious meal we ate in Mexico. Its setting was on a lake where a large fountain periodically became active and bright lights created a dazzling display.

The next day was Friday, and we took an all-day tour to Taxco, the Silver City. En route, we stopped at Toluca, the highest city in Mexico. In the farmer's market, everything raised on the farm was available for purchase - poultry, animals, fruits and vegetables. Pottery and woven baskets were for sale. All kinds of linens, embroidered material and clothes were offered. It was a beehive of activity.

Taxco was over 100 miles south of Mexico City in beautiful, hilly, rolling country with deep gorges. Ninety percent of the arable land was planted in corn (maize), with fields stretching for miles along the road. We saw farm animals in the yards surrounding small farm houses, but we saw no large plantation headquarters. When we returned after dark, these houses were lit by kerosene lamps and lanterns.

In Taxco, several silver mine entrances were visible above and below the highway. Several homes and business were located on the hillsides with access by narrow cobblestone roads. Our bus could not negotiate the curves and hills, so we parked by the highway below and climbed up about three blocks to a nice restaurant and had lunch. We passed an Indian woman leading two donkeys with large loads of wood on their backs. When we attempted to take pictures of her she chased us with a stick. I got one picture of her despite her objections.

After lunch, we visited the silver shops in the area and, finding beautiful jewelry of good quality, purchased some for our four daughters, for Dottie and for some of her friends. We boarded our bus about five o'clock for the long trip home.

Our return trip took us through the town of Cuernavaca at sunset. It is said to have the best climate of any place on earth, and is a favorite place to retire. It is a beautiful town with many luxurious homes and palm trees similar to what we see in Hawaii.

The trip back to Mexico City was long and tiresome. It was uphill all the way, and our bus seemed not to have much power. We finally arrived at 11 p.m.

Our last full day was Saturday, October 9th. We spent most of the day in the Pink zone stores and the Sabada Market where the stores are controlled by the government and the prices are reasonable. We walked through Chapultepec Park and bought a large painting from an artist who was displaying several of his paintings along the shaded walk. He insisted on bringing the picture to our hotel room and, eventually, four people arrived with the painting. It was well-wrapped so we could bring it home in the cabin of the plane. They were very excited about our purchase, and so were we. It was a beautiful picture of chrysanthemums in yellow, orange, red and brown shades. We have displayed it on a wall in our foyer ever since.

In Sullivan Park on Sunday morning we saw many more artists showing their paintings. Also, on the street corner by the park, there was a large array of cut flowers for sale. In fact, during the whole week in Mexico, we had seen beautiful cut flowers, especially roses, for sale almost everywhere. Nowhere else in the world have we seen such an abundance of flowers and it is one of our fondest memories of Mexico City. We caught a Western Airlines plane at 2:30 p.m. and arrived in San Francisco at 7:15.

We spent three days with Lois and John at Fremont and visited McLeod and Louise at Saratoga while we were there. I was busy most of the time doing house repairs for Lois, as John was not adept at doing such things. Finally, we left from Oakland on October 15th, visited with Ann at the Honolulu Airport and arrived home at 3 p.m. I worked the following day.

THE YEAR 1970 CONTINUED

Three days after we returned from our European and Mexican trip, Dr. and Mrs. F.W. Davison of the Geisinger Hospital visited us for a day. He was the chief of the Ear, Nose and Throat Department when I was an intern. He had guided me in taking out two pairs of tonsils, which was required of each intern. I have already described how I later became proficient at tonsillectomy working on the plantations. The Davisons were wonderful people who frequently entertained the interns and residents in their home. He was a Chevalier Jackson - trained bronchoscopist, and a leader in this field. He died recently in his late 80s.

Dottie slowly recovered from the fatigue of our long trip. The swelling of her ankles receded, and she was able to start playing golf. Within a month, she walked 18 holes and made 100. Par was 74.

OUR ONLY GRANDDAUGHTER IS BORN

In early December I got word from one of my obstetrician friends in Honolulu that he'd delivered a baby girl that was available for Lois and John to adopt. Lois came immediately and took this beautiful baby home with her. The baby received the name Carol Ann from her two aunts. John arrived a few weeks later and adopted Carol Ann legally in the courts. She has now graduated from high school and hopes to become a nurse. At the time of her birth, we had four grandsons and no grand-daughter and, for this reason, she was very welcome in our family. Eventually, identical twin boys were born to Carol and Peter Keck, and they would be our last grandchildren. So, Carol Ann remains our only granddaughter. She has grown more beautiful as she has matured into a young lady.

Our office was closed in the afternoon on New Year's Eve so Dottie and I played golf with our friend, Roy Savage. When the game was over I became very busy. I operated on a patient with a ruptured, ectopic pregnancy, delivered a baby, and did a dilation and curettage for an incomplete abortion. I was thankful for the relaxation I had gotten in the afternoon.

THE YEAR 1971

We were invited to Tamotsu and Mitsuko Omoto's home, less than a block away, for a New Year's Day feast and to watch the Rose Bowl football game with other guests. Tamotsu had taught all our daughters in high school.

It rained for three days during the first week of January, and Mount Haleakala was covered with snow down to about the 7,000 foot level. It was beautiful. The snow reminded us that it was wintertime up there, while we played golf in summerlike weather by the ocean.

I had rewritten my medical paper entitled, "Fetal Adrenal Hyperplasia," and sent it to the Journal of the American Medical Association for publication. It was re-jected. I then sent it to the American Journal of Diseases of Children, and again it was rejected.

Our nephew, Dick Graham, visited us for three days. He was the national sales representative for Bausch and Lomb Company. We took him to Hana and Lahaina sightseeing, and played golf at the Maui Country Club. While driving to the club, listening to the Super Bowl Game on the radio, I was stopped and given a ticket for speeding. This was the only ticket for a traffic violation I had ever received. It cost me $8.

During the last week of January, we spent two days with Ann at Kaneohe and five days on a golf safari on Kauai. Every day we played golf and cribbage with our friends from Kauai and Spokane and each evening we went to a different restaurant for a dinner party. One day, we played 36 holes of golf.

In February we saw the opera, "Tosca," at Baldwin Auditorium. It had been brought to Maui by the Honolulu Symphony who had imported singers from New York City for the leading roles. It was a delight to see and hear.

It seemed that I was forever busy and overworked. I tried to keep up with normal social life for Dottie's sake as well as my own, playing golf twice each week and going to church on Sunday morning. I had help to do the yard work, but still had much to do, such as caring for my orchids. Dr. Allred was a great help. I would still occasionally become overly tired and develop migraine headaches. One morning as I was delivering a baby, I vomited into my surgical mask. I could not stop work and rest, as it was the day for me to have the obstetrical clinic in Lahaina. During this clinic, I found a ruptured ectopic pregnancy. Luckily, Dr. Allred operated on her, and I had only to assist. My life was no different from any other obstetrician, except I may have tried to help my many patients in too many ways.

Dr. and Mrs. Clayton Mote, Dottie Jane's in-laws, spent a month in Taiwan doing missionary work. On their way home, they stopped on Maui and visited us for three days. They had many interesting stories to relate about their experiences and about the heroic efforts of Catholic sisters caring for the people in a very isolated area. No doctor was stationed there permanently. The sister in charge was able to take a month's vacation and come to the States while the Motes were there. Conditions were very primitive. Lula Mote, who was frail and weighed less than 100 pounds, worked fulltime as a nurse, housemaid and dietician. She was shocked when she saw the deplorable conditions where the people lived.

In May I operated on a patient with over a quart of blood in her pelvis. Normally, ovulation occurs each month with no bleeding from the ovary. This patient's ovary bled from the site of ovulation until she was almost exsanguinated.

I rewrote my medical paper and sent it to the Journal of Theoretical Biology. Just as before, it was rejected. This editor did make some very useful comments that helped me in the future. By this time, I had learned that an editor could quickly reject a medical paper and give a feeble excuse for doing so. Frequently he, or his reviewer, would give a reason for the rejection which showed that neither had read the entire paper. They would often contradict themselves. It soon was clear that the editors and reviewers did not know much about my subject and were not about to publish my paper. So far, I had sent it to the editors of nine medical journals, but I did not give up trying to get it published.

I continued to be very busy. In July I operated on a patient with a diagnosis of tubal pregnancy. At surgery, I found a pregnancy in each tube.

MAINLAND TRIP:
_____SEPTEMBER 4 TO OCTOBER 3, 1971

We left Maui at 8 a.m. for Honolulu and went to San Francisco, arriving at 6 p.m. We spent three days with Lois and her family in Fremont and visited McLeod and Louise briefly. On September 7th, we flew to Spokane, where Ada and Jim Blankenship met us. We arrived at Hayden Lake, Idaho, in time for 15 holes of golf. The next day I played with Jim, Grant Dixon and Dr. Sam Wallis of Kauai. Dottie played with their wives. The Hayden Lake Country Club Member-Guest Tournament started on the 8th and lasted for three days. There was a party each evening, either at the club or someone's house. I did not do well in the tournament.

On the day following the tournament, Jim took us for a ride on his speedboat on the lake. Hayden Lake is surrounded by tall mountains which, from a distance, appear to be pink and are known as the Pink Mountains of Idaho. Jim told us that in the winter when the lake freezes, deer come down out of the mountains and walk across the ice. The buck tests the ice first to see if it will support him and, if it does, the does will follow to the other side where the homes and golf course are located.

On this last evening, we attended a dinner party at the Grant Dixon home. A long table was filled with delicious foods, especially melons which were grown locally and were in season. This area produces the best melons in the United States - casaba and crenshaw melons, several varieties of cantaloupes, watermelons and others.

On September 13th we flew to Detroit, where Neff and Jane Graham met us. They took us to their home at Port Huron, Michigan. This was the fateful day of the massacre at the Attica State Prison in New York. We spent three days with Neff and Jane and played golf twice at the Port Huron Country Club.

We rented a U-drive and drove to Niagara Falls, the first time either of us had seen this famous spot. We stayed at the Sheraton Hotel and had dinner in a restaurant above the Canadian Falls. Next day we drove to Montreal, registered at the Holiday Inn, and had a very good lunch in the Rib Room of the Sonesta Hotel. The following day, Saturday, we toured the city in the morning and saw a baseball game between the Montreal Expos and the St. Louis Cardinals in the afternoon.

On Sunday we drove through northern New York State over the rolling hills on a superhighway. The scenery was as beautiful as we had ever seen. I was driving about 75 miles per hour when a patrolman suddenly appeared behind me. He passed us as though we were traveling at a snail's pace. I think the speed limit at the time was 70 miles per hour. We continued on to Naugatuck, Connecticut, where Carol and Peter lived. We played nine holes of golf the first afternoon and 18 holes each of the next two days on the golf course across the street from their house. We went shopping in the morning of our last day at the nearby Heritage Shopping Center in the uniquely designed Heritage Retirement Village. Here we found quality merchandise of almost every description. The village catered to wealthy, retired patrons. Before we left, I paid the professional at the golf course for a series of golf lessons for Peter.

Next day, we continued on to Philadelphia and spent two days with Dottie Jane and Michael. Little Gregory was only six weeks old and Timothy was sixteen months. We had a good visit with them and hired a baby sitter so we could take Dottie Jane and Michael to the famous Bookbinders Restaurant for dinner. Dottie Jane had to borrow a vacuum cleaner while we were there, so I bought her a new one.

We drove on to Lewistown and spent five days with our relatives. While we were there, Dottie Jane telephoned to tell me she had a breast infection and high fever. There was a pharmacy in their apartment building, so I called and prescribed a type of oral penicillin for her. I had an active Pennsylvania medical license at the time. She recovered promptly.

We spent our last night with Tony and Jo Artman near Penn State University and left early next morning for Pittsburgh. We encountered some fog, but arrived at the airport in time to turn in our U-drive and catch a plane for Portland, Oregon, via Chicago. I attended the annual meeting of Section VIII of the American College of Obstetricians and Gynecologists in the mornings for three days. We went sightseeing or shopping in the afternoons. On one trip up the Columbia River, we saw salmon spawning in a small tributary. The water flowed in a small stream above the road and then fell vertically for about 30 feet to a shallow pond 30 to 40 feet in diameter. When the salmon reached the pond, they could go no further. The females proceeded to dig depressions in the gravel at the water's edge and deposit their eggs. A male fertilized them. There were many dead salmon that had already spawned. We saw every step in the spawning process, from the time the fish arrived from downstream until they accomplished their last act and died. It was very interesting. The tour drivers communicated with other drivers, so that all tours headed to this one spot. Rarely was one able to see the whole spawning process so clearly. We were told that bears would come in the night and eat the dead salmon.

One evening we ate at the famous Canlis Restaurant in our Hilton Hotel. This same restaurant had a branch on Kalakaua Avenue in Honolulu, which is closed now. On the second evening we attended the banquet of the meeting and on our final evening we ate at Danny and Louis's Oyster Bar. We returned home on Sunday, October 3rd.

THE YEAR 1971 CONTINUED

Nothing very exciting happened during the last three months of the year. I was deeply involved with my research project, studying four hours or more on it each day. The various facets of it were slowly evolving. I was impatient, but was making definite progress toward my goal.

Michael, Ann and Michael II spent three days with us at Christmas. It was difficult to visualize that little 2-year-old Michael would eventually be six feet tall and weigh 190 pounds, his statistics as of this writing in 1989. He is much taller than his father and both grandfathers.

THE YEAR 1972

The year started the same as many before with a midday feast at our neighbors, the Nittas, followed by the Rose Bowl football game. My partner, Dr. Allred, left on New Year's Day for a three-week vacation in New Zealand.

A 30-year-old woman who worked in our pharmacy had severe high blood pressure, which was well controlled with medication prescribed by one of our internists. She became pregnant against the advice of the internist, who recommended she have an abortion. She was referred to me, and I also recommended a therapeutic abortion. She refused. She was doing well until two weeks before her due date, when her husband found her unconscious on the floor at 4 a.m. When I saw her at the hospital an hour later, she was having convulsions. I assumed she had eclampsia and treated her for such. Her convulsions stopped, but she also stopped breathing. She was given cardio-vascular-resuscitation and put on a pulmonary machine that produces artificial breathing. At this time, I could not hear fetal heart sounds. I called her internist and he visited her at 6:30 a.m. He thought she might have had a cerebral hemorrhage, and a spinal tap produced very bloody fluid. Her condition remained the same for the next 48 hours. I had been hearing normal fetal heart sounds for some time. She was declared brain dead. I did a cesarean section under local anesthesia and delivered a healthy eight-pound baby girl. The mother's heart stopped a few hours later, though the pulmonary machine had been continued. The baby grew and developed normally. She is now 17 years old.

On January 20th I gave a talk at the Maui Memorial Hospital staff meeting on the genesis of high blood pressure during pregnancy. It was well received.

We had almost six inches of rain in 18 hours on January 24th, the first rain in four months. Our winter rains usually started in early October, though some years we had rain almost every week. I remember one year we had no rain in Wailuku for eight months.

We visited Ann in Honolulu for two days and bought a white rug from her to cover all the floors in our home except in Dottie's bedroom and the kitchen area. It is nylon and has been very satisfactory. Luckily, it will not burn when hot coals from the fireplace land on it, which has happened twice. The nylon underneath has melted and charred. I was able to patch the areas with pieces of the original carpet, and they are not noticeable.

We went to Kauai for a five-day golf safari and played at Princeville for the first time. We returned many times over the years as several of our Spokane friends built homes in the newly developed resort. While we were away, a large eucalyptus tree from the nearby forest fell into our yard during a storm. I used my chainsaw to cut the tree for firewood.

We had guests in for dinner before going to Baldwin Auditorium to see the opera, "Cinderella." It was brought to Maui by the Honolulu Symphony Society, who brought in the singers from San Francisco and New York to play the leading roles.

Our long-time friends, Jack and Bennie Lightner from Virginia, spent two weeks in our guest cottage. We had a big party for them and attended many other parties on Maui held in their honor. We played golf many times. We had been good friends since before the war, 31 years ago.

I took our German shepherd-collie dog, Bonn, back to the Humane Society where I had gotten him 14 years before. He was severely infested with heartworm, had chronic heart failure and was losing weight. He had been unable to take medicine for heartworm for several years. Our children had loved him and so did the children in our neighborhood.

CHAPTER XVII

New Zealand and Australia Tours:
April 4 to 27, 1972

We left Honolulu at 1:30 a.m. on Air New Zealand for Auckland. Over the public address system on the plane, Auckland was pronounced the same as Oakland, so we made a double check to be sure we were on the right plane and not headed for California. We crossed the International Date Line soon after we crossed the equator and arrived in Auckland at 8:30 a.m. on April 5th. The distance from Honolulu to Auckland is 4280 miles. We stayed at the Hotel Intercontinental where my sister, Velma, and her husband, Marcus Lawrence, had stayed the night of April 4th. Velma left a letter to be given to me upon my arrival. When we planned our trips, neither couple knew of the other's plans. Velma and Marcus assumed they would visit us on Maui, but, of course, we were not there.

After a rest, we took a city tour in the afternoon. We were impressed by the beautiful harbor and the cleanliness of the city which reminded us of Honolulu. We visited a wooded area where we saw a kiwi, the national bird, in an enclosure containing many small plants. This timid bird is about 12 inches tall, is tailless and has rudimentary wings. There is also an edible green fruit by the same name.

The next morning we left by bus for Roturua and spent the night at the Continental Hotel. We loved the beautiful, green countryside and its lovely pastoral scenes, one after the other. Vast, green pasture lands contained hundreds of cattle and even more sheep. Every mile or so, there was a farm house, usually painted white. In almost every yard there was a well-groomed horse in a small wire enclosure or tethered with a rope. The horses had blankets covering them from neck to tail. The bus driver said the purpose of the blanket was not to keep the horse warm and dry, but to prevent the hair from growing long. At races, the horse's coat would be sleek and beautiful. It seemed that horse racing was popular in New Zealand, and that many farmers owned a race horse.

We learned all about sheep, which seemed to be everywhere. This was the breeding season, and I soon learned that the pattern of breeding sheep is much different from that of cattle. As we drove by the pastures filled with sheep, we saw that most of the ewes had a patch of red or green coloring on their backs. I learned that 50 ewes were put in a corral with one ram. The ram's abdomen was covered with paint-like material that stained the back of each ewe when he mounted her. In the morning all the ewes with color on their backs were allowed to leave the corral. Estrus occurs in sheep every 17 days, so, by the end of 17 days, all the ewes were bred.

In Rotorua we found steam everywhere, coming from cracks in the earth and bubbling from pools of mud. I remember seeing a pipe sticking out of the groud near our hotel and emitting steam just as a safety valve does on a commercial boiler when the pressure builds up too high. The steam not only provided heat for cooking, but provided an unlimited source of power to generate electricity. The area around Rotorua reminded us of the Kilauea Volcano area on the Island of Hawaii and the area in Yellowstone National Park near Old Faithful Geyser.

Rotorua was the headquarters of the Maori Empire or Nation. The Maoris were

Polynesian people very similar to the Hawaiians and had arrived in New Zealand hundreds of years before in canoes. The income from all the activities at Rotorua was used to enhance and preserve the Maori culture.

We visited the Government Gardens and a museum where we saw beautiful Maori wood carvings and other artifacts. In the evening we were entertained at our hotel by Maori dancers and warriors.

The next day we were off early on a direct flight on Mount Cook Airlines to the South Island. It was a beautiful day with bright sunshine. We flew directly over the Tasman Glacier with high mountains on each side, covered with snow many feet deep. The white mountains and the white glacier below us created an unbelievable sight. Suddenly, a New Zealand Air Force plane came along beside us, probably not more than a few hundred feet away, and we waved to the airmen. It flew with us a minute or so and then sped away. We landed on a small airstrip at the foot of Mount Cook in the Tasman Valley.

We stayed at the Heritage Hotel for two days and nights. This area was very peaceful and quiet and reminded us of our trips inside Haleakala Crater on Maui. The only noise was that of the engines of Piper Cub ski planes as they gained altitude to land on Tasman Glacier, 7,000 feet above. Sometimes the planes left their passengers, usually skiers, on the glacier and returned for them several hours later. Occasionally, the weather would turn bad so the planes could not return. There was an emergency hut equipped with blankets high on the glacier. The week before we were there, some skiers had to remain in it overnight. A favorite trek of the skiers was to fly to the head of the Tasman Glacier at the 7,000-foot level and then ski downhill 15 miles to Ball Hut in time to catch the afternoon bus back to the Heritage Hotel.

I refused to fly up and land on the glacier. Instead, Dottie and I took a 12-mile trip up the mountain on a bus along Tasman Glacier to Ball Hut. As we walked on the glacier, we could hear the river flowing beneath the ice. The glacier is up to two miles wide and drops nine to 18 inches daily. The milky-colored water could be seen at the terminal face of the glacier in the valley. From there, it flowed across Tasman Valley to Pukaki Lake. The ice at the 7,000-foot level is 1,500 to 2,000 feet thick and has been accumulating for centuries.

On our second day, we took a four-hour hike to Kea Point and saw Mueller Glacier. There was bright sunshine, and the scenery was beautiful. Just as we arrived in the area, there was an avalanche of ice and snow from the tip of the glacier only a few hundred yards away. It sounded like thunder. We also saw Hooker Glacier and the Hooker River, which is formed by the waters from the two glaciers.

While we were hiking, we heard many noisy kea parrots although we were not able to get very close to them or see them.

The mountains in this area are known as the Southern Alps. There are 17 peaks over 10,000 feet, and Mount Cook is the highest at 12,349 feet. Its ice-capped summit always appears very majestic, usually piercing the clouds.

We were very fortunate to have beautiful weather at Mount Cook. Others on our charter flight were not so lucky. Next morning the skies cleared after an early fog and Mount Cook again was bright and majestic. We left by plane for Queenstown at 11:30. In the afternoon, we took a cruise on Lake Wakatipu and stopped at Mckenzie Dude Sheep Station. After a guided tour of the home of the owner we were served tea and scones. Then the owner and his collie dog demonstrated how a sheep dog works. It was unbelievable for those of us who had not seen it before.

We had dinner at the Skyline Chalet, 1460 feet above Queenstown. The chalet is reached by a gondola cableway and offers an excellent view of Queenstown,

Wakatipu Lake and the surrounding mountains from the restaurant.

We visited the Scott Memorial, built in memory of explorer, Robert Falcon Scott, who reached the South Pole on January 17, 1912. He and his party perished on the return trip.

From Queenstown, we flew to Christchurch, a well-groomed, clean city. We visited the beautiful Angelican Cathedral.

Christchurch Airport is the takeoff point for New Zealand and American bases in Antarctica. It is the only airport in the world which has a specific arrival and departure counter for that southernmost continent. A sign above the counter reads, "Operation Deep Freeze," and below that, "Antarctica Flight Desk." It was not manned when we were there. I had Dottie stand behind the counter and took a picture of her and the sign.

On our third day, we rented a private car and driver and took an all-day tour of the countryside including Akaroa and Lyttleton Harbor. We spent some time on a beach where precious stones were occasionally found among the pebbles although we did not know what to look for. I bought a green semi-precious stone to give my sister-in-law, Jane Graham. In the afternoon, the driver stopped at his home and served us tea. We enjoyed our evening dinner as guests of Mr. and Mrs. James Murray of Maui. They were on our charter flight, but we had gone our separate ways since arriving in New Zealand. After dinner, we packed to leave for Australia the next day.

AUSTRALIA: APRIL 12 TO 27, 1972

We left for Melbourne at 1 p.m. on Air New Zealand and arrived within three hours, as I recall. We stayed at the Park Royal Motor Court. A tram (street car) passed the motor court, and we took it to the center of town, a few blocks away. We ate downtown in an underground boutique the first evening.

The second day we took an all-day tour to Ballarat and Sovereign Hill Gold Mine. This entire town and gold mine had been restored as it had been years ago as a working mine and was now a leading tourist attraction. We were shown the whole process of extracting gold from the soil. Near Ballarat we toured beautiful flower gardens filled with blooming begonias.

Early next morning, we visited the Melbourne Botanical Gardens which were enormous. There were many varieties of tall trees. Near the gardens was a magnificent art museum, which we visited. The architecture of the building was unusual and internationally famous, probably equalling the Archaeological Museum in Mexico City for splendor and uniqueness.

About noon, we flew to Hobart, Tasmania. The planes were all new DC-9s and we felt very safe in them. I had heard of Tasmania, an island south of Australia, and, because it seemed to be so far away, I thought it would be fun to visit. There was one complication. Our hotel reservation was in Launceston, and we landed in Hobart, 100 miles away. The next plane for Launceston was scheduled to depart about 8 p.m., but there was a bus at 4 p.m. We chose to take the bus. During the time before the bus departed, we explored Hobart and the surrounding area. We saw the remains of prisons that had been used to house habitual criminals from England in the 1800s. In Port Arthur, a ship from Europe was being loaded with delicious apples, one of the principle exports of Tasmania.

The bus trip to Launceston took over four hours. People living along the road had gone to town to shop, and we made many stops dropping them off. It was very interesting to see them, including children, returning home with their purchases. The scenes were very similar to those seen in rural America. The next day we took a taxi tour of the countryside around Launceston and saw Batman Suspension Bridge. This was April 15th, Dottie's birthday, and we had dinner at the Launceston Hotel. A delicious French onion soup was served. Later, Dottie wrote for the recipe, but they would not give it to her.

We were off early next morning for Adelaide with a brief stopover in Melbourne en route. It was Sunday, and the streets were filled with people. We took a boat ride on a lake and then visited the zoo where we saw the largest collection of exotic tropical birds we had ever seen. There were birds of paradise of all colors and sizes, including many colorful, noisy parrots.

On Monday we went shopping and saw beautiful opals though none were more beautiful than Dottie's which, we were told, had come from Australia. In the afternoon, we took a three-hour tour of the National Park and beaches in Adelaide.

We left the airport at 9 a.m. on Tuesday for Canberra. Again, we stopped at Melbourne en route, arriving at Canberra at 3:30 p.m. It is located halfway between Melbourne and Sydney. The new Nation of Australia was established in 1901, and there was great competition between Sydney and Melbourne to become its capital. Finally, virginal pasture land was set aside as Australian Capital Territory at Canberra. In the 1920s, American landscape architect, Walter B. Griffin, presented an award-winning plan for the seat of the federal government.

On the day we arrived, we walked through the business district. Next, we took an all-day tour of Canberra, which included a launch ride on a large artificial lake that entwined itself about the official buildings. A large fountain in the middle of the lake frequently sent water high into the air and then stopped. The Capitol building could be seen from most of the buildings and vantage points around the lake.

We visited all the official buildings. Just outside the Capitol, there was a medium-sized tent with a canopy and a table with several chairs. A sign read, "Aboriginal Embassy." Leaflets being passed out protested about the way the government had seized the Aboriginal lands. We were asked to sign a petition.

Inside the Capitol, we visited the chambers of the Senate which was in session. Outside, we saw the prime minister's car, a Rolls Royce with license plate number 1.

The architectural design of the capital grounds was outstanding. I was reminded of our capital at Washington D.C., but the design here was more beautiful with more room. There was just one main difference. The capitol building itself was only a temporary structure, one or two stories tall. It was not a large, magnificent edifice that dominated the scene locally and also contained the activities and records of the government of a large and growing nation. The cost to build now or in the future will be astronomical compared to what it would have been originally. I feel sure that those in charge have thought about this many times and wish that an elegant capitol building could have been started long ago. (A new capitol building was completed in 1988 at a cost of 10 billion dollars.)

Other buildings about the lake were the Library, the War Memorial and the Bell Tower. They were beautiful, especially when viewed from across the lake. All were of stone construction and a part of the permanent capitol complex. In the War Memorial Building, there were actual scenes of the battlefields just as they had existed in Vietnam, with life-size replicas of troops. It was jungle warfare. The troops were advancing with their equipment. The fronds of the palm trees had been shredded by shell fragments. It was very realistic.

We left the airport the next morning at 7:30 for Brisbane and arrived in three hours. The climate was subtropical and similar to that of Hawaii. We went shopping the day we arrived, and I bought a boomerang and shield. The shield had been made and decorated by Aborigines and was sold at an outlet that featured their handicrafts. I displayed it in my medical office as long as I practiced.

On our second day in Brisbane, we took a 50-mile tour up the Sunshine Coast north of the city. We visited a ginger root cannery which was very similar to a pineapple cannery. Large fields of ginger plants were harvested and brought to the canneries in large trucks. Lots of girls dressed in blue uniforms worked in the canneries, cutting and sorting the ginger root. It was then put in large tanks and cooked. Some was canned, while part of it was treated with sugar and sold as candied ginger.

We visited a pineapple museum set amid fields of pineapple, which looked just as they do in Hawaii. The museum contained pictures and movies showing how pineapple was grown and canned. Nearby were orchards growing all the tropical fruits that were grown in the area. We saw banana plants, macadamia nut trees, papaya trees (known as papaws), soursop, guavas and others.

This day was my 60th birthday, Australian time.

The following day, we took a three-hour city tour. The people were very friendly and unsophisticated, just as they are in Hawaii. Fred Lilly, a friend of our daughters, had married an Australian girl and they lived in Brisbane. We telephoned them and they visited us in our hotel. In the evening we saw the movie, "Fiddler on the Roof," in a theatre nearby. It is one of the most outstanding movies I have ever seen, and it left a deep impression on me.

This day was my birthday, Hawaiian time.

We went to Brisbane Airport to leave for Sydney. An airplane museum there contained the famous plane, Southern Cross. Sir Charles Kingford-Smith, along with co-pilot, navigator, and radioman, flew this plane around the world. It was a three-engine Fokker monoplane with the fuselage and two of the engines suspended under one long wing. The body appeared long and slender compared to modern aircraft. Small generators with a propeller were suspended under the wing on each side. The wind turned the propellers and generated the electricity for the plane.

Sir Kingford-Smith and his crew left Oakland, California, on May 31, 1928, and landed in Honolulu safely. From there, they went to Fiji and, after other stops, reached Australia. They continued slowly and finally reached London, England, in 1929. More money had to be raised for the trip to continue. Two of the crew were replaced by Americans. They made the first westward crossing of the Atlantic by airplane. Dense fog was encountered over Newfoundland, and they almost ran out of fuel before landing safely near the coast. They continued on across the United States and landed safely on July 4, 1930, at Oakland, from where they had started. It had taken them two years, one month and four days to fly around the world. I was sixteen years old when they started. As I recall, it was reported that over the Pacific, the plane had to fly low, just above the waves, to conserve fuel. It was a thrill to see this plane sitting in a museum. I had already seen the first plane to fly (by the Wright Brothers at Kitty Hawk, N.C.) and the Spirit of St. Louis, in which Lindbergh flew alone across the Atlantic from west to east. The latter two planes are in the Smithsonian Institute in Washington, D.C.

On the day we arrived in Sydney, we took a ferry trip across the harbor to the zoo. We stopped at the opera house and briefly went inside. Construction was not yet complete, but we could easily visualize what a wonderful building it would be. Since completion, it has received great acclaim. The people of Sydney and of all Australia can justly be proud of having one of the most unusual, most beautiful, and best opera houses in the world. It seems they should have a capitol building befitting such a large and wonderful country.

In the zoo, we saw many of the animals found in Australia. There were kangaroos, of course, which we had seen everywhere, including in the wild. We saw koala bears which really are not bears, but are beautiful, cuddly little animals resembling bears. They are marsupials and live in trees and their diet consists entirely of eucalyptus leaves.

The most interesting animal on earth is the duck bill platypus, found in eastern Australia. It was on display only a few hours each day at the zoo, and, luckily, we were there at the right time. It has a flat beak like a duck, webbed feet and a rudder-like tail. It lays eggs and suckles its young. When not in the water, it lives in burrows along stream banks, where it raises its young. The one we saw in the zoo was in a water tank about six feet long and was continually swimming. It would come to the surface at one end of the tank and inhale air through its beak. Then as it swam, bubbles of air escaped from an opening on its back just in front of the tail. The platypus is usually about 20 inches long and is covered with fur. I was particularly interested in it because of my research project on the cause of high blood pressure in pregnancy. I had to study the phylogeny of reproduction and particularly placentation in animals. The platypus is a mammal, yet it lays eggs, and there is no placenta.

On our second day we walked through the downtown area and shopped all morning. In the afternoon we visited the large museum at Hyde Park. Again, I was particularly interested in seeing the displays of preserved animals and to learn about the way they lived in the wild. There was a display showing the burrows and nests of the platypus on a bank near a stream. The entrance to the burrows was under water.

I was particularly interested in seeing an opossum, which had been mounted along with a dozen young. I used the opossum as an example when I discussed the phylogeny of embryonic nutrition and development in my monograph on fetal adrenal hyperplasia.

The opossum is a marsupial and is found in many places around the world. They are nocturnal and are fetid; they are scavengers. When I was a teenager, I would go "possum" hunting in the fall with my friends, boys and girls, in the woods near our home at Coats, N.C. A hunting dog would soon find the scent of an opossum and track it down. When the animal climbed a tree, the dog stood at the base and howled in a tone that told his master he had "treed a possum". Sometimes we were able to climb the tree and get the opossum; other times, we had to cut the tree down. When confronted, the opossum plays dead. It is easy to take it by its long tail and put it in a burlap bag.

Occasionally an opossum will be blinded by automobile lights on the highway, and is easily caught.

We would take our opossum home and keep it in a cage for about two months, fattening it primarily with table scraps. Opossums are about 15 inches long and might weigh 15 pounds. After a couple of months, they don't smell so bad. We made "possum stew," which was a delicacy for some although I found it to be very greasy. The best part of opossum hunting is going out in the crisp fall air on a moonlit night with one's friends. Good opossum dogs are trained not to chase rabbits at night, just like good coon dogs are trained not to chase opossums. The gestation period of the opossum is about 13 days, the length of the luteal phase of the menstrual cycle. At birth, the mother places the young in a pouch on the under side of her body, where the nipples are located. Opossums weigh only one-half gram at birth, but are able to breathe and to hold on to their mother's nipples to nurse. When born, the young are still in the embryo stage and pass through the stage comparable to the fetal stage in animals higher in the evolutionary scale while they are in their mother's pouch. They, necessarily, must use innate hormones in their metabolism. They remain in the pouch for several weeks until they are able to walk and eat solid food at which time they venture out of the pouch. At times, as many as 12 baby opossums can be seen riding on the mother's back, clinging to her fur.

April 25th, our third day, was Anzac Day, a national holiday honoring the Australian-New Zealand-Army-Corps-Troops who fought so bravely in all the previous wars. We went downtown to catch a bus for an all-day tour through the state park and had to wait for a large parade to pass. Thousands of veterans, some crippled, in uniforms with medals marched past.

Because of the holiday, the road was packed with cars parked along one side for miles. Our bus could not pass until, finally, we lifted some cars to the side. We boarded a ferry which took us to Palm Beach near Sydney. Many beautiful boats under sail shimmered in the radiance of the sunset.

Our final day in Australia was spent with Jim and Elizabeth Murray on a full-day tour of the Blue Mountains National Park, west of Sydney. We visited Katoomba, Penrith, and Echo Point. I have color photographs that show the mountains actually appear blue from a distance.

Late in the afternoon of April 27th, we departed from Australia after shopping in the morning and touring the Argyl Center at the Rocks. This is an area on the beach to the left of the opera house, where English prisoners had been discharged many years ago. Crude prisons were made and many prisoners did not survive. The area has been restored as a major historical tourist attraction. The local people are not ashamed of their heritage, pointing to their achievements and successes which attest to their intelligence and industriousness.

We were soon on our way back to Auckland, New Zealand, and after a two-hour stop, left for Honolulu at 11 p.m. We arrived at 9:30 a.m. the same day, as we had recrossed the International Date Line. The Air New Zealand charter flight we were on offered an open bar. Although we were tired and wanted to sleep, many of the passengers drank, yelled and celebrated all night long, making it impossible for anyone to rest. I think they drank all the alcoholic beverages on the plane. It took me two days to get rested, though I returned to work the day after I arrived home.

THE YEAR 1972 CONTINUED

I was busy from the moment I returned from Australia, it seemed. On my second day back, I delivered a patient who had had kidney X-rays before she knew she was pregnant. She was a school teacher and a sterility patient. After having one child several years before, she could not conceive again. She had heard about the dangers of X-rays during pregnancy and thought she should have a therapeutic abortion. I advised her to go ahead with the pregnancy, and she delivered a healthy baby boy. He is now a normal 17-year-old and his mother is very grateful she took my advice.

Another patient had an acute gallbladder attack one week before term. We did not operate on her at that time.

Ann and Michael II visited us for a few days. Little Michael, four years old at the time, loved driving nails with a hammer and managed to use most of my nails during their visit.

Ann called me on July 3rd after they had gone home and told me that Michael had asked her for a divorce. This upsetting news caused me to lose a couple of nights' sleep, for no one in my immediate family had ever been divorced, and I was not prepared for such. In retrospect, some of Michael's behavior could not be explained. I recommended a lawyer for Ann to consult.

Our business was good. In addition to our monthly living allowance, our bonus every six months was over $5,000.

My former yard man died. He had been unable to get all the work done in the hours that social security allowed him to work and would be penalized if he made more money than was allowable. He wanted to work the extra hours without pay but I refused to allow this. I paid him the maximum and gave him IOUs for the remainder. After his death, his widow sent me the IOUs and I paid them.

I played in the Maui Country Club's first Member-Guest Golf Tournament. There was one practice round on Friday and 18 holes on Saturday and Sunday. Although my partner was a much better player than I, he did not take the game seriously and made several bad plays. I did my best and won low individual net. The prize was a Panasonic nine-inch television and has served me for 17 years without needing repairs. It was very useful when I was a patient in the hospital. Since that time I again won the low individual net score prize, a $100 merchandise certificate from the pro shop. After this, the low individual net prize was discontinued because it was a team-effort type of tournament.

On September 5th, 11 Israeli athletes were killed in their dormitory at the Munich Olympics by Arab terrorists. One policeman and five terrorists also were killed. This event shocked the entire world. The feud between the two factions rage to this day, and members on each side are killed almost every week.

Dottie had had several attacks of upper abdominal pain on the left side radiating to her back. Several years before, she had been diagnosed as having a stomach ulcer and had had her stomach X-rayed on two occasions. After suffering severe abdominal pain and vomiting all night on September 7th, she called me at 4 a.m., and I took her to the hospital. Eventually, X-rays showed a large stone in the common duct of the gallbladder, and at surgery the gallbladder also was found to be filled with stones. She stayed in the hospital nine days after surgery. Two days after coming home, she was found to have atelectasis of the lower lobe of the right lung. This recovered on medication.

The Honolulu Symphony Society presented the opera La Boheme at Baldwin Auditorium using artists from the mainland for the leading roles. These musical events were always welcome entertainment for us.

President Richard Nixon was re-elected by a landslide on November 7th.

One of my patients had a ruptured appendix at 39 weeks gestation and Dr. Rockett operated on her successfully for me.

I played golf with a friend who made even par 74 for 18 holes. Seldom did I have the opportunity to play with such a good golfer. The next day, he developed a gastric hemorrhage and eventually died from it.

On December 13th, I made 40-37 in golf. My handicap was 13, giving me a net score of 64 - 10 under par and the best score of my life.

Ann and Michael II arrived on December 22nd and spent a week with us. New Year's Eve was on Sunday and it rained all day. We went to church and spent a quiet evening at home.

266

I had been sick with sinusitis for two days, but after a good night's sleep New Year's Eve, I felt fine.

Dr. Allred left for California when a member of his family became ill. I soon became very busy. On Tuesday, January 2nd, I was up the entire night, doing one cesarean and operating on another patient with a ruptured ectopic pregnancy. I slept Wednesday afternoon and skipped my usual golf. On Thursday, I operated on another patient with a ruptured ectopic pregnancy.

I was still rewriting my monograph, sending it to various editors who rejected it. Finally, I sent it to Charles C. Thomas Co., publishers.

The world-famous pianist, Philippe Entremont, presented a concert at Baldwin Auditorium and we attended. He is a Frenchman who has received wide acclaim since his debut at age 17 in Barcelona, Spain. He first played in America at 19 in 1953. Since then, he has played as soloist with most of the great orchestras of the world, has given many recitals and made many recordings. In 1988 we watched him on Educational Television.

Dottie and I spent four days with Ann and little Michael at Kaneohe. I bought Michael a model ship kit of the U.S.S. Constitution, and took more than a day to glue it together. Dottie developed the flu with a bad cough while we were with Ann and remained in bed.

Despite Dottie's illness, we went to Kauai for a golf safari for four days as planned. Dottie spent two of those days in bed, but was able to play golf twice. We played at Princeville, Wailua and Kauai Surf golf courses with our Kauai and Spokane friends. Merrill Carlsmith of Hilo and Dr. Ralph Cloward of Honolulu also played with us. We had our usual cocktail parties and then dinner at restaurants.

I heard from Charles C. Thomas Co. after two weeks and my monograph again had been rejected. It was returned by fourth class mail in an unsealed envelope and when it arrived, after three weeks, parts of it had been damaged. It had cost over $100 to have it typed.

Jim and Ada Blankenship visited us for five days, and we gave a party for them to meet our Maui friends. We played golf twice at Wailea and once at the Maui Country Club. They were wonderful guests. We had enjoyed our many visits with them on Kauai and at Hayden Lake, Idaho.

We attended a concert at the Baldwin Auditorium presented by the prestigious and world-renowned Juilliard Quartet of New York City.

I delivered twins to a mother who already had one normal child. The first twin was a stillborn due to a strangulated umbilical cord. We had thought we heard two fetal heartbeats, but, obviously, heard only one. The mother was more upset over losing this twin than most mothers without any living children would have been. At first I could not understand why she was so disturbed. Now I realize that she had experienced the joy and love of her first child, and she knew what she was losing when the twin was stillborn. A mother who has never had a living child could not know this sense of loss.

Dottie and I attended a concert given by four Russian harpists. A harpist quartet was most unusual, but very enjoyable. Harps seem to be the musical instrument of angels, and are seldom heard except in large orchestras.

I had operated on a patient for a dermoid tumor of her ovary a few years previously. She had two children at that time. I warned her that women who have a dermoid ovarian tumor are more likely to get another in the other ovary than the average woman. I told her that she should have any more children she might want as soon as possible in case this should happen. She had two more children during the next two years, which completed her family. When she developed symptoms of gallstone colic, X-rays showed gallstones. I removed another dermoid tumor, and at the same operation, Dr. Rockett removed her gallbladder and stones. Twenty years have passed, and she remains in good health.

On April 26, all Hawaii was hit by an earthquake that measured 6.2 on the Richter Scale. No tidal wave was generated, and there was no major damage. Paint on houses was cracked, and dishes were toppled. We feel minor quakes every few weeks, but one of this magnitude is unforgettable. Four days later, I found one of our toilet's water-supply-lines was leaking, apparently shaken too much by the earthquake.

I received my monograph back from an editor for the final time. A reviewer had gone over it in detail and made many useful suggestions as to form. He had had my monograph for so long I developed a peptic ulcer. The epigastric pain I experienced after eating food was relieved immediately by antacids and anticholinergic drugs. This was the first time in my life I had had symptoms of a stomach ulcer. It wasn't until I told the editor about this that he finally returned the monograph with the review.

We had a special staff meeting on leprosy (Hansen's Disease). During the past year there had been 40 new patients in Hawaii compared to the previous year when there had been only eight. These new patients were all aliens recently immigrated to Hawaii.

On June 2nd, I sent a check to a travel agency to pay for a trip for Dottie and me to go to Moscow to attend a meeting of the Federation of the International Congress of Obstetrics and Gynecology (F.I.G.O.) which convened there in August. I had never thought we would visit Russia. I was a member of the Congress through the American College of Obstetricians and Gynecologists and, as such, was an invited guest. We decided this would be the time for us to go.

On June 12th I made 43-37 on our nine-hole course at the Maui Country Club, the third time in my life that I had made par for nine holes.

I gave a talk to the medical staff at Maui Memorial Hospital on the actions of vitamin K and its use to prevent bleeding in the newborn. Vitamin K is necessary for prothrombin formation, which, along with other factors, is necessary for blood clotting. It acts inside the cell in respiratory chain phosphorylation directly affecting the mitochondral pathways. My paper was later published in the Hawaii Medical Journal31.

We planted three strawberry guava trees in our front entrance as part of the landscaping. They have beautiful light beige trunks. I had picked the plants from the wild in Iao Valley. When they grew and produced fruit, I picked a peck at a time and could do so about twice a week for two months. Dottie made delicious guava jelly from some of the fruit, and we gave much more to friends.

PUBLICATION OF MY MONOGRAPH

I was convinced that my monograph should be published and finally decided to publish it myself. No medical paper had ever been presented on fetal adrenal cortical hyperplasia which is present in about 89 percent of human newborns. About 11 percent of newborns who die of trauma or accidents have normal, adult-type, adrenal cortices. Most everyone assumed that hyperplasia was normal although it disintegrated immediately after birth by dissolution, and, by about two weeks of age, infants have adult-type cortices. Some primate animals have fetal adrenal hyperplasia in the first half of pregnancy which always disappears before term. Other primates may or may not have adrenal hyperplasia at birth.

My main research subject was to explain the cause of high blood pressure developing during pregnancy. I showed that there was a direct relationship between fetal adrenal cortical hyperplasia and high blood pressure. I tried to explain how this came about, but there was not enough information known at this time about the causes of high blood pressure for me to explain this fully. My monograph was correct. The final answer and proof were a few years away.

I made arrangements with Tongg Publishing Company of Honolulu to print my monograph, and had it copyrighted under my name, December 24, 1973. It was 81 pages with five figures and was hardbacked. Of the 2000 copies I ordered, which cost me $6,000, I gave away about 800 copies and sold about 200 at $6.00 each. I still have the remainder. I received many favorable comments about the monograph and still get an occasional order[32].

My practice kept me active with unusual cases and I had been very busy getting my monograph published. I was preparing for our trip to Russia in August. Two weeks before we were to leave, the visas for our group of 40 doctors were all canceled by the U.S.S.R. The State Department intervened and got them reinstated.

I was not feeling well. Severe pain in my right thigh awakened me every night for a month. A week before we were scheduled to leave, I developed a large area of herpes zoster (shingles) on my right thigh. I took six injections of Protamide in five days, and the shingles improved remarkably, though Protamide is no longer thought to be effective for this condition. One of the herpetic blisters became secondarily infected, and I had to take an antibiotic for it.

CHAPTER XVIII

Finland, Russia, Denmark
and U.S. Mainland Tours:
August 1 to 29, 1973

Dottie and I left home at noon and arrived in San Francisco at 9 p.m. Lois and John met us at the airport, and we stayed with them at Fremont for two days. McLeod and Louise visited us for lunch one day.

On August 3rd we flew to Asheville, N.C., arriving at 5:30 p.m. Velma and Marcus had a home at Waynesville, 25 miles west of Asheville, where we stayed for three days. Neill and Pearl lived beside them. Maisie and her sons, Tommy and Pat, arrived on Saturday and we played 36 holes of golf. After church on Sunday, we played another 18 holes and then visited with O.F. Patterson Jr. and Sally.

Ausgust 6th, we flew to Washington, D.C. My sister, Dorothy, and her husband, Jack, drove up from Richmond and spent two hours with us at the airport. Dottie Lawrence Lichtwardt, who lived in Fairfax, Virginia, also came for a short visit. We arrived in Hartford, Connecticut, at 2:45 p.m. and spent a day with Carol and Peter who then drove us to Kennedy Airport. Our plane to Copenhagen was two hours late, so we spent the time having dinner and watching the air traffic.

HELSINKI AND FINLAND TOUR

We arrived in Copenhagen at 9:30 in the morning, changed planes immediately and left for Helsinki, arriving at 1 p.m. We were now 12 hours ahead of Hawaiian time and far north, where it gets dark at 10 p.m. and is light again at 3 a.m. I had never experienced such an early sunrise. We were tired from the overnight flight, so we went to bed soon after dinner.

The weather was beautiful on our first day in Helsinki with the temperature in the 50s. We took a city tour which included the immediate surrounding area. We first visited the shipyards, famous for building the icebreakers that are put to use as soon as winter arrives.

We continued our tour to Finlandia Philharmonica Hall. Near it is a large sculpture of a pipe organ about 24 feet tall, which honors Sibelius, the great Finnish musician and composer. He and Richard Strauss are considered the last two giants of Europe's glorious musical past. Sibelius's two most popular works are Finlandia and En Saga.

Our tour took us to a special area on the Baltic Sea in Helsinki which is set aside to wash rugs. There are boardwalks leading to the water's edge, and large tables and racks where the rugs are scrubbed and dried after they have been submerged in the Baltic Sea. They remain on the racks for days to dry, and no one steals them.

Lutheranism is the predominant religion in Finland, and we visited both the large church in the town square and another, unusual, Lutheran church. A large rock, about 40 feet high, covered more than a city block in the middle of town. It was surrounded by paved streets and what appeared to be apartment buildings, six to nine stories tall. An architect had designed a church inside the rock, which had been hollowed out and fitted with a domed roof. The outer third of the dome was made of glass panels that allowed light to enter. The walls inside were natural rock and water seepage was collected at the base of the walls and drained away. The entry to the church was at street level. The interior of the church was beautifully designed and accommodated hundreds.

The Olympic Games had been held in Helsinki sometime before, and we visited the Olympic Stadium.

On our second day, we took a farm and forest tour. The highlight of the day was visiting architect, Eero Saarinen's home, which had been turned into a museum. Saarinen is to their architecture what Sibelius is to their music. Both were great Finns, and their countrymen are justly proud of them.

We had a memorable dinner at the Intercontinental Hotel. Crayfish was their specialty and, as it was in season, we ordered it as a first course. They were cooked in wine and dill and served beautifully. The orange crayfish were arranged vertically around an inside core of green vegetables. Large red cloths were tied around our necks and we were encouraged to take the crayfish in our hands and suck the meat out of the claws and body. Etiquette allowed us to make noise while sucking the meat from the claws. They were delicious. For my main course, I had reindeer filet steak, and Dottie had salmon. We will never forget this meal.

On August 11th, we went shopping in the morning. At a factory outlet we bought several pieces of beautiful Marimekko material, a new Finnish fabric that soon became very popular in the United States. It was used in many ways, even framed for wall hangings. Arabia was the name of their pottery. We bought two coffee mugs and two plates, which we have used ever since.

_____MOSCOW AND LENINGRAD VISITS

We left in early afternoon for Moscow on an Aeroflot plane, an old jet prop plane similar to a DC-4. I was interested in the way the luggage was handled. We checked the luggage as usual and it was put on a cart. When we were ready to board, each passenger took his luggage off the cart and handed it to a bag boy, who loaded it as the passengers embarked. This prevented any extra pieces of luggage being loaded which could have explosives in them, unless someone was planning suicide. We were served a meal aboard the plane, which consisted of cold cuts of meats and vegetables. The stewardesses were nice enough, though we could not converse with them. They never smiled.

We arrived at an airport before dark. After trying for some time to determine what kind of vegetation we had been flying over, I realized it was large fields of cabbage, mostly red and purple in color. We ate cabbage at most every meal while we were in Russia.

There was great confusion - followed by long hours of waiting - when we landed because we had landed at the wrong airport. Buses were waiting for us, but not at this particular location. Finally, old buses were sent to transport us to Moscow, a two-hour drive from where we landed. The bus that we rode in made an unusual noise in the transmission and almost didn't made it to our hotel. Although we had landed before dark, we did not reach our hotel until midnight. Our luggage arrived at 2:30 a.m.

We were preregistered at the Hotel Rossia. We were lucky. It was the largest hotel in the world and was very nice by Russian standards. Conveniently located near Red Square, the hotel covered a large city block and had four lobbies - North, East, South and West. A large restaurant adjoined each lobby, and we were given tickets for our meals. The meals were wholesome, but unappetizing - too much fat pork, fat fish, butter, bread and cabbage. We did have caviar every morning for breakfast.

The hotel had 6,000 rooms, enough for every delegate when the U.S.S.R. Congress was in session in the Palace of Congresses. As I recall, most of the hotel was about 14 stories high, but there was a center tower of 21 stories. The top floor contained a quality restaurant, on par with any restaurant, where Dottie and I had an excellent dinner one evening. We tipped the waiters 15 percent, and they gladly accepted it. They would not serve a second seating at the tables, although many customers were waiting outside the door. Each evening thereafter we tried to make reservations at this restaurant and also waited in line at the door, but we were never successful again.

Our hotel room was fair, with a telephone and a television. Sometimes the television offered good classical music; other times, the programs were extolling the virtues of the working man. Interesting farm scenes were shown. The beds were poor, with thin mattresses and sheets of unbleached muslin. There was an unusual arrangement to get into a pocket in a blanket. The towels were large- and small-sized washcloths that reminded me of an old, worn dishcloth. They were totally inadequate.

The room had a private bath, but it was awful. The water seemed to run in the toilet all the time, yet it would not flush, leaving a pervading odor of rotten fish in the bathroom. Apparently, the heavy fish diet caused this, and there was not enough water to flush the sewers thoroughly.

Soap was furnished, but it could not be called soap by American standards. Luckily, Dottie had brought our own.

Our room was immediately adjacent to the office of the floor supervisor. Our telephone calls had to go through her, and she always knew what was happening in our room. We think our room and all others had electronic listening devices.

The medical meetings were held at the University of Moscow located on Lenin Hills, about five or six miles from our hotel. A very good shuttle bus service ran between the University and our hotel. The doctors staying in outlying hotels were not so lucky, but everything was well-organized. They, too, had transportation to the University.

On August 12th, I registered at the University for the meeting. I got our tickets for the social events and the tours that Dottie and I would take. Dottie would go on some tours without me while I was at medical lectures. Each of us received a badge to wear at all times which stated that we were invited guests attending an official function. The badge gave us special privileges and we were treated as VIPs everywhere. I don't think I would care to be in Moscow without such a badge.

The official program of the meeting contained 1039 medical papers to be presented and scientific and commercial exhibits to review. Six thousand doctors and guests attended, many from foreign countries. There were simultaneous translations into Russian, English, French and German at the opening and closing sessions, as well as at the plenary sessions. All other sessions had simultaneous interpretations only in English and Russian. The opening and closing sessions were held in the Palace of Congresses of the U.S.S.R. inside the Kremlin. There were 19 dialects listed on the dial on the armrest between the seats, each representing a language spoken in a section of the U.S.S.R. Earphones transmitted the language of choice of the listener.

The opening ceremonies of the VII World Congress of Obstetrics and Gynecology were very impressive. The participating members were formally dressed and appeared tall and stately on the stage before this huge audience. I particularly remember Professor L.S. Persianinou, president of the congress and also Sir John Peel of Great Britain and Professor B.N. Purandare of India, president and president-elect respectively, of the International Federation of Obstetrics and Gynecology.

When the opening ceremony ended, the ballet, "Cinderella," was performed on the stage by the Bolshoi Ballet. The meaning of the word, bolshoi, is "the best," and indeed this ballet was very good. During intermission, there was a buffet served on the ninth floor.

The Palace of Congresses of the U.S.S.R. is in a new building inside the Kremlin walls. When it was built, it was decided that it could not be any taller than the surrounding buildings, which were four stories. To offset this, five stories were built underground.

When I was at the University I saw many American athletes, both black and white, practicing on the athletic fields. They were preparing for a world track meeting to be held there soon. Their t-shirts had U.S.A. in large print on the front and it made me feel good to see them.

In the morning of our second day, Dottie and I took a tour of the Scientific Exhibition area. This was a massive exhibition of Russian scientific successes, especially in space exploration: the rockets that took the cosmonauts into space, the memorial to the first astronaut, a replica of the first Sputnik put in space. We had seen one of the Sputniks in the sky over Hawaii several years previously. There were exhibitions demonstrating Soviet successes in engineering and agriculture. We saw a cinerama of the Soviet Union.

In the afternoon I attended medical meetings, and in the evening we had dinner at the twenty-first floor restaurant that I have already described.

On the third day Dottie and I took a tour of the Pushkin Art Museum, located inside the Kremlin. We saw many outstanding paintings of French, Italian, Dutch, Greek, and Egyptian art. Dottie had already been on a tour of the museum the day before with the ladies and was shown the czar's crown jewels. She said they were far more beautiful than any we had seen in London or Germany.

During our tour of the Pushkin Museum, Dottie became tired and started to lean against a bare wall to rest. An attendant, an elderly woman, quickly struck her with a stick and indicated that this was not permitted.

Soon after lunch, we visited the GUM Department Store, a government-run store covering a city block on Red Square, opposite Lenin's Tomb. To purchase something, one was required to wait in line for a chance to inspect the item. If it was to be bought, the purchaser was given a slip of paper to take to the cashier. After paying, the customer brought the receipt back, stood in line again, and finally got the merchandise. The quality of the goods in the GUM store appeared poor, and we made no purchases. We did buy several items - jewelry and a walking, talking, metal bird that was very clever - in Berioski stores, which were open only to tourists.

We were told we could buy artwork in an outlying art center on Oktober Square, which we could reach by subway. The subway stations were beautiful and clean, with decorative sculptures and escalators to take us up and down. We bought one picture of a peasant farm scene, which was labeled for export. I had thought it would fit into my luggage, but later discovered I had to remove the frame, as it was too large. We got on the subway again to return to our hotel, but did not know where to get off. None of the passengers spoke English. Finally, I showed a student the name of our hotel, and he showed us where to exit.

We took a tour of an art gallery inside the Kremlin that contained works of only Russian painters. The pictures were not noteworthy except for the icons, an art form that originated in Russia. They depicted the portraits of Jesus, Mary, Saints, royalty, or even relatives whom the artist wanted to immortalize.

We toured the Kremlin, and I took many pictures of the buildings inside the red brick walls. I also took pictures of parts of the buildings that showed outside the walls including the quarters where President Nixon had stayed during his State visit. I recorded scenes of the old palace and the beautiful new Palace of Congresses. I took a picture of a very large old bell that had one broken side. It must have been four times larger than our Liberty Bell in Philadelphia. We were told it was too heavy to be moved.

On August 16th I took a city tour of the Community Maternal Centers with the doctors. I was surprised to find that all the doctors in these centers were women, some of them older and holding the rank of professor. The general idea of the community health center was good, though I did not agree with some of their practices. During the prenatal period, the pregnant woman was treated with an electric current by placing electrodes to her head. Then during labor, this current would again be applied to relieve the pains of childbirth. If a woman were found to have high blood pressure during a visit to a health center, she would be sent to a central hospital for specific observation and treatment. This was good management.

We had heard about a good Georgian restaurant, Aragvi, at Number Six, Gorki Street, so we went there and waited in line. When we were admitted, the only table available was with a Russian couple. We accepted seats at this table and proceeded to have an interesting evening. Neither of the Russians could speak English, but the maitre d' could and he came to our table frequently to interpret for us. The Russians had a quart bottle of vodka on the table. They ordered two more glasses for us and insisted that we 'bottoms up' with them after each new course was served. We explained that we did not drink vodka like that, but they insisted we try. I swallowed a jigger of it and chased it with soda water. It was very strong, penetrating my sinuses and entire head, it seemed, although the taste with the soda water was very good. We refused to drink any more, but the Russian couple continued until the bottle was empty.

The man gave me his business card printed on one side in Russian and in English on the other. I still have the card. He was a photo correspondent for the Tass News Agency. He told me he had visited Washington, D.C., and California during Nikita Khrushchev's State visit several years before.

We followed their recommendations in ordering from the menu. First, we had a large plate of fresh vegetables with a delicious sauce followed by a fondue with unleavened bread. The maitre d' showed us how to serve ourselves the fondue. By this time we had had enough, but the main dish was yet to be served. It was called chicken-on-brick. Half of a two- to three-pound chicken had been broiled between two hot bricks, just as we would broil a young chicken in America. It was delicious. As it was near midnight we bade our Russian friends goodnight and left.

The restaurant was about two blocks beyond Red Square opposite Hotel Rossia. I remember walking home after midnight, across Red Square, past Saint Basil's Cathedral, and to our hotel. There were very few people to be seen, but we were not afraid.

On August 17th, our 35th wedding anniversary, I spent nine hours at the

University attending lectures and viewing exhibits. In the evening Dottie and I saw the ballet "Giselle" at the Palace of the Congresses in the Kremlin. We finally had dinner in the restaurant at the East Lobby in our hotel at 10:15 p.m.

The next day was Saturday, our last day in Moscow. We toured the Kremlin again in the morning and saw the cathedral where Ivan the Terrible had buried many of his wives as he discarded them. We were in the cathedral where Katherine the Great and about 50 other czarinas were buried. We toured Saint Basil's Cathedral, located just outside Red Square, after waiting in line for about an hour. This cathedral, with its many onion-shaped domes or minarets, is symbolic of Russia. The exterior of the building has been restored, and it is very beautiful with its many spirals of different colors. However, when we were there, the interior was in a sad state. Originally, all the interior walls to the top of the domes were covered with beautiful religious paintings. After the revolution, religion was outlawed and the cathedral had deteriorated. Paint was peeling from all the paintings on the walls. The cathedral was a great tourist attraction, and the wear and tear on the steps and floors was extensive. As I recall, some of the steps had been worn down four to six inches.

Saint Basil's Cathedral was built by Ivan the Terrible for the Common Man. It was placed outside the Kremlin and Red Square so anyone could visit it at anytime. Its beauty is unsurpassed. When it immediately became internationally famous, the English asked if it would be possible to duplicate it in England. Ivan the Terrible asked the architects who designed it if this were possible. When they told him it could be, he had their eyes removed, so that its duplication would be impossible.

We crossed Red Square many times, and it is exactly as it appears on television. Lenin's Tomb is the prime attraction, located beneath the second-story exhibition area where the members of the Politburo are usually shown on television. There was always a long line of people, extending around the corner, waiting to get in to see the body. We did not have time to wait, so we never saw it.

On the side of the Kremlin by Red Square, there was a monument to the unknown soldier. Bridal parties often go there to pay homage and leave flowers at the monument.

The concluding ceremonies of the meeting took place on August 18th in the Kremlin Palace of Congresses. Afterwards, there was a reception in the banquet hall on the ninth floor for the 6,000 members and guests. There was standing room only. Tables were laden with an abundance of delicious food, enough for all 6,000. There was plenty of caviar. A delicious ice cream in a large goblet was served for dessert. Waiters came in holding trays of 24 goblets high above their heads until they reached their designated tables. A doctor from South America tried to take a goblet from a tray as the waiter passed, upsetting the whole tray and spilling ice cream on the formal clothes of several guests. It caused much confusion. Apparently, the South Americans were often rowdy at the receptions of these international meetings.

The Russians had certainly put on a very good meeting. The scientific program and the social program were excellent. The banquet for 6,000 persons was lavish. We were made to feel that we were special, invited guests and had nothing but praise for the Russians as hosts.

Next day was Sunday, August 19th. We gathered in one of the hotel lobbies where we waited for buses to take us to the airport. We had been there about 30 minutes when the buses came. One couple had three children between the ages of six and ten with them. When we were halfway to the airport, about 20 miles away, the lady noticed that she had left her purse in the waiting area at the hotel. It contained their passports, traveler's checks and tickets. We stopped immediately at a wayside telephone where a call confirmed that the purse had been found and was being held at the hotel. The husband took a taxi and went back for the purse. The rest of the family was allowed to go on to Leningrad with us, and the husband arrived the next day. We were all relieved when we saw him.

We arrived in Leningrad at 1:00 p.m., and registered at the October Revolution Hotel. This was a very poor hotel. Half of us had been assigned to a newer, nicer hotel, but Dottie and I were not lucky this time as we had been in Moscow. There was something wrong with the bathroom plumbing. We were in a noisy location near stairs. We were near a busy streetcar track intersection. Less than a block away was some type of industry. Every few minutes, night and day, a loud noise sounded like piles being driven deep into the earth. The food was better than that in the regular restaurants in Hotel Rossia, but this was the only thing that was on par with a second-rate hotel elsewhere.

The Hermitage Art Museum was the main attraction in Leningrad, and it was closed on Monday. As we were leaving early Tuesday morning, we had only two and a half hours Sunday afternoon to see as much of it as we could. I am unable to describe what I saw. Katherine the Great had sent buyers over Europe to purchase as many masterpieces as were available. Hitler apparently confiscated more during World War II, particularly from France. At war's end, Russia got possession of these, and now they are in the Hermitage. In the usual art museum, one can see at least one painting of each great master of the past. In the Hermitage, there are entire exhibition halls devoted to a particular master, with two to three dozen of his paintings. This includes many of the masters of the past. It was bewildering, particularly to an unknowledgeable person like myself.

The Hermitage is located on the banks of the Neva River, and the building is several blocks long. Originally the winter palace of czars, sometime after the revolution in 1917 it was converted to a museum.

On Monday we took a city tour of Leningrad. On our way into town from the airport the day before, we saw the shells of many buildings that had been destroyed during World War II. The hollow walls without windows or roofs remained. Some buildings had been restored, but many had not. On this tour, we saw a World War I destroyer that now was a museum.

During World War II, Leningrad was under siege by the German army from about September 1, 1941, until January 27, 1944, a total of 871 days. During this time, it is estimated that of a population of about three million people, one million died as a result of war acts, starvation and disease. Our guide's father had died fighting in the war, and her mother, who lived in Leningrad, had died of an infection from a rat bite. The stories we were told of the horrors of Leningrad during World War II were almost unbelievable. Because of its past, Leningrad is now designated a Hero City. A large gold medal on the front of city hall denotes this.

In the afternoon we drove to Petrograd (St. Petersburg), the summer palace of the czars, built by Peter the Great. The palace and the fountains on the grounds had been severely damaged during the war, but had been restored. The dome of the palace was made of solid gold. The hundreds of fountains were gold-plated, creating a dazzling sight. Paths led down a steep hill from the palace to a water-filled canal at least 100 yards away. The whole area was covered with fountains, which turned on and off automatically. It was a beautiful display. Peter the Czar had delighted in having this created for his children.

We returned to our hotel, and I bought a quantity of postage stamps for my friend, Brig. Gen. Ernest Holmes, Ret. He was not allowed to visit Russia because of his army career.

In the evening we attended the Kirov Ballet. There were only 27 tickets available for 40 of us. Someone was kind enough to give us tickets, realizing that we were so isolated in Hawaii we should be given the opportunity to see it. The Kirov Ballet produces many of the world's leading ballet dancers.

During the last night in Leningrad, we got very little sleep because of the construction noise. We left early next morning on an Aeroflot plane for Stockholm, Sweden, and then immediately boarded a S.A.S. plane. The stewardesses were beautiful blondes with great smiles. As the S.A.S. plane lifted off the runway, great applause went up from the passengers, showing our relief to be out of the Soviet Union. We soon got the feeling that we were returning to friendly territory among good neighbors.

FOUR-DAY VISIT TO DENMARK

We arrived in Copenhagen the morning of August 21st. Our three-and-a-half-day stay at the Sheraton made us feel like we were home. About 7:30 a.m. on the 22nd, I heard fire engines outside. I looked out our fifth floor window, and saw firemen busy on the ground floor. Later I learned there had been a grease fire in the kitchen, which was quickly controlled. There was no general alarm, and we got our breakfast on time.

I have always been afraid of fire in old European hotels, many of which are over a hundred years old and not fireproof. Several have burned with loss of life.

On our first day, we took a boat cruise around Copenhagen Harbor and saw two large cruise ships, one of which was Russian. We circled it twice and made some waves about it. We passed the Royal Yacht and saw a hydrofoil boat en route to Sweden, which we could see in the distance. Similar boats were soon in use between the islands in Hawaii, but have been discontinued. From the waterways, we could see many of the landmarks of Copenhagen. One tall church spiral could be seen from many vantage points.

During the morning of our second day, we took a city bus tour. We saw one old windmill, though there were not many inside the city. We stopped and took pictures of the Queen's quarters with the handsomely dressed police guard and stopped again at the Little Mermaid statue poised on a large rock at the water's edge. Recently, vandals had painted her with yellow paint and maybe broken one of her arms. Our guide, who was a lovely middle-aged lady, had some difficulty choosing her words in English. She said that the mermaid had been violated recently, which got a big laugh from the doctors.

In the afternoon Dottie and I went shopping. There were walking streets and many beautiful small stores with internationally famous, quality merchandise.

We had dinner with Dr. and Mrs. Frederick Hofmeister and Dr. and Mrs. Paul Hodgkinson, and then went to a circus with them. We had seen many circus buildings in the Soviet Union and in Europe, where they have performances year-round.

The next day we went on an all-day tour of the countryside. We visited Elsinore Castle, the scene of Shakespeare's Hamlet, toured Fredericksburg Castle, and saw many more. We passed Hans Christian Anderson's home and saw country homes with thatched roofs. One home with a red tile roof was 250 years old. The roof sagged at places, but was still useable. The small towns were clean and picturesque.

On our last day the doctors of Copenhagen put on a medical seminar in the morning for us. Current topics were discussed, and this included my research subject on the relationship of fetal adrenal hyperplasia and the high blood pressure of pregnancy. I felt comfortable entering the discussion and did so.

After the meeting Dottie and I went shopping, and I bought a beautiful Danish bracelet made of enamel on silver, a swan and a trio of attached geese, which are very fine Bing and Grondal (Denmark) china. The swan is over six inches tall and eight inches long. All of them have broad, gold bands on their sides. They are very beautiful and have a permanent place on our etagere.

We left Copenhagen at 3:30 p.m. on S.A.S. and arrived in New York at 7:00 p.m. We rented a U-drive and drove to Philadelphia, arriving safely at the Motes at 11:30. This is probably the most foolish thing I ever did. I was too tired to drive on the six-lane New Jersey Turnpike at night and still remember the thousands of headlights coming toward us in the opposite three lanes.

We spent two days and nights with Dottie Jane and her family, just visiting. I had a migraine headache for two days as a result of the drive from New York. We gave them presents from Russia including the cleverly designed walking, talking, metal bird.

On August 27th we were off early and arrived in Lewistown at 11:30 a.m. We visited all the relatives in the area and spent the night with Jo and Tony Artman near Penn State University. The temperature was 94 degrees and the humidity 92 percent, night and day. We left for Pittsburgh at 3:00 the next afternoon. After a night at the Holiday Inn at the airport, we flew to Chicago and on to Honolulu, where we arrived at 2:00 p.m. After a couple of hours with Ann and little Michael in Honolulu, we arrived on Maui at 4:40 p.m. We had been away for 28 days. We had visited all our children, all our brothers and sisters and many relatives and friends. We had taken short tours of Finland and Denmark and had spent 10 days in the U.S.S.R. I had attended my first meeting of the International Federation of Obstetrics and Gynecology. In the future, I would present lectures on my research project at two of the annual meetings of this organization.

_____ *THE YEAR 1973 CONTINUED*

I returned to work on August 30th. We had a hospital staff meeting at 7:00 a.m., Dr. Allred and I did a cesarean at 8:00 a.m., and I delivered two more babies during the day. I worked 15 hours this first day before I could get to bed. The second day, I did one more major operation and delivered two more babies.

I learned that our good friend, Dr. Sam Wallis of Kauai, had died while we were away. He had many friends and was a beloved doctor. A large portrait of him hangs in the lobby of the Wilcox Hospital on Kauai, where he is held in great esteem. He was the leading doctor on that island for many years. He, too, came from North Carolina.

Dottie prepared a delicious dinner on September 3rd, serving leg of lamb. I described it as the best meal we had had in a month, including meals of some unusual foods such as crayfish and reindeer filet.

Dr. Allred was away on vacation. Two women decided to have their babies at the same time I had scheduled a cesarean. Within 30 minutes I had delivered three babies. I packed the episiotomy wound of the first to control the bleeding while I did the cesarean and then packed the episiotomy wound of the third while I repaired the first. The cesarean patient had received spinal anesthesia before the other two had, unexpectedly, become ready for delivery.

Our jeweler, who was Japanese, had redesigned Dottie's opal ring and had done an excellent job with the two opals and six diamonds. His wife was Caucasian and, after several years of difficulty conceiving, she finally had a boy and a girl. The girl had very blond hair and almost all-Caucasian features; the boy had black hair and mostly Japanese features.

On October 10, 1973, Vice-President Spiro Agnew resigned because of his questionable financial transactions before his election. Senator Gerald Ford was appointed by President Richard Nixon to replace him. Recently, I read that a final appeal of a court decision in this case was denied.

I gave a talk to the staff of Maui Memorial Hospital about the medical aspects of our trip to the Soviet Union and especially the way they were using electrical currents to treat the pain of childbirth.

On October 19th, we had an inch of rain, the first we had had in six months. During such droughts we are lucky to keep our plants alive. Fortunately, where we live, droughts occur only about every five to ten years.

I had to do a cesarean on a patient who had severe high blood pressure and weighed 290 pounds. She was only five feet tall. The baby had an omphalocele, which was repaired immediately. The baby survived. This is the type of patient that causes doctors' hair to turn gray.

Ann and four-year-old Michael were with us a few days. Mike and I hiked up the mountain beyond the resevoirs above our home to about the 1200-foot elevation. I had a rope I kept attached to him. He was always afraid of puas (wild pigs) or of falling. I laughed at these fears and almost had to force him to come with me. Since then, 300-pound wild boars have chased people up trees in this area more than once. They have even come down into our yard for mangoes and guavas. When our neighbor's dogs broke their leashes and went up the mountains to chase them, two of the dogs (pitt bulldogs) were killed by boars. The third returned alone after three days with deep lacerations on its body. When he went after the boars again he failed to return.

Ann and Michael had confirmed reservations to return to Honolulu at 4:00 p.m. on November 25th. This would allow them to reach home at Kaneohe well before dark. However, the airline had overbooked the flight, and they were delayed three hours. which meant they would not reach home until 10:00 p.m. When Ann complained, the airline, by law, was forced to give them a free dinner at the airport restaurant, free passage to Honolulu and a $50.00 bonus. Several other passengers, similarly delayed, received the same free services.

Carol and Peter Keck arrived December 21st to be with us for 10 days. Besides the usual Christmas activities, I was very busy at this time mailing the first copies of my monograph to leaders in the field as well as to research centers. Ann and Michael arrived on December 23rd for four days. I gave Dottie a sapphire ring for Christmas, which she likes very much.

THE YEAR 1974

The year began quietly. Carol and Peter were still with us, and we saw the Rose Bowl game on television. I received my first response on January 3rd to my monograph that I had mailed and my first order arrived on January 8th.

The leading authority in the U.S.A. and the world wrote me a letter about my monograph. He said he would be lecturing in Honolulu in February and wanted to talk to me. I got a second order for a monograph from Pakistan January 25th, and thereafter received one or two orders every week.

Eddie Page of Princeville, Kauai, invited Dottie and me to his 65th birthday party, a celebration to include about 100 mainland guests and two days of golf. A special golf horse race had been set up after the first day of golf, and I was matched up with a low-handicap lady golfer. Our team was lucky to be in contention until the last stroke. I had a chance to win by sinking a 12-foot birdie putt, but I missed. In the three-way play-off our team came in second. There was heavy parimutuel betting, but I had put all my wagers on our team to win. My friend, Merrill Carlsmith, and his partner won.

We had six inches of rain on January 21st, enough to end our drought.

On February 9th, I went to Honolulu at 4:00 p.m. and had a 30-minute conference with the international authority who had asked to talk to me. He was very nice and complimentary about my monograph. When I explained my problems getting it published, he said he would try to help me get a manuscript published if I wrote a suitable paper on the subject. He, himself, was the editor of a leading journal, so I was much encouraged. I returned home at 8:00 that evening.

Dr. Richard West, who was just finishing his orthopedic training, came in for an interview. I was chairman of the recruitment committee and had recommended him to the group. We hired him and he has proven to be a great asset. Ten years later, I would benefit from his expertise.

The Maui Philharmonic Society brought the opera, "Louise," to Baldwin Auditorium, which Dottie and I attended.

I began writing a new paper entitled, "Etiology of Eclampsia," to present to the editor whom I had seen in Honolulu. I planned to use my monograph on fetal adrenal hyperplasia as a reference. I was encouraged by his statements and hoped to finally get a paper in the medical literature.

When I had originally mailed my monographs, I sent one to a classmate, Dr. Saburo Kitamura, who lived in Tokyo. I had not seen or heard from him since my residency at the Pennsylvania Hospital in 1939. At that time, he was a resident in obstetrics and gynecology while I was the resident in newborn pediatrics. He had spent about 15 years in the United States attending high school, college, medical school, and taking additional training to become a specialist in obstetrics and gynecology. His visa had expired in 1940, and he had to return to Japan. He had married a Philadelphia girl who went back with him.

Dr. Kitamura became the liaison officer between the U.S.A. and the atomic-bomb victims in Japan and served in that capacity for many years. He made frequent trips to Honolulu and to Washington, D.C., and had made many friends. He was delighted to receive my monograph and wrote that he would like to visit me on his next trip to Hawaii. We received word he would be arriving on April 17th, but nothing was said about traveling companions. We planned a dinner party so he could meet some of our friends. He came as announced, except his secretary and his housekeeper - who spoke no English - were with him. His wife had died some years before.

As is customary, Dr. Kitamura brought us a lovely gift. It was an original picture of a Noh actor, the leading drama form in Japan. We had our party and invited three local Japanese couples. Our guests from Japan left the next day. Within a few years, I saw Dr. Kitamura again when I attended a medical meeting in Japan.

Dr. and Mrs. Clayton Mote, Dottie Jane's in-laws, visited us for three days in

June. We had a dinner party for them.

Dottie and I attended a first birthday luau at Ulupalakua Ranch for Richard Greenwell's son. I had delivered him. The ranch house was in green pastures on the slopes of Haleakala about 3,000 feet above sea level. We looked down on the blue Pacific Ocean towards Molokini and Kahoolawe Islands at sunset. The luau was a real Hawaiian feast prepared by Hawaiian cowboys. It was an honor to have been invited to this lovely occasion. This was the real thing and not a luau put on for tourists.

I got an order for a copy of my monograph from England and received word that it had been reviewed in a British medical journal. I was always encouraged when someone ordered a copy.

Lois, John and the two Uranga children arrived for a week with us. I took off from work for three days. We drove to Hana and the seven pools at Kipahulu one day and to Lahaina and Napili the next. Following this, we had a steak fry and picnic at Kamaole Park Number Three at Kihei. It was full moon and reminded us of the times we had picnics there when our children were small.

CHAPTER XIX

The Organisation Gestosis-Press Publishes My Monograph, "Etiology of Eclampsia"

After five weeks, my manuscript, "Etiology of Eclampsia," was returned by the editor who had asked me to write it. He had refused to publish it. He sent along the comments of a reviewer, as is customary, though he, himself, actually was the world authority on the subject. He had promised he would give me his opinion, but preferred to let someone else write a meaningless report for the rejection. After doing hundreds of hours of research and writing a manuscript, it is very discouraging to receive such reports. So far, I had received over 40 rejections. I would not be denied; I continued my efforts to get my opinions published and before the medical profession for consideration.

My editor friend, who also had refused to publish my manuscript, originally had asked me to send copies of my monograph on fetal adrenal hyperplasia to researchers around the world who were studying high blood pressure and pregnancy. One of them was Dr. Jeffry W. Theobold of Eastbourne, England. He was a senior statesman who had studied this subject for 50 years. He had studied high blood pressure during pregnancy in England, during both World War I and World War II, when all of England was on a borderline starvation diet. Curiously, there was less toxemia and blood pressure problems during both wars than at other times. (From what I know now, I would explain this by saying it was the quality of the food the pregnant women ate during the wars, rather than the quantity, that determined if they developed toxemia. Less refined, rich food was available, which meant more green, leafy vegetables and dairy products were consumed. Both of these have a high calcium content, a deficiency of which I will later explain is the critical factor in developing high blood pressure.)

I wrote Dr. Theobold many letters and, later, went to see him personally. We had a four-hour conference, and he gave me copies of many of his writings. My wife and I spent a day in Eastbourne and took Dr. and Mrs. Theobold to dinner. It was a rewarding experience. He stated that in 1934 there were 400 maternal deaths from eclampsia in England and Wales, while in 1974 there were only four. No new medicines were used in treatment. The only differences to explain the dramatic fall were better nutrition and more prenatal care. Bed rest was prescribed more often, which he said improved nutrition by reducing the physiological demands on the woman's metabolism.

I had asked Dr. Theobold if he could help me get my manuscript, "Etiology of Eclampsia," published in England or Europe. He told me about Professor Dr. E.T. Rippmann of Basel, Switzerland, who had formed the Organisation Gestosis in 1969. This was an international organization created to study the pathophysiology of gestation and especially the development of high blood pressure during pregnancy. Dr. Theobold said he would send my manuscript to Dr. Rippmann and ask for his help in getting it published.

I wrote Dr. Rippmann myself. The Organisation Gestosis was barely organized. Publishing the manuscipts and the proceedings of the meetings presented a problem. I offered to buy 500 copies of my manuscript if he published my monograph. Soon after, he formed the Organisation Gestosis-Press and hired a printer. The proceedings of the 1975 International Meeting was its first publication. My monograph, entitled "Etiology of Eclampsia," was publication number two. It consisted of only 48 pages, three figures and 53 references. (By 1985, there had been 24 publications by the Organisation Gestosis-Press, and four of them were mine.) Soon the Organisation Gestosis had many thousands of members from all countries of the world. I bought 500 of each of my monographs and distributed them to medical libraries in the U.S.A. and Canada and to research institutions throughout the world. Many others were purchased by members of the Organisation Gestosis. Eventually, I will discuss the contents of each of my monographs, which finally explain the exact pathophysiology of high blood pressure in pregnancy.

My sister, Maisie Parker, and her second son, my namesake, arrived on July 25th to be with us a week. We had a glorious time. Maisie did not play golf, so Dottie set up an art studio for her to use to paint while we three played golf. She painted a beautiful scene of Mount Haleakala from our home, which will eventually be given to her son, William.

VISIT TO SPOKANE EXPO '74 AND ASPEN MUSICAL FESTIVAL

Dottie and I left for San Francisco and Spokane on August 5th. We attended Expo '74, which was held in Spokane that summer. Our friend, Rodney Lindsey, was president of the exhibition and gave us VIP treatment. He drove us over the grounds in a golf cart, and we got to see and visit everything without becoming too tired. We were not accustomed to such luxurious treatment. The Lindseys spent the winters on Kauai, and were golfing friends.

We were house guests of Ada and Jim Blankenship at Hayden Lake, Idaho, and I was Jim's guest in the annual Member-Guest Golf Tournament at Hayden Lake Country Club. On the first day of the tournament, I had a 62 net. My gross score was two under par on the second nine holes, the first time I had ever been under par in a tournament, even for nine holes. As a result, I qualified for the golf horse race which my partner and I lost on the second hole. During the remaining two days, I did not play well. We had a lot fun seeing all our friends.

On August 11th we flew to Denver, changed planes and went on to Aspen. The plane that we boarded for Aspen was a Rocky Mountain Airline Otter, carrying 16 passengers and two pilots. The cabin was not pressurized. We had to fly over mountains with peaks of 14,500 feet and over the Continental Divide. The pilots had tubes in their mouths to furnish them extra oxygen. I became very sick at my stomach, and Dottie almost lost consciousness. I remember flying only slightly above the mountains, which were partly covered with snow. Cattle grazed just below us in the areas between the snow fields.

We landed at Aspen, relieved to breathe air with more oxygen. We rented a U-drive and drove to Snowmass, about ten miles from Aspen. This was primarily a ski resort, but in the summer many activities were available such as golf, hiking, tennis, biking, etc. I had registered for a five-day course on perinatal medicine put on by the University of Colorado. We stayed at the Wildwood Inn which had a dining room and was near a shopping area. Many hotels and condominiums were being built on the slopes just above our hotel, and they would be ready in time for the ski season. There were several ski lifts near the condominiums. Aspen is about 7,000 feet above sea level, while Snowmass is 8,000 feet, as I recall. The mountain tops at Snowmass were covered with ice and snow and were just above our hotel. Normally, I take cold baths, but had a chill after my first one and switched to hot baths. The only other time I have had to abandon my cold showers was at North Cape, Norway, which is above the Arctic Circle.

On the first day in Snowmass, I attended medical meetings until 3 p.m., then Dottie and I drove to Maroon Lake. We attended the music festival in Aspen where we saw and heard "St. John's Passion" by Bach, put on by the musicians in attendance. A large tent had been erected over a stage and seats. At that time, there was no charge to attend the performances.

The next day, I was in meetings until 12:30 and then we played golf at Snowmass Country Club. I found I could drive the balls much farther than usual, due to the altitude. After golf, we drove up the canyon to Ashcroft.

On Wednesday, I attended meetings until 3:00 and then we went shopping in Aspen. On Thursday, we played golf again and had dinner at the Refectory Restaurant in Aspen.

The medical meeting ended at noon on Friday, and we again played golf, then heard a chamber orchestra at the music festival; a soprano named Seibel and others sang. We had dinner at the Pomegranate Restaurant.

Next day was our last, and we drove to the small, mountain towns of Marble, McClure Pass, Paonia, and Carbondale. We were interested to learn that the white marble used to build Lincoln Memorial in Washington came from Marble.

At the music program we attended on our final day, Pincus Zukerman, Itzhak Perlman, and several others performed. This was one of the highlights of our trip. I have since seen them many times on television and always remember hearing them there in the tent that summer.

Another feature of this music festival was the many musicians one encountered in the wooded areas near the tent, each one practicing on his or her own instrument. They were oblivious to the passers-by. All kinds of music drifted from all directions.

August 17th was our 36th wedding anniversary and we celebrated with dinner at the Steak Pit Restaurant in Aspen.

We were scheduled to get an early plane on August 18th from Aspen to Denver and then another home. Unfortunately, I left the car's parking lights on all night and found a dead battery next morning. A hotel employee took us to the airport and we left the U-drive at Snowmass. The Hertz U-drive employees had not arrived at their airport office before we had to leave so I left the keys with the airline employees. When I eventually got the bill for use of the U-drive, there was no extra charge for the dead battery or for their retrieval of the car from Snowmass.

THE YEAR 1974 CONTINUED

I played in the Maui Country Club's Member-Guest Golf Tournament on Labor Day weekend with Tommy Hines Jr., age 15. His father was supposed to have been my partner, but could not come to Maui due to the illness of his wife. Tommy Jr.'s handicap was two, and we were ahead until the last hole, the 36th. We came in second. We each won a tape recorder and several golf balls. I refused to wager any money, but others, who knew Tommy, won large amounts on us.

I talked to the obstetrical staff meeting at the hospital on what I had learned at the Perinatal Conference at Snowmass.

My work was very erratic. Within four days in September, I delivered 10 babies and did four major operations. Then on the last day of the month, after a busy morning in the Wailuku office I treated 23 patients in our Lahaina office and delivered two babies that night.

Dottie spent two days in Honolulu with Ann, and they attended the opera. Dottie always enjoyed this change of pace and I was happy to do my own cooking while she was away.

We took a five-day vacation on the Island of Hawaii, starting November 30th. We stayed two nights at the Kona Surf Hotel. The day we arrived, we played 18 holes of golf at Keauhou Golf Course. The next day, we played 18 holes at Keauhou in the morning, had lunch at the pro shop, drove to Waikoloa and played 18 holes there. We were back in the hotel at 6:30.

On the third day, we drove to the City of Refuge National Park at Kona before going on over the lava fields to Naalehu where we had lived for 14 months in 1939 and 1940. The home we lived in appeared the same although our friends had moved on. We have fond memories of Naalehu, where we had started housekeeping and had our first baby, Lois.

A residential development with a golf course had been built near Punaluu, a nice beach about halfway between Pahala and Naalehu. The area is known as the Sea-Mountain Resort, because the golf course extends from the ocean to the mountains. There are many large mango trees along the fairways, and it is a challenging course. We played 18 holes and, after visiting Pahala, drove to the Volcano House Hotel, where we stayed two nights. We had stayed there many times, the last with our four daughters, and it was fun to be back. The hotel is at 4,000 feet elevation and the nights are cool.

Next morning, we played 18 holes of golf at the Volcano Golf Course, starting about 9:00 after the morning fog dissipated. We never experience anything like this on Maui, where most of the courses are near the ocean. We quickly learned to keep the balls on the fairways, otherwise they took a zigzag course, bouncing off the lava rocks.

We toured the volcanic area and saw some new cinder cones and lava flows, then drove into Hilo past the lush vegetation and flowers. We had dinner at the Waiakaea Village Hotel and returned to the Vocano House Hotel for the night. We returned home next morning in time for my regular Wednesday afternoon golf game.

In December we had a new hi-fi stereo-radio-phonograph combination installed. This was my Christmas present to Dottie. The house had been wired for music by Professor Charles Barbe when it was built, but we could never afford to buy the proper equipment. Finally, I got excellent equipment, including a Gerrard turntable. I am told by suppliers that machines of this quality are no longer available. Twelve speakers are scattered throughout the house, one by the front entrance and two directed toward the guest cottage. After 14 years of use, the turntable functions normally. The stereo receiver had its first maintenance check recently. We have relay stations atop Haleakala and can get excellent classical music on the Hawaii Public Radio Station. Good music is good therapy for Dottie, especially now that she has severe physical limitations due to cervical disc problems.

Dottie Jane and her family of four arrived on December 24th for 10 days. Ann and Michael II also came for Christmas and stayed for four days. I continued working and on the 27th, delivered five babies. That evening we had guests in for dinner, and I became very tired. Dottie also became exhausted, preparing food for everyone. I played golf a few times with Michael. We had a wonderful Christmas. At the time, we knew we were lucky to have children and grandchildren to help us celebrate Christmas. We still cherish these times and have fond memories of them. My main goal in life, since the death of my father when I was eight years old, was to have a happy home with children and grandchildren. I cannot understand why everyone does not have the same goal. It makes me sad when I see some of my older friends and acquaintances who have no one to love nor anyone to love them. It is even sadder when one member of a childless marriage dies. However, I have lived long enough to know that everyone is not suitable for marriage, or parenthood.

THE YEAR 1975

We were exhausted after a busy holiday season with grandchildren, but we soon were back into our routine. The Maui Medical Group bought me a new Skylark Buick with a V-6 engine. We were allowed up to $4,400 for a new car, and that is exactly what this one cost. Within a few years, the group's policy on cars changed. Each member bought his own car, and the group paid for gasoline and oil. Taxwise, my car had been written off, so the group sold it to me for $1. I still am driving it with 87,000 miles on the odometer and have no plans to buy a new one.

We had intermittent rains in February. Then on the 13th, it rained six inches. With this much rain, water runs off the mountain in all areas just like streams. The gulch beside our property becomes a roaring river and the ditches by the sides of our three lots flow continually.

The Pan Pacific Surgical Conference convened in Honolulu from February 16th through the 21st. This was an excellent medical meeting which I was attending for the first time because we usually combined my medical meetings with vacations far from home. Dottie and I attended the opening ceremonies and the banquet. We stayed with Ann at Kaneohe, and I commuted each day. I played golf twice, once at the Pali Course and once at Waialae Country Club, and managed to do a lot of yard work for Ann.

On Saturday after the meeting, I went to Kauai and spent the night with Ruth and Eddie Page while Dottie stayed in Honolulu with Ann. I played 27 holes of golf on Saturday and 18 holes on Sunday. I remember that on Sunday, most of my putts fell into the cup. My opponent, Grant Dixon, finally realized he couldn't beat me on this particular day. I had a lot of fun.

By Monday, I was busy at work. One of my patients failed to reach the hospital in time and delivered her baby in the car at Spreckelsville. Everything was fine when she arrived.

I applied to the Organisation Gestosis to give a talk at its international meeting to be held in Prague, Czechoslovakia, and was accepted. The talk would be based on what I had written in my monograph. The meeting dates were September 21st to the 26th. Dottie and I were excited about going and about my giving a talk to an international group.

Dr. Allred and I were overworked, especially when one of us went on vacation. When the Medical Group gave us permission to hire a third obstetrician-gynecologist, I communicated with Dr. William Gintling, who was in the U.S. Army on Okinawa. He was interested in practicing in Hawaii. He had excellent recommendations and when he came for an interview we hired him, though it would be a year before his discharge.

I delivered triplets to one of my patients. She had not taken fertility drugs. When her uterus enlarged very rapidly between the third and fourth months of pregnancy, I suspected an hydatidiform mole. I could not hear any fetal heart. In an X-ray of her uterus I saw three, small, fetal skeletons. Ultrasound was not available in our hospital at that time.

The patient did very well at home. She had an eight-year-old daughter who was a great help. While this daughter was at school, her neighbors took turns staying with her. She was bedridden during the fifth and sixth months and, at about six and a half months, I hospitalized her for care. Her abdomen was very large, and she could not get out of bed unassisted.

On the third day of hospitalization, she went into labor. One fetal head was deep in the pelvis, and the cervix dilated to about four centimeters. Then, for four hours there was no progress in spite of good contractions. I convinced Dr. Allred we should do a cesarean.

I found there was sacculation of the uterus just above the bladder. A fetal head and fluid were in the sac, and its wall was paper thin. Rupture was imminent. I incised the sac and removed baby A, who weighed three pounds, four ounces. Then I removed baby B whose head was deep in the pelvis, and it weighed three pounds, six ounces. Finally, baby C was removed from the top of the uterus. It weighed one pound, 14 ounces. All were girls and breathed spontaneously. Dr. John Briley was in charge of the babies and had two pediatricians assisting him.

The mother recovered rapidly. On the third day, baby C had a breathing problem and was sent to the Children's Hospital in Honolulu. She did not gain weight for about two months and had to be on a respirator continually. As I recall, her weight was one pound, 12 ounces when she was two months of age. I was very pessimistic about her survival. However, she improved, began gaining weight and, eventually, was home with her family. She was slightly smaller than her two sisters and, when she became of school age, she was sent to a special school. She laughed, played and talked almost continually when I last saw her at about eight years of age. I always am happy to get their pictures at Christmas.

On March 26th I made 35 on the second nine holes at Maui Country Club. This was the first time I had ever been below par (37) at the club.

A pair of francolin partridges live in our yard and usually raise one or two families of baby chicks each year. On April 1st we saw a mother, with 12 chicks following her in a line, walking across our yard. During the first three weeks after hatching, the chicks cannot fly and are easy prey for cats and mongooses .

Dr. H. Brody, professor and chairman of the Department of Obstetrics and Gynecology of the University of Calgary, Canada, had received one of my monographs on fetal adrenal hyperplasia. He was impressed. While he was on vacation in Lahaina, he telephoned me for an appointment to discuss it. This long discussion took place in my office on April 8th. I promised to keep him informed of any progress I made in my work and send him any future publications. Later in the year I sent him a copy of my monograph, "Etiology of Eclampsia." It was returned by his secretary who stated, sadly, that Dr. Brody had died on October 18th after a week's illness. I had lost my strongest supporter.

I made the first eagle of my life playing golf. I sank a 10-foot putt on Hole Number One at Maui Country Club. Since then I have made one other eagle on this hole. I can only do this when the wind is reversed from its usual pattern and is blowing from south to north.

I gave Dottie a new golf bag and a flower lei on April 15th, her 58th birthday, and took her out to dinner.

One of my patients almost died of preeclampsia and hydrops fetalis. After doing a cesarean it was nine days before I reported that she had improved. In spite of all my study, I was barely able to keep this patient alive and had asked for many consultations.

Golf was my favorite pastime. I experienced many unusual occurrences in my game including this: After hitting my drive out-of-bounds on Hole Number Four at Maui Country Club - a par four - I hit a second ball and then sank it from 180 yards for a par.

We usually played a few games of cribbage after golf, teamed with the same partners we had in golf. Once I double-skunked my favorite opponent at $1 a game and five cents a point. Then I beat him a few more games. A few weeks later he did the same to me. It is amazing how often the losers at golf win at cribbage.

A baby I delivered, who was 12 days overdue, weighed only three pounds, 12 ounces and appeared wrinkled and malnourished. The mother was the wife of the manager of a large hotel. Each evening she attended a cocktail party with her husband to help entertain hotel guests. Her pregnancy had been normal, labor started spontaneously, and the baby gained weight rapidly and soon appeared normal. I have often wondered how the child has developed.

I applied for and got visas for Dottie and me to go to Czechoslovakia to attend the meeting of the Organisation Gestosis in Prague.

The talk I gave at our staff meeting, "Etiology of Eclampsia," was the same that I would give at Prague. I needed the practice and hoped to get some useful input from our staff.

On our 37th wedding anniversary, I gave Dottie a red carnation lei and took her out for dinner.

During one day in August three severe complications occurred in three of my patients. One had a ruptured appendix, another had a strangulated hernia, and a third required a cesarean. These cases were in addition to my routine work, which meant I was tired for days.

CHAPTER XX

Tours of Begium, The Netherlands, Prague and Scotland (Isle of Skye): September 17 to October 11, 1975

We made reservations on a charter flight from Honolulu to Brussels with a return flight from Amsterdam. I arranged our itinerary so we would have time for sightseeing in Belgium. We planned to spend four days and nights in Prague, where I would attend the annual meeting of the Organisation Gestosis and give a lecture. After this we would go to London, get a U-drive, and spend 10 days in Scotland. Then we would spend three days and nights in Amsterdam and the Netherlands before returning home.

BELGIUM: FIVE DAYS

We left Maui September 17th at 7:30 a.m. and Honolulu at 10:00 for Anchorage, Alaska. After a brief refueling stop, we were on our way at 4:40 p.m., flying over the green forests and snow-covered mountains of Alaska. As we passed over northern Canada and Greenland, 600 miles south of the North Pole, there was snow as far as we could see in all directions, shining in the bright sunlight. Occasionally we passed over a river. When we flew over Iceland we could see mountains with snow-covered pinnacles.

As the sun set there was an orange glow on the horizon on the left side of the plane for a short while. On the right side, it was dark and there was a full moon. Shortly, it was dawn and we were in bright daylight and then we saw the sun rise on the right side. Never before had we experienced such a rapid change from night to day.

We had very favorable winds flying over Canada and the North Atlantic and arrived in Brussels at 1:30 p.m., two hours ahead of schedule. We did not have to stop in Scotland to refuel as was expected. Because we were so early, the bus that was supposed to meet us had not arrived so we took a taxi to our hotel, The Europa, and went to bed at 4:30 p.m.

A complication arose. We had overeaten on the plane and did not eat anything before going to bed. When we awoke after six hours, we were ravenously hungry. It had been over 12 hours since we had eaten. It was 11 p.m.; there was no place where we could eat or buy food. We went back to bed, hungry, and slept another six hours.

We had not known what we would find in Brussels. Formerly, it was a leisurely city, especially known for fancy, hand-woven lace, Gothic spires, open fish markets, charming small cafes, and city squares filled with beautiful flowers and surrounded by quaint, old buildings. Now it was the center of Europe, financially and strategically, as headquarters of the Common Market and NATO. A rapid transformation was taking place. The older buildings were being demolished and replaced with high-rises almost everywhere. A new subway was being installed through the center of the business district, leading to traffic tie-ups and other problems.

Luckily, Hotel Europa, which was new, was on the outskirts of the business district near the headquarters of the Common Market. There was no construction nearby. The area was silent and peaceful. The Common Market buildings and grounds were beautiful. A subway entrance was less than two blocks from our hotel and we soon learned how to get around town.

On our first day we took an all-day tour to Ghent and Bruges where we saw many cathedrals and museums. The highlight of this day was seeing older women weaving the beautiful lace we had heard so much about. They used many spools of thread, shuttles and pins to make the lace. Dottie bought a tray cover, six by eight inches, for $16. She says it is more valuable now, as the lace is no longer made by hand.

The next day we took a city tour in the morning. We had an excellent guide who gave us the history of many of the beautiful, old buildings, some dating back to the 15th century. In the afternoon we took a circular tour that first went to the site of the former World's Fair. A structure about 10 stories high, called the Atomium, represented an atom with electrons and a proton. After visiting several historic sites, we arrived at Waterloo where Napoleon was defeated. We saw the Lion of Waterloo Monument commemorating this battle. It sits atop a hill about 75 feet high.

In the evening we went to the Sablon Market Square and had dinner in a small restaurant on a side street. As I recall there were only four tables and room for 12 to be served. We had difficulty ordering because neither the proprietor nor his wife understood English. Our French was poor but we finally ordered a veal dinner. It was simply divine.

Each morning I studied for a couple of hours before we went exploring. I was nervous about giving a lecture to a group of professors. The next day, Sunday, we took the subway to the end of the line and walked back to the central station. We visited Saint Catherine Square, a market with vegetables, beautiful flowers and many species of colorful birds for sale. We continued on to Grand Sablon Square where we had lunch. Most of the shops were closed, but it was fun looking through the windows and deciding where to shop the next day.

On Monday we went back to Sablon Market Square. This is, no doubt, one of the quaintest places in Europe. The buildings are old, dating from medieval times, and most are four stories high. The fronts of the buildings facing the Square consisted of many windows with columns of stone in between. Life-size statues lined the roofs' edges. Many of the columns were gilded. There were all types of decorations and many large flags on the buildings. The surface of the square was cobblestones. Numerous containers of flowers for sale were positioned about the square, some with large, multi-colored umbrellas to protect the flowers from the sun.

Every conceivable type of specialty shop could be found on the square or on one of the adjoining streets. I bought several beautiful neckties.

We passed a small restaurant at noon that had a picture on the window of a large pot of mussels, which were in season. We decided to try them. Again, we had a language problem but finally our order was understood. We were both served a large potful of mussels and an empty pot for the shells. The mussels had been steamed in wine and herbs and were delicious, and the pot liquor in the bottom of the pot also was delightful. We could eat only half of what we were served. After this unforgettable lunch we walked through a nearby park and then returned to our hotel to pack for Prague.

Hotel Europa had a fancy French restaurant where we had eaten after an all-day tour, but had not really enjoyed our meal because of fatigue. On this final night in Brussels we decided to eat there again and enjoy the food and the service of the many waiters. We had one of the best and most enjoyable meals of our lives.

Next morning we left the hotel at 6:15 for our flight to Frankfurt. There, we changed planes and arrived in Prague at 10:30. We were staying at the Intercontinental Hotel, where the medical meeting was to be held. It was 3 p.m. before we got settled in our room.

PRAGUE: FOUR DAYS

The annual meeting of the Organisation Gestosis started on the day we arrived, September 23rd. We attended the reception that evening and I met Dr. E.T. Rippmann, the general secretary. He had finally published my monograph, "Etiology of Eclampsia," and had brought me six copies. I was very pleased with it. (It was the first of four monographs he published for me. As new information became available as to the cause of high blood pressure, I incorporated it in my writings and explained how it affected the blood presure during pregnancy. My last monograph, published in 1985, explained the exact microbiology of high blood pressure during pregnancy.)

I was allotted 20 minutes to give my talk the following morning and was very relieved when the ordeal was over. It appeared what I said was well received, though it was something new and would have to be studied. I had presented everything in my monograph, which the members eventually received. Meetings took up the entire day and I entered into many discussions.

While I was attending the meetings the first day, Dottie took a tour of interesting and historical sights in the vicinity of Prague. The most notable was Karlstejn Castle which dates from the middle of the 14th century. Dottie said everything she saw was very primitive. The roads were unpaved. The farm houses were very small and no modern farm equipment was seen. Dottie met Dr. Tibor Klacansky on this tour; he became a very good friend of ours. He lived in Bratislavia and, as he had not been to Prague since university days, was more interested in seeing the area than in attending all the medical meetings. Eventually, we visited him and his family in Bratislavia and, on another European visit, he and his wife, Elena, were our guests in Vienna.

Arrangements had been made for us to eat in the very old Loretto Monastery on the evening of the first day. After dinner we were taken on a tour of its library. Some of the books were 500 years old. It was difficult for an American to realize that such a library had existed for so long and that there were scholars at that time to create and use it.

After our library tour we gathered in a hall and were entertained by a Czechoslovakian string ensemble. Its quality was superior and we were indeed fortunate to hear them. To get to the monastery, we had come by taxi, crossing the Charles Bridge and proceeding several miles. We were told that when we were ready to go home, about 11, we could get a taxi at the street corner nearby. We walked to the corner, but there were no taxis. Finally, a street car arrived and we got aboard. The conductor could not understand English so we showed him the name of our hotel, and he realized where we wanted to go. When he finally let us off he told us to get another street car that would take us to our hotel. The street car with the correct number arrived and we boarded. The conductor indicated that our hotel was at the end of his line and that we would arrive in due time. When we finally arrived, we found ourselves at the International Hotel. Our hotel was the Intercontinental. There were several taxis at the hotel, though the drivers were all inside at a tavern. I was able to get one to take us to our hotel, which was still quite a distance. It was now about 1 a.m., and we were exhausted from our unusual adventure.

On the second day I attended meetings until 1 p.m. and we then went on a city tour. Everything in Prague seemed to be old except our Intercontinental Hotel. Prague dates back to the prehistoric era. It was the center of the Bohemian state in the 9th century; in the 11th and 12th centuries it was the largest city in central Europe. Now it has over one million inhabitants. The section called Old Town contains Old Town Square. This was near our hotel and we went there many times after our initial introduction during the city tour. Everything around the Square is old. As I recall, the buildings are about six stories tall, all about 500 years old, and made of stone, some gray and some brown. There are all kinds of shops, restaurants and arcades. The center of attraction is the medieval town hall with its mechanical clock, constructed in 1490. As the end of the hour approaches, people gather in front of town hall to see the parade of statues of Jesus and his disciples. Doors, about 40 feet above the street, come open on the hour, and the statues pass in procession out one door and in the other. A bell, representing Death, tolls, and a brass cock crows the hour. There is a large, regular clock with Roman numerals on the side of the building about 20 feet above the street. Below the mechanical clock are two colorful, circular decorations about 12 feet in diameter. One is somewhat like a geometrical figure of the Universe and the other like a medallion with three figures in the center.

Our city tour took us to the many different section of Prague. One area is called New Town, though it was founded in 1348. Wenceslas Square is a half mile long and contains modern shops, banks, restaurants, department stores and night clubs.

A few blocks from Old Town is the historic Jewish Quarter where daily services have been held in the Old-New Synagogue since 1270. Four other synagogues are now Jewish Museums. The most intriguing place in the Jewish Quarter is the cemetery. When all gravesites were used, no additional land was available so fresh earth was brought in and placed on top of the old graves. The new graves were installed on top of the old ones, until they now lie 10 to 12 layers deep in a mound of earth. More than 12,000 graves are located in this small cemetery.

Dr. Rippmann, his wife and two small sons were on the same bus with us making the city tour. He had noticed in the references of my monograph that I had done research at the Geisinger Medical Center at Danville, Pennsylvania. He had been a resident at this hospital in 1952; I had been there from 1936 to 1938. It is an odd coincidence that two of Geisinger Medical Center's residents from different parts of the world would eventually be collaborating on the same research project, high blood pressure and pregnancy.

In the evening the official banquet of the meeting was held at the Intercontinental Hotel. Dottie and I were the only ones present from the United States, though several Canadians attended.

I gave a four-minute talk on the third day, on my views as to the causes of the edema of pregnancy. During the two previous days there had been long discussions among the professors on this subject. At that time I was on the right track, but my work was not complete. It would be another 10 years before all the information would be available to explain the exact pathophysiology of the edema.

After the conference ended, at noon on the third day, Dottie and I went shopping for several records of classical music composed by Czech musicians. Our new friend, Dr. Klacansky, had given us several records and told us where we could buy more.

The next day was Saturday, September 27th. We reported to the Prague Airport, exchanged our money and cleared customs. I thought they returned too much money to me so imagine my surprise when, four weeks after we returned home, my bank received a draft for $30.00 from Czechoslovakia. The customs people stated that they had shortchanged me. The officials were courteous and treated us with great kindness. Our only problem during our stay in Prague had been the language.

_____SCOTLAND (ISLE OF SKYE): ELEVEN DAYS_

We reached London's Heathrow Airport at 2:40 p.m., and by 4 were on the road in our U-drive. We asked an English couple for directions, and they had us follow them for 20 miles, getting us through the maze of roads out of the Heathrow area. I had difficulty driving on the left side of the road and had to learn to use the roundabouts at intersections. Luckily the car had a sign on it warning that the driver was a tourist. Our plan was to go directly to the Isle of Skye, do some exploring, play as much golf as time permitted and do some sightseeing. We had no hotel reservations except for the last two nights in Edinburgh.

We had enjoyed our time in Brussels and Prague, but we were so happy to be in England where we could talk to people and be understood. The small towns were beautiful, with nice houses and well manicured yards. There was no roadside litter. We were surprised to find so many towns with the same names as places in the United States, forgetting that ours were named for these and that originally the U.S.A. was a colony of England.

We reached Oxford and drove on to Stratford-upon-Avon for the night where I was able to get two adjoining, single rooms in the Shakespeare Hotel. This building is the 1564 birthplace of William Shakespeare and has been carefully restored to what it was in his time. Although the building was not fireproof, it was a thrill to stay in such an historic place. It has three stories and is half timbered, as so many old homes in England were. We visited Ann Hathaway's cottage, a farmhouse with a thatched roof about one mile from Shakespeare's house. She was his childhood sweetheart and later became his beloved wife.

We left Stratford at 2 and reached Preston for the night, staying at the Crest Hotel. We were now about 100 miles from Scotland., having passed Birmingham, Liverpool and Manchester.

On Monday we drove from 9 a.m. to 6 p.m., passing Glasgow and reaching the lake country, where Dottie's father's ancestors had lived. We passed Loch Lomond, the lake that harbors the monster, Nessie. After driving through heavy afternoon rains, we finally reached Fort William where we spent the night at the Mercury Motel.

The next morning I got a haircut, which cost 50 cents - the price on Maui was $3.50 - and Dottie got her hair washed. We were about 50 miles from Kyle of Lochalsh, where we would board a ferry to the Isle of Skye. The Isle of Skye was only a few hundred yards from the mainland of Scotland.

We crossed on the ferry before noon and were told to be back by 5 for the last ferry of the day. Dunvegan Castle, headquarters of the MacLeod clan, was on the opposite side of the island and about 50 miles away. We proceeded there immediately. We were anxious to see the part of the world where my hardy, Scottish ancestors had come from and try to learn about the conditions that had made them so tough.

We drove across the Isle of Skye, through rolling, pastoral scenes somewhat like those of Maui. Heather grew everywhere. We saw small farms with picturesque farm houses, many sheep and some cattle. Frequently the sheep were on the highway, and we had to stop and wait while they moved out of the way, sometimes aided by a sheepherder with a dog. The ewes had green paint on their backs, which told us that breeding season had just passed. Dottie remarked that the day was similar to a beautiful day on Maui - the sun shining brightly in a very blue sky dotted with billowing, white clouds.

The many mountains of Skye vary in height from 2,000 to 3,000 feet and outcroppings of rock make the terrain very rough in places. Between these rocky areas are many lakes, inlets and sounds. In the areas between the mountains and the sea is beautiful, relatively flat, farm land. A labyrinth of roads connected all parts of the island.

The few villages we saw were usually located by inlets. The only industry we saw was a distillery where famous Scotch whiskey was made. We observed many truckloads of marble being transported to a port to be shipped and were told that this high-grade marble was one of the few exports of the island. The other exports were wool, lamb, beef, and a variety of farm products, whenever an excess was produced.

Dunvegan is located near the northwest tip of Skye on Loch Dunvegan. Only the Outer Hebrides Islands lie between Skye, the North Atlantic and the Arctic Circle, which is 500 to 600 miles away. Although the Gulf Stream has a warming effect on the climate of Great Britain in the wintertime, the Isle of Skye is so far north that the cold winds out of the north, no doubt, offset this.

I remember my maternal grandmother, whose father was a MacLeod from the Isle of Skye, talk about the harsh winters in Scotland, though she never lived there. As an example, lambs born in early spring would not always survive the cold. I can also understand the farming practices of my relatives in North Carolina whose ancestors came from the Isle of Skye and other parts of Scotland. They raised cotton and tobacco as money crops and raised many other crops for their own use, selling only what they did not need. No doubt, on the Isle of Skye where there were no major industries, the people had to raise most of the food they ate. They sold the excess for income. All the women knew how to make woolen thread and cloth and every family had a spinning wheel. Fish, including salmon, formed a good part of their diet because of the many streams, lakes and sounds.

It is easy to understand that just to live on the Isle of Skye, or in Northern Scotland, meant that one was successful. The hardships these people endured made them hardy and tough. Children started work early in life to help their parents eke out an existence. The work ethic was the norm and I have inherited this love for work, sometimes doing more than is neccesary. However, the act of work itself is beneficial and I do not consider my time wasted, even if I received no immediate tangible benefit or return.

We proceeded to the town of Dunvegan and on to Dunvegan Castle, about one mile north of the village. We were disappointed to learn that Dame Flora MacLeod of MacLeod was spending a few weeks elsewhere in Scotland and was not in residence at the time. A secretary met us and took us on a tour of the castle. I left a letter for Dame Flora, which she promptly answered upon her return and which we received soon after we arrived home. Her letter was written in longhand and dated 14 October 1975. It read:

Dear Dr. and Mrs. Patterson,

I am deeply touched by your kind memory of me, kind and most generous gift of superperfect maple syrup. I wish I had been at Dunvegan to see you and welcome you, and to thank you.

I am glad you love Scotland. I love your country too. I remember vividly the lovely lunch in your home and the thrashing of the Pacific

296

breakers. You must forgive this untidy letter. I am nearly 97 and nearly blind.

With very good wishes and many thanks.

Yours cordially,
Flora MacLeod of MacLeod

Dame Flora MacLeod, of MacLeod

Dame Flora died at age 98 in 1976. Her grandson, John MacLeod of MacLeod, succeeded her as 29th head of the MacLeod Clan.

The castle, which is built on a rock, is reached by a bridge that spans the former moat. On the side opposite the entrance is the Loch Dunvegan. A sea gate on the loch side originally was the only entrance. The castle grounds have many trees and flowering shrubs and, although the exterior of the castle is very old, it is in good repair. The interior of the castle has been changed and modernized somewhat and is used as the living quarters of the head of the clan.

Many relics are on display in the large entry room. One is a two-handed sword known as the Rory Mor's Sword that dates back to the middle of the 16th century. It had been used during the funerals of former clan chiefs to initiate the new chief.

Another treasured possession on display is the tattered and worn Fairy Flag, dating backing to the 14th century. Made of silken fabric of Eastern origin, it is thought to have come to the MacLeods of Dunvegan through their Norse ancestry. Legend relates that this flag was handed to a MacLeod at Fairy Bridge as a charm to take into battle. It is said to have the power to work three times if unfurled at the moment of dire need; so far it has been used twice to turn the tide favorably for the Clan MacLeod. Dame Flora MacLeod gave me a three-by-five inch photograph of this flag when she visited our home in 1955. She autographed it and wrote the clan motto, "Hold Fast," below her signature. A new tower was added to Dunvegan Castle in the 14th century and named the Fairy Tower for this flag.

One of the things that most intrigued me was the dungeon. As I recall, it was a circular enclosure about 12 feet in diameter with no doors and only very small windows. The upper end, three stories high, was open though covered with a roof. A rope pulley was used to lower prisoners into the dungeon. I do not know how often it was used.

Dottie and I were soon on our way and took the ferry back to the mainland. We reached the area of Inverness and spent the night in the only hotel available.

We had bought a golf catalogue published by the Scotland Tourist Bureau. Over 300 courses were listed, many of them indicating they had carts available, which we would need. We had brought golf shoes with us, but no clubs. When we came upon a golf course at Nairn about 9 a.m., we rented two sets of clubs and one handcart. This was the only golf cart of any kind we saw in Scotland at the six golf courses we visited. Dottie used the cart, and I carried my clubs; no caddies were available. I was pleased with my score of four pars and five bogies on the second nine. We were now on the coast of the North Sea and really needed our sweaters for warmth, even in the sunshine. It was October 1st.

After golf we drove through beautiful farmland to Aberdeen and spent the night at the Imperial Hotel. The next morning we played golf at one of the Hazelhead courses. As there were no carts or caddies we had to carry our clubs. Dottie carried hers for six holes, and then I carried both. I remember I had to pawn my watch until I returned the clubs which, I also recall, were not a matched set.

By this time I had learned how to get starting times at the golf courses. Many of the courses are public and starting times are determined by lottery. Twenty-four to 36 hours ahead, I would call to make room reservations at the hotel at the golf course where we were going to play. I would then ask the hotel clerk to put our names in for a starting time. The lottery for starting times was held at 9 p.m. for the next day. It was very simple. Sometimes we would start early and other times it might be as late as noon. We still finished in time to drive to our next hotel and golf course, as distances were short.

We next called Gleneagles Hotel and readily booked their one remaining deluxe suite, as we were hungry for some luxury after several motels and second-class hotels. On our way there, we drove by Balmoral, the Scottish home of the English Royal Family. Its setting, in the beautiful Dee Valley, is surrounded by mountains slightly over 2000 feet above sea level.

Gleneagles is a golfer's paradise in the highlands. There are three courses and everything is first class including the hotel and its dining room. We were very pleased with our deluxe suite, which had an outside room on the third floor overlooking one of the golf courses. The ceilings were high and all the rooms were large. Even the dressing room was about 12 feet square. In the dining room we ordered Chateaubriand steak for two, and it was delicious.

Next day, we played on the King's course using the services of a caddy who carried both our bags. We enjoyed playing this course very much, though it rained before we finished.

We were so pleased with Gleneagles that we opted to spend a second day there and play the Queen's course. Our deluxe room was already reserved, but we were given a regular room on the second floor, opening onto a central court. We hired a caddy for the second day and again it rained although we played in spite of the rain and enjoyed it. I made a birdie and three pars. That evening I called ahead to the Bruce Hotel at Carnoustie and reserved a room and got a starting time for the following day.

Carnoustie is a public course, and the separate hotel is not as fancy as Gleneagles. However, we had a pleasant surprise at dinner. A local couple had just been married and were having their wedding reception in the hotel. There were about 25 guests. The bride and the girls in the wedding party all had beautiful dresses with a sash across one shoulder with the tartan of their clan on it. The groom and the men wore kilts and, also, had a sash over one shoulder with their tartans on it. A group of bagpipers, also dressed in kilts, furnished Scottish music for the occasion. It was a very colorful affair and all the hotel guests thoroughly enjoyed it.

Carnoustie is by the North Sea and the weather was cold in spite of bright sunshine. We played golf the next day in gale-force winds of 40 miles per hour. When we reached the 18th hole, we found the sea had come over the fairway for the last 100 yards just in front of the green, due to the strong winds at high tide. We played our balls up to the water's edge, hit onto the green over the sea, and then had to go back several hundred yards to get across to the green. Our scores were not good.

I had made reservations at the famous old St. Andrew's course and the Old Course Hotel for the next day, our last day of golf. This is the first golf course ever made and is said to be where golf originated in the year 1100. A primitive course existed in 1414 when St. Andrew's University was opened. It still serves as a standard for golf course construction world-wide, and major tournaments are held there frequently. Much of the original layout remains, with nine holes going out and nine holes coming in. Our tee time at St. Andrew's was at noon so in the morning we went shopping. I bought several woolen items including a red coat of the Stewart plaid to wear in the Christmas season and another woolen coat that was forest green with brown threads. It still is the best coat I own. Dottie bought several yards of woolen cloth of the Graham clan plaid and some of the MacLeod clan plaid. She had a nice jacket made for herself and gave the rest to our daughters and her sisters. It was interesting to watch the customs officer in Honolulu inspect my luggage and check my woolen coats. I'm sure he felt I was hiding a cashmere coat.

We hired a caddie and had a nice 18 holes of golf with a few surprises. There were deep sand traps with vertical walls in the middle of the fairway. These traps could not be seen from a hundred yards away. Our caddie was a great help: He would warn us and tell us where to drive the ball. Some of the greens were enormous and had two holes with flags in them, one for a hole on the first nine and the other for a hole on the second nine. One could be on the green and still be 100 yards from the cup. I had two long shots on number 17. My second hit went across the road into trouble. I had gone about 450 yards.

We were amazed by the knowledge of the greens shown by all our caddies. One caddie did not play golf, but all of them knew exactly how much the ball would break from any position. They would indicate in half-inch distances where to aim the ball, and usually they were correct.

When we finished playing at St. Andrew's, I gave our caddie my golf shoes - which were good shoes but didn't fit me well - and all the balls we had.

After golf at St. Andrew's, we drove to Edinburgh where we had reservations for two nights at Hotel George. We had dinner in the hotel and, afterwards, were entertained by Scottish dancers and bagpipe music.

The next day we turned in our U-drive car, did some shopping and took a city tour. We visited a famous church, the Queen's Palace, and toured the Edinburgh Castle high on a hill from where we got a good view of the city. Returning to our hotel, we packed for our trip to Amsterdam the next day.

THE NETHERLANDS AND AMSTERDAM: OCTOBER 8 TO 11

We took an early flight to Manchester, England, where we had only 40 minute to change to our KLM Airlines flight to Amsterdam. When we arrived in Manchester, our plane was already loaded and sitting on the runway, ready to leave. We were rushed through customs, taken out to our plane and, as soon as our luggage came, the plane took off. Never again have I allowed so little time between flights. We were very unpopular at the moment.

We were registered at the deluxe, new Marriot Hotel. It was centrally located and so new that its name did not appear in the catalogue of hotel listings.

We had read about and wanted to see many things in Amsterdam: the museums, the music concerts, the countryside, the windmills and the reclaimed land that was below sea level. I arranged an itinerary that was action-packed.

The music season had just begun. I hiked down to the concert hall, six blocks away, and got tickets to hear the Danish Odense Symphony Orchestra for the evening of the first day. There was a great, young violinist as soloist. I learned that Artur Rubinstein was giving a piano concert the next evening, but it was sold out. In the afternoon we went to the Modern Museum of Art and the Van Gogh Museum, both of which were within walking distance of our hotel.

The next morning we took a three-hour tour of the low dyke area, north of Amsterdam. We learned how the windmills had been used to pump water from the drainage canals which crossed all the fields. When the water was high enough it was dumped into the ocean. I took a picture of three windmills in tandem, each raising the water to a higher level. At one place, the road passed between two canals: The one on the right was 15 feet higher than the one on the left. Very few new windmills are being built; electric pumps are now used to remove the water.

On this tour we visited a shop where the famous wooden shoes of Holland were made from poplar wood imported from Norway. We also stopped near Edam and walked across the canals into the shopping district. We bought some of the world-famous Edam cheese for Ann.

We saw acre after acre of beautiful flowers, planted in rows with alternating colors like a rainbow. We also saw many hundreds of hothouses, where the flowers were cultivated during adverse weather conditions.

In the afternoon of our second day, we spent two hours in the Rijkmuseum, one of the great art museums of the world. Someone had vandalized Rembrandt's "Night Watch" three weeks before and it was in the process of restoration when we saw it.

I decided to make another effort to get tickets to hear Artur Rubinstein that evening. I had been lucky in the past. While Dottie was resting after a busy day, I hiked back to the concert hall in the rain at 5 p.m., just in case any unsold tickets had been returned. Much to my surprise, there were tickets available. Extra seats had been placed on the stage where members of an orchestra normally sit. I got seats seven rows behind the piano and about 10 feet above. I was overjoyed. Dottie could hardly believe our luck.

At that time Artur Rubinstein was 88 years old, but was still giving concerts. He was one of the greatest pianists of all times. We sat just behind him and looked down on his hands as he played. It was one of the greatest thrills of our lives. Recently, we recorded a program about him on public television, narrated by his son. He related many fascinating stories about his father and his musical career. As I recall, he died at age 92.

On our last day we took an all-day tour. We first went to Aalsmere, where we saw many beautiful flower farms, then drove on to Delft and visited the pottery factory where the unusual blue and white pottery of Holland is made. We soon reached Rotterdam, which has the largest and busiest harbor in the world. Many large ships, both freighters and passenger cruise ships, were in the harbor. In 1939, Hitler's Luftwaffe had destroyed every building in Rotterdam except for three, which we saw. Today, this city of 700,000 people had been rebuilt and is very busy. It serves as the major transhipment center of the Rhine Valley and is a terminus for air and railroad freight. It tranships or exports almost every conceivable commodity. Shipbuilding is a major industry as is oil and sugar refining.

Our next stop was the Hague, the administrative capital of the Netherlands and the site of the International Court of Justice. We visited the Peace Palace, where important decisions had been made affecting world peace in the past. I remember studying about The Hague in high school. Though an important center of government, it is also a center of art and culture. In one of their museums we saw Rembrandt's "Lesson in Anatomy."

In the evening of our last day, we heard the Amsterdam Symphony Orchestra at the concert hall. We had had a busy three days, but had enjoyed every minute of it.

We packed for home the morning of October 11th and then learned our plane would be three hours late. Finally, we took off at 3 p.m. I took good pictures of the snow caps over northern Greenland, Canada and Alaska. There was snow as far as one could see. On our way to Europe over this area, I had seen some rivers. Now, the rivers were frozen, and fresh snow had fallen on the ice although they were still recognizable from their level surfaces. We were flying 600 miles south of the North Pole, as we had on our way to Europe.

After nine hours, we arrived in Anchorage, Alaska, refueled, and arrived in

Honolulu six hours later. It was 10:15 p.m., Honolulu time, when Ann met us at the airport. We were tired and ready for sleep. The next day, I relaxed while Dottie and Ann went to the Blaisdell Center to hear an opera with Eileen Farrell in the leading role. We returned to Maui on October 13th and I started work the next day. I was soon busy delivering babies night and day.

THE YEAR 1975 CONTINUED

I drew plans for and had mahogany book shelves built for one side of my bedroom, where my desk is located. Now all my books and papers were together, a real luxury for me.

I applied to the International Federation of Obstetrics and Gynecology to give a lecture at their meeting to be held in Mexico City in 1976. I was accepted and started preparing, though the meeting was a year away.

Dottie's mother died on November 8th at age 94. She had become confused a few months before her death and had spent about a month in a nursing home. She was a grand old lady who never complained. She had had ten children, five of whom are still living, and had been a widow for the last 45 years of her life.

I remember calling her on the telephone from Hawaii when she was 92. She remarked that she was fine except she had some trouble with her memory. She never mentioned death or admitted that there was such a thing. When she was 90, she had a new roof put on her home, commenting that she would not have to worry about another roof for 20 years. We all miss her very much.

Dottie Jane and Carol represented our family at mother Graham's funeral in Lewistown. It had been years since they had seen all their relatives on that side of the family. In spite of the sadness of the occasion, they had a real reunion and enjoyed seeing all of their aunts, uncles and cousins. There was one complication. When my brother-in-law, Neff, heard about his mother's death, it upset him so much that he promptly had a heart attack and could not attend the funeral. Luckily, he recovered and is still living at the time of this writing. He had to have cardiac by-pass surgery about eight years ago.

My supply of my monograph, "Etiology of Eclampsia," arrived from Switzerland with a $630 air freight bill. This was a surprise. I think I was overcharged, but I paid the bill.

For Dottie's Christmas present, I sent my Phi Rho Sigma Medical Fraternity pin to a jeweler and had it mounted on a ring. It has many small pearls on it. Dottie was very pleased.

Michael II and Ann spent the Christmas holidays with us. We bought ourselves a Kodak Carousel slide projector. For each of the next ten years, little Michael flew alone to California to spend Christmas with his father.

THE YEAR 1976

I attended a Perinatal Mortality Study Committee meeting in Honolulu in January and afterward had dinner with Ann. I returned on a late plane and brought a suitcase full of 150 pounds of hardware tools and supplies with me. Michael Senior had left them behind when he moved out.

Dr. and Mrs. William Gintling, our new partner in the O.B.-Gyn deparment, arrived February 18th. By the 26th, they had settled into their Wailuku Town House and Dr. Gintling began working. They had stayed in our guest house for a few days.

Dottie and I went to Kauai early February 28th and played golf for two days at Princeville. We were house guests of Grace and Grant Dixon. It was great fun playing golf with our friends there.

Michael Senior had given Ann their home, but she could not make the payments on the mortgages. She sold the home, paid off all indebtedness, and had enough money left to make half the down payment on a condominium. Dottie and I joined her on a 50 percent basis, and we bought a nice, new condominium at Haiku Woods. The developer had gone bankrupt after completing the condominiums. There were about 83 units. We bought a choice unit for $70,000, which originally had a $112,000 price tag. It had two bedrooms, two and a half baths, and was very plush, of Mediterranean design, with outside walls of stucco. I thought we had gotten a terrific bargain. Ann had watched this condominium being built and was very happy with it. We would not have believed what the future had in store for us.

I was very busy in my medical practice. Now with Dr. Gintling with us, I felt a responsibility to see all the patients I could so that I could keep him and Dr. Allred busy in surgery. Most of the women on Maui knew me and more came to my office than I could care for.

After a busy day on Monday, April 27th, which included the clinic in Lahaina, I attempted to wash my bedroom windows from the outside. When I looked up, I became dazed. After several attempts, I abandoned the window-washing and decided to irrigate my plants instead. I still did not feel well, so I came in the house, took a bath and had dinner. Afterward, I felt normal and had a normal sleep.

The next day I had my nurse take my blood pressure about mid-morning and it was 225/135. She became excited and said I must see one of our internists which I did immediately. He started me on medication and the next day my blood pressure was down to 170/108. He did a complete exam and had a series of tests done. His diagnosis was physiological hypertension due to overwork. Thereafter, if I were up at night working and failed to get my normal sleep, my blood pressure would be elevated the next day. Under normal conditions it was 140/90.

Dottie's sister and husband, Josephine and Tony Artman, spent six days with us. They had planned to come two years earlier but, just before they were about to leave, Tony had a heart attack. We had a very busy time sightseeing and entertaining them although I continued working most of the time they were here. The day before they arrived, I had a subconjunctival hemorrhage in my eye, which did not clear for about 10 days. I had had several of these during the past year.

We had applied for a charter flight to Oslo, Norway, and had made a down payment. However, the flight was canceled. We already had confirmed hotel reservations, so we decided to go anyway and made reservations on Pan American World Airways. They had a flight that originated in Honolulu and terminated in Oslo, though there was a plane change in London.

On July 4, 1976, we celebrated the 200th anniversary of the Declaration of Independence of our country. I flew our country's flag from our balcony. After church, we played in a golf tournament and had dinner at the Maui Country Club. I had just bought a new 1976 golf bag, which was red, white and blue.

Later in July I attended the Perinatal Mortality Committee meeting in Honolulu. While there I visited Pan American Airways and got our tickets for Europe. I brought Ann's garden tools home with me, some of which I had bought for her originally. I fashioned a box out of cardboard for the tools, and the airline allowed me to bring them to Maui without extra charge.

CHAPTER XXI

Tours of Norway, Sweden and England:
July 26 to August 27, 1976

I assisted with a cesarean during the night before our departure. We left Maui in the morning and Honolulu at 1 p.m. and arrived in San Francisco at 9:30. We spent the night with Lois and John at Fremont and then left for London at 11 a.m., stopping in Seattle for more passengers and fuel. We had an uneventful flight to London, arriving at 7 a.m. After changing planes, we were off to Oslo, though we did stop to discharge passengers in Bergen. The temperature was 35 degrees. We finally reached Oslo at 1:30 p.m., and the temperature was a warm 65 degrees.

We registered at the Grand Hotel which was centrally located and only three short blocks from the famous City Hall. This was a twin-towered, red-brick building located on the Oslo Fjord and the terminus for all bus and boat tours.

The following morning we took an hour-long cruise of the harbor. We visited the Norsk Folkemuseum, 160 wooden buildings that had been transported from their original sites and restored. A primitive village had been created just as it had been in 1150 A.D. The most outstanding building was the famous Norwegian Stave Church.

Three very old viking ships were on display. These had been found near the Oslo Fjord where they had been submerged since the ninth century. As I recall, one of them was in fairly good condition while all showed some deterioration. They are now housed in a museum.

We saw the raft, Kon-Tiki, on which Thor Heyerdahl and five companions drifted across the South Pacific Ocean from Peru to Polynesia in 1947. Their trip lasted 101 days and I remember reading about it in the newspaper.

In or near the Maritime Museum, we saw the polar exploration ships, Fram and Gjoa. They had been used about the end of the 19th century to explore large areas north of the American Continent and the Northwest Passage. Ten years later the Fram was also used by Roald Amundsen to explore the South Pole.

On one of our tours we visited the Vigeland Sculptures. As I remember, they were on a beautifully landscaped area on a slight hillside that covered 75 acres. Gustav Vigeland created many sculptures of humans and animals in stone, iron and bronze and displayed them in 150 groups on the 75 acres. They are most unusual and are universally regarded as unique.

One of Norway's great artists was Edvard Munch. The Munch Museum displays 350 of his paintings in addition to some sculptures and drawings. We bought a copy of one of his paintings and have it hanging in our home.

We were taken to the renowned, 168-foot Oslo Ski Jump. It is used only once a year, in March, for the final European competition, preventing local skiers from having a home advantage.

We toured Norway's Resistance Movement Museum, a display of about 100 exhibits of the resistance movement in Norway during the German occupation from 1940 to 1945. What we saw was most interesting.

On our second evening we had dinner in our hotel. Afterward, we were entertained by folk dancers in their native costumes.

On our harbor tour we saw a beautiful, three-masted sailboat. The manufacture of oil rigs is a major industry in Oslo. The ones we saw in the harbor were bright orange and were large, high structures. As we had never seen oil rigs before, these structures were impressive.

We went shopping after the harbor tour and again next morning before we left for Bergen. Shopping tours in foreign cities are very interesting. One quickly learns how the populace lives, what they eat and wear, and how they amuse themselves. Occasionally, we find an item that would fit nicely in our home, and we purchase it.

In the Heritage Section (Chapter I), I state that in the 8th century, Norsemen first invaded and raided the islands of Scotland. Later, they settled on the islands and intermarried with the Scots. They had come on viking ships similar to the ones that we had seen in the museums. My great grandfather, Neil MacLeod, was a descendant of the royalty of Norway. The name, Leod, is derived from the Norwegian name, Ljotr and Mac denotes that the person is the son of Leod. When we were in Norway, I did not know that any of my ancestors had been Norwegian.

Friends had recommended we take the Bergen Express train from Oslo to Bergen, which we did, leaving at 3:30 p.m. and arriving at 10:30. We crossed mountains 4267 feet high and for 60 miles the tracks were above the timber line. There were glaciers and perpetual snow on the mountain heaths. This is one of the most exciting train trips in the world, rivaling the train ride from Vancouver to Calgary, Canada. Unusual engineering skills were required to build both railroads. We enjoyed a lovely dinner en route while watching the unusual, beautiful scenery. It was still light when we arrived.

We were unable to get reservations at a downtown hotel in Bergen and, instead, stayed at the Fantof Summer Hotel, a university dormitory on the outskirts of Bergen. A streetcar line nearby provided frequent service to the center of the city. Our room was the usual college dormitory room with a private shower. It still contained some personal effects of the students who occupied it during the school year. There was an excellent dining room, where we ate breakfast. The room rate was about half that of the downtown hotels. It was a nice experience staying there for three days.

Bergen is a beautiful city. It is built on hillsides by fjords not far from the Atlantic Ocean on the west side. The mountain range on the east causes frequent rains in the summer and lots of snow in the winter. To offset the glare of the snow-covered roofs, the houses are painted different colors, creating a patchwork quilt-effect on the hillsides. There was no litter, and, because of the frequent rains, everything was clean. We came prepared with raincoats and rubber overshoes.

On our first day in Bergen, we were greeted by bright sunshine and took two sightseeing tours. We visited the home of Edvard Greig, Norway's great music composer. He wrote mostly Norwegian folk songs, but also is known for his world-famous song, "I Love Thee," written for his fiancee who later became his wife. He also wrote "A Swan" and "In a Boat," both which are universally popular. We have several of his recordings in our library, and our daughter, Lois, frequently sings "I Love Thee" as a solo at weddings.

In the afternoon we went to an art musem and saw many of Munch's paintings and heard several recordings of Greig's music.

It rained throughout our second day. We visited three more museums and the fruit-vegetable-flower market. I bought Dottie a pewter alloy ring with a viking design.

On our third and final day, the sun was shining again. We visited the aquarium and a nearby park in the morning and browsed through some of the shops before going to our hotel. After a rest, we checked out of our hotel and boarded the government-operated, 2,500-ton coastal steamer, Erling Jarl, for a trip to northern Norway.

Our destination was Kirkenes, beyond North Cape and as far as one can go in Norway. It is only a few miles from the Soviet Union border, over four hundred miles above the Arctic Circle and is above the tip of Finland. On the trip north the steamer navigates in and out of the fjords and makes about 16 stops before reaching Kirkenes on the seventh morning. Occasionally, the steamer goes into reverse to make the turns in the fjords. At other times, the ship must go into the Atlantic Ocean for short distances, times I recognized immediately because I became seasick. On the seventh day, these steamers head south, stopping at different ports, and reach Bergen on the twelfth day. They carry general cargo, mail, medical supplies, and passengers. We had booked first-class passage from Bergen to Kirkenes only and flew from Kirkenes to Stockholm on the seventh day.

As soon as we arrived aboard, we learned there had been a major engine breakdown. It was being repaired and our departure would be delayed a few hours. The occupants of the 16 to 24 staterooms ate their meals in the dining room. In addition, there was a large, enclosed area on the deck where many passengers spent their time without going to bed.

It was late before we went to bed, and I did not get much sleep. The ship was bobbing up and down all night, and I assumed we were underway. However, the next morning we were still tied to the dock in Bergen. We finally left at 9:30 a.m., missing the first scheduled stop.

We made good time this first day, with several short stops. The second day, we had several hours in Trondheim and visited a musical instrument museum. At 6 p.m. we were in the open ocean, so dinner was delayed until 8 when we were back in a fjord.

A delightful young courier was traveling with us. She kept us informed about the places where we stopped and what we should see. She was to be married after this trip, so Dottie gave her a puka shell necklace from Hawaii as a wedding present.

We met an older couple from Tel Aviv and a young Norwegian, a traveling salesman. The five of us played bridge and cribbage. The Norwegian was very interesting and made our trip much more enjoyable. He had a car aboard, loaded with samples and stocks of cloth, etc., which he would drive from Kirkenes back to Bergen, calling on his merchant customers en route. I remember his telling us about making this same trip in the winter. He said the waves would break over the bow of the ship, and the water would freeze. Finally, when the accumulated ice became too heavy, seamen would cut it away and throw it overboard.

We crossed the Arctic Circle on our third day at 6:30 a.m. I happened to be up on the deck at the time and saw the special marker on land, a metal world globe with an Arctic Circle. Later in the day we had a party aboard, celebrating the event.

At noon we arrived at Bodo where we had about three hours to visit. A beautiful polar bear, mounted by a taxidermist, stood on the sidewalk in front of a store. I took a picture of Dottie standing beside the bear with her hand on his shoulder. We then went immediately to a beautiful new cathedral and heard a 30-minute organ recital.

Soon after we left Bodo, we passed the Lofoten Islands where there were many fishing villages. We saw row after row of codfish hanging on racks, drying in the sun. These codfish were salted and, along with salt herring, had served as a major food source for the Norwegians as well as for other European countries for centuries.

On our last day our steamer stopped at Honninsvay, where we took a bus to North Cape, the northernmost point in Europe. We bought a special diploma stating we had been there. On our way back to the steamer, we visited a Lapp settlement which was a demonstration project for the tourists. To our surprise, the Lapps we saw were blue-eyed blonds.

Lapland is a broad belt of land above the Arctic Circle extending across the northern parts of Norway, Sweden and Finland and adjoining the Soviet Union. There are no trees as it is above the timber line. The Lapps are a nomadic people who follow the reindeer and are almost wholly dependent on them. In the summer, the reindeer live in the mountains where the grasses are good. In the winter, they move to the lowlands and survive on lichens, a plant that flourishes there in the cold months.

There are great herds of reindeer and a herdsman rides one to control the herd just like a cowboy rides a horse. The Lapps have domesticated the reindeer and use it as a beast of burden to pull sleds loaded with their belongings from one camp to another. The meat of the reindeer, along with reindeer milk and cheese, constitutes the greatest part of the Lapp's diet. The furs are used for clothing and to make tents. On the way to North Cape, we saw herds of reindeer grazing on the treeless tundra. Modernization has encroached on the lifestyle of the Lapps, so that it is being replaced.

Also on our last day, we set anchor opposite a village of several dozen buildings. We were told that the coastal steamers were the only connections this village and several others had with the outside world. When a launch came out to meet us, several items of freight, including lumber, were unloaded, and then freight from the launch was brought aboard. One woman passenger from the launch embarked. We were soon on our way, watching with interest the farms and occasional homes along the coastline.

In one of the towns where we stopped, we saw a special boat used for hunting seals. It had a loft about 40 feet above the deck where a rifleman would sit and shoot seals as they surfaced nearby. Other seamen would then retrieve them.

We reached Kirkenes on the morning of the sixth day. There had been daylight 24 hours a day throughout our trip. Whenever I awakened at night, I would go up on the deck to see the terrain. Dottie did the same and witnessed the ship engineering through some of the narrowest passages. We agreed that the food on the steamer had been good, although it was not of the gourmet type. After breakfast we disembarked and walked about Kirkenes until it was time to go to the airport to get our plane to Stockholm at 11:25 a.m. The plane made about 12 stops before it reached Oslo, then flew directly from Oslo to Stockholm.

STOCKHOLM, SWEDEN: AUGUST 9 TO 14

We reached our hotel, the Continental, in the evening. It was located in the middle of the city, conveniently located within walking distance of the major shopping area. On our first day we were still very tired from the unexpectedly long plane trip from Kirkenes. On a city sightseeing tour in the afternoon, one of the places we visited was Millesgarden, the house and gardens of the famous Swedish artist and sculptor, Carl Milles. It is on the island of Lidingo, across from Stockholm. Many of his magnificent sculptures, as well as paintings and sculptures he had collected from around the world, were displayed. He donated everything to Sweden. We also did some shopping and bought many pieces of beautiful Marimekko fabric, which is made in Finland.

On our second day we took the morning city tour and visited the outstanding city hall and Skansen Park. In the evening we went to Old Town to shop and for dinner.

We visited the Museum of Natural History on day three and also went to the Wasa dockyard, where the warship was being restored. The Wasa was launched in 1628 and sank on its maiden voyage in several hundred feet of water in the harbor in Stockholm.

The saga of the Wasa as related to us by our guide is as follows: The King of Sweden at that time had decided to have a large man-of-war built that would be invincible in battle on the sea. He appointed an officer in charge of planning and construction, but the king rushed the project and interfered with both the plans and construction. He warned those in charge that, if the ship were not completed by a certain time, they would all be disgraced.

There was confusion concerning the ship's design. It is said that the center of gravity was four feet too high. With many heavy cannons on deck, this created a dangerous situation. Also, the location of the ballast was improper. The officer in charge died before completion, and the project was left without leadership.

The Wasa was similar to the Mayflower in design, except it was one and a half times larger. It was 200 feet long, had a beam of 30 feet, and displaced 1300 tons. Its three masts flew 13,000 square feet of sail. It was equipped with the best of everything and even had a cow aboard to furnish fresh milk for the sailors.

On the Wasa's maiden voyage, a stong gust of wind hit the ship before it sailed out of the harbor. It capsized and sank immediately in several hundred feet of water where it lay on the bottom of the harbor for 233 years, until it was raised in 1961. The ship and its contents were in remarkably good condition. Restoration efforts were started immediately. When we were there, we were taken on a guided tour through it. A sprinkler system kept the ship wet until the lumber could be treated with preservatives. It was a great thrill to see this relic.

On the morning of the fourth day, I had an appointment with Dr. E. Diczfalusy at the university. I visited with him for about an hour, and we discussed my research project on high blood pressure and pregnancy. He was one of the leading authorities on endocrinology and I had often referred to his work in my medical writing. I was scheduled to give a medical paper at Mexico City within a few months and I wanted to get his opinion on some things. He was very gracious. I was very nervous about this appointment and finally asked him for a glass of water, because my mouth was so dry. After discussing my project, he told me all about acid rain and how it was killing the fish in the Swedish lakes. He thought the acid rain was coming to the Scandinavian countries from the manufacturing plants of central Europe.

In the afternoon Dottie and I played golf at Lidingo Golf Club. It was said to be one of the finest in Sweden, but we found it was not very good, by American standards. This was the end of our activities in Sweden. We had only one short tour outside Stockholm, and the next morning we left early for the airport to fly to London.

_____LONDON AND ENGLAND: AUGUST 14 TO 24

We arrived in London at 11 and were settled in the Tara Hotel by 1 p.m. This was in the Kensington district and just two blocks from the double-decker bus line. We soon knew how to make connections and get around London. The first evening, we saw the musical, "Irene," at the Adelphi Theatre.

When we were downtown near the theatre district, I would check the theatre box offices and get tickets for shows that we wanted to see while we were in town. On our second day, after sleeping late and getting rested, we went to Buckingham Palace in time to see the changing of the guards. We again saw Big Ben, the famous clock, and visited Westminister Abbey. In the afternoon we toured the National Art Gallery. We had dinner in our hotel that evening.

On our third day, we had lunch at Harrod's Department Store where even the butchers wear formal, long tail, morning frock coats while working. We always shop there when we are in London. We visited the Tate Art Gallery and I bought Dottie a book on Cezanne's art. In the evening, we saw a play, "The Pleasure of His Company," at the Phoenix Theatre.

The next day, we shopped at Fortnum and Mason and went to the Museum of Natural History and the Science Museum. That evening we saw the show, "Liza of Lambeth," at Shaft's Theatre.

Our wedding anniversary was August 17th, but we waited a day to celebrate. We visited the old Kensington, or William and Mary, Palace. We had lunch at Piccadilly Circus and then saw a comedy, "The Bed Before Yesterday," in the afternoon at the Lyric Theatre. We had a special anniversary dinner at a restaurant in the theatre district.

We rented a U-drive and left London on August 19th. We drove directly to Eastbourne in the morning and registered at the Cavendish Hotel. I spent the afternoon discussing my research project with Dr. Jeffrey Theobold, which I have already mentioned. In the evening, Dr. and Mrs. Theobold were our guests for dinner in our hotel.

We played golf the next morning at the Royal Eastbourne Golf Course, which was in poor condition due to a drought in the area. Wild rabbits had dug holes on several of the greens. The weather was hot that afternoon when we drove to Winchester and checked into the Royal Hotel.

The next day was most eventful. First we toured the 17th century Wilton House. Then we visited the Winchester Cathedral with its gracful spire and beautiful, stained glass windows - an example of the architecturally beautiful English cathedrals. Next, we went into the Winchester Castle, where King Arthur and his knights had met. We crossed the moat on the original drawbridge and entered the castle just as King Arthur and his knights had done. The Round Table was suspended from the ceiling to protect it from visitors. We saw the armor that the knights had worn as well as the armor for the horses.

From Winchester, we drove across the Salisbury Plains to Salisbury. We parked at the Stonehenge and inspected the enormous stone structures that were made by man between 1800 and 1400 B.C. They are one of the Seven Wonders of the world. We also saw Old Sarum, a mixture of Roman, Saxon, and Norman stone ruins that are very old. This area was settled after the last Ice Age and long before the time of Christ. We continued on to Bath and registered at the Beaufort Hotel.

The Romans arrived in Bath in the year 44 A.D. and developed it into a spa of great proportions. We visited the large pump room and the area where the hot baths were taken. It is used today just as it was in Roman times. It was most impressive to me as I had never seen a spa, nor had any of my family or acquaintances used spas for rejuvenation or for the treatment of chronic ailments as is done in many countries. We walked the streets of Bath and did some shopping.

We left Bath in early afternoon and arrived at Oxford in time to visit the 325-year old botanical gardens. The next day was one of the most memorable days of our lives. We toured Oxford on foot, visiting many of the colleges, cathedrals and art galleries. We saw the original copies of Aesop's Fables, Longfellow's Poems, Dicken's Tale of Two Cities, Shakespeare's Hamlet, the original poems and writings of Chaucer including the Canterbury Tales, The Magna Charta, Dante's works, and many other original copies of illustrious writings. In just one short day, we had seen the original copies of many famous writings that we had studied previously in school. It, indeed, was a thrill.

After a full day at Oxford, we drove to London's Heathrow Airport and registered at the Post House Hotel where I turned in my U-drive. The next day we boarded our plane at 12:15 and arrived in Seattle at 2:45 p.m. We took another plane to San Francisco, where Lois and John met us. I got to bed at 9 p.m. and slept ten and a half hours.

The weather was delightful in Fremont, with bright sunshine. McLeod and Louise drove from Saratoga the next day and had dinner with us. It was so nice to have a day to relax after the long plane ride and the activities of the past month.

On the following day, John, Lois, Dottie and I took the Bart commuter train from Fremont (its last stop on the peninsula) into San Francisco and got off at the Hyatt Hotel Station. John was a train enthusiast and told me all about Bart. He took me to the front car where a lone, black female operator was in charge. The speedometer showed that we were traveling between 75 and 84 miles an hour.

We took a cable car to to Fisherman's Wharf where we had a delicious early lunch, then returned to the downtown area and went shopping. It's always a thrill to be in this lovely city.

The next day we went to Oakland early and left for Honolulu where Ann met us at the airport. We were home on Maui at 2 p.m.

_____*THE YEAR 1976 CONTINUED*

We returned home on Friday. I played golf on Saturday and made 39 on the first nine holes, which was only two over par. I was back to work and my usual routine on Monday. On September 13th, a patient had her third son. I had delivered her other two sons, had attended her own birth 26 years before, and had delivered her husband 30 years ago. Today, when I go shopping on Maui, the clerks frequently tell me that I delivered them or their children. They are often surprised that I can't remember their names although I usually recall their faces.

On Sunday morning I helped one of our surgeons operate on a patient with intestinal obstruction. In the afternoon, I did an appendectomy and, in the evening, a dilation and curettage. The next day I complained of being tired. I was 64 and for the first time began to feel fatigued after working long hours. In the past, I could work continually for two or three days and nights and not be tired.

CHAPTER XXII

Visits to Mexico and the U.S. East Coast:
October 16 to November 6, 1976

I had applied and was accepted to give a medical paper at the meeting of the International Federation of Obstetrics and Gynecology (F.I.G.O.), which was to meet in Mexico City from October 17th to 22nd. The title of my talk would be, "Etiology of Eclampsia." This would be my first talk before this international organization, though I had given a paper at the annual meeting of the Organisation Gestosis in Prague in 1975. This would be our second trip to foreign countries in 1976.

Dottie and I left Maui October 16th at 7:15 a.m. and arrived in Los Angeles on time only to discover our connecting flight had been delayed. When we arrived in Mexico City at 1 a.m., we were met at the airport by a representative of the travel agency, who arranged for our transportation to our hotel, the Fiesta Palace. We were in bed by 2 a.m. Next day, I registered for the meeting at the medical center and attended the opening ceremonies. In late afternoon, we went to the Museum of Anthropology to attend a welcoming reception held in the lobby and adjoining courtyard. The fountain and the large inverted dome at the museum provided a beautiful setting for the reception.

The following day, meetings were held until 3:30. That evening, Dottie and I attended the Mexican Folklore Ballet, a performance of which we had seen on our previous visit. It is such a remarkable show that it was worth seeing a second time.

I gave my talk on the second day at 9 a.m. The lecture hall, seating about 150, was full by the time my talk was over. There was a high incidence of eclampsia in Mexico, and the practicing physicians were eager to learn all they could about its cause. Many came expecting me to give the final explanation for the cause of eclampsia. At this time, I did not know that the real culprit was a deficient calcium intake during pregnancy.

On the third day, I attended meetings until 3:30 while Dottie toured the pyramids with the ladies. That evening, we went to a Mexican festival held at the Colegio de las Vizcainus. The streets were filled with people and traffic was so dense our bus reached the location barely in time. The festival was extraordinary. The waiters were dressed in lavish clothes, the music was simply heavenly, and the food was delicious.

The plenary session on the fourth day was devoted to high blood pressure and pregnancy. Dr. Frederick Zuspan, world authority, gave a talk.

On the final day of the meeting, Dottie and I spent the entire afternoon in the Anthropology Museum. This is a sophisticated, contemporary building housing Mexican artifacts and monuments depicting the various Mexican and Central American cultures from the remotest past up to the present time. In my opinion and from what I read, it could be the greatest anthropology museum in the entire world.

That evening, the official banquet of the meeting was held in the Palace of Mines, an old building designed in classical, Spanish architecture. The dinner was very formal and the food was superb. There was excellent music, both on the stage and by musicians who strolled among the tables. It was a glorious affair.

After the meeting, we took a four-day motor coach tour of colonial Mexico with about 15 other passengers. By lunch time we were in Queretara, a city of 100,000 inhabitants, located about 6,000 feet above sea level. Gem cutting, especially of opals, was a major business in this industrial and agricultural center. Neither taxis nor the motor coach were allowed in the center of town, so we went sightseeing by foot.

By late afternoon we reached San Miguel Allende, in hilly terrain 175 miles northwest of Mexico City. As we approached, we passed a large aqueduct, similar to those we had seen near Rome. The town was a National Monument, full of Spanish colonial buildings. No new buildings were allowed. We stayed at Hotel Pasada de San Francisco.

Before we left next day, we went shopping in the excellent shopping areas which had an abundance of handcrafts.

En route to Guanajuato the next day, we stopped at a unique cemetery. The bodies had become mummified by a gas in the soil that preserved them and they had been removed from their graves and exhibited in a large building. It was unbelievable. They had died more than 50 years before, yet they appeared lifelike although the clothes on the bodies were starting to disintegrate. I remember seeing a French doctor who had been buried in a tuxedo. Another corpse was that of a mother who had died at childbirth. The baby had been removed from the uterus and was lying on her abdomen. Dottie and I hesitated before going inside the building and, later, were very sorry that we had. The attitude of the Mexicans was the opposite of ours.

Our hotel in Guanajuato was the Hotel Real Minas. We visited a beautiful university which had hundreds of steps leading to the main entrance. It was built in 1945, but the style of the buildings conformed to the older Spanish-Mexican architecture. We also toured a large silver mine nearby.

The next day we drove through the lake country and reached Morelia, where we stayed at the Hotel Virrey Mendoza. This city, founded in 1541, was 195 miles west of Mexico City, had a population of 129,000 and was 6,186 feet above sea level. Its main industry was textiles. Seventy of the buildings in the city were made of rose-colored stone. There was excellent shopping for needlework, handmade clothes, etc. I bought a thin wooden plate, nine inches in diameter, that had been decorated by a famous Mexican artist. It has a beautiful floral design trimmed in gold. We display it on our etagere, along with other objects of art.

On Tuesday, October 26th, we drove through the mountains and reached the Spa San Jose Purua and our hotel of the same name. The setting was very tropical and warm, with lush vegetation similar to the Hana area on Maui. We saw many of the same plants that thrive in Hawaii, such as bird of paradise, tulip trees and bougainvillea. The hotel and spa were built on the brink of a canyon with unbelievably beautiful scenery all around. The hotel itself was very plush and first-class in all respects - a beautiful place to end our colonial tour. The next morning, we returned to Mexico City and prepared to leave.

At the airport shops, I busily searched for merchandise that Dottie might like. We are so isolated on Maui that I have to buy presents in advance of special occasions whenever I visit foreign countries. I found a beautiful 18-carat gold ring with 30 beautifully cut rubies. Dottie had always wanted a ruby ring and was very pleased with my selection. Reluctantly, she agreed that I should buy it.

We left Mexico City at 2 p.m., but did not reach Asheville, N.C., until 11 that evening. When we went through customs in New Orleans, we discovered the name tag had been torn off one of Dottie's bags. I had it replaced. Then, only one of Dottie's bags arrived at Asheville. We waited an extra day in Waynesville, near Asheville, with my brother, Neill. A smart baggage handler at the airport called Atlanta and found the luggage still on the carousel. The name tag had been torn off, but Dottie's name was on the bag. By the time it arrived a few hours later, Dottie had already bought a new wardrobe, but was able to return what she didn't want.

While we were visiting Neill and his family, my sister, Maisie Parker and son, Pat, came to see us. We played golf on their mountainous course, and Pat reached a green with his drive from the tee, 400 yards away.

On October 30th we left for Connecticut to visit Carol and Peter Keck. En route, we stopped in Washington for several hours with our niece and her husband, Don and Dotty Lichtwardt. They took us on a tour of part of the city, including the new Kennedy Theater.

We continued on to Storrs, Connecticut, where Pete was studying for his doctorate. Carol was supposedly seven months pregnant although I commented that she was too large and predicted she would deliver December 1st instead of January 1st. I did not examine her. We had a lovely two days with them, which included an early Thanksgiving dinner.

The next day we flew to Philadelphia, got a U-drive at the airport and spent the night with Dottie Jane Mote and her family. We were off the next afternoon for Lewistown, where we saw all the relatives in two days.

We encountered a half-inch of snow near the Penn State University and temperatures of 30 to 40 degrees. Next day, we drove to Pittsburgh through snow flurries. We spent the night at the airport in the Holiday Inn. The temperature was 28 degrees when we left for Honolulu next morning. We arrived home at 6 p.m.

THE YEAR 1976 CONTINUED

On the weekend of December 4th and 5th, I called Carol several times without getting an answer. I felt sure she would go into labor about this time as she was so large when we saw her at Halloween. When I finally talked with her on December 7th she said she was fine.

On December 9th Dottie and I heard pianist, Gary Graffmann, at a concert of the Maui Philharmonic Society at Baldwin Auditorium.

On December 14th I sent an official letter of resignation to the Maui Medical Group to be effective June 30, 1977. I would be 65 years old in April and had decided I should retire from most of my work because of fluctuating blood pressure. I asked to be allowed to do office work for five half-days each week. My request was granted.

I was at the hospital Christmas Eve delivering a baby when Peter Keck called Dottie to tell her that baby boy A had been born at 12:05 a.m. on December 24th and weighed six pounds, nine ounces. Baby boy B followed at 12:06 and weighed five pounds, ten ounces.

Alan and Todd Keck, age 1 year

Carol and the babies were fine. When Dottie got the call, it was about 9 p.m. Hawaiian time.

We eventually learned that Carol had spent the weekend of December 4th and 5th in the hospital in mild labor. At that time, her doctor found that she had twins and gave her medication to stop labor. They did not tell me about the twins, thinking I would worry. Real labor started three weeks later. It turned out I was correct when I said she was larger than normal when I saw her at Halloween.

I talked with Carol on December 29th and learned that she was feeding both babies - named Adam and Todd - completely at breast. I knew this could not last very long. As a gift, Dottie and I gave them a diaper service for one year.

THE YEAR 1977

As usual, my sleep was disturbed on the last night of the year by my neighbor's firecrackers. When I finally learned to put in ear plugs on New Year's Eve, the noise no longer awakened me.

I had to induce labor on a patient with severe preeclampsia (high blood pressure) on New Year's Day. She delivered between 6 and 7 on the morning of January 2nd.

Our good friends, Ruth and Eddie Page of Spokane, Washington, and Kauai, visited us for two days. We played golf at the Maui Country Club and at Wailea. The Pages built one of the first homes on the golf course at Princeville and influenced many people to buy land and build homes there. In return, the golf course gave them special privileges. Eddie owned his own electric golf cart and I think he was allowed to play golf without fees.

On January 15th I began riding a golf cart regularly at the Maui Country Club. I had always walked for the exercise, though I did most of my own yard work. Now at age 65, I realized that I got too tired walking and could not sleep afterwards.

I made 35 and 39 in golf for a gross score of 74, even par, at Maui Country Club. This was the best score of my life. I had made 35 on nine holes on three different occasions.

Dottie was playing in a local golf tournament for two days, so I went to Kauai with Eddie Page for two days. On my way home, I stopped for a few hours with Ann and Michael in Honolulu.

My niece, Dottie, and her husband, Don Lichtwardt, from Washington, D.C., visited us for two days. We went to Lahaina sightseeing and for dinner.

Alice and John Hallet of Kauai and Hayden Lake, Idaho, were our house guests for two days. They were delightful people. He had been a very successful engineer, working for Kaiser Development Company on the mainland. He worked on the original construction of the Hoover Dam.

Ann and Michael II were with us for a few days in March. I took Mike to an automobile show at the gymnasium, which he enjoyed.

On April 5th we had five inches of rain at our home. On the other side of the mountain in Lahaina, 25 miles away, the sun was shining brightly all day.

The fall meeting of District VIII of the American College of Obstetricians and Gynecolgists was to be held in San Francisco. I applied to the program committee to give a paper entitled, "The Etiology of Preeclampsia." I worked diligently for many weeks and thought I had prepared an outstanding paper. My application was not accepted. The chairman of the program committee told me the committee received so many papers from resident doctors competing for prizes that they could not consider my paper. Yet, my paper contained original thinking about the etiology of high blood pressure during pregnancy. Recent developments have proven that I was on the right track to solve this dilemma. The chairman of the program committee suggested I send my manuscript to the editor of the College journal, which I did. He, also, rejected it. I was discouraged by the rejection and decided not to apply to the College to publish any more of my writings.

I made my first hole-in-one on the 140-yard seventh hole at the Maui Country Club. The wind was blowing 30 miles per hour. The ball took two bounces and fell into the cup. Eleven months later, I made another hole-in-one on the same hole from the 114-yard tee. These are the only holes-in-one I have made in 48 years of golf.

I won a $60 pair of golf shoes in the weekend tournament. Too much money had accumulated in the kitty, so large prizes were given to winners.

My first day of partial retirement was June 18, 1979. For the next two years I worked half days in the office.

CHAPTER XXIII

Tours of Switzerland, Austria, Bratislavia (C.S.S.R.) and Liechtenstein: June 21 to July 14, 1977

Michael Mote was visiting professor at the University of Zurich for one year. While there, he set up a research laboratory similar to the one he had at Temple University to study the retina. Dottie Jane, Timothy and Gregory, ages five and six, were living in Zurich with him, and the boys were attending school. Dottie and I decided to take another European vacation and visit them. We left Maui on June 21st and spent one night in Los Angeles. Next day, we left on a charter flight for Zurich, stopping in Bangor, Maine, to refuel. Dottie Jane met us at the Zurich Airport at 7 p.m.

Dottie and I rented a nice apartment at Muhlenbach and Krenze Strasse, only a few blocks from the center of town and easily reached by trolley.

On June 24th we met our friends, Dr. and Mrs. Tibor Klacansky, in Zurich and made final plans for our visit with them in Bratislavia, Czechoslovakia. They happened to be in Zurich that day on business.

The next day we took a boat excursion to Rapperswil, near the distant end of Lake Zurich. A thunderstorm brought a heavy downpour while we were there. We returned by train. That evening we had a very appetizing fondu dinner with Dottie Jane and her family at their apartment.

The next day was Sunday and Michael was free, so I rented a large Fiat sedan and we took an all-day tour. We visited many quaint Swiss hamlets, the most notable of which was Appenzell. The stores were closed so we were unable to do any shopping.

We drove to the principality of Liechtenstein, one of the smallest countries in Europe and located between Austria and Switzerland. When we stopped on the road above the Liechtenstein Castle, Timothy and Gregory got out of the car and climbed on the wrought iron gate at the entrance to the castle grounds. Suddenly, a car arrived and the gate swung open with the boys on it. In the car was the Prince of Liechtenstein who laughed and drove inside.

By the time we reached home, we were tired. The six of us more than filled the car.

The next day we rested and made plans for an escorted, motor coach and cogwheel train trip to Jungfraujoch for the following day.

Next morning we left early on the motor coach and eventually boarded the train to ascend the steep mountain. The train went through many tunnels to reach its destination at 11,333 feet above sea level. We arrived in a fairyland of ice and snow. Passages were cut in the ice, where we could walk. Outside, the scene was of majestic, ice-covered mountain peaks in all directions. Some brave skiers were trying their luck skiing down the mountain. Since we had left Zurich that morning, we had not seen a cloud in the sky and did not until about 4 p.m. on our way home. We had never seen such beautiful snow scenes as we did this day. We were so impressed that we bought tickets for Dottie Jane and her family to go up Jungfraujoch the next weekend. Unfortunately, it rained during their entire trip.

We spent the next afternoon with Dottie Jane and the boys, strolling through a large park in the rain. We stopped at the train station and bought tickets to Basel and then Geneva in the days ahead.

We made the 50-mile trip to Basel in the morning. After some sightseeing, we went to see Dr. Rippmann at his office, the headquarters of the Organisation Gestosis. He was very busy with many duties but took time to drive us in his new Jaguar to a private club for lunch. In the afternoon we visited a museum at his suggestion. We were back in our apartment in Zurich at 7 p.m.

The next morning we took a train to Geneva and arrived at 11:30. It was about 75 miles. The scenery on the 75-mile route was spectacular. We saw Mont Blanc and other high peaks in France as well as thousands of acres of vineyards.

When we left Zurich, everyone was speaking German. After a couple of hours on the train, no German could be heard, only French. The guttural sounds, so typical of German had been replaced by the melodic, romantic sounds that characterize the French language. Now I was able to hear the different tones that my teachers had talked about when I studied both languages in school.

We had a very delightful lunch at a French restaurant near Lake Geneva and then visited the government buildings. We returned to Zurich at 9:30 that evening.

On July 2nd Dottie and I went shopping in both the old town and the new town districts of Zurich. We bought Timothy and Gregory a children's book written in German, which they could both speak and understand.

The next day was Sunday and the last day of our long visit in Zurich. Michael, the boys and I hiked up the 1200-foot mountain by the park, near Dottie Jane's and Michael's apartment. In spite of the all-day hike, Timothy and Gregory wanted to play soccer when we returned home.

July 4th was a beautiful day. Dottie and I went by train through the Alps to Salzburg, Austria, where we stayed for two days at Hotel Europa. This was the third spectacular train ride of our lives. In the evening, we saw the marionette opera, "The Magic Flute."

July 5th was another beautiful day. In the morning we went on a city tour and then took a tour of the countryside where the movie, "The Sound of Music," was filmed. This musical was based on the lives of the members of the Trapp family who had visited in our home on two occasions, and we were especially interested in this tour. In the evening we heard the Vienna String Quartet at the old Capitol building.

The train ride to Vienna on July 6th was three-and-a-half hours. For three days we stayed at the Stephenplasse Hotel, just across the street from the Stephens Cathedral with its high spiral. We toured the cathedral on the day of our arrival and, during our stay, used the spiral for a landmark to find our way home.

The following day we went to the Sacher Hotel and tried some of their famous pastries, then took a city tour on a motor coach. We bought tickets for the symphony that evening and the opera the next day. The symphony was to be performed outside, but because of the rain, it was moved inside the theater. There were not enough seats for everyone, so we had to miss it. Instead, we heard an orchestra play Strauss's music at a bandstand in a park. I remember hearing Strauss's beautiful music most anytime and anywhere in Vienna.

On our last day we spent three hours in an art museum and visited Mozart's last living quarters. It was a single room, a very humble place where he died in extreme poverty and pain. That evening we saw the opera, "La Gazzetta," at the castle.

Before leaving Maui we had obtained visas to travel to Bratislavia, Czechoslovakia, only 40 miles from Vienna, where we planned to visit Dr. and Mrs. Tibor Klacansky for two days. We left by bus at 8 in the morning but were held up by a two-and-a-half hour delay at the border. A former citizen, who had immigrated to the United States, was under special surveillance. Everyone on the bus had to open his luggage for a second time for inspection. When we arrived at noon and were met by our friends they told us they had been worried by our delay.

Special arrangements had been made for us to stay in the six-story Devin Hotel, across from the Danube River. A suspension bridge with a very long span crossed the Danube near our hotel. We could see Hungary in the distance. All our expenses had been paid in advance by our friends and they would not allow us to pay for anything. Finally, they reluctantly agreed to be our guests for one meal in a revolving exposition restaurant in a lovely setting in the nearby hills.

On the day we arrived, our hosts took us on a city tour after a delightful lunch at the hotel. We saw the walls of many buildings that had been destroyed during World War II and had never been rebuilt. Elena and their son, who lived with them, had prepared a special dinner for us. Their home was on the fourth floor of an apartment building which had no elevators. Outside, the building was in poor repair with broken window panes in the stairwells and some graffiti on the walls. However, their apartment was magnificent, furnished with beautiful antique furniture and heirlooms handed down from several generations.

The next day was Sunday, and Tibor took us on a tour of the art museum. Of the many treasures in it, most notable were the old wool and silk tapestries dating back to 1630. During World War II, they had been hidden so that they would not be confiscated.

In the afternoon we took a ride in the countryside and by the Austria-Czech border. I remember seeing two barbed-wire fences separated by a few feet, and sentinels carrying rifles and leading police dogs on leashes. The sight of this was very obnoxious and helped me decide that this would be my last trip behind the Iron Curtain.

Tibor and Elena had proven to be wonderful people, and we became the best of friends. They did not approve of the communist domination of Czechoslovakia and frequently mentioned it. They, themselves, were not communists. They blamed President Roosevelt and Prime Minister Churchill for betraying Czechoslovakia at Potsdam.

While we were sightseeing, they took us to see the Slavin Memorial which honors the Soviet soldiers who liberated Czechoslovakia from the Germans in World War II. This was a large, beautiful monument built on the most prestigious, elevated location overlooking the Danube. There were many similar monuments throughout the country honoring the Soviet soldiers. The Czechs hated these memorials to the Soviets.

On Monday we were up at 5:30 and took a 7 a.m. bus to Vienna. This time it took only one hour to cross the border. We flew to Zurich and by noon we were back in Muhlenbach Apartments for our final dinner with Dottie Jane's family. Next day, we went shopping and packed for home. Dottie Jane and the boys spent the afternoon with us and we said our goodbyes.

Our flight was supposed to leave at 11 Wednesday morning, but was delayed until 3 by a mechanical problem. We refueled in Bangor, Maine, and reached Los Angeles at 10 p.m. We had had good weather all the way, but it was a long trip. We got a good night's rest at our airport hotel and then reported for our flight to Hono-lulu. When I reached for my tickets they were not in my pocket where I usually kept them. I took a taxi back to the hotel and found I had left them in our room. I was back at the check-in counter in 20 minutes, and we left for Honolulu. We saw Ann and Michael II in Honolulu and arrived home in late afternoon. I returned to work in the office on my half-day schedule.

THE YEAR 1977 CONTINUED

My sister, Dorothy, and her husband, Jack Thornton, arrived on August 2nd for six days. We stayed busy playing golf, sightseeing and having parties to introduce them to our friends.

I had been feeling unwell because of my elevated blood pressure and had been taking three types of medicine, but could not get adjusted properly. I stopped all medication just to see if I would improve with rest alone. Needing a change of pace, I decided to go to the College meeting in San Francisco.

Dottie and I went to San Francisco for six days and stayed at the Hyatt Regency Hotel, where the meeting was held. I attended most of the meetings and also discussed my research project with some of the leaders in this field. I did not sleep much at night because of my elevated blood pressure, but I had not brought any medicine with me.

We rode a BART train to Fremont and spent an afternoon with Lois and John. After the meeting, we spent a whole day with them. We invited Dr. and Mrs. Clayton Mote, Dottie Jane's in-laws from Sausaslito, to the Hyatt for dinner. We were agreeably surprised at the quality of the food in the hotel restaurants and the low prices. Prices in Hawaii were much higher.

When we returned home I found that without medication my blood pressure had risen to a dangerous level. I promptly resumed my treatment, and my pressure was soon back to normal. I learned to work less and relax more. When I became too tired for any reason, I took a sedative to help me sleep. I also slept an hour or more each afternoon. I applied the principles of work and rest that I had had my patients follow. So far, I have been fine and though my capacity is not what it used to be, it is good enough for one of my age.

I hired a new yard man and, together, we installed an irrigation system with plastic pipes. This makes my work much easier.

Dottie and I attended a concert at Baldwin Auditorium and heard the Russian pianist, Ashkenazy.

On October 18th, Reggie Jackson hit three home runs in the sixth and final game of the World Series, which the Yankees won.

President Sadat of Egypt visited Israel on November 20th in a successful peace move.

For Christmas I gave Dottie a Steuben Prunus vase which I had seen advertised. She was pleased.

I resigned from the Maui Memorial Hospital staff on December 16th, no longer caring to go to all the meetings that were required of staff members.

Dottie and I spent four days at Christmas with Ann and Michael II in Honolulu.

THE YEAR 1978

In January, Dottie and I attended a luau on the first birthday of a part-Hawaiian baby that I had delivered. A cesarean had been required after a good test of labor. The mother was unmarried. We were surprised to see the father of the baby at the luau, accompanied by a wife and another baby, who was about one year of age. I was confused until I learned that the relatives of the unmarried mother insisted that the usual luau be held on the baby's first birthday. The father could be seen holding the honored baby and celebrating with the other guests. Later, he would be holding his wife's baby and talking with different guests. Everyone appeared to be having a wonderful time and the luau food was good. Shortly after eating, we came home.

On February 15th, Leon Spinks defeated Muhammed Ali for the world heavy-weight boxing title.

Dottie and I went to Kauai for three days of golf with our friends from Spokane and with Mr. and Mrs. Merrill Carlsmith of Hilo. I was fortunate to be able to play with a golf professional for 18 holes. He was a golf course architect doing some work for Princeville.

Our friends, Dr. and Mrs. Frederick Hofmeister of Wisconsin and their friends, the Walkers, arrived for a three-day visit. He was formerly president of the American College of Obstetricians and Gynecologists. We had attended meetings in Russia and Mexico with them, and they had been our house guests many times. We always enjoyed being with them.

I rewrote my manuscript on preeclampsia that I had written the previous year but had not used. I sent it to Dr. E.T. Ripmann, head of the Organisation Gestosis-Press in Basel, Switzerland. He accepted it and published it as a 32-page monograph. In it, I discuss the etiology, prevention and treatment of preeclampsia[34]. This was the second monograph he published for me on this subject. Unfortunately, I made an error in letting him publish it without my proofreading it. His native tongue was German, and he was unable to recognize when the printer skipped an occasional line, a sentence or a whole paragraph. I had to have three paragraphs printed on adhesive paper and inserted where the errors had been made. He mailed out copies to the members of the Organisation Gestosis, and I mailed out 200 copies to libraries and researchers.

On May 4th I developed acute gouty arthritis in my right knee which became hot and swollen. Even with rest, my knee did not improve. Finally, I visited my orthopedist who treated me for four days with Butazolidin. Within 24 hours I was much improved and could play golf. Since then, I have had two more acute attacks of gout in my right knee, both following too much work.

The Maui Management Incorporated voted to sell the Maui Medical Group building to the Maui Medical Group. Money in the doctors' retirement fund would be borrowed to pay for the building. This was very important to all of us. With a booming economy on Maui and property values escalating rapidly, all of us would benefit. We were required to sell our shares in the building when we retired, by which time the value of our holding would have increased considerably.

On June 10th I received word from the Organisation Gestosis that I was on the program for the annual meeting in Cairo, Egypt, for December 2nd. The meeting had been postponed until December, when the weather was cool enough for comfort.

We had a new roof put on our main house in June, replacing the old one which leaked in several places. The year before, we had had new shingles put on our guest house.

Our 40th wedding anniversary was August 17th. We helped Jim and Elizabeth Murray celebrate their 30th anniversary on the 16th with a big party at their home. We were tired afterwards and celebrated our own anniversary quietly. I gave Dottie a dozen red roses and a special anniversary card. I had planned a trip to Greece later in the fall for a belated celebration, after which we would attend the medical meeting in

Egypt.

Lois and her two children arrived on August 22nd and I gave them a royal tour of all of Maui except Hana. I showed them colored slides of our home and their mother when she was young. The children stayed for five days and then went to Honolulu to be with Ann and Michael II while Lois remained with us three more days.

On August 31st I got a call from my sister-in-law, Pearl, telling me that my brother, Neill, had died early that morning. He had been at home, but got an acute attack of difficult breathing. She rushed him to the hospital, but he died shortly after arriving.

Neill had developed chronic myelogenous lukemia, a children's disease, soon after retiring from 31 years in the Air Force. During his last 10 years of duty, he was in the atomic missile program. For two years before that, he flew in the Strategic Air Command, carrying atomic bombs in B-52 bombers. Although he was supposed to be protected from radiation, there are no doubts in my mind that he received enough to produce the lukemia, which led to his premature death at age 62. He had flown throughout World War II and the Berlin Airlift, had spent a month at an advanced base near the North Pole, and had survived flying through electrical storms and other dangerous missions. He was given the Legion of Merit decoration by Congress for his work as commander of a missile base in Missouri, where he had guided development almost from the start. He received a total of 23 medals and decorations. He was a full colonel during the last 10 years of his service and was buried with honors at Arlington Military Cemetery among the cherry trees.

Merrill Carlsmith of Hilo, twice the National Seniors Champion, was my partner in our Member-Guest Golf tournament at the Maui Country Club over Labor Day weekend. We scored 69 and 67 net, but this was not good enough to win.

My doctor had returned to the mainland to practice and I became sensitive to the Aldomet he had prescribed. I could not read or look at television. My new physician switched me to Minipres and my problems disappeared. He continued me on a diuretic and gave me Dalmane for sleep, which I still take during times of stress. I plan to stop taking it when I finish writing my story. My blood pressure usually is normal.

I found it almost impossible to get any information about the medical meeting to be held in Cairo in December. I sent in all my fees and had to guess at the date to return home.

I had a patient who spent her winters on Maui while her professor husband was here writing a book. She complained of severe pain in the right side of her abdomen radiating from the back, which was relieved as long as she lay flat in bed. By 11 a.m. each day, she had to go to bed and remain there the rest of the day. She had been studied by one of the largest and best medical groups on the west coast. They could find nothing wrong with her and gave her no treatment.

To me, it appeared that she had right kidney pain for some reason, which was relieved by the supine position. I demonstrated by x-rays that she had severe ptosis of the right kidney which caused blockage of the ureter, resulting in the pain. This could be partially relieved with a tight belt and a pad to hold the kidney up. I sent a report along with her x-rays to the professor who was her doctor. He operated on her, and the pain was relieved. She had some serious complications from the surgery but recovered.

CHAPTER XXIV

Tours of Greece, Egypt and U.S. East Coast: November 13 to December 9, 1978

I had been accepted to give a talk at the annual meeting of the Organisation Gestosis, which was to meet in Cairo, Egypt, in early December. My talk would be based on my latest monograph which had just been published by the Organisation Gestosis-Press.

Our 40th wedding anniversary had been on August 17th, and I promised Dottie that I would take her on a tour of Greece in celebration of it. We waited until November and combined this trip with the one to the medical meeting in Egypt.

We left Honolulu in late afternoon on November 13th and arrived in Chicago early next morning. We then took a plane to Hartford, Connecticut, where Carol and Peter Keck met us. They lived not too far away. The temperature was 43 degrees. We spent two days with them and then left for Philadelphia. We spent one day with Dottie Jane and Michael, rented a U-drive and drove to Lewistown. All the Graham relatives came to see us before we returned to Philadelphia the next day. In the evening, Dottie Jane had a party for us and we saw our old friends, Jack and Mildred Heyl.

A day later, we took a plane to Asheville, North Carolina, and were met by my sisters, Velma and Maisie, and Neill's wife, Pearl. We spent two days with them at Waynesville before leaving for New York City on our way to Greece.

_____GREECE: NOVEMBER 21 TO 30

We were flying on Trans World Airlines, and our baggage was loaded on a Boeing 747 for Athens. However, when the airline learned there were not enough passengers to fill the 747, they put us on a Boeing 707 for Rome. We arrived there next afternoon at 2:30, changed planes, and finally reached Athens at 4:30. It had been a long trip, and we retired early to our room at the Amalia Hotel.

The next day we took a morning tour of Athens. I had once taken a course in Greek history, and was looking forward to seeing the ancient buildings and historic areas. Athens had been in existence since about 3000 B.C., passing through many stages of greatness and then centuries of neglect. It produced geniuses in all forms of thought and art. Socrates, Plato and Aristotle were Greek philosophers who influenced Western reasoning and civilization to this day. It was a thrill to realize that we were visiting the city where much of what we know today had actually begun.

In the afternoon we took another city tour which took us to the Acropolis where we were allowed to climb the hill and enter the Parthenon. The public is no longer allowed to enter the ruins of this famous building. We visited the Olympic stadium, which was originally built in the fourth century B.C. It had 70,000 seats. Five hundred years later, it was rebuilt with dazzling white marble. Again, it was restored in time for the revived Olympic games in 1896.

In the evening we took a tour of Piraeus, the famous port of the City of Athens. The crescent-shaped waterfront is lined by open-air cafes and restaurants. We had dinner and were entertained by Greek folk dancers and belly dancers who had been imported from Egypt. They kept us wide awake with their gyrations well past midnight. This was the first time we had seen them, but we were to see more in Egypt.

The next morning we left on an all-day boat trip on the Saronic Star to the islands of Aegina, Poros and Hydra. The sun was shining brightly and we had a beautiful trip. We left the boat for about an hour at each island and did some shopping. When our boat docked at Hydra, hundreds of cats met us at the pier for a handout of meat scraps by the crew. Cats seemed to come from everywhere.

On November 25th we took an overnight bus trip to Delphi and again stayed at an Amalia Hotel. We saw many ruins, including those of the temple of the god, Apollo. We visited a museum. This was a very restful trip and gave us a respite from all the activity we had had.

Next day, we flew to the island of Crete on a new Boeing 737. There was only one runway, and, in spite of a strong crosswind, the pilot brought the plane in for a perfect landing. We stayed at the Atlantis Hotel.

On the day we arrived we took a tour of Knossos and visited a museum. The next day, we toured Phaetos, Gortys and Triade. Archaeologists were busy unearthing facts about early Crete and its past cultures.

There was a Neolithic period that dated to 5000 B.C. The Minoan period with its highly developed civilization dates from 2600 to 1100 B.C. The Greek period then followed for over 1000 years. Since then, there were invasions by the Romans, Venitians, Turks, and others. I remember the excavations showed features of the Minoan period, including ceramic jugs for storing wine and olive oil. The homes even had a primitive sewer system.

We learned that Crete was the most fertile and richest part of Greece. Its products were mainly grapes, wine, raisins, olive oil and citrus fruits. There were 40,000,000 olive trees on the island, some of them hundreds of years old.

On the third day we returned to the airport at 9 a.m. to return to Athens. Our luggage was loaded, but the plane could not depart due to a storm in Athens that closed the airport and all harbors in the area. We waited until 6:30 that evening and returned to our hotel. The next morning we departed at 7 a.m. for the 45-minute flight to Athens, but were too late to get our transportation to Corinth. We spent the day shopping and sightseeing.

_____EGYPT: DECEMBER 1 TO 7

On December 1st we packed and flew to Cairo, Egypt. I was surprised to see revetments around the airport with fighter planes, anti-aircraft guns, and tanks in them ready for action. I had not seen such since World War II days on Maui. It was obvious they were on a war alert, which made me feel uneasy.

We received a royal welcome at the airport by the president of the meeting of the Organisation Gestosis. Dottie was assigned a female senior medical student, who would be with her throughout the meeting and attend to all her needs. I was assigned a male resident in Obstetrics, who would accompany me to all functions. We were staying at the new Cairo El Salam Hotel in the Heliopolis district near the airport. The medical meetings also were in this hotel. The center of Cairo was about 10 miles away.

The hotel had been open only four months and was very plush. The architects and builders were English. It had been built next to a slum area and had a high stone wall around it. From our third floor window, we could see what went on outside the wall on the slum side, and it was very enlightening. About sunrise, we heard the chimes coming from the Moslem mosque as the crier called the people to prayer. We would also hear the chimes at other times during the day. Soon after, large herds of goats and sheep passed with women and children following them. They seemed to be going to distant grazing areas. Later, we saw many of these animals grazing on the medial strip between the two lanes of the highway. In addition to the sheep and goats, burros with various materials on their backs or pulling carts would pass. A man accompanied each burro, urging it to move ahead.

The area beyond the wall by the hotel was very desolate with no vegetation. A multitude of children and goats roamed everywhere among hovels and makeshift dwellings. As the day went on, large trucks arrived and dumped loads of garbage near the dwellings. Women and children immediately sifted through the garbage and salvaged what was edible or usable for them. Later, goats took their turn rummaging through it. Cairo had about 10,000,000 people, so the amount of rubbish and garbage was enormous.

In late afternoon the herds of goats and sheep and the procession of donkeys that passed in the morning would return. This routine was repeated daily.

On the opposite side of the hotel, things were different. The hotel grounds had many newly planted trees and flower gardens, and a large swimming pool. Beyond the hotel grounds, there was a large race track for horse racing. There were many affluent homes in the adjoining areas.

We were happy to meet our friend, Dr. Tibor Klacansky from Bratislavia, at the meeting. We had not known that he was coming.

At the end of the first two-hour session, I gave my talk on the cause, prevention and treatment of high blood pressure during pregnancy. The good applause and many compliments I received made me feel I had done a good job.

The second day, the meeting lasted from 8 to 2 and then we had lunch, followed by a talk given by the Minister of Health. In the evening a group of us, who were designated VIPs, was taken on an escorted tour of Cairo. Dottie and I will never forget this evening. There were about a dozen doctors with their wives from all around the world. Most of them were professors and presidents of national or international obstetrical associations.

First, we were taken to the pyramids at sunset. The camels were still available for riding, but we chose not to go. As I remember, the camels were a bit ornery. The doctor leading our group tipped the guides, and we were taken inside a pyramid and also taken inside the tombs beside the pyramids. One of the guides had a small flashlight, and the other had a candle, both of which produced very little light. We crawled over the stone coffins that were filled with human bones. It was an eerie experience and we were glad to get out. We saw the Sphinx, which was nearby, lit up by moonlight and artificial lighting.

Following this, we were taken up the Tower of Cairo. It is 187 meters high, and we got a good view of Cairo at night. It was 10 p.m. Our last stop was an Oriental Cafe for dinner. 'Oriental' in Cairo has a different meaning from what it does in the United States and the Orient. As we entered, we saw pens holding live chickens. Customers would choose the fowl they wished to have cooked for their dinner. Our dinner had already been ordered. I can't remember just what it consisted of but I do remember it was highly seasoned and included a crusty bread. There was wine available, which one needed to be able to eat the food. It was midnight when we arrived back in our hotel.

I had paid for a post-convention tour to Luxor and to the Aswan Dam, including fare for hotels. However, communication with the travel agent in Cairo was so poor that I could never learn the exact dates of these tours. I guessed they would start the day following the last day of the meeting, and I made my return reservations based on this assumption. When I learned the tours started two days after the meeting closed, I refused to try to change all my plane and hotel reservations back to the United States. I did not want to get stranded in Egypt. I had already found that schedules were not adhered to and anything might happen.

I learned that a group of twelve Italian doctors and their wives were going on an escorted tour to Luxor on the third day of the meeting. They were leaving about 6 a.m. and returning at 4 p.m. One of the doctors spoke English and, when he agreed to be our interpreter, we decided to accompany them. We left from the Cairo airport on a new, wide-bodied Airbus. I remember seeing two huge General Electric jet engines, which made me feel good. As we reached about 5,000-feet, the plane turned and flew over the Nile. I got good pictures of the beautiful sight below us. The green Nile delta stretched for less than a mile on each side of the river and was lush with vegetation. Beyond the delta were the forbidding sands of the Sahara Desert.

In Luxor we watched farmers irrigating their fields, using a very primitive system. A sump-type excavation was made near the river's edge, which filled with water. The farmer would then lift water from this sump with a bucket attached to a pole. He would transfer it to furrows that carried it to the plants many yards away.

After arriving in Luxor, which in ancient times had been known as Thebes, we spent the morning exploring three tombs. These tombs were deep tunnels in the earth that led to many chambers containing the mummified bodies of kings, queens or noblemen. They originally contained many treasures of precious jewels, gold and art. When they were built, the doors had been sealed and hidden so thieves could not pilfer and rob them. The most famous tomb was that of King Tut (Pharaoh Tutankhamun) which was discovered in 1922. I was 10 years old at the time and can remember the excitement that its discovery created. King Tut ruled from 1361 to 1352 B.C. His tomb is located in an area on the West Bank of the Nile known as the Valley of Kings, across the river and two miles from Luxor. Dozens of other tombs of kings are in this area. Likewise, nearby is the Valley of Queens, containing the tombs of many queens and noblemen. In addition to King Tut's tomb, we visited the tombs of Ramses and one other.

There is no way I can adequately describe what we saw inside the tombs. The art work is unbelievable. The colors are vivid and still beautiful after more that 3300 years. Messages are conveyed by a series of paintings, which scholars are able to interpret. I think this artwork is the most outstanding thing that Dottie and I will ever see. I recommend that everyone go to Egypt and get a firsthand look, if possible. Otherwise, one could read any of the many books published about the art found in the various tombs and about the Egyptian Museum of Antiquities and its contents in Cairo.

The mummified body of King Tut still lies in an open sarcophagus in the tomb. There are two coffins - one wooden and another made of 450 pounds of gold. A face mask with a long beard is made of gold-plated metal and the eyes are wide open and appear very real.

We spent the afternoon until 4 exploring the East Bank in Luxor, visiting the Temple of Luxor and the three Karnak Temples. Again, I was bewildered by what I saw. There were many tall stone columns and other massive stone carvings, the likes of which we had never seen before.

We all gathered at the Etap Hotel in Luxor as instructed and expected to go to the airport for our flight back to Cairo. The tour guide then explained that the plane would not come for us because of mechanical trouble and that we would have to spend the night in the hotel. We were given free lodging and food, but none of us were prepared to spend the night. The hotel was a new, beautifully decorated French hotel just across the street from the Nile. In the late afternoon, Dottie and I did some shopping. We bought a five-inch, hand-carved ivory bust of an ancient Egyptian man from a vendor who was working on the sidewalk.

The next day at noon, our plane finally came for us, and we arrived back in our hotel in Cairo at 2. The scientific meeting was in its last session and we doctors who had been on the Luxor tour were embarrassed because we had missed so much of the meeting. One could not depend upon the Egyptian Tourist Bureau.

In the evening we went to the official banquet of the meeting, held in a tent on the desert by the pyramids. There were low tables, seats, and gorgeous, hand-woven wool rugs on the ground. Great fanfare accompanied our arrival and the master of ceremonies arrived on a prancing Arabian steed. As soon as we were served our food, we were entertained by a troupe of belly dancers. It was an exciting evening on the desert in the moonlight.

Dottie and I had one day left in Cairo. We decided not to see the Aswan Dam and lost our hotel deposit and the air fare. We used the day to tour Cairo in a taxi and also went to see the Museum of Antiquities. Our taxi took us to a village about 10 miles outside Cairo, where we bought a beautiful hand-woven rug suitable for a wall hanging. We paid only half the price that the same rug was sold for in the hotel gift shop. The children in the village threatened the taxi driver, and he had to bribe them so that they would not damage his car. We left in a hurry.

On December 7th we reported to the airport in early afternoon. Our Trans World Airlines plane had come from Tanzania and had passengers on board whose countries did not have diplomatic relations with Egypt. They were not allowed out of the plane. We took off at 4:30 and stopped in Athens for refueling. We arrived in Copenhagen, Denmark, at 9:30 and spent the night in a hotel. The temperature was below freezing.

The next day we departed from Copenhagen at 1 p.m. There was snow on the roofs. We arrived in New York City at 3 p.m., where it was raining and the temperature was 56 degrees. After a night at an airport hotel we were back in the air at 8 next morning and soon arrived in Chicago. Our Honolulu plane was two hours late, which meant that we missed our Maui flight at 5 p.m. After visiting with Ann and Michael in Honolulu, we finally reached Maui at 7:30 p.m., exhausted. It took us 30 minutes to get a taxi, as there were none at the terminal. We were happy to be home from Egypt, though we had had a wonderful trip.

_____*THE YEAR 1978 CONTINUED*

I think the following could only happen in Hawaii. When our electric bill doubled in one month, I called Maui Electric Company, and they promised to send someone to investigate. About this same time, we noticed that the white ginger in the garden by our entrance had begun to bloom for the first time. I found that the soil by the ginger was wet and, when I dug down six inches, the soil was warm. Digging a bit deeper, I found a hole in the hot water pipe, from which water flowed continuously. The pipe was repaired, and our electric bill returned to normal. Maui Electric

Company then credited our bill for $76.54.

The Maui Medical Group had its Christmas party, at which I was given $200 cash and round trip tickets for Dottie and me to go to Kauai for golf. I had resigned as a regular member and would work part-time only for six more months. By then I would be 67 years old.

We bought a large Sylvania television for our Christmas present. It has been repaired and adjusted three times in ten years. The dealer has told me twice that I should discard it and buy a new one, while the technician who repaired it said there was nothing seriously wrong, and he fixed it for a few dollars. It is used every day and functions like a new one, including the VCR attachment. It is instances like this that have taught me to be wary of merchants and to use my own judgement.

THE YEAR 1979

This year seemed to be almost a repetition of previous years. I worked in the office for five half-days weekly until the end of June. I was not making a lot of money, but I was able to contribute to my Keogh plan. The tax-deferred status of part of this income would help with my retirement.

At the end of January I applied to give a talk at the meeting of the International Federation of Obstetrics and Gynecology, taking place in Tokyo in October. My application was accepted. In addition to my talk on the cause of high blood pressure during pregnancy, I was appointed chairman of a two-hour session of the meeting.

After giving a post-graduate course in Lahaina, Drs. Frederick Zuspan, E.J. Quilligan, and A.C. Turnbull (of Oxford, England) had lunch with Dottie and me at the Maui Country Club. We were supposed to play golf afterward, but Dr. Zuspan had to leave early because of the death of his father in Ohio. I discussed my monographs with all three doctors. Dr. Zuspan offered to give serious consideration to a paper that I would write on the same subject, to be published in the American Journal of O.B.-Gyn., of which he was an editor. I wrote a new paper, but it was rejected just as several of my previous papers had been. I sent it to two other obstetrical journals, who likewise rejected it. This discouraged me, but I did not give up in my efforts to try to explain the exact pathophysiology of hypertension during pregnancy.

It rained five inches on February 10th. The mountain we live on ascends at a 30 percent grade. When there is this much rain, the whole mountainside becomes a river. Fortunately, there are ditches to divert the cascading water to the sides of our property.

Dottie and I went to Kauai for golf and stayed with our friends, the Blankenships. It rained the entire four days we were there, and we never were able to play golf. Instead, we had a cribbage tournament every day.

On March 13th, a final peace agreement between Israel and Egypt was announced, an accord that is still recognized at the time of this writing. It had been accomplished with the help of President Jimmy Carter at Camp David, near Washington, D.C. Suddenly President Answar Sadat of Egypt had become a world figure and later would be assassinated because of his action. He won the Nobel Peace Prize that year.

On June 29th, the Maui Medical Group had a party to honor me upon my retirement. I was the oldest member and the first to retire. The nurses had prepared a nice memory book for me, and I received several presents. On July 1st I announced at the family-sharing-time in our church that this was the first day of my retirement. I had practiced medicine for 43 years, over 38 of them on Maui.

Michael McGovern II, age nine, arrived for a five-day visit. We installed several new irrigation lines in the yard and did other jobs around the yard. I paid him well for his work.

On August 17th, our 41st wedding anniversary, I gave Dottie 13 long-stemmed red roses. The next day, which was Saturday, I took her out for an anniversary dinner.

Merrill Carlsmith was my partner again in the Member-Guest Golf Tournament at the Maui Country Club over the Labor Day weekend. We made 67 net on the low ball each day, which was not good enough to win anything. He and his wife were very sociable people and it was an honor to have them as our guests. He had had a minor stroke, so his golf was not any better than mine.

I played in the Doctor-Druggist-Dentist Golf Tournament, sponsored by the drug companies. The participants paid reduced fees for playing and for dinner. Many nice prizes were donated by the drug companies and drug stores and I won two of them, one for being nearest to the pin on a par three hole.

Our mayor resigned and we had a special election to replace him. Mayor Hannibal Tavares, a native Mauian and a Republican, won and is still in office nine years later. There is only one other Republican in our local county government.

CHAPTER XXV

Tour of Japan: October 23 to November 8, 1979

We left home before 8 a.m. and saw Ann at the Honolulu Airport. We had chosen to fly on Japan Airlines because we wanted to learn as much about Japan as possible on this trip. Although we had lived with Japanese people in Hawaii for 40 years, we knew little about the real Japan. We departed Honolulu just before noon and arrived at Narito Airport at 2 p.m. the next day, after a flight of about 10 hours. Two hours later we reached our hotel in Tokyo.

We were in Tokyo to attend the meeting of the International Federation of Obstetrics and Gynecology. We had been assigned to the New Japan Hotel by the meeting's organizing committee, though we had asked to be in the New Otani Hotel where the medical meeting was held.

We attended the opening ceremonies of the meeting on the 25th, and everything was fabulous. Many dignitaries gave greetings, including Crown Prince Akihito. Following a short intermission, the NHK Philharmonic Orchestra gave a beautiful concert entitled, "The Planets," by Holst, featuring special lighting effects. After the concert there was a reception at the Keio Plaza Hotel. We had been transported to the concert hall and then to the reception in large buses. As I recall, there were more than 3,000 visiting doctors and spouses from around the world. Our host was well-prepared, and the large numbers of people were cared for without a flaw.

The reception was most exceptional. Food was served, buffet style, on three floors of the hotel, connected by escalators. Both the halls and some adjoining rooms were used. Different types of delicious food were available on different floors. It was unbelievable how easily this mass of humanity was fed. It was obvious to visitors from this first day that this was going to be an outstanding, enjoyable meeting for all attending.

The scientific sessions started early the next day, which was Friday, and I attended all day. This was an enormous meeting, and one had to choose the lectures of greatest interest. For example, on Friday, there were 32 continuous lectures in 11 separate halls.

My former classmate at the University of Pennsylvania, Dr. Saburo Kitamura, invited us to dinner at the Japanese-American Club along with Dr. and Mrs. Yuki Nakaizumi. Dr. Kitamura was committed to go to Australia the next day as physician for a girl's swim team, so he had arranged for Dr. Nakaizumi to entertain us while we were in Tokyo. Dr. Nakaizumi owned a four-story medical building in the Ginza district. He was a fourth-generation ophthalmologist. His grandfather had created the Nishihara Eye Chart, which is in common usage world-wide to determine colorblindness. I had used it for years while doing physical examinations. The third floor of the building was a medical library, open to all doctors. In a safe in the library were several books on the eye, dating back to the 15th century, containing beautiful, anatomically correct drawings of the eye. The pages were worn and very fragile. Obstetricians and gynecologists also had offices in the building.

It was interesting to talk with Dr. Nakaizumi about the war years in Tokyo. He was 12 years old when the war ended. He said the contents of the medical library had been moved to Kyoto for safe keeping during the war. His building was one block from the tall (20 stories) Canon Camera building, located on a main street in the Ginza district. The building had a large sign on top which we used as a landmark when we were in the area. He said at the war's end, he could stand at this area and could not see a building in any direction. They had all been destroyed by American bombs. Now there are many skyscrapers and so many people that one could barely walk on the sidewalks.

Following the lectures the following morning, Dottie and I went shopping in the Ginza district in the afternoon. The weather was beautiful with a temperature of 72 degrees.

In the evening we attended a Japan Night held in the Fumonkan Concert Hall. As described by our host, it was a full ensemble of traditional, classical art performances and folk dances as well as traditional melodies by a modern orchestra.

The program was divided into three parts. The first part consisted of a rhapsody by the NHK Orchestra; a lantern dance with hundreds of lanterns; war drums with an unusual beat, apparently of a religious nature; koto music; and a deer dance in which the participants wore deer antlers on their heads.

The second part was a dance, Sagi-Musume (Heron Girl), a most unusual art form that we had never seen before. A man made up as a girl and wearing a kimono, headdress and face paint performed a very graceful dance. It brought a great applause from the audience.

The third part consisted of four dances by two dance groups who were from other prefectures. One dance was the umbrella dance of Inaba and, another, the Awa dance. We were late arriving back at our hotel, but had had a wonderful evening. Again, just as in the opening ceremonies, our host had entertained us in the greatest style. There is no way to describe it better than to say it was excellent and exactly what we foreigners wanted to see.

There were no scientific meetings on Sunday, so we took a 12-hour tour to Nikko. However, heavy traffic slowed the trip so by the time we reached Nikko, it was almost dark and time to return to Tokyo. We did see the beautiful shrines and took pictures of them. We also saw the stables of the sacred horses with the carvings of the three monkeys above the doors: hear no evil, see no evil, say no evil. It was autumn and the leaves of the trees were changing color, creating beautiful scenery.

On Monday afternoon I gave my lecture, entitled, "How Exhaustion and Other Stresses in the First Half of Pregnancy Produce Preeclampsia in the Second Half." In this two-hour session, 10 speakers from eight countries gave short lectures. My talk involved steroid hormone metabolism in the fetus and was well-received. The next day, Dr. Konbai Den of Tokyo gave a lecture on steroid metabolism in the fetus, and we exchanged information on this subject. I found his work more advanced than any I had read in the medical literature. We became friends and continue to communicate.

Dr. and Mrs. Nakaizumi took us to a fabulous, American-style dinner at the Imperial Hotel on Monday evening. I still remember the delicious roast beef. Our Japanese hosts always took us to restaurants where the food was prepared in the American style although we would have preferred more Japanese food.

After dinner the Nakaizumis took us to their home, which was not far. By American standards, it would have been considered a modest house with a little yard and barely enough room to park their car. The house was furnished with standard, Western-style furniture with no Oriental features. They were proud to have this type of furnishings and seemed to be striving to get away from everything Oriental. We met their daughter and son, who later graduated from medical school.

On Tuesday morning I heard a lecture by Dr. Diczfalusy, of Sweden, and later talked with him. I had met him previously in Stockholm and had discussed my research with him. In the afternoon Dottie and I took a city tour and saw the Imperial Palace, which had been carefully avoided by American bombers during the war. It was amazing that a city could recover after the war as Tokyo had.

I served as chairman of a session on Wednesday, October 31, which was the last day of the meeting. A young doctor, Dr. Masaki Imoto of the Kanazawa Medical School, gave a talk prompted by his professor, Dr. E. Nishida. After the session I told them we would be visiting Kanazawa on a post-convention tour. Dr. Imoto said he would meet our bus and entertain us while we were there.

Dottie and I took two post-convention tours. The first started on November 1st from Tokyo and ended in Kyoto five days later. The second started on November 6th in Kyoto, went to Hiroshima and Miyajima, and then returned to Kyoto within three days.

We boarded the famous bullet train in Tokyo. Our guide knew exactly where to stand on the platform to board the train near our reserved seats. In less than a minute the train was off at speeds of over 100 miles per hour. In two hours we were in Nagoya, over 200 miles away, though we had stopped several times. A retinue of waiters walked the aisles of the cars with food and drink and we were served a box lunch during our ride to Nagoya.

We boarded a tour bus and drove to Seki, where we watched a sword maker transform a steel rod into a beautiful samurai sword. These sword makers are now considered National Treasures. En route to Gifu we passed fishermen using cormorants to catch fish. A ring around the neck of the pelican-like seabird prevented it from swallowing the fish. The fishermen pulled the bird in by a tether, removed the fish from the cormorant's mouth, and then let it return to the water to catch another. We spent the night in the Nagaragawa Hotel.

From Gifu we went by train to Takayama and stayed at the Green Hotel. In Takayama we visited a manor house of the Edo period, a Folklore museum, and an old restored house of an earlier period.

The next day we left for Kanazawa by motorcoach and arrived at noon. It is located in beautiful mountainous terrain, known as the Japan Alps. Dr. Imoto and his wife met us as promised, and took us to a famous tea house for lunch. Just the four of us occupied the tea house, in addition to the waiters, and we sat on floor mats by a low table, as is customary. We were served raw, sweet shrimp, wild mushrooms and other delicacies we had never eaten before. Afterward, we were given a beautiful ceramic vase which Dottie displays in her room.

After lunch, Mrs. Imoto excused herself and took a taxi home to nurse her young baby. Professor Nishida then joined us and took us on a tour of the famous Kenrokuen Japanese Gardens. These had been nominated as one of the three most famous gardens in Japan. We also visited a shrine and then went to an auditorium to hear a concert of Indian music. Dr. Nishida was a tall, stately person who carried an umbrella on his arm and was the typical professor, full of knowledge and wisdom. He was happy to entertain us and we appreciated sharing an afternoon of his valuable time.

The next morning we boarded the train for Kyoto and arrived in early afternoon. We toured Sanjusangendo Temple, which housed 3,000 man-sized, bronze images of Buddha, and also visited several shrines. My friend in Tokyo, Dr. Kitamura, had arranged with a Miss Ueno for us to visit the Katsura Imperial Vilage. We called her and received the official tickets. When we visited the village there was slight rain, and the clouds drifting low over the trees produced scenes very similar to those we had seen in paintings.

We spent two nights in the Kyoto Hotel and prepared for our three-day tour to Hiroshima. We could not take our luggage, so I had to buy a small suitcase for this trip. As we were not returning to the Kyoto Hotel, but would end up at another hotel some distance away, the tour director offered to transfer our luggage to our new hotel while we were away and assured us it would be waiting for us upon our return. It was there and was intact.

On November 6th we caught the bullet train from Kyoto to Hiroshima. We took a tour of the city and saw a four-story stone building with a domed roof that had been only partially destroyed by the atomic bomb. All other buildings had been totally destroyed, and now they had been rebuilt. We saw the monument to a brave, 10-year old girl who had died of leukemia. She had attempted to make 1,000 paper cranes, believing she would survive if she succeeded. She lacked more than 100 when she succumbed. We toured the Peace Memorial building and saw the large mound of earth containing the remains of thousands of unknown dead. This humbling sight made one pray that it would never happen again.

Next morning we took a hydrofoil boat trip through the Japanese Inland Sea. There were extensive shipbuilding yards in the Japanese Sea where the Japanese naval ships had been built before World War II. There were many interesting islands and shrines, and large oyster farms near the water's edge, where cultured pearls were grown. We disembarked at Mihara and took a bullet train back to Kyoto.

Next day we went shopping in the morning and took a bus to Osaka in the afternoon. Our plane left at 8 p.m. for Honolulu. We were again on Japan Airlines and were given seats in first class which helped make the six and a half hour flight seem very short. We were on Maui at 9 a.m., our long-awaited Japan trip now over. Forty years had passed since we came to Hawaii and learned about Japan and the Japanese people. Many changes had occurred since the war with Japan.

THE YEAR 1979 CONTINUED

The World Health Organization knew of my research through my monographs published by the Organisation Gestosis-Press. A letter from them asked me to help get the Organisation Gestosis and the International Federation of Obstetrics and Gynecology (F.I.G.O.) to join forces. Their goals were the same and it seemed that there was a duplication of efforts. I wrote Dr. Rippmann, secretary-general of the Organisation Gestosis, and made suggestions. I doubt there will be a merger. The Organisation Gestosis meets annually, with the meetings on alternate years being held in Europe. F.I.G.O. has very large meetings every third year in cities around the world. I have attended meetings in Moscow, Mexico City and Tokyo, and was on the program at the latter two. I attended meetings of the Organisation Gestosis and gave papers in Prague, Cairo, Vienna, Japan and Spain. I think both organizations are worthwhile and are contributing to the welfare of women and each new generation of newborns.

We had a solar water heater installed in December. The cost of $3,000 was tax deductible and, after a few months, I was able to show a 10 percent return on our investment. At the time of this writing, we have had it 10 years and there have been no problems. On a cloudless day in January, 1980, the water from the solar heater was 183 degrees.

At the Maui County Medical Society's Christmas party, I received a plaque honoring me for my 38 years of service, including president, past president, councilor and delegate to the Hawaii Medical Association and chairman of the program for most of those years. I had also served in other capacities. Later I was elected an honorary member of the Hawaii State Medical Society, the American Medical Association, and the American College of Obstetricians and Gynecologists. I appreciate the respect of my fellow practitioners now that I have retired, and also appreciate the respect of my former patients and the newborns that I delivered, who are now scattered around these United States. I frequently see some of my former patients in the supermarket and many individuals whom I delivered.

Dottie and I spent four days with Ann and Michael II in Honolulu at Christmas and saw Michael baptized by the Reverend Abraham Akaka at the Kawaiahao Church.

THE YEAR 1980

The year started with a beautiful, warm day, though the temperature was 56 degrees at 6 a.m. We were invited to the Britt's for the afternoon and dinner. Our host was from Fayetteville, North Carolina, only 30 miles from where I was reared. His family's custom was to eat cornbread and blackeyed peas on New Year's Day and he continued this custom in his own family and always invited his friends. In my youth and before the days of electrical refrigeration, cornbread and blackeyed peas formed a large part of the diet of many rural people in the South. Both corn meal and peas could be stored through the winter without refrigeration when other food might not be available.

On January 3rd, Dr. Yuki Nakaizumi, with a group of six from Tokyo, arrived on Maui and spent the day with us. We asked what they would like to see and they said that in Japan, the Sugar Cane Train in Lahaina was very popular, so they would like to ride it. First we stopped at the Maui Coral Factory, where black and pink coral are designed into jewelry. They spent $3,000 in about 30 minutes. Then we took them to Lahaina, and they rode the train. Dottie and I met them at the terminal at the distant end (three miles) and took them sightseeing in Lahaina. We returned home and had a fabulous lunch, as Dottie is known to prepare. We invited some of our local Japanese friends who talked to our guests in their native tongue.

In the afternoon we drove to the Kula area, but did not have time to go up Haleakala. They left for Honolulu on a 5 p.m. plane and were back in Tokyo three days later. Dr. Nakaizumi brought me the customary gift, a Canon camera, which still functions perfectly.

On January 5th President Carter announced a very stiff policy against the Russian invasion of Afghanistan. At the time, I was very interested in our government's attitude towards this invasion. Now, eight years later, it has paid off, and the Russians are withdrawing.

We had a severe storm which lasted four days, starting on January 7th. Strong winds with some rain was followed by over three inches of rain on the 8th, over six inches on the 9th, and over six inches on the 10th. The rain gauges overflowed after six inches. We lost 20 banana trees. Many other trees and a lot of trash from the forest fell into our yard. The electricity and water supply were out for 20 hours at one time.

On January 15th I strained my knee doing yardwork, and the orthopedist prescribed a Depuy splint for two weeks. I was fine afterward, but doomed to need the splint again in a year.

The U.S.A. hockey team beat the Russians in the Winter Olympics, and two days later beat Finland to win the gold medal. This was the first time we had ever beaten Russia in hockey. Another American, Eric Heiden, won five gold medals in speed skating.

On February 27th I had a 28 hand in cribbage - my one and only. I have never had a 29 hand.

Dottie and I owned one-half of Ann's condominium at Haiku Woods and Ann owned the other half. The development had gone sour after eight years due to poor planning, improper construction and severe termite infestation. The homeowners' group sued everyone concerned with planning, construction and financing the 83-unit project. A settlement of 2.3 million dollars was agreed upon but this was not enough for repairs. When we were assessed $40,000 to complete the restoration project we put it on the market and finally got all our equity out. I think there are more problems in store for that condominium development.

An aborted attempt to rescue our hostages from Iran on April 24th and 25th left several of our troops dead when one of the rescue planes burned. All America was saddened. Three days later Secretary of State, Cyrus Vance, resigned.

CHAPTER XXVI

The Grand Patterson Reunion, Sanford, N.C: July 20, 1980

There had been talk of a Patterson reunion for years. Finally, O.F. Jr. and Sally Patterson agreed to have it at their home near Sanford on Sunday, July 20th. All the relatives on both the Patterson and Fuquay sides of the family were invited along with a few special friends. Many of the relatives still lived near Sanford or Broadway, N.C., where the two families had originated.

Dottie and I had not visited Dottie Jane or Carol for two years, nor had we visited our relatives in Pennsylvania and North Carolina. We decided to see all our relatives and close friends on the east coast, and end our trip in North Carolina with the big reunion. We left Honolulu on the evening of July 2nd and arrived at Rochester, N.Y., at 9:30 a.m. the next day. Neff and Jane Graham lived nearby at Lake Canandaigua and met us. After sleeping all afternoon, I felt fine. We spent three days with them, during which time our niece, Nancy, and her husband, John Griebling, visited. Also, Jean and Steve Graham, our niece and nephew, came to see us.

We continued on to Islip, Long Island, near Stonybrook, where the Brookhaven National Laboratory was located. Pete Keck was doing postdoctoral work there. I took Pete 25 volumes of "Vitamins and Hormones" I had packed in our old fiberglass American Tourister bag. It was very heavy. I still remember the look on the faces of the airline baggage handlers - especially the girls - when they tried to lift this bag .

Carol drove us around Long Island the next day. Her four-year-old twin boys were with us and got very tired. Along the highway, we watched ospreys (fish-eating eagles) in their nests feeding fish to their young. In an effort to keep the birds from building nests on the telephone poles, the phone company had built platforms on other poles. The ospreys had eventually gotten the message and used the platforms to build their nests on rather than the telephone poles. We had a delicious crab meat lunch in a popular seafood restaurant that had been built on an old, grounded barge.

The next day we flew to Philadelphia where we spent two days with Dottie Jane and her family. Timothy and Gregory were ten and nine. We took our lunch and fishing poles and spent a day by the Wissahickon Creek in Fairmount Park near their home. In the evening we went to the Bookbinders Restaurant for a lobster dinner. I had been fond of this restaurant since my medical school days.

We rented a U-drive and drove to Lewistown, Pa., where we spent four days with Dottie's sister, Helen. We visited another sister, Martha, and also some cousins. We planned to spend Saturday with a third sister, Polly, and her family at Mount Union. When we arrived we found the entire Graham Family there except for a few cousins. Neff and Jane had come as well as all of Dottie's four sisters. We had a fine reunion.

On July 14th we drove to Washingtonville to see Jean Bush and on to Danville to see Geisinger Medical Center. Dottie and I had met and courted there 42 years ago.

We spent the next day with Dottie's sister, Jo, and her husband, Tony, near Penn State University. The temperature was an uncomfortable 92 degrees.

I had promised our friends, Jack and Bennie Lightner, that we would be at their home near Round Hill, Virginia, by noon on July 16th, and that we would play golf in the afternoon. We got there at 11:40 a.m. We played at their home course, again complaining of the heat which had reached 95 degrees.

The next day we played at the Evergreen Country Club, about 20 miles away, where Jack had been manager at one time. By 11 a.m. we seemed to be the only golfers on the course. The temperature was 110 degrees and the rest of the golfers had decided it was too hot to play.

The weather cooled off during the night and was pleasant when we left the following day for Chapel Hill. We got lost en route and went through Charlottesville, Va., but it was nice to see this beautiful university town again. We arrived in Chapel Hill in late afternoon.

The guests were beginning to arrive for the big reunion which was two days away. Maisie had 20 for dinner that evening. Velma had made a beautiful flower arrangement for the table and her daughters, Peggy and Dottie, had helped with the food along with my sister, Dorothy Thornton. Luckily, Maisie had a window air-conditioner unit, which kept the temperature comfortable. The guests were all brothers and sisters, their spouses and a few of their children. I remember this as one of the nicest dinners I have ever attended, primarily because of the occasion and those present. Most of us stayed at the Carolina Inn, a short distance away.

On the following day we had brunch at Maisie's home at 11 and later went to the Carolina Inn for dinner. Maisie's sons, Pat and Tommy Parker, had arrived with their families.

Finally, the day of the reunion arrived. with a temperature of 100 degrees. Just as we were leaving Maisie's home about 9 a.m., I got a telephone call from Michael Mote. He was calling from a hospital in Port Jefferson, Long Island, New York. The Mote family had gone to Montauk, which is at the very outer end of Long Island, for a week's vacation. Dottie Jane had fallen and injured her neck, partially paralyzing her arms. The doctors were not sure how badly she had been injured. At first she was in shock, but had recovered enough in three days that the doctors said she would be allowed to go home to Philadelphia in about three more days. I told Michael that we would return to Philadelphia when she came home and then decide on a course of action. Dottie and I were upset about her injury.

We proceeded to the reunion at Sanford, about 30 miles away. Of the 100 people present, ninety-eight percent were close relatives. O.F. Jr. and Sally's home was ideal for such a gathering. A double-car garage opened onto a large yard covered with shade trees. At lunch, food was served from tables in the garage, and then the guests sat at tables about the yard to eat. Most of the guests had brought various types of food and there was plenty for everyone. Dottie and I had sent a dozen Hawaiian pineapples several days ahead.

Some notable guests were there. The matriarch of the family, Mrs. O.F. (Verl) Patterson Sr., was present. She was ill, but was able to sit in a chair inside the house and greet all the guests. I had lived with her family for eight summers during my high school and college days. She was a loving person and dear to everyone who knew her.

Rear Admiral Alex M. Patterson, U.S. Navy (Ret.), of Raleigh was present. He had written a heritage book about the Highland Scots Pattersons of North Carolina, which I referred to earlier. Dottie and I came the farthest distance, while McLeod and Louise Patterson with their son and two grandsons were from California. Richard Fuquay, a first cousin, was from Florida.

I met many of my first cousins, some of whom I had not seen for 40 years. Pearl

Patterson (Neill's widow) and several of her children attended. There were so many people present, I cannot remember just who was there. Some of them have visited us here in Hawaii, but I could not remember having seen them at the reunion.

Many children of the third generation were present. They were particularly interested in a fish pond about 200 yards away, where they used fishing poles to catch quite a few.

At the end of the day, everyone was tired. We returned to Chapel Hill for a good night's rest at the Carolina Inn. The next day I played 18 holes of golf with Pat Parker at the new Chapel Hill Country Club. Dottie and I were very worried about Dottie Jane and were anxious to get back to see her so I changed our reservations to return to Philadelphia in two days.

Dottie Jane returned home on July 23rd, and we arrived there the same afternoon. I called her doctor, Jack Heyl, and he referred her to a neurologist. Next day when he examined her, he said she might have a disc syndrome causing the partial paralysis in her arms. He chose to treat her, hoping she would improve.

Dottie and I took over the housework for a week. Dottie Jane went to see the doctor several times and had a CT scan x-ray of her neck. The diagnosis was still brachial plexus strain and physiotherapy was prescribed. She seemed to improve.

I did many odd jobs about the house, including vacuuming every rug, until I became exhausted.

I will never forget talking with Michael when we arrived in Philadelphia. He told me of his predicament and asked me how I would feel in a similar situation. They had been staying in a motel in Montauk when Dottie Jane fainted, fell, and struck her chin on the arm of a chair. She was unconcious and remained that way for over two hours. This was in the late afternoon. There was no doctor or hospital within five miles. Finally, an ambulance came, and he rode in it with her to the hospital at Port Jefferson. She remained unconcious and in shock. It was the next day before a specialist could see her, and then he could not make a diagnosis. She regained conciousness and complained of pain, paraesthesias, and partial paralysis in both arms. She was now much improved, but obviously had a major injury to her neck.

On our fourth day in Philadelphia, Michael, Tim, Gregory and I went to a baseball game at Veterans Stadium. We had a tire blowout on the freeway, but reached the stadium before game time. The Phillies beat Atlanta 17 to 4, their highest score of the year. The winning pitcher was Steve Carlton and Pete Rose got three hits.

The next day Dottie and I spent in the city. We had lunch at Wannamaker's store, heard the organ recital, and visited Gimbel's and other stores. We had lived in Philadelphia the first year of our marriage, so it was nice to be there again.

Dottie Jane's condition had stabilized after a week, and the neurologist recommended she continue her therapy. She still had severe involvement of her arms, but was able to do some housework. We returned home to Maui after being away 29 days.

_____*THE YEAR 1980 CONTINUED*

We finally bought a new indoor-outdoor carpet for our guest cottage after using our old rugs in it for 20 years. I had learned to install rugs and had put in the old ones myself. The new rug was a great improvement. The guest cottage was now completely furnished and had a new stove and refrigerator.

Merrill Carlsmith was my guest again at our Member-Guest golf Tournament at the Maui Country Club. We did not play well. He, Maxine, Dottie and I played at Kapalua on Labor Day.

Dottie Jane sent her mother a Cuisinart food processor as a thank-you present for our help during the week after her injury. We did not realize at the time that Dottie was fated to get three disc syndromes in her neck, which would leave her arms permanently partially paralyzed. Without the Cuisinart, she would have been unable to prepare meals and, while I can fix my own breakfast and lunch, I have a hard time with dinner.

WE PLAY IN THE MEMBER-GUEST GOLF TOURNAMENT AT SPYGLASS COUNTRY CLUB AT CARMEL, CA

Merrill Carlsmith was a charter member of the Spyglass Country Club at Carmel, California. He and his wife invited Dottie and me to Carmel for a week of golf, to include their member-guest tournament. We stayed at the Tally Ho Inn, in the center of Carmel, where we had a suite with two bedrooms. The first day, we played at Spyglass and had dinner at the Pebble Beach Lodge with our old Maui friend, Dr. Ian Kinnear.

The tournament then started, but we didn't play well. There were too many large pine trees along the fairways for the golf balls to hit. After the first day of the tournament, we ate dinner at Cannery Row in Carmel. The second day, we attended the banquet which was held in the clubhouse of another course about 10 miles away. The day after the tournament, we played in a mixed tournament with the ladies at Spyglass. We had dinner later at a French restaurant, the Felix. While in Carmel, we tried to get a starting time at Pebble Beach but the earliest we could get was 2:30 p.m., and the fee was $60. We played elsewhere.

After eight days in Carmel, we left for Fremont with the Carlsmiths. We stopped with Lois and John, and the Carlsmiths went on to San Francisco. During the next two days, I did many odd jobs for Lois and John, and we also drove to Mount Diablo on a sightseeing trip. We left from Oakland on the 25th, and I arrived home at 2:30 p.m., leaving Dottie in Honolulu to visit with Ann for a few days.

THE YEAR 1980 CONTINUED

On November 2nd, Iran announced it would deliver the U.S. hostages under certain conditions.

President Reagan beat incumbent President Carter for the U.S. presidency by a landslide on November 4th. This was the beginning of an eight-year term by the great communicator.

We attended the 80th birthday party of Dr. Alfred Burden on November 15th, at which his second marriage was announced. He is still living at the time of this writing, nine years later.

Ann and eleven-year-old Michael II arrived for Thanksgiving. Michael did several hours of yard work for me while he was here, for which I paid him $2 an hour.

Dottie is very fond of birds. I had ordered a special bird vase for her some weeks before Thanksgiving. Before sitting down to Thanksgiving dinner, I placed the vase on the table and carefully covered it. After several speeches I lifted the cover and presented the beautiful vase to Dottie. She liked it and appreciated the presentation, but commented that one was enough. The unveiling ceremony added a flair to a beautiful dinner.

Ann spent Christmas with us while Michael went to California to be with his father. My gift to Dottie was a digital electrical clock which would make it easy for her to determine the time during the night.

Drs. Jon and Jan Graham, our nephew and his wife, arrived at 7 a.m. on December 30th. They had come from Washington, D.C., and were with us for two days of golf. They were very happy to be here and said they would probably be back the following year. He was in training at the Walter Reed Army Hospital and she at Johns Hopkins Hospital.

CHAPTER XXVII

The Incidence of Eclampsia Shown to be Inversely Proportional to Calcium Intake

A very important discovery was made about the relationship of calcium intake to the incidence of eclampsia. Dr. Jose Belizan from the Institute of Nutrition of Central America and Panama and Dr. Jose Villar from the Johns Hopkins Hospital and I had corresponded and exchanged our publications about the cause of eclampsia and high blood pressure during pregnancy. They had a paper published in the American Journal of Nutrition in October, 1980[35], which showed that, world-wide, the incidence of eclampsia was inversely proportional to the intake of calcium. They sent me a reprint immediately and my life has not been the same since. I embarked upon a course of study at once to solve the mystery of how a calcium deficiency might produce eclampsia. I had already explained much of the pathophysiology of eclampsia in my publications. If I could show how a calcium deficiency produced the abnormal physiology, the research project that I started in 1936 would be completed.

Doctors were teaching that poor or no prenatal care and malnutrition were the main causes of eclampsia and the so-called late toxemias of pregnancy. Now, Belizan and Villar showed that in Ethiopia and Guatemala, where prenatal care often does not exist and malnutrition is rampant, the incidence of eclampsia was very low. It was lower in Guatemala than in the U.S.A. and only half as high as it was in the United Kingdom. They also showed that the calcium intake of the population of these two countries was high, primarily because they used lime (calcium hydroxide) in preparing and cooking their food. They showed that the calcium intake was a gram or more daily, almost as much as there is in a quart of milk.

The physiology of muscle cell contraction was known to require ionized calcium. Just how calcium deficiency could result in excessive contraction of the smooth muscle cells in arterial walls, producing a rise in the blood pressure, had to be elucidated. There seemed to be a paradox because, in spite of a deficient calcium intake, there was an excess of ionized calcium entering the muscle cells.

I studied all aspects of intracellular metabolism of the muscle cell, working four hours daily, seven days a week for seven months on this project. I presented a rough draft of a paper to Dr. Peter Keck, my son-in-law who is a biophysicist, for evaluation. He was able to help me clarify some parts of the problem. In the next seven years, I would write two more monographs and three medical papers, all of which were published. I gave lectures at three international meetings of the Organisation Gestosis.

THE YEAR 1981

I was excited about the new developments in my research field and continued my studies at full throttle. However, life continued, and there were many occurrences not related to my research.

On New Year's Day, we went to the Britt's as we had the year before for the afternoon and for dinner. Again, we were served the traditional cornbread and black-eyed peas.

Our yard seemed to be overrun by wild cats and mongooses. They killed many of the birds that frequented our property and especially the baby francolin partridges. I borrowed a cat trap from the Humane Society and caught a mongoose. Then I made my own trap, modeled after the one I borrowed, and within a year had caught between 30 and 40 cats and a number of mongooses. Occasionally, I caught a cat at night and a mongoose the next day. I took them to the Humane Society to be disposed of.

President Reagan was shot in the chest on March 30th in an assassination attempt by a mental patient. Luckily, he was near a hospital, where doctors were able to operate on him quickly and save his life. His condition was very critical at first and, without immediate surgery, he probably would have died.

On television, we saw the manned space ship, Columbia, take off into space April 12th and safely return to earth on the 14th. Our country was the first to accomplish this.

The Keck family of four arrived on April 18th. Peter left after six days to return to work, but Carol and the four-year old twins stayed 12 days. I took them up Haleakala, to Hana and the Seven Pools, to Lahaina, Kihei, the zoo and elswhere. I became exhausted, developed diarrhea, and spent two days in bed.

Dottie Jane's neck and partial arm paralysis had not improved after eight months of conservative treatment. Finally, she was examined by a neurosurgeon and operated on for two dislocated cervical discs. She made a good recovery and had very little residual effects from the injury.

Parts of the Island of Oahu had 20 inches of rain on May 8th, producing local flooding. Islanders must always be prepared for this type of natural occurrence.

Our Hayden mango tree was loaded with fruit this year. On many occasions, I picked 100 at a time - each weighing between 10 and 16 ounces - and gave them to friends. Frequent rains during flowering time often cause an increased fungus growth which destroys all the blooms.

I won the President's Cup at the Maui Country Club. My award was a merchandise order for $100 at the pro shop and prestige at the club. My name is engraved on a permanent plaque displayed in the clubhouse.

On July 29th Dottie and I saw the marriage of Prince and Lady Diana at St. Paul's Cathedral via television. Later, on one of our London trips, we would hear an organ recital in this cathedral.

On August 10th Dottie and I drove to Hana to visit McLeod and Louise, who were on vacation at Hotel Hana Maui. He was the doctor at Hana from 1934 through 1938, and married Louise during his last year there.

We received an announcement of the marriage of my sister, Maisie, to George Briner. He was 82 and she was 74; both were widowed. As of the time of this writing seven years later, they are enjoying a cruise on the St. Lawrence Waterway.

I played as Merill Carlsmith's guest again at the Spyglass Country Club Member-Guest Tournament in Carmel, California. Again, we did not win anything but we had fun, and later played in a special tournament with our wives. This time, we stayed in the Jim Murray home at Del Mesa. McLeod and Louise Patterson were our guests one evening for dinner at the Quail Lodge. Again, the Carlsmiths drove us to Fremont, where we stayed with Lois for three days. Lois drove us to the San Francisco Airport. We had a flat tire just before we entered the airport area, but had started from Lois's home 30 minutes early, which gave me plenty of time to put on the spare tire. We arrived on Maui via Honolulu at 3 p.m.

On November 12th, the Columbia space shuttle went into orbit for the second time and we watched its launch on television. It made an early landing at Edwards Air Force Base in California two days later after one of its three generators had given out.

Michael McGovern II, now 12, spent a week with me at Thanksgiving. I planned to build a lath house for my orchids while he was here. Since the age of three, he always wanted to hammer nails during his visits with us, and often used all my new nails. Getting ready for his visit, I prepared the foundation for the lath house and cut the timbers for the frame. On Monday and Tuesday, we put up the frame. On Wednesday, while I was playing golf, Michael put the redwood slats on the entire south side, the side that would be seen from the house. His work was almost perfect, and he was proud of it. I think he got to drive all the nails that he wanted to that day.

Ann came for Thanksgiving and we had a gourmet turkey dinner at home. Michael and I finished the lath house on Friday. When he returned home on Saturday, he had made $84 plus his air fare for his week's work.

We had heavy rains for several days, followed by strong winds. My macadamia nut tree, which was about four years old, was blown over but not damaged. I was able to restore it to its original position and kept four guy wires on it for three years, and it is now securely rooted. It is nine years old, and I harvested over 50 pounds of nuts this year (1988).

Jon and Jan Graham arrived from Washington, D.C., on December 9th for five days. Dottie and I played golf with them three times during their stay. Jon had fallen in love with Hawaii and planned to spend his three-year payback time to the Army at Tripler Army Hospital in Honolulu. He had been born at Wahiawa, but his family moved to the mainland when he was about four.

Dottie and I spent four days with Ann in Honolulu at Christmas while Michael was in California with his father. We visited many of Ann's friends and had a festive time. I gave Dottie a diamond pendant necklace for Christmas.

During the last two days of the year, I painted the lath house green, using a water-based paint sprayed on with my garden spray.

_____*THE YEAR 1982*

I had applied to the Organisation Gestosis to give a lecture at its next meeting, to be held in Vienna, Austria, December 5th to 10th. My application was accepted. I had studied the entire past year on the relationships of calcium, muscle contraction and high blood pressure. I state in my diary on January 3rd that I started rewriting a paper on the subject, which I hoped to get published.

In the meantime, my life continued the same. I planted a vegetable garden and did much of the yard work, including caring for several hundred orchid plants. I played golf with my friends on Wednesdays and Saturdays, and Dottie and I often played on Sunday after church. Once when the wind was blowing 30 to 40 miles per hour from the south, I made an eagle on Hole Number One and birdies on Number 10 and 13 at Maui Country Club. My golf had improved and, during the year, my handicap would get down to nine for the first time in my life. I made five birdies once in 18 holes.

Dr. and Mrs. Frederick Hofmeister, former president of the American College of Obstetricians and Gynecologists, visited us for 48 hours. It rained the entire time they were with us - seven inches in three days - and as soon as they left the sun shone beautifully. They did not play bridge, cribbage or any other games so we just had a talking marathon and found them to be a very amiable couple. We had a dinner party for them to meet some of our friends.

Maisie and her new, 82-year-old husband arrived for a five-day visit. They had driven across the southern part of the United States because George did not like to fly. There were severe storms along their entire route, which they tried to avoid by going further south, finally driving several hundred miles in Mexico before reaching California. They visited McLeod and Louise and left their car with them while they came to Hawaii.

I took them on the usual tours of Maui: Lahaina, Kapalua, up Haleakala and to Kihei. George had traveled considerably and had seen many things in his 82 years so I found it interesting that he was so impressed when we drove up Haleakala. We had a dinner party so they could meet some of our friends. Both of them were avid bridge players and had met at a seniors bridge club. They would have played late into the night, but Dottie and I were exhausted after about three hours. They went to the Island of Hawaii for two days to see the volcanoes and then returned to the Royal Hawaiian Hotel in Honolulu for several days.

Merrill and Maxine Carlsmith and Dottie and I went to Molokai for three days of golf and bridge. We stayed at the Sheraton Hotel and played golf at the new Kalua Koi Golf Course. The first day was very rainy and the wives would play only nine holes. The second day, Merrill and I played in the rain, but the wives refused to venture outside. The rain continued and the course was closed the third day. We played bridge until we were tired of it. When we returned home, we found there had been over three inches of rain on Maui while we were away.

Michael McGovern II spent three days with me during his Easter vacation, helping me with my yard work. On March 22nd while he was here, the Columbia spaceship made its third trip into space, and we watched the launch on television.

Dottie and I saw the last two hours of the Kemper L.P.G.A. Tournament at the Kaanapali Golf Course in Lahaina. Amy Alcott won with a score of six under par, Joanne Carner was second at minus five, and Nancy Lopez was third at minus four. Watching these professionals play was inspirational to an amateur golfer.

On April 1st we had over three inches of rain during the night, then from 1 to 3 p.m. it rained almost four inches. The gulch by our property was filled and roaring like a big river. Two large trees in the forest fell into our yard, breaking the six-inch county water line leading up to the reservoir. We were out of water for a few hours until repairmen fixed the main.

Argentina invaded the Falkland Islands on April 4th. War raged for weeks before the British droved them out. Afterward, the Argentine government changed due to mishandling of this invasion attempt.

We had 16 guests for a jarts party, followed by dinner, to celebrate our April birthdays. Most of the guests were about our ages and had some chronic ailments, some of which were aggravated by throwing the jarts. It was interesting watching Tommy Tompkins, who had been athletic director at Colorado State College for many years. Although he was old, he was very competitive and played to win, showing the attributes that had made him an athletic director.

A descendant of one of the misssionary families, who belonged to our church, gave a deacon's bench to the church. It had been made in Hilo in 1850, of beautiful, matching koa wood and contained no nails or screws. It would seat only two people and was placed in the chancel by the altar. There were three chairs on the opposite side of the chancel.

It occurred to me that there should be a matching bench opposite this deacon's bench and got permission from the minister to have this bench duplicated. I got in touch with the Wooden Stitch, a Maui company that specializes in the duplication of antique furniture, and took the proprietor to the church to see the bench. He made an exact replica, which Dottie and I donated to the church. Now there is a deacon's bench on each side of the chancel and both are used each service.

The space shuttle took off on a fourth trip on June 27th. A few months later it completed a fifth mission.

Dottie and I saw a full eclipse of the moon on July 5th, starting at 7:33 p.m. and ending at 8:33. This was also the 43rd anniversary of our arrival in Hawaii.

I saw the All-Star baseball game on television on July 13th, which was won by the National League. My favorite pitcher, Steve Carlton, struck out four in the two innings he pitched.

We had dinner with Dr. Andrew's family to meet Governor Ariyoshi who arrived with bodyguards. He was very personable and appeared different in person than he did on television.

I received an invitation to give a medical paper in Halle, East Germany. Although the offer included all my expenses except transportation, I had to decline as I had already agreed to give a paper in Vienna, Austria, in December. I met Dr. Woraschk, who had extended the invitation, at the meeting in Vienna. We had to converse through an interpreter.

The battery in my car finally wore out after 86 months. The replacement lasted only 8 months, though it had a four-year warrranty.

We had dinner with Dr. and Mrs. Tom Whaley of Zimbabwe (formerly Rhodesia), whose daughter had married a Maui boy. They were of British descent, but had been born and reared in Rhodesia. Later, we met his brother, Senator Sam Whaley of Zimbabwe.

Three professors from West Germany had taken a postgraduate course in Lahaina, and asked to have a conference with me about my research. Dr. H. Kaulhausen, Dr. T.H. Lippert and Dr. P. Brockerhoff came to our home for a two-hour discussion. I met Dr. Kaulhausen again at the medical meeting in Vienna in December.

On November 11th, Leonid Breshnev's death 24 hours before was announced. He was the commissar of the U.S.S.R.

CHAPTER XXVIII

I Write a Monograph Explaining How Calcium Deficiency Leads to High Blood Pressure

I continued my studies three to four hours daily. New medical information in my field was continually appearing in the medical literature and I correlated the new material with what I already knew about the pathophysiology of high blood pressure and pregnancy. By the end of March, I had written a manuscript entitled, "How Malnutrition, Primarily of Calcium, and/or Stress lead to Edema-, Proteinuria-, and Hypertension-Gestosis, an Hypothesis." I sent it to the American Journal of Clinical Nutrition that had published Belizan and Villar's paper on calcium deficiency as a cause of high blood pressure in pregnancy. The editor of this journal returned the manuscript without having it reviewed, saying it was not suitable for the journal.

By this time, I was tired of rejections. I felt secure that I was on the right track to explain the cause of high blood pressure during pregnancy. I decided to submit my manuscript to the Organisation Gestosis-Press to see if it would be accepted as a monograph, and it was. They received it in early May.

On August 11th, I received a letter from Dr. Rippmann that had been mailed on May 29th, notifying me that the Organisation Gestosis-Press would publish my monograph provided that I bought the usual number of copies to help defray the cost of publication. The letter had taken over 10 weeks to arrive by fourth-class mail. First-class mail usually arrived from Switzerland in 10 days. At 10 p.m. on the day the letter arrived, I telephoned Dr. Rippmann in Basel and told him to proceed with publishing my monograph. It was about midmorning there. The next day, I mailed him a check for $1500 to pay for 200 copies. I would distribute these to medical school libraries and special research institutions in North America, as well as to several researchers in this field. In my studies on calcium metabolism I had learned that when there is a grossly deficient calcium intake, the calcium content of the extracellular fluid that bathes the muscle cells and the nerves supplying them will be below normal. When this state exists, there is an exchange of sodium into, and potassium out of, the cell that creates an electric current (action potential). During the action potential, calcium ions enter the cell, creating an imbalance. Any minute increase above normal of the calcium content of the nerves to muscle cells, or of the muscle cells themselves, will cause spasm of the muscle cells. Spasms of the smooth muscle cells of the arterial walls lead to an elevation of blood pressure, though there are many modifying factors as I will point out. In my monograph, I explain in detail how all this comes about[36]. During pregnancy there is a great demand for calcium to form the rapidly growing fetal skeleton and for the increase in maternal metabolism by one third.

CHAPTER XXIX

Visits to the U.S. East Coast, London and Vienna: November 19 to December 14, 1982

We left Maui on November 19th and arrived in Philadelphia at 9 the next morning. Newspapers headlines told of a hurricane in Hawaii that had hit after we left. We telephoned our neighbor, Toshi Nitta, and learned that our home had no serious damage although several of our banana trees had been destroyed. There was severe damage on the Islands of Kauai and Oahu. This was only the second hurricane to hit Hawaii in 43 years.

We spent three days with Dottie Jane's family in Philadelphia, and I played golf once with Michael. We rented a U-drive and went to Lewistown, where we spent three days. We had a Graham family reunion on Thanksgiving Day at Jo and Tony Artman's home near Penn State University. All five Graham girls, brother Neff and their spouses were present. We had a gourmet dinner and a glorious time.

The temperature was 30 degrees in New York on November 27th. We drove to Kennedy Airport,spent the night in a hotel, and left for London at 10 a.m. on a British Airway plane. I chose this airline because it had the only daytime flight to London. We arrived in London at 10 p.m. By the time we went through customs and got our luggage, the buses had stopped running for the day. We went by subway and taxi to Dolphin Square Apartments, where we were staying for a week. Taking the subway was a big mistake, because we had to walk more than a mile in underground passages to reach the station. However, riding a London subway train at 11 p.m. was very interesting. We saw some weird characters, including a group of about a dozen boys and girls going to a nightclub. Their clothes did not indicate the sex of the individual, nor did their hairdos which were very unusual and colorful. I was uncomfortable in their presence.

We slept late the next morning and then visited the Tate Art Museum which was within walking distance of our apartment. We had been there on previous trips, but enjoyed it just as much this time. The paintings of many masters were on display and we were especially interested in the paintings of clouds by Turner.

In the evening we went to the new Barbican Centre to hear the London Symphony Orchestra present Berloiz's "L'Enfant du Christ." Six soloists sang with a chorus. It was the most spiritually-moving program that Dottie and I had ever heard. We went to the Barbican Centre by subway, allowing enough time so we would arrive 30 minutes early. However, when the train stopped at the second station before the Centre, we were told there would be a delay. We left the subway and took a taxi, arriving in time for the performance. The next day we read in the newspaper that the delay had been caused by the death of a child who had fallen onto the train tracks.

Dottie was unable to sleep the second night due to leg cramps, indicating that we had been too active. We rested in our apartment all the next day while I studied for my presentation in Vienna. I prepared breakfast and lunch, and we ate dinner in a French restaurant in the building.

Dottie was fine the next day. We went shopping at Fortnum and Mason's where the clerks wore red morning coats during the Christmas season. We visited the National Gallery of Art in the afternoon and saw paintings by Titan, Raphael and more clouds by Turner. Afterward, we went to the Covent Gardens for dinner and shopped in chic shops catering to the young.

We spent most of the next day, Thursday, shopping at Harrod's. It is a thrill to shop there, where one can probably see more quality merchandise than in any other store in the world. We bought a beautiful crystal decanter, which I carefully hand-carried 10,000 miles back to Maui.

When we first arrived at Dolphin Square Apartments, I checked with the ticket agent in the office about shows during our week in London, including the musical comedy, "Cats." We had read in American newspapers that this show was sold out for several months in advance. We were able to get tickets and thoroughly enjoyed this musical. All the seats in the theater were the same price, $30, and every seat offered the same view. The stage revolved. Between scenes, the lights went out and when they came on again, everything had changed.

We visited St. Paul's Cathedral, arriving in time to hear an organ recital. This is where the marriage of Prince Charles and Lady Diane had taken place. It was beautiful and more tasteful than Westminister Abbey.

We shopped in several stores in the Oxford Circle area and bought a recording of Berloiz's "L'Enfant du Christ" at His Master's Voice music shop.

In the evening we saw the play, "The Mouse Trap." It was in its 30th year of production and was delightful. We had considered seeing it on our earlier trips to London and are glad we saw it this time.

British Airways called on Saturday morning to say that our afternoon flight to New York, on December 11th, had been cancelled and that we were being put on an 11 a.m. flight. We would still be in Vienna at that time, and we were scheduled to return to London on a group flight in midafternoon. British Airways rescheduled us on an Austrian Airline flight at 8 a.m. to London, entirely at their expense. This surprised many airline agents along the way, but the airline did it to be sure we flew with them to New York.

We saw Sir Richard Harris, one of Britain's foremost actors, in "Camelot" on Saturday afternoon. This was a good way to end our vacation in London. We had been lucky to see such wonderful shows and especially to hear the London Symphony program at the new Barbican Centre. We packed and got ready to leave for Vienna early Sunday.

We left Dolphin Square Apartments at 7:30, while it was still dark. There was a light rain on the way to Heathrow Airport, the first rain we had had in London. We arrived in Vienna at 1:30 p.m. and registered at the Hilton Hotel where the medical meeting was to be held. Dr. Rippmann met me and gave me several copies of my latest monograph, which had just been published. I was very glad to get them as I could distribute some to leading researchers present at the meeting. Anyone could order a copy from Dr. Rippmann.

I was on the program the first day and was pleased at the reception my presentation received. The lecture room contained two screens for the projection of two lantern slides at the same time by an individual speaker. I had never seen this used before and found it very helpful. Of the six slides I had to show, the last three were based upon the information shown in the third slide. I was able to keep slide number three displayed on one screen and referred back to it while I discussed the other slides. I had learned by this time that, between the showing of lantern slides, it is necessary to have the auditorium lights turned on to full brightness. Otherwise, the audience tends to fall asleep.

This was the Christmas season, and I was very interested in observing the differences in the celebrations in Vienna and in the United States. The population of

Austria is almost entirely Roman Catholic. I developed a great respect for the way they celebrate the season. The four Sundays before Christmas make up the Advent season, which means the coming of Christ. To them, this season is a holy time, and they respect it. As one walked about the streets, some Christmas decorations were seen, but there was no garish display of flashing lights as is seen in the cities of the United States. Near the entrance of each store or restaurant, an Advent wreath with candles was usually seen in a display area. Each store had a counter with Christmas specialties, gifts, decorations, etc., and this counter itself was decorated just as it would be in America. However, this was the only Christmas display in the store.

Our church on Maui (Congregational) also has an Advent wreath with four candles. Only one candle is lit each Sunday during the season until all four are burning. A fifth is lit on Christmas.

During the entire Advent season, there is religious music available every evening in Vienna, in a concert hall, church or auditorium. One can ask at any hotel or tourist bureau office and learn where to go to hear this music, which is always superb. On our second evening, we went to a concert at Votivkirche (church). The temperature was below freezing, and our lightweight coats were not enough to keep us warm. There was no general heating in the large church, but there were heaters under the seats, which eventually helped warm us. It was so cold, one could see the condensation of the moisture in the conductor's breath. To get home, we had to walk about a block to a taxi stand and wait for a passing taxi. By the time we arrived at our hotel, Dottie could barely walk because of her leg problems. However, we agreed that the concert of Bach's music was worth all the trouble.

On our second day I attended meetings all morning, then Dottie and I went shopping in the fabulous walking street area. These are malls where cars are not allowed. We bought Dottie a beautiful Petite Point purse, which she uses often, and pastries from the bakery at the Sacher Hotel. We had lunch in a second-floor restuarant overlooking the walking street.

The next afternoon, we visited the St. Stephens Cathedral, a picture of which we have on our breakfast room wall at home. On our previous trip to Vienna, we stayed at the Stephenplatz Hotel, across the street from the Cathedral.

In the evening, we heard a beautiful program of Bach music at the Concert Hall, featuring four outstanding flute and harpist soloists.

The following day, Dottie rested while I attended meetings in the morning and afternoon. At 7 we went to see the opera, "Pique Dame" (Queen of Spades). It lasted over three hours, and we liked it very much. The singing was excellent.

On the next to the last day of the meeting, I attended sessions all morning. In the afternoon we took a tour through the Vienna Woods and to Baden and Mayerling. We visited a cathedral, which had beautiful glass windows and wooden hand carvings of Christ's life.

We had invited Drs. Tibor and Elena Klacansky from Bratislavia to visit us while we were in Vienna, but we doubted they would be allowed to do so. He had just returned from a meeting in India and thought the Czech authorities would not permit another trip so soon. However, they were allowed to come and stayed with friends in Vienna. Dottie and I entertained them at dinner in the grand dining room of the Hilton Hotel. We had a wonderful time, and we were so happy we could return some of the kindness they had shown us.

On the last day of the meeting, Friday, December 10th, I attended lectures most all day. I asked for and received permission to take Tibor and Elena to the official banquet in the evening. First we went to an Advent concert at the Augustiner Church and then to the banquet at the nearby Palais Pallavicini, the very opulent town palace of a former ruler. We were seated at tables for 10. All the furnishings, dishes, silverware, etc. were regal. The waiters wore long formal coats. The ladies were dressed in evening wear. Many courses of delicious food were served, all fit for a king. This was probably the most elegant meal Dottie and I had ever had.

Tibor and Elena thoroughly enjoyed themselves. They lived only 40 miles from Vienna, but after World War II they were not allowed to visit often. They saw many of their old friends and medical acquaintances.

We were up early next day and left Vienna at 8 a.m. on Austrian Airlines. At 9 we flew by the Parliament building in London in bright sunlight. Our flight to New York was routed further north than usual to avoid bad weather and took seven hours and 40 minutes. We flew over Iceland and Greenland. The captain announced that it was snowing at Kennedy Airport, but when we arrived there were only scattered patches of snow between the runways. We spent the night in a hotel at the airport.

When we looked out the window next morning, all we could see was snow. It was falling in great sheets, and the ground was covered. When a car drove around the hotel, its tracks were obliterated with new snow in a few minutes.

Pete Keck drove from Setauket, Long Island, to get us that morning. We were soon on the road returning to their home but it took two hours to drive the 40 miles. There were four inches of new snow on the road and more following. Snow plows had not yet started removing it. Pete had to guess where the road was by the banks on the sides and the utility poles. As I recall, there were also extra marker poles along the highway to show drivers where to go. This was the first time we Hawaiians had driven through a snow storm since 1947.

We spent two days with Carol, Pete, and Adam and Todd, their five-year old identical twins. The temperature was 24 degrees in the sunshine in midafternoon, but dropped to 10 degrees by 9 p.m. We enjoyed the snow and cold, but obviously this was no place for Hawaiians.

The second morning we were up early and left for La Guardia Airport. The snow had been cleared from the highways, and we had no problem reaching there in two hours. All our planes left on time, and we slept in our own bed on Maui that night. We saw Ann and Michael II at the Honolulu Airport.

THE YEAR 1982 CONTINUED

We found much evidence of the hurricane in our yard when we returned home. Trash from the surrounding forest was everywhere and several large eucalyptus trees near our property had been blown over. Many banana trees, some with yellow fruit, had been destroyed. I was busy for days giving away bananas and cleaning the yard. Although the hurricane had not hit Maui, strong winds accompanying it had.

Nancy Welch, my niece, arrived from Australia with her five-year old son. She had spent a year there teaching school and was returning home to Denver, Colorado. Ann and Michael also arrived for Christmas so we had a very nice holiday with two children to help us celebrate. All four visitors left the day after Christmas.

CHAPTER XXX

I Fell Off a Wall, But Unlike Humpty Dumpty, The Doctor Was Able to Put Me Together Again

The 1983 New Year began as usual. While Dottie could not sleep because of the noise of the neighbor's firecrackers, thanks to my ear plugs I was not awakened by the clatter.

The next day was Sunday. After church I felt rested and decided to cut the hedge at the edge of our property. Our neighbor had graded the earth in his backyard 20 feet and had built a stone wall to support the soil on our side. I walked along the space - about two feet - between the wall and our hedge, trimming as I moved along. Finished, I started walking behind the hedge to reach our backyard and noticed a clump of tall grass that I had missed. I needed to change the angle of the weed cutter to reach it. I was hot and tired. The weed cutter was running full throttle. Unconsciously, I stepped to the right to reach the clump of grass. With that step, I went off the wall into space and fell 20 feet to the ground below. I remember holding on to the weed cutter firmly with both hands. It seemed to take me a long time to reach the ground, all the while I was envisioning that I would break a leg, arm, hip, or injure myself otherwise. Luckily, I fell beside some banana plants which had been irrigated earlier in the day. The soil was wet and moderately soft.

As I fell, I remained upright. I was wearing good, high-top, leather working shoes that were tightly laced. My feet struck the ground first and my left knee buckled. Then, my left buttock struck the ground. Finally, the weed cutter hit the ground horizontally with me still holding on to it.

I was somewhat shocked by the fall and realized that I must have broken some bones. The weed cutter and I, including my shoes and clothes, weighed well over 200 pounds. I was surely falling at a high speed when I struck the ground.

My neighbor owned two pit bulldogs - a male and a female. The male was secured on a leash, while the female was free to roam in the yard. When she occasionally came into our yard, I would scold her to go home. She was not vicious, supposedly, and we had had only friendly confrontations. After I fell into her yard she came over and licked my face, went away and then returned. I was out of reach of the male, though I think we were friends also.

I rested for a while after I fell, trying to regain my composure. I had severe pain in the middle of my back and tried to find a comfortable position. I leaned against the wall in a sitting position, but the pain in my back continued.

I was more comfortable lying flat. I examined my extremities and could not find any evidence of broken bones. My left knee was painful, but otherwise I had no pain or limitation of motion in my arms and legs.

My neighbor was not home. Dottie was in our library, about 100 yards away and 40 feet above where I lay. I recovered from the initial shock in about 15 minutes. I decided I would try standing and walk up the hill to our house in spite of the severe pain in the middle of my back.

I got up and took the weed cutter in my hands. The engine had stalled when it hit the ground. As I began walking, I noticed my left knee was flail and I had to be careful not to twist it. After I emerged from our neighbor's yard, I sat on the stone wall by our drive to rest. I still had to walk up the hill, which rose 44 feet from where

I was sitting. After a short rest, I was able to continue until I entered our home. My back hurt severely, and I felt sure that I had a compression fracture of a vertebra. I had treated several of these when I worked for the sugar plantations and knew my fall was typical of the type that would produce one.

I walked into the library and told Dottie what had happened. I was not alarmed, but I was convinced that I had a fractured vertebra and had torn the internal ligament of my left knee. I knew I would need to see a doctor for treatment. It was 5 p.m. on Sunday, and I did not care to go to the hospital emergency room. I telephoned my orthopedist, Dr. West, explained what had happened and what I thought was injured. He offered to come to see me, but I told him to wait. I would use the Dupuy's splint on my left leg that I had from a former injury and I had some Dalmane on hand to take for sleep. If I had no further problems, I would go to his office the next morning. He offered to come to see me during the night if I needed him.

Dottie gave me a bath while I stood in the tub, fed me, and put me to bed. I slept about four hours during the night and reported to Dr. West's office at 8:30 in the morning. I ordered x-rays of my lumbar spine and then waited for the doctor. He examined my leg and said I had torn the internal ligaments of my knee, which he would have to repair in surgery the next day. He saw the x-rays and said there was no fractured lumbar vertebra, just severe arthritic changes. I insisted that there must be a fractured vertebra causing my pain. He then took a picture of the twelfth thoracic vertebra and discovered it was compressed by half. I am now a half-inch shorter than I was before. He sent me to the hospital and operated on my knee under general anesthesia the next morning. The first medication I received for pain was at 7 p.m., after the operation.

The tissues about my left buttock were sore. There was blood beneath the skin of my thigh down to my knee. A plaster cast was put on my leg from the hip to my ankle and I had to use crutches to walk.

I was soon able to be out of bed and walk. I was fitted with a back brace that extended from high on the front of my chest to my pelvic girdle. This prevented me from bending forward. I also had to wear a tight girdle around my waist, which gave me an erect posture. The doctor said I would have to wear the leg cast for six weeks and the back brace and girdle for 12 weeks. He advised that my knee would be well long before my back. I remembered it took 12 weeks for compression fractures of the spine to heal. I found this to be true. My back hurt continually until about the middle of the twelfth week.

I remained in the hospital for six days after surgery. I was given medication for pain twice daily and Dalmane for sleep while I was there. When I came home, I rested most of the time and took frequent naps.

My vegetable garden concerned me and I felt I had to water and maintain it although I was walking on crutches. I worked too much, and my chronic gout flared up. The pain in my left knee worsened as I became tired and overactive so I hired a boy to do most of the yardwork and help me with my garden and orchids.

After two weeks I noticed that I had a left footdrop and could not raise the front of my foot. When I walked with the crutches, my toes dragged on the floor and tripped me. I called Dr. West who was upset at this news. Footdrop frequently occurs in patients who have had cerebral strokes. He removed my cast and found my knee and leg swollen tightly due to an acute attack of gout in the knee, which had been precipitated by the trauma of the injury and operation. The cast had caused undue pressure on the peroneal nerve which runs down the outside of the leg, resulting in paralysis of the muscles of the leg. He put on a new cast and padded it carefully and the footdrop soon disappeared. I was more careful therafter and tried to avoid fatigue.

I drove my car - an automatic shift with no clutch - for the first time 18 days after my injury. I found that I slept better if I worked at something part of the time. However, as is my nature, I usually overworked, waxing our cars, spraying my plants and fruit trees, and doing repair work about our home.

During my 12-week recovery period, I watched many sporting events on television. I saw Japanese professional golfer, Aoki, chip in with a wedge from 130 yards for an eagle on the last hole of the Hawaii Open Golf Tournament to win by one stroke. I spent a lot of time on the very comfortable punee, a thick foam rubber pad on top of box springs, in our living room. After six weeks, my cast was removed. The muscles in my thigh and leg had atrophied, but my knee was still swollen about the operative site. I found that when I bent my knee in my sleep, I would awaken with pain. I began wearing the Dupuy's splint during the night and rested better.

I gave Dottie a dozen roses and a special valentine on Valentine's Day. She loved flowers and certainly deserved those roses because she had nursed me through my injury.

With physiotherapy, my knee became mobile, and the atrophied muscles of my thigh and leg returned to normal. Everything was much improved after a month of treatment.

I went to church on March 13th for the first time since my injury. It was the first time I had been to church without a tie, which I could not wear because of my back brace. I took the Christmas star off the roof on March 14th. Usually I removed it immediately after the New Year. Michael McGovern II came over at Easter to help me with the yard work and he used the chain saw for the first time. He made $65.00 plus his plane fare. It was always delightful to have him with us.

I was able to sleep through the night without Dalmane by the end of 12 weeks. My backache seemed to have disappeared overnight. I went to the club and hit some golf balls for practice, then, on April 9th, played in a scramble tournament and made four birdie putts of 30, 20, 10 and 4 feet. Our team still did not win anything.

As I continued to play golf twice weekly in addition to my home chores, my gout became worse. Both knees swelled as well as the first joint of my left big toe. I had to take a course of Butazolidin for four days and the gout promptly improved. My left knee continued to be sore.

THE YEAR 1983 CONTINUED

Dottie and I gave ourselves a new dining room table to celebrate our birthdays. The top measured 46 by 88 inches, and it was made of wavy-grained koa wood. We could easily seat 10 persons for dinner, which is the number of guests we usually entertain.

On June 13th, we heard a dog barking all day up the mountain behind our home. In the late afternoon one of our neighbors came into our yard from the woods. He said he had been trying to find his young dog in the area of the reservoirs at 1100 feet elevation when a 400-pound boar chased him. He quickly climbed a tree for safety. The large Doberman pinscher dog with him was no match for the boar, and he was concerned that the boar would kill and eat his younger dog before he could get him. He had not taken his rifle as he thought he would find the dog quickly, so he returned home and got his rifle. I loaned him a strong flashlight, and he hiked up the mountain toward the sound of the barking dog which he found at an altitude of 2000 feet, about 1000 feet above our home. When he returned at 1:00 a.m. he said he had not seen the boar again.

Dottie and I spent three days in Honolulu with Ann in July. We had never seen the Arizona Memorial, although we had heard the original explosions when Pearl Harbor was bombed on December 7, 1941. We went directly to the Memorial from the airport. Seeing this ship lying on the bottom and the long list of names of seamen who lost their lives was a sobering experience. The Japanese Nation had paid dearly for this exercise in wanton destruction and murder. It seems that nations never learn the follies of war. During the remainder of the three days, we went shopping and sightseeing around Oahu.

Dottie Jane and the Mote family arrived on August 13th for a week. We played golf, went sightseeing, had beach picnics and went swimming. We enjoyed a case of nectarines and a case of grapes I had bought from the Woolworth store at wholesale prices. Michael read my latest manuscript and gave it his approval.

I was invited to a Puunene camp reunion held at the vacated Puunene school on August 20th. Former residents of the camps of the original Puunene plantation, before the merger with Maui Agricultural Company, were invited. The merger had taken place 35 years before. I had lived in Haole (white man) Camp, which was really not a plantation-style camp. People came from all over the U.S.A. to attend this reunion, and there were great joy and comradeship among all those present. As I recall, only three doctors were invited and I was honored to have been included. I had worked long hours under difficult circumstances to take care of these people during the war and for almost 18 years while I was at Puunene. They had not forgotten me. There were drawings for door prizes and I won a $20.00 merchandise order. Most of those present had become successful in business, and some had reached high levels in society. Two of the attendees were mayors of large cities on the mainland.

August 31st was a banner day. After golf, my partner and I double-skunked our opponents at cribbage.

I played in our Member-Guest golf tournament at the Maui Country Club with Dr. Ian Kinnear. He was a retired dentist who had been reared on Maui and practiced dentistry at Monterey, California. He told me that on my second day of work at the Puunene plantation, February 2, 1941, I had set his broken arm with a perfect result. He was a teenager at the time.

I got estimates varying from $166 to $591 to have Dottie's 1965 Impala Super-Sport Coupe painted. I did the necessary rust removal and accepted the $166 bid, tax included. Now, six years later, it still looks like new.

We went to the post-season golf tournament at Kapalua, beyond Lahaina, and saw 40 professional golfers play, including Arnold Palmer, Peete, Erwin, Stadler, Norman, Charles and Tommy Hines Jr. Hines had been my partner in our Maui Country Club Member-Guest Tournament when he was 15 years old.

My manuscript, "Calcium Deficiency as the Prime Cause of Hypertension in Pregnancy: A Hypothesis," had been rejected by the American Journal of Obstetrics and Gynecology. Without changing it, I sent it to my friend in Japan, Dr. Konbai Den, to see if he could get it published in the Japanese literature. He was successful, though it was a year before it appeared[29]. I was very pleased with the high quality of the printing.

We had an earthquake measuring 4.4 on the Richter scale on Maui. On the Island of Hawaii, it measured 6.7 and did over $8,000,000 in property damage. No one was seriously injured although it was a reminder that earthquakes can be lethal.

During Michael McGovern II's five days with me at Thanksgiving, we cut down many trees behind the guest house and transplanted a large camellia. Ann arrived for Thanksgiving dinner and we invited my partner, Dr. Allred, whose wife had died recently following a stroke. Michael made $100 for his work during this visit and I was tired by the time he left.

The spacecraft, Columbia, was off again on a successful trip, its sixth, I think.

Dottie Jane called to tell us her husband, Michael, probably had a brain tumor and would need an operation.

The temperature was 52 degrees at 6:00 a.m. on one morning in December. I think this was a record. The temperature in Hawaii varies with the elevation above sea level.

During three days with Ann at Christmas, we saw the Christmas Star Program at the Bishop Museum Planetarium and attended church at Central Union. We were invited out to dinner two evenings, and Ann invited several guests in for dinner on the third day. With all this acitivity, I became tired and my gout bothered me a lot. It rained while we were there and when we returned home, I found both my rain guages had overflowed. I estimated we had 11 inches of rain on Maui while we were away.

THE YEAR 1984

Jon and Jan Graham arrived from Washington, D.C., on January 1st. We played golf at the Makena Golf Course and found it almost deserted. In spite of this, the marshal held us up and let several twosomes play through. We were not duffers; all of us had played for many years. Because of this treatment, we have never been back to play at Makena. Jon and Jan missed their plane to Honolulu on January 2nd, so I went back to the airport and got them. They left early the next morning.

We bought four swivel wicker chairs and a glass-top table for the breakfast room. They came directly from Red China and are of superior quality. Recently, we replaced the ceiling light fixture in the breakfast room with a beautiful lamp and shade. I think this about finishes furnishing our home.

Michael Mote had a brain tumor (acoustic neuroma) removed on January 9th in an operation lasting seven hours. The surgeon was unable to remove all of the tumor. Michael's condition was critical for several days with pneumonia developing and then he improved. In a second operation six weeks later, more of the tumor was removed. He has since recovered, but has residual facial paralysis. He has returned to his teaching duties as a professor at Temple University and is fine now after more than four years.

Barbara Keck, Carol's mother-in-law, arrived for a four-day visit. I showed her the usual attractions of Maui, and Dottie had a luncheon for her so she could meet some of our friends. She is a delightful person.

Michael McGovern II spent five days with me during his spring vacation. I bought a new chain saw, and we trimmed the hedge between our yard and our neighbors's yard on both sides. The hedge had been allowed to grow unrestrained for 24 years. We worked many hours together, then I completed the job after he left. He made $62 plus his airfare in five days. We took off some time for practicing golf and played 18 holes with my group.

Rain fell on April 6th. This would be the last rain for seven months, the longest dry spell in my memory.

CHAPTER XXXI

U.S. Mainland Trip:
April 11 to May 7, 1984

My sister, Velma, had breast cancer with metastases and had not been doing well. I promised her that as soon as the weather got warm in the spring, Dottie and I would visit her. I assumed it would be warm enough by the middle of April, so we left Maui on April 11th for North Carolina. I soon learned that we had gone one month too early. The temperature was in the high 30s in Southern Pines, North Carolina, in late April. It was in the 50s in Philadelphia the first week of May when we went to baseball games to see Timothy and Gregory Mote play.

While in North Carolina, we visited all our close relatives and made a trip to Coats, where I was reared through high school. We played golf in Chapel Hill and Southern Pines. The flowers were in full bloom everywhere, especially the azaleas, wisteria and crepe myrtle. Velma's two daughters, Peggy and Dottie, had arranged a special dinner on her 81st birthday, April 19th, at a fancy restaurant in a large, converted, colonial home a few miles out of Wilson. This was Velma's last birthday, though she lived to within 17 days of her next. She appeared fine, and was encouraged when I told her I thought she would live a few more years. She had regained the weight she had lost while taking chemotherapy and was enjoying life. However, she said she had lived her life and was ready to depart.

From North Carolina, we drove to Richmond and visited Dorothy and Jack Thornton. Again, we saw their yard filled with beautiful azaleas. We went on to Purcellville and had a golf game with Jack and Bennie Lightner. From there, we drove to Mt. Union, Pennsylvania, and visited Polly, Paul and Lee Prough. We visited the rest of Dottie's relatives in the Lewistown area and then drove to Philadelphia where we stayed with Dottie Jane's family for five days. This was the first time we had seen Michael since his brain surgery. While we were there, the Keck family drove down from Massachusetts to see us. On our last evening, we took the Mote family to the Bookbinders Seafood Restaurant for dinner, as we usually did on our visits. We left on May 7th at 7:45 a.m. and arrived home at 4:00 p.m.

THE YEAR 1984 CONTINUED

Carol and Pete Keck bought a 125-year-old farm house at Millbury, Massachusetts. It needed some remodeling, but Pete was smart enough to know that this would be good training for his boys who were now seven years old. When I asked him about the cold winters in this area, he said they would also be good for the boys. I had promised to help them finance the loan if necessary and sent them $6,000 by Western Union and the deal was closed. They repaid my loan within a few months.

I was continuing my work on a new monograph, which the Organisation Gestosis-Press had promised to publish for me. Its title would be "The Cellular Basis of Hypertension of Pregnancy."

On Memorial Day, an unknown soldier of the Vietnam war was buried at Arlington Cemetery along with the others. This was some time before the Vietnam Memorial was constructed.

Dottie was beginning to have severe pain in both arms. Her doctor ordered a cervical myelogram which showed a marked defect of the interspace between her fifth and sixth cervical vertebrae as well as degenerative changes in all the vertebrae and interspaces. She fainted during the procedure and was sick from it for several days.

She was referred to Dr. Ralph Cloward, who admitted her to the Queen's Hospital on June 26th. A discogram confirmed that she had a herniated disc, and she was operated on June 27th. All the symptoms in her arms disappeared and she came home three days after the surgery. The second night home, she slept 10 hours, eight hours without even awakening. This was the first uninterrupted night's sleep she had had in two years. She continued to improve for two weeks, and then the pain recurred although she was still able to drive her car and play bridge. After six weeks, her local doctor took x-rays which showed the bone graft in place, and all appeared normal. However, the pain worsened.

Dr. Cloward returned from a two-week trip to Europe and readmitted Dottie to Queen's Hospital. A discogram showed another herniated disc between the fourth and fifth cervical vertebrae. This was removed in surgery on August 23rd, and she returned to Maui on the 26th. The pain in her arm disappeared, and she recovered within a few weeks. She played nine holes of golf on December 18th, the first golf she had played since the operation.

Many of the trees in the forest surrounding our home had died from the drought. About 5:00 p.m. on September 16th, a fire broke out near the bottom of the ridge between our home and Iao Valley. The wind was blowing about 25 miles per hour, spreading the flames rapidly up the mountain until they were opposite our home. By twilight, live embers were falling on both our houses and over the yard. They looked like fireflies on the mainland in the summer. The roof of our guest cottage was made of cedar shingles treated with oil and there was a chance it would ignite. I tried to keep it wet using a garden hose. The main house had a tar and gravel roof, which was not apt to ignite from the small embers but I kept it wet also.

The fire reached to within 50 yards of the first home on our street, about 200 feet below us. It raged on the ridge opposite our home, but there is a gulch, 75 feet deep, between us and the ridge. By 9:30, the wind stopped blowing and the fire stopped advancing. The police forced us to vacate our home about 9 p.m. We took our cars and spent the night with our neighbors, the Claytors, who lived more than a block away from the woods. All I took with me was my diary, which I had kept for 54 years at that time. Dottie took our flat silver in her car. Our home could have been destoyed had the wind continued blowing, as the forest came within 30 yards of our home on three sides. Since that time, I have been moving it 30 yards further away. It is a tedious process, but well worth the effort. Our own plants thrive better without so much shade, and our yard is not constantly filled with trash from the trees. We hope we never experience another forest fire.

The fire smoldered for more than a week. Tree stumps had ignited and continued burning. The fire department's helicopter dumped water on the hot spots for several days. We could see and hear it make round trips to the reservoir a mile or so away. It was a welcome sound.

With the excitement of the fire, my gout flared up. For the third time, I had to take a four-day course of Butazolidin.

I finally finished writing my last monograph and mailed it to Dr. Rippmann in Basel, Switzerland, on October 2nd. His board approved publishing it after I agreed to add EPH-Gestosis to the title. The final title was "The Cellular Basis of Pregnancy

Induced Hypertension (EPH-Gestosis)[37]." This monograph, containing my explanation of the cause of high blood pressure, clarified how the calcium channels participated in this process. I would present it in Valencia, Spain, in 1986, and at the annual meeting of the Organisation Gestosis in Sendai, Japan, in 1985.

In the general election on November 6th, President Reagan and Vice President Bush won 325 electorial votes to only 13 for the opposition, an unprecedented victory.

The spacecraft, Challenger, retrieved two satellites from space within two days in November. This was a milestone in our space program.

I had kept my orchids in the shade of trees ever since we moved into our new home 24 years earlier. They produced nice flowers, but I thought I would have much better results with an orchid lath house. When Michael and I built one I filled it with my Cattleya orchids. For three years, there were no blooms. When I realized that the plants needed more sunlight I put them outside, and they began blooming regularly. We are in the shade of the West Maui mountains by midafternoon, and the orchids needed more sun than they could get in the lath house.

We spent two days at Thanksgiving with Ann and Michael II in Honolulu. All four of us had dinner with our nephew and niece, Drs. Jon and Jan Graham who gave us a large suitcase full of macadamia nuts from their trees. I was busy cracking them for quite a while and eventually bought a special nut cracker. Now, I have my own trees producing.

We got 1.27 inches of rain on November 26th and 27th, the first rain since the first week of April. It was an unbelievably long dry spell.

I gave Dottie a Zenith television with remote control for her bedroom as a Christmas present. I think this has given her more enjoyment than anything I ever gave her.

Michael II and Ann arrived December 24th for Christmas. Then, Dottie Jane and the Mote family arrived on the 26th for four days after a week on Kauai celebrating Michael's father's 80th birthday.

We had a glorious four days. The boys and men played golf together, and the women played golf together. Everyone went to the beach and swam in the ocean. The boys went to Hana and around the island with friends. The highlight of the visit was the dinner the evening after they arrived. We had an 18-pound prime rib roast and many other delicacies that Dottie excels at preparing. The boys could eat only about half the food at this meal, so they finished it up at another dinner. It was a delight to see their youthful appetites.

Dottie and I enjoyed a quiet and peaceful last day of the year alone. It is a joy to have all these children and grandchildren with us, but it takes days to recover after they visit. Someday, we plan to entertain all of them somewhere away from any of our homes.

THE YEAR 1985

Dottie and I started the year exhausted from having six guests for the four days after Christmas. We gradually returned to our routine of golf, playing bridge and doing house and yardwork.

On January 14th we had winds 60 miles per hour and heavy rains. A large trunk of one of our rainbow shower trees was broken. Luckily, there were two trunks on the tree, and the other one was not damaged. Other trees in the forest were blown over and fell into our yard.

President Reagan and Vice President Bush were scheduled to be inaugurated outside the White House, but the chill factor was minus 25 degrees in Washington. Instead, they were inaugurated in the Capitol rotunda and we viewed the ceremony on television.

I renewed my driver's license on January 31st, scoring 100 percent on the test. My vision was perfect. This would be the last time my vision would be normal because of developing cataracts.

The temperature was a cold 51 degrees at 7 a.m. on February 1st after a very chilly night. When it gets this cold, I build fires in the evening in our fireplace using the wood from the trees that fall into our yard.

I had applied to give a talk at the meeting of the Organisation Gestosis in May in Sendai, Japan, and became very busy preparing for this meeting. My talk would be based on the information in my last monograph[37], which was still at the press. I was also asked to lead an hour session. I sent the 329,600 yen registration fee for this meeting. The U.S. dollar was worth about 190 yen then; now it is worth about 60 percent of that.

The galley proof of my latest monograph was mistakenly delivered to the Maui Medical Group, and I did not receive it for a week after it arrived. I quickly made corrections and returned it to Dr. Rippmann in Basel.

A small lesion developed on the skin of my left ankle that was never exposed to sunlight. The dermatologist at the Maui Medical Group called me a few days after he removed it to tell me it was a skin cancer, but he had removed it thoroughly. He rechecked the site a couple of months later and confirmed that it had not recurred.

I had had lesions before on the backs of my hands and arms that I thought were skin cancers. I treated these areas with care and avoided exposing them to direct sunlight. They have since disappeared. I wear long-sleeved shirts while doing yardwork and gloves while playing golf. It was quite a shock to be told that I had any type of cancer. I know skin cancer can usually be treated easily and successfully, and I had treated many during my plantation practice.

Dottie had a picture taken at age 67 and gave it to me. It sits on my desk by the one taken just after we were married when she was almost 22 years old. Time leaves its marks, but she is still beautiful.

We drove to the Kaanapali Golf Course to see the end of the Kemper Open which Jane Blalock won at minus five.

Dottie's brother, Neff, and his wife, Jane, were with us for two days. They had lived on Maui about 25 years ago, when he worked for Libby's pineapple plantation. We went sightseeing to show them the changes on Maui and also had a dinner party for them to visit with their old friends.

On April 13th I played in a three-man scramble golf tournament at Maui Country Club. Our team won by one stroke and we each won a $50 merchandise prize plus $43 from the jackpot winnings. I always play my best golf in tournaments, but do not always win. In this tournament, all three of us contributed to our winning game.

CHAPTER XXXII

Visits to Sendai and Tokyo, Japan:
May 14 to 28, 1985

We took an early plane to Honolulu and checked in at Pan American Airway's ticket counter about one hour before we were to depart at 11. Our travel agent had told me we did not need visas to enter Japan, but Dottie thought we did. I could not remember anything about visas on our previous trip to Japan. When the ticket agent told us we needed visas, Ann quickly drove us to the Japanese consul's office in downtown Honolulu, and we were politely and promptly issued visas. I was so nervous about missing the flight I could barely fill in the application. We returned to the airport just as the last of the passengers checked in. I will never forget this nerve-wracking incident.

We arrived at Narita Airport at 2:15 p.m., and an agent of the tourist bureau was waiting for us with our names on a poster. It was already the next day, as we had crossed the International Date Line during the trip. We spent the night at the Holiday Inn at Narita and took a train to Tokyo next morning. There we changed to a Bullet Train and arrived in Sendai at 2 p.m. Dottie's arms were partially paralyzed at this time, and she could not help me with the luggage when we changed trains. A Japanese traveler saw my plight and helped me carry our luggage up and down the stairs at the station.

We stayed at the Sendai Plaza Hotel, which was not far from the shopping center. Dottie bought a beautiful lacquered hot plate to use on our buffet and I bought my secretary a double strand of Biwa pearls, which she liked very much.

The first evening, we were invited to a catered dinner at the home of Dr. Masakumi Suzuki, president of the meeting. It was a very elegant home of Japanese style. The second floor contained priceless oriental furnishings. Mrs. Suzuki was a master of flower arranging and had created a superior arrangement complementing an antique screen. Dottie had studied Japanese flower arrangement, which surprised Mrs. Suzuki, and they had a long discussion on the subject. The dinner was prepared and served in a beautiful Japanese garden. We had a lovely evening.

The next day I registered for the meeting, and Dottie and I went to the opening ceremonies at a park opposite Sendai Castle. By this time, Dr. Rippmann had arrived from Switzerland. After the dignitaries gave short speeches we had a chance to move about and meet one another. I will never forget a professor from Indonesia. He introduced himself and complimented me on the monographs I had written. He said he especially liked my illustrations, which helped him understand the contents of the monographs. I was so pleased that, the next day, I gave him one of each of my monographs, including the one just published and the hardback monograph on fetal adrenal hyperplasia.

I attended the medical meetings all the next morning, then all of us, including wives, left by bus for Matsushima. For hundreds of years this has been considered one of the most beautiful places in Japan. We visited a Buddhist monastery and saw many historic relics and scenic spots. In the evening, we boarded a boat and moved offshore for several miles into Matsushima Bay. We were served an early dinner aboard, allowing us to arrive back in Sendai at 8:30.

The main speaker on Sunday, May 19, was Dr. Claus B. Goecke of Germany who had just written a book on the cause of high blood pressure in pregnancy. He gave me a copy. In the evening, half the out-of-country guests were invited to the home of Dr. Hideo Imaizumi for entertainment and dinner. We were included.

Dr. Imaizumi's home was on the top floor of a six-story, private obstetrical hospital. We were served a delicious dinner in a solarium on the street side. The view of the city from here was beautiful. After dinner, we moved into an auditorium and were entertained with a musical program. First, two musicians played the koto, a Japanese musical instrument with 13 silk strings stretched over an oblong box. Then Dr. Imaizumi's daughter, who was studying piano at a conservatory, played a concert of classical music.

I gave a 30-minute lecture on Monday morning and it was well received. Dottie and I went shopping in the afternoon and then to the official banquet in the evening, held in the Sendai Plaza Hotel. After a good dinner, we were entertained by a dance troupe. As part of the finale, many of us attending were asked to go up on the stage and participate.

The next morning, I was chairman for an hour session ending at noon. I distributed monographs to the officials, who seemed pleased to get them. Soon after lunch a tourist bureau guide took us to the train station where we caught a bullet train to Tokyo. We checked into the Prince Hotel near the tall television tower. Our first two days at the hotel were part of the tour package that included the week in Sendai. We were put in a small room on the back side. After two days, we were moved to a very comfortable, deluxe room on the front side of the hotel overlooking a large court.

We spent our first day in Tokyo in the Ginza district, shopping in the morning and having lunch with Dr. Yuki Nakaizumi. He took us to a French restaurant named E'scoffiers, near his office. It was as though we were in Paris. I still remember the unusual and delicious soup that we were served.

On the second day, we had lunch with my former classmate, Dr. Saburo Kitamura and his charming wife, Dr. Michie Kitamura, at the Tokyo American Club. Michie was driving a new, red Mercedes Benz, which she had had only two days. She was a smart driver but riding with her made Saburo nervous, as he was much older and couldn't see well. The car was a convertible and had every possible accessory. Many of the employees of our hotel came out to inspect it. There was only one other in Tokyo like it.

On May 24th we went to Expo '85 by bus, a drive of about 40 miles from Tokyo. We spent the entire day there, going through many exhibits including the one from the United States. We were especially impressed by the South Korean exhibit and a dance troupe that performed there. All the exhibits were interesting and we learned much about many lands that we hardly knew existed. We saw, but decided not to ride on, the world's largest ferris wheel. In one exhibit, an artist was painting banners in water colors, using a combination of birds and flowers to spell out family names. We purchased one and in 30 minutes it was finished and dry. We have it hanging on a wall in our home.

The next day, it rained so we spent the day at the JapaneseNational Gallery of Art, where we saw many Japanese paintings, sculptures, and objects of art. We enjoyed an excellent Chinese dinner in a restaurant in our hotel.

On Sunday Dr. Nakaizumi took us by taxi to Hakone National Park, where the famous Fujiya Hotel with its spa is located. Dr. Nakaizumi had often taken his family there on vacations. They usually traveled by train, and he had bought train tickets for this trip. However, the weather was so nice, he decided we should travel by taxi, a drive that took over six hours. The Fujiya Hotel and its spa is where the movie, "The Tea House of the August Moon," was filmed. We were taken on a grand tour by the manager. During our drive around the park we saw some signs of volcanic activity.

After we returned to Tokyo, we invited the Nakaizumis to join us for dinner in a French restaurant in our hotel, a restaurant Mrs. Nakaizumi was unaware of. The dinner was excellent. Dottie and I will always remember this as an exceptional evening with dear friends.

On our last day in Tokyo we went shopping again in the Ginza District. Also on this day, Dr. Nakaizumi gave us a Seiko quartz clock shaped like a pyramid that, when pressed on the top, calls out the exact time in hours and minutes. The English-voice version had been available only one week. I keep this clock by my bed so when I press on it in the dark, a feminine voice tells me the time.

We had an early dinner at the Chinese reutarant in our hotel. At 7, we attended a concert by the Straussburg Philharmonic Orchestra at Tokyo Bunka Kaikan. The taxi driver got lost, and it took more than a half hour to reach the area across town. We enjoyed the concert which was strictly European classical music.

We packed for home on May 28th and left at 9 p.m. We arrived in Honolulu at 9 a.m. after a very nice flight, again crossing the International Date Line. It took me three days to get over jet-lag.

_____THE YEAR 1985 CONTINUED

My last monograph had arrived just as we left for Sendai. When I returned home, I mailed copies of it to all the libraries and research institutions as usual.

William Uranga, my oldest grandson, spent a week with us from July 12th to 19th. He rode in the golf cart with me on Wednesday and Saturday, but did not play. We did a lot of yard work and he made about $100 for the week. It was nice having him with me. I showed him many lantern slides of his mother when she was young.

I played in the Maui Country Club Member-Guest Golf Tournament with Dr. Ralph Cloward on the Labor Day weekend. We played poorly, but both won a dozen golf balls.

I began studying for a new medical paper on voltage and calcium influx in nerve and muscle cells. I bought a new book[38] which had much useful information in it, just what I needed to finish my study of the pathogenesis of high blood pressure.

For the first time in 17 years on the road, I had a flat tire. I had not watched my tires closely and the wires of a steel-belted, radial tire had worn through, causing a leak.

Dottie and I attended the annual Hawaiian State Medical Association meeting at Kona and stayed at the Keahou Beach Hotel. We both played in the annual golf tournament. I won a $30 merchandise order from Liberty House and a Keahou Golf Course visor.

I played in the Doctor-Dentist-Druggist Golf Tournament and won a Mr. Coffee coffeemaker, nine golf balls, a Timex wrist watch and some minor gadgets.

On November 13th, 22,500 people were killed by mud slides following a volcanic eruption in Columbia, South America. The whole world was shocked.

I received word that Dr. J.W. Gordner of Danville, Pennsylvania, had died on November 1st. He had been a fellow intern and resident and best man at our wedding.

I played in the Hawaiian Commercial and Sugar Company's Harvest-Home Golf Tournament and had 68 net. I won another round of golf at the Wailea Blue Course.

We had had heavy rains for many weeks and our back yard had become a quagmire. Finally, I decided that there had to be a leak in our water pipes in this area. I made extensive excavations around all pipes, but could not find the leak. The soil was saturated and every hole I dug quickly filled with water. I cut some of the lines and plugged them shut, but the water still flowed profusely. When I remembered that the county's six-inch water line was in this area, buried about eight feet, I called the county water department and they, reluctantly, agreed that the water must be coming from their main. A week later, they excavated down to the pipe and repaired a large break.

I put in a new, Japanese-style walk to the guest house and to the utility area. It has round stepping stones in the center surrounded by pebbles that I brought from the beach. Three-inch boards treated with a wood preservative border the walk on each side, keeping the pebbles in place. It has remained stable for three years with no sign of deterioration. This is the last hard work I have done up to this writing. It took me several weeks to recover from my fatigue.

For Christmas, I had an extra band put on Dottie's ruby ring that I had bought in Mexico City. The original setting was so heavy it twisted on her finger but she can now wear this beautiful ring. The redesigning cost as much as the ring had originally.

THE YEAR 1986

Dottie and I played nine holes of golf on January 3rd. Dottie had begun having pain in her neck and arms after golf and was always in trouble for two hours. However, she was a good golfer and enjoyed the association with her friends. She continued playing until May 2nd when she and I played nine holes, not realizing that this would be her last golf.

I played in a three-man scramble golf tournament on January 18th, and we came in first. We each won a $40 merchandise prize plus $40 from the jackpot.

The first Martin Luther King Jr. National Holiday was celebrated on January 20th, though not in Hawaii. I flew our American flag from the railing on our balcony.

I had applied to give a talk at the annual meeting of the Organisation Gestosis in Valencia, Spain, in June. A postal strike in Spain made communicating with those in charge of the meeting very difficult. Finally, I heard from Dr. F. Bonilla-Musoles, president. I sent him my monograph "Fetal Adrena Hyperplasia: Its Relationship to High Blood Pressure in Pregnancy." He promptly asked me to give a second lecture on this subject in addition to my other lecture, which was entitled, "How Calcium Deficiency Acting Through Voltage-Sensitive Calcium Channels Leads to EPH-Gestosis" (high blood pressure in pregnancy)[39]. I was honored that he should ask me to give two talks and became very busy preparing for the lectures. I had to do much research on how electric current affects nerve and muscle cells, make several new lantern slides to demonstrate my talks, and then write the two papers.

The Challenger spacecraft exploded and killed the seven astronauts aboard on January 28th. I saw the occurrence on television. The whole world was saddened, and our space program was slowed down. I am happy to say at the time of this writing, the new spacecraft, Discovery, has made a successful trip.

Apparently I was doing too much work; my gout was bothering me more each day. I finally took a four-day course of Butazolidin during the first week of February and promptly improved.

Dictator Fernando Marcos of the Philippines was forced to resign and leave his country on February 25th. He was given political asylum in Hawaii and was flown to Hawaii on a U.S. Airforce plane. He is still residing here at the time of this writing. He has been accused by his home government of malfeasance in office and by the U.S. government of criminal acts. He will eventually come to trial in both countries.

Using binoculars, I saw Haley's Comet over Haleakala Mountain at 5 a.m. on March 8th, 10th, and 11th. The comet and its tail were very clear. Although visible other nights, it was often obscured by clouds.

On April 14th, the United States bombed Libya because of frequent terrorist attacks supported by that country. The attacks stopped after the bombing.

Dottie and I heard Vladimir Horowitz's televised piano concert from Moscow, Russia. He was born in Russia and came to the United States at about age 20. He was now 80 years old and this was his first visit to Russia since leaving. We have a VCR recording of this performance by one of the foremost pianists in the world and play it frequently.

The nuclear reactor in a power plant at Chernobyl, Russia, exploded and melted on April 26th. The radioactivity in the air was detected in surrounding European countries before there was any announcement of the accident by the Russians. Within a week or so, the radioactivity had encircled the globe in the upper layers of the atmosphere. Many dozens of workers lost their lives soon after the accident, and it is believed that millions of people in Russia and Europe were adversely affected by the radiation. There was a concerted effort of leading world authorities on the treatment of nuclear accident victims to give all the help possible to those affected. It will be years before the final assessment of the damage of this explosion can be made.

I gave Dottie a red carnation lei for Lei Day, which she wore to the duplicate bridge session. She loves leis and is very beautiful with a red carnation lei around her neck.

We had a tidal wave alert on May 7th. There had been an earthquake in the Aleutian Islands, and a wave was generated. However, by the time it reached Hawaii it was only 12 inches high, and no damage was done. People living in Hawaii have learned to respect such warnings; those who don't may perish.

CHAPTER XXXIII

Tour of Spain and Visits to U.S. West and East Coasts: June 7 to July 4, 1986

Dottie and I left Honolulu at 1:30 p.m. and arrived in San Francisco at 9:30. We drove our U-drive to a Holiday Inn in Union City, a few miles from Lois's and John's home in Fremont. It was 11:30 before we reached our room. I was very tired after the trip and dreaded driving after dark in strange territory. I guess this is a sign of age, but I avoid as much night driving as I can.

We spent four days in California and had lovely visits with Lois and her family. We drove to Saratoga and spent one day with McLeod and Louise. One evening, Lois's family had dinner with us at the Holiday Inn. On our last day, Carol Ann and I went to a pet shop and bought four young pullets, about four days old. She named each pullet for one of her aunties and her mother. Two of them were of a breed that was supposed to lay colored eggs, similar to Easter eggs, when they were grown. (Sure enough, they did.) I prepared a shoe box in a cage as an incubator, leaving one end open and putting a small electric light bulb in the other end for warmth. The chicks adapted to their new environment and soon were grown. A large pen was built for them in the back yard. They provided Carol Ann with a good project while producing more eggs than the family used.

We flew to Philadelphia and spent three days with Dottie Jane and her family. My sister, Dorothy, and her husband, Jack, were in town and had lunch with us one day. When I reconfirmed our reservations from New York to Madrid, I found they had been cancelled. Luckily, due to the time difference, I was able to contact our travel agent on Maui who got our paid reservations reinstated. Otherwise, I would have had to pay for new tickets at a much higher price.

On June 13th Michael Mote and I watched my grandson, Gregory, pitch baseball in the City League for 14- to 15-year olds. He was six feet tall and would be 16 in about two months. Some of the younger boys were barely five feet and did not weigh much over 100 pounds. The game was late starting, so it lasted only six innings. Gregory struck out 17 of the 18 batters for a no-hitter. One batter hit the ball to the infield. He went to bat three times and scored three runs, getting two hits and one walk. He was a senior in high school and hoped to play baseball in college. He also excels at soccer.

We flew to Kennedy Airport in New York City on June 14th and left for Madrid at 8:30 p.m. We arrived at 8 a.m. on Sunday, after one of the nicest flights we have ever had. We were on an Iberia Air Lines 747, with every seat occupied. It was 10 a.m. by the time we got to the elegant Palace Hotel, one of Madrid's finest. We went to bed immediately and slept for five hours.

About 4 p.m., I talked to the concierge about possible entertainment for the evening. He told me the opera house was only two blocks from the hotel and that the opera, "Pagliacci," was being presented that evening. All the tickets had been sold, but he said there always were ticket scalpers present about one to two hours before show time with good tickets. He offered to send a bellboy out to buy tickets if I wanted them. I agreed and gave him a $50 ceiling on the tickets. Fortunately, they cost less than $35 each.

Dottie was very happy that I was able to get the tickets. We had an early dinner in the hotel and proceeded to the opera house.

In the prologue to the opera, Carlos Chausson who played the role of the clown, Tonia, appeared before the curtain and introduced himself. He then briefly and vehemently outlined the purpose of the opera in song. I have been to very few operas and am not a musician, but I have never heard anything so great as this performance. When he had finished, the audience rose to its feet and cheered him for several minutes. It was an exhilarating experience. The role of Pagliacci was played by Jose Carreras, said by some to be a greater singer than Placido Domingo. We thoroughly enjoyed all of "Pagliacci," and it was a great introduction to Spain.

I had considered going to a bullfight to see how the Spaniards entertain themselves. Fortunately, I found one being shown on television and watched for a few minutes, which was enough for me.

The next day, we were bothered by jet lag although we did take a panoramic tour of the city. On the following day, we spent three hours in the Prado Art Museum, one of the most outstanding in the world. It was less than a block from our hotel. Art museums have become to look about alike to me: Most of them have pictures painted by the same old masters and resemble one another.

In the afternoon we went shopping and bought records. We also bought a beautiful silver necklace for Dottie Jane, who no longer wears gold. Silver is her preferred color.

On our last day we took another city tour, seeing the outlying areas of Madrid. It is a beautiful city.

One day while we were waiting in the Palace Hotel lobby for a tour, I found a money clip with $351 (U.S.) in it. There was no identification. I reported to the concierge and the hotel assistant manager that I had found money and would return it to anyone who identified it. I gave my forwarding address, but have never heard from the hotel.

We got up early on June 19th and flew to Valencia, where the Organisation Gestosis was having its annual meeting. We were registered at the Hotel Rey Don Jaime, located some distance from the medical school where the meetings were held. Buses transported us from our hotel to the meetings and to all social events.

Dottie and I got settled in our room, and then I took a bus to the medical school to register for the meeting. I had learned that we were to register at 5 p.m., but had never seen a program. When I arrived I was met by Dr. Bonilla's secretary and told that the meeting would start at 5:15 p.m. I was listed as first on the program, but I had not brought a copy of my speech nor my lantern slides. The secretary and I took a taxi back to our hotel, I picked up my speech and slides, and we returned to the school. By this time it was after 6 p.m. I soon gave my talk, "Fetal Adrenal Hyperplasia: Its Relationship to EPH-Gestosis"[40]. It was well received.

When I went to our hotel to get my slides, I found Dottie in dire distress. She was barely able to open the door to let me in. When she had returned to the room, the elevator jolted her when it stopped and she developed severe pain in her neck and arms. She did not want me to leave. I put her to bed and went back to the meeting, assuring her I would return as soon as I could. She had improved somewhat when I got back but we decided to have dinner in our hotel and miss the elaborate reception and dinner to open the meeting.

The second day, I gave my main talk entitled, "How Calcium Deficiency Acting Through Voltage-sensitive Calcium Channels Leads to EPH-Gestosis"[39]. I had lantern slides to demonstrate what I was saying. My talk appeared to be well-accepted, and I was pleased. This speech was a summation of exactly 50 years of research on my part, including clinical, laboratory and academic research as well as clinical observation while I was practicing medicine for 43 years. A summary, in lay terms, of all my research follows in the last chapter.

The morning session ended shortly after 1 p.m., and all participants and accompanying persons were taken by bus to La Marcelina, a fabulous seafood restaurant by the beach. Dottie was unable to go because of her neck. She was very envious when I told her about the wonderful food we had eaten.

The afternoon session started at 5 and ended about 8:30. Dinner again was served at 10 and we arrived back in our hotel after midnight. Dottie felt well enough to go to the dinner party this second evening, which was held at La Hacienda Restuarant. The food was simply divine, similar to the very best French cuisine but with a definite Spanish flavor. The ladies at our table, who came from different European countries, could hardly believe that Spanish food could be so good. Indeed, it was one of the best meals Dottie and I had ever eaten.

The last day of the meeting was Saturday, June 21st. I was the moderator from 10:30 a.m. to 1:30 when the meeting ended. In translating Spanish to English, the moderator was referred to as the president, so I was the 'president' for the last session. Actually, Professor M. Tortajada of Valencia was the president of the entire meeting, and it seemed strange that the moderators also were presidents.

In the evening of this last day, Dr. Bonilla invited all the out-of-country guests to his country estate, or villa, for swimming and dinner. It was located about 10 miles from Valencia and situated on a bluff overlooking the Mediterranean Sea. We traveled by bus over narrow, curving roads. The home was new with a large swimming pool and the surrounding areas were planted with almond trees just starting to bear nuts.

When we arrived many were watching the world championship soccer match on television. Argentina defeated West Germany three to two and the people present from Brazil and Argentina were as excited about the game as Americans get about football.

Our dinner was served at tables outside by the pool. A bright moon was shining. It was a lovely scene. Dr. Bonilla and his young, beautiful wife had two children about four and six years old, who were with us. They spent the summers at the villa to get away from the city. Again, it was after midnight when we arrived back at our hotel.

The next morning my ankles were swollen, which was something new. Every evening in Valencia, we had eaten dinner after 10 and it was always after midnight before we could get to bed. I could not get enough rest on this schedule. We rested all morning in our room this last day. In the afternoon we took a four-hour taxi ride through the area south of Valencia, passing many large rice plantations, Valencia orange groves and beautiful beaches. On our way home, we had to detour because of a large fire near the highway, and got stuck in a bad traffic jam.

Our itinerary included a five-day Andalucia tour. We were up early next morning, flew to Madrid and then took another plane to Malaga, arriving at 4 p.m. We were met at the airport by a tour guide who took us to our hotel, the Melia Costa Sol. As I recall, there was only one other doctor and his wife taking this tour; the remainder of the 40 persons were French, Italian, English and Dutch tourists. Ninety percent of them were young.

We got an early start the following morning on an air-conditioned bus. Our excellent guide was a Spaniard named Jose Louis. The countryside was beautiful.

We followed the Mediterranean coast over relatively flat terrain. Suddenly, the Rock of Gibraltar came into view. There is only one description for this sight: a huge, solitary rock, several hundred feet high, on the edge of the Mediterranean. Looking across the Strait of Gibraltar we could see the mountains in northwest Africa (Morroco). It was a thrill for me to see these places, the names of which I had known since studying geography in grammar school. My brother, Neill, had flown to north Africa in the Army Airforce in 1942 and later flew across the Mediterranean during the invasion of Italy.

We continued along the coast of Spain until we reached Cadiz, an Atlantic Ocean port. Here we turned inland and went north for 75 miles. We reached Seville at 6 p.m. and spent the entire next day sightseeing.

So much is involved in the history of Seville that only a relatively few things can be mentioned here. When Julius Caesar was in Seville in the year 45 B.C. it had already been under Roman domination for two centuries. It remained under Roman occupation for more than 500 years. The Islamic Moors took over in 712 A.D. and ruled until 1248, when Ferdinand III of Castille was triumphant. Then in the 14th century, Pedro the Cruel took over and made a lasting impression in the famous palace, Alcazar, which incorporated portions of a pre-existing Moorish castle. We toured this very beautiful palace.

After America was discovered, Seville was the principal port for the returning treasure galleons. Commerce and the arts flourished during the resultant Golden Age, but this all ended with the wars of Phillip IV and the loss of control over the colonies.

We toured the unusual Seville Cathedral. A mosque that originally stood at the same site was used as a church from the Christian reconquest in 1248 until the cathedral was built in 1401. The Courtyard of the Orange Trees remains from the mosque. Only St. Peter's in Rome and St. Paul's in London can compare in size and splendor to the Seville Cathedral. We had seen both and thought that Seville was more beautiful.

We also visited the '29 Expo buildings and several beautiful parks and went shopping at El Corte Ingles where we bought beautiful silver jewelry and other items.

On our drive to Cordoba on June 26th we passed many thousands of acres of sunflowers. These beautiful plants have large, yellow heads that turn throughout the day so that they are always facing the sun.

The Romans occupied Cordoba in the second century B.C. It already was a thriving community, though later it was eclipsed by Seville and Madrid. A half-million people lived in the city around the year 1000 although the population declined during the ensuing centuries. It is now making a comeback.

As we entered Cordoba, we crossed a long Roman bridge with many arches made of stone blocks, dating back about 2000 years.

The next day we drove to Granada over mountainous roads. Millions of olive trees grew in rows that seemed to go for miles and rose for several thousand feet over the hilly terrain. There were also vast wheat fields along the way.

In the evening we went to a Flamenco ballet. It was entertaining and different from anything we had seen: a ballet with lots of foot-stomping.

On the last day of our tour, we visited Alhambra, the ultimate architectural achievement of the Moors in Spain. It ranks in near-mystical exuberance with the Taj Mahal and the Parthenon. It is not a single building but a multi-level complex of castles, churches, fortifications and royal residences connected by tiers of gardens, gates, terraces, corridors and staircases. We walked through the palace of the Arabic Emirates and gardens. I am not qualified to describe what we saw nor the importance of it to Iberian culture. I am sure it has also played a great role in the development of other cultures in Europe.

After seeing Alhambra, we returned to Malaga and finished our five-day tour. Dottie and I were among the oldest on the tour and had difficulty keeping up with the younger ones at times. We tipped the tour guide generously, contrary to the wishes of our European comrades. They even told us that Americans tipped too much.

Dottie and I had an extra day in Malaga at the Melia Costa Sol Hotel. After resting more than 12 hours in bed, we enjoyed a day on the beach and shopping. About 10 percent of the women on the beach were naked above the waist, which was something new for us.

The next day, June 30th, we flew to New York after boarding an Iberian Boeing 747 in Madrid. The flight was full of noisy, partially intoxicated American college students returning from a summer in Spain. They often used obscenities and told of the sordid, social affairs they had had during the summer. They were certainly ugly Americans, and we were ashamed of them. Our flight to Madrid had been so peaceful without them.

We changed planes at Kennedy Airport and flew on to Boston, arriving before dark. Pete Keck met us and took us to the Grafton Inn in Grafton, Massachusetts, about eight miles from their home in Millbury. They had moved only a few days previously and were not ready to have guests. The Grafton Inn was more than a hundred years old and a very unique place to stay. Their specialty on Tuesday was lobster, and we enjoyed the delicacy.

We rented a U-drive and shuttled between the Grafton Inn and Millbury. Pete took a day off from work and told us of his plans to remodel the 125-year old house. It rained all day the second day. On the third day, we packed in the morning and were ready to go to Logan Airport in Boston by limousine at 1 p.m. We invited Carol, Adam and Todd to have an early lunch with us at the Grafton Inn. We all had a lobster roll sandwich.

We left Boston in midafternoon and spent a night in Minneapolis-St. Paul, Minnesota. The next day our plane stopped in Los Angeles for 20 minutes, and we arrived in Honolulu at 1:30 p.m. Ann took us to a wholesale rug outlet where we bought a new gray-blue rug for Dottie's bedroom, dressing room and bath.

While we were in Spain, I bought a beautiful silver necklace for my secretary who had toiled many hours for me, typing my manuscripts. I am still indebted to her for her hard work over the course of many years.

From a scientific point of view, I think my work is finished. I have done what I started exactly 50 years ago and am satisfied that I have correctly described the pathophysiology of high blood pressure in pregnancy. It is time to end this dissertation. The final chapter is an explanation in lay terms of what I have written in the five monographs and about 25 scientific publications on this subject over 51 years.

So far as my life's story is concerned, I think I should conclude it as well. If it is worthy, it should be apparent in my writings. My contemporaries are cognizant of anything that I am at this time. Our youngest grandchildren are about 10 years old now and will remember any significant events that happen hereafter.

One final thing I will mention: Dottie and I celebrated our golden wedding anniversary on August 17, 1988, in a week-long family reunion at Snowmass, Colorado. All 16 members of our immediate family were present.

I was 77 years old on April 21, 1989. I think it is time for me to accept the following aphorism as stated by General Douglas MacArthur: Old soldiers don't die, they just fade away.

CHAPTER XXXIV

Summary of Fifty Years of Research: How Calcium Deficiency Produces High Blood Pressure, Using the Pregnant Woman as a Model to Prove It

Paradoxically, a deficient calcium intake eventually leads to an excess of ionic calcium in the fluid of vascular muscle cells, which causes vascular muscle spasm and high blood pressure. The pregnant woman serves as a clinical model to prove this fact. However, the pathophysiology of high blood pressure is different in the first and second halves of pregnancy, but a calcium deficiency is the dominant factor in both.

In the first half of pregnancy, there may be adrenal cortex exhaustion, due to malnutrition and stress. Adrenal cortical exhaustion is accompanied by the production of a massive excess of cyclic AMP, which is an intracellular enzyme activator. This excess cyclic AMP will not be inactivated if there is a calcium deficiency, and some of it will be absorbed into the plasma. It is then carried to other tissues, where it could have a nonspecific swamping effect resulting in many abnormal reactions. Some of these are: 1) the formation of an excess of cholesterol and cholesterol endarteritis in small placental vessels, 2) an excess of renin-angiotensin, causing spasm and occlusion of placental vessels and villus degeneration, and 3) an excess of aldosterone, causing a retention of sodium and water and producing edema throughout the body.

In the second half of pregnancy, the adrenal cortex may become necrotic, and the formation of cyclic AMP will be low. However, in the second half, the needs for calcium are so great that there may be a severe, progressive calcium deficiency, resulting in hypocalcemia in the extracellular fluid. This, then, causes an excess of ionic calcium to enter muscle cells, leading to vasospasm and high blood pressure. The pathophysiology involved is as follows: Nerve and muscle cells have excitable cell membranes which produce action potentials (electrical charges). At rest, the electrical charge of the membrane is in equilibrium with that of the extracellular fluid. After stimulation, sodium ions pass into the cell and potassium ions leave. The membrane becomes positive compared with the extracellular fluid, and then is said to be depolarized. During depolarization there is an increased production of action potentials by the cell membranes. Also, during depolarization and the action potential, calcium ions from the extracellular fluid pass into the cells through specific channels that have voltage-controlled gates. This creates more current.

The extracellular fluid normally contains 5,000 to 10,000 times more calcium than the intracellular fluid. If there is deficient calcium ingestion for a long period, and especially during the second half of pregnancy when the needs are so great, there will be hypocalcemia in the extracellular fluid. The calcium in the extracellular fluid controls nerve and muscle cell excitability. This hypocalcemia depolarizes the cell membranes and increases the production of action potentials, allowing the entry of excess calcium ions into the muscle cells. In nerve cells, the increased action potentials first cause the release of acetylcholine. This, then, causes the release of increased catecholamines (adrenalin and noradrenalin) by other nerve tissue. The catecholamines, acting through alpha receptors, allow more calcium to enter muscle cells, producing more spasm and high blood pressure.

In the above manner, it can be seen that a deficient calcium ingestion during pregnancy will result in a continuous hypocalcemia in the extracellular fluid, which will have a continuous depolarizing effect on nerve and vascular muscle cells. There will be a continuous inward flow of calcium ions and current into vascular muscle cells producing acute spasm, arteriosclerosis, and high blood pressure. This is in contrast to normal physiology in which there are alternating periods of activity and rest. Normally, during the rest periods the ionic calcium that entered the muscle cells causing contractions is removed. If there is hypocalcemia in the extracellular fluid, this does not occur.

In addition, there is more irrefutable evidence that high blood pressure is due to chronic calcium deficiency. For instance, epidemiological studies show that the blood pressure is inversely proportional to the calcium intake in humans in both pregnant and nonpregnant subjects. Also, experimental animals develop high blood pressure on a calcium restricted diet, which is reversible by calcium administration.

The needs of the body for calcium in children and adults have been estimated to be about 1.2 grams per day, the amount in one quart (960 ml) of milk. During pregnancy this amount should be increased by 50 percent. If one is unable to take milk, calcium carbonate or other calcium salts in tablet form may be substituted. The absorption of calcium from the intestinal tract is controlled by the parathyroid hormone. If more is ingested than is needed, it will not be absorbed.

BIBLIOGRAPHY

1.   Beatrice Bayley Heritage Book, Beatrice Bayley, Inc., Pennsylvania, 1981.

2.   Patterson, Alex M., Adm. (Ret.), Highland Scots Pattersons of North Carolina and Related Families, 2425 West Lake Drive, Raleigh, N.C., 27609, 1979.

3.   Grant, I.F., The Clan MacLeod. Johnson and Bacon, Ltd., Edinburgh, 1953.

4.   Broadway Centennial Celebration 1870-1970. The Woman's Club of Broadway, North Carolina.

5.   Patterson, W.B., Hunt, H.F., Nicodemus, R.E., "The Etiology of Eclampsia: A Preliminary Report." American Journal of Clinical Pathology 8:120-35, 1938.

6.   Patterson, W.B., Hunt, H.F., Nicodemus, R.E., "Evidence that Most Thyroid Disease is Congenital." Western Journal of Surgery, Obstetrics and Gynecology 45:486-99, 1937.

7.   Hunt, H.F., Patterson, W.B., Nicodemus, R.E., "Placental Infarction and Eclampsia." American Journal of Clinical Pathology 10:319-31, 1940.

8.   Patterson, W.B., Nicodemus, R.E., Hunt, H.F., "Hypothyroidism - An Etiological Factor in Eclampsia." Pennsylvania Medical Journal 49:983-88, 1938.

9.   Patterson, W.B., "The Congenital Factors in Thyroid Disease." Western Journal of Surgery, Obstetrics and Gynecology 47:273-76, 1939.

10. Porteus, S.D., Calabashes and Kings. Pacific Books. Palo Alto, Ca. 1945.

11. Barber, J. Jr., Hawaii Restless Rampart. The Bobbs-Merrill Company, New York,1941.

12. Patterson, W.B., "The Importance of Complete Pelvic Examinations in Obstetrics." Bulletin Hawaii Territorial Medical Association 3:20-23, 1941.

13. Patterson, W.B., "Appendicitis During Labor." Hawaii Medical Journal 5:267-68, 1946.

14. Allen, G., Hawaii War Years 1941-45. University of Hawaii Press, Honolulu, 1950.

15. Patterson, W.B., "Blood Typing 30,000 Civilians." Hawaii Medical Journal 2:99-100, 1942.

16. Patterson, W.B., "The Need for Autopsies in Stillbirths and Neonatal Deaths." Hawaii Medical Journal 1:301, 1942.

17. Lightner, G.H., Patterson, W.B., "Trichinosis." Hawaii Medical Journal 1:320-3, 1942.

18. Patterson, W.B., "Bacillary Dysentery with Special Reference to the Epidemic on Maui." Hawaii Medical Journal 3:222-26, 1944.

19. Patterson, W.B., "Pregnancy Near Term with Prolapse of the Uterus." American Journal of Obstetrics and Gynecology. 48:722-23, 1944.

20. Patterson, W.B., "Management of Labor in a Patient with Diabetes Mellitus." Hawaii Medical Journal 3:291-2, 1944.

21. Patterson, W.B., "Thrombocytopenic Purpura in Pregnancy and in the Newborn." Journal of the American Medical Association 130:700-02, 1946.

22. Patterson, W.B., "Hemorrhage from Meckel's Diverticulum in Infancy." Hawaii Medical Journal 5:85-86, 1945.

23. Patterson, H.M., "Weil's Disease." Journal of the American Medical Association 134:1077-80, 1947.

24. East Maui Irrigation Company's 100th Birthday. Ampersand. Alexander and Baldwin Inc., Honolulu, 1976.

25. Patterson, W.B., "Plantation Medicine in Hawaii." Industrial Medicine and Surgery 18:426-27, 1949.

26. Patterson, W.B., An Explanation of the Biological Functions of the Body in Health and Disease. Published by the Author, 1950.

27. Patterson, W.B., "Vitamin Deficiencies and Disease." Hawaii Medical Journal 10:347-49, 1951.

28. Patterson, W.B., "Adrenal Dysfunction; an Etiological Factor in Late Toxemia of Pregnancy." Western Journal of Surgery, Obstetrics and Gynecology 59:610-18, 1951.

29. Patterson, W.B., "Calcium Deficiency as the Prime Cause of Hypertension in Pregnancy: A Hypothesis." Asia-Oceania Journal of Obstetrics and Gynecology 10:485-98, 1984.

30. Patterson, W.B., "Normal Pregnancy After Recovery from Metastatic Choriocarcinoma." American Journal of Obstetrics and Gynecology 72:183-87, 1956.

31. Patterson, W.B., "The Prophylactic Use of Vitamin K During Pregnancy and the Newborn." Hawaii Medical Journal 33:134-37, 1974.

32. Patterson, W.B., Fetal Adrenal Hyperplasia: Its Relationship to Late Toxemia of Pregnancy. Published by the Author. Wailuku, Hawaii, 1973.

33. Patterson, W.B., Etiology of Eclampsia. Organisation Gestosis-Press, Basel, 1975.

34. Patterson, W.B., EPH-Gestosis (Preeclampsia) Etiology, Prevention, Treatment. Organisation Gestosis, Basel, 1978.

35. Belizan, J.M., Villar, J., "The Relationship Between Calcium Intake and Edema-, Proteinuria-, and Hypertension-Gestosis: An Hypothesis." American Journal of Clinical Nutrition 33:2202-10, 1980.

36. Patterson, W.B., How Malnutrition, Primarily of Calcium, and/or Stress Lead to Edema-, Proteinuria-, and Hypertension-Gestosis: An Hypothesis. Organisation Gestosis-Press, Basel, 1982.

37. Patterson, W.B., The Cellular Basis of Pregnancy Induced Hypertension (EPH-Gestosis). Organisation Gestosis-Press, Basel, 1985.

38. Hille, B., Ionic Channels in Excitable Membranes. Sinauer Associates Inc., Sunderland, Mass. 1984.

39. Patterson, W.B., How Calcium Deficiency Acting Through Voltage-Sensitive Calcium Channels Leads to EPH-Gestosis (High Blood Pressure in Pregnancy). Revista Espanola de Obstetricia/Ginecologia 42:797-806, 1987.

40. Patterson, W.B., Hiperplasia Suprarenal en el Feto: Su Relacion con la EPH-Gestosis. Revista Espanola de Obstetricia/Ginecologia 47:1-12, 1988.